C000231985

Letters and Journals
by Robert Baillie

Copyright © 2019 by HardPress

Address:
HardPress
8345 NW 66TH ST #2561
MIAMI FL 33166-2626
USA
Email: info@hardpress.net

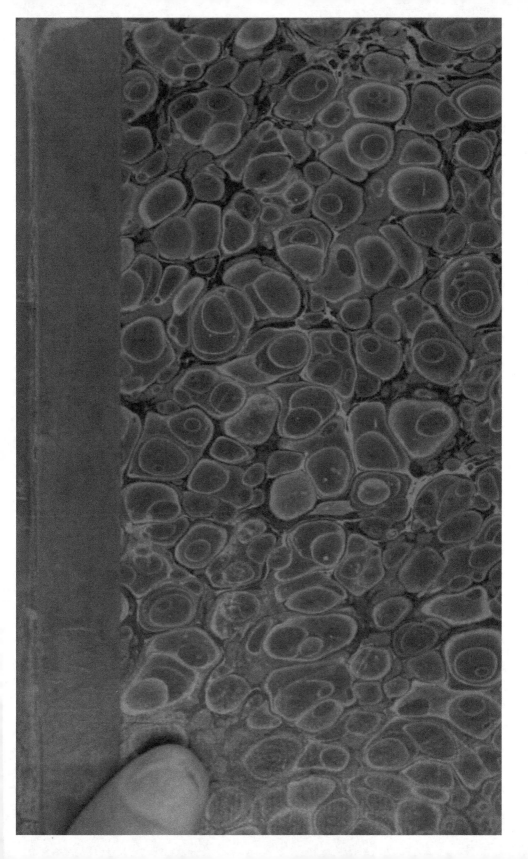

Brit
35 5 - 2

R. 352

BIBLIOTHECA
REGIA
MONACENSIS.

<36626300000018

<36626300000018

Bayer. Staatsbibliothek

LETTERS and JOURNALS,

Written by the deceafed

Mr ROBERT BAILLIE,

Principal of the Univerfity of Glafgow.

Carefully tranfcribed by ROBERT AIKEN.

Containing an impartial account of public tranfactions, Civil, Ecclefiaftic, and Military, both in England and Scotland, from 1637 to 1662; a period, perhaps, the moft remarkable that is to be met with in the Britifh Hiftory.

WITH

An Account of the Author's LIFE, prefixed;

AND

A GLOSSARY, annexed.

VOL. II.

EDINBURGH:

Printed for W. GRAY, Edinburgh; and J. BUCKLAND, and G. KEITH, London.

MDCCLXXV.

Bayerische
Staatsbibliothek
MÜNCHEN

LETTERS and JOURNALS

WRITTEN BY

Principal ROBERT BAILLIE.

50. *To Mr William Spang.*   *April* 19. 1644.

Reverend and Dear Cousin,

Yours of the 12th of this instant this day I received, whereby I perceive you had not received what I had written with the last post. That any of the assembly have written for Mr Durie, is more than I know; that the synod did never write for him, or any man else, I know assuredly; for smaller actions exceed their power. His letter to the synod I heard read with no great regard; for it favoured of somewhat. If he be pleased to come over to Oxford, he may resolve to be taken while he lives by us all here for a malignant; and if he should come to us with the least tincture of Episcopacy, or liturgick learning, he would not be welcome to any I know. As you love the man, persuade him to stay at this time where he is: he cannot be so well or honourably employed any where I know. As for Dr Forbes, you have done very well, in my mind, who have not given him your pulpit. As you desire not to be mistaken by too many, meddle not with him, or any who flee from our church-censure. I know there are sundry exceptions against that man, and that the last general assembly gave order to enter in process against him. No man did more for him in the assembly of Aberdeen than I; but it is my earnest advice to you, to send him away, and not to engage yourself in any of his affairs.

Our affairs here go very strangely. The disaster at Newark cast us much down; the victory at Winchester puts us as far up. We hoped Sir William Waller would shortly regain all the north; we feared Prince Rupert would make havock in my Lord Manchester's associations: but in both we were clean difappointed. Prince Rupert made a hafty march to Shrewfbury; Sir William Waller's forces melted quickly to a poor handful; the Londoners, and others, as is their mifkent cuftom, after a piece of fervice, get home: fo that Waller being weaker than the quickly-rallied forces of the enemy, were forced to retire without the conqueft of one foot of ground. We are exceeding fad and afhamed that our army, fo much talked of, has done as yet nothing at all. What can be the reafon of it we cannot guefs, only we think, that God, to humble our pride, and to difappoint the carnal confidence of our friends, has not yet been pleafed to af- fift them. Thefe bygone days there, has been the matter of our fhame and fear. We were begun to think, it was the General's wifdom, having Sunderland, a port open by fea, and having quartered by eaft and fouth to Durham, whereby he was provided in plenty of victuals and forage, to defeat the enemy without ftroke of fword. In this hope we were confirmed, when the other news we heard of the great victory of Sir Thomas Fairfax and Meldrum at Selby, which made our friends abfolutely mafters of the fields in Yorkfhire, and enabled them, without impedi- ment, to follow their inftructions, of going down to join with our army, or fall on Newcaftle's back. This put us in hopes quickly to be conquerors of all the north. Only this was our grief, that little honour would come to our army, which had fo long done fo little. Ungrate people did not confider that our lying there did keep off that great and very con- fiderable army of Newcaftle, who being free of us, had, without doubt, not only kept Fairfax in his old holes, but had, in all likelihood, been long ago at the gates of London. However, we were glad that God fhould end the work, how fmall a part foever we fhould have in the praife. But behold we have other thoughts this day put in our heads: Prince Rupert, we are advertifed, has gathered together an army of 12,000 men; and that, with all fpeed, he is marching northward to join with Newcaftle, and to crufh Fairfax in his way, that all together may thunder on our army. We are looking up to God. This, if he help not, may wrack us. We have fent to Manchefter to follow. We hope our army will be advertifed, that they may fight before Prince Rupert come. All here thought Prince Rupert would have come hitherward; but the fa- tal lazinefs of all, and treachery of the faction here, makes them all fecure at Oxford, and mifregard our threats.

threats. This day was appointed a rendezvous at Aylesbury for our forces, more than 30,000, to go seek the King where-ever he be. Oxford was said to prepare for a siege; the Queen and the children to be in the way to Bristol, and thence to Ireland or France: but not a man have we in readiness; Waller's army is molten away; Manchester's are mostly north; the General will be recruiting till doomsday; the city is on their new motions of levying, on their pay, 20,000 foot: but while these conceits are in daily debate, the enemy is in action. Your good ambassadors have so encouraged and strengthened the potent faction in both houses, and in the city, that we must be miserably spending all our thoughts and time in drawing up articles of peace, while the enemy is encompassing us for our ruin. It is said that a peace to the King's mind is drawn up already in private, which we must either be persuaded or forced to accept. Great jealousies here. One favourable blow in the north would make both the open and secret malignants despair, and take our too merciful conditions. They say the Queen's child is dead in her belly, and that she takes, now and then, convulsions of a palsy.

Our assembly at last has perfected ordination, both in the doctrinal and directory parts. I think, to-morrow, they shall present it to the Houses. It has cost us much labour, and above twenty long sessions. I hope it shall do good, and over all this land shall erect presently an association of ministers to ordain. Our presbytery shall shortly follow. The Independents are resolved yet to give in their reasons against us, and that will be the beginning of an open schism. Likely, after that, we will be forced to deal with them as open enemies. They have been here most unhappy instruments, the principal, if not the sole causes, why the parliament were so long in calling an assembly, and when it was called, why nothing in a whole year could be gotten concluded. In the mean time they, over all the land, are making up a faction to their own way, the far most part whereof is fallen off to Anabaptism and Antinomianism. Sundry also worse, if worse needs be: the mortality of the soul, the denial of angels and devils, and cast off all sacraments, and many blasphemous things. All these are from New England, where divers are in irons for their blasphemies, condemned to perpetual slavery, and well near by a few votes it went

for

for the life. They proclaim their fears of the rigours of prefbytery. Poffibly they are confcious of their unfufferable tenets, and certainly they know their own rigour againft the Prefbyterians. In all New England, no liberty of living for a Prefbyterian. Whoever there, were they angels for life and doctrine, will effay to fet up a different way from them, fhall be fure of prefent banifhment. Be diligent, we befeech you, with your fynod. While I am writing this, praife to God for evermore, a meffenger comes to us from our army, fhewing, that on Friday night the enemy hearing of Fairfax's victory, marched away from Durham towards the Tyfe ; that Saturday and Sunday we were following, and were within three miles of them, refolving to follow where-ever they went. The great God be with us. I muft clofe, for the poft is going.

51. *For Mr William Spang.*   *April 25. 1644.*

Reverend and Dear Coufin,

Yours of the 18th I received. You have fome of mine fince. The employments of Mr C. was procured by Mr Strickland's letters, calling for him oft by name ; befides, he is of very good efteem with us all ; neither had we any ready of fuch truft. The books you wrote for you fhall have all fhortly, and what more you defire. I wifh all odds in our counts were evened ; for I am too long behind ; wherefore I pray you write hither for what you pleafe. We are all very fenfible of your prudent diligence ; by all means go on with your divines for their anfwer. I wifh thefe whom you have engaged in Zealand were put on to engage with themfelves the divines of the other provinces, efpecially the prefbytery of Leyden, alfo Rivet and Voetius. There is great need ; for this is a very wavering and fickle people. Write what they pleafe againft bifhops and ceremonies *obiter,* for our confirmation ; for thefe are are now out of the hearts of all here almoft : but above all, and in earneft, let them exhort to be watchful againft anarchical fchifms, and the heretics of Antinomians and Anabaptifts. Thefe three come together cordially againft all the Reformed churches, and increafe fo much in number and boldnefs, as eafily they would carry all here to a lamentable confufion, if the fear

of

of our armies did not keep them in order; and, as it is, many fear they shall do much, if God prevent it not. We have given in to the parliament our conclusions anent ordination; whereupon, I think, we have spent above forty long sessions. To prevent a present rupture with the Independents, we were content not to give in our propositions of presbyteries and congregations, that we might not necessitate them to give in their remonstrance against our conclusions, which they are peremptor to do when we come on that matter. We judged it also convenient to delay till we had gone through the whole matters of the presbyteries and synods; to send them up rather in their full strength than by pieces; also we suffered ourselves to be persuaded to eschew that rupture at this time, when it were so dangerous for their bruckle state. The Independents having so managed their affairs, that of the officers and soldiers in Manchester's army, certainly also in the General's, and, as I hear, in Waller's likewise, more than the two parts are for them, and these of the far most resolute and confident men for the parliament-party. Judge ye if we had not need of our friends help. I with we had letters by some of your friends means from Switzerland and Geneva; and however the French divines dare not keep publick correspondence, and I hear the chief of them are like some of yours, so much courtiers, that they will not help us in the half they dare and might, policy and prudence so far keeps down their charity and zeal; yet I think some of the ministers of Paris, and their professors, if they were dealt with by some of your friends, might, in private letters, either to some here, or some with you, write so much of their mind in this publick cause of church-government, as might contribute to the encouragement of this fainting and weak-hearted people. In any letters that come here, I wish they may be sparing of the point of the magistrate; also in the enlarging of the power of particular congregations. I wish they might speak home to that you assure is their practice, of giving ordination only to the classes, and excommunication, at least for regulating of the process; albeit we make the chief parts of the process to be led before the classes, and gives them the power of the decree; for we count it a *musa communis*, and of so high a consequence as can be, to cut off a member, not from one congregation only, but the whole church and body of Christ. Our brethren here

are

are fo peremptor, that they will by no means tie themfelves
fo much as to advife any thing in the whole procefs with
the claffes; only when they have fentenced, if they be required, they will give an account to any whom they have
offended.   We have got letters this day from our army at
Wetherby.   The Marquis of Newcaftle ftole away from
Durham; we followed fo faft as we could.   He is now
with all his remaining forces, in York, and about it.   We
and Fairfax are joined, and lie about York, at fome diftance, at Selby, Wetherby, Tadcafter, &c.   Prince Rupert is expected, and Manchefter on his back.   Likely
there muft be blood fhed there, except God, without
blood, (as hitherto we have fhed very little, thanks to
God), make them melt away.   Waller could make no
ufe of his victory; for prefently the London foot would
home.   The General alfo called back his horfe.   The e-
nemy incontinent drew up fo ftrong, that Sir William was
forced to give ground, and return to Farnham.   Jealoufy
and lazinefs, and poffibly correfpondence with Oxford,
for all our great words to keep a general rendezvous on
Friday the 19th, makes that yet we are not near ready to
march.   We have, through your ambaffadors, and the
friends of Oxford among us their importunity, been more
fharply debating propofitions of peace than thinking of
war.   Yet as all other our enemies plots, fo haply this
fhall turn to our good: for that which feems was intended for divifion of the nations, and of the one Houfe from
the other, and of the Houfe of Commons among themfelves, and the city among themfelves, I hope fhall, before all be done, unite them all the more firmly; for we
are all like to agree to ftand to fuch articles of peace as
fhall give the contrivers of the motion fmall advantage.
The Queen is towards Briftol.   The reports of her health
are various.   Proclamations from the King call for the
victuals of the neighbouring counties to Oxford, or threat-
ens fire.

ROBERT BAILLIE.

London, April 26.

52. *To Mr David Dickfon.   April* 29. 1644.

Reverend and Dear Brother,
YOURS, in the beginning of April, we received yefternight.

hight. Your letters and memory, believe it, are very sweet to all here. I hope before this you have received many of mine since the 18th of February. You have here the doubles of my letters to Mr William Spang, and his to me. These are to yourself, Mr Robert, and Mr G. Young; also the paper the synod gave in to the parliament. Of this no copies are yet come out; so keep it to yourself alone. Disperse the rest as you think fit. For publick news that any may see, I have sent you printed papers to spare my writing. The most in the diurnal and intelligences are true. Aulicus and Britannicus are for jests only, and not worth the reading. You have in my wife's letter a paper for foreign news. I wrote to you my mind anent the motion of our coming down to the general assembly. I am still of that mind, and my Lord Wariston thinks so with me; yea, it is all our minds that Mr Henderson cannot be spared; for the matter of both government and directory, especially in the points of prayer, sacraments, preaching, which we have given in already; the catechism, which is almost ready, and the other parts also, will shortly be in such a maturity, that about the midst and end of May it is like our work shall be hottest. Mr Henderson's absence for a little might not only retard, but also put matters so far wrong, as would not in haste be gotten righted. For any other of us to come down to the assembly, we conceive, were not only very needless, but in some respects, which I will not write, disadvantageous to affairs here and there both; yet if you on the place think fit to send for any or all of us, we are all willing and ready to obey your calls. However, in this long anarchy, the sectaries and hereticks increase marvellously; yet we are hopeful, if God might help us, to have our presbyteries erected, as we expect shortly to have them, and get the chief of the Independents to join with us in our practical conclusions, as we are labouring much for it, and are not yet out of hope, we trust, to win about all the rest of these wild and enormous people. However, for the time, the confusions about religion are very great, and remediless. There were many bickerings, and fear of breaking, about the articles of peace; but, thanks to God, I hope that fear be past. The committee of both kingdoms has unanimously agreed the articles, which my Lord Wariston, for the far most part, drew up. I think he may come down with them himself one of these days, to

be

be agreed to by you there. Upon your first hearing of his coming to Edinburgh, make haste to be at him, for he cannot stay. The articles are such as doubtless the King will scorn, till his wicked council and party be broken, which, by God's help, will shortly be. Prince Rupert, so far as yet we hear, is to come south to join with the rest about Oxford. We hope ere long to be on the fields with a great army; Essex, Waller, and Manchester. In the mean time, Lesly and Fairfax, we hope in God, shall get York; and then we conceive the rest will faint and give over. The storm which long has been threatening you from Montrose and the rest in the south, Huntly, and these in the north, are like to break very seasonably. I hope it shall do no harm but to the contrivers. We look for a merciful and glorious end of all these troubles. I pray you remember my love and best affections to all our scholars, and to these most who give you greatest satisfaction. All of them, who will be gracious and learned, are likely to be well provided, if once we had peace. ——— The Lord be with you,

    Your Brother,   ROBERT BAILLIE.

53. *For my Lord Eglinton.* *April* 30. 1644.

My very good Lord,

    I am much refreshed to hear of your Lordship's good health in so hard and laborious services. I do oft joy to hear of your Lordship's personal valour and success. I pray God preserve your Lordship from all hurt. All our worldly hopes depend on the happiness of that your army. You are every day near the hearts of all the godly here. Next to the salvation of our souls, we wish that army prosperity. We esteem our lives and estates, and, which is more dear to us, our religion and liberties, both ours and the posterity's in all the three kingdoms, to be at this time in your hands. We trust in the goodness of our God, that he will furnish you with so much grace, wisdom, and courage, that you shall make to us, and after ages, a very good account of these greatest and most precious jewels which you now carry on the points of your swords. We are very hopeful here, that when God gives you a prosperous day against York, it shall be a real defeating of all the enemies both before and behind you. For occurrences here, I know your Lordship in that com-

    2   mittee

mittee receives them from much better and more legible hands than mine; only I do here present your Lordship with a copy of my poor sermon, and with my very hearty service; for well it becomes me, all the days of my life, to remain, your Lordship's very affectionate servant,

ROBERT BAILLIE.

54. To Mr William Spang. May 3. 1644.

Reverend and Dear Cousin,

Yours of the 18th of April I received. You had two of me since, and this is the third; so you are much in my debt; but I most freely forgive you. For that letter of your synod, a better turn could not have been done to us. It was read with very good acceptance, and a committee is appointed, not only to translate, and transmit it to the Houses, as the former, but to think of an answer; which, according to their woeful way, cannot be expected for some months. Doubtless the point of the magistrate will hinder the printing of it here; but we wish it were printed there, and sent over, with the former of Wallachren's. No man here can get the copy of either. We have printed our letter to you both in Latin and English, why should not you do the like with yours to us? also in your Walachren letter, if I remember, you profess your putting in print your former letter to the synod; certainly there is much more use of these two latter. What I wrote, of engaging your other provinces, professors, and other churches, you will do what you may herein. I sent to you by Thomas Cunningham my sermon before; but receive now another; also three of Goodwin's pieces, one at 5 s. another at 1 s. 4 d. a third at 1 s. 6 d. I cannot help the extraordinary dearth. They say, the great sum which the author puts on his copy is the cause of it. Also Huet on Daniel, at 2 s. 10 d. and a wicked piece, which one of the Independents wrote against D. Stuart, at 6 d. In all 11 s. 4 d. For the folio Bible, as yet I have not got any to my mind. I hear you may have better and cheaper there; so I would send none till you advertised again. Mr Samuel has sent you one of his sermons, and one of his great books which came out the other day; also other two to Voetius and Mr Forbes at Delft. Mr George also sends you his sermon. All these are bound up together, and delivered to Mr Teren's man, who undertook to get all safe to you what I sent him. I cannot tell how things go here. If God do not this work, it will perish of itself without an enemy. Extreme inlack of money for all occasions, which yet daily are many and great; a mighty party in the Houses, in the city, and every where, who mind their own things, and cause such distrusts, and fears of treachery, as are formidable; in all the armies great divisions, and extreme want of pay. When we have any truce with the Independents anent our presbytery, we fall in new wars with others. For our sessions, a great party in the synod, for fear of ruling elders, and in opposition to Independency, will have no ecclesiastick court at all, but one presbytery for all the congregations within its bounds. I cannot tell you our daily perplexities; yet we must trust in God, and not faint, for all the vexation which passes from far and near on all hands.

Our army, of 14,000 foot and 2000 horse at least, are joined with Fairfax his 2000 horse and 4000 of foot: they are about York on all quarters near the town. Before they came so near, Newcastle sent out all his horse, who are followed by all ours; but it is thought we will let them be gone. The design is suspected to go towards Shrewsbury to join with Prince Rupert, that all may come together to relieve the siege; but this we do no much regard. Albeit Manchester, with good 8000 or 9000, is in Lincoln to wait on these. But our greatest difficulty is want. No penny have we got since we came to England, except it have been a fortnight's pay at most. The country gives no victual; our discipline hinders the taking of it. The soldiers cloaths are worn; their extremity is great. Sundry think it was not well advised, that they staid not till they had taken Durham and Newcastle; yet we hope all shall turn to the best. Argyle, I hope, by this has gotten order of Huntly, and Callendar of Montrose; so I hope both shortly shall come to Newcastle as they purpose, and clear the north of England; while Lesly, after York is gotten, may go over Trent. My Lord Wariston is gone to Scotland with the articles of peace, whereto the committee of both kingdoms hath unanimously agreed, and transmitted them to the Houses. I am in haste. The Lord help us, and be with you.

55. *To Mr Robert Ramfay.   May 9. 1644.*

Reverend and Dear Brother,

I have got none from you fince February 11. I faw a
fhort one of Mr David's, without date, before you went
to the provincial. Since that, I think, he has fundry from
me long enough. You may fee our affairs in the papers.
The moft is true, and all are the common reports here.
The infide of our affairs, experience of God's carrying of this caufe from the beginning to this day, and ever
coming in with his feen and immediate help, make us that
we dare not but be confident of a happy iffue ; but were it
not for our hope in God, we oft would be put to black
thoughts, when we behold the carriage and difpofitions of
men. This people are fo divided, and fubdivided, in their
judgements and practice, that if ever either their church
or ftate fettle, it is God's miraculous mercy. Had not
God raifed our nation to join with all our ftrength, long
ere this, without all doubt, they had been fwallowed up
by their enemies ; yea, they had, without the hand of an e-
nemy, by their own broken and languid proceedings, been
loft irrecoverably ; and as yet it ftands, the dangers are
exceeding great.

For our affembly-matters, we are daily perplexed ; not
only we make no progrefs, and are far from the fight of
any appearance of an end, but alfo matters oft in hazard
of mifcarriage. The Independents, fo far as yet we can
fee, are peremptory for a fchifm ; and their party is very
ftrong and growing, efpecially in the army. The leading
men in the affembly are much at this time divided about
the queftions in hand, of the power of congregations and
fynods. Some of them would give nothing to congregations, denying peremptorily all example, precept, or reafon, for a congregational elderfhip ; others, and many
more, are wilful to give to congregational elderfhip all
and entire power of ordination, excommunication, and
all. Had not God fent Mr Henderfon, Mr Rutherford,
and Mr Gillefpie among them, I fee not that ever they
could agree on any fettled government. We expect the
favour of God to help us over the rocks, and through
the ftorms, in the midft whereof we fail at this hour.
The anfwer and return of your prayers we oft feel and

acknowledge.

acknowledge. All our company, bleſſed be God, have had perfect health, good courage, and hearty unanimity, in all things; great credit and reputation; ſenſible aſſiſtance in every thing, and hitherto very good ſucceſs, to all our motions, either for church or ſtate; ſo that we are hopeful to wreſtle through the preſent difficulties, as we have done many before, by the help of the prayers of God's people among you. The humour of this people is very various, and inclinable to ſingularities, to differ from all the world, and one from another, and ſhortly from themſelves. No people had ſo much need of a preſbytery. The affairs of the ſtate, marvel not that I and others write oft ſo diverſely of them; for there are many contrary and divers tides into them. We are ſtill feared that the King come, and ſet himſelf down in the parliament. If he had done ſo this twelvemonth bygone, or yet would, it would put our affairs in the greateſt hazard of confuſion. To croſs that dangerous deſign of the mighty faction among us, the engine of the articles of peace is turned on the face of the authors, to our great advantage. We have got ſuch articles paſſed the committee of both kingdoms, and tranſmitted to both Houſes, as Wariſton has brought down. They are of our own framing. Nine of the greateſt are conſented to by the Commons, and the reſt will ſhortly paſs, I truſt. Yeſterday the whole Houſe went to the Lords for a conference, and required the paſſing of three ordinances, which long had lien by. 1. The continuance of the committe of both kingdoms for other three months. That committee is the great bulwark againſt the faction. The firſt framing of it was over their heads. It has been their greateſt eye-ſore. It expires the morn. They thought either to hinder the renewing of the ordinance, or to add unto it ſuch other members of both Houſes, of their mind, as might have overſwayed the better party and us; but we hope this union of the Commons will counteract that plot. 2. The continuance of Mancheſter's ordinance for other three months; that Mancheſter ſhould have ſo many counties under him. It was the faction's grief; it made him a greater and better paid army than the General's. It and Waller's army were their great ſtrength, if any treachery had been uſed by any others; for unhappy, and, I hope, ungrounded jealouſies here, trouble all. However, it was the deſign of ſome to have Mancheſter and Waller's ordinance altered. The 3d was,

for

for the excluding of thefe from the Houfes that returned from Oxford. Sundry of them are here already, as Holland, Bedford, Clare, Kingfton, Trennant, and Conway; and many more are coming It was feared their errand was not good. To preveen the danger of their counfels, the Commons prefs they may not be readmitted to their places in hafte. An anfwer this day is expected from the Lords. The General one of thefe days will march out. He and Waller joined will have greater forces than any the King can oppofe in thefe bounds. The Queen is at Exeter, very big. It is feared the flip over to France. The wars of Italy are certainly ended. The treaty of Munfter at laft is begun. Sundry think, that either a peace, or a truce, is like to be taken between France and Spain. If this be, our condition is in a horrible hazard, if quickly we come not to an end of our bufinefs. Manchefter, with a pretty good army, of 8000 or 9000, has taken Lincoln by force, and fo could not hinder the plunder of it. We have ftraitly beleagured York. On the event of that fiege, the affairs both of this church and kingdom doth much depend. To-morrow there will be fhipped L. 20,000 Sterling for our army, and the next week L. 16,000 for Ireland; and more at once will follow. We truft God will arife, and do fomewhat by our Scots army. We are afflicted, that after fo long time we have gotten no hit of our enemy; we hope God will put away that fhame. Waller, Manchefter, Fairfax, and all get victories; but Lefly, from whom all was expected, as yet has had his hands bound. God, we hope, will loofe them, and fend us matter of praife; but blefled be his name that we are in fo good a pofture, and the enemy in fo bad, that without ftrokes we can overcome. It is beft. I muft end; for I am in hafte. My fervice to all who mind the caufe of God in hand, and to no other. Thefe for yourfelf, Mr David, and Mr George Young.

　　Your Brother,

ROBERT BAILLIE.

56. *Memorandum to Mr Buchanan.*

I conceive it very expedient, that you write to fome of the minifters of Paris, Geneva, and Bern, the true eftate of our affairs, how that a mighty faction is arifen, to prefer

fer liberty of confcience for all fects, at leaft a freedom for Morellius's popular government of the church; that the Scots, and moft of the fynod and parliament, are for the eftablifhing the government by fynods and claffes. It would encourage them much, if the divines of Geneva and Switzerland would, in their anfwers to the fynod's letter, as the divines of Zealand have done in their letter, and the divines of Heffe alfo, exhort the fynod at fome length, and in earneft, to beware of that pernicious liberty of all fects, in particular thofe who are enemies to the difcipline of all the Reformed. There is a golden occafion in hand, if improved, to get England conform in worfhip and government to the reft of the Reformed. If nothing dare be written in publick by the French, fee if they will write their mind, for our encouragement, to any private friend here, or in Holland. You would write for the fame purpofe to Moulin in Sedan, and Spanheim in Leyden. It were good, if they write, that their letters were conceived in the greateft names they could procure; the theologie of Bern would get a letter from the Switzerland church, thefe of Geneva from their whole ecclefiaftick claffes, Moulin from the univerfity of Sedan, and Spanheim from the univerfity of Leyden. It were not ill, that in all their letters they congratulated the abolition of Epifcopacy and Popifh ceremonies, and exhorted to fet up quickly the government of Chrift; that fo long an anarchy as has been here, is the mother of herefies, and fchifms, and many more evils.

57. *To Mr William Spang.*

Dear Coufin,

I wrote not to you the laft Friday; for what I wrote with your poft the three Fridays preceeding, I know not yet whether you have received them; neither dare I write any more by the poft, while I find you receive them unbroken up. I fent to you the Hooker you wrote for, and fome other. The letter of your claffes of Zealand, I fear it fhall here be drained, as well as that of Wallachren, becaufe the Independents, on the occafion of the claufe of the magiftrate, work, by their too many friends, on the parliament to fupprefs it. You would do well to caufe print it there, and fend over a number of copies
of

of it here : you did so with your other letter the last year;
and the synod has caused print, in Latin and English,
their letter to you ; who can justly offend, if you do so,
with your letter in answer ? I approve exceedingly well of
Apollonius's letter, to enquire of the Independents themselves their judgements in three heads he proposes. The
two books which I have sent you last, will inform him
more of their mind. Little D. Homes, the author of the
Cool Conference, M. S. against A. S. is John Goodwin of
Colman-street. He names you expresſly, and profeſſes to
cenſure the letter of Zealand. He is a bitter enemy to
preſbytery, and is openly for a full liberty of conſcience
to all ſects, even Turks, Jews, Papiſts, and all to be
more openly tolerate than with you. This way is very
pleaſant to many here. We are much obliged to that excellent divine Apollonius. We truſt he will, with all
diligence, go on in his avowed intention : there is nothing wherein he can do better ſervice to God and the
Reformed churches. To underſtand them better, I ſend
you herewith other two pieces. That faction increaſes
mightily in number, hopes, and pride; but if it pleaſe
God to give us good news from York, we will tell them
more of our mind. Our opinion of their piety and inge-
nuity is much diminiſhed, by that we ſee and hear daily
from the beſt of them. It is marvelled, that the reſt of
your provinces and profeſſors will not follow the gracious
and charitable example of Zealand. Shall they ſee both
the church and ſtate of all theſe three kingdoms periſh,
and ſtand aloof without the leaſt aſſiſtance by the ſtretch
of their pen, when they are called to it by our lamentable letters, and the gracious example of their compaſſionate brethren ? See how they will be anſwerable for
ſuch an apathy in ſo neceſſary a time. Mr Forbes, in
Delft, has ſent us over, in writ, a very pretty piece againſt
the Apologetick. I like it very well, I wiſh it were in
print. It is good you keep correſpondence with that
young man, and acquaint him with all you know in this
ſubject. We and Fairfax, with 20,000 horſe and foot,
are lying about York. Mancheſter, with more than 8000,
is in Lincoln. Prince Rupert, with all he can make, is
drawing near Newark. It is expected ſhortly, that thereabout the fatal blow will be given. Eſſex and Waller are
going out at laſt, they ſay, to-morrow, with 19,000 betwixt them. However, Prince Maurice, Ruthven, and
                                        Hopeton,

Hopeton, can make no power to withstand; yet we expect small action in these quarters. Montrose's foolish brava-do is turned to nothing. The gentlemen of Teviotdale, before Callendar drew near with the army, chased him in to Carslile, with the loss of most of his cannon. Huntly, with some 3000 men, run over the fields as far as Mont-rose; but we hope shortly it shall be otherwise. On Fri-day, after a week's debate, we carried, albeit hardly, that no single congregation had the power of ordination. To-morrow we begin to debate if they have any right of ex-communication. We gave in, long ago, a paper to the great committee, wherein we asserted a congregational el-dership, for governing the private affairs of the congrega-tion, from the 18th of Matthew. Mr David Calderwood, in his letter to us, has censured us grievously for so doing; shewing us, that our books of discipline admit of no pres-bytery or eldership but one; that we put ourselves in ha-zard to be forced to give excommunication, and so entire government, to congregations, which is a great step to In-dependency. Mr Henderson acknowledges this: and we are in a peck of troubles with it. In many things we had need of the prayers of our friends.

58. *Publick Letter.* May 14. 1644.

Since my last, the 9th of this instant, our affairs here go as you may see in the two inclosed diurnals, and busi-ness abroad as you may see in the paper. Yesternight Essex went out to his army; Waller will go to-morrow: they will be pretty strong. There is great fear at Oxford. Small hope of the relieving York, or saving any part of the north, from the hands of the Scots. Their hopes in force are near an end; they have therefore returned to their old ways of treacherous plotting. A great word here of the King's coming hither, and putting all in the will of his parliament; being, as is feared, confident of the one house, and a great part of the other, and of many in the city. This now is our greatest fear; and care, to provide for it: we hope the discovery shall prove the preventing of it. We expect daily the rendering of York. This day L. 20,000 Sterling is shipped for our army. We hope, before eight days end, to have near as much ship-ped for Carrickfergus. In our publick letter to the general affembly, fince we are commanded, all of us, to ftay ftill, we fhall give an account how the affairs of our fynod go. The greateft things, both in church and ftate, are prefently in hand. O if we had humbled hearts to deal earneftly with God, who hath granted us fo much of our defires, and hath put us in fo fair a way fhortly to obtain all, albeit in fo wife a difpenfation as to mix our hopes with very great dangers, that he may ftill be fled to and depended on. We keep a faft in the affembly on Friday next, for all the armies, and the great affairs which in that fynod are prefently in hand. We hope our Father will hear and comfort us. The Queen is at Exeter ; it is thought fhe can hardly be delivered ; it is fufpected fhe will go to France. Much of Wales is rifen for the parliament. A few days may produce great things. We had much need, and confidently we expect the help of your prayers to our very great and difficult employment. All our company, bleffed be God, are in health and chearfulnefs, feeling fenfibly, in God's continual affiftance, the anfwer of your prayers.

59. *Poftfcript to Mr Spang's Letter. May 17.*

While I had written thus far, yours of the 3d of May comes to my hand, fo I will venture to fend this yet by the poft. Apollonius's letter and queftions I had gotten before, by another fecret means. I fear thefe men fhall either not write, or delay too long, or write obfcurely ; for, as I conceive, they are not at a point, in their own mind, as yet, what to ftand at. Among themfelves are fundry differences, which time will bring out. They profefs to differ from thefe of England ; but who knows wherein ? The main feems to be in liberty of confcience ; for both feem to avow the divine right of fynods for confulting, albeit the deftroying of prefbyteries claffical ; for a prefbytery to them is our feffion, and our prefbytery is their fynod. Take herewith another of their apologies : it is old, namelefs, and as yet I have not read it ; only they in New England are more ftrict and rigid than we, or any church, to fupprefs, by the power of the magiftrate, all who are not of their way, to banifhment ordinarly, and prefently even to death lately, or perpetual flavery ; for one Jortin, fometime a famous citizen

here, for piety, having taught a number in New England to cast off the word and sacrament, and deny angels and devils, and teach a gross kind of union with Christ, in this life, by force of arms was brought to New Boston, and there, with ten of the chief of his followers, by the civil court was decerned perpetual slaves; but the votes of many were for their execution. They lie in irons, though gentlemen; and out of their prison write to the Admiral here, to deal with the parliament for their deliverance. The Independents here, finding they have not the magistrate so obsequious as in New England, turn their pens, as you will see in MS, to take from the magistrate all power of taking any coercive order with the vilest hereticks. Not only they praise your magistrate, who for policy gives some secret tolerance to divers religions, wherein, as I conceive, your divines preach against them as great sinners; but avow, that by God's command, the magistrate is discharged to put the least discourtesy on any man, Jew, Turk, Papist, Socinian, or whatever, for his religion. I wish Apollonius considered this well. The five he writes to will not say this; but M. S. is of as great authority here as any of them. Your course of engaging the other provinces is very good. I send this inclosed to a friend here, (vide p. 13.), who is well acquainted in Paris, Bern, Leyden, Sedan, and Geneva, who accordingly has written to all these five places for their assistance in the common cause. My correspondence with you is so secret as may be. Some of them suspect somewhat of you; but know little: however, they must be content that all the Reformed, whom they openly avow to oppugn, should declare what sense they have of their wounds and danger from them. I long for Morellius and Sadael, also if by Mr Paget, or any of your friends at Amsterdam, you could find any of the writs of Brown, the first sectary; for however I have used all possible diligence, yet cannot I find any of that man's writs here: they would, I conceive, be very useful to me. This day was the best that I have seen since I came to England. General Essex, when he went out, sent to the assembly, to intreat, that a day of fasting might be kept for him. We appoint, this day, four of our number to preach and pray at Christ's church; also, taking the occasion, we thought it meet to be humbled in the assembly, so we spent from nine to five very graciously. After D. Twisse had begun
with

with a brief prayer, Mr Marshall prayed large two hours, most divinely, confessing the sins of the members of the assembly, in a wonderful, pathetick, and prudent way. After, Mr Arrowsmith preached an hour; then a psalm; thereafter Mr Vines prayed near two hours, and Mr Palmer preached an hour, and Mr Seaman prayed near two hours, then a psalm; after Mr Henderson brought them to a sweet conference of the heat confessed in the assembly, and other seen faults, to be remedied, and the conveniency to preach against all sects, especially Anabaptists and Antinomians. Dr Twisse closed with a short prayer and blessing. God was so evidently in all this exercise, that we expect certainly a blessing both in our matter of the assembly and whole kingdom. They have sallied out of York, once or twice; but are beaten in with loss. Callendar, with 8000 or 10,000, is lying about Carlisle. We have 4000 or 5000 about Newcastle. David Lesly, with the most of our Fairfax and Manchester's horse, are about Nottingham. We hear nothing of Prince Rupert. Waller is out with 8000 or 9000 men: Essex with ten. The King with his forces are near. You shall hear more with the next; the post can stay no longer. Farewell.

    Your Cousin,

                  ROBERT BAILLIE.

    Our Admiral has taken a ship with L. 7000, and some thousand of arms, coming from you. No more notice here of your ambassadors. Our affairs here, blessed be God, are in an excellent posture every where. When we settle, your estates cannot hope to get any thanks. We might have perished, and they looked on us without any help. God will not be mocked.

     60. *For Mr Robert Blair.* *May* 19. 1644.

Reverend and Dear Brother,

    THE condition of our affairs here you will see in our publick letters. This is only a postscript which I was desired to write to you. We are advertised, that much more than the most part of my Lord Manchester's army are seduced to Independency, and very many of them have added either Anabaptism or Antinomianism, or both. We hear that their horse and yours are conjoined, and that

             C 2   occasions

occasions may fall out wherein more of them may join to you. We all conceive, that our silly simple lads are in great danger to be infected by their company; and if that pest enter in our army, we fear it may spread. We remember, that in our former expedition, on far less occasion than now is apparent, some of our soldiers were leavened, and at their return were the authors of trouble in divers parts of our land. We earnestly intreat you and Mr R. Douglas to advise of the most prudent and safe ways of preveening the danger of this evil; which we all apprehend to be very great, except God bless you our brethren there with wisdom and zeal to preveen the beginnings. Praying for the help of God to you in this particular, and all things else, I rest, Your loving brother,

ROBERT BAILLIE.

61. *To Mr William Spang.* May 31. 1644.

Cousin,

YOURS of the 3d of May, and that inclosed, I received yesternight. The books I sent with Mr Garet, the young man with whom Thomas Cunningham lay, by whom I send all my letters. As for the synod's acceptance of your Zealand letter, I assure you, after it was read, Mr Calandrin was called in, and it was solemnly declared to him, by the prolocutor, how thankfully the assembly took it, and how much they were obliged for it. As for returning an answer, they have no power to write one line to any soul, but as the parliament directs; neither may they importune the parliament for warrants to keep foreign correspendence. With what art and diligence that general one to all the churches was gotten, I know. You know this is no proper assembly, but a meeting called by the parliament to advise them in what things they are asked; so their not answering comes on no neglect I know very well. By all means encourage Apollonius, and whomever else you can, to assist in this common cause: if this season be missed, it will be hardly recovered. The Independents have no considerable power either in the assembly or parliament, or the General or Waller's army; but in the city and country, and Manchester's army, their strength is great and growing; yet by the help of God and our friends, if once we had the assembly at an end, and peace,

peace, we would get them quieted. Since our Friday faft we have made good fpeed in the affembly. Our church-feflions, to which Independents gave all, and their oppo-fites nothing at all, we have got fettled with unanimity in the Scots fafhion. Our great debate, of the power of ex-communication, we have laid afide, and taken in at laft the directory. Already we have paft the draught of all the prayers, reading of fcripture, and finging of pfalms, on the Sabbath-day, *nemine contradicente.* We truft, in one or two feflions, to pafs alfo our draught of preach-ing. If we continue this race, we will amend our for-mer infamous flownefs. Always I can fay little till once we pafs the directory of the Lord's fupper. In the commit-tee we found they were very ftickling; the Independents, and all, love fo well fundry of their Englifh guifes, which we muft have away: however we are in hope of a better fpeed than before. We have not heard from Scotland thefe twenty days. Warifton is down to the parliament, for their confirmation of the articles of peace. The Ox-fordian faction is now quieter here. I told you how it was preft to cite the King to a day for his compearance here; if that had been afked, he had appeared, as now we find. The next was to importune a draught of articles of peace, hoping about thefe to have divided us; but, God be thanked, we have made vantage of that plot alfo, and have agreed unanimoufly to fuch articles as we hope in the end to obtain. The laft was, for the King to come to the parliament without any conditions; for this we were a-fraid, as exceedingly dangerous: but upon the firft fufpi-cion of the defign, fuch courfes were taken as made that plot to evanifh alfo. At the expiring of the three months of the committee of both kingdoms, it was plotted that this committee fhould not be renewed, for it was the humour of the evil party, but that the General himfelf, with his very fufpected counfellors, fhould manage the war; or if it fhould be renewed, they fhould be ordered fo many, and fo fufpect perfons, that it fhould be an en-gine againft us. With this defire we were many days vexed. Let the Houfe of Commons and the city do what they would, if all fhould have gone to all, the Houfe of Lords was peremptor. The committee they would not re-new, without fuch alterations as made it ineffectual for its end: yet, by God's providence, a mean at laft was found, which, nill they will they, forced them to renew it as it

was

was before. I have no time to write it. By the direction of this committee all is guided. Essex and Waller are joined: they have half-chased the King and his army from Reading to Wantage, from Wantage to Abingdon, from Abingdon to Oxford, from this to Islip and Woodstock. We trust shortly to hear of their defeat. Manchester has above 12,000 very well appointed men; quickly he regained all Lincolnshire, laid a bridge over the Trent, has joined with our army. We and Fairfax, with above 20,000 brave men, lie about York: finding it has more victual than we expected, we are preparing to storm it. It is strong in works, has above 6000 armed men, and plenty of ammunition: their confidence is in Prince Rupert's succours. He is an ubiquitary; he holds both York and Oxford in full expectation of his coming daily: yet where he is, and what are his forces, no man can certainly tell. He has been long about Chester, waiting for the performance of the promise of 15,000 Irish. The King has granted them peace, oblivion for bygones, liberty of conscience, and all they desire for time to come. This horrible grant cannot but provoke God and man's indignation. We are grieved to hear nothing of Callendar. Montrose ravages at his pleasure in all Northumberland and Bishoprick: we hope it shall not be so long. I doubt if your book be Sadael against Morellius: I think it is a writ before that debate was heard of. Your translating of your Dutch notes is a purpose myself and many moe here do passionately desire. Diodati, I conceive, is not so good; yet it sells excellently. The stationers here would doubtless cause translate and print your Dutch notes, but they delay for their own gain. They have, on the press, large English notes by some divines. While that impression be sold, that cannot come out this twelvemonth, they will not meddle with the other; but we look for little good from these English notes. The authors were set on by Episcopal men; neither are they of such abilities or disposition as that work would require. If you can find a means to get these Dutch notes printed in English, it would, as I conceive, be a work exceeding profitable; but of this more hereafter. Will neither Rivet nor Voetius follow the example of brave Apollonius? Do your best in this. If men will forsake themselves and us, we will be the more obliged to God. All Glasgow quarrels are to my
joy

joy settled by Mr George Young's coming to them. Farewell.

62. *Publick Letter.* *June* 7. 1644.

WE are much rejoiced to hear, that our malignant countrymen, both in the north and south, are so easily compesced. It is the Lord that watches over that blessed land : a blessed land indeed, if compared with others. The miseries of England you may see in the inclosed print, and these of Denmark and Germany in the writ. Civil war wracks Spain, and lately wracked Italy. It is coming by appearance shortly upon France. The just Lord, who beholds with patience the wickedness of nations, at last arises in fury ; great is his mercy unto sinful Scotland. We trust God will send peace to this land by the ruin of the malignant party. Both the Spanish and French junto's are glad now to change the Oxford dialect, and speak to the Houses at Westminster as a true parliament. On Monday at night the King broke up, with all his horse, and so many of his foot, as he could mount, and, with all speed, made first as it were to Worcester, but thereafter turned towards Bristol. Essex and Waller are on his back : he will not be able to keep the fields. Very like, before he can come to Bristol, the small army he has will be routed. The only considerable force he has is with Prince Rupert in Lancashire, where great and barbarous cruelties are committed. We hope before this a course is taken with that insolent man ; for Meldrum in Manchester will be 4000 or 5000. Denbigh can bring him 3000 or 4000 ; and the armies now about York may spare 10,000 for that service, and keep good 18,000 behind. If God be pleased to bless, there are men enow to break that wicked faction shortly in pieces ; yet it is in God alone that we will put our trust. We hope his gracious Majesty will so much the more be pleased to look upon us, as no remorse at all appears in our enemies ; but horrible cruelty, rapine, and uncleanness, rages among them as much as ever. Their only trust is in the Irish butchers and Spain. France has given them over, and will be glad, if we please, to join with us. The Swedes have sent agents for a strict league with us. The Irish butchers have gotten peace, and all they desire. The Protestant commissioners from Ireland came all hither yesternight from Oxford. For the

encouragement

encouragement of our Irish army, there is gone away in coin L. 30,000 Sterling, and as much will be gotten for them ere it be long. We long much for Callendar's coming to Newcastle; doubtless the parliament here will take burden of his army also.

Our progress in the assembly, albeit slow, yet, blessed be God, is sensible daily. We have passed, but after a world of debate, all the directory which concerns ordinary prayers, reading of the word, singing of psalms, and preaching. Our toil is exceeding great; every day, from eight in the morning till near one, and oft in the afternoon from three to half past six, we are in exercise; only the Saturday free, and that for our Sunday's preaching, when single times any of us does vaik. All of us long much to be at home; but we are all commanded to stay, and attend this great service. Of a truth, to our power, we put spurs to their slow sides. We hope all, ere it be long, shall go according to our hearts desire. The Independents, our great retarders, it is like, shall not vaunt themselves in the end of their oppositions. The most of their party are fallen off to Anabaptism, Antinomianism, and Socinianism; the rest are divided among themselves. One Mr Williams has drawn a great number after him to a singular Independency, denying any true church in the world, and will have every man to serve God by himself alone, without any church at all. This man has made a great and bitter schism lately among the Independents. We hope, if once we had peace, by God's help, with the spirit of meekness mixed with a little justice, to get the most of these erroneous spirits reduced. The ministers of London, near six score, have their weekly meetings. They are all Presbyterians, except Burton, said to be a Brownist; John Goodwin to be a Socinian, and one scrupling Pædobaptism. Some of the Independents are lecturers, but none settled ministers. We had much need of the prayers of God's people there; by that help a very glorious work here may be hastened. All our company are in good health. Oft our spirits are overwearied; but God always by new favours refreshes us. No man here to speak a word either for bishops, or liturgy, or any ceremony. We are thinking of a new work over sea, if this church were settled. The times of Antichrist's fall are approaching. The very outward providence of God seems to be disposing France, Spain, Italy, and Germany; for

I   — the

the receiving of the gospel. When the curtains of the Lord's tabernacle are thus far, and much farther, enlarged, by the means which yet appear not, how shall our mouth be filled with laughter, our tongue with praise, and our hearts with rejoicing! My hearty service to all friends on whose spirit any piece of the burden of this great work doth lie. These on whose heart there lies no weight but of this world, I pity more, but regard less. The French General in Catalonia, after he had supplied the garrison of Lerida, would needs set upon the Spanish army that lay near by. The fruit of this rash and needless enterprise was the total rout of the French army, the strict beleaguring of Lerida, the great hopes of dinging the French out of all Catalonia. Yet the French are using all diligence to make up their loss. The Marshal of Turenne could not get his army made so strong as to relieve the siege of Uberlingen; so at last the Bavarian General Merci has gotten it, and come down nearer Brisack, to besiege other places in Alsatia. The great design of the French is on Gravelling, a sea-port betwixt Calais and Dunkirk. Many doubt of the event of that siege. Sundry rumours of bad designs in Monsieur's counsellors to trouble the state. The Protestents are in dool for Mr Coligni Chatillon his eldest son's untimeous death. The pity is, that his other only son Andelot revolted the other year to Popery; yet they speak now of some hopes of his return to the Protestant religion.

63. *To Mr William Spang.* *June* 9. 1644.

Cousin,

I wrote not with Friday's post. I have got no answer from you of what I wrote before. Lest this bearer should come to you with nothing from me, you have here what I sent the other day to our friends in Scotland. I can add little to it. Upon Tuesday at night, Waller, without order, followed the King. What is become of either party, as yet we know not, which is strange. General Essex was pleased to sit still, and after so long delay to send a small party of horse to make a fashion of pursuing. When he found Waller with all his forces was gone, he sent word to the Houses he would go for the relief of Lyme. This was not well taken; for it was to enter into the heart of

Waller's associations, and really to subvert his army. The Admiral, and the bravery of that poor garrison of Lyme, I hope will have resolved that question; for the other week, on our solemn fast-day, that unhappy prince. Maurice, having assaulted with confidence of carrying of that small town, was beaten off with so huge a slaughter, that they are in no more fear of him. We hear the Admiral has taken three ships, which were carrying from you to Exeter L. 45,000 Sterling. If it be so, it is a good prize. Manchester, with all his forces, have lien down before York. On Wednesday last they drew near the walls. They within put all the suburbs in a fire. We were favoured by the wind to quench it. We are now within pistol-shot of the walls, and are making ready to storm it; for they have much more victuals within than was thought. It cannot but be a bloody business. Prince Rupert rages in Lancashire; it is thought he will make a great army before he come to York. If God help us to take York, and defeat him, the business is ended in England. Send me Morellius, if you can get him. I have got Brown at last, Forbes is on the press. Hold Apollonius on. The Independents have set up a number of private congregations in the city. They are exceeding busy. We will have much to do with them. Edward's piece we expect the next week at farthest. Strange! that your divines of Holland will learn nothing from England. Do they sit still while we are a-dying! The calamity may shortly come over to them. Be assured, your state will follow the fortune of England. If the malignants prevail, all the force of this isle will be employed to put the Nassovian yoke on their neck, nill they will they; and if the democratick anarchy vex our churches, ye are blind if ye see not that pest incumbent to you likewise. Paper bids me say adieu.

64. *My Publick Letter.*

AFFAIRS here at this time stand thus. After the King broke up from before Oxford, Waller followed him beyond Worcester towards Shrewsbury, his foot being left in divers strengths by the way. Waller could not overtake him; only was careful he should not win to Prince Rupert, nor raise any new forces in these quarters. His Majesty finding this, turns about, and with all speed, with
what

what he could carry, returns to Oxford. Waller is ftill at
his heels: after fome days reft at Oxford, having joined all
he could make out of the neigbour garrifons, he got towards the affociate counties. This puts us in fome perplexity; yet we are informed this night, that Waller is at
his back, and the counties have caft 10,000 well-armed
men before his face; fo that much harm cannot be done
in thefe bounds. The General having gone of his own
head, yea, contrary to the direction of the Houfe of Commons and committee of both kingdoms, to the weft, Maurice rofe from Lyme. Weymouth rendered to us, and
fair hopes were made of a fhort recovery of the whole
weft; but wife men do not look for much good from that
airth. Prince Rupert, after the fpoiling of Lancafhire,
and the great increafe of his army there, has returned to
Chefhire. We were once much afraid he fhould have
gone to Scotland; but now that fear is paft. Left he
fhould do harm where he is going, there is a gallant army
now in purfuit of him. 10,000 from York, 6000 from
Lancafhire; Denbigh and others will join all the forces
they have. In the mean time, thefe about York will be
quiet. The ftorming of the town will coft much blood;
and if Rupert's army were once off the fields, all hope of
fuccour being cut off, it is hoped it will render. The
Queen on Sunday laft was delivered of a daughter. We
are proceeding in our affembly. This day before noon
we got fundry propofitions of our directory for the facrament of the Lord's fupper paffed; but in the afternoon we
could not move one inch. The unhappy Independents
would mangle that facrament. No catechifing nor preparation before; no thankfgiving after; no facramental doctrine, or chapters, in the day of celebration; no coming
up to any table, but a carrying of the elements to all in
their feats athort the church: yet all this, with God's
help, we have carried over their bellies to our practice.
But exhortations at tables yet we ftick at. They would have
no words fpoken at all. Nye would be at covering the
head at the receiving. We muft difpute every inch of our
ground. Great need had we of the prayers of all God's
people. We rejoiced at the peaceable conclefion of our
general affembly. By the printed papers you have the
common reports here; and by the writ which comes
weekly from Bruffels to my good friend Sir Robert An-
ftruther, you may fee how things go over-fea.
                    D 2   65. *For*

65. *For Mr Robert Ramſay. The end of June.*

I will continue ſtill to write unto you, though none of yours has come ſince that of February 11. Where Mr David is, I do not know: if he be in town, let this ſerve you both. We have here many ups and downs, great ſecurity and luxury in the city, and over all the land where the ſword rages not, which makes us afraid of further judgements than yet have appeared. We ſee very little zeal or mind in the parliament for the houſe of God. We are on occaſion telling them, that this neglect is a great cauſe of the continuance of the war; but for no purpoſe: the moſt of the people who are counted religious, are running to ways of error and ſchiſm of many divers kinds. The avowed diſobedience of the General, and his going the clean contrary way to his orders, what it may produce we do not know. No great appearance of getting York in haſte. The fooliſh raſhneſs of Major Crawford, and his great vanity to aſſault his alone the breach made by his mine, without the acquainting Leſly or Fairfax with it, and the killing of ſo great a number of his men, alſo the ſending away from the ſiege ſo great a party to follow Prince Rupert, will force us to look on theſe walls till hunger makes them fall, whereof as yet we hear not much. The delay of Callendar's incoming ſo long has given time to the Marquis of Montroſe to make havock of the northern counties, which will make the ſiege of Newcaſtle the harder; and without Newcaſtle, this city will hardly put off this winter. Very many of the aſſembly are departed for want of means. The allowance granted by the parliament is not paid. What we gave in concerning ordination yet lies ſtill, and, by the underhand dealing of the Independents, is like to come out from the Houſe ſo mangled, that if we get it not helped, it will much offend us both for the matter and the preparative, it being the firſt paper came from us to the Houſes. Very many things that come to be handled in the aſſembly are new to us all, and obſcure. We have to do with very many ſcrupulous and thraward wits. Whether we had need of prayers, or not, you may judge. We have overcome many difficulties; our God has extricated us out of very many labyrinths; we are confident therefore, by the aſſiſtance of
God's

God's people there, to fee a glorious work ended in thefe dominions, and begun elfewhere, ere it be long. The fear of this makes the devil and his inftruments fo bufy in their malicious oppofition.

66. To Mr William Spang.   June 28.

Coufin,

Your laft, June 1ft, and your former, wherein was a part of Rivet's letters, I received the other week. I write none, being diverted with bufinefs; for here we have very little fpare time. You have here what was written to our friends of Glafgow, and more privately to a fpecial one B. What Mr Buchanan, at my defire, wrote to Paris, produced a letter from Monf. Drelincourt, with the advice of the whole confiftory there, which had been printed, had I not ftayed it by this paper: we have fent it to have it rectified according to my motion. What Moulin wrote from Sedan, is more to the purpofe, and our mind, though we expected leaft from that man. Spanheim, I fee by his anfwer, is not difpofed to write at this time, except the univerfity would lay it upon him. Certainly Mr Rivet is very ill informed. As I am an honeft man, I never heard man, privately or publickly, fpeak either of his perfon, or any of his writs, but with honour: if he or any there will give ear to all that is written from London at this time, they will wrong themfelves. That of burning his, or any divine's book over-fea, is a malignant calumny. We cannot but regret, that both your ftatef-men and divines fhould fee and hear us fweating to the blood, under thefe burdens which concern all the Reform-ed alike, while they will obftinately fit ftill as neutral. It is clear, many of your good fimple people have no fuch mind. Their large contribution to the poor Irifh, fhew their affection that it fhould be diftribute to the poor people there, as well as to the foldiers: I think it great reafon, and for fatisfaction in this point, letters are gone already from the committee of both kingdoms, and more will go fhortly upon this your motion. But I hope your people will not exclude the foldiers of the Scots army al-together from their liberality: for I know it, there live not any more poor than the moft of them, being kept to-gether without one penny of pay for twenty-two months.

Something

Something is going from this for help, but within two months pay. Apollonius would do well to go on in his writing. What you speak of a voyage to Holland, would be good service to God and this church. For the over-swaying power of the Independents, you speak of, I know it to be a false fable; only this is true, that they and o-ther sects, joined with the strange backwardness of the most of these here to do in time, what they must, and are willing also oft to do, may be very dangerous, and calls for all the help can be obtained from our neigh-bours. We are vexed to the heart very often with these unkent and unexpected ways of some or other here. Yesterday my stomach was full of them, and this day more. I had need of patience, and not only of wisdom and courage. Not long ago, while I am visiting my good friend Mr Rous, I find the favour from him of that which then I suspected, and now have found, a dange-rous design. After very great labour, we gave in, as our first fruits, a paper for ordination to both Houses. Oft had they called for it before it came. When it had lien in their hands neglected for many weeks, at last it was committed to a few of the Commons to make a report to the House about it. We hear surmises, that this commit-tee had altered much of our paper; but I finding by Mr Rous, the chief of that committee, that the alterations were both more and greater than we suspected, and that the committee had closed their report, and were ready to make it to the House, without any further meeting. I persuaded him it would be convenient before the report was made, and either Houses engaged in any thing which was against the mind of the assembly, and of our nation, to confer privately with some of us anent these altera-tions. Upon this he obtained an order of the House for the committee to call for any of the assembly they pleased. This he brought to the assembly, and called out Marshal and me to tell us his purpose. We gave him our best ad-vice. On his motion the assembly named Marshal, Vines, Burgess, Tuckney, and the scribes, to wait on; and with-al requested us to be with them. Great strife and cla-mour was made to have Mr Goodwin joined; but he was refused by a vote. Marshal came not. At meeting we found, they had passed by all the whole doctrinal part of ordination, and all our scriptural grounds for it; that they had chosen only the extraordinary way of ordination,
                                                        and

and in that very part had scraped out whatever might displease the Independents, or patrons, or Selden and others, who will have no discipline at all in any church *jure divino*, but settled only upon the free-will and pleasure of the parliament. Mr Henderson, and the rest, reasoned against the dangerousness and disgrace of this their way, so clearly, that sundry of the gentlemen repented of their alterations; yet the most took all to advisement. We, in private, resolved we would, by all means, stick to our paper; else, this being the first, if we yielded to these most prejudicial alterations, which the Independents and Civilians underhand had wrought, the assembly's reputation was clean overthrown, and Erastus's way would triumph. What will be the end of this debate, God knows. If the assembly could stand to their deed, we hope to have the parliament reasonable; for they will be loth to lose the assembly and us, for the pleasure of any other party. But we fear the fainting of many of our House: this holds our mind in suspense; only we are glad we have taken the matter before it came to the House. This day we were vexed also in the assembly: we thought we had passed with consent, sitting at the table; but behold, Mr Nye, Mr Goodwin, and Bridges, cast all in the hows, denying to us the necessity of any table, but pressing the communicating of all in their seats, without coming up to a table. Mess. Henderson, Rutherford, and Gillespie, all three disputed exceeding well for it, with arguments unanswerable; yet not one of the English did join with us, only Mr Assessor Burges, who then was in the chair, beginning to speak somewhat for us, but a little too vehemently, was so met with by the Independents, that a shameful and long clamour ended their debate. This has grieved us, that we fear the end of our work, always we expect it shall be better. Prince Rupert is not gone south, but north towards Cumberland. I pray God save Callendar's army and Scotland from his bloody mouth. York seems to be so provided, that in haste it cannot be taken, neither can we spare any more from the siege, the garrison within is so strong, and our works so large. The Commons have written a sharp letter to the General, for his disobedience to the committee of both kingdoms. His army is not great, and we fear shall do little good in the west. The King is stronger than we expected, and is falling on the associations. Things go here every other week

wonderful

wonderful varioufly; yet by God's help, all will be well; and your ambaffadors in the end will not be commended for their bad offices they have, as is faid, done us. If your Prince will needs, without the parliament, make a fecond marriage with our King, it is feared it may haften the ruin of both families, which might be prevented if God would but touch the heart of your Prince to go another way to work. Had he and your ftates joined with our parliament their counfels, it might have faved all. While they fide with the King, and make your people neuters, they do what in hafte will not be forgotten. I muft break off here. My fervice to your wife, and Thomas Cunningham my good friend. Farewell.

The King is about Bedford, as they fay, with near 8000 men. Waller is near him. Some think that they will fight; others that the King is wheeled about again towards Oxford, and will wait for his Irifh fuccours. If your Prince had the wifdom and moderation I wifh, it feems, with all mens bleffings, he might attain all his ends both in England and Holland quickly, for the great benefit of all; but as he is like to proceed, he will mifs his defign, and lofe all.

67. *To Mr William Spang.*   *July* 5. 1644.

Coufin,

WITH the laft poft, you had from me, at length, how things went here. Since, we have been in great perplexity; but God the Lord, within this hour, has begun to fhine. The General, in the weft, was doing little, and as little is expected from him. The King had given an alarm to Bedfordfhire, and all the affociate counties; Waller had fkirmifhed with him at Banbury, loft eight cannon, and had gotten fome rub: but that which concerned the heart of the affairs, the unhappinefs of our countryman Major Crawford's precipitation, in his fpringing a mine by himfelf, and affaulting his alone, and lofs upon it, had fo difcouraged all the reft of the army, that they could not be brought to ftorm any more. Very many of our Scots foldiers were fallen fick; and, to bring our dangers to the top, Prince Rupert, above all mens expectations, had brought over the hills of Lancafhire, a very ftrong army, both in horfe and foot, 8000

2   horfe

horse at leaft, and 10,000 of foot; thefe were marching
directly to York. Within, it is thought, were 6000 good
foldiers, very many gentlemen and officers. When we
heard that ours had raifed the fiege, we were much afflicted, both with the difgrace and great danger of the perfons of our brethren, if they fought with that greater
power, and danger to the caufe if they fought not; for
the moft thought, fince Prince Rupert had got his point,
and raifed the fiege, he would prefently retire, and with
his great army go ravage in the affociate counties, where
Manchefter durft not fall on him, nor Waller meet him;
York at once would be revictualled; the Marquis of Newcaftle and Gen. King, being at liberty, would quickly gather an army and ftraiten us. As for the affembly, thefe
three weeks, Mr Nye, and his good friend Mr Herle,
has kept us on one point of our directory alone, the re-
commending of the communicants coming up to the table
to communicate. Their way of communicating, of fome
at the table, and fome about it, without any fucceffion of
companies to more tables, is that whereon we ftick, and
are like to ftick longer. Alfo the great appearance of
the parliament's mifleading, by a few, to change the papers
we gave in to them, fo that nothing fhall be eftablifhed
on any fcripture or divine right, did much afflict us. But
behold, in a moment, when our credit was beginning fenfibly to decay, God has come in. Our army has fought
Prince Rupert, has overthrown his forces, taken his cannon and baggage, killed many of his chief officers, and
chafed the reft into York. You have here the copy of
my Lord Fairfax's letter to the mayor of Hull, which
is feconded with two or three other letters to the Speaker
of the Houfe of Commons. Major Brown has joined to
Waller a pretty army. The King has run away again,
with his horfe only, northward. Waller is following as
he may. The General writes, that the Queen has left
Exeter, and is going to Pendennis caftle. I pray God
fave poor Hamilton from her malice. The gentry of the
weft are coming faft in. This people, yefterday and to-
day, were much difcouraged, and fainting; but this night
are triumphing. We dare not be too much exalted, only
we blefs God from our heart, who is beginning to fhine
on our army, and make it, after very long expectance,
and beating down of our pride, to be a fountain of joy
and hope to thefe who love the welfare of religion. We

hope things in the aſſembly and parliament may go more
after our mind. Our army oft ſignified to us, they conceived their want of ſucceſs flowed moſt from God's anger
at the parliament and aſſembly, for their neglect of eſtabliſhing of religion. We oft told them the truth, that
we had no hope of any progreſs here, till God gave them
victories ; and then, we doubted not, all would run both
in parliament and aſſembly. You have here, for you and
Mr Forbes, a dozen of the Anatomies, and two or three
of the anſwers : let him anſwer that poor piece if he
pleaſe : alſo receive a late piece of Cotton's. Edwards's
book is expected within two or three days ; it is excreſced
to near forty ſheets. Dr Stuart is not yet on the preſs.
I think my Lord has written to Mr Strickland and Mr
Cunningham, anent the Iriſh money, and will write alſo
to you. I am too long in your debt. I pray you write
me what I am reſting you ; alſo ſend me over Bechmare
againſt the Socinians, and Rivet's Critick, laſt edition, and
his *Inſtitutio Principis* ; alſo if his Catholick, laſt edition, at
Geneva, be yet come out, and his firſt piece againſt Grotius's Annotations on Caſſander : I have the poſterior. I
ſhall ſend over to you by exchange what I am reſting for
all. The claſſes of Amſterdam have written kind letters
to our aſſembly, and recommended conformity with Scotland. Hold on Apollonius. I wiſh Voetius engaged.
The Lord be with you.

68. *For Mr William Spang. July* 12. 1644.

Dear Couſin,

By yours, June 5th and 15th, I ſee you had not got
what I had written largely with the two laſt poſts. I hope,
before this, you have all. I did aſſure you of the great
falſehood of the informations which came to Dr River. I
wiſh again and again, that Apollonius and Voetius were
moved to write. They muſt not expect that this aſſembly,
or any member of it, will deſire them to do ſo : it is far a-
bove their power ; and if they eſſayed it, they would ſoon
be taken up by the parliament. Yet we are doing what we
can to get leave to anſwer, with great reſpect, all your
letters, both of Walachren, Zealand, and Amſterdam.
That engagement you write, of the parliament with Spain,
againſt the French and you, I give you full aſſurance of
                                                    my

my certain knowledge it was never intended. True, the Spanish ambaſſador made ſuch a motion to the commit-tee of both kingdoms, which they tranſmitted to the Houſes, and a prieſt cauſed print a paper, of the great hurt would come to England, if the ſea-coaſts of Flanders ſhould fall to the French; but that any living ſoul here e-ver dreamed to intermeddle with the ſiege of Graveling, it is as falſe as the other informations, which your ambaſ-ſadors have come over to coin, and vend them over ſeas to our prejudice: but thanks to God, and gra-mercy good Scot, that theſe men are like now in a ſud-den to change their note. On Friday, the certain news of Prince Rupert's routing came here. On Saturday the Dutch ambaſſadors preſſed for audience from both houſes of parliament, in as ample a form as either the Spaniſh ambaſſador or Imperial agent had uſed. We expect no good from their trifling propoſitions. There is no friend-ly word, ſo far as I can hear, come out of any of their mouths ſince their arrival; but it is generally thought here, that their deſigns have been wholly for the advance-ment of the malignant party. No man doubts but, in ſpite of the devil, Britain and Holland muſt join heart in hand for their common neceſſities; but for the courtiers of Oxford and Hague, it is very like, if they go on ſtill in their wicked ways, they may be taken both for com-mon enemies. Concerning Thomas Cunningham, I wiſh by all means you and he may keep entire correſpondence, otherwiſe I foreſee it cannot fail to fall out to both your great diſpleaſures. He is taken here, and at home, for a very honeſt man, and one who is diligent, and very cordial, to his utmoſt ability, for the common cauſe. You will not believe what ſcarcity there is of men whom we dare truſt with ſuch a matter. Never a miniſter was taxed by a committee, but many of us, in this time of great need, got on our credit, ſome 500, ſome 1000 merks, to lend to the publick; which will be returned, with the intereſt, according to condition, or elſe all will go to all. It is my earneſt advice to you, to keep faſt with that man. I ſend you, herewith, two printed ſheets of the paſſage of the battle. God was merciful to us. We were in a ſad condition: Prince Rupert had done a glorious piece of ſervice: from nothing, had gathered, without money, a powerful army, and in ſpite of all our three Generals, had made us leave York, after a long fiege: But the blood of Bolton would not let him reft, till all the glory he had got was loft in an hour: againft the mind of Newcaftle and General King, and all his council of war, he would fight, and purfue our army: where in half an hour he loft all. The Independents fent up one quickly, to affure, that all the glory of that night was theirs; that they, and their Major-General, Cromwell, had done it all their alone: but Captain Stuart afterward fhowed the vanity and falfehood of their difgraceful relation. God gave us that victory wonderfully. There were three generals on each fide, Lefly, Fairfax, and Manchefter; Rupert, Newcaftle, and King. Within half an hour and lefs, all fix took them to their heels; this to you alone. The difadvantage of the ground, and violence of the flower of Prince Rupert's horfe, carried all our right wing down; only Eglinton kept ground there to his great lofs; his lieutenant-crowner, a brave man, I fear fhall die, and his fon Robert be mutilated of an arm. Lindfay had the greateft hazard of any; but the beginning of the victory was from David Lefly, who betore was much fufpected of evil defigns: he, with the Scots, and Cromwell's horfe, having the advantage of the ground, did diffipate all before them. For a while no quarter was given. Lieutenant-General Baillie and Lumfden had the greateft burden of the conduct of all. Scarce one hour did the fight laft till an entire victory was gotten. Never fuch armies, this hundred years, met in England, large 50,000 men on the field. I pray God we make good ufe of this. We have a folemn thankfgiving on Thurfday next. You may fee what Lieutenant-General Baillie writes to me. We expect daily to hear of the delivery of York. The defign is to leave Newcaftle to Callendar, and to march fouth with their victorious army, if York were yielded.

In our affembly we go on as we may. The Independents and others kept us long three weeks upon one point alone, the communicating at a table. By this we came to debate, the divers coming up of companies fucceffively to a table; the confecrating of the bread and wine feverally; the giving of the bread to all the congregation, and then the wine to all, and fo twice coming up to the table, firft for the bread, and then for the wine; the mutual diftribution, the table-exhortations, and a world of fuch queftions, which to the moft of them were new and ftrange things. After we were overtoiled with debate, we were

forced

forced to leave all thefe things, and take us to general expreffions, which, by a benign expofition, would infer our church-practices, which the moft promifed to follow, fo much the more as we did not neceffitate them by the affembly's exprefs determination. We have ended the matter of the Lord's fupper, and thefe laft three days have been upon baptifm. We have carried, with much greater eafe than we expected, the publicknefs of baptifm. The abufe was great over all this land. In the greateft parifh of London, fcarce one child in a-year was brought to the church for baptifm. Alfo we have carried the parent's prefenting of his child, and not their midwives, as was their univerfal cuftom. In our laft debate with the committee of Commons, for our paper of ordination, we were in the midft, over head and ears, of that greateft of our queftions, the power of the parliament in ecclefiaftick affairs. It is like this queftion fhall be hotter here than any where elfe: but we mind to hold off; for yet it is very unfeafonable. As yet we are come to no iffue what to do with that paper. This day your ambaffadors had audience to their compliment in both Houfes. For anfwer, they will be remitted to the committee of both kingdoms, and there they muft ftand till they fetch over letters of credence, as well for Scotland as England: but fpending of time is their aim, to fee the event of affairs before they engage. If Apollonius, or any other, write at all, it were good it were done quickly; for the chief ufe, either of their authority or arguments, will be fhortly at that nick of time when the Independents give up their reafons againft us to the parliament. The chief point we wifh were proven, is the real authority, power, and jurifdiction of fynods and claffical prefbyteries over any the members, or the whole, of a particular congregation; alfo the right of ordinary profeffors to the facraments, though they can give no certain or fatisfactory figns of real regeneration. Thefe two are the main heads; alfo I wifh the power of prefbyteries claffical, to ordain and excommunicate, were cleared. Many befides the Independents, by Voetius's writs, are brought to give the rights of both thefe actions to the congregational prefbytery, much againft our mind and practice. The churches of Jerufalem, Corinth, and the reft of the apoftolick churches mentioned in the New Teftament, which can be proven to have practifed either ordination or excommunication, appear to us to have been claffical, confifting

fifting of more congregations than one, and of greater numbers, when they did exercife either of thefe acts, than could meet in one place. Alfo it is a great queftion about the power of jurifdiction in a congregation. We are not againft the people's power of election of the officers, or, at leaft, free confent thereto; but befide, they prefs all procefs and acts of cenfures to be done, if not in the name and authority, as the Brownifts, and thofe of New England, yet neceffarily in the prefence, and with the confent, not only of the prefbytery congregational, but alfo of the whole people, even every communicant male. If in thefe we were agreed, I think the difficulty would be fmall in any other matter.

69. *For   Lieutenant - General Baillie.*   London,   Tuefday, *July* 16. 1644.

Right Honourable,

I give hearty thanks to God for his work on the 2d of July, and to you for your true account of it. We hope that bleffed day fhall be the crifis of our affairs, which then were in fo dangerous a condition. Had Prince Rupert been profperous that day in his fight, or paffed by without fighting, we all conceive affairs fhould have been defperate. God, who in mercy to his people, who long have been waiting upon him, gave to you that moft glorious victory, we truft, will give you wifdom and courage to make ufe of it. On Thurfday next, in all our churches, we are to praife God for that unfpeakable favour, and, as we hear, the King has directed to do the like in Oxford on Friday. We are longing to hear news of York. This people here will never end any bufinefs either in church or ftate; all that honour is referved for you. Waller has been running up and down with the King for little purpofe. His London and affociate foot are all home; fo the King, with his horfe and foot, are ftronger than he, and are drawing towards Briftol. It is feared that, being joined with Maurice and Hopeton, he may diftrefs the General. The Holland ambaffadors have been heard in both Houfes. The only delay of a treaty is on the upcoming of our commiffioners, with the articles fent down to our parliament. No good is expected of that treaty. You muft give a fecond blow to that faction before it be in a

posture

pofture to receive fuch a peace as is neceffar.——So I reft,
your coufin to ferve you,

ROBERT BAILLIE.

70. *For Captain Porterfield.*   *July* 16. 1644.

Dear Coufin,

I long to hear what became of you and your company
on that perilous, but glorious, 2d of July.   As yet I can
hear nothing of you, though I have heard enough of many others, and of fome much more than I defired.   I pray
God you be all well.   Mr John Dickfon came here yefternight.   He told me, your wife, and all friends in Glafgow, were in health fome ten days before.   Let me hear
what you have deburfed for my foldier, that I may fend it
to you with many thanks.   Bleffed be the name of God
for evermore, that ftrengthened your arms that night.
Had our God deferted but one hour, it had been the
blackeft news that ever Britain got fince it was inhabited;
but now, bleffed be his name, we hope the back of their
pernicious faction is broken.   One other found blow will
beat out its brains.   All things, both here and in Edinburgh, both in church and ftate, would quickly have mifcarried, had not that bleffed day holden all right, and kept
many a wicked defign within breaft which was ready to
have broken out.   The Lord fend you York and Newcaftle.   Till then all things fticks.   Many a perplexed night
have we of it.   If our neighbours at Edinburgh tafted the
fauce wherein we dip our venifon at London, their teeth
would not water fo faft to be here as fome of them do.
Our hope is in the Lord, that he who has done fo glorious
things for us, will not give us over to the will of the moft
unreafonable and wicked men that ever were born.   Mr
Maxwell of Rofs has printed at Oxford fo defperately malicious an invective againft our affemblies and prefbyteries,
that, however I could hardly confent to the hanging of
Canterbury himfelf, or of any Jefuit, yet I could give my
fentence freely againft that unhappy liar's life.   It is good
he is no better to our parliaments than to our affemblies;
for in his other pamphlet, *Sacrofancta Regia Majeftas,*
he lays them abfolutely under the feet of a king's mere
pleafure, were he the greateft tyrant that ever was.   If
God go on a little with you, fuch flattering ferpents, incendiaries,

cendiaries, and overthrowers both of kings, parliaments, and churches, will be gotten charmed. Blessing God again and again for his mercies to us all in you, I rest, your loving friend to serve you,

ROBERT BAILLIE.

71. *To Mr Robert Blair.   London, July* 16.

Reverend and Dear Brother,

I think it for little purpose to write oft to you, since I know that Samuel writes largely at all occasions. Blessed be God for evermore, that has looked down upon us all in that glorious 2d of July. By that that I see here, and hear from Edinburgh, our affairs, both of church and state, both here and in Scotland, were in such a posture, that if you in that day had miscarried, whatever we have been building up these bygone years, in less than a month was like to have been overturned, to the unspeakable woe and wrack of all the godly in both kingdoms; but honour and glory to his name, who has established our tottering estate by that day's mercy. However shame hath fallen on particular men, when they turned their backs, who were most obliged, and most expected to have stood still; yet it was well, since God was glorified, and you are victorious in so full and splendid an overthrow of all your enemies. We were both grieved and angry, that your Independents there should have sent up Major Harrison to trumpet over all the city their own praises, to our prejudice, making all believe, that Cromwell alone, with his unspeakably valorous regiments, had done all that service; that the most of us fled; and who staid, fought so and so, as it might be. We were much vexed with these reports, against which you were not pleased, any of you, to instruct us with any answer, till Lindsay's letters came at last, and Captain Stewart with his colours. Then we sent abroad our printed relations, and could lift up our face. But within three days Mr Ash's relation was also printed, who gives us many good words, but gives much more to Cromwell than we are informed is his due. Let good Mr Ash know what is the use that generally here is made of his relations; much I know beside his intention; even this in plain terms, the Independents have done so brave service, yea, they are so strong and considerable a party, that they must

I   not

not only be tolerated, but in nothing grieved, and no ways to be provoked. It seems very neceffary, that since none of you of purpofe, and ordinarily, fend up relations, and Mr Afh fends to the prefs conftant intelligence of your actions, which, for the man's known integrity, are every word believed, your proceedings have a great influence here both of church and ftate; I fay, it feems needful that all Mr Afh's letters which are fent hither to the prefs, fhould be firft feen and pondered by fome of you there. Thefe are my own private motions, which I propone to you alone, to be made ufe of as you think fit. I blefs God, who gracioufly faved your life in that fo dangerous an hour. Glory to his name. Farewell.

See by this inclofed, if the whole victory, both in the right and left wing, be not afcribed to Cromwell, and not a word of David Lefly, who in all places that day was his leader. If his reports of Manchefter be true, you know the flight of fome is worfe and more fhameful than death.

72. For my Lord Eglinton. July 18. 1644.

My very good Lord,

AFTER the reports of your great battle, hearing, for all our victory, that the whole right wing, wherein your Lordfhip was, to be routed, I was for fome days in perplexity and fear, doubting much what was your Lordfhip's condition; but after Captain Stuart came up, and alfo your Lordfhip's large letter to Sir John Seaton, I was much comforted, and blefled God, who had faved your life, and of your brave fon Robert, from the greateft and moft apparent danger that ever you had feen. Blefied be God again and again, who did protect you, and brought you out of the jaws of death, and that with fo great honour, when fo many with cowardice fell in difgrace, worfe than death. This day we have been giving to God publick praife for that day's unfpeakable mercy. If God had not been with you at that hour, if you there had been broken, we all conceive our welfare in this world had been overthrown with you; our religion, our liberties, our children, our perfons, our eftates, our pofterity, had all been put in the cruel mercy of that wicked faction. Great is your honour and happinefs, whom God made the inftruments to conferve to all this ifle all that is dear to hem. We are hearing also, that the town is rendered to you without blood, another very great favour. O! if we were thankful to God for all these great mercies. I long to hear of the cure of Robert's wounds; also of Lieutenant Montgomery, that brave and gallant gentleman. I have sent herewith to your Lordship three weeks of the gazettes of Paris; for many I have oft received from your Lordship. I wish in any thing of the world I were able to do your Lordship, or any of yours, pleasure; by God's grace, while I live, I shall be very willing, as I am straitly obliged to serve your Lordship, and all yours. Praying God to be present with your Lordship in all your noble enterprises, I rest, your Lordship's, ever to be commanded,

ROBERT BAILLIE.

All affairs here, both of church and state, of war and peace, are much hindered by the too long and unexpected delay of the coming up of our commissioners from Scotland.

73. *To Mr David Dickson.*   *July* 23. 1644.

Reverend and Dear Brother,

NOT knowing where you were from April till the time of your son's coming hither, I directed my letters to Mr Robert. You have in my publick letter and papers the outside of our affairs; but the inside of the thoughts of many here is this. Our difficulties in all our affairs, both of church and state, are great and many, as they have ever been, from the beginning till this day; yet the Lord has carried us through hitherto. If his good hand continued not with us, we see no possibility of any tolerable issue. Our progress in the assembly is small; there is so much matter yet before us, as we cannot win through for a long time after our common pace. Our Independents continue and increase in their obstinacy. Much is added to their pride and hope by their service at the battle of York; albeit much of their valour is grounded on very false lies, prejudicial to God, the author, and to us, the true instruments, of that day's honour. The politick part in the parliament is the stronger, who are resolute to conclude nothing in the matters of religion that may grieve the sectaries, whom they count necessary for the time. Our

army

army is much diminifhed in number and reputation. Alfo here Callendar's army is called very fmall, and no ways able to reduce Newcaftle. The letters we have, both from the committee and prefbytery at York, are much for a fafe peace; which we wifh from our heart; but think their proponing of it is from the confcience of their prefent weaknefs. We fear the extraordinar long ftay of our commiffioners be from new factions and divifions among yourfelves. If the King fhould get any real vantage againft Effex, it would much change affairs here. This is an irrefolute, divided, and dangeroufly-humoured people. We long much to fee them fettled, and our nation honeftly rid of them. We fufpect the Queen may work us much mifchief in France. The articles of peace, which are concluded here, and, as we hear, with you alfo, are fuch as we think the King will never accept; and if we fhould begin to treat with him on the alteration of any of them, it will draw both to a great length, and a dangerous lofing of our ground. The fectaries of divers forts, Anabaptifts chiefly, increafe here. Very many are for a total liberty of all religions, and write very plaufible treatifes for that end. Sundry of the Independents are ftepped out of the church, and follow my good acquaintance Mr Roger Williams; who fays, there is no church, no facraments, no paftors, no church-officers or ordinance in the world, nor has been fince a few years after the apoftles. If our commiffioners were once come up, we mind to put them a little harder to it, and fee what they underftand by their uniformity, which they have fworn to us. We can make no certain conclu-fion, but that we believe God will work his own gracious ends by man's weaknefs. One week we have fair appear-ance to get all things quickly done according to our mind, another week fuch alteration in affairs, that nothing lefs can be hoped for. Thefe viciffitudes of hopes and defpair, when we look to the earth, are very frequent. If we had no need of your prayers, yourfelf judge. Communicate this to Mr Robert, and Mr George, if he be with you. I fhall have a care to fpeak with Mr Jo. and caufe Mr Alexander and Mr Samuel fpeak him in the purpofe ye wrote of. It would be very fweet to me to be at home, and ferving in my charge; but as yet no appearance of loofing for any of us. We are upholden by God's pre-fence with us, giving us all health, grace, love, and con-cord, and in all occafions opening the mouths of my col-

F 2   leagues

leagues to ſpeak what is convenient. Thanks be to God, that in nothing hitherto have we been a ſhame to our church and country. The things you deſired to be helped in our church, will all fall out according to your mind; but I may not enter into particulars till all be finiſhed. They put us always in hopes, if the malignant faction were brought down, and our army well advanced, then quickly all ſhould be ſettled, with ſmall regard to the ſectaries, whom now they dare not offend, at leaſt not put them to deſpair.

How our affairs go here, you may ſee in the four incloſed papers printed; and foreign affairs you may ſee in the written one. I can add little thereto. Our aſſembly being wearied with ſitting ſince the beginning of July was a-year, without any intermiſſion, was earneſt for a little relaxation; ſo fourteen days were obtained from the Houſes, of vacation. We ſit not till Wedneſday, Auguſt 7th. Some of us were earneſt to delay that vacation till we had cloſed the directory of baptiſm, which was near an end, and till the Houſes did return to us their ſenſe of our paper of ordination, whereupon they had ſpent already ſome time; but the dog-days and faſting-week coming on, and the particular affairs of divers our members admitted of no delay. As yet there is nothing concluded anent the diſpoſition of the army at York; but Humbie being now come up to us for that end, I think quickly they will be all diſpoſed on for our beſt advantage. My Lord Humbie told us, that the Governor of York ſhewed him, that he was going out to bury the old Biſhop of Glaſgow at the very time when word came to him of the fight; ſo he behoved, with the moſt with him, to leave the corpſe to be put in the earth by ſome few poor men. The Biſhop had nothing for his burial but as the Governor furniſhed. The judgements of God are to be obſerved and adored. Jacobus, as Humbie ſays, was killed long before at Bandouner. The army is at Doncaſter, willing to follow Prince Rupert whitherſoever he goes, if ſo they be furniſhed with neceſſaries for the march. General Eſſex is betwixt Exeter and Plymouth. The King is towards him. When Maurice and Hopeton are joined, they will be many more men than we. To help this, Waller is to ſend a great party of horſe and dragoons to Eſſex. The Queen from Falmouth was carried by ten ſhips of the Hollanders to Breſt in Bretagne. What the may work againſt us at the court of France, many

           ny

by doubt. Dr Mayern would make us believe, that her days cannot be many. The French and States ambassadors are urging a treaty, wherein we suspect deceit, and a continuance of their old arts; but nothing can be said to that point till our commissioners come from Scotland. We have been expecting them every week these two months. Their delay is exceeding prejudicial to all our affairs here, both of church and state. The victory at York, so far as we are informed, appears to us more and more miraculous. We cannot praise God enough for it. It was exceeding great, and exceeding seasonable, if all the truth were known. By the assistance of your prayers, we trust to obtain from God a happy conclusion of the whole work in his due time. All our company, praised be God, are in good health.

74. *For Glasgow.   August 7. 1644.*

The estate of affairs here, since my last, you may see in these printed papers, and of affairs abroad, in the inclosed writ. I can add little hereunto. This day we sit down in our assembly, after our vacance. The House of Commons have past the paper of ordination unanimously, with some alterations, which are to be considered by us. The right settling of that business will be a great step to advance our affairs. The little interruption we have had in our sitting, make both ourselves, the Houses, and the city, and all the world, to call on us for dispatch; and it seems God, disposing of all affairs, is making for our furtherance; so we hope for a farther progress quickly, than for a long time bygone we have made. We are afflicted with the delay of our commissioners upcoming. We know not what you are doing in Scotland. No man here has seen one line from Scotland since the 26th of June, which is a sottishness inexcusable. The publick suffers by the carelessness of some. By letters intercepted from Ireland, we here of Antrim's landing in Argyle, with 2500 men at most. We trust they shall not do much hurt, but that God, who has defended hitherto our land, shall deliver these idolatrous butchers to our swords. There is a great expectation here from Inchiquin, and the rest of the Protestant Irish in the south, who are risen for the parliament. This accident, if it please God, may do much

much good. Essex's army is in good case, praised be God, in Cornwal. The King, Maurice, and Hopeton, and all they can make, are upon his back, but are weaker than to fight. The most of Waller's horse are gone with our brave countryman, Major-General Middleton, to wait on the King's rear. Prince Rupert has divided the remnant of his beaten army. Himself, with the foot he can get, are towards Shrewsbury; and Manchester is to attend him. The most of his horse, with Clavering, Glenham, and Montrose, are towards Westmoreland: so our whole army, after refreshment at Leeds and Wakefield, by the hearty and unanimous advice of all the English committee, is sent north; for there is nothing worthy of their stay either in Yorkshire or Lancashire. Fairfax has the reducing of these castles committed to him. Newcastle is the only design of importance. We pray God deliver it in our hands. We are glad to hear of the recovery of our sick and wounded men, and that our army is so full of chearfulness. Much money is coming from the sale of the prime malignants lands. God is still very gracious to us. We feared the effects of the Queen's going to France; but our fears now are diminished. The King's affairs at the court of France are taken for desperate, and not to be meddled with; so much the less, as the Queen and her faction are conceived to be Spanish, and upon the design to trouble the affairs of France. But the evidence of God's care for us, is in that great stir that is quickly like to fill all France for our great advantage. The Duke of Orleans will not come to the court, but sends sundry articles to the Queen, which will overturn the Cardinal and all her counsels, if they be granted; and, if not, he has a victorious army wherewith he will command. This might be the beginning of a great commotion, if the lightness of the French spirit hindered not all men from building any thing on their motions. Lerida is taken at last by the Spaniard. Since Anguien and Touraine are joined, a bloody battle is expected about Friburg, betwixt the French and the Bavarians. That old fox Urban is at last gone to his place; yet the devil his father cannot die, and will never want a son to be the Pope's successor. At our sitting down this day, a great many of our brethren did complain of the great increase and insolency in divers places of the Antinomian and Anabaptistical conventicles. A committee was appointed for a remedy of
this

this evil, to be reprefented quickly to the parliament. Mr Edwards has written a fplendid confutation of all the Independents apology. All the minifters of London, at leaft more than 100 of them, have agreed to erect a weekly lecture for him in Chrift's Church, in the heart of the city, where he may handle thefe queftions, and nothing elfe, before all that will come to hear. We hope God will provide remeids for that evil of Independency, the mother and true fountain of the church's diftractions here.

75. *For Mr William Spang.* *Auguft* 10. 1644.

Dear Coufin,

I wrote none to you the laft poft, for it was our vacance, and we were abroad; neither, I think, the two pofts before, waiting while I heard you had received what I had written with the three former: and when your's came, I find that you had only then received my laft, July 12th; but not the two former. Of this enquire the caufe. I fent you long ago Mr Edwards's book. Dr Stuart has a call to Leyden, fo he intends not to put his reply to the prefs till he be going hence, left he fhould be retarded with a new anfwer. As for our affairs, thus they ftand. The parliament goes on after their old way, flowly in all things. The truft is in the Commons alone. They have a world of affairs in hand. They moft do by a member fince Pym died. Not a ftate-head amongft them. Many very good and able fpirits, but not any of fo great and comprehenfive a brain, as to manage the multitude of fo weighty affairs as lies on them. If God did not fit at their helm, for any good guiding of theirs, long ere this they had been gone. Callendar, with above 5000 foot and horfe, came over Tyne about the 20th of July, got Hartlepole and Stockton on the Tyfe the 24th, went thereafter to Newcaftle, took in Gatefide, and barricaded the bridge-port. The army in York, after having fent up my Lord Humby hither for direction, were advifed by the Englifh committee to go back to Newcaftle, the taking of it being judged the moft neceffary fervice; for the few caftles in Yorkfhire were not worth their labour. Alfo Fairfax was efteemed able enough for their reduction. Prince Rupert had fent the moft of his horfe, with

Clavering

Clavering and Montrose, northward ; and the few broken troops he retained with him were diftribute about
Chefter, where he purpofes to lie till men and ammunition come to him from Ireland.   However, Manchefter
was directed to wait on his wings.   We were the more
willing to be fent north, becaufe of Callendar's danger
from Montrofe, alfo to be near Scotland, if any need
were.   Our parliament, before the excife and loan-money
could be eftablifhed, fpent too much time ; alfo much debate and fecret working was about the commiffioners to be
fent hither.   If men knew the vexation we have here,
they would not be fo earneft for the employment as we
hear many have been.   Always at laft the better party prevailed, to get the Chancellor, Argyle, and Balmerino
named for the Lords ; Warifton, Sir Charles Arefkine,
and Mr George Dundas, for the gentry ; Sir John Smith,
Mr Robert Barclay, and Hugh Kennedy, for the burrows.   Their chief bufinefs will be about the articles for
pacification.   We expected their return, at fartheft, a-
gainft the midft of June, and yet they are not come ; only
Warifton is faid to be on his way with them : however
we have been much called for them, yet in my mind
they fhall not be of great ufe when they come, for fo long
as the King is able to keep up any face of an army, there
is fmall hope he will ever hear of them.   Our longfome parliament was haftened to an adjournment, by the fudden
and unexpected invafion of Kintyre, by Coll, Mr Gillefpie's fons, who, with 2500 runagates from Ireland, are
loppen over there.   Argyle is gone to wait on their fervice.   I truft God will make them repent of their voyage.
The chief action and expectation is now in the weft.   Effex, after his journey through all the weft, for little purpofe, has caft himfelf into Cornwall, as far as Foy near
Falmouth.   The King, with all he can make, is at his
back.   Many various opinions are here.   Many think his
voyage, as againft his orders, fo it was contrived by his
bad counfellors, for no good end.   Waller's army is deftroyed thereby.   No confiderable place in the weft has
been fo much as attempted.   The King might eafily have
been hindered to have come to fuch a ftrength, and yet
the General's army is much the better.   Always many
doubt the event.   A faft is appointed for God's help to
that army, on Tuefday next.   If God make all honeft,
we doubt not of a fuccefs.   The firft day after our va-
2   cance,

cance, a number of complaints were given in againſt the
Anabaptiſts and Antinomians huge increaſe and intolerable inſolencies. Notwithſtanding of Mr Nye's and others
oppoſition, it was carried that the aſſembly ſhould remonſtrate it to the parliament. Both Houſes took our complaint well, has ſent for the chief of the ſeditious ſectaries,
and promiſes a quick remeid to that great and dangerous
evil. A kind letter from the ſynod of Holland to us was
read. We have ended our directory for baptiſm. Thomas Goodwin one day was exceedingly confounded. He
has undertaken a publick lecture againſt the Anabaptiſts:
it was ſaid, under pretence of refuting them, he betrayed
our cauſe to them. That of the Corinthians, our chief
ground for baptiſm of infants, " Your children are holy,"
he exponed of a real holineſs, and preached down our
ordinary and neceſſary diſtinction of real and federal holineſs. Being poſed hereupon, he could no ways clear
himſelf, and no man took his part. God permits theſe
gracious men to be many ways unhappy inſtruments. As
yet their pride continues; but we are hopeful the parliament will not own their way ſo much as to tolerate it, if
once they found themſelves maſters. For the time they
are loth to caſt them off, and to put their party to deſpair,
left they deſert them. The men are exceeding active in
their own way. They ſtrive to advance Cromwell for
their head. They aſcribe to him the victory of York;
but moſt unjuſtly: for Humbie aſſures us, that Prince
Rupert's firſt charge falling on him, did humble him ſo,
that if David Leſly had not ſupported them, he had fled.
Skeldon Crawford, who had a regiment of dragoons in
that wing, upon his oath aſſured me, that at the beginning of the fight, Cromwell got a little wound on the neck,
which made him retire, ſo that he was not ſo much as
preſent at the ſervice; but his troopers were led on by
David Leſly. The ſectaries books preſs moſt in an uni-
verſal liberty for all religions. If Apollonius, Voetius,
or any other, intend to aſſiſt us, let them not delay. Try
what anſwer the Independents have given to Apollonius.
In my judgement they neither will nor can declare themſelves in the half of his interrogatories. Concerning the
Iriſh money, our commiſſioners long ago wrote at length
to Thomas Cunningham and Strickland. I muſt bid you
farewell. Anſwer my former letter.

76. *For James Mitchell.*   *August* 13. 1644.

James,

THAT since I came here I never heard from you but once, I was marvelling what could be the cause, till John Dick did tell me your condition ; but now my heart does much pity your great affliction. I have lost, with you, a youth whom much I loved. I cannot blame you to be thoroughly pained with so deep a stroke. In a sudden, he ripened more than ordinary, and above my expectation. I trust, long before this, the Lord has cured the wound of his own hand. The certain felicity of that glorious soul will not suffer you to mourn above measure, for his going home some hours before you. I am sure his eyes are closed from much woe, sin, labour, and danger, which was before him. He is the fourth of my scholars, excellent youths, whom God has translated, before our desires, in that spot of ground, Sir Henry, Mr John Bell, Mr Alexander Cunningham. We had much hopes of great service from them all ; but the Lord will find instruments of all the comforts he intends for us, and these fair blossoming plants will bring forth better and more fruit, when they stand in that good soil above, where the fountain of life continually waters their roots, and that glorious sun of righteousness shines in the full strength of all his beams upon them, night and day, summer and winter alike. God has left unto you divers gracious children, a favour denied to many, which ye would not undervalue. The publick is like to go well ; many wonderful and desperate hazards it has past through, and we are confident there are glorious days of the gospel at hand. What a glorious mercy was that at York ! how near was our army, and so all our wordly strength and hope, to shame, discredit, and very ruin ! Since, we were in great fears for Essex's army, in the west ; but now, as you may see in my publick letter, we are almost freed of these troubles. At these times, when the very being, not the welfare alone, of all the churches of these dominions, are in hazard, we must not let our minds be drowned in private affections. When the Lord shall triumph over that wicked party, which yet is full of strength and hopes, publick griefs shall be swallowed up in publick joys ; and if that party should get up the

head,

head, children would be the greatest burden and grief to all honest minds. Always when Christ and Antichrist are wrestling together, our eyes must be more upon this great and publick combat, than any thing within our doors. I trust that God, who has brought you through many and great troubles, will comfort you in this present and very great one. Praying for it, I rest,

    Your Compassionate Brother,

                ROBERT BAILLIE.

77. *Publick Letter. August* 18. 1644.

SINCE my last, our affairs here had this progress. We have gone through, in the assembly, the whole directory for baptism, except some little things referred to a committtee, also the whole directory for solemn thanfgiving, with a good unanimity. So soon as my Lord Wariston came up, we resolved on the occasion of his instructings, and the letters of our general assembly, both to ourselves and to this assembly, which he brought to quicken a little, who had great need of spurs.

Lord Wariston very particularly declared in the assembly the passionate desires of our parliament, assembly, army, and whole people, of the performance of the covenanted uniformity; and withal we called for a meeting of the grand committee of Lords, Commons, Assembly, and us; to whom we gave a paper, notably well penned by Mr Henderson, bearing the great evils of so long a delay of settling religion, and our earnest desires that some ways might be found out for expedition. This paper my Lord Sey took to deliver to the House of Lords, Mr Solicitor also for the House of Commons, and a third copy was given to Mr Marshal, to be presented to the assembly. On Tuesday last there was a solemn fast for General Effex's army. Mr Palmer and Mr Hill preached that day to the assembly, two of the most Scottish and free sermons that ever I heard any where. The way here of all preachers, even the best, has been, to speak before the parliament with so profound a reverence as truly took all edge from their exhortations, and made all applications toothless and adultorious. That style is much changed of late: however, these two good men laid well about them, and charged publick and parliamentary sins strictly on the backs of the

guilty; amongst the rest, their neglect to settle religion according to the covenant, and to set up ordination, which lay so long in their hands. This was a means to make the House of Commons send us down that long delayed paper of ordination. On Thursday it was twice publick-ly read, so much altered from our paper, that all of us did much mislike it. To encourage the assembly to reject it, we did add in the end of our paper an express disa-vowing of it; and at the committee's desire, we set down our reasons in writ against the House's alterations; which did so encourage the assembly, that this day, unanimously, they sent a committee to the House, to crave leave to con-sider their alterations; for without their express order they have not so much power as to debate a question. This leave is granted: we are confident of reason, second-ed by more plain and stout dealing than hitherto has been used, to make them take up their unreasonable altera-tions of our first paper; also we have the grand commit-tee to meet on Monday, to find out ways of expedience; and we have got it to be the work of the assembly itself, to do no other thing till they have found out ways of ac-celerating; so by God's help we expect a far quicker pro-gress than hitherto. The long looked-for propositions of peace, which my Lord Warriston brought down to our parliament, are now past the committee of both king-doms unanimously, with all the additions our parliament put to them; also this day they are transmitted to the House of Commons, and from thence it is expected they will quickly go to the Lords, that so they may be sent to the King. If he will accept them, our troubles will short-ly be ended; if he reject them, they will be published, that the world may see which party refuses, and which has been misguiding ignorant people with the shew of the desire of peace. There is not, so far as we can hear, any change in the mind of the malignant faction. Max-well, our excommunicate incendiary, is one of the chief preachers at court, and before the King. The King's de-claration to foreign churches, avows his resolution to stand by the hierarchy and liturgy. It will be no other-wise till that wicked faction, which still misleads him, be broken in pieces. Prince Palatine is landed this day. He has no design here but to live, which elsewhere he cannot do. We were afraid of the General's army in the west, and so we had reason; for great mutterings there has
been

been of correspondence betwixt the chief officers of that army with the King; but thanks to God, that is now broken, and this we have as the first answer of our Tuesday's prayers.   On Thursday the General sent up to the House a letter written to him, all with the King's hand, and subscribed, the most flattering and tempting of any thing ever I saw, offering to Essex and all his officers, and all his friends, what they could desire, if they would concur with him, to make the parliament accept of a just and equitable peace. The sending up of this letter is a demonstration of Essex's honesty, and will put off him all calumnies which long has burdened him.   His army and the King's have been within a mile of each other for some days.   There has been some strokes lately for our advantage.   Inchiquin's brother has delivered Warham to Middleton, which we take for a good advantage; but most because it is a clear evidence, that a party is arisen for us in Munster above all our thoughts.   After the taking of the town, with fifteen pieces of cannon, and fifty barrels of powder, Middleton went on to Somersetshire, and at his first coming routed 1000 of the enemy's horse, and took the most of their officers.   The House of Commons, on Saturday, has past all the propositions of peace, as they came from our parliament, without the least alteration; also, on the reading of our paper, they recalled, by vote, four of their chief alterations of the assembly's paper of ordination.   We hope we shall move them to recal the rest also.

There is a great stir in Rome upon the victory of Naples.   The Dukes of Florence and Parma sent their armies thither to have the election of the new Pope every one to their own mind.   The nephews of the last Pope have barricaded the town, and filled it with their own army. The Cardinals refuse to enter the conclave till the town be void of soldiers.   Lerida in Catalonia, and Freyburg in Alsatia, after long sieges, and many sharp assaults, were both about one time lost to the French: but, by a strange providence, they have regained the one; Duc de Anguien coming up with his army, and joining with the Marshal of Turenne, with a great slaughter of the Bavarians; and in a few days got back Freyburg in the poor terms of discretion.   Gallas, with the Imperial army, is joined with the Bishop of Bremen and the Danes.   They lay near to Torstenson in Holstein.   The Swedish and Danish fleets, after

after a hot fight, are making for a new onset. Great blood is feared fhall be fhortly fhed there, both by fea and land. The anger of the Lord againft all Chriftendom is great; and yet little humiliation of heart any where. In our affembly we cannot but quickly come to our greateft queftions, and our hotteft debates; alfo the propofitions of peace, as we have drawn them, will be fhortly fent to the King. All who love the common caufe, and would be glad to fee the church reformed, and the peace of the kingdoms fettled, would be diligent now, if ever, to ftir up their fpirits to deal with the God of peace and truth, that he would fo over-rule the hearts of our oppofites, that both church and ftate, in all thefe dominions, may be relieved from the grievous calamities and dangers which this day preffes very fore. I believe there is nothing wanting to the quick and happy ending of our troubles, but the diligence of the godly to wreftle with their Father for that very defirable bleffing. Expecting the affiftance of your prayers to God, both for the great work in hand, and the weak finful perfons who are employed about it, I reft, your fervant,

ROBERT BAILLIE.

Sir William Waller, this week, with all the reft of his forces, will follow Lieutenant Middleton, that they may gather up the King's rear, while Effex is dealing with his van. We wifh both may become happy inftruments to move his Majefty to pafs thefe propofitions of peace which both parliaments have found to be neceffary.

78. *Publick Letter.* *Auguft* 28. 1644.

How our affairs go, you may fee in the three printed papers; and foreign affairs you may read in the inclofed writ. Our affembly thefe days bygone has been bufy on the Houfe of Commons their alterations of our paper of ordination; at laft they have agreed to fend back our defires for changing the moft of thefe alterations, according to the papers which we gave in to the affembly and both Houfes. Concerning thefe alterations, we expect, without farther ado, the Houfes will pafs our defires; fo that prefently all the youths in England, who for many years have waited for a pure ordination, fhall be admitted to

churches:

churches: and when all thefe, and what moe Scotland can afford of good youths for the miniftry here, are provided, it is thought fome thoufands of churches muft vaik for want of men. Our next work is, to give our advice what to do for fuppreffing of Anabaptifts, Antinomians, and other fectaries. This will be a hard work; yet fo much as concerns us will be quickly difpatched, I hope in one feffion. It is appointed thereafter that we return to the government, and to hold to it till we conclude the erection of feffions, prefbyteries, and fynods. The moft of the directory is paffed, and the reft is given to proper hands to prepare the models for the affembly. All the world are fenfible of our neceffitated delays, and cry for expedition. All of us long much to be at home; but the daily unexpected difficulties, and the neceffitated length of our affairs, are incredible to any who is not on the place. What prayers to God, and diligence with men, can do, we are in our weaknefs effaying, and, praife to God, with fenfible fruit. The affairs of the ftate are in no worfe pofture than before. In all our churches, on Sunday laft, we prayed for Monro's hard condition. We were informed, that the greateft army which ever the Irifh had on foot was come down upon him to root all our people out of Ulfter; but this day we hear he has beat them. We pray God it may be true. Inchiquin in Munfter goes on for us. Prince Rupert lies ftill quiet in Chefter. He gets no men from Ireland, and has no munition. In Lancafhire, Meldrum has taken Prefton, and is mafter of the fields. The forces which Clavering had about Carlifle are making towards him, and Manchefter is fending fupplies to him. The condition of Newcaftle you know better than we. The King and Effex are yet looking the one upon the other. Middleton has ranged all thefe weftern fields for good purpofe. Waller is away to join with him. We expect good news from that airth. The tumults at Rome are compofed; the Cardinals are entered the conclave for the chufing another fury to trouble the world. Prince Thomas has an army for France in Milan, belieging little towns for fmall purpofe. The French in Catalonia, to regain their credit in the lofs of Lerida, are belieging Tarragon. What was believed at Paris, and here, of the retaking of Freyburg, is falfe. Duc de Anguienne and Turenne, with their gallant army, are down the Rhine as far as Philipfburg, which they are like to befiege. The Bavarian

rian army is following them. Gallas is now very near to
Torstenson in Holstein, and the two fleets are looking upon each other at sea. Great strokes are there feared.
The Transylvanians have broken through Poland towards
Silesia, and Coningsmark is going up to join there with
them. The Duke of Saxony lies in his way. The Prince
of Orange is battering Sas de Ghent; but the enemy has
opened the sluices, and drowned much land about it.
The French army at Graveling vex the Spaniards with a
number of strong forts, which they are building in these
parts of Flanders. It is thought Don Melos the Governor, a Portuguese, favours too much the French designs.
The Duke of Orleans is gone to Paris; the Cardinal flat-
ters him much. It is thought they cannot long agree.
Palatine is not yet come hither, but is daily expected.
Both we here, and all the churches abroad, have much
need of the prayers of all the godly there. My hearty
service to all the brethren of the presbytery of Glasgow
and Irvine. I pray God bless every one of them in their
service of Christ, and his people.

ROBERT BAILLIE.

79. *For Mr William Spang.* *September* 13. 1644.

Dear Consin,
You see what I have written here to our friends in
Scotland. We are for the time under a great and very
black cloud. While Argyle is entangled with one company of Irish in his bounds, another company lands in Seaforth's bounds, who lets them pass in peace. Many by
the way joined. Before they came to Strathern, Montrose
came from England disguised, and is now on their head.
Kilpont is gone to him, and Sir John Drummond. He
took, as is thought, with their own good will, Inchmar-
tin and Grandtully. Elcho, with the body of Fife, without officers or ministers, will rashly set on them, before
Gask, now Tullibardine, and Drummond join. At the
first stroke, sweet Reirus, and his brother, and more,
were killed. The rest fled, and cast away some thousand
arms, and left four pieces of cannon. A lamentable disaster! Montrose after fell on Perth. It abode the first
assault. What next, we know not. Lothian and his regiment are to guard Stirling bridge. All the weir and

south-east are running to Stirling. Argyle is marching, Callendar, Lindfay, Montgomery, Dalhowfie, Lawers, are pofting from Newcaftle, with their regiments of horfe and foot. Had this calamity befallen two months before, when Prince Rupert, with his 6000 horfe, might eafily fallen in on Edinburgh, and was fo refolved, had not the King called him fouth on other fruitlefs employments, they, by appearance, had drawn all our forces out of England, and once put all Scotland in a hazard. But God is our watchman. This whip, I hope, fhall do us good. All the armies here are pitifully filled with divifion. The General mifled, would needs go to the weft, in defpite of his exprefs orders to the contrary. This was to break, and did break Waller's army, and brought it to little or nothing. When he went there, it was for no fervice to run to the extreme end of Cornwall, and to lie there till the King gathered an army at his back, and belaid him on all fides, to be mafter of his victuals, and take up the paffage betwixt him and Foy, his fea-port. The greateft pity is if any treachery was here. The authors of it will have power to do it again in this our next and only army on this fide Newcaftle; but it is hoped all will be honeft; that Middleftone and Beir, Effex and Waller, Waller and Maffie and Brown, Cromwell and Crawford, will lay down their great and known quarrels to join againft the common enemy. Great fcarcity of money for any thing; great clamour every where of injuftice and rapine; church-divifions every where increafe. The fectaries wax bolder daily; yet we are hopeful all fhall quickly go better. It is time, I hope, for God to work, our extremity of danger is fo great. If Apollonius ftand on ceremonies, and wait for the authority of his claffes, or ftay till he clog his book with other treatifes, *De magiftratu*, as Callendrin was, his purpofe will come out of feafon here, and will be for little purpofe. One Mr Hoak is on the turning of your Dutch notes on the Bible. This day Cromwell has obtained an order of the Houfe of Commons, to refer to the committee of both kingdoms the accommodation or toleration of the Independents; a high and unexpected order; yet, by God's help, we will make ufe of it contrare to the defign of the procurers. We had need of your prayers in this hour of great darknefs; fince none of your help, nor any others elfe over fea, can be obtained. The unkindnefs of all the Reformed churches to us at thefe

times is great.   It is England's merit, but may be the great
sin of those who have no charity, nor so much zeal as
prudence.   The Lord be with you.   The next, I hope,
shall be more comfortable.

80. *Publick Letter.*   September 16. 1644.

OUR affairs here, thanks to God, go better than lately.
On Saturday last we went out to meet the Chancellor.   He
was welcomed by some appointed by both Houses.   Two
hours after his coming, that same night, we were much
afflicted with the miscarriage of Essex's army in the west,
and the disaster of the Fife gentlemen in Scotland.   Our
recourse, in these griefs and fears, was to our God.   On
Thursday we had a solemn humiliation, wherein we trust
the Lord did hear us, and already has comforted us in a
good measure.   Sir William Balfour, in the night, after
the setting of the moon, broke through the enemy with
all his horse, with no loss considerable.   Essex, Roberts,
and Merrick, had before gone by sea to Plymouth; Skippon had put his foot in good order about his cannon, resolving to die fighting, if good quarter was refused.   Tolerable quarter was given, but not kept; yet there was no
slaughter.   Middleton's horse are now joined with the General's; also the foot, naked as they were, are come to
them   Cloaths and arms are at them before this.   Waller
is also joined with them, and Manchester's whole army is
marching fast towards them; so, by the blessing of God,
that army will be stronger than ever, and that loss will do
us much good, to humble us, and draw us nearer God,
and unite our minds; for their divisions were shameful and
many, and jealousies great, of many men, which this mis-
accident is like to cure.   General Leven writes to us of his
dissipating the enemy's forces in Cumberland, and good
hopes to carry Newcastle in a short time; also of his sending up my Lord Callendar, with so many of his best horse
and foot, as, with Argyle's forces on the rebels backs,
and the country-forces on their face, with God's help,
may bring these wicked men to their deserved end.   When
we heard of Lord Elcho's disaster, we were much perplexed: and above all things in the world we long for good
news from Scotland.   We hope these things will further
our assembly; albeit we have made little progress these
                                                     fourteen

fourteen days. We fpent a number of feffions on fome propofitions of advice to the parliament, for fuppreffing Antinomians, Anabaptifts, and thefe who preach a liberty for all religions. Even in thefe our good Independents found us great difficulty; and when we had carried our advices againft their mind, they offered to give in contrare reafons to the parliament. We fpent two or three days on the matter of a remonftrance to the parliament of the fins which provoked God to give us this late ftroke; and here we had the moft free and ftrange parliament that ever I heard, about the evident fins of the affembly, the fins of the parliament, the fins of the army, the fins of the people. When we were in full hope of a large fruit of fo honeft and faithful a cenfure, Thomas Goodwin and his brethren, as their cuftom is to oppofe all things that are good, carried it fo, that all was dung in the howes, and that matter clean laid by. We are again on the government. We have paffed two or three propofitions, that the church may be governed by three forts of affemblies, congregational, claffical, and fynodical. We begin with fynods, and hope to make quicker difpatch than before, by God's help. We have fundry means of hafte in agitation with our private friends. One of our fpecial helps muft be the prayers of the godly there. This rage of the devil, both here and there, is a good fign to us of a glorious work in hand, which he fo violently oppofeth. The French make ftrange progrefs in Germany. They have, with great eafe, taken that great ftrength of Philipfburg; and with it almoft all the Nether Palatinate. Palfefield, Lorrain, and Beck, have joined their forces with the Bavarian army, and great fupplies alfo are come from France to the Weimarifh. There may be a battle there. The Swedes and Imperialifts are parted without any confiderable cuff. The Holland fleet is joined, they fay, with the Swedes againft the Danes. Our good Queen is negotiating the marriage of her fon with her brother the Duke of Orleans' daughter. She fold her daughter to the Prince of Orange for his money, and now would caft away her fon for an army from France againft us; but all will not do. The phyficians fpeak of her impoffibility to live long. By God's help we may make an end of this war before the French can be at leifure to engage.

81, *For Mr David Dickson.*   September 16, 1644.

Reverend and Dear Brother,

How affairs go here you may see in my publick letters and printed papers; but beside all these, you may know more. At this time we are put to live by faith; for so far as we can reach with the eye of our sense, there is one of the thickest clouds above us that we have seen since the beginning of our affairs. Besides your troubles in Scotland, which we fear are very great, and the small hopes of carrying Newcastle in haste, we walk here very heavily. We can get no money. Very vast sums are mis-spent. No man will contribute any more willingly, and compulsory ways brings not in what so many and great necessities as we have calls for. The dissolution of the General's army in the west, in itself is a huge loss both of strength and reputation: but the circumstances make it greater. These who affect the General, think it was procured by the parliament's willing neglect to send him timeous supplies; others fear their treachery in running to such a place needlessly, and staying in it till they were circumveened, which a little providence might have eschewed. Our greatest fear is, that the forces we have to oppose the King are full of jealousies and malice one against another. The most of the officers in the General and Waller's army have open and known quarrels. Manchester's is more pitifully divided. It is like to divide us all incontinent. Manchester himself, a sweet meek man, permitted his Lieutenant-General Cromwell to guide all the army at his pleasure. The man is a very wise and active head, universally well beloved, as religious and stout; being a known Independent, the most of the soldiers who loved new ways put themselves under his command. Our countryman Crawford was made Major-General of that army. This man proving very stout and successful, got a great hand with Manchester, and with all the army that were not for sects. The other party finding their designs marred by him, set themselves by all means to have him out of the way, that he being removed, they might frame the whole army to their devotion, and draw Manchester himself to them by persuasion, or else to weary him out of his charge, that Cromwell might be General. This has been the Independents

pendents great plot by this army, to counterbalance us, and overawe the affembly and parliament both to their ends. At this nick of time, while their fervice is neceffary to oppofe the King, they give in a challenge againft Crawford; they require a committee of war to remove him. Both the parties write up here to their friends the cafe. At laft, Manchefter, Cromwell, and Crawford, come up themfelves. Our labour to reconcile them was vain. Cromwell was peremptor, notwithftanding the kingdom's evident hazard, and the evident difpleafure of our nation; yet if Crawford were not cafhiered, his Colonels would lay down their commiffions. All of us, by my Lord Manchefter's own teftimony, and the teftimony of the minifters in the army, find Crawford a very honeft and valorous man, in nothing confiderably guilty, only perfecuted to make way to their defigns on that army, and by it on the parliament and kingdom; therefore all here of our friends refolve to fee him get as little wrong as we may. What the end of this may be, God knows. While Cromwell is here, the Houfe of Commons, without the leaft advertifement to any of us, or of the affembly, paffes an order, that the grand committee of both Houfes, affembly, and us, fhall confider of the means to unite us and the Independents; or, if that be found impoffible, to fee how they may be tolerated. This has much affected us. Thefe men have retarded the affembly thefe long twelve months. This is the fruit of their differvice, to obtain really an act of parliament for their toleration, before we have got any thing for prefbytery either in affembly or parliament. Our greateft friends, Sir Henry Vane and the Solicitor, are the main procurers of all this; and that without any regard to us, who have faved their nation, and brought thefe two perfons to the height of the power now they enjoy, and ufe to our prejudice. We are on our ways, with God and men, to redrefs all thefe things as we may. We had much need of your prayers. This is a very fickle people; fo wonderfully divided in all their armies, both their Houfes of parliament, affembly, city, and country, that it is a miracle if they fall not into the mouth of the King. That party grows in ftrength and courage. The Queen is very like to get an army from France. The great fhot of Cromwell and Vane is to have a liberty of all religions, without any exception. Many a time we are put to great trouble of mind. We muft make
the

the beft of an ill game we can. Marfhall' miskens us altogether : he is for a middle way of his own, and draws a
faction in the fynod to give ordination and excommunication to congregations; albeit dependently, in cafe of male-
adminiftration. God help us! If God be pleafed to fettle Scotland, and give us Newcaftle, all will go well. We
muft fee for new friends at laft, when our old ones, without any the leaft caufe, have deferted, and have half-
betrayed us. Thefe things to you alone, to ftir up your
prayers, by knowing our ftraits, and increafing your
thankfgiving when you hear of the falvation of the Lord;
which we do certainly expect. The Chancellor is here in
a very needful time. Bleffed be God, all our company
are in good health and chearful; trufting God, and refolving to do our duty with all the care and prudence God
will enable us, be the fuccefs what it may, as truly we are
hopeful it fhall be very good. Thefe things to you, and
Mr Robert, and Mr George. I reft,

     Your Brother,

                        ROBERT BAILLIE.

82. *Publick Letter. October.*

How affairs go here and elfewhere, fince my laft with
Mr John Dickfon, the fix inclofed printed papers, and
two in writ, may fhew. We were here for fome days under a cloud. The difafters lamentable in Scotland about
St Johnfton and Aberdeen, the prolongation of the fiege
of Newcaftle, the fcattering of Effex's army in the weft,
Sir Henry Vane, our moft entire friend, joining with a
new faction to procure liberty for fects; thefe, and fundry other mifaccidents, did much afflict us for a fortnight. At that time we endeavoured to live by faith;
but the goodnefs of our God has already begun to en-
lighten our darknefs. If it were God's will to crufh that
wicked infurrection with you, as we hear, praife to God,
thefe wicked men are not far from their ruin; and if
Newcaftle were taken, as we are informed it is like to be
fhortly; then all difficulties here, we hope, would eafily
be overcome. Thanks to God, things are in much better pofture than lately. The Chancellor has done a great
deal of noble fervice. The treachery in General Effex's
army was like to be the fountain of great confufion;
                                      but

but it will now do good: it will purge that army of all the dangerous knaves, and procure to Essex as much trust and more command than before, for which he may thank our Chancellor. It will reconcile him and Waller, it will compose tho irreconcileable differences betwixt Cromwell and Crawford, in Manchester's army; all these are now joining in one, above 8000 horse and 12,000 of foot, well armed and old foldiers. The King has got nothing by his victory: he is with his army about Bristol, not much above 10,000 horse and foot, and no other army he has on foot in England. We hope this posture may draw out a peace, and move his Majesty to accept the propositions whereupon both kingdoms have agreed. In the assembly, thanks to God, we have throughed not only our presbyteries, but also our synods provincial and national, and the subordination of all the four meetings, parochial, classical, provincial, and national. We are now to dispute upon the power of all the four. We have strange tugging with the Independents. The House of Commons have appointed a committee to consider of their differences with us, if they be reconcileable; or, if not, how far they may be tolerated. At first the motion did much perplex us; but, after some debates upon it, we are now hopeful to make vantage of it, for the truth against the errors of that very wilful and obstinate party. We are in hopes to get the directory brought towards an end, and the catechism also ere long, with which some of us are likely to be sent down. The Confession of Faith is referred to a committee, to be put in several the best hands that are here. By the help of God, procured by your prayers, our adversaries defigns may contribute to the happy closure of these longsome and wonderfully troublesome affairs.

83. For Mr William Spang.   October 25. 1644.

Dear Cousin,

I have not written to you these three or four weeks, not only to stay while I found you had got my last, but specially because I had not a mind nor a hand to write any thing to any while I saw what would be the pleasure of God to do with us; and howsoever we be yet under the cloud, yet left you should wait so long, I force myself

felf to write this to you. On the other fide you have what I wrote laſt to Scotland. Poor deſolate Ireland lies in the former miſeries. Monro, with all he could make, in July, made a road within ſixteen miles of Dublin; for want of proviſion he quickly returned without the fight of an enemy. Caſtlehaven, convoyed with all the Iriſh commanders of note, followed him at the heels, with the beſt army ever that nation had, above 12,000 well-armed and diſciplined men: they lay down under Charlemont, fenced in with water and bogs. Monro brought up to Ardmagh all he could make. Both were lying there September 19th, waiting who ſhould firſt, for want of victuals, diſband: ſince, we have heard nought of either. Inchiquin, and the Munſtermen, who declared againſt the Popiſh Iriſh, lie quiet. Ormond, with the King's advice, has prorogued the ceſſation for three months longer, holding out the hopes of a full peace. In the mean time Alaſter Macdonald, Colkittoch's ſon, with ſome 1500, the moſt part Scots highlanders, comes from iſle to iſle to Argyle, from the continent, with ſome Engliſh and Holland ſhips, take from them the moſt of their ſhips and boats; whereupon they run to the Lewis, and through paſſages where it is thought Seaforth (eſpecially being warned by Argyle for that effect) might have ſtopped them; but, without any oppoſition, they run through Lochaber. When they come to Athol, the moſt there joined with them. Drummond and Gaſk raiſed the low country againſt them; but Montroſe coming from England his alone diſguiſed, did join with them, and, by his letters, got many of Strathern and Perthſhire to join with him. Kilpont's treachery is revenged by his death, juſtly inflicted. Lord Duplin, now Kinnoul, Maderty, Fintry, Braco, and a number of note, did increaſe the army; yet they were but a pack of naked runagates, not three horſe among them, few either ſwords or muſquets: but the villainy of Lord Drummond and his friend, in the point of joining, exhorting to flee, according as by his letters he had appointed the night before, ſtruck the reſt with a panick fear, ſo that near 6000 of very good and brave men fled, leaving eight piece of cannon, and the moſt of their arms. In the fight not ten were killed; but in the flight ſome hundreds of the honeſt burgeſſes of Fife did fall. The villains gave no quarter; not a priſoner in the field was taken; Perth rendered at the firſt

2   ſummons.

summons. Argyle, after he had learned the way whither the miscreants had run, followed as armed men might, which was four or five days journey behind them. As he came near Stirling, Montrose left Perth, having extorted near 9000 merks of money, and what arms they had. His summoning of Dundee was in vain; but all the rest of the country was at his mercy. Had Argyle gotten him later, all Fife had been sacked. The bridge of Dee was manned, so he went over a ford, where Elcho's regiment had a hot dispute, and killed many of his men; but prevailing in number, he forced his passage. Marischal being malecontent, sat still in Dunnotter. Gordon, to whom, unadvisedly, the command of the country was committed, did not bring with him above thirty horse, and these nothing stout. The townsmen of Aberdeen essayed to defend their market-place; but 140 of them were killed: within two days after put the knaves to their best. Our greatest fears were, that Seaforth, Grant, and Murray there should have joined; but when they came to Spey, Seaforth and Sutherland, with the gentry of Murray, lay on either side, kept them from passing; Argyle was at their heels; they got up to the mountains. Many of their followers left them; yet Montrose, with 2000 or 3000 of most desperate and cruel villains, came back on the hills, so far as Athol, whither he was to break down on Argyle, and so to fisher-boats, to flee to Ireland; or to keep the hills till he came to Campsie, and then to fall down on Glasgow; and then to break through to England, as most did fear. We do not yet hear, only Kyle and Cunningham, with my Lord Montgomery, Clydesdale, with my Lord Lanerk, Renfrew, and Lennox, had their rendezvous at Glasgow the 11th of October. If he come that way, our greatest fear is, that a new army from Ireland fall on our west before Argyle can come back from the north. This is the greatest hurt our poor land got these fourscore years, and the greatest disgrace befell us these thousand. The reproach will stick on us for ever. It has much diminished our reputation already, being joined with the length of the siege of Newcastle. Many things there have deceived our hopes: The enemy within desperately resolute, with frequent sallies keep our people night and day in duty; our mines, the most part, after all our labour, were countermined or drowned; our soldiers, for want of pay and cloaths, were worn to rags;

sundry

fundry of our beft regiments and officers were of neceffity gone to Scotland; befide, winter and ill-weather comes now on. The Independent party lying always at the watch, finding us fo low, and the General in the weft fhamefully difgraced, began luftily to play their game. Their firft effay was on Manchefter's army; there they had caft their ftrength, under Cromwell. All fectaries who pleafed to be foldiers, for a long time cafting themfelves from all the other, arrive under his command, in one body. By many means they effayed to get Manchefter removed; finding they could not conquer him, when all had failed, they betook themfelves to our countryman Jordanhill's brother, Gen. Major Crawford, to have been cafhiered by a council of war, for a number of pretended faults; but we did fo manage that bufinefs that all their effays fo were in vain. Their next effay was to have laid afide the General, and remnant of his forces, that Cromwell and their forces might be the more confiderable: but confidering the hazard; and feeing, after all our trial, no guiltinefs in the General; and finding the underhand dealing to join the General to their party, when they could not overthrow him; God helped us to guard it fo, that the General keeps his place and credit, and knows who are his friends and foes. We had another bout with them about Shippon. They made the city crave him to be leader of their new levy of 5000 foot, and to be joined to Manchefter. This was by Shippon's foot and Cromwell's horfe to have made themfelves mafters of the field: this we alfo got croffed. But their greateft plot, wherewith yet we are wreftling, is an order of the Houfe of Commons, contrived by Mr Solicitor and Mr Marfhall, which they got ftolen through, to the committee of Lords, Commons, and Divines, which treated with us, to confider of differences in point of church-government, which were among the members of the affembly, that they might be agreed; or if not, how far tender confciences might be borne with, which could not come up to the common rule to be eftablifhed, that fo the proceedings of the affembly might not be retarded. This order prefently gave us the alarm: we faw it was for a toleration of the Independents by act of parliament, before the prefbytery or any common rule were eftablifhed. Our moft trufty friend the Solicitor had throughed it the Houfe before we heard of it. Mr Marfhal had evidently,

in

in the profecution of it, flighted us. Sir Henry Vane, whom we trufted moft, had given us many figns of his alteration; twice at our table prolixly, earneftly, and paffionately had reafoned for a full liberty of confcience to all religions, without any exceptions; had publickly, in the Houfe, oppofed the claufe in the ordination that required minifters to fubfcribe the covenant, and that which did intimate their being over their flocks in the Lord; had moved the muftering of our army, as being far lefs than we were paid for; had been offended with the Solicitor for putting in the ordinance the differences about church-government; and not only about free grace, intruding liberty to the Antinomians, and to all fects, he, without the leaft occafion on our fide, did openly oppofe us. Always God has helped us againft him and them egregioufly to this day. In the firft meeting of the grand committee, Mr Marfhal the chairman, by canny convoyance, got a fubcommittee nominate according to his mind, to draw the differences; Goodwin and Nye, other four with himfelf, who joined with the Independents in giving to the congregations power of excommunication and ordination. Vines, Herle, Reynolds, Temple, Seaman, and Palmer, of our mind, were named; but feeing us excluded by Marfhal's cunning, would not join. The next two or three meetings were fpent on the fubcommittee's draught of the differences. We found the Independents clear for the whole people, every communicant male, to have decifive voice in all ecclefiaftic caufes, in admiffion, depofition, excommunication of minifters, in determining of fchifms and herefies. 2. That no congregation did depend on any fuperior fynod, fo that a congregation falling in all the herefies and crimes of the world, neither the whole nor any member of it can be cenfured by any fynod or prefbytery in the earth, however it may be refufed communion by any who find no fatisfaction in its proceedings: but, which is worft of all, they avow they cannot communicate as members with any congregation in England, though reformed to the uttermoft pitch of purity which the affembly or parliament are like to require, becaufe even the Englifh, as all the reft of the Reformed, will confift but of profeffors of the truth in whofe life there is no fcandal; but they require to a member, befide a fair profeffion, and want of fcandal, fuch figns of grace as perfuades the whole congregation of their true regeneration. We were glad to have them declare this much under their

I 2 hands;

hands ; for hitherto it has been their great care to avoid any such declaration ; but now they are more bold, apprehending their party to be much more confiderable, and our nation much lefs confiderable than before. The The change of providence did nothing daunt our courage ; yet we were much in prayer and longing expectation that God would raife us from our lownefs, near to contempt, and compefce their groundlefs infolency. At our firft meeting, my Lords Sey and Wharton, Vane and the Solicitor, preffed vehemently to debate the propofitions of the fubcommittee. They knew, when they had debated, and come to voicing, they would carry all by plurality in the committee ; and though they fhould not, yet they were confident, when the report came to the Houfe of Commons, to get all they defired there paft. So, without the affembly, they purpofed immediately from this committee to get a toleration of Independency concluded in the Houfe of Commons, long before any thing fhould be got fo much as reported from the affembly anent prefbyteries. Here it was where God helped us befide our expectation. Mr Rous, Mr Taite, and Mr Prideaux, among the ableft of the Houfe of Commons, oppofed them to their face. My Lord Chancellor, with a fpirit of divine eloquence, Wariffon, with the fharp points of manifold arguments, Maitland, Mr Henderfon, Mr Gillefpie, and all, made their defigns to appear fo clearly, that at once many did diflike them ; yet Henry Vane went on violently. We refufed to confider their propofitions, except on two exprefs caveats ; one, That no report fhould be made of any conclufion of the committee, till firft it came to the affembly, and from them, after examination, fhould be tranfmitted to the Houfe of Commons ; another, That firft the common rule of government fhould be refolved, before any forbearance of thefe who differed therefrom fhould be refolved upon. The firft, after many hours fharp debate, we obtained : the fecond we are to debate to-morrow ; and, if we obtain it not, we have a brave paper ready, penned by Mr Henderfon, to be given in to the Houfes and affembly, which will paint out the Independents and their adherents fo clearly, that I am hopeful that the bottom of their plots fhall be dung out. While I am writing, we get the long-expected news of the taking of Newcaftle, and that by ftorm. Bleffed be the name of the Lord, who will not for ever contemn the prayers of his people. We were extremely dejected on

many

many grounds: we were perplexed for Scotland; beside winter, poverty, and strong, proud, obstinate enemies within Newcastle, the pest was beginning in our army; the King, with the greatest army he ever commanded, was coming straight upon us, being hopeful to dissipate our armies before they could conjoin, and it was but the miss of one day; yet Waller held him up skirmishing at and over till Manchester came to Newbury, and Essex to Alfort, whence all three, on Saturday, joined at Basing. The emulations and quarrels among all these three armies, both Generals and inferior officers, were formidable; yet such was the wisdom and diligence of the Chancellor and others, that Wariston and Mr Carew going down from the committee of both kingdoms, did move all the three Generals, and their armies, to join cordially against the enemy. The most true and real fast I ever saw here, was kept on Tuesday; also the House of Commons desired us in the assembly, to pray upon Wednesday, thinking the armies both these days to be in action, and expecting the determination of the great quarrel hourly, neither party having any other considerable forces on this side Newcastle. Great were the frays of this people, and their tears to God plentiful. The answer was not long a-coming. Before we had ended our prayers on Wednesday, in the assembly, the House of Peers sent us a message by my Lord Admiral and Pembroke, with all diligence, to haste the church-government, for heresies did spread mightily over all the land; also they told, the King had turned his back on us, and was retiring towards Oxford, finding, against his expectation, that all our armies were joined. He sent his foot and artillery away, and with his horse drew near, as resolute to fight; but shortly drew off, and followed his foot: we are at their heels. It will be hard if we get not a hit of them before they win to Oxford. Hurry is come back to us, and received; he promises the coming over of a better soldier than himself: but above all, the news of Newcastle, in these two hours, has filled the city with extreme joy. The great God be blessed again and again for it. This people would have perished of cold without it. Had we got it by composition, it had not relieved our credit, nor the necessity of our most deserving and worse rewarded army. God, in clear justice toward that most wicked town, and great mercy to us all, hardened that people, that they should
reject,

reject, with infolence, the faireft conditions that ever people in their condition could have expected; fo that any lofs they have, the world will excufe us of it. That our joy may be the greater, the Admiral at the fame time receives a letter from one of his fhips on the Irifh coaft, that Monro has defeat Caftlehaven with all his proud army in Ulfter. We truft to hear next of the vengeance of God on Montrofe, and his followers in Scotland. All thefe things lift us not up, but haften us to fend our propofitions to the King, without any addition to thefe articles which were debated and agreed on in our parliament. The admitting of thefe articles is the greateft ufe we defire to make of thefe great favours our God has thefe two days poured upon us.

The books you wrote of are not come to me; I hear nought of them as yet. What you wrote for I delivered to Mr Garret, to be fent in the next fhip. Downham's guide is 18 s. and Hooker's 3 volumes is 15 s. I know I am much in your debt; but I intreat, fo far as either your papers or your memory can ferve you, let me once again know my fum what it is: by any means fatisfy me in this. I fhall the more freely fend for any thing I defire from thence, and fhall fend you what you defire from this. If God will blefs us with the overthrow of thefe evil men, friends will yet live comfortably together. Apollonius's book will not be delivered to the affembly till it come off the prefs. We are extremely obliged to him, and as much difobliged to his oppofites. The letter of the fynod of Utretch was read the other day in the affembly, but had not one word either of Epifcopacy or Independency. We would have expected other things from Voetius; but the Independents diligence far and near is great; yet I believe God will not blefs their ways. Rivet, in all our controverfies, refolves to be mute and filent alfo; yet Moulin has written very honeftly his mind; but Diodati and the Parifians are not as we expected. The Switzers, and lately the reft of the divines of Geneva, have given us fatisfaction. We hope fhortly, when God has put our enemies under our feet, thefe our Reverend brethren who have been laft in appearing for us, fhall be moft ample in their encouragements. We are loth to cenfure any man, only, in fo great conflicts, we would have expected from brethren in a common caufe, greater affiftance than we have got from any over fea, except only worthy

worthy and noble Apollonius; but I must end abruptly, or lose my late supper.   Farewell.
    Your Cousin,

                    ROBERT BAILLIE.

84. *For Mr William Spang.*   *November* 1. 1644.

Dear Cousin,
    ——Of the taking of Newcastle I wrote at length. The routing of the Irish by Monro is not seconded; but the routing and flight of the King's army here is very true. His foot are all dissipated; few slain.   His horse got away at midnight towards Oxford.   Monday last, himself, and the Prince, with some 500 horse, towards Bristol.   The remnant of his cannon and baggage, which was not taken that night, were left in Dennington castle, a mile from Newbury.   We expect to hear this night, or to-morrow, that the castle, and all in it, also General Ruthven to the boot, now weary of the King, shall fall in our hands. Our committee at Newcastle wrote up to the Houses, to haste the settling of the church.   This motion was well received by all but Sey, Vane, and some few Independents. To comfort them, six or eight of the chief Lords came this day in message from the House of Peers with that letter, intreated the assembly to haste; also in that letter the Commons voted, over the Independents bellies, the dissolving of that dangerous committee which these five weeks has vexed us.   The preface of our directory, casting out at doors the liturgy, and all the ceremonies *in cumulo*, is this day passed.   It cost us divers days debate, and these sharp enough, with our best friends.   Apollonius's book is not yet off the press, and so I have not seen it; only the preface I read, which I like exceedingly well. One thing I must recommend to your serious care.   We are informed from thence very credibly, that the agents of the Independents have so far prevailed with Voetius, as to make him publish his approbation of the Keys of the kingdom of heaven, as consonant to truth, and the discipline of Holland.   If he should be so evil advised as to do any thing of this kind at this time, he will wrong himself, and us, and all the Reformed churches, exceedingly, and do what in him lies to mar the most great and gracious work here; which, by God's help, after so great opposition,

tion, we are carrying to a happy conclusion. You would write to him, and all you can join with you, to obtest him he do not any such work, so unworthy of himself. We could never have suspected any such things, if a very good hand had not confidently assured us of it.

Your Cousin,

ROBERT BAILLIE.

85. *Publick Letter.* November 21. 1644.

OUR languor here is great to hear of the crushing of that wicked crew which troubles your peace. That as yet you have not got order with them, is the matter of our greatest grief. If the Lord had humbled and softened the hearts of your people, and wrought them by that rod to a real reformation, which I trust he is doing, I am confident, by the blast of his vengeance, these grashoppers should be carried out of the land. The condition of affairs here you, may read in the printed papers, and of things abroad in the writ. The fruit of our victory at Newbury was not so great as we expected. Within ten days thereafter the King rallied his forces, and, with the addition of what Prince Rupert brought him, became stronger than we: for the custom of the soldiers here is woeful; they cannot bide from home a month together on any condition. This unamendable abuse diminished much our army; so that the King came safely from Oxford to Dennington castle, and brought off his cannon and baggage, and all he had left there. Our army were content to look on him in the bygoing, without minting to fight. This was ill spoken of here. The King marched towards Basing to relieve that longsome siege. Our army followed, much incensed with the obloquy they had received for their sitting still at Newbury. The Houses, fearing their rashness in fighting, and seeing the necessar dissolution of the King's army of its own accord in a few days, having no pay, and the winter being rainy, sent them word to be very wary in fighting: so ours returned to Reading, and the King's to Newbury; whence it is expected, that, without more ado, both will go to their winter-quarters, leaving the ending of the war in the spring to the Scots army, if peace cannot be had before. Three of our commissioners, Maitland, Sir Charles Erskine, and Mr Barclay,

clay, went yefterday, with the Earl of Danby, and four commoners, to the King, upon his fafe-conduct, with the propofitions of peace agreed upon by the parliaments of both kingdoms. We pray God give them good fpeed. There is fmall hopes of the King's acceptance of them; yet many think they may draw on a treaty; and who knows but that may bring us to a peace? However, the difficulties as yet feem inextricable by the wit of any man.

Our church-affairs go on now apace, bleffed be God. Our letters from Newcaftle moved the Houfes to call once, twice, thrice, to the affembly for expedition. They fent up our propofitions concerning prefbyteries. The Independents gave in the reafons of their diffent therefrom. Thefe are in the hands of a committee. The anfwer is like to be full and fatisfactory to the world, and poffibly to the parties themfelves. In a few days, all we have done about government will be fent up to the Houfes, againft which the Independents will have nothing confiderable to fay more than is in their papers againft prefbyteries. But that which moft comforts us is the directory. All that we have done in it is this day fent up, with a full unanimity of all. Many a wearifome debate has it coft us; but we hope the fweet fruit will overbalance the very great toil we had in it. The laft paffage was fenfibly from God. After, with huge deal of ado, we paffed the parts that concerned prayers, reading of fcripture, preaching, both the facraments, ordination, and fanctification of the fabbath, there were many references to the preface; one, to turn the directory to a ftraight liturgy; another to make it fo loofe and free, that it fhould ferve for little ufe: but God helped us to get both thefe rocks efchewed. Always hereyefterday, when we were at the very end of it, the Independents brought us fo doubtful a difputation, that we were in very great fear all fhould be caft in the hows, and that their oppofition to the whole directory fhould be as great as to the government; yet God in his mercy guided it fo, that yefterday we got them, and all others, fo fatisfied, that, *nemine contradicente*, it was ordered all together to be tranfmitted to the Houfes, and Goodwin to be one of the carriers; which was this day done, to all our great joy, and hope that this will be a good ground of agreeance betwixt us and them, either foon or fyne. What remains of the directory, anent marrying and burial, will foon be difpatched. The catechifm is drawn up, and, I think, shall not take up much time. I fear the Confeſſion of Faith may ſtick longer. However, we will, by God's help, have ſo much work done in a month, that it ſeems neceſſar to have a general aſſembly in Scotland ſhortly, that ſome of us may bring there what here has been ſo long in doing, to be reviſed, and, I hope, without great difficulty, to be paſſed. If it pleaſe the Lord to perfect this work, it will be the ſweeteſt and moſt happy buſineſs that ever in this iſle was enterpriſed. The hope of it comforts us in the midſt of our perplexities, which ſometimes are not ſmall. The chimes for midnight are ringing at Weſtminſter, ſo I muſt crave leave to go to bed ; only, remembering my beſt affections to my brethren of both my preſbyteries, and deſiring their prayers for the advancing and perfecting the great work in hand, I reſt, the ſervant of all thoſe who with the weal of Zion.

86. *Publick Letter.*   *December* 1.-1644.

ALL our company, thanks to God, feel the fruit of Scotland's prayers. We all, ſince our coming to this day, had good health, and perfect concord, and, in greateſt perplexity, faith in God. After two days tough debate, and great appearance of irreconcileable differences, thanks to God, we have got the Independents ſatisfied, and an unanimous conſent of all the aſſembly, that marriage ſhall be celebrated only by the miniſter, and that in the church, after our faſhion. There are whiſperings of good appearance, that the Independents will be gotten contented to take up their reaſons, and ſubmit themſelves to the aſſembly. If this be, it were better than a new victory over the King's army. Who knows what reward the Lord may give us for our great patience, and love to theſe, however very good, yet very dangerous and unhappy men, who have been the great and mighty inſtruments to keep all things here looſe, both in church and ſtate, theſe two years bygone, for the increaſing of their party to ſo great a ſtrength, that they might, by fear and threats, obtain their deſires. But theſe four months bygone, ſince we ſet our face againſt them openly, their plots are ſo broken, and their ſtrength decayed, that I hope God will make them more pliable to reaſon, than otherwiſe they were inclined. You ſee I am careful by all occaſions to let you
know

know how the world does go. With our post, by land, I
sent large information, November 21. With this bearer
you have a journal; and, for affairs abroad, two papers;
the one, what Sir Thomas Dishington sent me last from
Paris; the other, what Sir Robert Anstruther got the last
week from Brussels. Matters here stand thus: The House
of Commons have passed, without any variation to count
of, all the directory we sent them, and I hope to-morrow
will send it to the Lords to make an ordinance upon it. In
the assembly we have stuck longer than we expected on
marriage: but I hope to-morrow we shall end it; and before this week end we shall pass the two remanent parts
of the directory, fasting, and burial, or visitation of the
sick; also, that we shall one of the days of this week send
up the rest of our votes of government, except we fall in
debate of some passages of our too large answer to the Independents reasons against presbyteries. Believe it, for as
slow as you may think us, and as we pronounce ourselves
to be, yet all the days of the week we are pretty busy. We
sit daily from nine till near one; and after noon till night
we are usually in committees. Saturday, our only free
day, is to prepare for Sunday; wherein we seldom vaik
from preaching in some eminent place of the city. Judge
what time we have for letters, and writing of pamphlets,
and many other businesses. We would think it a great
ease both to our bodies and spirits to be at home. There
are two new businesses fallen in, which will make some
stir for a time. Our commissioners are returned from Oxford. In the few days they were there, they saw, and
learned from their secret friends, that however the soldiers, and most both of nobility and gentry, be extreme
miserable and poor, and have great need of peace; yet
the Queen's party, that guides still the King, Digby,
Hyde, Ashburnham, Rupert, and Maurice, Richmond,
and Southampton, the junto that makes cyphers of the
other Lords and Commons, few and poor, who now sit
in the two Houses of parliament at Oxford, are as far a-
verse from any just and equitable peace as ever. They
think Montrose is master of Scotland, that from Ireland
and France they will get wonders; therefore they but
laugh at us and our propositions. Only to increase our
divisions, they have sent for a safe-conduct to Richmond
and Southampton, to come with the King's answer to our
propositions. What these two will offer, we know not;

but we expect little good from them. The other matter is, Lieutenant-General Cromwell has publickly, in the House of Commons, accused my Lord of Manchester of the neglect of fighting at Newbury. That neglect indeed was great; for, as we now are made sure, the King's army was in that posture, that they took themselves as lost all utterly. Yet the fault is unjustly laid on Manchester. It was common to all the general officers then present, and to Cromwell himself as much as to any other. Always Manchester has cleared himself abundantly in the House of Lords, and there has recriminated Cromwell, as one who has avowed his desire to abolish the nobility of England; who has spoken contumeliously of the Scots intention of coming into England to establish their church-government, in which Cromwell said he would draw his sword against them, also against the assembly of divines, and has threatened to make an army of sectaries, to extort by force, both from King and parliament, what conditions they thought meet. This fire was long under the embers; now it is broken out, we trust, in a good time. It is like, for the interest of our nation, we must crave reason of that darling of the sectaries, and in obtaining his removal from the army, which himself, by his own rashness, has procured, to break the power of that potent faction. This is our present difficult exercise. We had need of your prayers.

87. *To Mr William Spang.*　　December 6. 1644.

Reverend and Dear Brother,

You have here what I have written to Scotland. Besides, I let you know, we never go so quickly in the assembly as we expect. This week, after many sharp debates, we have agreed, and sent up to the Houses, our directory, for marriage, and days of thanksgiving; also we have, with much difficulty, passed a proposition for abolishing their ceremonies at burial: but our difference about funeral sermons seems irreconcileable, as it has been here and every where preached. It is nothing but an abuse of preaching, to serve the humours only of rich people for a reward. Our church expressly has discharged them on many good reasons. It is here a good part of the ministers livelihood; therefore they will not quit it.

After

After three days debate, we cannot find yet a way of a-greeance. If this were passed, there is no more in our directory, but fasting and holidays, wherein we apprehend no difference. Upon these, with our votes of government already passed, and our answers to the Independents reasons, the next week, I think, will be spent. The letter of your classes before Apollonius's book was read the other day, and a printed copy of his book given to every member of the assembly. It was not only very well taken, but also, which is singular, and, so far as I remember, *absque exemplo*, it was ordered, *nemine contradicente*, to write a letter of thanks to Apollonius. Surely he has done a piece of good service to God, and his churches here. I have not yet had leisure to read it all; but I approve what I have read. This matter of Cromwell has been a high and mighty plot of the Independent party to have gotten an army for themselves under Cromwell, with the ruin, and shamefully unjust crushing, of Manchester's person, of dissolving the union of the nations, of abolishing the House of Lords, of dividing the House of Commons, of filling the city, and most of the Commons, with intestine wars, of setting up themselves upon the ruins of all; but God, who has drawn us out of many desperate dangers, is like to turn this dangerous mischief on the heads of the contrivers. I hope it shall break the far more supposed than real strength of that party, and unite us more strongly; but we are yet wrestling with them. By the next you may have more. Whether the King will send Lennox and Southampton, we cannot yet say; for in our answer we have put, we think, the thorn in their foot. By a letter from our General to their General, we have signified, that a safe-conduct shall be sent to Lennox and Southampton, if so be the King will send them to the houses of parliament, with his answer to the propositions sent to him by the parliaments of both kingdoms. Things on neither hands seem yet mature for any real pacification; but the Lord knows what he is doing.

88. *Publick Letter.*   December 26. 1644.

THE last week I wrote at length how all went. What is more since, you may see in the three printed and two written papers. It seems there will be a present entry in a
treaty

treaty of peace. There is very great need and defire of it on both fides; but the difficulties are yet infuperable to human reafon, albeit there be a fairer beginning on both fides than was expected: for though the hope of either party of a peace, fuch as they can accept, be yet but fmall; yet both ftrive by all means, in the profecuting of it, to approve themfelves to the people as men who are moft defirous thereof. The fafe-conduct is fent from this to Oxford; fo one of thefe days we expect Richmond and Southampton. The Holland ambaffadors and French agent are as bufy with the parliament to put themfelves in a way of furthering that treaty; but the thing which now is moft fpoken of here, is the fudden and unexpected work of yefterday. The Houfe of Commons, in one hour, has ended all the quarrels which was betwixt Manchefter and Cromwell, all the obloquies againft the General, the grumblings againft the proceedings of many in their Houfe. They have taken all office from all the members of both Houfes. This done on a fudden, in one feffion, with great unanimity, is ftill more and more admired by fome, as a moft wife, neceffar, and heroick action; by the other, as the moft rafh, hazardous, and unjuft action, as ever parliament did. Much may be faid on both hands, but as yet it feems a dream, and the bottom of it is not underftood. We pray God it may have a good fuccefs. We daily now make good progrefs in the affembly. We have fent up our directory for marriage and thankfgiving; we have alfo got through burial. We have fome little thing to fay of fafting, and vifiting of the fick; and fo our long-looked for directory will be clofed. It is exceedingly liked by all who fee it. Every piece of it paffes the Houfes as faft as we fend it. Our anfwers to the Independents reafons are now ready, and I hope this week may be fent up to the Houfe. We have alfo put together all our votes of government, and will fend them up to-morrow to both Houfes. The Independents have entered their diffent only to three propofitions: " That in Ephefus was a claffical " prefbytery; That there is a fubordination of affemblies; " That a fingle congregation has not all and fole power of " ordination." Their reafons againft thefe three propofitions we expect to-morrow. Againft the end of the next week we hope our committees will have anfwers ready to all they will fay; and after all is fent up to the Houfe, by God's help, we expect fhortly an erection of prefbyteries

                                                                    and

and fynods here; for there appears a good forwardnefs to
expede all things of that kind in both Houfes fince the taking of Newcaftle.   If the directory and government were
once out of our hands, as a few days will put them, then
we will fall on our great queftion of excommunication,
the catechifm, and confeffion.   There is here matter to
hold us long enough, if the wrangling humour which long
predominated in many here did continue; but, thanks to
God, that is much abated, and all incline towards a conclufion.   We have drawn up a directory for church-cenfures and excommunication; wherein we keep the practice
of our church, but decline fpeculative queftions.   This,
we hope, will pleafe all who are not Independents; yea, I
think even they needed not differ with us here: but it yet
appears they will to feparation, and are not fo careful to
accommodate, as confcience would command peaceable
men to be.   However, we hope to get the debates of thefe
things we moft feared either efchewed or fhortened.   We
have near alfo agreed in private on a draught of catechifm;
whereupon, when it comes in publick, we expect little debate.   I think we muft either pafs the Confeffion to another feafon, or, if God will help us, the heads of it being
diftribute among many able hands, it may in a fhort time
be fo drawn up, as the debates of it may coft little time.
All this chalking is on the fuppofition of God's fingular affiftance, continuing fuch a difpofition in the affembly and
parliament as has appeared this month or two bypaft.   On
this fuppofition, two months, or three at moft, may do
much to put on the cope-ftone of our wonderful great
work.   For this end, we had much need of all your earneft prayers to God; for, we truft, many living, and many more not yet born, fhall eat with delight, and blefs the
Lord for the fweet fruit of our very toilfome, and fometimes heavy and bitter labours.   But of all thefe things
much more, if it pleafe God I may be permitted to come
down to that general affembly, which, according to our
late advice, I hope before this be indicted in our church.

    I truft this fhall be the laft which I fhall write from
this; for Mr Gillefpie and I being appointed to attend
the general affembly, purpofe, if God will, fhortly to
take journey.   We hope this day to clofe in the affembly, the remainder of our directory, and to fend it up
to-morrow to the Houfes; fo the next week we expect
an ordinance of parliament for the whole directory.   We
                                                    have

have tranfmitted our anfwers to the Independents reafons
againft our prefbytery. They are well taken, and now
upon the prefs. We hope, in the beginning of next week,
to fend up alfo our anfwer to their reafons againft fynods.
We make no queftion but fhortly thereafter the Houfes
will pafs an ordinance for the government; what is behind,
a good part of it, will be ended, and follow us to our general affembly; and all the reft, by all appearance, will be
clofed in a month or two thereafter; for all men now incline to a conclufion. God, in his good providence, has
made many things, efpecially the counfels of our enemies
and retarders, to co-operate for his ends.

The King's commiffioners, Lennox and Southampton,
are gone. We can fay little yet. If any that come from
Oxford might be trufted, we might have fome little hope,
but truly I dare fay nothing yet; for the great hopes they
put us in at firft, by their confident affurances of the
King's willingnefs to give us fatisfaction in the hardeft of
the propofitions, concerning the church and militia, before their departure they fomewhat blafted, by their needlefs lingerings here, and ufing, as we fufpected, fuch
courfes as favoured of their old unhappy and unprofitable
way of hen-wiles, to make and increafe parties among us.
But this will not do it. They refolve here quickly to put
the matter of the treaty to a point; to have it in a mid
place betwixt this and Oxford; to limit it to a nineteen or
twenty days, in the which, if two or three prime articles
cannot pafs, they mind not to delay more. They are
now on a fair and probable way to get a good fum of money to our army for the prefent, and to have them better
paid hereafter; fo that quickly in February they may
come fouth to better quarters. If it pleafe God to affift,
this evil faction here may be broken, and caft out of England, in fome months: a courfe alfo will be taken both for
fea and land, that will give the Irifh rebels fome other
work than to run over, in any confiderable number, either to England or Scotland. No appearances of any forces
or great fums of money from France. Good appearance
here of a more vigorous proceeding, and greater correfpondence with us in all things both of church and ftate,
both of peace and war, than hitherto has been. Might it
pleafe the Lord to be gracious to you there, to humble
your hearts under the rod that lies on you, that unanimoufly you might join to fling that handful of vermin in
the

the fea, we would quickly expect a glorious conclufion of
the great work in hand.   Our moft earneft prayers are
for this.

89. *For Mr William Spang.*   December 27. 1644.

Dear Coufin,

YOURS with Col. Fullarton I received, and three books.
The reafon I write not weekly to you, is not only the
multitude of our affairs here, but alfo a maxim I had refolved to keep, not to deliver to the Dunkirkers two
of my letters in end.   For thefe three months we have
heard noife of intercepting of letters, or opening of them:
however, we have not felt any fuch thing in truth, but only the laft week, when the packet-boat going from this to
you was taken by a knave; yet it was my refolution to
write none to you till I had found my former had been
delivered fafely: but hereafter you fhall have no fuch
caufe of complaint; for I purpofe to write to you the next
week, and no more at this time from this place, for the Monday thereafter at fartheft, Jan. 6. Mr Gillefpie and I muft
take journey for Scotland, to give an account of our
labours here to the general affembly, which, at our defire,
they have called to meet at Edinburgh, Jan. 22.   We
have ended this day the directory in the affembly.   The
Houfes are through the moft of it already.   Before we go
they will pafs all.   What remains of the government
concerning the hard queftions of excommunication, Mr
Henderfon has drawn it up by way of a practical directory,
fo calmly, that we truft to get it all paft the affembly next
week, without much debate.   The men whom moft we feared,
profefs their fatisfaction with that draught.   It is certainly true of what you wrote, of the impoffibility ever to
have gotten England reformed by human means, as things
here ftood, without their brethrens help.   The learnedeft
and moft confiderable part of them were fully Epifcopal.
Of thefe who joined with the parliament, the greateft and
moft countenanced part were much Epifcopal.   The independents had brought the people to fuch a confufion, that
was infuperable by all the wit and ftrength which was here;
but God has fo guided it, that all has contributed for the
main work.   The wickednefs of the Popifh and Prelatical
faction ftill continuing and increafing; the horrible ex-

VOL. II.   L   travagancies

travagancies of the sectaries; the unreasonable obstinacy of the Independents; the strange confusions of this long anarchy; and, most of all, God's good hand on us here in the assembly, and on our armies in the fields, has contribute to dispose this land to a very fair reformation above all their hopes. If their treaty bring us not to the substance of our propositions, we will early go to a more vigorous war, and hope in God, before harvest, to put these evil men out of Britain. The continuance of our troubles in Scotland, from a most naughty and despicable enemy, is from God, to humble our pride, and to prepare us for greater service. The means of it was, and is, some improvidence in some of our guides; but well I know no crime. The envy and emulation of some, and, as some think, the idleness and perverseness of some late covenanters, made Argyle to be almost deserted in his pursuit; but I hope all these things are, or shortly will be helped. My Lord Wariston and Mr Barclay went from this yesterday to our parliament, that fits January 7. If God be pleased to remember his mercy, we are in a fair way of prospering. As to Cromerus and Rivet, I wrote to the college to receive them. Rivet, I have it all before in parcels. I thank you that at last ye have sent me my account, yet you must close it, for I understand not guilders and stivers. Rutherford's last book was sent to you by the author. Edwards's book was the author's gift to me; so it is gratis *accepistis*. Diodati I gave to Mr Garret. I shall get the prices of the other. That any of my Canterburians or Parallels sells, it is well; for neither here nor in Scotland they give money, they are out of date. I am sorry I cannot come over to see your wife, to whom I pray you remember me. Your advice about the boy I will communicate with my wife, and after consult with you farther. Try what stirs are these which the divines of Saumur and Paris, Cameron's scholars, are moving. Write no more to me hither. When it pleases God I retire to my old corner, keep promise of paying me your debt of intelligence with great increase, for I cannot deny my creed. The Lord be with you. Pardon my evil hand; for usually I am in haste. You have a double here of my last two to Scotland. Farewell. Your Cousin,

JAMESONE.

90. *For Mr Buchanan at Paris.*

Monsigneur,

At my first sight of your papers, if I mistake not the sense, I remark sundry passages which I conceive would much prejudice our cause, if the writ went abroad without some alterations.

1. In the 12th, 13th, and 14th propositions, however the divine right and tyranny of Episcopacy be disclaimed, yet the lawfulness of a moderate Episcopacy, established upon an ecclesiastical right, is plainly avowed. This assertion our church judges both wrong in itself, and extremely prejudical to our present affairs.

2. In the 5th, 7th, 8th, and 9th, the divine right of our ruling elders is evented; they are made only the deputies of the people, and they alone also are called the church-representative; the preachers and deacons, exclusive and opposite to ruling elders, are made to be the only divine and apostolick officers in the church. We admit of no officers in the house of God, on a human and ecclesiastick right.

3. In the 6th, the divine right of the whole congregation, to give voice and suffrage in matters of government, is avowed. This is one of the greatest grounds of the Independents. What the word of God grants to the people we may not deny to them, and no posterior canon of the church can take from them.

4. Of all that here is said against the Independents, there is very little to the point; for they will grant it all, and deny they maintain any such independency as here is impugned. They avow a dependency, and that by divine command, on all the neighbour churches; only deny a superiority of jurisdiction of any church or synod over another church. In my judgement, these and such-like grounds, give much more advantage to the Prelatical and Independent party against us, than we can get of all the rest of the writ against them. I could not communicate it to Mr Henderson as yet; but ye will consider of these my extemporal and possibly misgrounded thoughts. So, till meeting; and ever, I rest your servant,

ROBERT BAILLIE.

P. S. Since, I have conferred with Mr Henderson. We are both in opinion, that you in your own way, the best you can, would essay to get your friends so informed, that they, in forenamed points, would write according to the mind of our church; or if this cannot be obtained, with all thankfulness to themselves, for their hearty affection to our cause, you will so guide it, that they may be silent till they see what it may be the will of God to do with these poor distressed churches.

91. *For Mr Buchanan.*

Monsieur,

It were good that our friends at Paris were made to understand our hearty and very kind resentment of their demonstration of zeal and affection towards the common cause of all the Reformed churches now in our poor weak hands; that, since they offer to take information of the points in question from us on the place, to whom they intend this brotherly and very timeous assistance, we present to their wise considerations,

1. That the covenant of Scotland rejects absolutely all kinds of Episcopacy: That the covenant of the three kingdoms, is expressly for rooting of all Prelacy, not the tyranny alone of that office: That the Royalists would be well content to keep in any imaginable kind of Episcopacy, being assured, in their own time, to break in pieces and rend all the caveats we can put on it; so it is necessary to hold to that ground, wherein all here do agree, and to which the Royalists themselves are on the point of yielding, That no Episcopacy here is tolerable, as being a mere human invention, without the word of God, which, where-ever it lodged, has been a very unhappy guest. The total extirpation of it would be applauded and congratulated without any distractions or any reservations, or else nothing would be spoken of that point.

2. That ruling elders are conceived here on the old French grounds, by all of our side, to stand on a divine right; and that an ecclesiastick right alone is no just foundation for any officer in the house of God.

3. That the Independents common tenets are these: 1. That the power of ecclesiastick censures is alone in the congregational presbyteries. They grant the divine right,

and

and many excellent uses, of synods, lesser and greater; only deny their power of jurisdiction over any congregation. Ordination of all officers, also their deposition, and excommunication of all members, they give to the congregational consistory. They give so much authority to a synod, and to every neighbour congregation, when they receive no satisfaction from any scandalous congregation, to abstain from communion with it, and to pronounce their sentence of that non-communion with it. 2. They will admit of none to be members of their congregations of whose true grace and regeneration they have no good evidences. By this means they would keep out all the Christian church, forty for one of the members of the best reformed churches. 3. They make it necessary to have all the men who are communicants, present at every act of jurisdiction of the consistory : though they give them not suffrages, yet nothing must be done without their consent. 4. They give liberty to any man who is able, though he never intend the ministry, to profess and preach publickly, in the face of the church. 5. They do not censure, in their churches, the denial of pædobaptism, though they profess their dislike of that error. 6. Many of them preach, and some print, a liberty of conscience, at least the great equity of a toleration of all religions ; that every man should be permitted, without any fear so much as of discountenance from the magistrate, to profess publickly his conscience, were he never so erroneous, and also live according thereunto, if he trouble not the publick peace by any seditious or wicked practice. They have a number of more singularities, which I take no time to relate. They profess to regard nothing at all, what all the Reformed, or all the world, say, if their sayings be not backed with convincing scriptures or reason. All human testimonies they declaim against, as a Popish argument. So far as yet we perceive, they will separate from all the Reformed, and will essay, by all they can either do or suffer, to have their new way advanced. The sooner all the Reformed declare against them, it will be the better.

92. My Assembly-Speech.

Right Honourable, Right Reverend Fathers and Brethren,

IT is the joy of our heart, and the refreshing of our
weariness,

weariness, after a long and troublesome journey, to behold the chearful face of this most venerable assembly; whom we pray God to bless, and all these honourable companies we are come from, does heartily salute in the Lord.

Our main errand hither at this time is, as you all know, to give some account, as God shall enable our weakness, of the employment of your servants and commissioners, and our Honourable and Reverend Brethren at London, who now a whole year and divers months have, with all care, attended the assembly and parliament there, for the furthering and advancement in that uniformity in divine worship and church-government, which both nations have sworn in their solemn league and covenant. The success which God, according to your prayers, hath been pleased to grant to our labour, you will better see than we can report, in the papers which we have brought from the Honourable Houses of Parliament, to be communicate when your wisdom shall think it seasonable to call for them. The sum of all, as we conceive, is well expressed in the letter of our dear colleagues to this venerable meeting, which here we offer; as also in that other letter of that Reverend assembly at London to that same meeting, which here likewise we present.

We can add nothing to that which from these letters you will hear read; only with your Reverences permission and favour, we are bold to profess, that God has done great things for poor Scotland, wherein our hearts doth rejoice; and we are confident, that the hearts of the godly posterity will not only rejoice, but wonder, when they look back on the footsteps of the Lord in his glorious work. When the bishops of England had put upon the neck of our church and nation the yoke, first of their Episcopacy, then of their ceremonies, 3dly, the whole mass of a service-book, and with it the body of Popery; when both our church and state did groan under an unsupportable slavery; to have been freed of these burdens; to have been restored unto the purity of our first reformation, and the ancient liberty of our kingdom; to have had bishops, ceremonies, book and state slavery reformed, we would lately have esteemed it a mercy above all our praises: but now, beholding the progress of the Lord, how he has led us by the hand, and marched before us to the homes and holds of our injurious oppressors; how

there

there he has made bare his holy arm, and brought the wheel of his vengeance upon the whole race and order of prelates in England, and has plucked up the root, and all the branches of Episcopacy in all the King's dominions; that an assembly and parliament in England unanimously, but which is their word, abolished not only these ceremonies which troubled us, but the whole service-book, as a very idol, so speak they also, and a vessel full of much mischief; that in place of Episcopacy a Scots presbytery should be concluded in an English assembly, and ordained in an English parliament, as it is already ordained in the House of Commons; that the practice of the church of Scotland, set down in a most wholesome, pious, and prudent directory, should come in the place of a liturgy in all the three dominions; such stories lately told, would have been counted fancies, dreams, mere impossibilities: yet this day we tell them as truths, and deeds done, for the great honour of our God, and, we are persuaded, the joy of many a godly soul. If any will not believe our report, let them trust their own eyes; for behold here the warrant of our words, written and subscribed by the hands of the clerks of the parliament of England, and the scribes of the assembly there. We will not descend into any particulars; for that were to take up more of your precious time than now you can spare; and it were needlessly to anticipate by discourse these things which presently, in particular and length, must be read unto you. Only it is our earnest desire, that the mercies whereof we are speaking, may be matter of thankfulness to all, a door of hope to fainting and feeble minds, who are oft miscarried with fear what yet may be the event; a certain ground of clear despair to all the enemies of Zion, that they may give over their vain labour, and cease to oppose the work of God, whether by their secret obstructions, or open hostility; knowing that it will be hard for them to kick against the pricks, and that there is neither wisdom nor strength against the Lord. Since the beginning of this work to this present moment, an observing and faithful eye may clearly remark the Lord still advancing like the morning-sun, ever advancing towards the meridian; it is great folly to fear, that any man, that all the worms of the earth, can stop the progress of the sun in the firmament. Clouds may arise from the earth, and thick mists may darken the face of the sky; but the sun goes on in his course, and at last by his strength will dispel

pel thefe vapours, and make them fall to the ground, not without the benefit of the earth. This will doubtlefs be the end of thefe clouds that now fill our air. Let them yet further break out in more ftormy winds, in greater fires and claps of thunder than ever; yet at laft this muft be their deftiny, to the ground they muft fall, and fill the ditches and pits of God's vengeance. Our fun will fhine, and our air will clear again. This we muft believe, and, according to our faith, we fhall certainly find it. It was indeed very needful that we fhould be humbled; our nation lately was advanced to a high pitch of honour; we might have perifhed worfe, if we had not perifhed thus. We judge truly, that all our prefent troubles are not fo much interruptions of the work, as very fit and feafonable preparatives to make us capable of more honour than yet we have attained; to fit us to be inftrumental in greater works and fervices than yet we have been employed in. We all hope, that the chariot of the Lord will not here ftand, nor be arrefted within the compafs of this ifle.

93. *To Mr William Spang.*   London, April 25. 1645.

Reverend and Beloved Brother,

YOURS, with my coufin James Baillie, I got, and thank you for it. This is the firft I wrote to you fince I came from London. It pleafed God to give us a very profperous journey. However, the ways were very deep, and the excurfions of the enemy from Newark hazardous; yea, much more than we knew; for we learned thereafter that we were purfued, and efcaped fcarcely one hour. The reft was alfo in many places of our way; yet God brought us both to Edinburgh fafe, without a fall or great wearinefs, on the Wednefday at night, the firft day of the affembly. I wanted not my fears of oppofition in the affembly to fundry things we had brought down. I would gladly have had time to have informed privately our friends of all things before we had brought them in publick. As for the changes in our church, I had laboured with my colleagues to have efchewed them all, and found Mr Henderfon not much from my mind; but others were paffionate for them, and at laft carried, firft Mr Henderfon, and then me, to their mind. The belief in baptifm was never faid in England, and they would not undergo

2   that

that yoke. When they urged, we could not deny, but the saying by many was a fruitless and mere formality, and to others a needless weight; and that the saying the commands was no less unneceffary. We got the affembly to equivalent interrogatories, much againft the mind of the Independents, and we were affured to have the creed a part of the catechifm. All, both they and we, would gladly have been at the keeping ftill of readers; for we forefaw the burden which the removal would bring on the minifters back: but, after all our ftudy, we could find no warrant for fuch an officer in the church; and to bring in the church a man to be the congregation's mouth to God, and God's mouth to the congregation, without a clear warrant of the word, we faw the intolerable confequences of fuch a maxim. For bowing in the pulpit, whether by cuftom, or becaufe of the late confequent abufe of it by the prelatical party, to bow to the eaft and the altar, it was univerfally, by all forts of men, fo unanimoufly diffufed, that we were not able to make them alter. I think they would have taken our difference here in good enough part; but the conveniency of uniformity in this point, and our willingnefs to have that matter of debate removed out of our church, made us the more condefcending to their defire of our coming to them here. Alfo about the conclufion of the pfalm, we had no debate with them; without fcruple, Independents and all fang it, fo far as I know, where it was printed at the end of two or three pfalms. But in the new tranflation of the pfalms, refolving to keep punctually to the original text, without any addition, we and they were content to omit that; whereupon we faw both the Popifh and Prelatical party did fo much dote, as to put it to the end of the moft of their leffons, and all their pfalms. Of the laft two there was nothing in the directory, only in the letter of the Englifh affembly; alfo in our colleagues letter to the affembly there was a defire of them in a general courteous claufe, which we were inftructed to make particular. I preffed much, that this defire fhould be delayed till Mr Henderfon had come home, fearing we had more burden already than our weak back would bear; yet fuch was the importunity of others, fearing not to get fo good a feafon afterward, that we behoved to venture.

On Thurfday we were brought to the affembly. I fpoke what you have in the inclofed. Mr Gillefpie fpoke there-after

after much to the fame purpofe. Becaufe of the longing
defire of all to know what we brought, and to deliver the
minds of fome from their fears, left we had other things
than we at firft would bring forth, all was prefently read ;
the letters of the Englifh affembly, our commiffioners letters, the directory from end to end, the directory for ordination, the votes of government fo far as had paffed the
affembly, and fome other papers. All was heard with
great applaufe, and contentment of all. It was one of the
faireft affemblies I had feen ; the choiceft of the miniftry
and elders of all Scotland well conveened ; almoft the
whole parliament, nobles, barons, burghs, and all the
confiderable perfons who were in town. Our meffage was
exceeding opportune, and welcome to all. It was a great
refrefhing to them in a time of languifhing and difcouragement. A numerous committee was appointed to examine
all punctually, which we were defired to attend. In five
or fix days we went through, and, by God's affiftance,
gave all men fatisfaction in every thing. The brethren
from whom we expected moft fathry were eafily fatisfied ;
all did lovingly condefcend to the alterations I had fo
much oppofed, whereof I was very glad ; only Mr And.
R. was oft exceeding impertinent with his oftentation of
antiquity, and Mr D. Calderwood was oft fafhious with
his very rude and humorous oppofition : yet we got them
all at laft contented ; and the act, which Mr Gillefpie drew
very well, confented to, in the committee firft, and thereafter in the affembly, with a joy unfpeakable, bleffed be
God.

Thereafter we gave to the committee like fatisfaction a-
nent the other papers whereupon they were to have the
affembly's opinion, but no act till they had paffed the houfes of the Englifh parliament. When we had thus far
proceeded, I went to Glafgow, to fee my family and
friends, after fixteen month's abfence ; where, to my great
joy, I found all in health and welfare as I could wifh ;
our mother alfo, and fundry friends whom I faw, bleffed
be God. I had left with fundry in the affembly to deal
for my abode at home ; but there was no remeid ; both of
us were ordained with diligence to go back ; fo all that
concerned myfelf in private and publick went according
to my mind. But for all this, my wine was incontinent
mixed with much wormwood from fundry finiftrous accidents both in England and Scotland. The Independents,
with

with Mr Marſhall's help, were very near to have carried, by canny conveyance of ſome propoſitions in the matter of church-cenſure, a fair and legal toleration of their way; but their legerdemain being perceived, was got cruſhed, to their ſmall credit, and to the break-neck of that accommodation betwixt us and them, which was far advanced, but now, by their ſchiſmatick practices, is made deſperate.   Alſo the diviſion of the Houſes about the militia is great; for, however contrare to our expectation, the Houſe of Lords have paſſed the ordinance for Sir Thomas Fairfax to be Generaliſſimo; yet it is againſt their mind, and there is great grumblings both in the houſes and country, and eſpecially in the armies, that ſpare not whiles openly to mutiny.   This has cauſed the loſs of Weymouth, and lets Hopeton and Goring do in the weſt what they will.   Alſo Sir Thomas Fairfax leaving of Yorkſhire, has given Langdale from Newark occaſion to beat his father at Ferrybridge, and raiſe the ſiege of Pomfret, and, which is worſt, has broke up the treaty.   We were aſſured by Richmond and Southampton, that both the King and Queen were ſo diſpoſed to peace, upon the great extremities wherein their affairs ſtood, and ſmall hopes from any place to get them helped, that they would embrace the ſubſtance of all our propoſitions, with very ſmall and tolerable modifications.   This ſeemed to us not unlike.   But the new diviſions at London, and the great alterations in Scotland, has ſo far revived the malignity of the court, that they have returned to their old minds on new hopes, which, we truſt in God, will ſhortly deceive them.   The moſt debate in the treaty was on the point of Epiſcopacy, wherein, we hear, Mr Henderſon has diſcharged himſelf to his great credit.   However, nothing could be yielded. Biſhops, books, and all, muſt ſtand; our covenant, directory, and all we have been doing, muſt be aboliſhed; peace with Ireland is juſtified as honourable: ſo all muſt return to a bitter war.   That which has been the great ſnare to the King, is the unhappy ſucceſs of Montroſe in Scotland.   For however there be a beginning of a levy in France for the Queen, and many Iriſh are expected to land in Scotland and England, and the Engliſh diviſions promiſe much to them; yet that which has blown them up moſt, is the unexpected ſucceſs their deſigns in Scotland have had to this day.   It ſeems to many wiſe men, that God has rained this ſnare on the court to avenge on them their former practices.   Matters on all hands were in that posture, that the King was on the point to have been restored to all in reason he could have desired; but now, on the foolish hopes of a most eminently wicked crew, to continue the miseries of all the three kingdoms, will enrage, and make implacable, those who were panting for peace on any equitable terms.   So when God has cast out these grashoppers from Scotland, and broken the small remainders of that malignant party in England, what the next propositions may be which shall be treated on, he is wise who can conjecture; only it fears me, they be of a harder digestion than any yet named; or, so far as I know, yet thought upon.   However, our present state here is thus: When the canniness of Rothes had brought in Montrose to our party, his more than ordinary and civil pride made him very hard to be guided.   His first voyage to Aberdeen made him swallow the certain hopes of a generalissimo over all our armies.   When that honour was put on Lefly, he incontinent began to deal with the King. And when we were at Dunse Law, had given assurance, and was in a fair way of performance, (had not the honesty and courage of Marshall preveened it), to have given over the whole north to the enemy.   When our voyage to Newcastle came in hand, by his damnable band he thought to have sold us to the enemy.   Thereafter he was ever on correspondence for our ruin.   Allaster Macdonald was the smallest string in his bow, and a design which he least trusted in; but God resolving to humble us, who were beginning to swell with our great success in England, and, on base partialities, to be filled with emulations and factious heart-burnings, he would demean us with no more honourable rod.   Some 1500 naked Scots Irish having leaped from isle to isle, till at last, getting away through Badenoch, they brake down on Strathern.   The country-forces of Fife and Strathern were three to one well armed on Tippermuir, had horse and cannon: but the treachery of Kilpont, and especially Sir John Drummond, together with Elcho's rashness, delivered all that tumultuous people, and their arms, in the enemy's hand, without stroke.   A great many burgesses were killed, twenty-five householders in St Andrew's, many were bursten in the flight, and died without stroke.   At Aberdeen, 400 of the Fife soldiers well near routed the whole enemy; but being ill seconded by the burgesses of Aberdeen, they

fled

fled alfo.   Marifchal, and the gentry of the country, the
Forbeffes and Frafers, lay by as malecontent ; Gordon,
by Argyle's great miftake, having the commandment,
whereof, through his own haughtinefs, and treachery of
his followers, he made no ufe at all.   A great many A-
berdeenfmen were killed,.and the town ill plundered. You
heard what followed that ftrange courfing, as I remember, thrice round about from Spey to Athol, wherein Argyle and Lothian's foldiers were tired out ; the country,
haraffed by both, and no lefs by friends than foes, did nothing for their own defence.

Whether through envy and emulation, or negligence,
or inability, Argyle's army was not relieved as it fhould,
himfelf was much grieved, fo that he laid down his commiffion ; which neither Lothian nor Callendar, for any
requeft, would take up ; fo Baillie was forced to take it, or
it muft have lien.   In the mean time, the enemy, after
this long ftorm, fhoring to fall down on Glafgow, turned
to Argyle, and went through it all without oppofition ;
burnt Inverary, killed and fpoiled what they pleafed. The
world believed, that Argyle could have been maintained
againft the greateft army, as a country inacceffible ; but we
fee there is no ftrength or refuge on earth againft the Lord.
The Marquis did his beft to be revenged, with an army fufficient overtook the rogues in Lochaber at Inverlochy. We
hoped they might have been eafily defeated ; but, behold
the indignation of the Lord ! Argyle having a hurt in his
arm and face, got by a cafual fall from his horfe fome
weeks before, whereby he was difabled to ufe either fword
or piftol, his coufin Auchinbreck took the leading of his
army.   No appearance but of courage and fuccefs ; yet no
fooner did the enemy fet on, but all our people, overtaken
with a panick fear, without any neceffity, turned backs,
and fled.   Auchinbreck, a ftout foldier, but a very vicious
man, and many fpecial gentlemen of Argyle's friends,
were killed.   This difafter did extremely amaze us.   I verily think, had Montrofe come prefently from that battle,
he fhould have had no great oppofition in all the highlands, in the Lennox, and the fheriffdom of Ayr, Glafgow, Clydefdale, fcarce till he had come to Edinburgh.
But God, in mercy to us, put other thoughts in his heart.
He went incontinent northward ; did what he pleafed as
far as Murray ; got the Gordons, Grants, and many of
the clans, to join.   Seaforth alfo came to his camp.   His

hopes

hopes were, and we had reason to fear it, that having near the one half of Scotland in his power, he would, with a great army, march the high way southward.

Before this time our people did not well awake; our parliament had trifled much time in needless debates. Sir John Smith, and divers burgesses, had debated too much for their own ends upon the excise. Lindsay by the burrows, to please the Treasurer, was made President, in Lauderdale's place, whom the stone had removed, to our great loss and regret. He was not so able to dispatch business. Emulations, and heart-burnings about particulars, hindered much our affairs in a most dangerous time. The country was exceedingly exhausted with burdens; and, which was worst, a careless stupid lethargy had seized on the people, so that we were brought exceedingly low. In this lamentable condition, we took ourselves to our old rock; we turned ourselves to God. The assembly sent out a printed warning to the country, very well penned by Mr Gillespie. We wrote a free admonition to the parliament, of their jealousies and divisions; which, although it took not away the root, yet did it sned many of the branches, of the evils complained of. Baillie was enabled to move, and written to by the assembly; Marischal also. All was put in the best posture might be. The parliament was adjourned, that the war might the better be followed. And in this case left I Scotland, with a heart full of perplexities.

You know how graciously the Lord brought me through the seas. The storm, a little before, had been so extraordinary, that many here thought we had been cast away. When we came from you, we were exceeding welcome; but found our affairs in an exceeding ill posture, the credit of our nation impaired, sensible neglects and real grounds of complaint daily offended us in many occurrences private and publick, that would have tempted greater wisdom and patience than was national to us: yet we resolved to go on as we might, waiting when God would blink upon Scotland; for we knew, as God helped us there, our affairs here would amend. It was a matter of exceeding joy unto us, to hear of the great and first real disaster that Montrose got at Dundee, and of the posture of our country at last, according to our mind, after the flight of the enemy, the killing of 400 or 500 of the best of the Irish, the dissipating of the most of the Scots highlandmen,

landmen, the lofs of their ammunition and moft of their arms, the returning of the remnant to the hills and woods. Baillie, with one half of the army, is gone to Athol, to keep them from that ftarting hold. Hurry, with the other half, with Marifchal and the north country, is towards Aberdeen. Lawers, and the Murraymen, are to keep in another turn. Argyle, with a regiment of his own, aud 1500 from Ireland, are to the highlands. So, by God's help, in a little time, we hope to get fuch order of thefe our troublers, that Scotland fhall be in peace, and fend back the foldiers now it makes ufe of, with fuch increafe, that Leflie, with a better army than yet he has commanded, fhall march over Trent, and Monro to Connaught and Munfter. The Englifh look on us already much more chearfully than of late. We pity their rafh and unadvifed feeblenefs; and yet, thanks to God, we have been conftant to do all duties to them; in the midft of all their ingratitude and provocations, we refolve they will, by our actions, fee at laft their obligation to us.

Their new-modelled army confifts, for the moft, of raw, unexperienced, preffed foldiers. Few of the officers are thought capable of their places; many of them are fectaries, or their confident friends : if they do great fervice, many will be deceived. Some have great fears, not only of their defigns to ftrengthen the party of the fectaries, fo that it may not fafely be difpleafed; but alfo of componing with the King, to the prejudice of us and all our friends here : yet I hope thefe fears are groundlefs. Sundry wife men whom I fpeak with, believe that the new army is not fo full of fectaries as is faid; and however, are affured of their honefty and obedience to the parliament; alfo if any difafter fhould befal them, which we, with our daily prayers, do heartily deprecate, they hope that our army, well recruited from Scotland, and much ftrengthened by a multitude of good officers, which partly have left, partly are put out of the Englifh army, fhall by God's help, be enabled to do their bufinefs, and fettle peace here ere it be long.

We heave great toil here in the church-bufinefs. We are on the point of fetting up prefbyteries and fynods in London; but all the ports of hell are opened upon us. Of thefe things ye fhall hear an account with the next occafion; for now I am weary with writing, though the moft of this letter was written before I left Scotland.——We all
love

ove Thomas Cunningham, and are doing for him what
re can.   The thefes of Voetius, you have befide you,
nd Spanheim againft the Anabaptifts, fend me.   It hath
een a mighty neglect that no man hath anfwered Eraftus's
reply to Beza.   The moft of the Houfe of Commons
re downright Eraftians : they are like to create us much
more woe than all the fectaries of England.   If you
vould fet Apollonius, or Voetius, or Rivet, or Spanheim, when he has done with Amirant, or all of them,
o write againft Eraftus, it would be a great fervice to us and
he Reformed churches alfo ; only it would be done well and
fatisfactorily, and alfo fpeedily ; both which I fear be impoffible.   L'Emperour promifed to write againft Selden, for
he Jewifh ecclefiaftical Sanhedrim, and their excommunication.   This man is the head of the Eraftians : his
glory is moft in the Jewifh learning ; he avows every where,
that the Jewifh ftate and church were all one, and that
fo in England it muft be, that the parliament is the church.
L'Emperour is well able to beat down the infolent abfurdi-
ty of the man with his own arms ; and, if he would do
t quickly, it were a very good office to us and to all the
Reformed churches.   Do what you can, by your friends,
o put him on.   Send me no books by the poft, as John
Henderfon did the laft week ; for the pamphlet I bought
n Rotterdam for fix ftivers, Mr Gillefpie behoved to give
he poft for it five fhillings.   My fervice to your good
wife, and to Apollonius.   My only regret and Mr Gillefpie's both, is, that we faw him not in Middleburg.   It
was only Mr Gillefpie's wilfulnefs, which he acknow-
edges out of time.   At laft farewell, I reft,

    Your Coufin,

                      JAMESONE.

94. *A Publick Letter.*   *London, April 25. 1645.*

AFFAIRS here ftand thus, fo far as I underftand.
The affembly hath now, I may fay, ended the whole body
of the church-government, and that according to the doctrine and practice of the church of Scotland, in every
thing material.   We have been thefe two or three weeks
on additional propofitions, which feemed to be wanting,
for the making of the reft practicable and perfect ; thefe
alfo we have ended, except one or two, which I truft at
    I   our

our next seffion we shall pass. There will then remain no more for the government, but the methodizing and wording of thefe matters, that they may be tranfmitted to the houses of parliament for their authority. The catechifm, and Confeffion of Faith, are put in the hands of feveral committees, and fome reports are made to the affembly concerning both. We expect not fo much debate upon thefe, as we have had in the directory and government. The Independents, thefe fix weeks, have not much troubled the affembly; for after we had been a long time troubled with their oppofition to all things, it was found meet to put them to declare their mind pofitively what they would be at. This they have fhifted to this day, as it was thought not fully agreeing among themfelves; but now being put peremptorily to it, they could not get it declined. Since, they have been about that task, and we expect daily when they fhall prefent to us their platform of church-government. The affembly purpofes not to take it into publick debate, but to give it to fome committee that they may frame an anfwer to it, if fo it be found convenient. The Houfes have paft of our votes of government, purpofing quickly to erect the ecclefiaftical courts, of feffions, prefbyteries, and fynods, and thereafter to pafs fo much of our government as they think neceffary. We will have much to do with them to make fundry of our votes pafs; for moft of their lawyers are ftrong Eraftians, and would have all the church-government depend abfolutely on the parliament: for this end they have paft a vote in the Houfe of Commons, for appeals from feffions to prefbyteries, from thefe to fynods, from thefe to national affemblies, and from thefe to the parliament. We mind to be filent for fome time on this, left we mar the erection of the ecclefiaftick courts; but when we find it feafonable, we mind to make much ado before it go fo. We are hopeful to make them declare, they mean no other thing, by their appeals from the national affembly to a parliament, than a complaint of an injurious proceeding; which we never denied.

As for other bufinefs, this long time the reputation of our nation hath been much lower than before. The lafting troubles, which a handful of Irifh hath brought upon our whole land, was the beginning of our difgrace. The much-talked of weaknefs of our army in England did add unto it: our neceffity to lie upon the northern fhires, almoft exhaufted by the King's army before, and their daily

Bayerifche
Staatsbibliothek
München

butcries of our oppreffion, made it to increafe. But that which highly advanced it, is our delay to march fouth-ward, after all their importunate calls. Thefe things have made us here almoft contemptible, and this contempt hath occafioned jealoufy and provocations, which may, if not provided for, prove dangerous. Upon their jea-loufy they caft their old armies in a new mould, and left out the moft, both of our nation, and of our friends in their own nation, and put in divers fectaries, who much increafed our malecontentment. Our commiffioners have not been wanting in all that diligence, prudence, and pa-tience could work. All who are wife, finds the union of the nations neceffary for both their fubfiftence, and who-ever would brangle it are moft unhappy inftruments; but there is no human means for us, were we all angels, to keep our reputation, and the hearts of the people, but by ftrenthening our army. Many advertifements hereof hath been given from time to time to Scotland, but all in vain hitherto. Had it been provided that we might have marched with 20,000 men, we might quickly have got here all we defired. If it hath been the defign of any, to keep the enemy at home on foot, that fo our army in England might be made weak and for little fervice, I vow they have been the bafeft traitors that ever Scotland bred. Befide all that is come out of Ireland, and all raifed in the country, there are, we hear, eight regiments of foot, and fome of horfe, brought home out of England, and not one man fent in their place. All who love either the honour or fafety of our nation with this amended. None need to talk of any ficklenefs or ingratitude of the Englifh towards us, of any advancement of the Indepen-dent party; for no man here doubts, but if once our ar-my were in fuch a condition, as eafily, if we were dili-gent, might be, all thefe clouds would evanifh, and we would regain this people's hearts, and do with all fectaries, and all things elfe, what we would : but if quickly we take no courfe to fend back the Englifh regiments, and recruit what is wanting of their due number, our hazards are great and prefent. The King, with Rupert and Mau-rice, are north by this as far as Chefter. Many fufpect his intention is for our army, knowing its weaknefs, and malevolence of the fhires wherein it lies. Our officers are doing what they can to prepare for the worft, and the commiffioners here are doing their utmoft endeavours to

get

get provisions and forces also sent to them ; but the only remeid, under God, is forces from Scotland. We have men in abundance : they will be allowed entertainment on the country, and in time they will not want a groat of their pay, though for the present it cannot be had. We hear also, that by no means will come to the army any ministers ; that in twenty-two regiments there is not one minister : so this day's letters bear. This is a wonderful lethargy, and if God help it not, it prognosticates strange things ; but our eyes are towards God, waiting when he will arise for us. We know many godly hearts there join with us in daily praying that God would crush that unhappy enemy at home, and give us wisdom in time to supply our English army, to send up to it the best of our ministers, and a strong honest committee ; for in these days there is great need of faithful and incorruptible men. In many discouragements we have here, we are comforted with the good progress we make in the matters of God, and good appearances we see to get the naughty enemy at home shortly crushed : if we could, in faith, draw near to God, he would make his work run apace, and hasten the confusion of all its opposites; in whatever way, whether secret or open, and discover villanous underminers.

The Turk still menaces Italy. The Swedes and Transilvanians are like to undo the Emperor. Denmark is plagued with the Swedes; their treaty is broken. The Bavarian's victory over the French was great ; but now the French are set on their feet again by the help of the Hessians, and a new army from France. The French on the one side, and the Hollanders on the other, are on their march against Flanders. The French ambassador, and most of the nation, at the King's command, have left Rome, to declare their miscontent with the Pope for his siding with Spain.

You see, in my publick, the best side of our affairs. The church-matters go well, blessed be God; but truly our state-matters are in a very dangerous posture. This people's jealousy, contempt, and injurious provocations, daily increase. The King is bending toward our army, which is called exceeding weak, evil provided, and miscontent. You there have been wonderful ill-advised, that what soldiers you took from it, you sent not plowmen or others in their room. If quickly you reinforce them not

with

with men and honest ministers, in a clap you have the King and all the north of England on your back. If it should be so, there is no help to be expected from this; for here they are so wise, as to let all their army lie down before Oxford, when the King is going where he will. In this they are peremptor'. Our strait is great, and we had never more need to run to God. If matters be not past helping before this come to you, there is great need of supply to the English army. It were much better fighting the King in Yorkshire than in Lothian. However Montrose and the Independents have brought us to this pass; yet if it be God's pleasure to make you able and willing, after all your neglects, to supply the army in England, all in a short time will flow according to our mind; but if you be unable or unwilling, for whatsoever cause, to do this, we were never in a greater and more present hazard. Our fears here who know how things go, are great; yet we dare not think that God will desert his people and cause. Too much glory hath been spent on us these seven last years to be so easily lost. We must return to our old rock.

95. For Mr Robert Ramsay.   May 4. 1645.

Reverend and Dear Brother,

I long to hear from you. I have got some from Mr David and Mr George, but none from you. I shall have a care of your memorandum. How matters go with you in the town I know not. The lamentable losses you have still by the hand of that wicked enemy, and the increase of the pestilence, together with the great security we hear yet to lie on the hearts of the most, make clear such a measure of the wrath and desertion of God, that oftentimes sads our hearts exceedingly: and however the affairs of the church, which is our talk, go according to our mind; yet the great danger of the state, wherein the foolish and malicious counsels of some few here has cast it, and whether the not marching of our army, upon what causes we yet much doubt, has contributed not a little; these things have made our lives here for a time very bitter to us. We see no remeid but in God's mercy, and blessing of our army. If this people had prospered in
their

their way of exceeding folly and ingratitude, it might have proven ſhortly very hurtful to themſelves and us both; but now a little diſcipline makes them begin to enquire about the authors of theſe diſaſters, and fearful dangers wherein they ſtand, and look back on their old deliverers, whom they were begun too much to forget. If the Lord will be pleaſed to uphold our army, I believe we ſhall cloſe all church-affairs ſhortly according to our mind, and eaſily call in the wantonneſs of the ſectaries; but the Lord ſave us from the rage of the roaring malignants, and their crafty counſels, of which we are much afraid. God ſave our army, and make all therein ſo pious, and honeſt, and wiſe, as our preſent dangers require. Coll-Kettoch's and Montroſe's troubles are little to theſe that are coming, if God ſhould not bleſs this much decreaſed and enfeebled army. Prayer, counſel, and activity, were never more requiſite among you. We have done the utmoſt of our endeavours, both here and to our friends at Edinburgh, and with the army, to give warning and advice. Remember my ſervice to your two colleagues, alſo to the Principal, to Mr Edward, and Mr Hugh, to the regents, and to the brethren of the preſbytery, and whoever mind, in their prayers, the work in hand, your neighbour Mr Zachary and his wife: but I muſt break off. Diodati you ſhall get: neither the Engliſh nor Dutch notes are yet come out. Pamphlets I will ſend you none, there are ſo many, and I cannot chuſe; for I have ſome hundreds to myſelf, all which ſhall be for you and your brethren.

Our hearts are much grieved for the great troubles of Scotland, that the Lord is yet pleaſed to ſtrike us ſo ſore both with the ſword and peſtilence. Oh! if at laſt we could awake, and turn to him, who by all theſe means is ſeeking our repentance and ſanctification. We cannot but ſee the loving countenance of a father in the midſt of all that wrath. Church-work here, bleſſed be God, goes on with leſs difficulty than it was wont. The aſſembly having put the Independents to ſhew what poſitively is their judgement in things controverted, we have been quit of their cumber theſe ſix or ſeven weeks. Every day this month we have been expecting their poſitive tenets, but as yet we have heard nothing of them; only in their ſermons in the city they are deviating more and more towards old and new errors, eſpecially liberty of conſcience. Their ways are daily more and more diſliked. The directory is ſo far
from

from being cried down, as fools fay there, that there is an
ordinance of parliament coming out for the practice of it,
if it be not changed, that I will be caution few fhall dare
to contemn, either that whole book, or any part of it. We
have thefe fourteen days been upon our advice to a fubcommittee of the Houfe of Commons, anent the execution
of our votes of government : for it is the work of that
fubcommittee to draw two ordinances; the one, for the
practice of the directory, wherein their punifhment is as
rigorous, if it be not mitigated, for the contemners of a-
ny part of that book, as it was before to the contemners
of their religion. For preachers, or writers, or publifh-
ers, againft it, were they Dukes and Peers, their third
fault is the lofs of all their goods, and perpetual imprifonment. The other ordinance is for the erection of ecclefiaftick courts over the whole kingdom. For their help
herein, they called the minifters of London to advife them
for their city, and they fent to the affembly for their advice anent the reft of the kingdom. The city-minifters
have fent them their unanimous advice (for of 121 city-
minifters, there are not three Independents) for planting,
juft after our Scottifh fafhion, an elderfhip in every congregation; of fourteen prefbyteries within the lines of communication, every one confifting of minifters betwixt
twelve and fixteen, and alfo many ruling elders; and of a
provincial fynod for London and ten miles round about.
The affembly have prefented their advice this day. We
went through this forenoon-feffion unanimoufly what concerns provincial and national affemblies, as yefterday what
concerned prefbyteries, and the days before congregational elderfhips. They have concluded provincial fynods
twice a-year, prefbyteries once a-month, and national affemblies once a-year; and after, every one of thefe as it
fhall be needful. Herein the greatnefs of this nation forces them to differ from us with our good liking. Their
provincial affemblies cannot confift of all the minifters,
but of fo many delegated from every prefbytery; for in
fundry of their provinces will be above 600 churches,
which would make at leaft 1200 members in a provincial
fynod: alfo their national affembly is conftitute of three
minifters and two ruling elders, deputed, not from every
prefbytery, but as it is in France and Holland, from every
provincial fynod, whereof there will be at leaft fixty. We
fhortly expect an ordinance according to our advice, and
the

the execution presently upon the back of it. Our next work will be the Confession and Catechism, upon both which we have already made some entrance. The matters of the estate were in a worse condition; but now I hope they are recovering. These that guide here, having easily raised the siege of   they thought meet to besiege Oxford; making account, that our army, with the forces to be joined with them, were more than able to have marred the King's progress whithersoever he should turn. But our army not being accommodated in provisions for a long march; and also not very well content that their chief army should in the time of action lie down before Oxford, which was impossible to be taken for many months; and being informed by Sir William Brereton, that the King's purpose was to come to Lancashire, and from thence to send Prince Maurice to Scotland with a party of horse, himself and Prince Rupert having recruited his army in Lancashire and Yorkshire to come back on the associations: on these and the like motives, our army thought it meet to march back towards Westmoreland, to be in the King's way at the foot of Lancashire, for the safeguard of Scotland, and the besiegers of Carlisle. This our march, and that their siege of Oxford, gave the King fair liberty to march where he would, to raise the siege of Chester, to take the town of Colchester by storm, and to become terrible both to Yorkshire and the associations, or whithersoever he should go. Hence a great clamour of all here, first against our army, and then more against the authors of the model, and of the unhappy siege of Oxford. We excused our army the best we could. We obtained to it all we could desire; free quarters on billet where-ever it came; an ordinance for pay as to any of their own armies; an ordinance for all the northern forces to join, and of 4000 horse and dragoons to be constantly with them, and under their command; also the besiegers of Oxford to rise and follow the King; and intreaties to us to march south in so great a need, with assurance to send a party of English and Scots horse stronger than any the King could send towards Carlisle or Scotland. Hereupon we sent Daniel Carmichael post to our army, to haste them back from Westmoreland; and to-morrow we send down Mr Kennedy and Mr Gillespie for that same end. We hear they are already on their way towards Yorkshire to our great joy; for truly we have had eight days as sad

hearts

hearts as any living men. Upon the fuccefs of that army, all here think the whole affairs of Britain doth depend. It is all the pities in the world, that it fhould have been fo much neglected; that for fo many months there fhould not have been three able minifters into it; not a committee at all; that befide the feven regiments which were in Scotland, the reft were decreafed to fhameful numbers, without any recruits at all. If any love the caufe in hand, or defire either Scotland or England to be preferved from quick ruin, let that army be provided for with all diligence; for if it be but a little neglected, this people will faint, and be over-maftered. The King's whole ftrength will be upon that army, and their weaknefs quickly will draw the heat of the war into Scotland. As yet the parliament's forces are entire. If our army march quickly, they will have 4000 or 5000 horfe to join with them, and a great army to follow the King's rear; if they delay, they muft ftand alone. However, you cannot be anfwerable to God, if you do not your beft quickly to fend up an able minifter to every regiment, and at leaft one half-dozen of the moft gracious, wife, and couragious minifters of the kingdom: for that is the head of the bufinefs; and where-ever that army is, Scotland, and the Proteftant party of this ifle, muft be faved or loft. Alfo a full, able, and honeft, committee of nobles, gentry, and barons, muft be there. Their abfence has been extremely prejudicial; and if it be continued, may prove fatal. Alfo it were exceeding requifite, that the regiments were recruited with 5000 or 6000 foot. I believe, upon the tuck of drum men would be gotten, if the great neceffity were demonftrated; alfo if it were believed, which is verily truth, that every foldier will get meat his fill, much more than at home, and for the prefent fome money monthly; and if God blefs but a very little, fair rewards. If by any means we would get thefe our regiments, which are called near thirty, to 16,000 marching men, by the blefting of God, in a fhort time, we might ruin both the malignant party and the fectaries. The only ftrength of both thefe is the weaknefs of our army. The ftrength, motion, and fuccefs of that army, in the opinion of all here, is their certain and quick ruin; wherefore we muft teftify, before God and the world, that if any among you, of what degree foever, either upon private defigns and emulation, or our fottifh carelefs ftupility, or backward thrawart malecontentment, do contribute

2   bute

bate for the keeping the army of England in a weak condition, that they are cursed traitors to God and their poor suffering country, and to the whole Protestant cause, that is on the very point of great success, if God be with us; of a great disaster, if God be tempted by mens either treachery, or sottish negligence, to leave that poor army. These that can do no more, I hope will pray; and that truly is much, and the most; for it is the Lord that puts wisdom and courage in the hearts of foolish people, and who takes away, when he is not sought, wisdom and courage from the most valiant and wise. Any discourtesy that has been put on any of our nation, or any clamour has been made against us, we need not care for it: for if it please God to assist us but a little, to be at this time serviceable, not so much to defend this people in their present danger, as to fight for Scotland in the midst of their land, at their charge, and with all the assistance they can make us, we may be assured of satisfaction for any wrong in word or deed that any of our friends pretend to have received, and the full payment of all any can crave, beside all the contentment we can desire of them in any matter either of church or state But if at this time we draw back, or if it should be God's will not to assist us, all our bygone labours are lost: but this we will not fear. The rash and imprudent courses of these who have miscarried matters for a time, becomes now palpable when they come to be executed. Some losses got already, and more feared, are likely to prove happy, by opening the eyes of many to see their error, and to return, albeit a little too late, to a wiser way. It is our only desire to have the favour of God, and to hear of the speedy march of our army. The enemy is more wicked and cruel than ever. It is a wonder if God revenge not their barbarous inhumanities. If their carriage have been, as we hear, at Leicester, they cannot go long unpunished.

96. To Mr William Spang.

——The condition of our church-affairs is good. We are at a point with the government, and beginning to take the Confession of Faith and Catechism to our consideration. These eight days we have been on our advice for the manner of chusing of elders in every congregation,

nd divifion of the country into prefbyteries and provin-
ial fynods. We hope now fhortly, by God's help, to fee
fynod and fourteen prefbyteries in London, and a fef-
ion in every church, juft after the Scots fafhion. But o-
her matters are in a dangerous pofture. Hurry and
Montrofe have fought a moft bloody battle. We have,
hey fay, 1000 killed on the place, and he near as many,
of the beft of his men; but he had the beft, fo far as we
hear. Baillie, with the body of our army, came fhortly
after to Spey. Our fear is, that Montrofe efcape to the
hills, and ftill keep our country in trouble. The peft increafes in Edinburgh, and divers other places. Our army
here is in a prefent diforder. The King went from Oxford northwards. It was our much-prefied advice, that
their army might follow him, and ours might meet him.
The authors of the new model were peremptor to lay their
army down before Oxford, and have our army, with a
good part of their horfe, joined, to march againft the
King. While this is expected, and our army on their way
fouthward as far as Rippon, on a fudden, upon a letter
from Sir William Brereton, that the King was to march
through Lancafhire, and fo into Scotland, either himfelf,
or Prince Maurice, with a party of horfe, arofe with diligence, turned backwards to Weftmoreland to ftop the
King's pafiage. They here (confcious to themfelves of
manifold needlefs provocations given both to that army,
and to many perfons of our nation) fear this march to
have fomewhat of malecontentment into it. We hope it
is nothing fo; for indeed we have no fcruple from any of
them what they mean by it; but to-morrow they are to
fend an exprefs, to try how all goes. However, this puts
all their affairs in a great perplexity. The King has turned from Lancafhire towards Newark. Some fear the affociations, and fome Yorkfhire. In neither is any fufficient
ftrength to oppofe him. The huge imprudence and rafhnefs of the new model is now vifible. All that it can attain to, when the befiegers and Cromwell, and the party
in the weft, and　　　　　　　with his northern party, are
joined, will be within 14,000, horfe and foot, many of
them new levied, and ill commanded. They wifh now
they had made more of us, and are on ways of amending
former neglects. If it pleafe God to bring up our army
in time, all will be well; however, their long delay is
much regretted, and marvelled at. For Mr Eleazar Gilbert,
what

what we wrote was on our beft information, and fome experience of the man, whom we have heard preach, and have been fatisfied with his conference, and fome of his printed treatifes, both Latin and Englifh. We never heard of any fuch thing as you are informed of; but howfoever, fince you are fo informed, we think it no way expedient to fend him over to you. If that regiment vaik, I think Mr D. Dickfon could fend you one of his fcholars, who would ferve you well; one Mr Robert Auld, if he be not yet provided, would in my mind be very fit for fuch a condition. Mr Henderfon recommended Mr Hume to Mr Forbes; but moft upon your coufin, Mr David Buchanan, a moft honeft and worthy man's teftimony, whom I fhall caufe write to you the next week what he knows of the man; to me he is a mere ftranger. It is certain your two ambaffadors did all the time of their abode here carry themfelves as induftrious agents for the King. I hear there is come to your eftates before this a publick declaration of the proceedings with us. I fear we cannot fend an ambaffage fo foon over as we would. The Eraftian party in the parliament is ftronger than the Independent, and is like to work us much woe. Selden is their head. If L'Emperour would beat down that man's arrogance, as he very well can, to fhow, out of the Rabbins, that the Jewifh ftate was diverfe from their church, and that they held the cenfure of excommunication among them, and a double Sanhedrim, one civil, another ecclefiaftick; if he would confound him with Hebrew teftimonies; it would lay Selden's vanity, who is very infolent for his Oriental literature. Alfo if any of you would meddle with Eraftus, whom Beza, they fay, durft never anfwer, it would do us a great deal of good. I have fent you over one of Mr David's books; if you can make a bargain for him there, it will be a great encouragement to him. Mr Rutherford has fent you over fix of his books to be diftribute according to his letter. Thus far I had written the laft week, but it miffed the poft; you have for recompence, here inclofed, what I wrote to Scotland this week. We are ftill in perplexity for the not marching of our army. In the taking of Leicefter, our lofs was not fo great as we fuppofed at firft. Only the half of our officers were there; few of them are killed; the reft got quarter, whereof we are glad. The King is marching thitherward. He is thought to be as far as Northampton.

O 2

97. *Far*

97. *For David Dickson.*   *June* 10. 1645.

1. You would remonstrate, that the Independents treating with Oxford is under trial, and that it is suspected it flows from their practice with the Queen by Harry Perry, of which we have been oft advertised.

2. You would remonstrate, that this is the party whose principles, and known constant carriage, is to settle the state, without any King at all; and so they are for the ruin of the whole royal family.

3. Beside, their dealing is utterly disliked by the body of the English, and the whole Scots. The Queen's entertaining of them will make her the more irreconcileable with the rest of both nations.

4. You would assure the Queen's dealing with that party is to put the King in his old posture, to be guided by Digby and the Spanish faction; to have dependence on the Papists and sectaries, who have need of liberty to be in a perpetual jealousy with the rest of his subjects, who mind the ruin of the Austrians, the setting up of the Palatine, and the interest of France.

5. That the discovery of the Independents negotiation at Paris or Oxford, with a great furtherance to settle a firm peace in a more solid way than the Independents intend, or can attain, for the good of the King and his allies; and above all, for the interest of France against Austria and Spain.

6. That William Murray cannot do better service, than to search and communicate what can be found of these negotiations, that whoever of the French can contribute any thing for this, they will further much the conjunction of these kingdoms among themselves and with France; otherwise these unhappy men may deceive the King, and, for their own ends alone, draw him to particular treaties, which may ruin his kingdoms, or destroy his family, to which they are no friends; or at least put him in his old condition, to reign, but hated by his people, and necessitate to be guided by the counsels of the Popish and Spanish party.

98. *For*

98. For Mr. Cranford.   June 17. 1645.

1. Inform me where our army is. See what they will do if Fairfax be beat, or what if Cromwell be victor, if at this nick of extreme danger they should not put their forces in a posture.

2. Only Essex is able, and may get officers. Our three Majors are going, and on small conditions, if loving, may be kept. They will get abundance of officers. By this means you join the hearts of the nations, which, by the Independents craft, you have near broke asunder; you make yourself able to stand till the Scots army come up and join, or you may be considerable for treating; also you put yourself in that case, that you may not be enslaved by the Independents, but may be their masters; you may capitulate so with Essex, that he be not able to betray you.

3. How will you put on the ordinance for government, that else will linger? How will you provide Burton's and Goodwin's church? And if there be any more Independents, good they were removed by the parliament before the presbytery were erected.

4. What encouragement so hastened Bastwick Edwards to print Borough's Sermons, and his own Tractates? also the other books against libertines?

5. How this plot, of capitulating with Oxford, may be found out?

99. For my Lord Lauderdale. Worcester-house, June 17. 1645.

My Lord,

We were all glad of your safe arrival. We have had great missing of you here already. Your presence was never more necessary here than at this time. How all goes, you may see in the inclosed packet, which I have left open for your Lordship's reading. You will close it, and send it to Glasgow with the first clean hand. We have been in a peck of troubles, many of us, these days bygone. Mr Henderson kept his chamber from Thursday to this day: a languishing but not sharp pain of the gravel troubled him. Mr Kennedy and Mr Gillespie are not yet returned

turned from the army. I hope their labours there have
been happy. A pity they had not gone a month ago,
that some part of the late victory might have been ours.
How little are we obliged to the unhappiness of some
men! I have also been much sashed in my own mind upon this occasion. An intercepted letter of my Lord Digby's bore expressly the offer of propositions to the King.
As my custom was, I made a visit to Mr Cranford; in
the end we fell to speak of that letter in a free and friendly way. I was not well gone from him, till in the Exchange he falls out very rashly and imprudently to com-
ment upon that letter, and to say little less than some
members of both Houses were banqueting with the King.
Some of the Independents overhearing it, presently complain of it to the committee of both kingdoms. Harry
Vane and the Solicitor exaggerate the matter, and report it to the House of Commons. They sent for poor
Mr Cranford, and examined him at their bar for some
hours, and referred him after to a committee of Lords
and Commons to free himself. He gives me up as informer of much in his discourse, in a paper under his
hand; which the committee gave to our commissioners,
not requiring any answer *. Yet, in duty, I thought meet
to give this inclosed answer to our commissioners, which, at
my desire, was this afternoon given in to the committee
of both kingdoms; and I think it will satisfy, and no
more will be of this matter. Yet when you read my paper, you may see what need there is of you here. Keep
it to yourself, for I desire no speech of it. There is a
second part of my persecution come out this day worse
than the first. My Lord Fairfax sent up, the last week,

* Mr Cranford's information of my speeches to him is as follows. "He
told me, that there was a letter intercepted, intimating some propositions sent to the King, and a committee of seven Lords and fourteen
Commons appointed to examine and search out the author; and said,
that if the matter were thoroughly examined, much might be done;
and said, that suspicion fell very hard upon three Lords and some Commons, whom he named; and that one of the Lords had named another
of the House of Commons as to be suspected to have hand in such propositions; but he more suspected the former, as having more opportunity to send and receive intelligence from Oxford than any other, because they were a subcommittee unto which, though the Lord Wariston, and another of their commissioners, and Mr John Crew, were added, they were never yet called to any business. He desired these things
might be imparted to some citizens; for it was convenient that petition
should be made, that this business might be thoroughly examined."

an

an horrible Antitriaftrian; the whole affembly went in a body to the Houfes to complain of his blafphemies. It was the will of Cromwell, in the letter of his victory, to defire the Houfe not to difcourage thefe who had ventured their lives for them, and to come out exprefsly with their much-defired liberty of confcience. You will fee the letter in print, by order, as I think, of the Houfes. You have here alfo the laft fifty of Mr Roufe's pfalms. They would be fent to Edinburgh to the committee for the pfalms. Mr And. Ker will deliver them. When your Lordfhip goes thither, you would ftir up that committee to diligence; for now the want of the pfalms will lie upon them alone; for if once their animadverfions were come up, I believe the book would quickly be printed and practifed here. I know how lazy foever, and tedioufly longfome, they be here, yet that they will be impatient of any long delay there in this work. If ever ye did God or your country, or the whole ifle, fervice in your life, hafte up thefe recruits to our army. There is no other way to make the King take reafon in patience, alfo to bridle the infolency of wicked men. If we fettle affairs here, Montrofe will melt like a fnail. Let them be marked with infamy to all pofterity, who are not honeft to their heartroots at this time. I avow he is not worthy to breathe in Scots air who has not compaffion on that much-diftreffed country. Your Lordfhip will not only be a witnefs to men, but alfo a phyfician to the difeafed, and a pedagogue to thofe that will not be fchooled by others. All withdrawing of heart or hand now, upon whatever provocation, is villanous treachery, and a betraying of their poor dying mother-country. No imaginable mean fo good for attaining all intentions as real honefty. All pultroons will be difcovered and perifh. My Lord, make hafte hither, for I tell you there is great need of you here. We muft wreftle a fall with fome kind of creatures before our covenant be abolifhed. But truly, if we could make hafte to do our duty, I believe, with little ado, we fhould perfuade many to be reafonable. You may fee, my Lord, I am the old man. My fervice to your kind lady, and to yourfelf, fo long as you remain honeft, but not an hour longer. So I reft, &c.

ROBERT BAILLIE.

My Lord Irvine, this day, took a fit of an apoplexy: it is thought he cannot live.

100. *To*

100. *To the Right Honourable the Commiſſioners of the king-dom of Scotland, by Mr Baillie.*

Your Lordſhips having communicate to me a paper concerning ſome paſſages of a late diſcourſe of mine, with a Reverend miniſter of the city, I have thought meet to acquit myſelf, by giving you the true and ſimple account thereof, to be made uſe of as you ſhall find moſt expedient.

I acknowledge, that on Tueſday the 10th of June, I made a viſit to Mr Cranford, as often we had mutually done before, being very confident and intimate friends ever ſince our firſt acquaintance. I profeſs I did not conſult with any living man about that my viſit, neither did I acquaint any with the purpoſes we diſcourſed upon, till I had heard he was publickly challenged. I alſo profeſs, that notwithſtanding of any importance might be in the matters we were to ſpeak of, which oft was great enough, yet I had no particular deſign with him at that more than at other times ; for it was ever our cuſtom, when we met, to diſcourſe freely, as familiar friends, and lovers of the publick, of the affairs of church and ſtate, according as our particular occaſions gave us intelligence.

At that time our meeting was but about an hour; for before I entered his houſe, I told eleven, and when I returned, I told upon the water twelve from ſome clocks.

We ſpent more than the firſt half-hour upon the ways of ſettling the church-government, which now at laſt, by God's mercy, was well nigh fully and finally agreed upon in the aſſembly. This, in all our meetings, was the principal part of our diſcourſe ; for the continuance of ſo many years of a total anarchy in the church did burden both our ſpirits, we conceiving it to be a fountain-evil, and an evident cauſe of the loſs of many thouſand ſouls, ſeduced, ſo far as we could judge, irrecoverably, to pernicious hereſies and ſchiſms.

Thereafter we fell to ſpeak of another point, which I confeſs was the chief cauſe of my viſit that day. The week before, my Reverend brother had called me out of the aſſembly, to underſtand if your Lordſhips had diſclaimed the late printed paper, intituled the *Scots manifeſta.* I told him, though ye underſtood nothing either of the

I   preface

preface, or title, or printing of it; yet the paper itself you did not disclaim, being the same, word by word, which you had lately given in to the Houses. I said also, that in my judgement no good man could be discontent with that paper; for it reflected upon no man's person, neither did it contain any thing but a mere vindication of the Scots army from the injurious aspersions, which, for a long time, without all cause, had lien upon it.

I did also communicate unto him the anxiety of my mind for the present posture of affairs; Goring and Hopeton appearing to be the stronger in the west; the King marching southward with an advantage from Leicester; thought our danger very great if any cross accident should befal Sir Thomas Fairfax, which in my most earnest prayers I intreated God to avert. My Reverend brother told me, that the county of Essex and the city of London were upon ways for raising great forces for our defence if any unexpected accident should require them; my chief errand therefore with him, that following Tuesday, was, to understand the fruit of these consultations for the quieting my own perplexed mind. He told me, that these counsels were still on foot, albeit now they seemed not so necessary as before; for he had learned from some who had lately come from the army, that the King was neither in a condition nor mind to fight, till he had got more forces from the west. Of this I was very joyful; trusting, that before any considerable party could come to the King from the west, the Scots army might be upon his back; and so, by God's help, that wicked army of malignants should easily be brought to an end; the English and Scots army making it their only strife who should be most forward, first to bring down the common enemy, and thereafter to embrace one another in love, for the settling of these much-troubled kingdoms in a solid and everlasting amity.

Having spoken of these and sundry other purposes at length, a little, and but a little, before my Reverend brother was called to dinner, we came to speak of the purpose in the paper. Finding that he had not heard of my L. Digby's letter, I told him what I knew of it, and withal my opinion that it deserved an accurate trial; for to me it seemed to hold out clearly, that there were some here that kept such correspondence with the King as to offer him propositions. I conceived none would dare to

ake ſo much on them, who were not either very powerful amongſt us, or very fooliſh.

Hereupon, as oft at other times, being intimate friends,
in a private conference, we took the liberty, which is
known to be ordinary in theſe times among ſuch as affect
the publick, to ſpeak of divers names, who, as many
thouſands do know, though they agree in the end, the
welfare of the church and kingdom, as lines in the centre,
yet they differ in their opinion about the midſes to that
end, as the ſame lines in the circumference : but that I did
lay the framing of the propoſitions upon any of the perſons names, I do utterly deny, neither doth the paper lay
ſo much upon me.

I ſaid, indeed, that a noble Lord of the Houſe of
Peers had ſaid, that my L. Savile had averred to a certain lady, that a noble gentleman of the Houſe of Commons did keep weekly correſpondence with my Lord Digby, which I took for a great untruth. I ſaid alſo, that I
heard of a ſubcommittee appointed by the committee of
both kingdoms, to treat concerning the rendering of gar-
riſons to the parliament, and bringing over any of the enemy's forces, which at firſt was not obſerved by any of the
Scots commiſſioners, and for a time none of them were
named to be of that ſubcommittee ; and afterward, when
ſome of them were added to it, they were never called to
any meeting, nor acquainted with the proceedings of that
ſubcommittee, till after my L. Digby's letter was intercepted, and brought to the committee of both kingdoms ;
though the rendering of Oxford, and the coming over of
Goring, with his forces, were in agitation, betwixt one of
that ſubcommittee and my Lord Savile, whom many do
think to have kept ſo great correſpondence with Oxford,
all the time ſince his coming hither, that I did eſteem all
privacy with him not to be ſo fair as I could have wiſhed ;
but that I did faſten the ſuſpicion of framing the foreſaid
propoſitions on that honourable member of the ſubcommittee, or that I required any one word of what I had
ſpoken concerning that ſubcommittee to be communicate
to any living ſoul, I do expreſsly deny, neither doth the
paper aſſert it. I grant, indeed, it was my deſire to have
Digby's letter tried to the uttermoſt, conceiving it to contain matters very dangerous to both nations ; but for the
particular ways of furthering that trial, I being a ſtranger,
could not but be ignorant of them. I heard of the city's frequent

quent petitioning the Houſes for matters that ſeemed to me of leſs importance. Therefore, if in a convenient way, they would have been moved to petition for this, I thought it would not be amiſs. My Reverend brother told me, that in the afternoon ſome of the common council were to meet with a committee of the Houſe of Commons, about money for Taunton; and that he would inform ſome of them about Digby's letter, that they might deſire the gentlemen of the Houſe, with whom they met, to look after that buſineſs. To this I acquieſced : and that Captain Jones, or any other whom my Reverend brother thought fit, ſhould be ſpoken to for this end, I did not diſallow; but that any other part of our diſcourſe, except that of my Lord Digby's letter, which was then the talk of thouſands, ſhould be communicate to any whoſoever, or that even this much ſhould go to any as from me, and in my name, to my beſt memory I heard nothing at all; but truly, had I ſuſpected any ſuch thing, I know that very earneſtly I would have deprecated it by all the laws of friendſhip.

This I have ſet down as my memory can furniſh the chief matters that paſt betwixt us; but the formal end and poſitive words, as in a familiar converſe, whereby I did not expect to be called to an account, I cannot confidently report.

I confeſs to me it ſeems very ſtrange, that at theſe times of ſo great liberty, when ſo many go away without the leaſt cenſure, with their horrible railings againſt whole churches and nations, and them of our deareſt brethren; yet my private diſcourſe to my boſom-friend being all very true and innocent, and, as I conceive, containing nothing but what was my duty to ſpeak, and which any man who had a ſpark of zeal to the common cauſe, and preſervation of the nations engaged in the brotherly covenant, from the bloody plots of malignants, could not but have ſpoken upon the like occaſion, ſhould be thus ſearched after, this to my mind hath been the more heavy, becauſe of my utter unacquaintance hitherto with all apologeticks for any part of my coverſation; for it hath been the great mercy of God towards me, that to this day I was never called by any authority, civil or eccleſiaſtick, to the leaſt queſtion, for any of my words or deeds. Yet all this I ſhall digeſt with the greater contentment, if it may pleaſe God to bleſs it with the double fruit, whereof I am in good hope ; first, that my Lord Digby's letter be so exactly urged as the authors of the propositions he speaks of may be found out, and so the whole island delivered from the danger of that treacherous design ; next, that hereafter (if with permission I may say so much) more notice may be taken of all, of whatsoever quality, who shall take the boldness to asperse either the parliament or the assembly, or the neighbour churches and nations, without cause, as too many for a long time have done too freely, without so much as any real inquiry after their misdemeanours.

101. *For Glasgow.* *June 17. 1645.*

SINCE my last, June 3d, there is, by God's mercy, a great change of affairs here. Our progress in the assembly is but small. We fell in a labyrinth of a catalogue of sins for which people must be kept from the sacrament, and ministers be deposed. When we had spent many days upon this, we found it was necessary to have an and a general clause, whereby the presbyteries and synods behoved to be intrusted with many more cases than possibly could be enumerated. This retarded us so much, that yet it will be some days before the body of our government go up to the Houses. We have sent down the last fifty of the psalms. We wish they may be well examined there, that we may have your animadversions and approbation. Doubtless these new psalms will be a great deal better than the old. The King is turning his head southward, to my great joy ; for I was much afraid, that the north of England should have joined with him, and fallen first on our army, and then on Scotland. He took Leicester by storm ; and much rapin, and ravishing of women, was committed there ; which was, in my judgement, the last and most immediate cause of God's vengeance on that army. After he had for a week fortified a part of that town, he marched towards Northampton. It was uncertain whither he intended. However Sir Thomas Fairfax gathered together all he could, to the number of 11,000 or 12,000 horse and foot. The King was much weaker in foot, yet we were exceedingly afraid for the parliament's forces : albeit lusty, well-armed, and well-paid men ; yet without officers of experience. The King
finding

finding them stronger, after three or four days lying
near together, began to draw off towards Oxford, to wait
for Goring from the west; but Sir Thomas followed so
close, that one Saturday morning both drew up for battle.
About twelve they engaged. Rupert, on the King's right
wing carried down the parliament's left wing, and made
the Independent Colonels Pickering and Montacue flee
like men; but Cromwell, on our right wing, carried down
Prince Maurice; and while Rupert, in his fury, pursues
too far, Cromwell comes on the back of the King's foot,
and Fairfax on their face, and quickly makes them lay
down their arms. Rupert, with difficulty, did charge
through our army. The King, in person, did rally again
the body of his horse; but they were again put to flight.
The victory was entire: the whole foot killed or taken:
the horse routed: all the cannon and baggage lost: some
of ours hurt; but few killed. We have a publick thanksgiving on Thursday. This accident is like to change
much the face of affairs here. We hope the back of the
malignant party is broken. Some fear the insolency of
others, to whom alone the Lord has given the victory of
that day. It was never more necessary to haste up all possible recruits to our army. What next shall be done is
not yet certain. The city will be careful to send a month's
pay to our army. I am sure our army will be in better
condition by much in the south than it was in the north.
Likely there may be once again sent to the King, to accept
the three propositions agreed on by his parliaments, about
religion, the militia, and Ireland. If these, without delay, be yielded to, the rest may be treated on. But if
this offer, which I hope may be made, be refused, I am
feared for the sequel.

We hear the French got Dunkirk the last Tuesday, by
surprise: this shortly will confine the Spaniards to the
south side of the Pyrennees. The Swedes and Transylvanians are lying in Hungary, before Presburg. After the
taking of Brin, the Danes will force their old wilful King
to a peace: he must demolish Elfineur, and give over toll,
and leave all he has on the north of the Baltick for a
pledge to the Swedes. All would go well if it might
please God to blink upon Scotland, to remove the three
great plagues we hear that continue there, hardness of
heart, the pestilence, and the sword. Our fasheries here
are great and many; we wish, from our heart, to see a
happy

happy end, and to be at home. My Lord Chancellor
takes journey the next week.

102. *To Mr William Spang.* *June* 17. 1645.

Coufin,

THOUGH in your laft ye complain of my not writing
for three pofts; yet before this comes to you, you will
find your error. I wrote at length, which I hope before
this you have received. It is not my purpofe to write with
every poft, for fear of intercepting, but to be fure that
you received the former, left two at once be intercepted:
yet your earneftnefs makes me at this time break that order. You fee what this week I wrote to Glafgow; alfo
what I wrote to L. Lauderdale; alfo you have a copy of
the paper I gave in to be tranfmitted to the Houfes. I
hear it has given good fatisfaction. I know it has been a
great means to make the trial of Digby's letter more accurate than elfe it was like to have been. We have got Leicefter back by compofition. Our army is come up to Not-
ingham. What way we fhall profecute the enemy is now
in deliberation. It will be hard for the King to ftand any
more in the fields. This day the Chancellor took his
leave with the affembly, and exhorted them to expedition.
They are in hopes to put the government off their hands
one of thefe days. It is exceeding falfe, that there has
ever been the leaft appearance of difcord betwixt our commiffioners and the parliament, neither I hope ever fhall
be. What ufe the Independent party may make of this
very great and entire victory, wherewith God has been
pleafed to blefs thefe counfels which they took againft the
mind of moft here, and by appearance againft all reafon,
we cannot yet fay. However, our danger was very great,
and God now has made us fecure from the malignant
party; for their ftrength feems to be broken, except God,
contrare to all appearance, as oft he has done, raife them
yet again to fcourge us more, who truly are not in our
hearts humbled in either nation. I do not love Mr Dane's
notion. If it be his mind to draw from the profeffors a
declaration for our behoof, I think he would have propo-
fed far other queftions. I pray you fee he do us no evil.
Advertife Dr Stewart to keep his colleagues filent, if they
be not willing to declare flatly againft all the branches of
Independency,

Independency, as Apollonius and Spanheim have done, and for the rooting out of all kinds of Episcopacy, according to our covenant : why else should they trouble us with their untimeous declarations, who have trouble enough already in our great and dangerous wrestlings with the common enemy ?

103. *Concerning Lord Savile's business.*

April 12. 1645.

Ordered,

That my Lord Sey and Seal, Mr Pierpoint, Mr Solicitor, and Mr Carew, have power to treat with such as shall be employed by them for delivering up any considerable garrison of the enemy's, or bringing over any considerable force, and for discovery of such as give the enemy intelligence.

May 6. 1645.

The Lord Sey, Mr Carew, and Mr Solicitor, shall have power to treat with any for bringing in any of the forces or garrisons of the King, or to find out such as give intelligence.

May 7. 1645.

That the Earl of Loudon be added to this subcommittee, or in his absence the Lord Wariston.

Tetbury, the 26th *May* 1645.

Dear Governor,

Just as this messenger was taking horse, I received yours of the 22d, for which I thank you, assuring, that nothing can come more welcome to me than your kindness. The reason of my limitation in your order concerning the oath, was chiefly not to give umbrage to my L. Southampton, if it had been general. I have not time to write at large both to you and my brother secretary in cypher, and therefore I must refer you to his letter ; wherein you will see, hard designs by the letter to LLL contained nothing but a dislike of my answer to the propositions you wrote of, as not at all satisfactory. All is villany and juggling among them. Dear William, adieu. Let us hear from you often. I am, your faithful friend and servant,

GEO. DIGBY.

For my noble friend, Col. William Legge,
Governor of Oxford.

Die

Die Saturni, 12 *April* 1645.

Earl Northumberland,	Mr Pierpoint,	Earl of London,
Earl Manchester,	Sir Hen. Vane fen.	Mr Barclay.
Lord Sey,	Sir Arthur Hafelrig,	
	Mr Brown,	

May 6. 1645.

Earl Effex,	Mr Pierpoint,	
Earl Northumberland,	Sir Gilbert Gerard,	
Earl Manchester,	Mr Solicitor,	Mr Kennedy,
Earl Warwick,	Mr Wallop,	
Lord Sey,		
Lord Wharton,		

April 28. The fubcommittee went to Windfor.

June 6. 1645.

That upon the report of the fubcommittee, to whom power was given for to treat with any concerning the delivering up of any towns, or part of the enemy's horfe, and for finding out any that keep intelligence, that order be vacated, it being declared by the fubcommittee, that there is no more hope of the delivery of Oxford, the fiege being raifed.

Paper given in by my Lord Wariston to the Committee of both Kingdoms, June 12. 1645, together with the Lord Chancellor's declaration.

ALL my knowledge concerning the fubcommittee is this only, That this fubcommittee was made firft, and then renewed, without putting any of our number upon it; yea, none of us remarking that fuch a thing was appointed.

That within two days after the renewing of it, fome of the members of the Houfes of this committee called for the order, and defired fome of our number to be added.

Whereupon, about the 7th of May, my Lord Chancellor was added, and I in his abfence.

That until the afternoon, wherein the report was made to the committee, being the 6th of June, I was never called to that fubcommittee.

That day, before the report, my Lord Sey was pleafed to tell me this in general,

2   That

That the busine/s was some overtures for the surrender-
ing of Oxford, and bringing over to the parliament some
of the King's horses, and that he would take some time to
communicate the particulars to my Lord Chancellor, and
to me.

That at that meeting, immediately before the report,
my Lord Sey told me, that it was Goring's horse should
have been brought over.

That Col. Legge was the man that should surrender Oxford; and that the Lord Savile was the man that dealt
with the one and the other, and who assured him of it;
as also, that he had revealed to a lady, by decyphering a
letter came from him to Oxford, that Mr Hollis was the
man that kept weekly correspondence with Digby; but
withal, that now he heard the busine/s would fail. Whereupon we all resolved, for preventing jealousies and misre-
ports of the subcommittee, to make our report to the committee, and to desire the vacating of that order, and to
speak nothing; because we conceived there was no suffi-
cient ground to bring any man's name in question, or
make it good; and so the report was made.

Since the report ye/ternight, my Lord Sey was pleased
to tell me, and the rest, of the circumstances, which now
his Lordship reported to the committee and us, and shewed
to me my Lord Savile's letter to my Lady Temple.

My Lord Chancellor of Scotland did further declare,
that he did not know there was any such committee appointed, nor when it was again appointed; but his first
knowledge of it was upon the 7th of May; at which time,
he and my Lord Wariston were added to that subcommittee; but that he was never called to that subcommittee,
nor did meet with them, nor knew any thing at all of that
busine/s, till the subcommittee was vacated; after which
time, my Lord Sey was pleased to acquaint him therewith.

These inclosed, being the Lord Savile's own writings,
are put into your hands for publick use by a well-wisher
of the parliament. They came but a few days since to his
knowlege that presents them. Now you have them, let
them not be kept long without a due improvement. He
cannot deny them to be His writing, if he be duly examined; which is left to your wisdom by,

Your's and the publick's servant.

These

These were found amongst Mr Howard's papers.

SIR,   *Worcester-house,* July 14. 1645.

THESE three papers inclosed, which came to our hands
yesterday after eight of the clock, as written by the Lord
Savile, and found amongst the papers of Mr Howard, we
found, upon our perusal of them, to contain matters of
so great importance and publick concernment, that we resolved, according to our obligation in the covenant, and
that duty which our place and trust require of us, to take
the first occasion to communicate them to the Honourable
House of Commons, the Committee of both kingdoms
not sitting this morning, that in their wisdom, with all
speed, and before the matter be divulged, make the best
use of them for the publick good.   As we doubt not but
this our service will be acceptable to the Honourable Houses of Parliament, so are we willing, what farther we know
of this business, and by this occasion is brought to our
remembrance, to communicate also, in such a way as may
give most satisfaction to the Honourable Houses, and acquit us of our duty; who continues,

Your affectionate and humble servants.

Then the Independents began to court me again, and
did assure me, if I would quit Essex's party, and join myself to them, and make a protestation not to betray them
by any design, nor by joining in arms against them, they
would quit their vote, call me to London again, and treat
and advise with me concerning the peace of the kingdom.
Which being so just according to my own heart, (all the
power being in them), I am now in London again, in a
more probable way to do good, if I may for my Lord D.
what way to do it.

Essex is now of no power at all of himself to do any
thing.   The admiralty is in commission.   They are confident of a great navy this summer.   Young Sir H. is going
to bring up the Scots army, which, by reason of the good
success lately in Scotland, they assure themselves will come.
Sir Thomas Fairfax will get an army, a great one, they
think.   One part thereof is designed to go to Taunton
presently.   They say they have certain intelligence from
France, that the King can have no hopes of any   forces
                                                   from

from thence, nor from Ireland neither, where they fhall have 18,000 men to keep them doing.

That being never weary in defiring the peace of this poor kingdom, notwithftanding all his former endeavours, which God knows he hath continually ufed, he cannot but once more, in a time when there are no arguments to perfuade him, but his unfeigned love to his people and their peace, to reflect again upon the three propofitions made at Uxbridge, and once more to make thefe offers.

1. That the bufinefs in Ireland, he will leave it as it is already fettled by act of parliament.

2. As for the militia, he will agree to the time, not doubting but that fuch perfons fhall be named on both fides as both may confide in.

3. For the church-government, if that which he hath offered do not fatisfy, he fhall come up to his parliament, and advife with them about it, where you may hope to receive all reafonable fatisfaction from him in the third, that he hath fhewed fo great a defire to comply with you in the two former.

Our friends fay, D. hath fent no anfwer to the meffage defired, but that it is unreafonable at any time, and unfeafonable at this; that the King is gone, and nothing of all they fear was intended; that S. hath had ill grounds, or worfe advice, for his hopes. They wonder that fo much reafon fhould not be hearkened unto better. They confefs D. faith moft rationally, that many things may be hearkened unto upon a certain conclufion, the very overture of which before might weaken the hands that muft fight for them; but the fame ground they alledge from the treaty, that many things for the church, at a treaty here, after other things are agreed, might be condefcended unto, the overture of which before might weaken their party, and deftroy their caufe.

They are in conclufion fo much unfatisfied with that part of the anfwer which S. acquainted them withal, concerning the meffage defired, that being in fuch a diftemper, S. thought it neither fafe for him, nor the caufe, hereafter to make them any new offers for their own particular fatisfaction or hopes; or to defire (as D. requires) from them any probabilities for the undertaking at this time; becaufe S. is confident, if he fhould, they would look upon them, not as offers, but as baits, to make them obnoxious to the other party, to act againft them when it

Q 2
was

vas known; and it would deftroy S. in their fufpicious
breafts, that he fhould never be able to refume it again
hereafter if there fhould be occafion.   If you can beat or
difgrace Fairfax's army of Independents, Effex and the
Scots will be greater than ever, which I affure you they
look for certainly; and if they be, S. knows they will be
wifer than they were, and affures D. S. will not only revive, but improve the former defign, and do the King's
bufinefs the fafeft, fpeedieft, and nobleft way; and fhall
not omit neither, when they are in a better temper, to offer what is defired to this other fide.   And albeit S. will
have as many witneffes as you have friends here, of his unfeigned endeavours to ferve you, though with hazard of
all he hath; and let not D. imagine, that ever it came into the heart of S. to do any offices for him but what a
juft man might, and an innocent man fhould defire. Pray,
defire the Duchefs of Buckingham to fend the man fhe
did to Nonfuch as foon as fhe can.

     Coufin,
  Upon conference this night with my L. Sey, it is held
fit that we fhould not fend a pafs to Jo. Cary before your
return.   When we fhall underftand how far (L) will communicate himfelf unto him, and whether he will be willing
to put the bufinefs into his hands.   The parliament's forces are now about Wallingford, fo as I am doubtful whether he will come to that place he appointed; but I am
fure you will do that which you think fitteft, and your return will be much wifhed I affure you.   I wrote, that they
of Oxford need not fear the advance of Fairfax's army
fpeedily; but now I believe the contrary, of which I
thought fit to let you know.   If you would this evening
ftep up hither, it would not be amifs.   Adieu.

          Die Lunæ, July 14. 1645.
  Sir Hen. Mildmay, Mr Bainton, and Mr Herle, are
appointed to go to the Scots commiffioners, to defire them
to be prefent at the committee this afternoon appointed to
examine the Lord Savile.
          HEN. ELSYNGE, Cler. P. D. Com.

  As the confcience of our folemn league and covenant,
and the fenfe of that duty, which, from our fpecial truft
and intereft, we owe to the publick, and is expected from
                                                  us,

us, did lay a neceffity upon us to communicate fome papers of publick concernment, which came to our hands,
unto the Honourable Houfe of Commons ; fo do we, upon the fame grounds, and upon the defire of the Honourable Houfe of Commons, imparted to us by this committee, offer for the prefent fuch other particulars as did
make us apprehend there hath been fome underhand dealing about propofitions of peace, contrare to the covenant
and treaty ; and before thefe matters come to publick agitation, to exprefs our thoughts thereof to feveral members
of this committee of both kingdoms, and will give light to
the former paper.

Firft, about the 23d of April, the Lord Chancellor
made known unto us who are joined with him in commiffion, that the Lord Savile, after his coming hither from
Oxford, fent one unto his Lordfhip, to fhew his defire to
come and fpeak with him ; unto which my Lord Chancellor returned his anfwer by Mr Traill, That he was lately
come from the enemy's quarters, and was not reconciled
to the parliament ; and therefore could not grant his defire. Upon this occafion, he difcovered himfelf thus far
to Mr Traill, that fome here had made their addreffes by
their agents to his Majefty upon thefe terms, That if his
Majefty would make good what he had declared concerning toleration in matters of religion, they would adhere
unto him, and come and refide in his quarters ; and that
he had a way of intelligence with the Queen for bringing
about an accommodation betwixt King and parliament.

After the Lord Savile had taken the proteftation for
the parliament, he came unexpectedly upon my L.
Chancellor, when under phyfic ; and after prefacing
of his reconcilement to the parliament, and of his taking
the oath, whereby he was now a free man, and might be
fpoken with, he entered immediately upon a difcourfe,
that he wondered why the Scots commiffioners were fo
averfe from the peace of the kingdoms, which others
both here and at Oxford were fo much inclined unto ;
that for himfelf he came from Oxford with the King's
knowledge, and as much truft and favour as ever he had
before, and that he came to this place with no other intention, but to ufe his beft endeavours for bringing about
a peace, wherein he wifhed his Lordfhip's concurrence.
My L. Chancellor anfwered, That the commiffioners
from Scotland had concurred with this kingdom, in propofitions

pofitions of peace, and that it was a great unhappinefs in the King to refufe the three propofitions offered to him at Uxbridge, without the granting whereof it was but folly to think upon any treaty, or to entertain any hope of peace. At this my L. Chancellor was forced, by his phyfic, to break off abruptly. This the Lord Savile is faid to have taken as an affront to himfelf, and a fign of the L. Chancellor's averfenefs from his intentions of peace, and therefore did neither come nor fend thereafter unto him; which may give the meaning of that which he writeth in one of his letters, " that the Scots would be wifer " than they were." My L. Chancellor had refufed to treat with Savile, had informations from perfons of truft, and well-affected to the parliament; that he kept frequent meetings with others, and with their knowledge fent meffengers divers times to Oxford; and that he treated with them upon the three propofitions; concerning the militia, that they were willing the King fhould have the choice of the third or fourth part of the commiffion; concerning Ireland, that the King fhould reftore all things to the condition they were in before the beginning of the troubles, and fome way fhould be thought upon for repairing the loffes of the Proteftants, without deftroying the natives; and concerning church-bufinefs, all things to be delayed till the King's coming up to London. That if they agreed to this treaty, the Queen was to have the honour of it, and was to be moved to write to the King, and that fhe herfelf fhould receive fatisfaction and liberty alfo to Henry Jermyn; that the perfons who treated fhould have the power to difpofe of all places; that when he queftioned, What if the people here fhould grumble at it? it was anfwered, That there an army was fure againft fuch: and the queftion being made to him, What if the King fhall refufe it? was anfwered, That Goring and his officers would be for it, and join with their forces. All thefe particulars were, by L. Chancellor, related to divers of us, and written down at this time by fome of us in our diurnals, which may be a fufficient ground againft all fufpicion of fiction or forgery upon our part. The fame alfo were by his Lordfhip repeated afterward, upon the occafion of the bufinefs of the fubcommittee, and of Mr Cranford's relation, and certain interrogatories were drawn up upon them.

The information which my L. Chancellor received,
and

and did relate to us concerning the privy way of treating, was mightily confirmed by some letters of intelligence, written from France about the same time, which did contain the same articles of giving content to the King concerning the militia, and delaying the church-business, and all other matters, till his coming to London: and that it was moved to the Queen to deal for this effect with his Majesty, upon these considerations.

That the Scots had no power here, and were averse from peace; that their opposites had all power in the houses, in the city, in the army, and in the navy: That Presbyterial government would be more powerful, permanent, and prejudicial to monarchy, and to the recovery of regal power in church-matters; but Independency being weak in itself, and so near into disorder and confusion, would call quickly for a remedy, and open a way for the King to return to his own power; and that the one side was in their principles for liberty of conscience, and therefore would be compliant with the Catholicks of his Majesty's party in the three kingdoms; but the Presbyterians were more rigid, and would oppose toleration of divers religions in his Majesty's dominions.

· Those discoveries made formerly by Savile's propositions, by information from others, and by letters from France, were renewed to our sense, and further confirmed unto us by other emergents; as by Digby's intercepted letter to Legge, mentioning the dislike of his answer to the propositions sent to Oxford, as being not at all satisfactory; by the naming and meeting of a subcommittee, without our knowledge, as is more fully expressed in the papers given in by the L. Chancellor and the L. Wariston, the 12th of May, to be reported to the Houses; and by the King's intercepted letters, especially that to the Queen, concerning a proposition from a person at London, whom he calls one of the most considerable London rebels, for renewing the treaty upon her motion, with a preassurance of submitting to reason.

We add also, when some of our number went to Oxford, with the propositions of peace, it was told them, that there was one there agenting privily for a party at London; which, when some of the English commissioners were acquainted with, they told, that there was one come from London to the L. Cottington at that time, as at several times before. We have also been advertised

from

from the Earl of Lauderdale, that the secret, concerning the surprise of Oxford at an advantageous place, communicated by Mr Napier to a subcommittee of three persons, of which number his Lordship was one, is found now by the intercepted letters to have been discovered at Oxford to some, and by them particularly written to the King, which his Lordship wonders how it comes to pass, and we now hear to be a truth, although the letter itself, which beareth so much, was not communicated unto us with the other letters.

These particulars so much cleared and confirmed unto us, we conceive to be of so great importance, that (were the persons concerned never so dear unto us) we could not, without great guiltiness, conceal them from the Honourable Houses; which they will therefore take to their consideration, and do what in their wisdom may seem most for the well of the publick.

July 24. 1645.

We being desired, by a message from the Honourable House of Commons, to be present at this committee, appointed for the examination of the L. Savile, and having heard his elusory answer concerning his intention and pretension, we have thought fit, for acquitting ourselves of the trust put upon us, to represent our thoughts concerning that answer of his, the only seeming strength and advantage in all his defences.

That his real intention was to do the King's business, and to bring about new and unsafe propositions of peace; and that the business of Goring and Legge, and the finding out the King's intelligencer here, were but pretensions, it may thus appear.

1. By Mr Howard's flying out of the kingdom, when the L. Savile was challenged upon underhand dealings; it being clear, by the L. Savile's letter to Mr Howard, that Mr Howard knew of the reality of his intentions; which is also confessed by Savile himself: so that there had been nothing to fright away Mr Howard, and make him flee, if the real intention had been to do service to the parliament, and not to the King.

2. The L. Savile's own papers (which we did formerly communicate) do testify against him, that he endeavoured to do the King all possible services; for he kept ordinary correspondence with those at Oxford, and gave

I

                them

hem intelligence of such things as might be most for their
dvantage and our prejudice. As that concerning the
cots army's march southward, and that Sir Thomas
airfax was to get a great army, and a part thereof de-
gned to go to Taunton. He wrote also what intelligence
as here at this time from France and Ireland, the par-
ament's forces being about Wallingford; he did intimate,
1 his letter to Mr Howard, John Gary's danger if he
hould adventure to come to the place appointed. And
aving formerly written, that they of Oxford should not
car the advance of Sir Thomas Fairfax's army speedily,
e did thereafter recal that intelligence, and wrote the
ontrary, left his former intelligence had made the ene-
ay flack in their preparations. He wrote also concern-
ag divisions and factions here; that Essex had no power;
hat the Independents are the prevailing party: where-
pon he recommendeth the beating or disgracing of Sir
Thomas Fairfax's army. He puts the enemy in hopes, that
Essex and the Scots army will be wiser than they were,
nd will hearken more to peace than they did; and in-
orms, that in the mean time the Independents were court-
ag him, and treating with him concerning the peace of
he kingdoms; and when they were unsatisfied with the
.. Digby's answer concerning the message, he gave notice
ow unsatisfied they were, and promiseth to deal with
hem at a fitter season. These things being laid together,
leclare, that he did both really and intentionally endea-
our to strengthen the enemy, and to weaken the parlia-
nent, by acquainting these at Oxford, with the condi-
ion of our affairs, our intelligence, our intentions, the
osture and motion of our armies, our strength, our
veakness, our divisions, and such other things as might
nost encourage and be useful to the enemy; and endanger our affairs, so that when he tells us, that all these
vere but pretensions, it calls to mind Solomon's observa-
ion, " As a madman that casteth fire-brands, arrows,
' and death, so is the man that deceiveth his neighbour,
' and saith, Am not I in sport ?"

3. In the end of his large paper he bids assure Digby,
hat he will do the King's business the safest, the speediest,
nd the noblest way; and that they at Oxford shall under-
tand from their friends here, his unfeigned desires to
erve them, though with the hazard of all he hath; those
riends of theirs whom they will trust, being witnesses of

his proceedings. But if he had been doing service to the parliament, as now he professeth, why did he either fear the hazard of all he hath, or acquaint the Oxfordian intelligencer here with what he did ?

4. In the beginning of his first paper, he intimates to them at Oxford, that the protestation that some here offered unto him, and that which they desired and advised, was all according to his own heart. No wise man would write so to them at Oxford, if they at Oxford had not real testimonies of his desires to serve them; otherwise it had been a ready way to break his credit and trust at Oxford.

5. He did most really, seriously, and with great asseverations and assurances, deal with some persons here toward the making of a peace, and bringing about a new message from the King, which might be accepted here; and particularly he endeavoured to persuade the L. Chancellor to this business, as is expressed in our other paper. This not being well relished by the L. Chancellor, he applieth himself unto others whom he designeth in these papers. And the whole course of his proceedings do declare, that he came hither from Oxford to gain a party for the King, whomsoever he shall find most willing and useful for his ends, concerning new propositions of peace.

6. That which he calls his pretension is found to have been really acted, and diligently prosecuted by him, as appears not only by his own hand-writ, which is instead of many witnesses, but also by the Lord Digby's letter, relating to the same business, and by the King's letter to the Queen, the 13th of March 1645, intimating the Lord Savile's purpose to go to her, in order to a new treaty. But for that which he calls his real intention, there appears no real evidence for it, neither by his own papers, nor by any letters of his correspondents; nor doth he shew any warrant from the subcommittee for making a pretension of peace.

7. The L. Savile confessed, before the committee, that the propositions which he sent to Oxford, and which he desired might be sent hither in a message from the King, were such as he really desired might be sent from the King, and which he is confident should be accepted by those whom he calls his friends here, and the prevalent party. And whereas he saith, that he thought these propositions to be the same with the three propositions which were

were treated upon at Uxbridge, it would foon appear, that the propofitions were fubftantially different, if they be compared together: yea the L. Savile himfelf could not be ignorant that thefe propofitions of his were not the fame with thofe treated upon at Uxbridge; for he well knew, that the King had abfolutely refufed to grant thefe propofitions, except they be mollified and altered; fo that he could never have made that a colour or pretext for another defign, to defire that the King fhould fend back the parliament's own propofitions, and now offer what he had refufed at Uxbridge.

8. The L. Savile faid before the committee, that the end why he fent thofe advertifements to Oxford, was to find out the party on which the King relies here, he having heard much at Oxford of two parties here; and that the L. Digby faid at the L. Dorfet's houfe, that the King hath a party here greater than all his armies; and being employed, as he faith, by the fubcommittee, to try out who are the King's party here, this, he faid, was the ground and reafon of writing thefe papers, whereupon he is now challenged: yet this his pretence is overthrown by his own papers, by which he himfelf communicates to thofe at Oxford, intelligence concerning two parties here, and which of the two parties courts and treats with him about peace, and hath the power in their hands, and what party it was that had defired him to join himfelf to them by proteftation; and to quit the other party. But how can this be a way to make them at Oxford to difcover to him the King's party here, while he himfelf difcovereth to them which is the party here that is both weakeft and moft unwilling for peace? neither doth it at all appear that he wrote to any at Oxford for finding out the King's party here.

9. That which the L. Savile faith was but his pretenfion, is really coincident with the defign which the enemy hath been driving on all this while paft, as is evident by the Queen's letter to the King, for cafting of religion to be treated of in the laft place, the fame is found in Savile's papers and propofitions fent to Oxford. It is alfo evident by the King's letter to the Duke of Richmond, putting him in mind to cajole the Independents and the Scots, which is the very fame that Savile endeavoured to do; and when he could not prevail one way, he applied himfelf another way. It doth farther appear by that let-

　　ter

ter to the Duke of Richmond, and by some of the King's letters to the Queen, that although it was not the Queen's mind, yet there were thoughts of bringing the King to London, and divers about the King were for it; which is another circumstance coincident with the Lord Savile's papers.

10. There can be no such credit given to what the L. Savile alledgeth, when he was a prisoner under examination, and fearing to lose a party whose protection he desireth and expecteth, as for that which is found under Savile and Digby their own hands, having past between them in a secret way of correspondence, and now discovered and brought to light by a secret providence of God, without their knowledge, and against their desire; and Digby's intercepted letter agreeing with Savile's papers, in the progress and way of the business, and the one answering the other, as face answereth, both shewing that propositions were sent to Oxford, that Digby sent an answer thereunto, and that this answer was communicated by the L. Savile to those here whom he thought most willing to make peace : whereupon Savile perceiving they were not satisfied with Digby's answer, did intimate to Digby that they were not satisfied, but displeased and distempered, and gave this occasion to Digby to write his opinion in that letter which was intercepted, in which CCC signifieth John Cary, who was Mr Howard's correspondent, which the L. Savile himself confesseth. Besides all this, the L. Savile's answer and expressions before the committee were contradictory one to another, and therefore the less to be trusted.

11. The 4th article of the solemn league and covenant, bindeth us to endeavour the discovery, trial, and condign punishment of all such evil instruments as hinder the reformation of religion, divide the King from his people, or one of the kingdoms from another, or make any faction or parties amongst the people, contrary to the covenant. This article must be applied, and performed, either according to the reality of mens actions, or according to the interpretations which men will put upon their own actions. If the former, then the L. Savile falleth within the compass of that article, his actions being really a hindering of the reformation of religion, and a dividing the King from his best subjects, and of the kingdoms one from another, and making a faction or party contrare to
the

the covenant. If the latter, then the greatest incendiary or traitor may shelter himself under this evasion, that he did intend some great good, and to do service to the parliament, which, that he might the better do, he did insinuate himself in a handsome way of compliance with those of Oxford, to make them trust him the more. It is not to be forgotten, that the thing which he calls his intention here, he persuadeth them at Oxford to be but a pretension; and that which he calls a pretension here, he persuades them at Oxford to be his real intention; so that in this case he must needs be examined according to the nature and reality of his actions and divisive motions.

104. To Principal Strang. *July* 1. 1645.

Reverend and Beloved Brother,
—— Since my last there is little more news here. The King's cabinet being taken in the battle is sent up here. Yesterday all day the House of Commons was reading his letters. A world of things there, under the King's hand, to increase his disgrace. I am afraid for the consequence of these secrets. Many foul things are found, which cannot but much increase our distrust, which before was great enough. ——

105. Publick Letter. *July* 1. 1645.

How this fortnight bygone affairs have gone here, the two inclosed diurnals will show. Little more progress is made in church-affairs. The assembly has been forced to adjourn on five divers occasions of fastings and thanksgiving lately, every one whereof took from us almost two days. When we sat we had no real controversy; only petty debates for alterations of words, and transposition of propositions, in the whole body of government, took up our time. Our luck will be very evil, if once this week, by God's help, we do not at last put out of our hands to the Houses all that we have to say of government, the whole platform there really according to the practice of our church. Farther, order for the directory, after many debates, at last is passed the House of Commons; very near as severe an ordinance as that against the neglect of
the

the service-book. Wednesdays and Fridays are set apart
by the Houses for church-affairs, so we hope very shortly
to see presbyteries and synods erected: yet what retard-
ment we may have from this great victory, obtained most
by the Independent party, and what that model of government, whereupon Thomas Goodwin and his brethren
these three months have been sitting so close, that they very rarely, and he never at all has yet appeared, we do not
know; only we expect a very sharp assault, how soon we
know not, for a toleration to we wot not what. This we
know, that we had never more need of your prayers for
wisdom and grace, to get the dangerous and evil designs
of very crafty and diligent men overthrown, and turned
on the head of the contrivers. For our own parts, we
have strong enough mutual affections to be at our own
homes in so stormy times; yet we were unworthy of the
trust put upon us, if we did not declare, that the necessity
of men here for our church, and the cause of God, was
never so palpable as at this hour. The King, since the battle, has been in Worcestershire, and now in Hereford and
Monmouth shires, on the borders of Wales, recruiting
his foot; but comes small speed. Our forces in Taunton
were in hazard to have been overmastered by Goring; but
Massey got near 4000 horse together for their relief. Goring is thought yet to be the stronger. Sir Thomas Fairfax is marching with all the speed he can to join with Massey. It is much feared Goring fight before Sir Thomas
can come up. This is a day of prayer in the city for help
from God to Massey. If Goring were broke, it is thought
that party were undone. The King expects forces from
Ireland to land in Wales. But that which now is most
spoken of, is the King's cabinet, sent up hither by Sir
Thomas Fairfax after the battle. Some make it of as great
value as the victory; I pray God it may be so. It doth discover under the King's hand many great secrets, which I
fear will make all peace with him, and hopes of him, more
desperate. Our commissioners gave in a paper before the
Chancellor went, to make three uses of the victory; the
present settling of the church, the active prosecution of
the war, the sending to the King in his low condition for
peace on the former propositions. We expect to-morrow
an answer to these important motions. Our army, blessed
be God, is well, and has rested itself at leisure about Nottingham. I hope they are now on their march for Worcester

cefter and Hereford. Their quarters there will be good,
and their service for the time not hard. It is exceeding
necessar, that the promised recruits should come up with
all diligence. All that love either God or Scotland would
bestir themselves in the places where they live to haste up
these men. If they be put in garrison in Newcastle, their
labour is not great; if they come up to Worcester, tho'
the journey be far, yet the way is safe; no enemy by the
way, and they are sure of good maintenance. If it might
please God to make you there so wise as to strengthen this
army to 14,000 or 15,000 foot, that the whole might be
18,000 or 20,000 men, horse and foot, then we would be
so looked upon as to be reverenced by our friends, feared
by our foes, be well entertained of all, and be able to keep
all here in church and state right, according to our mind.
But will we sit still, and neglect the army here; it will be
contemned, and our whole nation with it. The consequences will be deplorable to both the kingdoms. Now a
little wisdom and diligence will help all. Our hearts here
are oft exceeding sorry to think, that it is God's will to
continue his plagues on our dear country; that not only
these bloody miscreants are permitted to rage among us,
but that God immediately should strike the chief parts of
our land with the pestilence, and that under both these
plagues a stupid, blind, lethargick stupidity should be upon us. For these things we mourn, and oft our eyes
trickle down with water: but if, with all these evils, there
be any unmerciful men among us, who now will follow
private interests, and be for emulations and factions, for
the upholding of the common enemy, and casting of this
whole island back in the gulph of deeper misery than yet
we have seen, at this very time when God's mercy has
brought us very near to the shore and end of all our troubles; I cannot deny but my heart does detest and curse
the wickedness of all such men; and I am confident God
will discover, and make their base designs so visible, that their
names shall rot and stink to the generations following. I
hope many honest ministers, and others, will countenance
this session of parliament. My L. Chancellor and my L.
Lauderdale will there fully inform the posture of affairs
here. I hope there will be none there so evil a countryman as to be upon any design which evidently may put
things either here or there in a confusion. Private ends
are ever base; but at this nick of time, mens self-interests
may

may be deſtructive both to themſelves and the publick.
Time will not fail to reveal many ſecrets. If God may be
pleaſed to make you there wiſe and unanimous, and a little active, we are likely ere long to have all ſettled in the
whole iſland according to our mind; otherwiſe our miſeries in all the iſle are but beginning. What I wrote about
the ſurpriſe of Dunkirk was reported confidently here for
four or five days; but it is falſe. Duke de Orleans is lying about Mardike, and has burnt the ſuburbs of Dunkirk. Torſtenſon has not yet got Brin. The Prince of
Orange, with all his army, is in Flanders, but yet not lies
down before any town. The State's fleet is joined with the
Swediſh. The ſtraits of Denmark are great. They ſay
Harcourt has got a great victory in Arragon.

106. To my Lord Lauderdale. July 1. 1645.

My Lord,
I forgive your firſt fault in not anſwering mine, that
you may fall the readier in the next. I hope you got the
laſt fifty pſalms, and have ſent them to the committee.
There is longing here already for your animadverſions.
Mr Rous has twice in this ſhort time been ſpeaking to me
about it. You will not fail to put the committee in mind
to uſe what diligence conveniently they may. Your Lordſhip may ſee what I write to my wife. Cloſe all, and ſend
all away with the firſt occaſion. If you be a good Scotſ-
man, remonſtrate what neceſſity there is to make our army here ſtrong in men and miniſters and a committee. For
the time it is like to have little ado; for the Independents
and Cromwell are like to put a quick end to all here without any other help. What will be next, if we, by our e-
ternally unanſwerable ſottiſhneſs, will make ourſelves in-
conſiderable but for a little time longer, who can tell?
Our church-buſineſs drives on wonderful heavily, and is
like to go on more and more heavily if this world laſt.
The letters of the cabinet have been ſtrangely ſhuffled. It
is ſaid now they were rifled by the ſoldiers, and caſt here
and there, and hardly one got gathered together. However, the box was in ſome hands at fartheſt on the Sunday. The committee of both kingdoms had leiſure to
write for them to Sir Thomas Fairfax; but no anſwer at
all was returned to that letter; only the letters came all

here open, on the Friday, to Mr White, who did with them what he pleased till Monday morning; at which time they were given in as a huge great secret to the House of Commons, and there all the forenoon and afternoon, and the day following, read over in the audience of the House. They are this day, as I think, but to be read in the House of Lords, and on Thursday by a great committee of Lords and Commons to be read in a common council at London; thereafter we will have the favour to see them. It is very like that new advisements here will be taken upon them. What they who love an anarchy in the church, as it is feared in state also, do intend, we will shortly know. Only they who have any love to God, or their covenant, or Britain, among you, let them at this diet of parliament, or never, see to our army here, and to our London commission. Are there any pedantick fools now talking of removing of the commission? The necessity of continuing and increasing it was never half so apparent as now. If there be any fitter men than the former, let them in God's name have their turn; but a lamentable pity it is, that men should so far mind their own open interests, as to hazard the publick safety, for to revenge the just miscarriage of their unreasonable desires. If there was any trinketing with the King, it seems the evidence of it was in that box; but, by canny convoyance, these men in whose hands the open box so long remained, might destroy whatever concerned their friends. This is done in such a way as cannot be gotten questioned. Savile and Sey have oft been before the committee of examination; but all is like to turn to nothing. Except you be unanimous, this poor isle is farther from peace and happiness than ever. When we have put the King to Wales and Cornwall, and printed all his shameful secrets, as it is like shortly we will, what then shall we do next? The like of this consultation never yet came above your table. Make haste hither you and the Chancellor, except you also love to drown yourselves in your private affairs, till both you and they be lost with us all in the publick. An agent for the army is most needless; we are at charges enough already. That needless office will find us all faggots to heat our waters more than we can suffer. Suppress that motion in time, or it will hurt us all, and most the first movers. I am as busy as I may with our sectaries. If I had some time, readily I may give an account

o the publick of my studies under your Lordship's patronage, if you continue honest, (a great if in these days of
notion); but my progress yet is but small. Mr Hender-
on feared me much the other day by stopping of his water; but now, blessed be God, he is well. We expected
George and Mr Kennedy this night from the army at farthest; but we have heard nothing of them, or it, since
Friday. We send to the army to-morrow L. 20,000. Remembering my service to your good kind Lady, and her
glowming son, whom I pray God to bless, and make fa-
therbetter, I rest,
Your Lordship's servant.

107. *Publick Letter.* *July* 8. 1645.

WITH the last post all I would say beside what was in
my publick letter, you and Mr Robert did see in my letter to Mr David. Let me know if you received what I
wrote to you with James Nisbet. I got Mr Robert's and
Mr Zacharias's. You had great need to further up recruits to our army. It may shortly have much to do. If
you will send to it what you ought and may, it will have
little or nought to do. I see by Mr Robert's letter, that
you are misinformed of our numbers. The King and Goring together will have triple our number of horse, and
double of foot. The parliament, if they labour, can make
Sir Thomas Fairfax's double our number in foot as he is
already double in horse. Under God the welfare of Scotland depends on this army. The Chancellor can inform
how necessar it is to have a strong committee and presbytery there to keep better discipline than has been. Ravishing, and plundering of friends, unpunished, will make God
to punish all for a few. Men of suspected faith are very dangerous to be there. The parliament is wise to make,
in a canny and safe way, a wholesome purgation, that it
may be timeous. You will remember me to the magistrates of the town, and have a care that my publick letters, and printed papers, be communicated to them and
to my colleagues. If this be neglected, I pray you let them
know it is not my fault. However our opposition is mighty, yet daily, blessed be God, we get ground. All the
ministers in London now without exception are for our
presbytery. Thomas Goodwin and Burton, that were a-
gainst

gainſt it, are put by the parliament from their places. Some other few preachers are but lecturers. The Independents yet preſent not their model. We ſuſpect their domeſtick diviſions, or their perplexity, whether to take in or hold out from amongſt themſelves the reſt of the ſectaries. If our army were in good caſe, by God's bleſſing, all would ſettle quickly in peace; elſe, we are but in the beginning of confuſions and troubles. The troubles in Scotland are but ſecondary evils. Your right eye would be on the affairs here, if you have either wiſdom, or any love to yourſelves. Mr Henderſon is much tenderer than he wont. He and Mr Rutherford are gone this day to Epſom waters. So long as any thing is to do here, he cannot be away. I hope the reſt of us ere long may be well ſpared, if once we had through the Catechiſm and a part of the Confeſſion. If I write not the next two poſts, the cauſe will be my employment to preach to the Houſe of Lords the next faſt-day. What our conſultation about ſending of articles to the King will produce, we cannot tell as yet; only we expect great events. I pray God they may be good, and for ending of our troubles. I think you and Mr David both will be at Stirling. Let it be your care, that Lauderdale be ſent back to us with all expedition. No living man fitter to do ſervice for Scotland againſt the plotting Independent party, which, for the time, has a great hand in the ſtate. Alſo, if the affairs of Scotland may any way permit, it were neceſſar the Chancellor returned. He is very much regarded and loved here. Take heed, as ye love our affairs here either of church or ſtate, that my L. Wariſton be not called back. Whoever and whatever pretence will offer it, they, for private and corrupt deſigns, would diſgrace one of the moſt faithful, diligent, and able ſervants that our church and kingdom has had all the times of our troubles. There is no need at all for an agent for the army, if there be any commiſſioners for our ſtate here. It is not only a needleſs office, but it is ſought merely for private ends, and will be occaſion of evil. In all theſe things miſken me, and all information from this.

108. *To my Lord Lauderdale.*   *July 8.* 1645.

My Lord,

So long as the plague is in Edinburgh, you must be content to be our postmaster-general. How all goes here, you will get it from many hands. If you please to read what I have sent to my friends, you may close the utmost cover, and send it to some Glasgow man there. Mr Henderson went this day to Epsom. He is better than he was, but not yet well. Many here stumble at our offer of propositions to the King; but to me the offer seems very necessary. You know the temper of our army, and I think of the parliament also. If they be offered and received, we attain our end; if rejected, all will be the more encouraged to go on. But if they should not be offered, and yet upon the letters a summons, a certification go to the King, what should be next? The Prince and York are with their father. Gloucester is put in Northumberland's keeping. The kingdoms behoved to be guided by the parliaments, and so England by these who now prevail; whose government how sweet it would be either to church or state, no man knows better than you. And what would Scotland's condition be, if, beside Montrose, they had any other factions to deal with, striving for the government, and possibly a rupture with England, beside an immortal war so long as the King or Prince had any friends either at home or abroad? I would therefore think it simply necessary for the good of Britain to send offers of peace to the King, but withal that they may be real. Many here that can condescend to send them, mind no more than a bare paper to be accepted or refused, not only without any treaty, but without any words. If we desire to deal truly with the heart of a man obstinate near to enduration, we would use some probable means of persuasion. If you condescend to send propositions, by all means let Mr Henderson be one to go with them, with an express to him, and all whom ye will send, to deal to the uttermost of their power to persuade the King's conscience to go on no farther to his own evident ruin, and possibly ours also. No man on our side so meet as Mr Henderson, and you know he will not go without express commands both from church and state. This much remember I forewarned you
of,

of, albeit possibly for little purpose; for if Goring get over
the Severn with his 7000 horse and three of foot, as they
call him, the King and he will make a powerful army, and
in reason they will march directly on us at Worcester.
There we are our alone. The English forces which were
promised to join, I hear not of them. Sir Thomas Fairfax, appointed to follow Goring, it is feared shall lie still
to refresh his weary foot; and the present condition of
our army I doubt it much. By all means haste up our recruits to lie still in the northern garrisons, that the old soldiers may come to our army. O! if you could get one
sound blow of Montrose, that the body of that army might
come up to England. We are hated and despised daily by
many here. No means but by a miracle either of safety
or reputation, but the strengthening of this army much
above what it is. If you take not a course in the parliament, that justice may be done on unclean, drunken, blasphemous, plundering officers, noblemen, as well as o-
thers, we will stink in the nose of this people deservedly,
and God will plague us; and if any thing should befal
this army, what were Scotland's condition? The face of
affairs convinces you, that there is a necessity you should
lay by your private affairs, and haste up hither so soon as
the English commissioners are dismissed; for before, I
think, you must not stir. Wharton is the leader of this
negotiation. You know his metal. He is as fully as ever
for that party, who grows in hopes and insolency against
all that are in their way. Their designs are very high;
yet pride dwells on the brink of ruin. I thought to have
written but six lines at most; yet old freedom with you
has made my pen run thus far. Please your Lordship,
farewell. Your servant,

                               ROBERT BAILLIE.

209. *To the Earl of Eglinton. Worcester-house, July 8. 1645.*

   My Lord,
   I thank your Lordship for your kind letter by Hugh
Kennedy. I saw no other of your letters this twelve
months at least. All the news I have ever sent to Scotland, it was my direction they should go from Glasgow to
your Lordship's house at Kilwinning. How all goes here,
                                                    our

our fecretary writes to your committee. Yefterday we
fent up to both Houfes the whole body of the church-
government; fo it is once out of the affembly's hands.
Bleffed be God, all the minifters of London are for us.
Burton and Goodwin, the only two that were Independents, are by the parliament removed from their places.
Seven or eight preachers that are againft our way are only
lecturers in the city, but not minifters. We hope fhortly
to get the Independents put to it to declare themfelves either to be for the reft of the fectaries, or againft them. If
they declare againft them, they will be but a fmall inconfiderable company; if for them, all honeft men will cry
out upon them for feparating from all the Reformed
churches, to join with Anabaptifts and Libertines. The
Lords this day named Rutland and Wharton for their
commiffioners for our parliament, as the Commons before
had done Sir Henry Vane elder, Sir William Armyne,
Mr Hatcher, and Goodwin. I hope their friendly debate
with our parliament about Carlifle fhall end in a ftraiter
union betwixt the nations, and fhall be a mean to remeid
many of our grievances; but the only hope we have to
prevail in any thing, either in church or ftate, is God's
bleffing on that your army. We fear that Goring crofs
the Severn, and join with the King. You then will be
neareft the danger. I doubt not but you prefs with all diligence to have your recruits from Scotland, and what you
can draw from your northern garrifons. That which affrays us moft is, your neglect of difcipline, if it be true
which very many have told us, that ravifhers of women,
and plunderers of people; that blafphemers, and profa-
ners of the fabbath, and fuch like enormities, are unpu-
nifhed among you; that fundry new covenanters have
place among you alfo. Thefe things will make God to
withdraw his affiftance from you. Your Lordfhip was
wont to have the beft ordered and moft pious foldiers in
the army; if this be not ftill your Lordfhip's care, you
will lofe much of that honour which before you did enjoy
upon juft defert. I muft here abruptly break off. Our
prayers here are for all your profperities. We truft God
will honour you all by notable fervices to God and both
the kingdoms. When you have feen the copy of the
King's writs, you will believe your own eyes, that our
hopes of peace by any treaty can be but fmall fo long as
                                                          the

the King has any army on the fields.   But I muſt ſay, A-
dieu.

Your Lordſhip's, to be commanded after the old
faſhion,

ROBERT BAILLIE.

My ſervice to the Colonel, of whom I hear much good.

110. *Publick Letter.*   *July* 15. 1645.

SINCE my laſt, with the former poſt, July 1ſt, we have,
thanks be to God, at laſt finiſhed the whole body of government, and after all our reviews, ſent it up to both
Houſes on Monday; ſo it is once out of our hands.   We
expect the parliament, when it lies on them alone, will,
with expedition, ſee much of our advice put in practice.
Since, we have entered on the Confeſſion of Faith; as
yet I cannot pronounce of the length or ſhortneſs of our
proceedings therein.   If God be pleaſed to aſſiſt us, as
ſometimes he does, we may, ere long, be at an end of
our whole work.

So ſoon as Sir Thomas Fairfax had overtaken Maſſey,
the clubmen that made ſo great noiſe, did ſhrink away.
Goring drew off from Taunton; and, as it is thought, is
gone towards Briſtol.   The King is beyond the Severn,
gathering in Wales what recruits he is able.   It ſeems he
and Goring will join, and ſo make up a great army betwixt them.   If Goring go over the Severn to the King,
it ſeems they will fall upon our army, who now, as we
think, are about Worceſter; but if the King come over
the Severn, it ſeems they will fall on Sir Thomas Fairfax,
who is following Goring ſo faſt as his wearied foot are
able.   There is great need, that with all the ſpeed may be,
theſe 6000 foot we hear of be ſent up from Scotland, and
with them ſome gracious miniſters.   If our army were ſo
much ſtrengthened with men and miniſters, and a committee, as eaſily by a little care it might be, it would
be a pregnant mean to end the troubles of Scotland, to
ſettle all theſe dominions according to our mind; but if
diligence for this end be not uſed, and that quickly, we
hurt the common cauſe, we much endanger both the honour and ſafety of our own nation. Montroſe will be cheaper
and more eaſily defeat here than he can be there.   The

placing

placing of a Scots garrison in Carlisle is taken ill here
by the most part. The parliament has named two Lords
and four Commons to go to Stirling to require reason in
this point. They who are seeking division betwixt the nations, blow much at this coal. I am hopeful our parliament will be able to satisfy the English commissioners in
any thing they will demand, and that Carlisle, which many fear, and some expect, shall be the apple of strife,
will be the band of a straiter union betwixt us, and a little
reckoning and friendly debate betwixt the parliaments.
Union has been, and is our subsistence; it must be entertained at whatever rate; all divisive motions are destructive,
and never more than now. The King's writs I saw the
other day, for the parliament sent them to us to be all
seen, and so many of them copied as we thought meet.
In divers letters under his hand, he presses Ormond to
make a firm peace with the Irish, gives him full power to
recal all laws against Papists, also Poyning's statutes,
which they say are for the dependence of Ireland on the
parliament of England; likewise to join with the Irish
for casting the Scots out of Ireland. All this he presses
may be done quickly, that so powerful supplies may be
sent over to him against the rebels of England, and an army to Scotland to land in Cumberland before the end of
March last past. There be many letters to the Queen, that
she may procure, from Popish princes, help to him on
very favourable conditions to Papists. In one of her letters, all in cyphers, but decyphered by the King's hand,
she assures him of the Duke of Lorrain's service with
10,000 men. Thanks be to God, all these designs have
been crushed by God's hand. Before the Chancellor
went, we had given in a paper, as for other things, so for
sending to the King, after his overthrow at Naseby, the
former three propositions of peace. The parliament returned a civil answer, that after the consideration of the
King's writs, they and we behoved to advise how to proceed. We are to press again the sending of the propositions so much the more of the writs, for we think they
will contribute to the humbling of the King's mind, and
disposing him to do reason both to us and to himself.
Some fear the King's obstinacy; others with it to increase; but the best and the most here think it exceeding
necessary to essay if we can have peace on the former propositions. If the Lord harden his heart, that our offers

2   be

be refufed, one other ftroke may break his party without recovery. But when that is done, and we freed from all fears of them, we fee a new fea of troubles, wherein we muft enter. Though in it we feel no bottom, and can fee no fhore, however, we muft do our duty, and truft in the Lord. Our hearts are exceedingly grieved that yet the wicked enemy there doth fubfift, and that the Lord is pleafed to ftrike us fo fore with the peftilence. Oh that his hand were not heavy on our hearts! that many were not ftupified and hardened! We cannot but expect a glorious iffue out of all thefe troubles, whatever be the perfonal fins of thoufands, and fo our juft defervings of worfe than yet has befallen us; yet truly we muft take God to witnefs, in the midft of the flames of his wrath, that the publick intentions of the godly in the land have been and are for the glory of his name, for the advancement of piety, truth, and righteoufnefs, without the hurt of any flefh, except fo far as our neceffary defence does compel; fo we cannot but confidently hope of the Lord's glorious falvation in the end, and we hope it is near. The Lords this day have nominated their commiffioners, Rutland and Wharton. The Commons, the other day, named theirs, Sir Hary Vane elder, Sir William Armyne, Mr Hatcher, and Mr Goodwin. My Lord Chancellor and Lauderdale knows all the men well. I hope their meffage may ftrengthen the union of the kingdoms, and help to redrefs many of our grievances, if God give you grace to manage well.

111. *For my Lord Lauderdale.* London, *July* 15. 1645.

My Lord,

WE think the dolorous condition of Scotland has hindered you and others to write unto us with the laft poft. Our hearts are deeply wounded with Baillie's defeat. As yet our army here has done nothing. If its credit be not relieved with fome fuccefsful action quickly, the clamours of this people will arife againft it. Cromwell's extraordinary fuccefs makes that party here triumph. I wrote to you of L. Digby's intercepted letter, intimating the fending of propofitions from fome peer to the King, and my difcourfe with Mr Cranford thereupon. It was the Independents ftudy to caft all the odium of trinketing with

Oxford on Hollis, while Savile refuses to decypher the letter wherein he said, it was written to him from Oxford, that Hollis kept weekly correspondence with Digby : he is sent prisoner to the tower.   So soon as he comes there, he sends his daughter-in-law, the Lady Temple, with a letter to Mr Gordon, (but first to be communicated to my Lord Sey), requiring him to declare to the House of Commons, that when you were last at Oxford, Hollis had given a paper of propositions to Lindsay and him, to be communicated to the King, according to which the King had framed an answer to your demands : this made din enough.   Some would have had Hollis removed the House presently.   He declared ingenuously what the matter was, That all of you having conceived the expediency of receiving and returning visits, he, with Mr Whitlock, had visited Lindsay, with whom Savile was ; that in discourse he had said, it was in vain to speak of a treaty, unless the three propositions were granted by the King ; that Lindsay desired him to set down in what terms he could with the King to pass these propositions : he did so in presence of the whole company ; and when Lindsay had taken a copy of it, he took back his paper, and acquainted Wenman and Denbigh thereafter with all.   The House appointed a committee to inquire into this action, how innocent soever it was.   Hollis's friends have been in great fear for his undoing by it.   His only relief was apprehended to stand in bringing forth the Independents real trinketing with Oxford by Savile.   They who were able to demonstrate this, were the still committee, your good friends.   The one, whose hatred is perfect, was for some days very willing to witness the Bruslean would not come on the stage ; yet at last was persuaded : but then the other refused.   While Mr Hollis is resolute to ruin, before he will bring any of them forth against their minds, behold a strange providence put in our hands three writs of Savile's hand, which evidences his trafficking with Oxford, by my Lord Sey and the Independent party's advice.   These we sent to the House of Commons, offering to declare what we knew further to that purpose.   The House presently appointed a committee to examine Savile and these writs.   He has acknowledged his hand ; but by strange juggling evasions.   Our fault of you, at such a time, is great.   The matter is so clear, that if it had been rightly timed, a little either sooner or later, by all appearance

pearance it had removed that party, which long has obstructed the reformation both of church and kingdom : but their present favour with the city, and all on their double victory, and our neafeance is so great, that all can be brought against them will not prejudice them. And indeed, it seems they have altered a principle, that as, before Leicester, their trafficking was to bring back the King on very dangerous terms, so now, after their great success, it is to cast him clean away. Whatever miseries may follow, yet this conclusion would for once put all power in their friends hands; but the God of justice and truth will not permit them to turn states at their pleasure. Since Marshal is appointed, and willing, to go with the commissioners to Scotland, I am apprehending they have some other business with you than Carlisle. You have now enough of my evil hand. The great God give you courage, wisdom, and success, in this your great strait. So I rest, &c.

ROBERT BAILLIE.

112. *Publick Letter.* *August* 10. 1645.

WHEN the singular favours of God do lift up our hearts in praises here, and in confidence of a happy issue of this troublesome work, our spirits are deeply wounded within us, and broken by what we hear from time to time from dear Scotland. We are amazed that it should be the pleasure of our God to make us fall thus the fifth time, before a company of the worst men in the earth; and beside all the calamity which the sword of these barbarous men does bring, that our angry God should send upon us a more furious pestilence than ever I heard of in our land : for these things we weep; our eyes run down with water : we cannot but think there is love at the bottom of all this bitterness : the cause here and there is one. If there be any odds, surely the enemy in Scotland, for all kind of wickedness, has it. That the Lord should cast them down here, and set them up there, it is one of the depths of divine wisdom, which we will adore. The constant practice here, on the least appearance of any publick danger, is to flee both to publick and private fasting. Truly the godly here are a praying people, and the parliament is very ready to further this disposition. If the

T 2

godly

godly there have the like care, and if the magiftrate be alike induſtrious, to crave the affiſtance of gracious people's faſting and praying, I know not; only it is my wiſh that God would make clear, what the caufe may be that ſo long he deſerts us. Whatever the matter may be, were I this night to die, my heart does not ſmite me for any wrong I know our nation has done, in lifting arms a-gainſt the malignant party, either the firſt, ſecond, or third time; for daily more and more it appears to the world, that the deſign of the miſled court was, and is, by all means out of hell, to faſten the yoke of tyranny on the necks both of our bodies and fouls, for our times, and the days of our poſterity; and therefore, what we have done we were abſolutely neceſſitated to it; and whatever troubles God has caſt upon us for our preſent trial, we expect, ere long, a comfortable concluſion; albeit no thanks to them, be who they will, who either by their treachery, or cowardice, or untimeous diviſions, or groundleſs jealouſies, or neglect of the publick, are the inſtruments of Scotland's woe. If yet they will not wa-ken, they will periſh, not only without any wife man's compaſſion, but with a mark of infamy on their perfons and families for ever. This my great heavineſs for the report of my unhappy couſin's defeat has drawn from me: yet let our friends there know for their comfort, the ene-my here is going down the wind apace.

Goring's army, in the weſt, the King's greateſt hope, is totally routed by Sir Thomas Fairfax. The remainder of that army, we hope, will not be able to keep the fields in the weſt long. Wales then only will remain to the King. Our army, bleſſed be God, is in good cafe. They are now making over the Severn; for they think it not fit to lie down before Worceſter, or any other town, for a long ſiege, ſo long as the enemy have any army. We hope the few forces which are with the King in Hereford-ſhire, ſhall not ſtay for them. If theſe, and Hopeton in the weſt, were diſſipated, the next care will be of the gar-riſons, if offers of any equitable peace from the King pre-vent it not. It ſeems Montroſe ſhall prove fatal to the King. His victories hitherto have been powerful ſnares to his hard heart. A little more continuance in this diſ-poſition is like to undo him. We proceed in our church-buſineſs alfo; only the affairs of Scotland torment us. We hope the Lord will not forget to be merciful for ever,

and

and will do it for his name's fake, whatever be our defervings. We are looking when he will be pleafed to
draw us out of that fiery furnace, as gold tried in the
fire, and filver purged more than feven times. We will
lie ftill at his feet; our petitions are nailed to the throne
of his mercy; we will wait patiently for our anfwer.

We have fent down to this meeting of the commiffion,
the whole body of the government, as it is fent up to the
parliament from the affembly. You will find few confiderable differences from the practice of our church. The
other day an order paft the Houfe of Commons, for the
erection of twelve prefbyteries within the lines of communication.

113. *A Publick Letter.*

In the affembly we have gone through a part of the Catechifm, and a part of the Confeffion of Faith; but as
many hinderances, when leaft we expect them, comes in
our way, fo the other week we were diverted by an occafion which may do us great harm, if God provide not for
it. Since April we have not much been troubled with the
Independents; for fince that time they have been about
the model of their way, and have not fince much minded
the affembly; and what they have done yet, all is a fecret.
Many think they cannot agree among themfelves : but if
we fhould be quit of them, we have no fcant of fectaries
to the common caufe. Paul Beft, the Antitrinitarian,
took up fome of our days. Mr Archer's blafphemous
book, called *The Author of the very finfulnefs of Sin,* took
up more of our time before we got it burnt by the hand
of the hangman. Mr Colman's fermon to the Houfe of
Commons, the firft faft day, exhorting them to keep all
the church-government in their own hand, and to give
churchmen none of it, took up fome days alfo. The
Lords preffing to have their chaplains and families exeem-
ed, as before, from ecclefiaftick jurifdiction; fuch things
are a little fafhious to us : but that which is like to vex
us, is another matter wherein we have need of your
earneft prayers to God; for a far lefs matter may be occafion of great evil. The moft part of the Houfe of Commons, efpecially the lawyers, whereof there are many, and
divers of them very able men, are either half or whole E-
rastians,

raftians, believing no church-government to be of divine right, but all to be a human constitution, depending on the will of the magistrate. About this matter we have had, at divers times, much bickering with them : now it is come to a shock. Ever since the directory came out, we have been pressing for a power to hold all ignorant and scandalous persons from the table : with much ado this was granted ; but so as we behoved to set down the points : this we agreed. But for the scandalous, when we had long essayed, we could not make such an enumeration, but always we found more of the like nature, which could not be expressed ; therefore we required to have power to exclude all scandalous, as well as some. The general they would not grant, as including an arbitrary and unlimited power. Our advice was, that they would go on to set up their presbyteries and synods with so much power as they could get ; and after they were once settled, then they might strive to obtain their full due power. But the synod was in another mind ; and after divers fair papers, at last they framed a most zealous, clear, and peremptor one, wherein they held out plainly the church's divine right to keep off from the sacrament, all who were scandalous ; and if they cannot obtain the free exercise of that power which Christ hath given them, they will lay down their charges, and rather chuse all afflictions than to sin by profaning the holy table The House is highly inflamed with this petition, and seems resolute to refuse it. The assembly is as peremptor to have it granted ; for upon this point, they say, depends their standing, all the godly being resolved to separate from them, if there be not a power, and care, to keep the profane from the sacraments. If the Lord assist us not in this difficulty, it may be the cause of great confusion among us. The House has appointed a conference with us to-morrow afternoon, and we purpose to require a grand committee thereafter, that we may press our interest of uniformity. We are hopeful, by God's help, to obtain our point, if this jar delay it not. We expect this week, that over all London, elders and deacons shall be chosen for every congregation, and then in a week or two, that the thirteen presbyteries, and the provincial synods, within the lines, shall be set up ; and so without delay in the other shires ; for orders are drawn already for this effect. All here are full of hope, that with the settling of these orders the heresies, refics, the fchifms, the ignorance, and profanity, which do exceedingly every where here abound, fhall quickly, if not evanifh, yet be diminifhed.

Sir Thomas Fairfax, after the taking of Bridgewater, and of Bath, and Wells, lies about Sherburn, waiting for his recruits. It is thought Maffey and he will make a great army. The Prince, Hopeton, and Goring, are raifing what power they can, beyond them, in the Weft; but it is not likely they can keep the field, except it be in a piece of Cornwal Our army is lying at Hereford; and hopes, by God's help, in a few days to carry it. The King hath, in Wales, fome thoufand horfe, but few foot. They fay he has gone to Chefter, and from thence intends, as fome fay, to Ireland, and others to Scotland. If he come to Scotland, I truft we fhall be fo wife and Chriftian as to remember our covenant, and remove thefe wicked inftruments from him, that have brought fo much evil both on him and all the three kingdoms. If God would difpofe his heart to accept of thefe neceffary propofitions whereupon both parliaments did agree, we might yet have peace; but if thefe wicked men will put him upon new defigns, our troubles will yet for a time continue. If it might pleafe God to look upon Scotland, all here go very well, bleffed be God.

We hear that the Great Turk is fallen with his naval army upon Creta, and with his land-army upon the other territories of the Venetians. They fpeak of a peace at laft betwixt the Swedes and the Danes, to the Danes great prejudice. The Prince of Orange lies ftill in the fields, and yet hath enterprifed nothing. After Linken, the French have taken in Borborough; fo there remains now nothing betwixt them and Dunkirk. Duke d'Anguien and the Bavarians are near one another; but yet have not fought. It yet holds that Forftenfon and Ragotfki are joined; but have done nothing more of importance againft the Emperor. All they in Italy join with the Venetians againft the Turk. Affairs in Europe, thefe many ages, were not in a greater and more dangerous fituation than at this hour. Our thoughts are, that the Lord is fhaking the foundations of kingdoms and ftates, to make way for the great propagation of the gofpel, which the godly here and elfewhere are expecting fhortly, according to the Lord's promife.

114. *A Publick Letter.*

SINCE my laſt on Monday by ſea, I can add nothing for the matters of our church.   All this week, both publickly in the aſſembly, and more privately in our committees, we have been preparing our papers for the ſatisfaction of the Houſe of our divine right to keep ſcandalous perſons from the holy table, and of our neceſſity to ſtand to a general rule for ſcandals, a particular enumeration being in itſelf impoſſible, and never required in any church in any time.   Bleſſed be God, we gain ground on the minds of ſundry of the parliament ; yet how long we may ſtick here, we know not.

Sir Thomas Fairfax is yet before Sherburne.   We heard little or nothing of the King for two or three weeks ; but behold, for one twenty-four hours, and no longer, he put us all aghaſt.   By very ſwift long marches he came from Wales to Newark, with 2000 or 3000 horſe.   We were much afraid he would go to Yorkſhire from Newark, with 4000 too, good horſe.   We ſaw no oppoſition to him till he had gone through all the north.   Our army being ſo engaged at Hereford that it could not riſe.   Sir Thomas Fairfax being far in the weſt, and having a ſtrong enemy on his hand, might not for the time look north.   All our intelligence aſſured the King's intention was for Scotland, where we feared his oppoſition ſhould be ſmall, having Montroſe, and the peſt, and many falſe-hearted men there to join with him.   While yeſterday all day we were tormented with theſe thoughts, and ſaw no help but in God ; behold, at nine o'clock a poſt from our army did fully conſent, for they knowing of the King's motion, had preſently ſent after him the moſt of their horſe.   David Leſly and Middleton, with near 4000 horſe and dragoons, were, on Wedneſday, within twenty miles of him.   The Engliſh have ordered to join as many to them, all to be under David Leſly's command ; ſo our fears are ſecured on that ſide, bleſſed be the gracious name of the Lord.   We hope a few days ſhall put Hereford in our hands.   Already four of the beſt ſhires in Wales have ſent to our general to offer their ſubmiſſion to the parliament.   We are preſſing to ſend the propoſitions of peace to the King, hoping, when all

I   things

things conjoin to crofs his defigns, it may be the will of God to foften his heart, to pity himfelf and his fuffering people. I hope the Lord will give you courage and patience for a little time; for we truft it fhall be the pleafure of God to anfwer our prayers, and to remove from us his fore rods of war and peftilence. O! if it may be his pleafure to bring us as gold out of the fire, and to make all our fad afflictions be means of fanctifying the land: we cannot think that the Lord will deftroy Scotland. I hope there is more of the fpirit of grace and fupplication upon us than before did appear. We got fundry advertifements from France, of Col. Cochran's fending of a fhip of arms to Montrofe, from the Queen, from Nantz in Bretaigne, to Murray frith, and that now himfelf has followed. Whither may not apoftafy carry men of the faireft hopes! ——

115. *To Mr William Spang.* *London, Auguft* 15. 1645.

Reverend and Dear Brother,

I have not written for fome weeks. My fermon to the Lords the laft faft-day, the preparing and printing of it was a fafhry to me, being added to our ordinary tafk. But the chief caufe of not writing was fear of intercepting. Savile's bufinefs for a time made a fell ftir among us. Cranford had overlafhed, I fufpect, fomething in the matter, but much in form; however, the witnefs deponed againft him, words that indeed were falfe and fcandalous, but which he peremptorily denies that ever he fpoke. Your friend's part was well taken by all; the moft malicious had nothing to reprove in it. He got his defire, that the matter was put to a more accurate trial than ever it would elfe have been. Savile and Sey brought Hollis on the ftage; but he did acquit himfelf with a great deal of credit, both to himfelf and his friends, and of mifcontent to his oppofites. By that occafion our commiffioners gave in to the Houfe fundry papers, which to our mind evidences Savile's trinketing with Oxford, by the advice and knowledge, as he writes with his hands, of the Independent party; and names my L. Sey; but with ftrange juggling would elude it. The moft of the Houfe being gone to the country for their health, it was thought fit to adjourn that committee of examinations for five

weeks. We refolve to do our beft to find out the truth.
Mr Cranford's fentence did fleep without fo much as any
intimation of it to him till Friday laft, when on a fudden
he was commanded to the tower. We think it was for
his neglect to petition, and are hopeful within a day or
two to get him free. *The Rife and Reign of the Antino-*
mians of New England, you fhall have with the firft occafion. I pray you write for fo much as may once put me
out of your debt. I think, Mr Rutherford and I may go
home within a month; for our work here is drawing near
a period. I got my Scots letters: commend me to Har-
rie. Jo. Henderfon writes to me, that you had written
to me of his defign; but furely I know nothing of it.
His brother has written twice to me to underftand it; but
I cannot anfwer but by conjectures. Send this letter to
him. Eraftus is the book vexes us moft. None of the
affembly, for their life, can do any thing of moment.
Were we free, there is above a dozen would beat him to
duft. If you would move Apollonius or Cabellarius to
give him a fuccinct and nervous anfwer, it would be a
feafonable fervice both to us and to Holland. They are
both engaged, and well verfed in that caufe. See what
you can do with both, and with Voffius, if he have any
leifure. I wifh he had never meddled with the Independents. If Spanheim's book were come out, I wifh he were
intreated to go on with his Anabaptifts. Voffius faid to
me he had a large treatife againft them, and would put it
out. It is the prevailing fect here. I have written to D.
Stewart, to put Spanheim and Voffius on the Anabaptifts,
and L'Emperor on Eraftus. My hearty fervice to your
wife. I reft.

ROBERT BAILLIE.

116. *To Mr Cranford, prifoner in the Tower of London.*

Reverend and Dear Brother,
YOUR affliction has been one of the heavieft burdens
that ever came upon my mind, and will be fo ftill till you
be fully delivered. The reafon of my not vifiting you was
from no unkindnefs, for that is very far from me; but
from an information of a wife and good friend to us both,
who told me, that my vifiting you was againft your laws,
                                                        and

and would be evil taken. However, so soon as I heard of
your imprisonment, I resolved to venture, come of it
what might. But yesternight, after I had told so much
to some of your friends, and had resolved to have been
with you this day, I went to Mr   to enquire the cause of your imprisonment, and the best way
of getting you free. He told me, that after he had
thought your business would have slept and died without
any more hearing, it had come in abruptly; by whom, or
which way, he could not tell; that the sentence was for
no words you had confessed, but for the words that three
or four witnesses had positively deponed, which I believe
you never thought, much less spoke, viz. That the subcommittee had assumed a power to themselves to treat for
their own safety, and to deliver over to the King the parliament forces and garrisons. He told me, that the framing of the words which the House would require of
you for satisfaction, was given to a committee, wherein
he and Mr Selden had a chief hand, and that they were
agreed to require no more of you, but a general acknowledgement of your sorrow, that from any thing you had
spoken, any had been offended; something to this purpose, without putting you to confess any words which
might be against your mind. He wished you to petition
for your freedom so soon as you can; that he himself
would second it, and hopes your desire will be granted.
I told him, that as yet I had not seen you, for fear of offence; but was resolved to see you, and carry you his information. He desired me to write it; but, as I would not
do you harm, that I should not visit you; for again and
again he assured me, that my appearing at this time in your
cause would make it much the worse. This is the only
reason, why, sore against my heart, I do not this day
come to you, lest I should be so unhappy as to be occasion to you of farther evil. There is nothing that either
myself or any of my friends are able to do for you, but
we will be most willing to do it, when we know when to
apply ourselves so as we may truly help you, and not procure you more trouble. What was given in to the House
about my Lord Savile, cannot be communicate by any of
us without great offence. I trust the Lord God, who is
witness to the honesty of your heart, will furnish you
with comfort and strength, and ere long will deliver you,

to all our joy. So do I pray, and rest your loving brother and fellow sufferer.

ROBERT BAILLIE.

117. *To Mr William Spang. September 5. 1645.*

Reverend and Dear Brother,

I got yours with Apollonius, and   I hope
both will testify our great respects to them so far as you
could wish. Send me the rest of Forbes. I like the book
very well, and the man much the better for the book's
sake. I marvel I can find nothing in its index against the
Millenaries. I cannot think the author a Millenary. I
cannot dream why he should have omitted an error so famous in antiquity, and so troublesome among us; for the
most of the chief divines here, not only Independents, but
others, such as Twisse, Marshall, Palmer, and many more,
are express Chiliasts. It is needful, if his judgement be
right, that he should amend that omission, by an express
and large appendix. I like Croius's learning passing well.
But I pray put the price to these eight. Let me know
once my debt; how oft shall I call for it ? If Harry be
there, tell him it is not my advice he should go home till
he hear farther from Glasgow. The case of that land is
wonderful evil. This day we had a publick fast in all the
churches within the lines for the miseries of Scotland. I
confess I am amazed, and cannot see to my mind's satisfaction, the reasons of the Lord's dealing with that land.
The sins of all ranks there I know to be great, and
the late mercies of God, spiritual and temporal, towards
them to have been many; but what means the Lord,
so far against the expectation of the most clear-sighted,
to humble us so low, and by his own immediate hand,
I confess I know not. I never expected the clear and solid
fruit of our reformation, till we had some time to work in
our churches without distractions and fear, which these
seven years we never had. Of the causes which some cast
in our teeth, our consciences absolve us. We have not opposed the King, nor bishops, nor sects, farther than was
our duty. We were necessitated, in piety, charity, and
prudence, to assist England. I have not yet seen the
grounds of that which some exaggerate so much, of the
divisions, much less of the treachery of our nobles. I
                                                      hear

hear of a great deal of impenitency and hardnefs of heart in the beft, and a world of backwardnefs, terror, and cowardice, in the moft. I hope the Lord will not deftroy that nation in the very act of maintenance of fo good a caufe. However, I believe, fince William Wallace's days, or rather fince Fergus the Second, our land was never in the prefent condition.

The peft hath laid Leith and Edinburgh defolate, and rages in many more places. Never fuch a peft feen in Scotland. That this fhould have tryfted the enemy at that time and place, when we had moft to do with Leith and Edinburgh, is evidently God's hand.

The particulars of this fixth victory I yet have not fully heard. The flaughter, captivity, and flight, was moft fhameful. Glafgow came out, and componed, as fome fay, for 18,000 lib.; as others, for 10,000 merks. Some fay, that after he got the money, he plundered the town, fortified the caftle, took with him 500 of their men, and left 500 of his own. For my books, and all I have, I care not much; but I long much to know what is become of my wife and children, and my dear colleagues and friends. After Glafgow, the moft of Clydefdale and Linlithgow-fhire componed. Edinburgh fent him out Crawford and Ogilbie, and all the prifoners, and, they fay, 30,000 lib. The Marquis of Douglas, Queenfberry, Hartfield, Annandale, took commiffions to raife men; the fheriff-dom of Ayr keeps together in a body of 4000 or 5000 men; they expect affiftance from Galloway; Buccleugh has 2000 or 3000 together in the fouth; and Seaforth fome in the north.

But our firft hopes are from David Lefly's horfe. On Tuefday was eight days, when we had fpoiled the King's northern exceeding dangerous defign, and chafed him back to Newark and Oxford, where in his way the King fpoiled much the affociations; upon letters from Scotland, he rofe prefently from Nottingham, with his 4000 horfe, and went in hafte towards Carlifle and Scotland. If the Lord be with him, he may put Montrofe again to the hills: yet his rafhnefs has been very great; for he has left our foot-army naked about Hereford, and now the King is gone thither; albeit it feems it had been much more needful for him to have gone and joined with Goring for the raifing of the fiege of Briftol, which is in hazard of being taken, and Rupert in it. Our army having refolved their march

to

to Scotland, did excuse yesterday their not storming of Hereford. That is but a small disgrace, in respect of the rest that the Lord has heaped upon us. We pray, God give wisdom and courage, and continue fidelity in our officers, if the King should pursue them with his large 5000 horse. If the King misken them, and join with Goring, he will be large as strong as Sir Thomas Fairfax; and if he should beat him, which the Lord God avert, he should in a trice overthrow our affairs; and if he be beat again, Montrose will not be able to support him.

Yet all here is in the balance. In the assembly we are going on languidly with the Confession of Faith and Catechism. The minds of the divines are much enfeebled by the House their delay to grant the petition, a power to seclude from the table all scandalous persons as well as some. Mr Prin and the Erastian lawyers are now our *remora*. The Independents and sects are quiet, enjoying peaceably all their desires, and increasing daily their party. They speak no more of bringing their model in the assembly. We are afraid that this shameful and monstrous delay of building the Lord's house, and their ingratitude and unkindness to us in our deep sufferings for them, will provoke God against them, which we oft earnestly deprecate; for their misery will be ours, and their welfare will profit all the Reformed churches. I believe in time they will do all we desire. You shall get some of my sermons with Apollonius. I thought to have been going home about this time; but now whether to go I know not. The greatest mischief is, that Montrose puts people to a new oath. This will be a seed of great trouble when he is away. I am afraid for our friends miscarriage. Farewell. The committee at the army has sent us orders to answer Thomas Cunningham 5000 lib. Sterling, whereof I am glad. My service to your wife.

Mr Cranford, on his first motion to the House, was let free, without any word of acknowledgement. If our Scots affairs had not put such things out of our heads, we might have put Savile and others hard to it. The recruiting of the House, procured by the cunning and diligence of that party, what it will produce, we are yet in doubt. Some think it will bring many favourers of sectaries and malignants into the House; some think otherwise.

118. *A Publick Letter. London, October* 14. 1645.

FOR the great and seasonable mercies of God to desolate Scotland, our afflicted spirits do rejoice in God.   Since he has begun to stretch out his arm for our deliverance, we hope he will not draw it back till he give us more matter of praise.   We trust he will call back the destroying angel, and persecute the cruel enemy till he be no more.   We hope the Lord will give repentance to that land, that after all these troubles we may be a holy and sanctified people ; also, that those who ever have been but false-hearted, and now are discovered, and taken in the snare, will be so disposed upon, that they be no more able to serve the enemy.   How matters go here, the last three diurnals will shew.   The war here seems to be near an end.   The taking of Bristol brought in to us several other places about it, and has lost Prince Rupert to the King.   Whether the flagrant reports of his deliverance of Bristol to us be true or not, yet it is like he is so far in disgrace at court, that he will serve no more.   The King's total rout at Chester, at Prins, wherein the Duke of Lennox's brother, Bernard, the captain of the guard, was killed, and Sir Thomas Gleinham taken, has put the King in that condition, that he neither has, nor is like to have, any more the face of an army in England.   Goring's forces in a corner of the west are decreased.   Sir Thomas Fairfax, with the most of his army, are going towards him.   Cromwell, with the rest, are taking the places about Winchester.   It seems, the field being cleared, they intend Massey to block up Exeter, and Fairfax to lie about Oxford, and our army about Newark.   It is hoped, by God's blessing, these places will be gotten, all hope of relief being desperate.   It is thought Chester before this time is gotten.   Prins purposes to attend the King.   The Prince's letter to the parliament is not yet taken into consideration ; yet we think, that it and our earnest desires will bring on a treaty of peace.

Great wrestling have we for the erecting of our presbytery.   It must be a divine thing to which so much resistance is made by men of all sorts ; yet, by God's help, we will very speedily see it set up, in spite of the devil.   We have great difficulties on all hands ; yet if the Lord continue to
                                                                        blink

blink in mercy upon Scotland, they will diminish.   I long extremely to hear the condition of Glasgow, what the e-nemy has done in it, and how now it fares; what is be-come of my dear brethren and colleagues, and their fa-milies; and what of my own.   We hear particularly from almost all the parts of Scotland weekly; but since that black day at Kilfyth, we have got nothing particularly from Glasgow.   I hope some good friend will satisfy my desire, in letting me know the condition of that town; which, whatever the world speaks of some persons in it, I must love while I live, and pray for its welfare.   You have here a copy of the papers which we gave this day in to the House.

Affairs here go, by God's blessing, so prosperously, that there is no more fear of the malignant party.   Many now leave Oxford daily.   The Marquis of Hereford, Lord Lovelace, and others, came hither last week; also the Lord Abercorn, Sir James Hamilton of Priestfield, Sir James Galloway.   Legge, the Governor of Oxford, is laid fast, and Glenham put in his place.   The commission of Ge-neralissimo is taken from Prince Rupert.   Cromwell has taken Winchester castle, and Basing also.   Sir Thomas Fairfax is not yet come up to Goring.   We expect Che-ster daily.   Prins waits about Newark on the King's mo-tions.   There are here very great exceptions taken, at our ar-my's doing nothing all this year but plundering the country as they went through it.   Some exaggerate this very much. If we come not up ere long to quarter about Newark, and when we come, if our army be not more considerable, and better disciplined, it will not be possible to keep matters long here fair.   It is like they will not enter seriously on any treaty for peace till the time of action be past, and the armies go to their winter-quarters; then, I believe, they will try the King if he will accept of the propositions. We fear much his obstinacy.

We were in a long expectation of a model from the In-dependents; but yesterday, after seven months waiting, they have scorned us.   The assembly having put them to it, to make a report of their diligence, they gave us in a sheet or two of injurious reasons why they would not give us any reasons of their tenets.   We have appointed a com-mittee to answer that libel.   We think they agree not a-mong themselves, and that there are many things among them which they are loth to profess, which, by God's

2   help,

help, ere long I mind to do for them in their own words. But our greatest trouble for the time is from the Erastians in the House of Commons.   They are at last content to erect presbyteries and synods in all the land, and have given out their orders for that end; yet they give to the ecclesiastick courts so little power, that the assembly finding their petitions not granted, are in great doubt whether to set up any thing, till, by some powerful petition of many thousand hands, they obtain some more of their just desires.   The only mean to obtain this, and all else we desire, is our recruited army about Newark.   The inlacks of that army is the earthly fountain of all our difficulties here.   If our distressed land be able to remeid it, it would be done quickly; else evils will grow both here and with you at home.

119. *For Mr George Young.   October 1645.*

Reverend and Dear Brother,

If I should be silent, I might be excused by your example.   We hear weekly from all the parts of Scotland; only I in all the company have no friends.   I pray you amend this fault.   I write at least with every other post. Think you not that I have reason to desire to know, and you to satisfy me, in the estate of my friends, after so fearful a storm?   Let me know who are your magistrates, and how; what is become of the Commissar, the Principal, Sir Robert Douglas, the old magistrates, the ministers of the town and presbytery, regents, and other my friends; what have been their actions and sufferings in the time of great trial.   The packet runs weekly.   Strange! not so much wit among you as to get a letter convoyed to the packet.   If ye would send to Berwick to my Lady Argyle, or Lady Loudon, I would not miss them; but you are forgetful of your friends, who have too much mind of you.

Our hearts here are oft much weighted and wounded by many hands.   Our wrestlings with devils and men are great.   However the body of this people be as good as any people, yet they that rule all are much opposite to our desires.   Some very few guide all now at their pleasure, only through the default of our army.   For this long time they have not trusted us; but have had their secret fear of our colluding with the King. Our doing nothing since the taking of Newcaftle; our lying ftill in the north too long; and when we moved, our running back to Carlifle; when we were drawn up to Hereford, our lying there for no purpofe; and when we returned, our plunderings all the way, are much exaggerated. We anfwer for all the beft we can: but truly the letter fent by Digby to the General, and by him to us this night, importing the King's defire of an anfwer of a former letter; in confidence of the good effect whereof, he was come with a body of horfe to Newark through many difficulties; which former letter the General profeffed he never faw, make us fear there has been fome defign with fome in our army which is not honeft. However, the army's want of fuccefs, by the miferies of our country hindering their recruits, by the injuftice of this people to furnifh them with pay, have put all our affairs out of frame. The faction that here prevails, minding liberty of confcience, and finding it impoffible to gain us to overfee that fo great a fault, have made that their work to be quit of us. They have occafioned many provocations, to vex us, and make us vex others. I cannot write the half of their unjuft, proud, and unjuft dealings.

The mifcarriage of our army they exaggerate. We fay, by their withdrawing all the promifed pay the feven laft months, not giving one month's pay, have forced us to take by violence for our fubfiftence, and difabled us to do any fervice, of purpofe to make us odious; that their own army, which they have put in the hand only of fectaries, or their confident friends, they have furnifhed with men and money every fortnight, and were fure in all enterprifes to have it ever the ftronger; fo that it was an eafy matter for them to do all their fervices, and be cried up. The affembly is much difcouraged; they find their advice altogether flighted; a kind of   *   prefbytery fet up; fects daily fpreading over all the land, without any care at all to reftrain them; a clear aim in the prevailing party to have a liberty univerfal; an utter diflike of our nation for oppofing their defigns, and driving it fo high, that ways are ftudied, if no better may be, to break the union of the nations, and have us, for the carriage of our army, declared the firft breakers to them, and dealt with us as fuch. We do what we are able to prevent mifchief. We cry to God, who knows the honefty of our hearts, and the dif-

honefty

honefty of theirs; the caufe of our engagement, and our huge fuffering; their great ingratitude to us, and our great patience to them. It is gone already very high. We fear that they make Digby feem to deal with us, while they in truth know how to get the King from us to themfelves on their own terms; and if we be not willing to compone in what terms, both for religion and ftate, they pleafe, to caft us off; and for the recompence of all our labours, to turn on our poor, broken, diftreffed country the armies of both. The beft way we know to prevent this, is to hafte up our army, well recruited and difciplined, to Newark, having cathiered all who are the known inftruments of debauchery, or can be proven to have kept correfpondence with the enemy. This, in fpite of the Independent plots, would help all: for the body of the parliament, city, and country, are for the prefbytery, and love us, and hate the fectaries; but are all overwitted and overpowered by a few, whom the fervice and activenefs of our army would undo. Thrice unhappy are thefe men who have difabled that army from fervice: they have facrificed the honour of their country, and profpering of religion in thefe dominions, to their own bafe defigns; they have put us on the brink of lofing all our intentions, and bringing a worfe war on our kingdom than ever we feared: yet God will help all, if we can clear the honefty of our army, by finding out fome few ill perfons, and laying them afide; if we will, by after diligence, help former negligence; if we will govern well the garrifons we find neceffary to keep, as it will be neceffar for a time to keep three. But of thefe things much more than I purpofed; only I thought good to let you know the infide of our affairs. If we be able to fend up to Newark a reafonable army, we will be very welcome to this people; we will without difficulty, in my mind, get that ftrong place; for all relief being defperate, they will not long ftand out. Whatever be to do, either for the Prefbyterians here, who are incomparably the ftrongeft, or at home, we will always have that army ready; but if we for any reafon be unable or unwilling to fend up that army, this people's jealoufies and angers againft us will increafe; they will give us nothing; the Prefbyterians here will fuccumb and faint; our army will difband and evanifh, and a long and will follow. Thir things to you only and Mr David, and to whom you think expedient. Remember what I wrote about the pfalms; hafte up the committee's animad-

X 2   verfions.

verfions. Mr Samuel and Mr George are bufy with the prefs, and I will be fo for one five or fix weeks thereafter. I could wifh to be at home, not before, except I would lofe my former labours.

120. *For Mr William Spang. October* 17. 1645.

Reverend and Dear Brother,

Not only incident affairs fometimes by expectation on the poft-day, but efpecially grief of mind for the ftate of affairs, makes me more fparing to write than otherwife I could wifh. You have here a double of my laft three to Scotland. I can add little. However, the Lord has fhown us a great mercy there; yet the miferies of that land is great, and the dangers greater. The Lord made thefe men fo mad as to ftay for our army's coming to them in a plain field. Above 1000 were buried in the place; whereof fcarce 15 were ours. Mr Macdonald, with fome 400 or 500 fome days before, were gone to Argyle; for his friends in the ifles were wracked by a party of the Marquis of Argyle. Montrofe, with 200 or 300 horfe, got to Athol. Gordon was before in the north. David Lefly went ftraight to Glafgow, where he borrowed from that people 20,000 lib. as the annualrent of 50,000 they gave to Montrofe. Neither the one nor other army did any violence in that town, to my great joy. Mr David and Mr Robert Ramfay fled to Houfton, and there remained fafe; all the reft ftaid. The Commiffar was too bufy for Montrofe; for which, they fay, he is now faft, and it is thought will not come off while he leave his place, and a great fine befide. I fear the Principal's cafe fhall be little better. It is good to be honeft at the heart. It is marvellous how few handfuls of the enemy went, after the fight of Kilfyth, through Fife, Lothian, fhire of Ayr, without any oppofition but a general fubmiffion of all who did not flee. This fhame for an age will not be put off us. The Englifh contemn us much the more. They have fent commiffioners to crave Newcaftle and Carlifle from us, and all our places of garrifons but Berwick. They are angry, that yet we have not given them a meeting. At this very time we are treating with them at St Andrew's. What to do with them we know not. If we now give up thefe places, it will make them the more infolent; if we
refufe

refufe them on never fo fair terms, it will increafe the occafion of them who are feeking a quarrel. Yet I hope God will direct. To clear our reputation, we have printed fome of our late papers to fatisfy the ignorance of the people. In anfwer to our laft paper, the Houfe of Commons have paffed fundry very ftrange and unkind votes, wherewith the Lords have yet refufed to concur. The King's party here is taken for irrecoverable. They fpeak of Pirno and Montbafon levying of 10,000 French underhand, to be fent over to Falmouth by a convoy of the Prince of Orange's fhips. We take this for a fable. Fairfax is expected daily to be at Goring, and fo to get back all the weft but Exeter at one ftroke.

Give one of my fermons to Apollonius, one to Thomas Cunningham, and one to Mr Strickland, with my fervice. At St Andrew's now they will advife how to recruit and reform our Englifh army. It is thought Sinclair, Montgomery, Livingftone, and others, have had fome dealing with William Fleming for the King. Very great profanity has been in that army. God will never blefs it as it is; it has never been attended with minifters. Many would have attended that fervice; but they could get no maintenance. It is thought Johnfton, Ogilbie, Sir John Hay, Spotfwood, and divers others of the prifoners, will, at that meeting, lofe their heads, that once fome juftice may be done on fome for example; albeit to this day no man in England has been executed for bearing arms againft the parliament. David Leflie muft go quickly back with the moft of the army to England; for Scotland is overburdened with them long ago, and cannot maintain them; fo we fear that Montrofe, Gordon, and Macdonald, run yet again over an extremely weakened and divided country. The peft continues yet to rage. The divifions of our people are not yet cured: the hearts of our people are not foftened with all our plagues. The Lord be merciful to us. I muft end.

Your Coufin,

JAMESONE.

121. *For Mr William Spang. October* 24. 1645.

Reverend and Dear Brother,
WITH the laft poft I wrote to you at length. I can
tell

tell you little more fince. I think we cannot prefently give over all our garrifons in England: and upon our refufal, or but delay to the   of our parliament in December, what evil courfe this people will take with us, I know not ; for fundry of the leading men are not well difpofed towards us. It is true, our army's fruitleffnefs this whole year, and their too great plunder in their marches, irritates them ; and, what is worfe, the great appearances that the King has been tampering with them, gives them great jealoufies of us ; and their extraordinary fucceffes, with our extraordinary prefent weakening by the peft, fword, and want of trade, blows them up to a great contempt of us, fo that our union with them is not fo infringible as need were : yet the moft and beft of them will be loth to forget our kindnefs to them in their diftrefs, and our recovering them from their miferies by cafting ourfelves in the pit of all our prefent woes. That we may remeid and remove the prefent matter of their irritation, we have fent my Lord Wariston and Mr Barclay away poft this day to the army, and thereafter to Scotland, to caufe our army come to block up Newark, and take their winter-quarters about it. My Lord Chancellor, the next week, will go home for that fame end. Mr Henderfon and I are appointed to follow within a fortnight, to fee if we can further a better union and correfpondence among ourfelves at home than has been this twelve months. It feems Digby and Langdale intended to have kept Montrofe's parliament at Glafgow, but God laid a ftraw in their way. In their route, Digby's coach was taken, and fundry of his writs ; which fhews the King's refolution to have no peace but on his own terms ; albeit this people, for all we can fay, are yet backward and unready to make any fuch motion to him.

Unhappily Amirant's queftions are brought in our affembly. Many more love thefe fancies here than I expected. It falls out ill that Spanheim's book is fo long acoming out, whileas Amirant's treatife goes in the affembly from hand to hand ; yet I hope this fhall go right. The city and affembly are on a better way than before, to make the parliament for more liberty to fufpend from the table fcandalous perfons, than they would willingly grant. We expect daily to hear of Goring's defeat, and fo the King has not any face of an army in England, nor appearance of any poffibility to keep the field more for the

the time. He, Rupert, and Maurice, are almoſt beſieged in Newark : they dare hardly venture to come out ; and if they ſtay a little longer, they may be beſieged cloſe. Shew me if you deſire the Engliſh Annotations. I pray you, without farther delay, in your next letter, let me know what Engliſh money I am in your debt. I think I can receive no more of your letters, after this coming to your hands, than one. Only Mr Henderſon, againſt my mind, is reſolved to go by ſea. I hope the wind will not the ſecond time miſcarry us. My hearty ſervice to Apollonius, and to your kind wife. So I reſt your couſin.

My piece againſt the Independents is on the preſs.

122. *A Publick Letter.   November 25. 1645.*

THINGS here go on proſperouſly, bleſſed be God, as you may ſee by the incloſed diurnal. The King, with much ado, is come from Newark to Oxford. He has no part of an army for the fields, but ſome with Goring in the weſt, of whom Fairfax hopes ſhortly to make a good account. My Lord Chancellor, Mr Henderſon, and I with them, thought, before this, to have been on our journey for Scotland ; but with great importunity the Chancellor yet has been kept, the greateſt affairs coming preſently in hand that yet we have treated of, and my Lord Balmerino's health not permitting him to attend the committee. The other two, Sir Charles Erſkine, and Major Kennedy, being ſimply unwilling to take the burden of ſo weighty affairs on them, as the matter of the garriſons, which the Engliſh are very inſtant to have ; the marching of our army to Newark ; the propoſitions of peace, which the Engliſh are like to alter more than we deſire ; eſpecially the renewing of the committee of accommodation, wherein the toleration of the Independents will come in agitation ; no man of our nation, either for abilities, or credit with this people, is ſo fit for theſe great things as the Chancellor. However, the affairs of our kingdom, and his own private affairs and vehement deſires, do preſs him to go home ; yet all of us, and all that love us, are earneſt for his ſtay for farther time. The ſame cauſe I fear may keep Mr Henderſon here alſo longer than I could wiſh ; for we have reſolved all of us, that he ſhould go down when my L. Wariſton went.

went. But since other emergents have interveened for the time, we are irresolute. We expect an express from Scotland; for with this post we have no directions.

In the assembly, we are going on with the Confession of Faith. We had long and tough debates about the decrees of election; yet thanks to God all is gone right according to our mind. That which has taken up much of the assembly's time and mind, these six or seven weeks, is their manifold petitions to the parliament, for a full liberty to keep from the holy table all scandalous persons. The parliament calls this an arbitrary power, and requires the assembly to make an express enumeration of all the sins for which they intend to censure. After many returns, we gave them in an enumeration of many particulars, but withal craves a general clause to be added. We have some more hope to attain it by God's help than before. This has been the only impediment why the presbyteries and synods have not been erected; for the ministers refuse to accept of presbyteries without this power. Had it been God's will that our army this summer had done any service, we had long before this obtained all our desires; or yet, if we could send any considerable strength to Newark, we would have great influence in their counsels. All good men here desire the continuance of the union of the nations, and know, as well as we, that in that union the happiness of both doth consist, and in the breach of it the lasting miseries of both are certain ruin.

This much I did write to be sent with that post which was taken; but by good luck it fell by, and did not then go. Since, our affairs here for the state are in some better posture. The Chancellor's labours have been so blessed, that the desires of these who seemed to be seeking a breach with us, are for the time either broken or laid aside; so, upon the pressing necessities of our land, he is dismissed, and this day takes journey. No living man is fitter to deal with this people; none of our nation is so much beloved, or of so much credit with them. We are now hot on the committee for accommodation. I tell my mind freely of it in my preface to my Dissuasive from the errors of the time, which now is abroad, and whereof I shall send some copies with the first occasion. We never expected any good of it, and less now than ever. The ministers of London sent from their meeting some twenty of their number to intreat, that the Chancellor and Mr Hen-

I　　　　　　　　　　　　　　　　　　　　derson

derfon might stay for some time. After advisement, we
thought all that Mr Henderson's stay was simply necessary,
so much the more as the Chancellor behoved to go. We
had never so much need of your prayers. The city, both
magistrates and ministers, are now engaged, blessed be
God, in very home and earnest petitions for the erection
of general and provincial assemblies, of presbyteries and
sessions, and all with their full power. The Independents
in their last meeting of our grand committee of accommodation have expressed their desires for toleration, not
only to themselves but to other sects. The parliament has
no great inclination to satisfy either. What may come
of this, we know not ; only it were our heart's desire that
our army at Newark were recruited. Nothing is better
for the good of Scotland, for the welfare of the whole
isle, and the Protestant religion. If God make us either
unable or unwilling to this, the loss will be great to us
and all.

We go on daily in some proposition of the Confession
of Faith : till this be ended we will not take in any more
of the catechism. The psalms are perfected : the best that
without all doubt ever yet were extant. They are on the
press ; but not to be perused till they be sent to you, and
your animadversions returned hither, which we wish were
so soon as might be. The Lord give our poor land the
fruit of their grievous troubles, and haste their deliverance.

123. *To Mr William Spang.*   *November* 29. 1645.

Dear Cousin,

I think you were never so far behind with me as now I
am with you. I think these six or seven posts I have
heard nothing from you. I see the English Annotations
and my Sermons, which, four or five weeks ago, I gave
to Mr Tirence, are not yet gone. I have sent you seven
of my Dissuasives ; only one for yourself ; the rest, with my
service, to Thomas Cunningham, Mr Strickland, Apollonius, Spanheim, Dr Stuart, and Voetius. As you have
occasion to send them, send always a Sermon with a Dissuasive. I expect a shower of Independents about my
ears ; but I am not feared : I have a reserve of more stories, and I think they will have more to do shortly, for

their elusory denial to the assembly, of their model they,
caused print under the name of a remonstrance, to which
the assembly has made a large and sharp answer, which
lays them more even ; also their rejecting of all accommodation, and pleading for a toleration, not only of their
separate churches, but for the other sects, gives great offence, and will draw out bitter writs quickly against them.
The city continues zealous for to press their petition ; more
hopes we have from them than ever. The parliament is
laying the assembly and city's petition more to heart. Our
condition in Scotland is not good ; but you know all there
as well as I. Upon the city's earnest desires, and some o-
ther considerations, Mr Henderson's voyage and mine to
Scotland is stayed. I pray you let me be once out of your
debt, and write to me what English money I am resting.
Gomarus and Rivet goes to the college-count. You would
do well to set Dr Forbes on a supplement, wherein he may
handle Anabaptism, Antinomianism, the Erastian, and
the rest of the modern sects. Will you intreat him to
press his friend Voslius to print that he told me he had
ready against the Anabaptists, the greatest and most prevalent sect here. In tumultuous ways they provoke our
chief ministers to publick disputations for pædobaptism.
I thank you for Clopenburg. I wish Spanheim made this
his principal work. The Lord be with you.
Your Cousin,

ROBERT BAILLIE.

124. *To Mr William Spang.*

Cousin,

Yours with the last post I received, also your large one
with the former. I admitted your reasons for my long
want. All that I sent you is frozen in the Thames ; when
you may have them, I know not. I doubt much if my
debt be so little as 9 s. If you miscount, to yourself be
it said. Josephus you shall have with the first fair weather ;
for now there is here a vehement frost. The first impression
of my Dissuasive is away already. It is going again to the
press. I got thanks for it from many. I wish you might put
Forbes to go on with his history, especially of the Anabaptists, Libertines, and such as presently vex us. I wrote
to

to you to caufe fome prefs Voffius to print what he told me
he had befide him againft the Anabaptifts. When Spanheim is free of Amirant, I wifh he went on with his
Collegium Anabaptifticum. Thefe are the fectaries who
moft increafe amongft us. Thombes, a minifter of London,
has printed a large book for them, wherein he dares
us all. Dr Rivet required, by Mr Durie, our affembly's
teftification, that he had not fent to them any writ againft
Amirant, nor had ftirred them up againft his tenets, directly nor indirectly : this was granted to him. But I
think fince Amirent has been fo rafh, as without all
occafion to expoftulate with Dr Rivet, he fhould the more
be wakened to do that duty which he is obliged to do for
his love to the truth of God, and care of the churches of
France, which Amirant only by his amity and pride has
troubled, and will do more if God be not merciful. We
all commend Spanheim for his diligence and zeal, though
yet his writs be not come to us. We hope Dr Rivet and
others there will fecond him in the defence of the truth
againft vain innovators.

Our affairs ftand thus : It was refolved that Mr Henderfon fhould have gone home for doing his endeavour
for knitting together the minds of fome whofe divifions
did much trouble our ftate. He was the fitteft inftrument for it on earth ; but the weather fell fo ill, and he
fo unhealthful, and the bufinefs here is fo great, that he
behoved to ftay ; and fo my voyage, who was appointed
to be his convoy, was ftoped. Some fix or feven weeks a-
go, the humour of the faction who guides here, towards
us feemed not to be friendly. The crufhing of our nation by the peftilence, and Montrofe's victories, made us
contemptible to them ; their unexpected fucceffes made us
needlefs to them ; the King and his party were no more
confiderable ; with their hearts they wifhed to be free of
our burden, and rather than to have us lie upon them
more, it feems fome of them were bent to have a quarrel.
Hence their unkind votes for the difgrace of our army,
and the reftitution of their garrifons. But the wifdom
and diligence of the Chancellor brought them, before his
going, to a much better temper ; yet what fhall be the
iffue, I cannot fay. We were content to have the committee for accommodation renewed for our oppofition to
their defigns : in this was the main fountain of their evil
talent againft us ; albeit we do not fee what alfo their

mind

mind is for matters of the ftate. We have had fundry
meetings with them for accommodation both in the grand
committee and fubcommittees. We would, for peace's
caufe, difpenfe with them in very many things; but they
are peremptor they will not hear nor fpeak of any accommodation, but they will by all means have their feparate churches. They plead for a toleration to other fects
as well as to themfelves; and with much ado could we get
them to propone what they defired to themfelves. At laft
the gave us a paper, requiring exprefsly a full toleration
of congregations in their way every where, feparate from
ours. In our anfwer we flatly denied fuch a vaft liberty,
and backed it with reafons, and withal are begun to fhew
what indulgence we could, for peace fake, grant. Here
Mr Marfhal our chairman has been their moft diligent a-
gent, to draw too many of us to grant them much more
than my heart can yield to, and which to my power I oppofe. As yet we are not come to exprefs our rafh boun-
ty, and fome things have interveened from God, that I
hope will ftay the precipitancy of fome whom I expected
fhould have been more oppofite to all toleration of feparate congregations, than when it comes to a chock I found
them. 1. Thomas Goodwin, the laft meeting, declared
publickly, that he cannot refufe to be members, no cenfure when members any for Anabaptifm, Lutheranifm, or
any errors which are not fundamental, and maintained a-
gainft knowledge, according to the principle in the Apologetick. This ingenuous, and moft timeous, albeit merely accidental profeflion, has much allayed the favour of
fome to their toleration. 2. Some good friend has informed the city-minifters, that they in their meeting at
Sion college, have refolved unanimoufly to petition the
affembly againft all fuch tolerations. 3. The other day
Sey and Wharton moved in the Houfe of Lords to adjourn, that is really to diffolve, the affembly. 4. The Independents are ftickling too openly to have the common
council of London modelled to their mind. 5. Inftead of
their long-expected model, they prefented a libel of invectives as reafons why they would prefent no model to
the affembly. This, underhand, they caufed print; and
when the affembly had drawn up a fober and true anfwer,
and got an order from the Houfe of Lords to print it,
they make their friends in the Houfe of Commons as yet
to keep it in. All thefe are alarms to make us, if we be
not

not demented, as many the best men here are, to be the more wary of their toleration.

We go on in the assembly now with pretty good speed in our Confession of Faith. We have passed the heads of scripture, God, Trinity, decrees, providence, redemption, covenant, justification, sanctification, free-will, sacraments in general, a part of perseverance, and of the Lord's supper. It seems the King's party would now be glad of a peace; but as yet I see no possibility of it. The Prince of Wales's letter for a permission to send two of his council to his father for that end, got no answer. The King, therefore, without farther circumlocution, sent the other week a trumpet, with a letter, requiring a safe-conduct for commissioners with propositions. While they and we are debating on the answer to this letter, behold a second trumpet, bringing a very pathetick and conjuring letter from the King for peace. The truth is, his secret letters written about the last treaty makes them trust him no more, and resolve to treat no more at all with him; only they will send him propositions, and require his positive answer. We are content that all the former propositions be sent, and that a positive answer be required to them all, without any treaty; but they are altering many of them, and adding more and more hard. These we cannot consent to be sent, till the parliament of Scotland see and assent to them, and declare their mind, whether they will deny or refuse the King all treaty upon every one of these. Also it seems to us, that the faction here intends no peace in haste, and we much doubt the sincerity of them who to this day rule about the King; but our condition is such, that we would with all our heart have a good peace. Always, in prosecution of it, we resolve to cleave to our covenanted union with this people, how ingrate soever the body of all estates here are in our mind. But what the small handful who guides all will do, we yet know not. The city is kind to us, and readily have provided L. 31,000 in money, and L. 6000 in cloaths, for our army. We oft are in great perplexities; but our eyes are towards God, and we resolve, in all temptations, by his help, to do our duty. The condition of Scotland is very hard. Wariston, with the help of Argyle and the ministers, have yet kept the parliament right against a powerful party. Sir John Smith's second fault, far worse than the first, albeit a lurdane to defend all he had done, and to draw the

most

moſt of the barons to ſide with him, was a very dangerous deſign. I hope it is near broken. If Glaſgow be made the only example of the ſtate's ſeverity, I fear it will do no good ; but if the like courſe be taken with Edinburgh, and the reſt, whoſe fault was greater, all will be digeſted. When Montroſe the other week came down to Angus, Middleton was appointed to go towards him. He quickly retreated ; but Middleton in St Andrew's fell in an inſtant in a deadly fit of the iliack paſſion, that troubled all exceedingly, and was taken for a terrible ſtroke of God ; yet our laſt letters ſay there was hopes of his recovery. Callendar has accepted his charge of Lieutenant-General of all the forces, which puts us in good hopes of reconciliation of differences, and active managing of the war.

125. *A Publick Letter.* London.

HOWEVER we wait daily on the aſſembly, yet our progreſs in the Confeſſion of Faith is but ſlow. We have many diverſions, many days of faſts and thankſgivings, with the days preceding them for preparation. The providing miniſters to all vacant churches, even to remote ſhires, their trial and miſſion, lies on the aſſembly, and takes up almoſt every day too much of our time. The printing of the Bibles faſhed us much before we could fall on the way to get them printed well for eight groats in octavo, with the marginal quotations, and for ſix or ſeven groats at moſt in 12mo unbound. This we hope will encourage poor people to buy Bibles. Alſo we are oft diverted with many by-queſtions from the Houſe ; yet we hope, by God's grace, ere long to end the Confeſſion. We ſtick long ſometimes on ſcabrous queſtions ; but that whereupon the eyes and hearts of all are fixed, is the ſettling of the government, and with it the toleration of ſects. The greateſt part of the parliament have been hitherto very to do leſs in the one, and more in the other, than we could wiſh. Great ſtruggling have we had, and yet we have much to do. God has helped us to get the body of the miniſtry of all the land to be cordially for us, and the city is now ſtriking in ; which we hope ſhall carry it, and get up a ſtraighter government, and alſo exclude toleration of ſects more than many men here do deſire. We have had many bickerings with the Independents

ents in the grand committee about an indulgence for their separate congregations. We have spent many sheets of paper on both sides. They have given in writs thrice, and we have as oft answered in writ. They are on their fourth writ. To these we must give a fourth rejoinder, and then come to debate verbally. For this point, both they and we contend *tanquam pro aris et focis.* Had it been God's will to have made our army here this last year succesful, we should have had few debates for any of our desires; but the calamities of our country, and weakness of our army, make the sects and their friends bold, and very insolent. The King's party here is brought almost to nothing. The taking of Chester keeps out the Irish. The Queen's letters in France are not much feared; they are but by connivance; they cannot be many. All her begged money will not keep long a little army. The King's last letter for peace takes off our greatest objection, the shameful capitulation with the Irish by Glamorgan. This he disclaims, and offers so much to the parliament, that we are in some little hope of peace. If he come but a little farther, it is hoped so much may be granted as we may be contented. We expect every other day from the parliament their seven propositions, that we may send to Scotland, that upon their consent they may go to the King; who, if he will grant them, shall presently thereafter come to London, and treat on all the rest at leisure, and in place. We dare not promise to ourselves that peace yet is near, it hath so many both visible and invisible impediments; especially the crying and evident sins, not only of the people, but of all, or the most, in eminent place, on both sides, in all the three kingdoms. We fear our furnace must yet be hotter before the lump be purified. Appearances one day are good, and another bad. What the Lord will do, he knows. France would be glad that we broke with England, and, on that condition, it seems would give us great assistance; but of all mischiefs that would be the greatest. There is no unkindness yet so great, but, if God please to keep the managing of it in happy hands, it may turn as the jarring of friends to a greater familiarity. The Turk is like to be terrible to Italy. France is like in earnest to yoke with the Pope; who is so perverse and foolish, that he will force France to restore the barbarians to their places, whence they are ejected with the force of arms. The Venetians will join

with

with France. The Florentine and the other petty princes are foxing already for fear. The Emperor and Spain have so much ado, that they can make the Pope small help. France has many irons in the fire; great designs and successes both in Spain, Flanders, Germany, and Italy. This forces them to lay so great taxes on the people, that it is expected every year they will make great insurrection. A very little thing would set all that state in a fire. The Hollanders are setting out a great fleet to Brazilia against the Portuguese, who have almost undone their West-Indian plantation. It were great wisdom in us at last, without more delay, to send up to our army before Newark a committee, and a number of ministers, with all the forces we could spare: who knows but the Lord may deliver our poor land sooner than we expect?

126. *To Mr William Spang.*

Dear Cousin,

I have not written to you these three or four posts, of purpose, waiting till I find you have received the last. There is so great intercepting of letters, that I am loth that more than one of mine should miscarry. Though I have got three of yours since I wrote any, yet I find not that you have gotten my last. I got Grotius's last piece. The Annotations I allow you for Forbes; you shall have the price of Josephus on it. I cannot think but I am much more in debt than you speak of. How things are here, you may see by the former leaf, which went lately to Glasgow. Matters are near some crisis. I pray God it may be happy. I count the King's party utterly undone. Yesternight, at our thanksgiving for Chester, the news came of the routing of Hopeton, the only army the King had remaining in England. Oxford, Exeter, and Newark, having no hope of relief, cannot long hold out. As yet there is no appearance of the parliament's answer to the King's last four letters. However, twenty days ago they resolved to send the three propositions of Uxbridge, and other four additionals; upon the grant whereof, the King should be permitted to come to London. All the stay that was imagined was upon our part, who behoved to send these additions to Scotland for their approbation. Yet that might have been gotten in one three weeks; but

I   as

as yet they are not come to our hands, neither know we when they shall come. Peace is disadvantageous to sundry here; so it seems it will be their work to shun it, if they be able. Their present pretext is, that their third proposition of Uxbridge, concerning the militia, is yet in controversy among themselves: they have altogether altered. All the interest that Scotland and London had therein is annihilated, and all that power is put in the hand of the Houses solely. London is not willing to quit what both parliaments granted to them before, and therefore did offer petition upon petition to have their own militia, as in the propositions agreed to by both kingdoms was settled. The Lords were willing to let it go so. The Commons, foreseeing that such a power in the hands of London, though under the parliament, yet makes them masters of the parliament, also gives them power over the city of Westminster, and all the suburbs, which they had not before, do demur upon the matter, and are not content to hear the contrare petitions of Westminster and the suburbs, which may draw the business of the propositions to so great a length as they please. In the mean time, the King's extremity makes him very impatient of such delays. The city is much grieved, that what before was without a question granted to them, should now be taken away. This controversy makes them the more willing to look into the ways of the sectaries. Howbeit truly the body of the city is a zealous and understanding people, fully apprehensive of the mischief of the sectaries among them. Their ministry are faithful watchmen; and some late books have done them good; especially Mr Edwards's Gangrena; which must either waken the parliament, and all others, to lay to heart the spreading of the evil errors, or I know not what can do it. The city is in so good a temper these two months as we could wish. The other week our commissioners went to their common council, with a letter of thanks from our parliament, for their care to furnish great sums of money for our army whenever they were intreated. To this short, fair, and very innocent letter, my Lord Lauderdale spake some few words, intimating the resolution of the kingdom of Scotland to be constant to their covenant, notwithstanding all the calumnies which malignants have invented against them, and others, for their own base ends, do spread. Great signs of love were expressed by the mayor, aldermen, and common council.

One Allen, a goldsmith, a professed Presbyterian, and at first a great friend to us, but since some fell off us, a busy and diligent agent for the Independent party, becoming a late member of the House of Commons, made presently in that House such a misrepresentation of that action in the common council, as much did commove many of our own friends. An order passes, to require the production of our letter, and reporting of our speeches. For this my Lord is miscontent with Allen as a false informer, and this day appears against him in the House of Commons in a high enough strain. Also this same day, the letter of our parliament is read; which, in high and peremptor terms, but yet wise and unchangeable terms, requires the settling of religion at last, according to the advice of the assembly, without all toleration of any schism; also the payment of their debts to our army against the 3d of May, and the making up of our losses sustained by sea, through the want of their ships appointed to attend our coasts, and by land, by our Irish invasion against it, which they were obliged to secure us, for their demand of the garrisons we possess against the 1st of March. They referred their satisfactory answer to their commissioners; which will be thought, so soon as peace can be obtained, and the church settled, and our debts paid or secured, they shall have all gladly; but so long as our army remains, it cannot want places for retreat, and for magazines. What this clear and punctual dealing, both of Scotland and the city in one day, will produce, we cannot yet say. The sectarian party would gladly be at a breach with us; but the affection which France and the city declares towards us, does a little bridle them.

127. *Publick Letter.*   *London, December* 2. 1645.

Since my last there is no more news here to count of. Our army is come to Newark. I hope before the spring you will recruit it. General Goring is to France. They speak of the Prince's intention to follow. This will do no good to the King's affairs. It may help much to destroy the hope that was remaining. There were some speaking of Admiral Dorp's hiring some thirty-six war-ships in Holland for the King of France's service; but the last week's accidents will blow up that design.   has re-
                                                                        gained

gained Mardyke, the greatest conquest the French made this summer in Flanders; and the Hollanders are so circumvened by the Portuguese, that they are on the point to lose many years great labours, to be cast out of all Brazil. All their thoughts now are turned hither. If God would take order with Montrose, the troubles of this isle might quickly be at an end. We make good progress in our Confession of Faith. It would be very satisfactory when the Lord gives it a conclusion. Our two great high businesses for the time, are the obtaining from the House a power to exclude all scandalous persons from the communion. We have stuck some months on that work. The city, both ministers and magistrates, have come down to put off our   We expect, by God's help, satisfaction in this. The other is our committee of accommodation, which will be a mighty business. The Independents here plead for a toleration both for themselves and other sects. My Dissuasive is come in time to do service here. We hope God will assist us to remonstrate the wickedness of such a toleration. Yet the assembly and city do cordially join with us in opposition to all such motion; and we hope the House shall never approve it. An accommodation in just terms we were well content with; but the Independents always scorned it. Yet ere long I think they will beg it when it will not be granted. But of this more afterward   · This will be our great   We had great need here of the help of your prayers. We hope ere long to get Chester. Exeter, Newark, Oxford, are blocked up. The King has no more considerable in England. The propositions of peace, and a declaration, in answer to many of our late papers, we expect this week, which, with an express, we will send down to the parliament.

128. *For Mr Roberts.*

Reverend and Beloved Brother,
· You have here inclosed some of our grounds whereupon we build congregational and classical elderships, and in the other paper our grounds for synods. Make what use of them you think expedient. Yesterday the assembly's petition was frowned upon in both Houses; notwithstanding we purpose, God willing, on Thursday to give in

a remonstrance of a more full and high strain, to be communicate to both Houses, and the assembly, on Friday, by the hand of the grand committee. What necessity there is of hastening your petition also, you may consider. I heard yesterday, that Mr Lilburn has a petition for the sectaries, subscribed with the hands of a great many thousands. I do not believe it; yet it would be tried. If your city will countenance Mr Peter's sermon on the day appointed, they do but go on as they have begun. Send back this letter with the bearer; for we had need to beware what papers lie in any of your studies, since the other day it was earnestly pressed in the House, that Mr Jenkins, Mr Cranford's, and, as I think, Mr Fisher's studies, should be presently sealed up, and searched. These be but the beginnings of evils. The other papers I shall call for hereafter. Thus I rest,

Your Brother to serve you,

ROBERT BAILLIE.

129. *For the Right Worshipful my Noble Friend Mr Rous, my humble advice concerning the erection of the congregational elderships and classical presbyteries in the city of London, and within the lines of communication.*

1. THAT with so much speed as may be, the House be moved to appoint a committee of some few of the most orthodox and conscientious of their members, to prepare an ordinance for the foresaid end, or to refer that matter to the committee for the Directory, whereof Mr Tate was chairman.

2. That this committee may be pleased to consider the votes of the assembly anent classical presbyteries and congregational elderships, the chief whereof are contained in this inclosed paper.

3. Because the nomination of persons fittest to govern every congregation will be difficult, the committee may take the secret advice of some orthodox, pious, and wise ministers, acquainted with the condition of the city congregations, especially the minister of the congregation to be provided for, if he may be trusted, that they may first inform themselves, and then the committee, what names are fittest to be put in the ordinance.

4. It

4. It seems, that the smallest congregations would have at least four elders and deacons, and that the greatest would not have above twenty of both.

5. It is to be provided, that no man be named for an elder or deacon, against whom any of the congregation can justly object any scandalous sin, or disaffection to any part of the reformation in hand. For this end some notice must be given to the congregation of the names, before they be put in the ordinance.

6. The ordinance may appoint the meeting of the eldership to be once a-week; and after, upon occasion, to consult and determine, by most votes of the minister and ruling elders, the ecclesiastick affairs belonging to that congregation, which the ordinance commits to them. The deacons ought to be present to give their advice anent the poor, and the ecclesiastick goods.

7. The ordinance must express so many acts of power as the House will think expedient to be put in the hands of that eldership, with a clear proviso, that it shall be without prejudice of what power the parliament, after farther consultation with the assembly of divines, shall find meet to be added thereto.

8. That besides the power of holding from the Lord's table of any scandalous person within the bounds of the parish, it must be enjoined to the eldership, to take care that all within their bounds may live as it becomes Christians. That for this end they may be appointed to visit the families, and to call before them any who are scandalous either in life or judgement, to instruct, admonish, and rebuke them, and to convent them whom they find disobedient, before the presbytery and synod, that so, where need is, in meekness all may be reclaimed from their enormities. But if the church counsels and censures do not prevail, then recourse must be had to the magistrate, to have the obstinate offender, by his civil power, brought so far as may be, to do duty.

9. The committee would advise with the forenamed brethren, how many classical presbyteries it is meet to be set up within the lines of communication; whether all the ministers in office may be admitted as members; and if any of the congregational elders may be put in the ordinance to attend the presbyters for the first year whom the eldership shall chuse. It seems that thirty is a great enough number for one presbytery; so if there be 120 parishes

riches within the lines, and from every parish there come
at least one minister and one elder to the presbytery, there
must be eight presbyteries; which might meet ordinarly
once a fortnight; and all in a synod once in a quarter, or
at least once in the half-year.

10. The ordinance may express all the acts of power
voted by the assembly to belong to classical presbyteries
which the House does not much controvert, with a proviso, that it shall be without prejudice of what farther power
the Houses after consultation with the assembly of divines
shall find meet to be added.

11. It seems needful that the House would call upon the
assembly to hasten what remains of government; and require them, out of all their votes, to draw up a directory
for government, wherein the uniformity promised in the
covenant may be so far advanced as may be for the present.

130. *A Publick Letter.*   *January* 20. 1646.

Reverend and Dear Brother,

AFTER much longing for your letters, also some anger
and much both grief and fear expressed in sundry of my
letters, that for a whole quarter of a year I could learn
from none of you any thing of my poor wife, her estate,
at last, yesterday the 19th of January I received yours of
the 25th of December, and Mr George's, and my wife
her own, which has removed fully all my anger, grief,
and fear.   I thank God heartily for his gracious care of
you all, and his goodness to all mine, and gives you thanks
for your large kind letter. I thank God my Dissuasive has
done no evil here.   I hear no word of any answer for it;
albeit it be on the subject most here in agitation.   The
whole first impression is sold : the second I expect to-morrow. When Thomas Young comes home, he has a dozen
for friends; and as many of my late sermons, and forty
of his own, to be sold.   He will give you and Mr George
the Annotations, which I pray you accept without any
scrupulosity. Mr Alexander Dickson shall have what he
wrote for, with the first conveniency.   My obligation to
you all is great for your comfortableness to my poor wife
in this her desolate time.   I am rejoiced with the kindness
she writes to me God has poured on her spirit all this
time.

me. It is oft my refolution, for all this goodnefs of
God towards unworthy me, to be willingly, while I live,
ferviceable to the meaneft of the faints, with gifts, means,
perfon, and whatever God has given me, and fhall give
me : blefled be his name.   When I compare all our informations from Scotland, Ireland, France, with our know-
edge of things here, I affure you our affairs are in a
hopeful, yet very dangerous pofture, which I will relate
to you, Mr David, and Mr George, and to you only fo
far as I conceive of them.

The hearts of the divines here who are wife, of the affembly, city, and elfewhere, are fet only on the point of
government.   We are going on in the affembly with the
Confeffion, and could, if need were, fhortly end it.   We
are preparing for the Catechifm ; but we think all is for
little purpofe till the government be fet up.   The affembly has delivered their full fenfe of all its parts to the parliament half a year ago.   The Independent party, albeit
their number in the parliament be very fmall, yet being
prime men, active and diligent, and making it their great
work to retard all till they be firft fecured of a toleration
of their feparate congregations ; and the body of the lawyers, who are another ftrong party in the Houfe, believing all church-government to be a part of the civil and
parliamentary power, which nature and fcripture has
placed in them, and to be derived from them to the minifters only fo far as they think expedient ; a third party
of worldly profane men, who are extremely affrighted to
come under the yoke of ecclefiaftick difcipline ; thefe
three kinds making up two parts at leaft of the parliament, there is no hopes that ever they will fettle the government according to our mind, if they were left to
themfelves.

The affembly has plied them with petition upon petition,
the city alfo, both minifters and magiftrates ; but all in
vain.   They know that fchifms and herefies daily increafe
in all the corners of the land for want of difcipline ; yet
the moft of them care for none of thefe things.   Had our
army been but one 15,000 men in England, our advice
would have been followed quickly in all things ; but our
lamentable pofture at home, and our weaknefs here,
make our defires contemptible.   Had the King been of
any confiderable ftrength, fear would have made them
careful to do duty ; but their great fuccefs, the King's extreme

treme weaknefs, and our miferies, make them follow their own natural humours, to the grief of fundry gracious men of their own number. In this cafe our laft refuge is to God, and under him to the city. We have gotten it, thanks to God, to this point, that the mayor aldermen, common council, and moft of the confiderable men, are grieved for the increafe of fects and herefies, and want of government. They have, yefterday had a publick faft for it, and renewed folemnly their covenant by oath and fubfcription; and this day have given in a ftrong petition for fettling of church-government, and fuppreffing of all fects, without any toleration. No doubt, if they be conftant, they will obtain all their defires; for all know here that the parliament cannot fubfift without London: fo whatfoever they defire in earneft, and conftantly, it muft be granted. Wherefore, albeit they gave them a baffling anfwer to their former petition a month ago; yet confidering the addrefs of this in all its progrefs, they have thanked them for it, and promifed a good anfwer fpeedily. The Independents, and all fects, are wakened much upon it, and all will ftir; which way, we do not know yet. We had much need of your prayers. They are but very few of the city-minifters about the firft and fecond wheels of the bufinefs. I make it my tafk to give them weekly my beft advice and encouragements; and, bleffed be God, with fuch fuccefs hitherto, that it is worth my ftay here. The King being brought to fo low a condition, has been fending thefe weeks bygone meffage upon meffage, for a treaty of peace. It is true, the leading party of the parliament feems much to fear and be averfe from all peace for the time, as prejudicial to their private defigns; yet our affairs in Scotland, yea the ftate of this land alfo, calls for peace in any equitable terms; which has made our commiffioners have many long and unpleafant debates upon the anfwers to the King's meffages, while they laboured to efchew that which fome endeavoured, the impoffibility of any farther treating with the King: yet we did ever at laft agree in good terms. The fum of the anfwer was ever the inexpediency of farther treating, and refolution to fend propofitions to the King, whereupon they expected his pofitive anfwer: but here the defperate cafe of both hands; the former propofitions agreed on by both kingdoms we have required this half year to be fent, and the King's an-

I   fwer

swer to be required thereupon, without treaty. Since Naseby field, their thoughts have been higher: they profess they will alter and add to the former propositions. We desire to know what to this day they have not told us. We know they have altered all which concerned our interest in the militia of England and Ireland, and that yet they have not concluded their alterations, neither in haste are like to do it. On the other hand, we see no appearance that the King, for all his desperate condition, is minded to yield what both kingdoms have concluded to have; but is still going on in his old plotting way, to destroy the remainder of his subjects: His messengers are still dealing with Denmark, for men to come over; the Queen is daily agenting with the clergy and court of France, and the Prince of Orange, for men, money, ships, and arms; and we are advertised by many, that she has got from both too great assistance, which shortly will trouble us, if God prevent it not. Yet the great army which D'Anguien is preparing for Italy, for Milan, and the Pope, we hope is not to come over to us; albeit, if the three years negotiation at Munster could conclude a peace, there is no doubt but both Spain and France send in powerful armies upon us: but we think that peace is impossible for the time, albeit the Turks invasion of the Venetians, and the Swedes success in Saxony, makes the Emperor and Spain willing to it upon any tolerable condition.

But that which troubles us most is Ireland. The Pope, this half-year bygone, has had a nuncio there. Both the Spanish and French Kings have had their residents at Kilkenny. We had a rumour of it before, but this night the copies of the writs from the English commissioners in Ireland have been read in the committee of both kingdoms, and to-morrow are to be reported to the Houses, wherein the King gives ample commission to the Earl of Glamorgan to give full liberty to his loyal Catholick subjects of Ireland of their religion, restores them to all the church-lands in Ireland, and recalls all the laws against Popery there. We fear this shall undo the King for ever; that no repentance shall ever obtain a pardon of this act, if it be true, from his parliaments. The fear is, albeit the rebels be expelled from Ulster and Connaught, yet that, according to their capitulation, they send over to Alaster Macdonald 10,000 men, compleatly armed, half-muskets and half pikes, which are designed first to run through the low-ands of Scotland, and then to raise the malignant north of England ; while the King of Denmark's son, Woldemar, bring over to the north of Scotland, some 3000 or 4000 of old Dutch soldiers, and from France they come over some 8000 or 10,000 French, with a convoy of Holland ships, to join with the King's army in Cornwal. These are the present designs, as likely as any the King yet ever had ; but we trust God, who blasted all the other, will blast all these also. However, if God be not with us extraordinarily, they are too likely to wrack Scotland, considering our weakness already, our divisions, discouragements, and the great power of the enemy in our bowels. This is a powerful people ; but very feeble. The sectaries are too like to stir ; the malignants and malecontents are many. It is God who keeps all right, and I am very hopeful will do it ; for I know there are a great many here and there also of real saints, and the enemy's designs to this hour are nothing but oppression both of church and state. Always I thought myself obliged (for your last very comfortable letters) to let you see the inside of our affairs, I am sorry for the condition of my friends there. I adore the unsearchable judgements of God, and submit to his righteousness ; only, in these times of wrath against the whole land, and dangers, I wish justice may be mixed with mercy towards any of whom there was any ground of hope. The commissary is my dear friend ; his crimes I do not know distinctly, only I wish he were not killed by a prison, as I am informed he is very near to be. I dare not take upon me to give advice in such a distance ; but I cannot dissemble my grief. If that man be lost, if any of you three can save, I do not say his place, or his fine, but his life, by procuring him the free air, it would be to me a great favour, which, if I were present, I would earnestly beg from any who could procure it. There is another of my special friends, who I hear is also in danger, Mr William Wilkie : my interest in him is very great since my first acquaintance : though I differed in sundry things, yet I always did much love him, and I ever found him a very fast and steadable friend, I knew, in the worst times. At my desire, he helped to keep storms off my brethren. His father, at the beginning of these troubles, was oft cordial, and I am witness of sundry his good services. My cousin, his poor wife, I know has ever been a good

and

and gracious woman. What his faults are whereupon he is challenged, I do not know. If they be matters of an unpardonable ſtrain, I am not to ſay any thing ; but if o-therwiſe, I would intreat all you three, as earneſtly as I can do for any thing of that kind, to do for him what you may with a good conſcieuce. I pity much his mo-ther, who ever loved this cauſe, and his good-mother, whoſe grace and virtue for many years I have highly e-ſteemed. Her caſe is deplorable. She has loſt well near all that belongs to her, and, which makes it the more grievous, through their own default. Mr Matthew and Mr David long ago loſt ; Mr James died a baniſhed man ; Mr John depoſed, and his ſon alſo ; Mr John Creighton really baniſhed ; her ſon Alexander little better ; her huſ-band caſt out of his place ; the commiſſar. wracked ; Mr Gavin and Mr John Hay, both in hazard. I wiſh from my heart that ſhe might get ſome favour in the caſe of her ſon-in-law. I am certified, by theſe whom I think I may truſt, that he may be gained ſo fully to our cauſe, that I may be caution for him, he ſhall never publickly or privately oppoſe (as too oft to my grief he has done) any of your deſires. I propone to you, in his behalf, if his faults be not great, and there be appearance he will amend, as I have aſſurance of it under the hands of three whom I do much truſt, that you would conſider if this be a time of putting all from their places who deſerve it, when the ſtorm is not yet ended ; but if you believe all the company wherein I live, the miſeries of Scotland, if God work not above all we can ſee among men, are but beginning. 2. If God would ſettle Scotland, I think the caſe of that town is not like in haſte to ſettle. There is there a good but a great change made by violence, otherwiſe than in any other towns, as yet I hear, whoſe delinquencies at this time was every way as great. I think it will be need-ful to have ſome to be good inſtruments to lenify the rankled hearts of many there. I know none fitter to do ſervice in that kind than the man I am ſpeaking of. I am in opinion his depoſition will increaſe the evil humour of many conſiderable perſons there, as much as any one thing. 3. If my private affections may have any place with you, I cannot deny but it is my very earneſt deſire that he may have favour ; and if it go ill with him, I profeſs it will be a great grief unto me. I under-

and that you and Mr David were his so good friends; both at the firft committee in Glafgow, and there-fter in St Andrew's, you kept his name from publick hearing; if you may think it fit to do fo ftill, at leaft to keep him off the ftage a little time till I may be at home, I will take it for a great obligation. I hope, for my caufe, you will do in this what you may with a good confcience.

I could have dealt with others for help to him at this time; but I have thought meet to recommend him to you three alone, that whatever favour he gets, I may owe it all either to you only, or elfe to none other. Pardon the extraordinary importunity of my affection in this cafe. I leave it to you; do as God will direct.

—— Thefe two days our hearts are oppreffed with di-vers paffions. The King's laft letter for peace is fo full of defperate paffion, that I fear it hafte on his ruin. The prevalent party have ftill harboured jealoufies againft us, and the other day have produced, in the committee of both kingdoms, letters from unknown hands, full of horrid calumnies, both againft our nation and commif-fioners here. Our vindication will coft us a peck of troubles. Upon the city's petition for government, the Houfe of Commons have gone on to vote a committee in every fhire to cognofce on fundry ecclefiaftick caufes, which will fpoil all our church-government. This night our fubcommittee has voted fo much toleration for the independents, that if to-morrow the grand committee pafs it, as it is too like to do, this church, by law, will be gi-ven over to confufion, notwithftanding all we can do to the contrary. But that which vexes us moft of all, is a report that is whifpered, of the King's purpofe to go to our army. What this can mean, we do not yet know; but if he be able to debauch it, it will be a fountain of moft dangerous and horrible evils. We will be proclaim-ed the moft wicked traitors that ever were born. All their calumnies will be taken for truths; that unhappy prince will, without any profit to himfelf, haften our fhameful ruin; for if we fhould in fo bafe and treache-rous a way join with him, we would be able to do him no real help at all: but I hope there is nothing of the report true. However, all thefe things to you three alone. We are in a mighty perplexity; help us with your prayers. The Lord that knows the great fufferings of our nation

for

or their honesty, affist us in this time of our great tur-
moil.

Your Brother,

ROBERT BAILLIE.

131. *To Mr David Dickfon.* *January* 31. 1646.

Reverend and Dear Brother,

WITHIN these ten or twelve days I wrote to you at
great length how all affairs here went. Though I can add
little more, yet an exprefs going from us, I could not but
write falutations. The King fends thick meffages for a
perfonal treaty. The parliament anfwers as they may in
their way. So at this time they have three of the King's
to anfwer together. What the matter will produce, we
know not yet. The lofs of Dartmouth, the well near dif-
fipation of the Prince's army in the weft, the capitulating
of Chefter, the extreme wants of Oxford, and all the
King's foldiers, puts the King hard to it. The peace
which Glamorgan made with the Irifh, in the King's
name, in fo fhameful terms, the King difavows it, and
Glamorgan is made a prifoner in Dublin for it. The
King offers to give over the managing of the war of Ireland to this parliament. I hope this offer may ftay the I-
rifh forces from troubling this ifle; fo much the more, as
the parliament is like to fend over with Inchiquin and my
Lord Lyle (whom they have made governors of Ireland
for a year) fome confiderable forces. It is true the Queen
is very bufy, and has at laft obtained great fums of money, and makes a great deal of fhew to lift an army in
France, which Admiral Dorp is to convoy hither : but
here is fmall fear here of that enterprife. They write from
France, that no men, but only arms, are coming from
Denmark to Scotland; however, that which perplexes us
moft, is the unkindnefs of moft of this people, and too
too apparent defign of the leading party, to break with us
on a fmall occafion, which it feems they are feeking. The
ift of March is near, wherein they will prefs their garrifons, and we cannot render them fo foon. They require
us to keep no more horfe in England than 2000, and 1000
dragoons. They fay we have near 6000, and not half fo
many foot. There be many mutual jealoufies, which daily do rather increafe than diminifh. If there be a breach,

it

t is like to be deſtructive to both, and to the whole Pro-
eſtant party in Chriſtendom.   However, for the time, it
s like that both they and we will have our thoughts buſied
ipon the matter of peace with the King.   The Houſes are
ipon a ſhorter way than we expected, to our joy, and
ome little hope of good.   They are willing to ſend ſome
ix or ſeven propoſitions to the King, which, if he will
iaſs without treaty, they are content he come to London,
s he deſires to treat at leiſure on the reſt, the three treat-
d on at Uxbridge, concerning religion, Ireland, and the
iilitia.   The other four is for a power to the Houſes to
aiſe money, to keep new-made Lords from ſitting in par-
ament, for puniſhing the named delinquents.   I have
orgot the fourth.   Theſe will be ready the next week,
nd ſent to Scotland for our concurrence   I think the
iifficulty will be only that of the militia; for it is much
ltered from what it was.   They have clearly the great
and of the nations union; for of the thirty-ſix commiſ-
oners for the militia in either kingdom, there was a third,
ven twelve Scots to be of the Engliſh militia, and twelve
ingliſh to be of the Scots militia, which is now altered,
iving to every kingdom their own.   This miſtruſt will be
grief and a ſtick, but hardly a total and final ſtop.   I
hink, if no better may be, we muſt yield.   But whether
ver the King will paſs theſe things without a treaty, and
iodification, and ſome mutual condeſcenſion, we yet much
oubt.   A little time will ſhew if peace be poſſible or de-
perate.   The leading party here ſeem to be very careleſs of
:; for it indeed makes not for their ſuppoſed ends; albeit
he King, in his laſt letters, among many of his great of-
ers, offers a great liberty for all Proteſtants to ſerve God
i their own way one by one.   I was earneſt with you in
iy former for your favours, ſo far as you were able with
good conſcience, for my two dear friends, the commiſ-
ar and Mr William Wilkie.   I intreat ſtill for the ſame.   I
m much deceived, if both theſe men might not do you ſer-
ice, both in your general gracious purpoſes, and in your
articulars, worth all the favour you ſhall beſtow upon
hem; and if you ſuffer them to be undone, you will repent
: afterward.   All church-buſineſs goes very croſs.   Our
earts are oft overburdened; albeit on Monday the matter
f toleration went better with us than we expected, yet we
re ſo deceived, that we will ſay nothing yet.   We proceed
ut ſlowly in the Confeſſion of Faith.   This muſt be ended

d before the Catechifm be refumed. The parliament will have a court of civil commiffioners erected in every fhire, on pretence to make report to the Houfes in every new cafe of fcandal, but really to keep down the power of the prefbyteries for ever, and hold up the head of fectaries. It is our prefent work to get that crufhed, and I hope we have done fome good in this. Our hearts ake for grief and fear for that poor land. The calamities on you, and the greater danger, feems yet to us to be above our head. The Lord arife ere we perifh.——The King's defign on our army here, if it was real, we hope we have timeoufly prevented it. Sinclair feems to be fcarce a good man. We are on vindication of ourfelves from fcurvy afperfions, to the fhame of the foolifh contrivers.

132. *Duke William's letter to Mr Baillie from Linlithgow, February 26. 1646. Duke Hamilton, then Earl of Lanerk.*

Reverend Sir,

THE occafion of writing with this bearer procures you this trouble, elfe I fhould have continued filent, and at this time, as formerly, trufted to your charity; but calumnies grow fo new upon me, that I muft beg you would not deny me the continuance of your favourable opinion, (in defpite of my traducers, how eminent foever they be), until either ye hear myfelf, or God fo blefs my endeavours, that my actions force them to confefs themfelves liars; for though none dare or can juftify themfelves before God, yet I will profefs my intentions of affectionate defires, have ftill been to ferve my country in this caufe, according to my covenant, without perfonal end, of advantage or benefit to myfelf, or prejudice to any who have been juftly ambitious of being inftruments in this caufe. I know good, wife, and impartial men, will not deny me charity; fo I will expect it from you no longer than I make it my ftudy both to be an honeft man, and

Your obliged friend and fervant,

LANERK.

133. For

133. *For my Lord Lanerk.*   *An anfwer to the former.*

My Lord,

I received your Lordfhip's of the 26th of February from James Hamilton, which, together with the kind and confident expreffions therein, I acknowledge as an new obligation. What your Lordfhip defires is very reafonable and juft. You may be affured to obtain it eafily of me, and all others with whom I have power; for, believe it, now of a long time, at leaft three months, fo far as I remember, I have not heard one word from any man to your Lordfhip's prejudice. By the contrary, the other day I heard a larger and more vehement panegyric to your commendation, and bitterer invectives to the difgrace of fome others, than I conceive was needful. If I were befide you, I could ufe my old, pedantick, and magifterial freedom; but papers at fo far a diftance, in this pofture of affairs, are unfafe convoys of free and honeft thoughts; only this much I muft fay, for all the world fees it, that matters are pitifully mifcarried in Scotland; that our fhame and fkaith was not fo great thefe 600 years as this laft year. We are nothing helped by banding the caufe of our miferies from one of you to another. The poor land bleeds and is deftroyed; I dare not fay with fome, large as much by the differences of your friends, as by the hand of the enemy; yet I am bold to fay too too much, and more than the beft of you fhall ever be able to anfwer, either to God, or the world abroad, or to the pofterity. It is a filly plea, that you are all united in the end, fince your debates about the midfes make the end among your hand to be loft. If I had any power among any of you, I would in all earneftnefs obteft, That if any love to God and religion, if any tendernefs to your poor, broken, difgraced country, if any fenfe of your own honour and fafety be yet remaining, that at laft you would all do what divers times has been affayed, promifed, and begun, by every one of you, but performed by none; I mean, that all our quarrels might for a time at leaft be laid afide; that every one of you would cede and fubmit to one another, and cordially join in the common defence. Albeit I be no prophet, yet I think I forefee, that whoever of you, in thefe fad times, are readieft to facrifice all your felf-inte-

2   refts

efts to the well of the publick, he fhall obtain, in defpight
if all oppofers, in the moft eafy and honourable way, all
iis defires. But if you refolve every one of you fo to
ook to your own defigns, and go on in your differences,
hough all fhould perifh; among many other unhappy
vents, this will be one, that the people who outlive
hefe troubles, will curfe all your memories, will gladly
onfent to that curfe which fomewhere in the world is
nuch defired, and far advanced, (though my heart did e-
er abhor it), that when kings and princes are brought
lown, the power and following of the nobles may be abo-
ifhed, as that which they have feen and felt, not at all to
:rve for the defence, but clearly for the dividing and
uining of a poor people. Of this enough. I am very
lopeful your Lordfhip will be as ready as any one to lay
fide whatever may concern yourfelf and your friends, till
our poor dying country may once be recovered, that in
he life and health thereof you may find yourfelf and
hem; otherwife you know well neither you nor they can
e fafe. I hope againft the general affembly to fee your
lordfhip, when I fhall be ready to tell you all my mind of
ffairs, both private and publick. In the mean time, I
emain,

Your Lordfhip's affectionate friend and fervant,
ROBERT BAILLIE.

POSTSCRIPT.

The Commiffar of Glafgow is my dear and fpecial
riend. I am forry he has mifcarried in the publick caufe.
fee you purpofe to proceed now no farther with him
han to a fine. Since this is the mind of the parliament,
think it a great pity his life fhould be loft by a long and
lofe imprifonment. I marvel he has lived fo long, know-
1g the temper of his body. I muft intreat your Lordfhip
o get him fo foon to the free air as may be: by fo doing,
ou fhall fave a life which the ftate intends fhould be fafe,
nd preferve a man, who I hope may yet do good fervice
1 the place where he lives; and whatever your Lordfhip
an do for him, without prejudice to the publick, I will
cknowledge it all as done for myfelf.

The Prince's arrival in France, the ftate of affairs here,
s with this packet they will be reprefented by divers hands,

hat dangerous and unhappy remonstrance of Seaforth's, call aloud to all who have a drop of kindness to Scotland, to join hearts and hands quickly, without any farther delay; else our woes are but beginning.

134. *A Postscript to Mr David Dickson's letter. London, March 6. 1646.*

THIS much I had written a fortnight ago, but on the post-night was hindered to send it away. Since, Fairfax has routed Hopeton again; and now it seems, without any impediment, will go to the utmost part of Cornwall. Where the Prince will lurk, it is hard to say. The King's forces thought to have surprised Abingdon; but were repulsed. The King has sent us a fifth or sixth letter for a treaty, without any answer. His extremities are said to be great, and his fears no less. Where-ever he goes, he may be besieged and taken. He has lost all his sea-ports but Falmouth. We are masters also of the seas. It will be hard for him to flee any where. If he can have a little patience, it seems a treaty will be obtained. They have at last given to us all the propositions they mind to send, but two, that of London and the delinquents, which they are hastening. Likely our debates with them about the alterations will not be long. Also I hope it shall not be needful to send them to Scotland; for Wariston and Mr Barclay are come, and the Chancellor will be here to-morrow, who, I think, have instructions to conclude upon the additions and alterations. It is much hoped, that the King will pass the propositions, were they worse and harder than they are: so, except some evil spirit interpose, there is some appearance of peace shortly; albeit we dare not yet be confident. The sectarian party is very malicious and powerful. They have carried the House of Commons, and are like also to carry the House of Lords, to spoil much our church-government. They have passed an ordinance, not only for appeal from the general assembly to the parliament, for two ruling elders, for one minister in every church-meeting, for no censure, except in such particular offences as they have enumerated; but also, which vexes us most, and against which we have been labouring this month bygone, a court of civil commissioners in every county, to whom the congregational elderships must

bring

bring all cases not enumerated, to be reported by them, with their judgement to the parliament or their committee. This is a trick of the Independents invention, of purpose to enervate and disgrace all our government, in which they have been assisted by the lawyers and the Erastian party. This troubles us all exceedingly. The whole assembly and ministry over the kingdom, the body of the city, are much grieved with it; but how to help it, we cannot well tell. In the mean time, it mars us to set up any thing; the anarchy continues, and the vilest sects do daily increase. Many are afraid of God's judgement. Argyle is to Ireland for 2000 old foot to land in Argyle, to cast out these unhappy men who possess peaceably all his estate. Callendar, after all could be done to him, has refused what all pressed him to: he would be at a greater sovereignty than could be granted, thinking he could not miss it in any terms he pleased. Heart-burnings there continue still. This people, what they will do on the refusal of the garrisons, we do not yet know. If God would send us peace on any tolerable terms, it would be very welcome. When all is tried to the utmost, there is not the least treachery found in Baillie, though great unhappiness, the fault whereof is seen to have been in other men, more than in him.

135. *To Scotland. To Mr David Dickson.* March 17. 1646.

Since my last, this day fortnight, all the account I can give of our affairs here is this. In the assembly we are fallen on a fashious proposition, that has kept us divers days, and will do so divers more, coming upon the article of the church and the church-notes to oppose the Erastian heresy, which in this land is very strong, especially among the lawyers, unhappy members of this parliament. We find it necessary to say, "That Christ in the New Testament had institute a church-government distinct from the civil, to be exercised by the officers of the church, without commission from the magistrate." None in the assembly has any doubt of this truth but one Colman, a professed Erastian; a man reasonably learned, but stupid and inconsiderate, half a pleasant, and of small estimation. But the lawyers in the parliament, making it their work to spoil our presbytery, not so much upon conscience, as

upon

upon fear that the prefbytery fpoil their market, and
take up the moft of the country-pleas without law, did
blow up the poor man with much vanity; fo he is become
their champion, to bring out, in the beft way he can, E-
raftian arguments againft the propofition, for the contentment of the parliament. We give him a free and fair
hearing; albeit we fear, when we have anfwered all he can
bring, and have confirmed with undeniable proofs our
pofition, the Houfes, when it comes to them, fhall fcrape
it out of the Confeffion; for this point is their idol. The
moft of them are incredibly zealous for it. The Pope
and King were never more earneft for the headfhip of the
church than the plurality of this parliament. However
they are like for a time by violence to carry it, yet almoft
all the miniftry are zealous for the prerogative of Chrift
againft them. We are at this inftant yoked in a great and
dangerous combat for this very thing. We have been
often on the brink to fet up our government; but Satan
to this day hindered us. The minifters and elders are not
willing to fet up and begin any action, till they may have
a law for fome power to purpofe; all former ordinances
have been fo intolerably defective, that they could not be
accepted. The Eraftian and Independent party joining
together in the Houfes to keep off the government fo long
as they were able, and when it was extorted, to make it
fo lame and corrupt as they were able; yet at laft yefterday an ordinance came forth to fupply the defects of all
the former, that fo, without further delay, we might go
to work. We laboured fo much as we were able, before
it came out, to have it fo free of exceptions as might be:
but notwithftanding of all we could do, it is, by the malignity of the forementioned brethren in evil, fo filled with
grievances, that yet it cannot be put in practice. We, for
our part, mind to give in a remonftrance againft it; the
affembly will do the like; the city-minifters will give the
third; but that which, by God's help, may prove beft
effectual, is, the zeal of the city itfelf. Before the ordinance came out, they petitioned againft fome materials of
it. This, both the Houfes voted to be a breach of their
privilege, to offer a petition againft any thing that is in debate before them, till once it be concluded and come a-
broad. This vote the city takes very evil. It is likely to
go very high betwixt them. Our prayers and endeavours
are for wifdom and courage to the city. I know to whom
this

his matter has coft much labour. The Independents have
the leaft zeal to the truth of God of any men we know.
lafphemous herefies are now fpread here more than ever
in any part of the world; yet they are not only filent, but
are patrons and pleaders for liberty almoft to them all.
We and they have fpent many fheets of paper upon the
toleration of their feparate churches.   At the laft meeting we concluded to ftop our paper-debates, and on Thurfday next to begin our verbal difputation againft the lawfulnefs of their defired feparation.   When we have ended,
the Houfes will begin to confider this matter.   The moft
here, and in the army, will be for too great a liberty;
but the affembly, the city, and the body of all the miniftry
in the kingdom, are paffionately oppofite to fuch an evident breach of our covenant.   What the Lord will make
the iffue, a little time will now declare.   We had great
need of your prayers.   We were never more full of weighty
bufinefs and perplexed folicitude of mind.   Alfo the matter of peace is now in the caulms.   The propofitions to be
fent to the King were given to us fome days ago.   Yefterday our commiffioners returned their fenfe of them.   Their
alterations of the former propofitions are fo many, that I
fear we fhall not agree in hafte; and the pity is, the King
will not be able to endure any long time.   Hopeton being
driven to the utmoft nook of Cornwall, has rendered himfelf, and whole army, without ftroke of fword, to Sir
Thomas Fairfax.   The Prince is fled to Scilly.   Falmouth
and Exeter, it is thought, will not hold out.   The army,
with fpeed, will come to lie down before Oxford.   The
King in a fortnight will not know whither to go.   Never
man did him worfe fervice than Montrofe, and all thofe
men who have weakened and divided Scotland.   I believe
the King feels that folly, among other errors, which now
he cannot remeid.   A few days will clear many things of
church and ftate that for the time are in great darknefs.

A Poftfcript.   March 31. 1646.

For the time our commiffioners can think on no private
thing; for every day they attend, five or fix hours together,
a folemn debate, with a number of the chief of both Houfes
of parliament, about the propofitions of peace to be fent
to the King.   A little time will fhew much.   We are in great
doubts,

doubts. The leaders of the people feem to be inclined to have no fhadow of a king; to have liberty for all religions; to have but a lame Eraftian prefbytery; to be fo injurious to us, as to chafe us home with the fword. Thefe things to you three alone. The Prince is landed in France, which will be a fentence of foreign war. This day the Houfe of Commons have appointed a committee to fecure the King's perfon, if he fhould come to London. Our great hope on earth, the city of London, has played nipfhot : they are fpeaking of diffolving the affembly. If we had not need to pray, you fee. That unhappy wicked remonftrance of Seaforth feems to us a clear preface to his joining with Montrofe. For all that, I hope we may have better news hereafter, and we hope that God will not leave us to the will of our enemies. This people are fwollen fo big with fucceffes, that they are impatient to hear reafon from any : the end can hardly be good. If my Lady Argyle be with you, remember my hearty affections to her, and to my Lord, and all his : for all that is come, he is my choice of all the noblemen I know. The Lord be with him, and affift him. Remember me to all friends. So I reft,

  Your Brother,

         ROBERT BAILLIE.

136. *To Mr William Spang.*   April 3. 1646.

Dear Coufin,

——— Matters here go very dangeroufly. The Prince ftaid long in Scilly. Six weeks they have been in debate in the Houfe of Commons, of a cold, flight, invitatory letter to him to come to their quarters : but it feems they defire not his prefence. Since his mother has got him in her hands, fhe may readily make him go to mafs, and marry the Duke of Orleans's daughter, which by all appearance will banifh him from Britain for ever. The laft letter of the King being more taking than the former, offering to be advifed by the parliament, if his followers may be fecured of their eftates, has drawn an anfwer yeafternight, which his five or fix former were not able to do. The anfwer is, That they conceive it not for his good, nor the good of his people, to come hither, till firft the propofitions be granted which they are preparing to fend.

                In

1 the mean time the city-guards are multiplied, and a
ommittee appointed to fecure his perfon, and feize on
is followers, if he fhould come hither. How foon the
ropofitions can be ready, we know not. It is not likely
1ey fhall go before Sir Thomas Fairfax have inclofed
)xford, and have the King in his power. In their de-
ates with us, God helps our commiffioners to demon-
:rate the great injuftice of their new alterations ; but for
ttle purpofe ; for we have no hopes of any reafon from
hem : yet we muft exoner our confciences. The city has
1uch grieved us by their unexpected fainting ; they will
uickly repent it, but out of time. It pleafes God to fa-
our Middleton's beginnings. Seaforth's new divifive mo-
ion is exceeding untimeous, unjuft, and dangerous. We
re vexed that we hear the King's defperate obftinacy, re-
olving to ftick to the militia and bifhops though he fhould
ie for it. Afhburnam, his grand counfellor, deceived
y his Independent minifters, does put, it feems, the poor
rince in vain hopes of the Independents concurrence to
hefe his defires, albeit it be evident they feek his ruin.
Iis mifregard and malice towards us continues, albeit the
ndependents go on to whifper our correfpondence with
iim. It is a marvel to me if thefe men fhould always
rofper, their ways are fo impious, unjuft, ungrate, and
very way hateful. Our eyes are towards God, and we
re as cautious and diligent to do all our duty as we are
ble. God has ftruck Coleman with death ; he fell in an
gue, and after four or five days expired. It is not good
o ftand in Chrift's way.

137. *To Mr William Spang.* *April* 23. 1646.

Coufin,

You fee what I writ for you the two laft pofts, though
hey miffed the packet through ill luck. Your letter to
he Principal I received on Friday laft. I fent it home on
Monday, with one who was riding journey ftraight to
Ilafgow. I could amend nothing in it. I feconded it
vith one of my own.

Matters here are in a very ambiguous pofture. Exeter
s capitulating, if not already rendered. The Prince is
et in Scilly. The Houfes have voted 10,000 foot and
,000 of horfe to be raifed in the north. Sir Thomas Fairfax's

Fax's 21,000 men are voted to continue other four months.
They are fpeaking of other 10,000 for the weſt : 40,000
men are a great army when there is not one man in the
fields againſt them.   The moſt think they intend to force
us to what they will.   The common word is, that they
will have the King priſoner.   Poſſibly they may grant to
the Prince to be a Duke of Venice.   The militia muſt be
abſolutely, for all time to come, in the power of the parliament alone.   The King and we muſt conſent to what
the Houſes have done and ſhall do in religion.   But for
any particular, neither he nor we muſt enquire after it.
The Houſes muſt have power of levying money without
the King.   A perpetual parliament is a perpetual army;
and means to entertain it, will keep all in quiet.   The city now is pretty tame.   A wicked and ill-invented calumny was written hither from Oxford, that the mayor of
London had correſpondence with the King, and had given him protection in the city, with 40,000 men; that he
would put fire in the town, and ſeize on the parliament.
A great din was made for this.   All ſee the fooliſhly-in-
vented calumny; and many think it invented here, to blaſt
the perſon of the mayor, who is too honeſt to follow the
way of the faction, and to try the pulſe of the city how
they will ſuffer the King's impriſonment.   They make the
word to go, that the King reſolves to go to the Scots army,
knowing their compaſſionate hearts, and love to the King,
if he would do his duty.   They have belaid all the ways,
that they may catch him if he ſhould eſſay to go any where
out of Oxford, till Cromwell come and take him up.   No
appearance of ſettling religion or the kingdom, yet God
may do both quickly.   We are in great grief and perplexity; we pity it that a very few perſons ſhould be enabled
to keep all in a dangerous confuſion, when all might be
ſo eaſily ſettled.   The body of both the parliament and
people are ſo good, religious, and wiſe, that I cannot
think but they will, ere long, take order with thoſe who
mind themſelves and friends more than either religion or
the country, rather than by their evil counſel alter their
undamental laws, and keep the country in awe by a perpetual army, and fall on us, who have deſerved ſo well of
them, and for their cauſe alone ſuffers our own country
to be publickly deſtroyed.   If we knew not there was a
God who over-ruled the counſels of all men, and had a
are of kingdoms and churches, our grieved hearts would
be

e much more grieved and faint. The affembly have gi-
en in a very honeft petition; but it is like fhall have no
ood anfwer. The city-minifters are to give in one much
igher, not fo much upon hopes of fuccefs, as refolu-
on to deliver their confcience. The citizens fay, they
ill give in another for the fame end, but we do not
elieve them. Their fainting has given our caufe one of
ie greateft wounds yet it has gotten. The next week
ill, it is thought, declare much. We are longing for
Apollonius againft Eraftus. It were good to put 'Span-
eim on the Anabaptifts; for that is the predominant fect
ere. I wrote to you to ufe means to make Voffius print
is treatife againft them, which is long ago perfect befide
im; alfo that ye would fpeak with Forbes to go on. with
is book, and to ufe diligence againft our prefent fects
ere. I marvel that your printers there will not be plea-
ed to put out in little form the Greek Septuagint and the
Chaldee Paraphrafe with the points and verfion. No
ooks would fell better; and fome pieces of the Talmud
nd Maffora pointed, and with the Latin. Give me fome
ccount of this. The devil makes fuch oppofition, that we
xpect here a great work; and truly there is great and
air appearances and beginnings, if it pleafe God to re-
ove fome impediments.

138. *For Scotland.* *April* 24. 1646.

How matters ftand here they are wife who well under-
tands. Exeter, Barnftable, and all the reft, are fully re-
uced; and, among other places, Michaelfmount: fo
Duke Hamilton is free, and on his way hither. The
Prince is yet at Scilly, and not in France. Whether, on
ie parliament's invitation, he will come hither or not,
re do not yet know. We have had divers ftrange tra-
erfes lately, not very comfortable. We are, for the
me, between hope and fear for the end. The Houfes
ut out an ordinance for the erecting of prefbyteries; but
o defective, that while it was in doing, the city drew up
petition againft it; which the Houfes voted a breach of
ieir privileges. While we were in great hopes that the
ity would for all that ftand to their petition, that we
iould learn to truft in no flefh, they fhamefully fuc-
umbed: by a few fair words from the Houfes, they were

made as mute as fish. Yet the assembly were bold to petition the Houses against that ordinance; for which also they are voted breakers of their privileges. The assembly yet say, they will be stouter than the city, and mind not, by a few, whether fair or foul, words, to acknowledge any fault where none was. And we also, for our exoneration, do give in a fair remonstrance against that ordinance; whereunto as yet we have got no answer, and scarce expect any good one. But the eyes of all are most on the propositions of peace. Our state-commissioners had many and long debates, both by word and writ, with a committee of the Houses, upon the alterations of the former propositions, whereupon both kingdoms had agreed long ago. It came at last to this, that however by treaty they were obliged not to make peace without us, yet they might send what propositions they pleased for their own kingdom; and that, for religion, they would send no particular at all, but only require the King's consent for a power to the parliament here to establish religion in England and Ireland as they thought fit; also they required him to consent, that for time coming the power of the militia should be in the Houses allenarly, and no part of it in the crown. To neither of these we would consent. The word was made to go far and near, that not only we retarded the settling of peace, but also that in our papers and debates we did press many unreasonable desires; yea, desires expressly contrary to our papers were generally imputed to us. Hence many of our friends thought it necessary to have our papers printed. Among others, Mr Buchanan, a most sincere and zealous gentleman, who has done, both in writ and print, here and over sea, many singular favours and services to this parliament, to his nation, and the whole cause, got a copy of our late papers by his private friendship, and hazarded to print them, with a preface of his own, and an introduction, both very harmless, and consonant to the three following papers, which we had given in to both Houses. In two or three days, 3000 or 4000 of these papers were sold. They gave immediately to the people satisfaction with our proceedings so great as was marvellous. Our small friends were thereby so inflamed, that they carried first the House of Commons, and then the House of Lords, albeit with the great grief and opposition of the better party in both Houses, to vote these papers false and scandalous, and as

such

ıch to be burnt by the hand of the hangman; the puᵬ-
lifher, Mr Buchanan, to be an incendiary betwixt the two
ations; and a declaration to be made for undeceiving of
ıe people. In all this they knew none of us; they
rounded their offence on the preface and introduction,
ot on our papers themfelves: fo we held our peace. The
urning of the papers, and the Houfe of Commons decla-
ıtion, very fly and cunning, has not yet done much pre-
ıdice to us; only it has made the extraordinary malice
nd pride of fome men fhine more clearly. Mr Bucha-
an is gone to a place fafe enough. If he come among
ou, he is a man worthy of great honour for many good
ervices. The minifters of London have fubfcribed a pe-
tion a great deal higher and larger than the affembly,
nd higher than our remonftrance. The city alfo has
ıken fome courage, and are again in the way to re-
ıonftrate all their grievances, not only for the matters of
ıe church, but of the ftate. What it will produce, their
ormer failing when moft was expected, will let us pro-
ıife nothing till afterward. This day we have given in
ıat we have further to fay both for matters of church and
ate, in ten or eleven fheets clofe written. It feems maters will come to a quick clofe. All the Royalifts in Scot-
ınd could not have pleaded fo much for the crown and
ıe King's juft power, as the Chancellor and Warifton
ıd for many days together. All will be prefently print-
ı either here or there. Sir Thomas Fairfax's army will
ow be near Oxford. They would have made us believe,
ıat the King had refolved to have broke through to our
rmy for protection from prifon; but I fufpect the chief
readers of thefe reports know well enough how they
eep him fettered in Oxford with 4000 or 5000 horfe, be-
de their daily treaties with Afhburnam, and thefe who
ave abfolute power over him, to keep him ftill till they
eliver him to Sir Thomas Fairfax, and to be difpofed up-
n as Cromwell and his friends think it fitteft for their af-
ıirs. The Scots army could not be very pleafant, fince
ıere was no fhelter there for any of the King's followers
hom the parliament had or fhould make unpardonable;
either for the King himfelf, unlefs willingly to take pre-
ently the covenant, and follow hereafter the advice of his
arliament. Hard pills to be fwallowed by a wilful and
n unadvifed prince; but at laft he muft determine. It
ems a very few days will bring him up hither; in

what quality it is hard to fay. That which has moft an-noyed the city at this time, is a malicious and cunningly-devifed fable, of a defign in the Lord Mayor to protect the King, and to cut off all his enemies in the parliament. With this my Lord Sey, the Solicitor, and others, were fent to acquaint him in an undue time of night. The ci-ty take their moft honeft Mayor's affront in no good part. You fee how things ftand here. We are on the brink ei-ther of a happy peace, or of a more unhappy war than yet we have felt. The madnefs of thefe unnatural men, who continue to let out the blood of their country, when it had moft need of ftrength, is inexcufable. Scotland, for ever, muft curfe the memory, not only of thefe wicked murderers, but alfo of all thefe unhappy felf-feeking fools who have or do contribute any thing to our divifions and heart-burnings. Let all honeft men embrace other as bre-thren, or elfe, I profefs, they will repent it. ———

Let thefe be fent weft to my Lady Montgomery. Whe-ther my Lord, and his father my good Lord Eglinton, be at home, I cannot fay; my hearty fervice to them. It is fpoken, and much feared, that Sir Thomas Fairfax's ar-my will be quickly at Newark. They do not queftion to carry Oxford and Newark without great difficulty. But the Scots muft go home, or elfe be made go with fpeed. Newcaftle muft be reftored. Fie upon thefe enemies of Scotland, who mar the fending up of men hither, who by God's blefling might fpare us a greater labour, and fave much blood, which cannot but be fhed if a war begin be-twixt the nations. It is neither reafon nor religion that ftays fome mens rage, but a ftrong army bridling them with fear. Weaknefs invites and provokes them to in-gratitude and mifchief.

You have here, with the two laft journals, the burnt papers, and the Houfe of Commons declaration. Crom-well came yefternight to town. It is hoped the city re-monftrance may be ready this day. Matters here are looking towards fome end, or elfe fome new beginning. The great God keep the nations from breaking, which fome fear.

139. *For*

139. *For Mr Henderſon, being at Newcaſtle with the King.*

SIR,

PERCEIVING by yours to Mr Kennedy, that mine had paſſed by you to Scotland, I marvel of the miſcarriage; or I delivered, with the books, two letters for you, to my Lord Balcarras's man, out of my own hand, with expreſs directions. I pray you ſearch for that letter, directed on the back *To Aliſter Mackay.* It is pretty free, and had incloſed one from Dr Burgeſs. The week after that I delivered to Mr Cheeſly one from Col. Jones to you. Mr Robert Blair's letter to us bore, that you were weakly. We wiſh to be delivered from that fear. You will have it from many hands, and I cannot but advertiſe you alſo, that the prevalent-party deſires nothing ſo much as the King's refuſing of any one of the propoſitions. It is the ſenſe of all I meet with, that if the King ſhould but delay to grant the propoſitions, this people will declare againſt him, and reject him for ever from being King. The Prince his going to France does much imbitter them, and further that which is the deſign of many, to aboliſh monarchy, and ſettle themſelves in a new kind of popular government. If the King will preſently paſs all the propoſitions, I find the moſt very willing that he ſhould return, and be received with ſo much power and honour, as may in a little time bring him to all his juſt and pious deſires. He deceives himſelf exceedingly, if he expect any diviſions here in haſte. All will agree, if he remain obſtinate, to ruin him and his family, and all who adhere to them. While this fear be ſecured, by appearance this people will be one. Divers, from whom leaſt I expected it, are for the putting away of the whole royal race. The natural reſpect I have to all great families, and the great love and reverence that I ever carried to the King's perſon, makes me grieve and fear much at this time. When I look upon the diſpoſition of all men I know, I ſee nothing but ruin for poor Scotland, except the God of heaven help you there to ſave that poor prince from deſtroying of himſelf and his poſterity, againſt whom he has but invocated too oft the name of God. Though he ſhould ſwear it, no man will believe it, that he ſticks upon Epiſcopacy for any conſcience. It was certainly reſolved, and

expected

expected by all, that the committee ſhould have conſiſted
of four of the prime Lords and eight of the chief Commons; but the inſuperable wilfulneſs of two of our friends
has ſent down the ſix that are named, in ſatisfaction of
their private emulations, without any deſign to harden
and irritate the King. This I know to be true. All men
are for the time in ſuſpenſe, but ready, upon the King's
declaration whatever way, to enter into new thoughts
and actions. I think you ſhall ſhortly have with you all
our three great men, Richmond, Hamilton, Argyle. I
doubt not but all three will join to perſuade, to their ut-
ermoſt, the King to do his duty. If this ſucceed, it
would be your next care, for the well of Scotland, to
make all theſe three more real friends than as yet I ſuſpect
hey are. The Lord help you. I reſt, Yours,
ROBERT BAILLIE.

It has ever been the King's perpetual fault, to grant his
people's deſires by bits, and ſo late, that he ever loſt his
thanks. Muſt we yet wait for oracles from France? A-
pril 28. 1646. at night.
[The preceding date, I ſuppoſe, is a miſtake.]

May 8. 1646.
The King, on Monday early, went as Aſhburnham's
man out of Oxford. For almoſt eight days, great fear and
gnorance here whither he had gone. Many did think he
was in London, many that he was for Ireland. At laſt he
was found in our army at Newark.

140. *For Mr Spang. May 15. 1646. From London.*

Couſin,
YOURS with the laſt poſt I received. I am glad of your
wife's recovery; let my ſervice be remembered to her.
Fear of intercepting makes me to write rarely. The other
week, by appearance by a ſecret inſtruction, our letters at
he city-guards were taken, and broken up, and read in
he Houſe of Commons. One of John Cheeſly's has cau-
ed much noiſe. For ourſelves we are all well; neither
to we fear any hard uſage for any thing that can fall out.
There is no appearance of any ſuch wrong; but there
was great appearance of ſurrounding our army at Newark,

rk, with all the forces they had, at leaft, with 20,000
well-armed men, to take the King from us to prifon, or
o cut us off. This made us, after the capitulation for
Newark, to retire with fpeed. We are now out of their
anger in hafte. The faction's great defign is to continue
he war; a peace is their quick and evident ruin. The
King's being with us makes them mad; but all good peo-
le are very joyful of it. Thanks to God, matters go much
etter. Thefe mens credit is much fallen already. The
ood party has now the plurality in the Houfe of Lords;
many in the Houfe of Commons are falling off our un-
riends. It is hoped the city may yet remonftrate againft
he fects, and that to purpofe, fhortly; but our great per-
lexity is for the King's difpofition. How far he will be
erfuaded to yield, we do not yet know. I hope Mr Hen-
lerfon is with him this night at Newcaftle. The Chancel-
or takes journey thither to-morrow by God's help. They
vill endeavour to make him take the covenant, be fully
lirected to follow the advice of his parliament. If he do
o, we expect from God prefently a happy peace; if his
nduration be remedilefs, our army will not fhelter him:
or, by God's grace, do what he will, we fhall be honeft,
nd ftick by our covenant, how greatly foever this people
ufpect, meafuring us by their own hearts. Hitherto we
have ftuck by our principles in many great and long temp-
ations. I wrote to you in my former letters anent fundry
hings, as the printing of the Targum, the Maffora, and
of other fuch books, in a fmall volume, with the points,
nd expofition. Alfo to ftir up Voffius to print his trea-
ifes, efpecially of Anabaptifm; albeit in his Thefes he be
oo much for dipping. Apollonius to put out his treatife
gainft Eraftus. Of thefe, and fuch like, you have given
ne no anfwer. Send me over Rivius Cabeljavius, and Ma-
ovius about Videlius's queftions. I reft,

ROBERT BAILLIE.

141. *To Mr Henderfon.* May 16. 1646.

SIR,

YOUR Sunday's letter came not to me till Wednefday
norning. This is the firft occafion I could get whereby
o fend you the papers you defired. This is the beft copy
ve had. With it you have Mr Wither's letter to me.
Many

Many here long to hear the King's refolution, and more to hear the refolution of our nation.   If God help you to make him quickly do his duty, this people feem ready to welcome him ; but if he fhall remain obftinate, or delay much time, it is very like all his people will join againft him, and all who will take his part.   The delay of a de-claration ·from him and us increafes jealoufies and cla-mours.   The great God help you to foften that man's heart, left he ruin himfelf, and us with him.   Be affured, he muft either yield to reafon, and altogether change his principles, or elfe he will fall in tragick miferies, and that without the commiferation of thefe who hitherto have ve-ry much commiferated his condition.   I hope with the next, at leaft fhortly, to fend you my thoughts, as you defired, on King James's declaration.   The Lord God be with you, and give you counfel, and a mouth convincing irrefiftibly.

Your Servant,

ROBERT BAILLIE.

The city-remonftrance had a ftop; but it is like to be for its furtherance.   If that man now go to tinkle on bi-fhops, and delinquents, and fuch foolifh toys, it feems he is mad.   If he have the leaft grace or wifdom, he may, by God's mercy, prefently end the miferies, wherein him-felf, and many more, are likely elfe to fink.   Let me in-treat you for one thing, when you have done your utter-moft, if it be God's pleafure to deny the fuccefs, not to vex yourfelf more than is meet : *Si mundus vult vadere,* &c.   When we hear of your health and courage, it will refrefh us.   Go matters as they will, if men will not be faved, who can help it !   And yet you know I was never among thofe who had greateft averfion from his perfon, or leaft fympathy with his afflictions.   If he be refolved to ftop our mouths, and bind our hands, that we may nei-ther fpeak nor do for him, let him go on fo to make him-felf and us miferable ; there is a better life coming ; but woe to thefe villains who have bewitched, poifoned, and infatuated a good prince, for his own, and fo many mil-lions ruin.   We are in a fair way, and daily advance into it, if his obftinacy fpoil not all the play.   God's will be done.

I

142. *For Mr Henderson.* May 19. 1646.

Sir,

The papers you defired I fent with Daniel upon Satur-
ay. I have no more to add unto that than I wrote, but
iat the Commons voted to-day, that our army fhall be
one : and that, when we go, L..50,000 fhall be given, and
ther L. 50,000 when the garrifons are delivered, is an e-
idence, among many moe, of this people's intentions to-
ards us. Every circumftance is written daily from the
orth to our unfriends. There is much talk here by all
irts of people of the King's obftinacy ; that he is the long-
: the worfe, and refufes all reafon. The faction rejoices
erein. This difpofition contributes exceedingly to their
icked defign. All our friends are very forry for it. Ex-
:pt God help you, that you have occafion to let us know
iortly there is a great change, we will not know whi-
ier to turn us. Our perplexity for him and ourfelves
ir the prefent is very great. If he would do his duty, in
iite of all knaves, all would in a moment go right ; but
God have hardened him, fo far as I can perceive, this
:ople will ftrive to have him in their power, and make
i example of him. I abhor to think of it, what they
ieak of execution. Every hour of his delay gives advan-
ige to thefe men, who make it their work to fteal votes
'ery day, to engage the nations, and to make him irre-
incileable. It has been his conftant unhappinefs to give
othing in time. All things have been given at laft ; but
e has ever loft the thanks, and his gifts have been count-
i conftrained and extorted. If Afhburnham be kept,
'e will not be able to abide this people's clamours. But
iough of this. A blind man fees, that if he refolve to
lay the madman longer, he will be forced to do it within
arrower bounds.

So many call upon us to fay fomething to Maxwell's
iok, that if Mr D. Calderwood would help us with fome
f his hiftorick knowledge, we fhould effay to give a poft-
:ript to Maxwell after Adamfon. If you think meet, I
ray you write a line to Mr Dav. with this inclofed, which
ou will clofe, and fend to him with the firft. The Lord
e with you, and help you in this hardeft paffage of this
reat work. I reft, your fervant, Robert Baillie.

143. *To Mr David Calderwood.*   *May* 19. 1646.

Right Reverend,

Your papers have been exceeding helpful to us for an
anfwer to K. James's declaration; which we are now ha-
tening fo foon as we may.   Many call upon us for fome
anfwer to Maxwell Bifhop of Rofs his fcurrilous treatife
against our church, printed two or three years ago at Oxford, and now reprinted here, under the name of *Iffa-*
char's burden; a copy herewith we fend you.   It is full of
odious hiftories, and matters of fact, whereof all of us are
utterly ignorant.   If you will be pleafed to be again at the
pains to fend us up fome informations for our help against
his wicked narrations, we fhall readily fay fomething in
anfwer to him.   Hafte is requifite, fo foon as you may.
We will expect to hear from you; whom we pray God to
affift in all your labours, especially in your Hiftory of our
Church, which is more neceffary than you, or many there,
would believe.   I reft,

Your Brother to ferve you,

ROBERT BAILLIE,

144. *For Mr Roberts.*

Reverend and Beloved Brother,

I marvel that Mr Edwards's book is not yet come a-
broad.   Its ftay is hurtful.   If you know not, as I cannot
think but you muft know that whereof this afternoon I
was informed, the order of the Houfe of Commons,
for commiffioners in every fhire, though it be not as yet
reported to the Houfe of Lords, is far advanced; that
the burgeffes of Southwark, and fome others of the neareft fhires, have named their commiffioners; that the burgeffes of London, before they would name theirs, were
pleafed to fignify to my Lord Mayor their purpofe; whereupon, yefternight, a common council was called, which
appointed a committee, the fame that drew the petition,
to confider of that bufinefs; and if they found it convenient, without any more ado, to advife with their burgeffes upon the perfons to be nominated.   This day they
met; they were like, unanimoufly, to find that court of
commiffioners

commiffioners contrary to the covenant, and to be difa-
vowed ; but Alderman Foulks did change them, and did
perfuade, that what had paft the vote of the Houfe fhould
not be called by them contrare to the covenant : yet the
bufinefs is put off till Monday. If your burgeffes have allowance, yea, were it but a connivance, from the city, to
name thefe commiffioners, they will be received in the
whole kingdom. It were needful to take this bufinefs to
ferious confideration. It admits not of much delay. Farewell.

145. *Mr Roberts's anfwer.*

You have made a clear narration of that bufinefs fpeci-
fied. But the longer that committee thinks upon it, the
worfe they like it ; and fo do other common-council-men.
I have good grounds to conceive that it will be quite difclaimed. It may conduce to make advantage. Mr Edwards told me, his book could not come out till the next
week, by reafon of many unexpected enlargements.

146. *For Mr Roberts.* 1646.

Reverend and Beloved Brother,
YESTERDAY Mr Rous and Mr Tate came to confer with
us. From them we learned, that the new ordinance,
whereby the moft of your grievances are remedied, is fent
up to the Lords ; that it is in Manchefter's hand to be reported fpeedily ; that if he will carry it fo as the Lords
fcrape out all that concerns the commiffioners for fhires,
and put in their room the claffical prefbyteries, to be re-
porters to the parliament of all the not enumerate cafes of
fcandals, they are confident to carry it in their Houfe, according to the Lords amendment. Confider, therefore,
if it were not expedient for you to fpeak with Mr Afh,
that, with all poffible fpeed, he might go to Manchefter,
and obtain of him to perufe with you and Mr Clarke that
ordinance. I am very hopeful that his Lordfhip will do
his uttermoft endeavour to make the Houfe of Lords affent, not only to the mentioned amendment, but to others
which you may find neceffar to move on the fight of the
ordinance. If Mr Afh think it more expedient for you

o go with him, left my Lord fcruple to give the writs out
of his houfe, you will do well in my mind to go. Allan's
bufinefs, and the city's zeal, has much altered, in a few
days, the temper of the Houfe. Our friends there lift up
their head; the fectaries are lower. Strike the iron while
it is hot. Let me know the refult of Monday's meeting.
It is now the great bufinefs of fome to fend recruits to
Cromwell's army. The end is vifible; the pretence to oppofe the landing of 8000 French. If the informations of
all your own agents in France, and of our friends there,
be true, this is but a fhadow to cover fomewhat elfe. If
God help you to keep on the city's zeal, more is like to be
done in a week than hitherto in a year. Be diligent in
this happy nick of time.

147. *For Mr William Spang.* · *June* 26. 1646.

Reverend and Dear Brother,

I am loth to write this till I be fure you have received the
former. We have, every week almoft, a great deal ado
for intercepted or feigned letters. What will become of
us, God knows! but certainly the Scots do yet continue
in the midft of all, and thofe very heavy temptations, to be
very honeft to the Englifh and the common caufe. We
thought the King his coming to us, would have quickly
fettled all; but yet the danger is great: this people are
very jealous, and the fectarian party, intending only for
private ends to continue the war, entertain their humour.
Let the Scots do and fay what they can, yet certainly they
cannot be honeft: they have a defign, with the King and
foreign nations, to betray and ruin England; therefore let
us be rid of them with diligence: if they will not immediately be gone, let us drive them home with our armies.
To thefe foolifh and moft mad counfels, the King's unhappinefs does daily contribute. Some twenty days before he came out of Oxford, he wrote to Ormond, of his
defign to go to the Scots army, upon confidence, to work
them to his defigns, fince the parliament were refolute to
ruin him. This letter is fent to Monro by Ormond, and
by Monro delivered to the Englifh commiffioners, who
fend it to the Houfe of Commons, where it is read publickly, and a vote paffed on it, that the King's intention in coming towards us, was to divide the nations.
                                    This

his was but a preface to a harder vote against him; and
had we not prevented it by a paper, contrary to that letter, declaring, with great confidence, the sincerity of our
ation, and freedom from any capitulation with the King,
is like, they who had stolen through a vote, of the use-
fsnefs of our army in England, had proceeded farther to
make us odious still, and to discredit our most solemn
roteftations of our innocency. Their committee, with
their army at Newark, make a most base report of our
army's miscarriages. The party intended to have had
that a part of a declaration against us; for the great work
f some was, by all means, to have us once engaged; for
this end they hemmed us in a corner of the north, and
made Pointz to lie in our nose, giving us not a sixpence of
money, being assured that being straitened in quarters,
and having no money, that the country, exhausted be-
ore, would be so grieved with us, that we and they would
all foul; and Pointz's army being at hand, there should
e a yoking, and so a necessity of war. Yet we abhor war
o far, that by the great mercy of God, our army hither-
o has given no provocation to those that watched for it,
ut has drawn from it many testimonies for our credit.
While we have almost wrestled through this great danger,
and given satisfaction for Ashburnam and Hudson's escape, as
indeed we were free of fault therein, behold the villain Hud-
on, as it is like by the King's direction, puts himself in the
parliament's hands, and makes grievous complaints of us, as
Ashburnam also did by his letters from over-sea, as if we had
drawn the King to our army by fair promises; and when we
had gotten him, we did use him roughly as a prisoner,
and in nothing gave him contentment. The second was a
refutation of the first. The truth is, we never had any
dealing with him for coming to our army, and would never enter in terms to make him any promise, farther than
that we know our duty, and would keep our covenant; and
had it not been that he foresaw he was ready to be taken
at Oxford, and either to have been execute, which is the
mind of too many here, or to have been clapped up in
perpetual prison, he had never come near us. However,
the carriage of our army, and all our nobles, even they
who were counted the greatest malignants, has been wise,
moderate, and honest, towards the King and this parliament hitherto; yet that party who were the diligent
watchmen of the commonwealth, were doing their uttermost to make it appear that we were but false men; and,
for

For that end, a number of poor inconsiderable delations were brought to the bar of the Commons, to make it evident that we minded no good; a new letter of the King's to the Prince, and sundry letters as from France, confirming them in these jealousies. We could never have abidden the half of their mad follies, had we not been retrained with the sight of the mischiefs which we saw were at hand upon the neck of both, if we should take fire at their daily provocations. The lamentable slaughter of Monro's army in Ireland, and Antrim coming over with 1500 men to Scotland, with our severe carriage toward the King, putting him out of all hopes of any compliance with the kingdom, also Argyle's authority and wise carriage here, has much stopt the mouths of our enemies here : but that which has done us most good, and brought greatest shame on them who most maligned us, is our passing the propositions without all delay, whereon they have stuck these ten months, and wherein they expected surely we would have made much greater difficulty. Also the scurvy base propositions which Cromwell has given to the malignants of Oxford, have offended many more than his former capitulation at Exeter ; all seeing the evident design of these conscientious men to the greatest conditions to the worst men, that they may be expeded for their northern warfare. Nothing so much affrays these men as a peace; albeit truly all men who are not nisled, see a very pregnant appearance of ruin to England, if they should war with us at this time. Our great fear is now from the King; his wilfulness is very great : if he should be so obstinate as to refuse the propositions, we will be put to a fearful perplexity. We resolve not to divide from England on any terms. If the King will not return upon just terms, what to do with him we cannot tell; but we hope our God will soften his heart to preserve himself and many others from great miseries. The Queen's counsels seem yet to sway all, and these to be still desperate. The French designs are, in my mind, contrary to the welfare of both kingdoms, and the Protestant cause : that monarchy will quickly be more terrible to us than Spain was before. Yet so mad are the sectaries, that they would be glad to drive us to the French. They are so blinded, that they think it a matter very easy to subdue our kingdom, though united and assisted by all the power which Ireland, France, Holland, Denmark,

and

nd all our friends in England, could make us. We pity
uch fury; and, by God's help, shall never tempt them,
s they needlefsly do us from time to time.

For the matters of our church, with much ado we got
he provincial commiffioners laid afide, and fo refolve to
&t.   The minifters of the affembly did meet with thofe of
London, and agreed upon a declaration for acting; fo
hat the next week they purpofe to fet up. I pray God
ie with them. It was defigned to fend nothing for religion but one line, that the King fhould ratify what the
arliament had or fhould vote. With much ado we rea-
oned them out of that ftrange motion; fo we expect all
heir ordinances fhall go. That for the directory, for or-
lination, for abolifhing Epifcopacy, for the prefbytery,
&c. What day, and by whofe hand, all will be fent, yet
we know not; but our confent fo quickly to fend the propofitions, though we affent not to all the matter, is much
cried up. We are afraid Montrofe and Antrim lay not
down arms; and if the King efcape to them, it will be a
woful cafe; fo much the more, as, in the leaders of this
people, we find no kindnefs nor wifdom. The parliament's queftions have retarded us much. Without them
we had ended the Confeffion of Faith. A committee has
prepared anfwers for them all, much for our advantage,
and contrary to the expectation of thofe who moved
them. All the fkill will be to pafs them without debate :
it will be endeavoured; but we fear great oppofition from
the Independents, who are as earneft as ever to keep
off all determinations, and make the confufions both of
church and ftate infinite. There are depofitions enow
in the prefbytery of Glafgow, Mr John Forfyth, Mr Gavin Forfyth, Mr Robert Tran; but their proceeding with
the Principal, Mr Wilkie, and Mr Edward, what it may
produce, I know not. I no ways love it. If thefe three
be depofed, peace in Glafgow in our days feems to me
defperate, whereof I am exceeding forry. God, in great
mercy, has kept me from among them all this while. I
am again on the prefs. I got never your opinion of the
former pamphlet. At this time I yoke with Maxwell and
Adamfon, who with bafe pamphlets have done our
church here much harm. The fectaries, of purpofe, reprinted their books, and carefully fpread them; but I
fhall make them repent it. Mr Henderfon had undertaken
the fervice; but being fent to Newcaftle, he laid it on me.

This

This much may serve you for one three weeks. I am glad of your wife her recovery; my service to her and kind Apollonius. We long for his book. Mr Gillespie has a large and learned treatise on his subject near printed. I am glad every other day to see Duke Hamilton and the Marquis of Argyle at our table. Long may these two gree well. We are in great fears of the King's obstinacy; if this mar us not, we are in a fair way to do well. You wrote for some things, but I forgot them, I pray you write again. Will you not put Forbes to write against the Anabaptists, Spanheim, Vossius, and Voetius also; these and the Antinomians plague our common people. I rest,   Your Cousin,

JAMESON.

148. *For Glasgow.*   *July* 14. 1646.

MATTERS here look better upon it, blessed be God, than sometimes they have. On Sunday, in all congregations of the city, the elders are to be chosen. So the next week, church-sessions in every parish, and twelve presbyteries within the city, and a provincial synod are to be set up, and quickly, without any impediment that we apprehend. The like is to be done over all the land. They go to this work unanimously and chearfully at last, I mean all but the sectaries. That it may the better succeed, there is on Thursday next a general fast over the city, which both the assembly and parliament do countenance. The work of the assembly, these bygone weeks, has been to answer some very captious questions of the parliament, about the clear scriptural warrant for all the punctilio's of the government. It was thought it would be impossible to us to answer, and that in our answers there should be no unanimity; yet, by God's grace, we shall deceive them who were waiting for our halting. The committee has prepared very solid and satisfactory answers already, almost to all the questions, wherein there is like to be an unanimity absolute in all things material, even with the Independents. But because of the assembly's way, and the Independents miserable unamendable design to keep all things from any conclusion, it is like we shall not be able to perfect our answers for some time; therefore I have put some of my good friends, leading men in

the

the Houfe of Commons, to move the affembly to lay afide our queftions for a time, and labour about that which is moft neceffary, and all are crying for the perfecting of, the Confeffion of Faith and Catechifm. If this motion take, I hope we fhall end fhortly our Confeffion, for there are but a few articles now to go through. It will be a very gracious and fatisfactory Confeffion when you fee it. We made, long ago, a pretty progrefs in the Catechifm; but falling on rubs and long debates, it was laid afide till the Confeffion was ended, with refolution to have no matter in it but what was expreffed in the Confeffion, which fhould not be debated over again in the Catechifm. If thefe two pieces, and the Catechifm, were out of our hands, our long work were at an end. All the corrections of Mr Rous's pfalms, and advices which come up from hence, were very friendly received, and almoft all of them followed. It is like the affembly and parliament here will, ere long, authorife the ufe of that oft corrected Pfalter. Whether you think meet to make ufe of it or not, it fhall be abfolutely in your own power. But that whereupon the eyes of all are fixed at this time, is the propofitions of peace. The fectarian party here are ftill very averfe from peace, if they could choofe. They made the propofitions fo ill as they were able, hoping we fhould never have paft them; yet, for many great caufes, we have fwallowed down the hardeft pills they prefented, to their great difappointment. So we have got at laft, with much ado, their commiffioners this day to Newcaftle. Argyle, to-morrow, will follow them. All that we heard before this day was, that the King would never take thefe propofitions; fo a worfe confufion than yet we have feen did prefent itfelf to our eyes, to our great grief and trouble, but to the joy and confidence of thefe here, whofe intereft it is to have war and confufion to continue: but, thanks to God, this day we are put in a pretty good hope that the King will follow advice. God's people had never more need to feek earneftly to him; for furely, if the King follow his nature and conftant practice, and but delay to pafs all thefe propofitions, how hard to him fo-ever, we cannot tell in all the world what to do next; and their fears and perplexities are greateft who underftand beft the prefent pofture of affairs in all the three kingdoms, and our neighbour nations. But if the Lord difpofe the heart of the King to do his duty, there is an appearance of a very gracious peace prefently. The Lord pour the fpirit of prayer on all his faints, in this fo needful a time. The city of London, and the whole land, continue and increafe in their defires of peace, and love of our nation, and hating of the fects, who, for their own wicked ends, would, with all their hearts, behold the deftruction of both nations. The city has avowed to the parliament, their defires to have the King back, and hardly has been hindered from fending fome of their prime men to him, with a petition to pafs the propofitions. Some of us, I think, muft, and I am fure one of us do long much to be at home. Mr Rutherford, Mr Gillefpie, and your friend alfo, are all on the prefs again, for the defence of our church, and truth of God, againft divers enemies.

The Turk is to opprefs the Venetians. The Emperor can make them no help. The French have taken in Orbitello in Tufcany, fcarce a day's journey from Rome. It is faid, the Pope, Florence, and Parma, are leaguing with Spain, to caft out the French there : however, neither Spain, Italy, nor France, can give any help againft the Turk. Pole is very willing, and has levied a great army to divert the Turk ; but the ftates of his kingdom are like to hinder his undertaking. The Swedes have joined their armies and their friends together near Marpurg. The Imperialifts and Bavarians, much of this month, have lien near them. Their forces are near equal : it is thought they will fight. Great appearance that the Hollanders will make peace with Spain ; for almoft all they could defire is offered them ; yet they are to the fields for this fummer very ftrong, and the French on the other fide as ftrong. The Spaniard is much ftronger than any one ; but will not be able to keep the field againft both. We are grieved and imbittered by the Prince's journey to Paris. It can produce no good ; yet God can bring light out of darknefs. Let this be fent weft to James Mitchell.

149. *To Mr William Spang.* *July* 17. 1646.

THIS I wrote to Glafgow on Tuefday laft, I can add no more news to count of. The French ambaffador got audience this day in both Houfes. So far as yet we can learn, his errand is good, to join the King and his parliaments

ments in our terms.   He applies himfelf moft to us.
Our hopes yet increafe that the King will do his duty.   Our
divifions among ourfelves are like to be too great ; but if
God give the countries peace, let men that feek themfelves
moft, divide the court among them.   Since neither grace
nor wifdom will learn them concord, they deferve no pity.
Let them beat one another as they will, there is never a
dint ftroke among courtiers. ——

150. *For Mr Henderfon.   Saturday, July 18. 1646.*

SIR,
I hope you got my laft with Daniel Carmichael.   You
have here one from Dr. Burgefs.   It now comes near the
choak.   I am trembling for your anfwer to our propofi-
ions.   I am grieved that your refolutions fhould depend
fo abfolutely upon France, and that upon a party there,
who have been fo evidently foolifh, wicked, and pernicious.   Your debates upon Epifcopacy I never took to be
confcientious, but merely politick, and a pretence to gain
time.   I hear France has, or will loofe that fcruple of
confcience very eafily.   Will fuch bafe hypocrify be bleffed ?   The French ambaffador is all compofed of honefty,
and has no other errand but peace ; yet I do no ways like
his his almoft abrupt running to you at fo unfeafonable a
time.   The paffing of the propofition for Epifcopacy will
not do your turn now.   You have that good property to
do all out of time.   Though you pafs the militia and Ireland, that will not do it neither.   We would beg of you
to ftand upon any one thing.   Let the French perfuade
you to do it, and we fhall blefs them ; for it is our only
fear, that you pafs all, and fo quickly return, and be our
mafters.   But ftick upon any thing we have fent, we fhall
quickly eftablifh ourfelves in a republick, and forfwear
kings for ever ; for you have been fo exceffively bloody
and falfe, that God and man calls for your extirpation ;
fpecially now, when the world fees your remedilefs obftinacy, and full refolution to go on in your falfe and hypo-
critick way.   Better once for all be rid of you, and all
who will take your part.   This, Sir, I find to be the heart
of many, whofe fenfe I expected fhould have been much
otherwife.   I marvel to fee the fimplicity of fome, who
think your condefcenfion in fome main things will do your

urn. I profefs, thefe men whom you will find flatter you
n fuch counfels, I fufpect their defigns are to ruin the
poor prince for their own ends. Sir, if you have any
power, let that man come off once very frankly in all
things, and he fhall have all he ought to defire. Will he
do it by halfs and quarters, he is running to utter deftruction; who can help it! Yet I muft be one of the mourn-
ers for it. Sir, give over your difputations; they are but
vain. It is now near the fool's faying, They will make
prince elector of thee. O the madnefs of blinded men,
that no experience will teach them to fave themfelves and
thoufands from evident mifchief. The Lord help and affift you to do and fay what becomes, be the event what it
may. All men I fee feek themfelves above all things, either publick or private.

.Your Servant,

ROBERT BAILLIE.

151. *For Mr Henderfon.* London, *Auguft* 4. 1646.

Reverend and Dear Brother,

YOUR ficknefs has much grieved my heart. It is a part
of my prayers to God, to reftore you to health, and continue your fervice at this fo neceffary a time. We never
had fo much need of you as now. I have fent you at laft
my pamphlet. It has ftuck on the prefs thefe feven weeks,
through the fottifhnefs of the printers. Our brethren are
all content with it. I was altogether averfe from intermeddling with it, till you at your departure fpoke to me
of it. But what do I fpeak of fuch toys? The King's
madnefs has confounded us all. We are in a woful evil
taking; we know not what to do, nor what to fay. We
know well the weight that lies on your heart. I fear this
be the fountain of your difeafe; yet I am fure, if you
would take courage, and digeft what cannot be got a-
mended, and if, after the fhaking off melancholious
thoughts, the Lord might be pleafed to ftrengthen you at
this time, you would much more promote the honour of
God, the welfare of Scotland and England, the comfort
of many thoufands, than you can do by weakening of
your body and mind with fuch thoughts as are unprofitable. George has been fhipping your things this day with
Robert Hamilton of the Pans, who goes with the firft fair
wind.

wind. The great God fill your heart with ftrength and
comfort from his own face. Thus I reft,

Your moft loving brother and fervant,

ROBERT BAILLIE.

152. *For Mr Robert Blair.　London, Auguft 4. 1646.*

Reverend and Dear Brother,

I caufed buckle up the laft winter fundry of my pamphlets for you. They fell by a miftake in the hands of
Humbie his fon's pedagogue. I hope he gave them to you,
as Mr Samuel directed him. I have neither a mind, nor
great fitnefs, to appear in print; yet it has been my fortune much ofter than I thought to come out in this kind.
At this time all my colleagues are my witneffes, how loth
I was to meddle with more printing; yet all thought it neceffar I fhould make this anfwer. In my Epiftle I thought
it my duty to let the world know my obligations to you.
I hope you will take this teftimony of the thankfulnefs
of my heart in good part, till I have occafion to declare
the fame by deed. I have burdened James Hamilton with
twelve copies; one is for himfelf, one for you. You will
be pleafed to deliver a third to dear Mr Henderfon, and a
fourth to my coufin, Lieut.-Gen. Baillie, a fifth to the
Governor, Sir James Lumfdale, a fixth to my Lord Crawford, a feventh to my Lord Lanerk. The other five I intreat you to knit together, and fend them to Mr Andrew
Ker, with my letter to him, who will diftribute them as I
direct him. The King's anfwer has broken our hearts.
We fee nothing but a fea of new more horrible confufions.
We are afraid of the hardnefs of God's decree againft that
madman, and againft all his kingdoms. We look above
to God; for all below is full of darknefs. The Lord affift you in your uncomfortable fervice. So I reft,

Your Brother,

ROBERT BAILLIE.

153. *For Mr William Spang.　Auguft 7. 1646.*

Coufin,

I am now two to the fore with you, albeit I wrote none
the laft poft; for I was at Oxford, the beft built and
booked

booked univerfity in the world, but the worft provided of
learned and orthodox men I know of any. We were lately in fome good hopes of an happy end of our long troubles, but now we are very near defperate of that. After
all poffible endeavours by all unanimoufly, Scots, Englifh,
French, fo far as yet we know, the King refufes the propofitions. We expect on Monday the Chancellor and Argyle, with the Englifh commiffioners. After their report
to the Houfes, we fear fad votes. It will be our endeavour to keep them from fudden conclufions. They take
very long time to the fmalleft affairs : I fear they be too
quick in depofing the King, and fetting a day to the
Prince. We are at a great nonplus, in very great grief
and perplexity. We know not what either to fay or do.
There is before us a thick cloud of confufion. Many of
the King's greateft friends think his obftinacy judicial, as
if, in God's juftice, he were deftroying himfelf. I fear
he will down with him all his pofterity, and monarchy.
Alfo in this ifle we have very fmall hopes of doing any
more with him, and many thoufands more of his beft
fubjects. This is the great joy of the prevalent party, the
thing they panted for with all earneftnefs. Our griefs and
fears are great, and for the time we are in a great ftupi-
dity and aftonifhment. It will be our endeavour to keep
the nations together, albeit we fcarce fee the poffibility of
it. Mr Henderfon is dying moft of heartbreak at Newcaftle. Our grandees are like to be ftate-fchifmaticks, and
the worft fide to be the ftrongeft. A truly pious and really publick man is a rare piece upon earth. Mr Gillefpie
will fend you over his learned book. My pamphlet, with
thefe pieces I anfwer, I give now to Mr Tirrence. I fend
three more, with my fervice, to Mr Cunningham, Mr
Stuart, and Mr Apollonius. I have feen the Paris Bible;
it is 50 lb. price. I think your printers at Amfterdam or
Leyden might give us the Arabick and Syriack Bible, alfo
the Chaldea paraphrafe, for a fmall price, to their own
great advantage. A marvel that no man there will perfuade thefe printers to do fo good a turn for their own benefit. A pity but Eyrenius's manufcript Arabick dictio-
nary were perfected. Grief and anxiety makes me cut
off. The Lord be with you. My fervice to your wife.
So I reft,

    Your Coufin,

                      ROBERT BAILLIE.

154. For

154. *For Mr Henderson.* *August* 13. 1646.

SIR,

THOUGH I have little purpose, yet I could not let George go without two or three lines. Your weakness is much regretted by many here. To me it is one of the sad presages of the evils coming. If it be the Lord's will, it is my hearty prayer oft times you might be lent to us yet for some time. Upon the great appearance of our full compliance with this people, the most seem to applaud our carriage towards the King; but how long, I doubt. It seems the most here are inclined to declare against the King, and that without much regret. I know no remeid, but a quick message from him to grant all. I wish our meeting at Edinburgh would yet send to him for that effect; but I fear it be too late. In all things he continues to be extremely unhappy. Montreuil and his letters were taken by sea. Believer's brother posting by land, after a a sore fall, sent his letters by an express, with the speaker's pass; yet the man was stopped, and his letters taken from him. The parliament's agents write still from Paris, that the Duke of Lorrain shall winter in England; that Bavaria is upon the league, upon an express condition, that the King shall meddle no more in the Palatine cause; that 100,000 crowns are sent into Scotland from France, by the way of Holland. The belief of these things, how false soever, is equivalent to their truth. Ormond's pacification with the Irish is very unseasonable; the placing of Hobbes (a professed Atheist as they speak) about the Prince as his teacher, is ill taken. In the assembly we were like to have stuck many months on the questions; and the Independents were in a way to get all their differences debated over again. I dealt so with Mr Rous and Mr Tate, that they brought us an order from the House to lay aside the questions till the Confession and Catechism were ended. Many took it for a trick of the Independents and Erastians for our hurt; but I knew it was nothing less. We are now near an end of our Confession. We stick on the article of synods, upon the proposition of their coercive power, or their power to excommunicate. If this were over, we apprehend no more long debates on the Confession. The committee for the Catechism has well near
ended

ended their work.   It must be perfected before any part
of it be reported.   The election of elders in the most of
the parishes of London is passed with a cordial unanimity,
and these who are chosen approved by the triers.   We
expect classical meetings speedily.   There is this day to be
presented to the House an honest and high petition, like
to the city-remonstrance, from Lancashire, subscribed with
12,500 hands and above.   The French are like this year to
have very bad success, both in Italy, Spain, and West
Flanders, and to break at home.   If you see not to it, I
fear great divisions among our own statesmen; but our
great God can help all these things.   His spirit strengthen,
comfort, and encourage you to the end.   So I rest in my
hearty love and reverence toward you.

155. *For Mr Robert Blair.*   *August 18. 1646.*

Reverend and Dear Brother,
   I am glad you take my dedication in good part.   None
who know my obligations to you, can offend that I should
acknowledge them.   When you have read the book, let
me have your judgement of the matter.   You must not so
weary of your charge as not to go about it chearfully, and
to do in it all the good you can for your short time.   It is
well that Mr Andrew Ramsay's treatise has done what Mr
Henderson and all the rest of you could not do.   But it is
a pity that base hypocrisy, when it is pellucid, should still
be entertained.   No oaths did ever persuade me, that E-
piscopacy was ever adhered to on any conscience.   I e-
steemed all your debates on that subject to be but ridiculous pretexts to gain time, till the last resolution came
from your masters beyond sea; and now, when it is come,
are you so wise as to dream, that the abolition of Episcopacy will give any satisfaction?   Will that plum please
Scotland so well, as to make them join with the malignants against England?   Will your new officers of state,
new Lords and Knights, draw that nation at your heels?
Have you been so long in the mortar, and beaten so much
with the pestle, and that folly is not yet driven from you?
All your friends here lament at your palpable extœcation;
but all abhor these ambitious madmen, who will destroy a
more than half-destroyed prince, by betraying him with
their flatteries.   With much diligence, and art, and great
                                                  perplexities,

perplexities, we ftrive every day to keep the Houfe of Commons from falling on the King's anfwer. We know not what hour they will clofe their doors, and declare the King fallen from his throne ; which if they fhould once do, we put no doubt but all England would concur ; and if any fhould mutter againft it, they would be quickly fupprefled. Do not expect, that ever any more meffages will come to you from this. If within a very few days you fend not hither a fimple and abfolute grant of all the propofitions, without any *if*, or *and*, you will quickly obtain your defire. A martyrdom, a perpetual clofe prifon at leaft, will be your portion ; and that without the pity of many. If yet you would do what within a few weeks you will on your knees beg to be permitted to do, but in vain, you might fave all. Why is no courfe taken to declare them infamous for ever that do enfnare the King, by taking any honour, place, or promife, from him in his prefent condition ? Shall fuch unhappy bribers be enabled by any more truft in their country to do mifchief ? Be obftinate but a little more, and all here, without any more vexing of themfelves, will let you take your will, and play the fool while you live. All that favour the King in England are not worth a button, if he make any more fcruple in any of our demands. Thefe falfe, traiterous whifperers, that would make the blinded prince believe, that the fectaries are not his extremely malicious enemies, burning for the day to caft him and all his pofterity out of England, they are impudent liars. I fometimes weep in fecret for the inexpreffible evils, which, moft needlefsly, that man is haftening on himfelf, and his whole houfe, and many thoufands of his poor fubjects ; but if fo it muft be, the Lord's will be done. The Lord make you faithful and wife at fo ftrange a nick of time. I reft, &c.

ROBERT BAILLIE.

156. *For Mr David Dickfon.   Auguft 18. 1646.*

IN the affembly we are returned to the Confeffion of Faith, and are drawing towards the end of it. The Catechifm is almoft all paffed through the committee. If thefe were done, likely the affembly may adjourn, that the members thereof may go down to their feveral fhires, to affift the erecting of feflions, prefbyteries, and

fynods. They have gone on in London, and have chofen very many gracious and able elders. The triers publickly have taken account of them, both of their life and knowledge, with their own confent. None have refufed to be tried: they are all chofen for life: they will be a great help and ftrength to the government. The King's unhappy refufal of the propofitions has put us here in a great deal of confufion and perplexity. The fectaries do exceedingly rejoice; the reft are in great fadnefs. The great danger was, that the Houfe of Commons prefently without any more, fhould declare againft the King. Our great care was to prevent that great mifchief; for if they once had paffed a vote to demand the King, to remove our army, to fend their army northward, there was no remeid. Therefore we made ready a paper before their commiffioners returned, and prefented it at the very back of their commiffioners report, of our willingnefs to difband our army, and give up the garrifons upon reafonable fatisfaction; and our defire to take, by common advice, a courfe for fettling of the kingdoms. The noife of our very good carriage at Newcaftle, the great equity of our paper, our private dealing with our friends in the Houfes, made our motions taken: fo we have got them to confider firft the matter of our army before they came to the King's anfwer. We hope to keep them on this for fome days, till the King have a little more time to be better advifed. And fuch diligence has been ufed, that we hear he is coming near us. Some farther inftructions are come to him from France, and the harmonious refolution of both nations, to take a courfe without him if he will not be advifed, is more apparent to him than before. The great hazard is, that he confent not fully to all, and quickly, fo a qualified confent, or a full confent a little delayed, will undo him. The running of unhappy men upon him, for honours and places, is a great fnare to him. Such untimeous honours are very hurtful both to the giver and taker. It is all our fkill to gain a little time. Their firft offer to us was of L. 100,000 Sterling for the difbanding of our army. We, this day, gave them in a paper wherein we were peremptor for more than double that fum for the prefent, befides the huge fums which we crave to be paid afterward. They have appointed a committee to confer with us; we are in fome hopes of agreement. The money muft be borrowed in the city, and
here

here will be the question. They are our loving friends; but before they will part with more money, they will press hard the disbanding of their own army as ours. If they obtain this, the sectaries will be broken; if they obtain it not, the pride of the sectaries will be intolerable. The advices the King gets from France, are the more moderate, because of their present misfortunes. Their army in Italy is with great loss and shame sent home. In Catalonia they have not much prospered this year. In West Flanders, the Spaniards from Mardyke, near Dunkirk, have killed a great many noblemen and commanders to them. The Hollanders do no good this summer; for they are bent, for fear of the French greatness, to take peace with Spain. The Prince of Conde is like to fall foul with the Cardinal, so the French have the less will to meddle with England. The Turk is incroaching sore upon the Venetians in Dalmatia. The Swedith and Imperial armies are yet looking one upon another, near Frankfort.

157. *For Glasgow. To Mr Robert Ramsay. London, August* 18. 1646.

Reverend and Dear Brother,

Yours, with Mr Legge, yesterday I received. I thank you for it. I have written to Mr David this once more for that matter I importuned you for. You and Mr George will be pleased to consider what I say there. For our affairs here, you will read them in the publick letter, which you will send west to James Mitchell. I purpose to send his informations to Paris to Dr Davison; so I wish with the first you let me know from himself his present condition. Whatever is in my power I would be glad to do it for that gracious man. We are here, by the King's madness, in a terrible plunge. The powerful faction desires nothing so much as any colour to cast the King and all his race away, to have a quarrel with us: this they will get if the King stick but for a few days many of the propositions. Many here will regret it; but none will oppose. With great difficulty we drive over a little time, and to our utmost labours with the King. He never did any good turn in due time; our people, I fear, be a snare to him. Divisions are like to increase, and the best to be borne down most. Worse evils hang above

                                                    the

the head of poor Scotland than yet we have suffered, except the Lord prevent, and such as I cannot see their end. Blasphemous heresies rage here every where, without any controul, to this day. Warnings are clear and zealous; but a few that make it their work to patronise and advance a horrible liberty, mars all. This nation also is in a temper to fall in a worse war than the former. God help us, we had need to pray. Never people nearer to a bottomless pit of horrible evils. I am exceeding weary of this life; and so soon as I can, will beg leave to be gone. Mr Henderson's absence, and the variable health both of Mr Gillespie and Mr Rutherford, has kept me the stricter; but I hope our work is near a period. By this time I think you have my last book. ———

So I rest,   Your Brother,

ROBERT BAILLIE.

158. *For Mr Tate.*

Right Worshipful,

THAT you may not forget whereof yesternight we spoke, I have sent you this memorandum. 1. That the ordinances for setting up the government in the country, and against blasphemies, after so much delay, may at last be expedited. 2. That when the matter of itinerant preachers comes again in hand, some rules may be made for their election and work; at least that they may be tried by the assembly, and be found not men infamous for errors, as many think your three first to be. 3. That you mind the Oxford committee, and see the rules already past be put in the ordinance: That all masters, fellows, and scholars, take the covenant, and be willing to act in their places, according to the ordinances of parliament; and why should not Oxford have the favour which Manchester shewed to Cambridge? That all the new masters and fellows be tried by the assembly. Consider if Mr Lee, a very able and deserving man, ought to be set aside, only for his zeal against Independents: the deanry of Christ's church is due. The ministers would be sent to Oxford with all speed. 4. The pious and honest petition of Lancashire, a speedy hearing and favourable answer. It is the work of some to have it slighted and disgraced. 5. We have great need that now and then, were it but one half hour in the week,

you

you should come to the assembly, and exhort us to diligence; also to clear handsomely the mistake of many, that your earnestness for the end of the Confession and Catechism, is nothing less than for the suppressing of the answer to the questions, or for the dissolving of the assembly. Sir, if such things be not minded by you, and some others, as your special work; that which is most dear to you, the honour, truth, and church of God, is like to suffer yet more. Your more than ordinary favour to me makes be bold to be your remembrancer.

159. *For Mr William Murray.*　　*September* 8. 1646.

Memorandum from your agent.

1. That what was promised to me in your name be really performed. I neither have, nor ever mind to have, any use of your service for myself; yet I should be glad to have that promise performed, (God will not ever be mocked): you shall never be a happy instrument for any good to yourself, or your friends, or the publick, if after so fair warnings, and great sparing, you will again run in rebellion against God's clear commands, and into treason against your own soul; doubtless a worse evil, if any worse upon earth may be, than what lately was near you, cannot but overtake and fall upon you if you return to your old ways. My care and diligence for you, in your hardest times, will excuse this liberty.

2. As you would be thankful to your master for all his favours to you, flatter him not now to his ruin. All with whom I converse, how willing soever to forget bygones if he will take the propositions, yet I assure you, so far as I can observe, are as willing, without any regret, to have him destroyed, if he will go on in his obstinacy. His partial and qualified grants, are taken but for tricks to make new divisions and parties for the compassing of his former designs, and these things will no longer be borne.

3. It is exceedingly provoking, that his resolutions should, at such a time, depend upon France. Shall nothing within himself, or nothing within this isle, be able to advise him? His kingdoms will not be governed by packets from over-sea. Such open indignities are at no time sufferable.

4. If

4. If he do not defire to ruin the innocent Prince with himfelf, bring him quickly out of France; or, if this now be not in his power, let Hobbes, and fuch wicked men, be put from about him, and the ill-beft there taken into his fervice.

5. If he will yet join with Ireland, and endeavour divifions in Scotland and here, to embroil all in a new war, rather than take the propofitions; then let him know, the remainder of love and pity, which in the heart of many yet remains towards him, is ready to be extinguifhed, and all I know will be moft willing to have him, and all who adhere to him, brought to their ruin, without any more compaffion.

6. If you have any love and pity towards poor Scotland, endeavour to divert its engagement in a new war, before fuch a defign can be fet on foot. The beft of that land, who cannot but oppofe it, muft be crufhed, and this oppreffion will cry to Heaven for more vengeance; and when all the power of that broken and defolate land is brought out, what will it do but deftroy itfelf, and become the infamous inftrument of lofing to the King and his pofterity for ever, that which, without their unhappy intermeddling, he might have been perfuaded to have accepted, without more trouble or hazard to himfelf or others. None but fools will dream of a party to any purpofe in this land. All with whom I fpeak, put it out of queftion, that if a new war fhould arife, the greateft malecontents here fhall either be quickly fatisfied, or elfe be fo ordered, as not to be able to make any oppofition to that party which is inclined, and on fuch an occafion fhall be greatly furthered, to exterminate royalty.

7. I have many good witneffes of my refpects to monarchy, and to King Charles's perfon, above many, if not all my fellows. This confcience makes me the more earneft to have fuch truths reprefented to him without difguife, and oft ingeminated in his ears, with freedom, as may prevent, if poffible, the evident and imminent ruin of his perfon and pofterity. Curfed be all thefe villains who now will be fo mad as to betray by their wicked compliances an ill-advifed and bewitched prince.

160. *For*

160. *For Mr William Murray.*

Right Worſhipful,

It was your pleaſure to give me two kind viſits in my chamber. What then I purpoſed to have ſaid to you, but was interrupted therein by thoſe who came in upon us, I have taken the boldneſs to write it to you in this memorandum, as my obſervation from my converſe with divers citizens and divines of the beſt note among the Engliſh. I doubt not but you know from many hands much more than all this, yet I thought meet that you ſhould have this much from me alſo, in teſtimony of my freedom with you, and of my love and compaſſion towards a periſhing prince, and three kingdoms ready to fall in extreme miſeries. Nothing doubting of your favourable acceptance, I reſt,

Your loving friend and agent,

ROBERT BAILLIE.

161. *To Mr David Dickſon.* September 22. 1646.

Reverend and Dear Brother,

—— We have ended the Confeſſion of Faith for the matter, and have perfected the moſt half of its nineteen chapters. The other ſeventeen, I hope, in a ten or twelve days will be perfected, and ſo all be ſent up to the Houſes. It will be, I hope, a very ſweet and orthodox piece, much better than any Confeſſion yet extant, if the Houſe of Commons mangle it not to us. We are now upon the Catechiſm. We hope that alſo ſhall be a very good and plain piece. We are now at work, thanks to God, in earneſt much more than ever. If the race hold, I truſt this alſo in a month ſhall be over, and then Mr Rutherford and I will ſupplicate the commiſſion for a demiſſion. Mr Gilleſpie will be abundance to attend the queries. It will be a great queſtion when you ſhall think meet to call a general aſſembly. We yet know not what to adviſe. It will be neceſſary to have the Confeſſion and Catechiſm approven in a general aſſembly, as the Directory was; but we fear the condition of your affairs at this time, will ſcarce permit you to hazard to call one. Always be

thinking

thinking on this; for it will be a great deliberandum
ſhortly.　To-morrow, the Houſe of Commons debate the
ordinance againſt hereſies and blaſphemies; we are very
ſolicitous for it.　The orthodox and heterodox party will
yoke about it with all their ſtrength, the Lord be among
them; for the right or wrong carrying of that buſineſs is
of a huge conſequence, and nothing beyond it but another queſtion which this day is handled, How to diſpoſe
of the King's perſon?　Great need had you there, as in
my laſt I warned you, to ſee to the election of commiſſioners to the parliament, both in the burghs and ſhires.
If that choice fall wrong, Scotland is in hazard to be
ruined.　It is like you may ſee the Marquis of Argyle
ſhortly.　The Lord help him out of his trouble; his
enemies are many, and friends for any purpoſe but few;
yet God is not dead.　My ſervice to Margaret, Mr John,
and all the reſt.　I reſt,
　　　　Your Brother,
　　　　　　　　　　　ROBERT BAILLIE.

162. *For Mr Spang.　October 2. 1646.*

Dear Couſin,
　THESE three or four poſts I did not write to you, partly through lazineſs, and partly upon expectation of farther and better matter; and now, when there is no better
purpoſe, I am ſomewhat alſo diverted: yet left I be too
long in your debt, I muſt write ſomewhat.　I was minded
to have certified you in ſome miſtakes of your former letter; but it is now fallen by, and I cannot find it.　The
falſe reports which went here of Mr Henderſon, are, I
ſee, alſo come to your hand.　Believe me, for I have it
under his own hand a little before his death, that he was
utterly diſpleaſed with the King's ways, and ever the longer the more; and whoever ſay otherwiſe, I know they
ſpeak falſe.　That man died as he lived, in great modeſty,
piety, and faith.
　Matters in Glaſgow go not well.　My advice, which oft
I ſent with intreaties, was never followed; but as yet I
think the refuſers, though they did not well, yet committed no great fault, all things well conſidered.　The former magiſtrates were more obſtinately oppoſite to every
thing which our gracious brethren did propoſe, for the
I　　　　　　　　　　　　　　　　　　　　　　　furtherance

furtherance of piety in that town, than I ever did fee any
where elfe. When their capitulation with Montrofe put
them in the reverence of the ftate, and the committee of
parliament found it expedient to remove all who had confented to that capitulation, I thought it had been better to
have removed from the magiftracy, feffion, and council,
rather fome than all; and if they had been fo ftrict, it
feemed juft to have dealt fo in Linlithgow, Irvine, Ayr,
St Andrew's, efpecially Edinburgh, whofe fault, in my
judgement, was much greater than Glafgow's. But fince
the ftate took that courfe, I thought it no fault in our
brethren to fuggeft the names of thefe whom they counted
moft ferviceable to God and the publick, and to countenance them in the difcharge of their office. That which
exceedingly augmented the malecontentment of that people,
was the great burdens. They were preffed by a great garrifon,
and the making of a very extenfive and unprofitable ditch
through their lands and yards; but in this our brethren
had no hand to count of. The challenges that came on
the Principal, Mr Edward, and Mr William Wilkie, and
others, they procured them themfelves. There was great
reafon to defire Mr Edward to be tranfported. I dealt
what I could to ftop all proceeding againft the other two;
and hopes, by our brotherly means, to obtain it. But
their laft bickering is like to be worft; James Bell en-
deavouring to have the former magiftrates and council
joined with the prefent in the new election; as indeed I
could not much blame him to defire it, confidering the general courfe which the ftate took with all other burghs
and fhires. I remember I advifed Mr David half a year
ago to take the very fame courfe; for without it I faw no
way of peace; and had it come from him, it would have,
in my mind, done well. But James Bell would
it too much, and would have added to the prefent council, not only the old, but alfo all living who had ever been
deacons of crafts. This put it in his hand to caft out all
the prefent magiftrates and council, and fo was eafily got
ranverfed, and that whole matter referred to the next feffion of parliament, where I wifh it may be determined to
the good of all.

We were here in a good way, and very great hopes, to
have clofed all quickly and well; but we are now fallen in
a very great cloud, and fear. I pray God bring us fafe
out of it. When the King's unhappy anfwer to the com-

miffioners of both parliaments did come hither, it was our great care to divert this parliament from all deliberation a-bout the King till he had yet fome more time of advice. We caft in the debate of our army's return, and render-ing the garrifons. With much labour we got that to a good point, to the contentment of all. We got the par-liament to put the affembly fo to it, that we expected a quick end both of our Confeffion and Catechifm. All our fear was of a too great compliance of Duke Hamilton and his friends with the King, of which there was too pregnant appearance; yet that fear proved groundlefs: for all thefe men have concurred as effectually to prefs the King to take the propofitions as we could have wifhed; though, in the carriage of it, they committed three or four flips of very grofs imprudence very needlefsly, where-by they offended a little both the King and the church, and the country and this people. But in fubftance they have hitherto, to the acknowledgement of all, done and fpoken honeftly enough. When thus all was running well, behold fuddenly many crofs accidents. We had la-boured much, and were in full confidence to have Alder-man Langham Lord Mayor of London; but, by the run-ning of fome, Gayer is the man, a greater malignant than fectary; yet many hope well of him. The affembly obli-ged themfelves by promife to fit before and after noon for fome time; but now, thinking they have fatisfied the Houfes, by fending up the half of the Confeffion, the firft nineteen heads, they are relapfed into their former negligence. So we will be able few days in a week to make an affembly; for if there be one fewer than forty, it is no meeting; and though the reft of the heads be alfo paft, yet, in the review, the alteration of words, and the me-thodifing, take up fo much time, that we know not when we fhall end. Befides that we have fome additionals, e-fpecially one propofition, about liberty of confcience, wherein the Independents offer to keep us long and tough debates; for long ago they have laid down in this their mafh, and plead for a liberty well near univerfal. Our long labours on the pfalms, when ready to be put in prac-tice, are like, by a faction, to be altogether ftilled. They will have a liberty to take what pfalter they will. The un-expected death of the brave Earl of Effex has wounded us exceedingly. He was the head of our party here, kept all together, who now are like by that alone to fall in pieces.

The

The House of Lords absolutely, the city very much, and very many of the shires, depended on him; but that which vexes us most is, that the King is so unhappy that he will do nothing till he have undone himself and us. Had he but granted the substance of the propositions, we would have guided it well enough; but his hopes of our divisions, and expectation from France, puts him further off than ever.   In Oxford he was willing to have taken all the propositions; also he gave commission to Ormond to pass these horrible propositions of peace with Ireland: so no man thinks his denial of our desires is either of conscience or honour.   This puts us to difficulties inextricable.   They have passed a vote of disposing the King's person as their two Houses shall think fit, without any reference to us.   We press, by many unanswerable reasons, our joint interest.   They deny it.   It is like we may join in advising, and get the question of power laid aside; but when we come to advise, we know not what to say.   We expect one of these days William Murray with the King's last answers.   We are certain they will not satisfy.   Their course thereafter with the King will be more summar than we readily can join in peace.   We see an inundation of evils; except the great God arise we are undone.   These things were the subject of yesterday's full debate betwixt the two Houses and our commissioners.   We expected L. 200,000 to have been put in our army's hand within a fortnight, and the sectarian army disbanded, and that party humbled, government presently set up, the ordinance against sects and heresies that now is in debate to pass, and be execute; but the King's obstinacy is like to mar all. And having done all we can, we know not what to do with him next.   The good Chancellor is distempered with grief, and I with him also, and others of us; God help us.   When we get better news ye shall get part; for the time I am not well neither in body or mind.   Farewell.

163. *For Mr George Young.   October* 13. 1646.

George,
———Things here are in a marvellous ambiguity betwixt great hope and imminent despair.   The King, by the conspiracy of all about him, without the exception of one, is driven to his particular answer of the propositions.   It is

resterday, as we expect, sent from Newcastle hither by William Murray. By many an express, by three or four :ven since Argyle went from us, we have given fair warnng of the mischief which every day evidently draws near, ind have been importunately begging the grant of the propositions, as that which alone is divertive of ruin ; but we have to do with the most careless and ill-advised person in the world. The evil party here is driving on their design to profligate monarchy every day by the King's hand more than any other. The unreasonable vote of disposing of the King's person as their two Houses of Parliament think meet, without the least reference to Scotland, they still adhere to. In three solemn meetings, the Chancellor, Warifton, and Lauderdale, did so outreason them, that all the hundreds of hearers did grope their infolent absurdities; but for no other purpose, than to draw from them another very unexpected vote, of keeping up the army for six months more. The keys, the sword, and money, and preferments, in the hands of the sectaries. With much ado have we kept the report of these three conferences from the Houses, to be made in four or five sheets, on Thursday, by ourselves. The King's answer cannot be here till Monday. In the mean time they are so peremptor, that they may pass a vote, declaring the King, for no scant of faults, incapable to govern while he lives. If this nail be once rooved, we with our teeth will never get it drawn. If we get it delayed a few days, till the answer come, it is well ; but when that much-expected answer comes, if it be not satisfactory, as we are extremely afraid for it, then, by all appearance, this people, without more delay, will strike the fatal stroke ; the consequences whereof I am oft troubled to think upon. If the answer were satisfactory, as some hope there is that at least in time it may be so, if the patience of this people, by all diligence we can use, may be kept but for a few weeks unbroken, all would go well.

For matters of religion, albeit for the time in an extreme ill posture, yet are in a case of thriving, if the accommodating of the King did permit men but to draw up their fainting spirits. The fear of that miscarriage lets no man mind any thing else. London and Lancashire goes on with the presbyteries and sessions but languidly. Sundry other shires are making to ; but all the errors of the world are raging over all the kingdom. God save Scotland

land from that pest! In the ordinance against that evil there is some little progress made. To-morrow, by God's help, we expect a farther. Our assembly for one twenty days posted hard; but since have got into its old pace. The first half, and more, of the Confession, we sent up to the House. The end of these who called for it, was the shuffling out the ordinance against errors: yet our friends have carried to go on with that. But others have carried the putting of scriptures to the margin of the Confession, which may prove a very long business, if not dextrously managed. It will be yet a fortnight before the other half of it be ready; for sundry necessar, but scabrous propositions, were added in the review. We have passed near a quarter of the Catechism; but we will not in earnest win to it till the Confession be off our hand. I am near ready to speak a word with the Anabaptists. I dare say, too much ease has not been hitherto in me or my colleague's disease. If any there desire any of our books, any of our merchants may send to James Parlane for so many as they think they will sell; for me, I will not meddle into it. My heart is at home long ago. The Lord knows, I am praying to God, and waiting for a door opened to return, which shortly I expect. This must serve you and your two neighbours. Tell Mr David his book is now selling, and in a good way of offgoing. The half sheet of the very encouraging Elogia of the prolocutor Herle, and the assessor Palmer, and of us three, he shall receive with the next. Copies of what we have done I may not send down; yet I shall do my best to have a copy of the Confession at you so soon as it is closed, if ye give me assurance of keeping it among yourselves three. For buying of books, I desire to supersede till you see to whom these shall belong you have already. I have said so much, that I think I ought to say no more to you three in the behalf of Mr Wilkie. I were inexcusably senseless if I put any doubt, that whatever comes on him by occasion of these letters, I, and I only, were the occasion of it; and I am sure all three of you, before the incident of these letters, assured me sundry times he was in no hazard. If I have any power with any of you, be intreated now at last to end that very great vexation of my mind, and let me hear that ye have settled him peaceably in his ministry. Whatever conditions you require of him, I will either make them good, or assure you to concur to punish the

breach

breach of them. If in this you be rigid, I cannot but be more grieved than I will exprefs. What great din is in all our univerfities and affemblies upon the Principal's dictates! to this day I could never hear the true grounds of it. I am fure none of you can have a thought of removing that man from his place, except ye know much more of him than we wont. Not any here has any fuch mind. Ding his bufinefs dead fo foon as ye are able. Some of the chief fticklers therein are in great hazard of drawing themfelves to them; for there be evil furmifes on them. However, it is a thing I cannot digeft with patience, to fee the preparative led to bring all profeffors dictates *in prima inftantia* to a general affembly, and the reft of the univerfities. This is a way to keep the church and fchools of Scotland in a perpetual unquietnefs. Is the Principal of that humour, to teach any thing which, upon his coleagues firft admonition, he is not content to keep to himfelf? For will the moft rigorous juftice call him to any cenfure? No man the other day in the affembly, when his cafe was on the table, did offer to contradict it; fo it is paffed in the Confeffion of Faith. I think, if I were one hour among you, I could, by God's help, make you all good friends. Believe it, I muft and will have it fo; or elfe you muft pardon me fome time in fecret to weep my fill, but never to leave off to do my own part to my power, and to ferve you all as God fhall enable me. If God will make us fo happy as to get the unhappy King and the parliament atoned, be affured I will fend a command to you three to bring, by God's blefling, that poor town and college to a better harmony, whereof I would defire, when you had the happinefs to make it to have the good hap to be its fequefter. The Lord be with you, and make my next to you fo comfortable as my hopes, wifhes, or more than my fears, prefage. However, I reft juft as when I left you, without any change,

      Your very loving Brother,

                  Robert Baillie.

POSTSCRIPT.

Dunkirk is in the hand of the French at a very cheap rate. Lerida they fhortly expect. The Pope, for fear of them, has given the Barbarins all their will. The
                          Emperor

Emperor offers to France fo much of Germany as they crave, and almoft to the Swedes alfo.   The Hollanders are very near agreed with Spain.   The Venetian is on the point of fubmiffion to the Turk.   All the world is on a-greeance, and miferable we are like to begin a new war; but I hope God will prevent it.   Ormond's three honour-able meffengers are here with his fubmiffion.

164. *To Mr David Dickfon.*   *October* 27. 1646.

Reverend and Beloved Brother,

By my laft to Mr George and you, I fhewed how things went here.   Since, there is no change.   My Lord Wari-fton will inform you fully how all goes.   Before he went, I dealt with him, and obtained his promife, not only to move, but to obtain from the commiffion of the church, a permiffion for me and Mr Samuel to return.   For this end alfo I moved my colleagues to write to the commiffion this inclofed letter.   I intreat you, and Mr Samuel intreats you alfo by me, to concur with my Lord Warifton for the obtaining of our defire.   He writes to Mr Robert Blair and Mr James Wood for this fame end.   It is true, I con-ceive it very neceffary, that fome of us would ftay till our work were nearer an end ;   but truly,   both Mr Samuel and I are fo overwearied, that pity will plead for a dimif-fion to us ; and we do think, fince matters are like to draw there fo extremely long, that it will be enough for one to wait on : and however Mr Gillefpie would be as gladly loofed as any of us, yet if any ftay, without all que-ftion, all things well confidered, he is the meeteft of the three.   But the commiffion poffibly will leave to ourfelves which of the three fhall be left ;   only I pray you to prefs a dimiffion for two.   We have been above three years ab-fent from our charges, and the affembly proceeds fo lan-guidly, that we were more profitable at home.   Mr Ru-thertord's large piece againft the Antinomians will in a few days come abroad ; and mine, againft the Anabaptifts, I hope to have out before the affembly end the Confeffion ; for that long I purpofe to ftay, though my permiffion to go were come.   The peace of the kingdoms is ftill in a great uncertainty.   We fear every other day, that the Houfes impatience of the King's infinite delays break off in a fury againft him, and then that he be brought to confent

ent to all but to no purpofe, unlefs to engage our poor kingdom in his quarrel, for the joining of our ruin to his own. It is alfo whifpered, that he is coming off to grant all things but the covenant and church-government, and that it is like the parliament here will clofe with him in thefe terms, without much regard to our complaints and mifcontentment this way. Alfo the King and they do us great wrong. Alfo there arifes fo many difficulties in fe-curing the city for their money, that before it can be pro-vided, there is great fears the country fhall break out in violence againft our army. It pleafes the Lord to keep us ftill in great perplexities and dangers. I wifh, if by any means you can, you might fettle the differences of that own among yourfelves; elfe the condition of the publick, however it go, is like to call upon the ftate to meddle more with that town than I fear fhall be for your contentment. My Lord Wariſton, I believe, will be willing to labour di-igently in it, according to your mind. Peace will be the beft of it ; elfe the fruit of your miniftry is ftopt towards many. But truly I know not what to advife you. My heart oft pities the cafe, and oft prays to God for it ; and were I befide you, I would, by God's help, do my beft to help you.

165. *To my Lord Wariſton.* *October* 27. 1646.

My Lord,

THESE are only to hold you in mind of our memoran-dum, and your promife. William Murray his difpatch, as it is intended on Thurfday morning, has put our fami-ly-faft off from Wednefday, as your journey did from Saturday. This day, yefterday, and Saturday, the com-mittee of the Houfe has fat on the fecond ordinance for the city's fecurity ; but they are like fo to clog it, that it will not be fatisfactory, and fo we fear the retarding of our money. If the King grant fatisfaction to all the propofi-ions, but that of religion and the covenant, and that be accepted by his people, as fome whifper it will be, then both his and their ingratitude to God and us will not pafs without a juft revenge, though we be not in a prefent po-ture to take it. I gave to William Murray my free paper; who read it all, and promifed to mind it. If you permit the Chancellor to be called for before your return, re-

I

folve

folve to extinguifh this commiffion. If God help William
Murray to draw from the King, at laft, a fatisfactory anfwer, I wifh my Lord Argyle and ye would come along
with it. Farewell.

Your Mafter and Servant,

ROBERT BAILLIE.

166. *To* ————. [*This letter is, I fuppofe, for Mr Robert Blair.*]. *November* 3. 1646.

Reverend and Dear Brother,

KNOWING your troublefome and fafhious employment
there, I will not trouble you much with my letters, only
at this time apprehending our affairs tb be drawing near
fome clofe, I have thought meet to acquaint you with
fome of my thoughts. Since Mr Murray's departure, I
have learned that the Houfe of Commons have given the
covenant to a committee to be put in an ordinance; that
the ordinance is drawn, and ready to be prefented to the
Houfes at the firft opportunity; alfo that fome of the
prime aldermen, and of the moft leading both of the common council and minifters of the city, have been with me,
and told me, that, as fome of them expreffed it, they will
be ready to fpend the laft drop of their blood in his Majefty's fervice, if he will take the propofitions; but if the
covenant be not at leaft approved as an act of parliament
and law, let all other propofitions be taken, and both the
Houfes agree with him as they pleafe, the hearts of the
city he would never get while he lived.

I hear alfo, that not only the chief of the fectarian
party, but fome others feem in private to give their readinefs to welcome the King, if the other propofitions be
granted, though the covenant be fhifted. The fectarian
party, and divers others who profefs moft to oppofe them,
feem to be in a way near a difpofition to admit, unanimoufly enough, of a charge againft the King's perfon,
which they fay is in readinefs, and that the great ftop to this,
all fear from the Scots and the city will be removed. If
they find that the King in his anfwer give not quick and
full fatisfaction in the covenant, I really believe the King
s greatly abufed if he dream that either the Scots or the
city will make any confiderable oppofition to any courfe

the parliament fhall be pleafed to take with his perfon, if there be any more hefitations in eftablifhing that covenant.

· It is to me marvellous, that no experience, how dear or frequent foever, will learn his Majefty that one point of prudence, to do in time for his great advantage, what he mult and will do ere long, without any thanks, and that with a great addition. The covenant now will do all his bufinefs. Will he fcruple it till the ordinance pafs, the next debate will be about his negative voice in the parliament; and very readily that fhall be put in an ordinance; and without it alfo there fhall be no admittance of him, or any of his, to the throne.

To many here it feems a great meafure of imprudence, and (as fome call it) induration and dementation, to be content that the parliament here fhould run out into the greateft extremities, and to hope that thofe fhall be the readieft means to obtain to the King all his defires; for I verily think, that if the parliament fhall once go on to the hardeft courfes with the King, upon his refufal to pafs the covenant, and to do thefe duties which the moft of the good men in both kingdoms are perfuaded he ought in reafon, he will never get, either here or in Scotland, any confiderable force for his defence.

We think it is the intereft of France to have our troubles continue till they do their bufinefs in· Flanders, Germany, Italy, Spain, and where they pleafe; and divers now begin to think that the King himfelf means a new war: but if it fhould be fo, I confefs it would be my great grief to fee him after all his misfortunes, in that new mifery of haftening the death and wrack of many thoufands more of his fubjects, for no purpofe but the accomplifhing of his own ruin.

We marvel that any fhould be fo ill-advifed as to think that Scotland will always be ready to join with the King whenfoever he pleafes to follow their advice. We think that a clear miftake: when their moft paffionate defires are flighted ever till the parliament of England have made their laft declaration, that then any thing the King is able to do will engage Scotland thereafter, no wife man does expect.

Colonel Cromwell is a-coming from Holland, to be General-Major of the Englifh foot. See if there be great appearance of difbanding of their army. The laft ordinance of the bifhops lands paft yefterday. It is now thought
the

the money for our army will be gotten. The other day orders were given to fee to the paffages on the Trent, that none may go north or come fouth but by their army's permiffion. We fear William Murray may be catched in his way. There is a high indignity here, that the King's refolutions for thefe things that concern the fafety both of his perfon and kingdoms fhould have all this time fo evident a dependence from French packets.

This people's patient waiting for the King's laft anfwer is very near a final period; and all are afraid that one of thefe days the Houfe of Commons doors be clofed, and fome high vote pafs that never fhall be recalled. I thought meet you fhould know this much from me. We are often praying to God for a more counfellable heart to the King than yet we can hear he has got. But if, when all is done, his obftinacy be remedilefs, we are preparing ourfelves for mourning and fafting for thefe things which feem unavoidable, and at the doors. The Lord affift you in your weariefome, and as yet, I fear, comfortlefs employment. I reft,

ROBERT BAILLIE.

Though all thefe things, and many more, are by many hands poffibly conveyed to the King himfelf; yet thefe two or three days I have had an impulfe of mind to have acquainted you from me of the prefent moft dangerous condition of the King, and of us all, through his unexampled obftinacy.

Again, I tell you, from all I converfe with, the covenant is his fafety; nothing lefs will do it; and this will do it, by God's help, abundantly.

There are here four or five juntos, all of divers, and fomewhat contrary cabals; but thefe who are little acquainted with the defigns of any of them, are the greateft, ftrongeft, and honefteft party. Whatever they caufe to be fuggefted, yet the body of honeft men, neither for their, nor his Majefty's pleafure, will let themfelves be long befooled; but if they find their hopes deluded, or near to ftrike the ftroke, which if once they had done, all the juntos, for their own ends, will comply, and leave the King and his family to deplore thefe lafting miferies which their falfe fuggeftions did much help to bring on.

167. *To Mr George Young.*   *December* 1. 1646.

Reverend and Dear Brother,

——— I think to obtain a dimiffion this week, yet it will
be above twenty days ere I can take journey, for I have
got out a dozen of fheets of my Anabaptifm from the
prefs.   With much ado we have gone through, at laft,
the reft of our Confeffion.   The firft part I fent to you
three only, in Mr David's letter, long ago.   The whole
will go up to the Houfe one of thefe days, and fo to the
prefs.   It is generally taken here for a very gracious and
brave piece of work.   We are now on the Catechifm, a
quarter of it is paft ; poffibly I may bring it all or the moft
part with me.   The L. 200,000 was all told on Friday laft.
All this day our commiffioners have been agreeing upon
the way of its receiving, and the going of our army.
Great hafte will be ufed upon all hands, no ftop is expected.   We have had fore labour thefe weeks bygone,
to put on many things in the Houfes, affembly, and city,
much ado to get the great fum ; but when once it was on
a way, it ran fafter than it could be received.   It was my
dear friend Dr Burgefs's fingular invention, that all who
contribute to this fum, would have as much of his old debt,
with all the annualrents counted to him, and for all make
a good pennyworth of the bifhops lands ; fo the bargain
being exceeding advantageous, the ftrife was, who fhould
come in with his money fooneft.   By this means we got
the bifhops lands on our back, without any grudge, and
in a way that no fkill will get them back again.   There is
fome progrefs made in the ordinance againft herefy ; alfo
in the ordinance for the covenant : there will be extreme
great oppofition, yet we are in fome hopes to carry them ;
and if fo, the horrible lift of errors here will get a deadly
wound.   The minifters of London have put out this day,
a very fine book, proving from fcripture, the divine right
of every part of the Prefbyterial government.   The morrow the Houfe of Commons have fet apart for removing
the obftructions of the government.   The treaty betwixt
Ormond and the commiffioners of the parliament are broken off, fo the foldiers which went from this to receive
Dublin, are towards Derry.   Imprudence, rather than
treachery, has fpoiled this good and great bufinefs.   We
                                                    expected,

expected, long before this, the King's anfwer to the propofitions, and a good one. We think it may come the
next week; but our hopes are not fo good as they were,
though the Queen and Prince be miferable in France, and
would fee an end of trouble at any price; yet the French
ambaffador, for all his profeffions, is conceived to mar
and retard our conclufion. The King, all his life, has
loved trinketing naturally, and is thought to be much in
that action now with all parties, for the imminent hazard
of all. Our greateft fear is, that the malignant Oxford
Lords have drawn him to the Independents, for the undoing of Scotland, and the Prefbyterian party here. We
are fure our army and parliament will be honeft to death,
and will not draw on themfelves, for any man's words,
vengeance from God and man. The body of this people
would gladly embrace the King and peace; but if one
month longer he go on to dally, they will reject him for
ever; and if he then run to us, to draw a perpetual war
upon our backs, he cannot be very wellcome. Our commiffioners here, twice every week, write fuch long, free,
and true fcrolls, as will abfolve them from any guilt, if
perfons obftinate in madnefs will needs deftroy themfelves.
I think all here fhall either come home with me, or at my
back. A bafe fcurvy pamphlet came out againft our papers, which by order of parliament this day was publickly burnt; yet the Houfe of Commons anfwer to us was
fent us this day alfo, little better than that which they
burnt. Always paper-debates are the leaft of our care;
we never loft yet at that game. The King's ways are our
only true vexation. I truft no confiderable men among
you will, for their own, endeavour to make their poor
country again miferable. I pray you, good George, write
to me three weeks, though your letters fhould mif-
carry. ——

Your brother, in grief,

ROBERT BAILLIE.

There is a new petition, almoft in readinefs, to come
from the city for thefe things we defire.

168. *For*

58. *For Mr James Roberton of Bedlay.*   December 8. 1646.

Worſhipful Couſin,

WITHIN theſe eight days I have received two of your
:ters, but none before ſince I ſaw you, as I remember.
t meeting, I ſhall ſatisfy your queſtions.   For the ſtate
' the much-noiſed hereſies here, you ſhall have account
ɔm me in a few days in the next part of my Diſſuaſive.
ɔme few of the moſt active men of the Houſe of Com-
ons and army are for too general a liberty for all con-
iences ; but the moſt of both Houſes are right and
und, and the body of the city are zealous againſt all er-
rs and confuſions, as the world will ſee in their new pe-
ion yet before this week end.   Generally the miniſters
er all the kingdom are orthodox ; and the ſectaries, ex-
pt a very few, are but heady, illiterate perſons.   If
ace were ſettled, and the army down, all here think
at the noiſe of hereſies, which now is very loud, would
aniſh.   This night 1 count us as good as agreed for the
ɩding down of our money, and the return of our army.
:hink, on Monday, and not ſooner, it will go.   We re-
ive, at Northallerton, L. 100,000, and the other be-
nd the Tine, when Newcaſtle is delivered.   Before a
ɔnth all this is like to be ended.   The King's anſwer,
ɩen it comes back from your great friends there, is ex-
cted here in haſte.   God forgive them that have made
at anſwer worſe than once it was.   Had it been ſo good
for ſome weeks we certainly expected, the King had
en received with great joy, and been put preſently
poſſeſſion but of too much power.   But as that an-
er is like to be, many think he and it will both be
jected ; and what that will bring on poor Scotland,
may eaſily conjecture.   Others think it poſſible he may
admitted by this people ; but without any love or truſt.
ɩcked, ſelf-ſeeking men have contributed much to hard the rooting out of the whole royal family, by the ob-
nacy and imprudence of the moſt unhappily adviſed
ince that this day lives.   I know and have been witneſs
at theſe here have done all that lay in men to prevent
ɩſchief ; but they have ſpoken to ſtones, and loſt their
ɔour, they have now given over, and looking what God
                                                       will

will make the event.   This is the incomparably beſt people I ever knew, if they were in the hands of any governors of tolerable parts.   A great ſtorm, if God prevent it not, is near and likely to fall moſt on the head of the contrivers.   The Lord be with you.   Within a twenty days ſundry of us will be ready to take journey.   Thus I reſt,   Your Couſin,

                                ROBERT BAILLIE.

169. *To my Lord* —————.   [*This, I ſuppoſe, is to the Earl of Loudon, Chancellor of Scotland.*]. *December 25. 1646.*

    My Lord,
    WHAT I was ſpeaking to your Lordſhip of Mr Blair, I wiſh it were taken in farther conſideration.   If it pleaſe God the King come hither, who ſhall be his miniſters? By all means it muſt be provided, that he be not permitted to have any ſervice either from Epiſcopal men or ſectaries.   There will be difficulty to get theſe eſchewed.   If the King have his choice, without rules from his parliament, he will take no other than Epiſcopal men.   If ſome have the power either of nomination or effectual recommendation, without doubt the prime ſectaries ſhall be planted about him.   For the preventing of this, were it not meet, while the King is with us, to be thinking what miniſters we could wiſh to wait on his family and children?   In the mean time, while the King is on his journey, and while he is a-ſettling here, were it not meet to move his Majeſty to require Mr Blair to attend him; and if it may be, to have the ſpiritual care of the children? The King cannot do himſelf a better turn.   Of all the divines that I know in both nations, I think none ſo fit for the education of the King's children, for piety, learning, and good manners.   I have had much experience of his ſingular dexterity in that art.   The man is ſo eminent in piety, wiſdom, learning, gravity, and moderation, that I think his employment would bring a bleſſing to the royal family and all the kingdoms.   His Majeſty would be aſſured, that there is no ſuch means to keep the Houſes from preſcribing rules to him in the choice of his chaplains, as with ſpeed to chuſe ſuch himſelf as may be above exception, and in whom all his ſubjects may have good ſatiſ-
                                        faction.

faction.   Of our nation, befide Mr Blair, I wifh no other but one at moft, my worthy brother Mr Gillefpie.   Of the Englifh, the ableft Herle, Marfhal, Vines, Burgefs, or Palmer; but I believe Newcoman, Ward, Afh, Perm, Seaman, Whittaker, Calamy, would give as good fatiffaction.   I wifh this motion were thought upon; as if it be approven, that the beft means for obtaining it muft be ufed in time.

170. *To Mr William Spang.*

Dear Coufin,

I know you marvel why I have been fo long in writing to you.   The truth is, I have every week thefe many bygone been expecting fome better matter; but that not yet appearing, I had ftill been filent, had not my journey to Scotland forced me to bid you farewell.   Being overwearied with the infufferable tedioufnefs of this parliament and affembly, I refolved to labour for a dimiffion.   My other two brethren were earneft alfo to be gone.   By our joint and feveral letters to the commiffion of the general affembly, and to our particular friends, we could not obtain more but permiffion for one to come home; who, and when, ourfelves thought expedient.   After fome debates, I, who truly may beft be fpared, got the favour: for however both the other two preffed for themfelves, yet both of them having their wives and families here, who in the dead of winter could not be got tranfported, and I producing a letter under the hand of Mr David Dickfon, Mr Robert Ramfay, and Mr G. Young, not only of the great need of my return to my charge, but alfo of the ficknefs of my wife and three of my children, I obtained at laft my freedom, to my great joy.   The treaty for our army, and fo the committee of both kingdoms, being ended, and the next deliberation about the King, being of that importance, that our commiffioners think meet to remit it to the parliament of England, the Chancellor and Lauderdale purpofe to go home the next week, and I, God willing, with them.   Our affembly, with much ado, at laft have wreftled through the Confeffion, and the whole is now printed.   The Houfe of Commons require to put fcripture to it before they take it to confideration; and what time that will take up, who knows?

2   We

We have passed a quarter of the Catechism, and thought to have made short work with the rest; but they are fallen into such mislikes, and endless janglings, about the method and the matter, that all think it will be a long work. The increase of all heresies here is very great, as you will perceive in the second part of my Dissuasive, which the next week will come abroad, but more in the third part of Mr Edwards's Gangrena: yet we think they will quickly fall; for it is a faction generally misliked, as composed of error, policy, pride, and insolent oppression. The city of London's notable petition would help all, did not the great unhappiness of the King spoil all our hopes. For many weeks together friends here did give him most free, wise, and friendly counsel. From Scotland the like duties were done. The only thing principally insisted on, was to approve the covenant. While we had great hopes of his yielding, whether emissaries from the Independents, who do like him the better because he rejects the covenant and Presbyterial government, or the French, who notwithstanding of all their contrare profession, yet for their own interest do endeavour the continuance of our troubles, has made him peremptor in refusing the article of religion. He drew up a particular answer to the propositions, and sent it privily both here and to Scotland; but finding it extremely unsatisfactory to both, he delayed to send any answer. The fear was and is great, that his evil designs continue either to go to France, where there is much speech of an army for England, as of one from Ireland to Scotland, or else to go to Scotland. It is much feared he shall be both able and willing to suppress the better party there, and draw the English armies on the rest. Always we have guarded so well as may be against his voyage and journey to these places. At last his answer is come to us, and this day was communicate to both Houses. It is but a mere general, that he desires to come here to be heard, for the loosing of his scruples. The Houses have voted his coming to Holmby house near Northampton, in quality little better than a prisoner; which he will never agree to. It will be endeavoured that the two parliaments may agree in some course of his restraint, if he continue in his unhappy courses. His warrant the other day was produced for 'stealing away the Duke of York to France. If either he could be moved to agree with his parliament, or they to agree among themselves

elves in any courfe for him, it feems we might have here, both in church and ftate, all our defires ; but neither of thefe being likely, our dangers both in church and ftate are very great and imminent. They fay the plague is ill in Glafgow : that poor town thefe two years has been a place of great trouble, and like to be of more : yet I will venture among them, albeit with fmall hopes of doing good ; for things feem to be fpoiled there irrecoverably in our days.

171. *To Mr William Spang.*

Dear Coufin,

I wrote to you at length before I came from London. I have had a long and tedious, but, thanks to God, profperous journey. I am now here well. I have made my report in the commiffion of the church to all their contentment ; our errand in England being brought near a happy period, fo far as concerned us the commiffioners of the church ; for, by God's blefling, the four points of uniformity, which was all our church gave us in commiffion to agent in the affembly at Weftminfter, were as good as obtained. The Directory I brought down before. The model of government we have gotten it through the affembly according to our mind : it yet fticks in the hands of the Houfes. They have paffed four ordinances at leaft about it, all pretty right, fo far as concerns the conftitution and erection of general affemblies, provincial fynods, prefbyteries, and feffions, and the power of ordination. In the province of London and Lancafhire the bodies are fet up. That the like diligence is not ufed long ago in all other places, it is the fottifh negligence of the minifters and gentry in the fhires more than the parliament's. That the power of jurifdiction in all things we require, excepting appeals from the general affembly to the parliament, is not put in ordinances long ago, it is by the coming of the Independents and Eraftians in the Houfe of Commons; which obftacle we truft will now be removed by the zeal of the city of London ; fo much the more, as our nation are taken away fooner and more eafily than any did expect. All grounds of jealoufy of our joining with the King, the greateft prop of the fectaries power in the Houfe. However, in the *Jus divinum* of Prefbytery, printed

ed by the miniftry of London, you may fee that burden
taken off our fhoulders; the body of the miniftry of England, not the affembly and Londoners only, being fully
leavened with our fenfe in all the point of government;
and become willing, and able abundantly, to manage that
caufe, without us, againft all oppofites.   The third point,
the Confeffion of Faith, I brought it with me, now in
print, as it was offered to the Houfes by the affembly,
without confiderable diffent of any.   It is much cried up
by all, even many of our greateft oppofites, as the beft
Confeffion yet extant.   It is expected the Houfes fhall pafs
it, as they did the Directory, without much debate.   Howbeit the retarding party has put the affembly to add fcrip-
tures to it, which they omitted only to efchew the offence
of the Houfe, whofe practice hitherto has been, to enact
nothing of religion on divine right or fcriptural grounds,
but upon their own authority alone.   This innovation of
our oppofites may well coft the affembly fome time, who
cannot do the moft eafy things with any expedition; but
it will be for the advantage and ftrength of the work.   The
fourth part of our defired and covenanted uniformity is
the Catechifm.   A committee has drawn and reported the
whole.

The affembly ere I came away had voted more than the
half.   A fhort time will end the reft; for they ftudy bre-
vity, and have voted to have no other head of divinity into it than is fet down in the Confeffion.   This ended, we
have no more ado in the affembly, neither know we any
more work the affembly has in hand, but an anfwer to the
nine queries of the Houfe of Commons about the *jus divinum* of divers parts of the government.   The minifters
of London's late *Jus divinum* of Prefbytery does this a-
bundantly.   Alfo a committee of the affembly has a full
anfwer to all thefe queries ready.   The authors repent
much of that motion.   Their aim was, to have confounded and divided the affembly by their infnaring queftions;
but finding the affembly's unanimity in them, the Independents principles forcing them to join with the reft, in
afferting the divine right of thefe points of government,
whereupon the parliament does moft ftick, the movers of
thefe queftions wifhes they had been filent.   There is no
more work before the affembly.   The tranflation of the
pfalms is paffed long ago in the affembly; yet it fticks in
the Houfes.   The Commons paffed their order long ago;

ut the Lords joined not, being folicited by divers of the
ffembly, and of the minifters of London, who love bet-
er the more poetical paraphrafe of their colleague Mr
Burton. The too great accuracy of fome in the affembly,
ticking too hard to the original text, made the laft edi-
ion more concife and obfcure than the former. With
this the commiffion of our church was not fo well pleafed;
but we have got all thofe obfcurities helped; fo I think it
fhall pafs. Our good friend Mr Zachary Boyd has put
himfelf to a great deal of pains and charges to make a
pfalter, but I ever warned him his hopes were groundlefs
to get it received in our churches; yet the flatteries of his
unadvifed neighbours makes him infift in his fruitlefs defign.

When I took my leave of the affembly, I fpoke a little
to them. The prolocutor, in name of the affembly, gave
me an honourable teftimony, and many thanks for my labours. I had been ever filent in all their debates; and
however this filence fometimes weighted my mind, yet I
found it the beft and wifeft courfe. No man there is defired to fpeak. Four parts of five do not fpeak at all; and
among thefe are many moft able men, and known by their
writs and fermons to be much abler than fundry of the
fpeakers; and of thefe few that ufe to fpeak, fundry are
fo tedious, and thrufts themfelves in with fuch mifregard of others, that it were better for them to be filent.
Alfo there are fome eight or nine fo able, and ready at all
times, that hardly a man can fay any thing, but what o-
thers, without his labour, are fure to fay as well or better.
Finding, therefore, that filence was a matter of no reproach, and of great eafe, and brought no hurt to the
work, I was content to ufe it, as Mr Henderfon alfo did.
For the far moft part of the laft two years, my writs did
conciliate to me credit enough, and my fenfe of unability
to debate with the beft, made me content to abftain; whereof I did never as yet repent. We ftaid eight or nine days
at Newcaftle. The King took very well with me. I might
have had occafion to have faid to him what I pleafed; but
knowing his fixed refolutions, I would not meddle at all
neither to preach nor pray before him. His unhappy wilfulnefs does ftill continue; and to this day he gets fome
mifchievous inftruments to feed his madnefs. Sundry
made us believe the Queen was content he fhould do any
thing, finding her difappointment in France from all hands.
'There

There were some whisperings of the sectaries plotting with him; but this I scarce believe; for each of them do really labour the others overthrow. The French ambassador, for all his fair protestations, has been no good instrument; but that which has undone him, has been his hopes from Scotland, to get them, by one means or other, to espouse his quarrel. Much dealings, some think, has been both with the army and parliament for that end. It is very like, if he had done any duty, though he had never taken the covenant, but permitted it to have been put in an act of parliament in both kingdoms, and given so satisfactory an answer to the rest of the propositions, as easily he might, and sometimes I know he was willing, certainly Scotland had been for him as one man; and the body of England, upon many grounds, was upon a disposition to have so cordially embraced him, that no man, for his life, durst have muttered against his present restitution. But remaining what he was in all his maxims, a full Canterburian, both in matters of religion and state, he still inclined to a new war; and for that end resolved to go to Scotland. Some great men there pressed the equity of Scotland's protecting of him on any terms. This untimeous excess of friendship has ruined that unhappy prince; for the better party, finding the conclusion of the King's coming to Scotland, and thereby their own present ruin, and ruin of the whole cause, the making the malignants masters of church and state, the drawing the whole force of England upon Scotland for their perjurious violation of their covenant, they resolved by all means to cross that design. *End of the year* 1646.

So when others proposed to the parliament the assistance of the King to recover his government in England, notwithstanding any answer he might give to the propositions, the better sort, before they should give answer to so high a question, desired a publick fast in the parliament, and the advice also of the commission of the church. Both with some difficulty were obtained. But after that fast, and the distinct answer of the church, that it was unlawful for Scotland to assist the King for his recovery of the government in England, if he approved not the covenant, the parliament was peremptor to refuse the King free access to Scotland, unless he satisfied the propositions. This much they signified to him by their commissioners, which we met at Newcastle. It was easy to be grieved, and to find

find what to reprehend in this refolution; for indeed it was clothed with many dangers and grievances; but to fall at that nick of time on any conclufion, free of more dangers and grievances, feemed impoffible. Notwithftanding of the great fums of money, yet the difbanding of our army in peace will be a great tafk : to fet on foot 6000 foot and 1200 horfe, to the contentment of all, will be hard; and the entertaining them will be harder. What the King or his Englifh parliament will do next, there is no certainty. The peft increafes in Glafgow. My heart pities that much mifguided place. All that may, are fled out of it. The Lord be with you. Foreign intelligence to me muft now be the larger; for all here live in great ignorance, and neglect of things abroad. So I reft,

      Your Coufin,

                         ROBERT BAILLIE.

Edinburgh, January 26. 1647.

       172. *To Mr Spang.*   *June 2. 1647.*

————— David Lefly and Argyle rofe from Dumblane the 17th of May, with a very fmall and ill-provided army. He made very long marches over the mountains in ftormy weather, without houfes or tents. Againft the 23d he came to Kintyre upon the enemy, fought and diffipated hem, took in all Kintyre, has fent a party after Alafter, who, with a few, are fled to the ifles. This quick and happy expedition may be to us of great advantage, if the Prince and Montrofe fhould come over to raife new broils amongft us, as fome furmife they intend; or if the King hould put himfelf on the head of the Sectarian army, which is not yet difbanded nor quiet, David Lefly being free of the highlanders, by God's help, will keep Scotland quiet for this fummer with the little army he has on foot.

      173. *To Mr Spang.* *Edinburgh, July 13. 1647.*

Dear Coufin,

I received yours, the 6th of July, this day, and another of yours, April 9th, within thefe two or three weeks, together with your *Honorius Reggius,* for which we are all
                            much

much obliged to your great pains in. That bufinefs which you fo earneftly recommended to Mr David Dickfon and me, was not feafible, had we ufed all poffible diligence : but the truth is, although I believe ye know my willingnefs to do to my power in things that concern you lefs than you write that matter did, yet it fell fo out, that I could ufe little diligence to fpeak of ; for your letter about that purpofe came not to my hand till near three months after it was written ; and when it came, our whole town of Kilwinning were kept up upon fome fufpicion of the plague ; fo I could have no effectual communication, neither by word or writ, with any ; and therefore I came to Edinburgh. That matter was fettled on Mr Arnot, who had divers of the chief Lords of the Seffion to folicit for him. For the great ficknefs of your good honeft wife I am forry ; but glad for her grace and patience. Thefe matters of England are fo extremely defperate, that now twice they have made me fick. Except God arife, all is gone there. The imprudence and cowardice of the better part of the city and parliament, which was triple or fextuple the greater, has permitted a company of filly rafcals, who call themfelves yet no more than 14,000, horfe and foot, to make themfelves mafters of the King, parliament, and city, and by them of all England : fo that now that difgraced parliament is but a committee to act all at their pleafure, and the city is ready to fright the parliament at every firft or fecond boaft from the army. No human hope remains but in the King's unparallelled wilfulnefs, and the army's unmeafurable pride. As yet they are not agreed, and fome write they are not like to agree : for in our particular I expect certainly they will agree well enough, at what diftance foever their affections and principles ftand. Always if the finger of God in their fpirits fhould fo far dement them as to difagree, I would think there were yet fome life in the play ; for I know the body of England are overweary long ago of the parliament, and ever hated the fectaries, but much more now for this their unexpected treachery and oppreffion. On the other part, the King is much pitied and defired ; fo if they give him not contentment, he will overthrow them. If he and they agree, our hands are bound : we will be able, in our prefent pofture, and humour of our highly diftracted people, to do nothing. And whom fhall we go to help, when none calls ? but the King, parliament, and city, as their

mafters

masters command, are ready to declare against us if we should offer to arm.   But if the King would call, I doubt not of rising of the best army ever we had, for the crushing of these serpents, enemies to God and man.   David Lesly has gotten all Isla, and old Colhittoch, without quarters. He is now over to Mull, and purposes within a fortnight to return, having no more to do in these bounds.   That things go well abroad, it is a comfort to us.   That Leopold lays a little the French pride; that all the Dutch princes, even Bavier, and the Ecclesiastick Elector, have left the Emperor, I am glad; but counts it a strange prank of ingratitude in Bavier, and of unkindness in the Swedes toward the poor Palatine, at whose charge most that neurality, I fear, be concluded.   I think your states wise in taking peace with Spain.

174. *To a friend in Kilwinning. Edinburgh, August 20. Friday night.*

LONDON, and the affairs of England, lie sore on the heart of many honest men; yet the prosperity of our own affairs here, both of church and state, gives us some relief.   Mr Cheefly sent us word, that he was detained at Newcastle; which did much perplex us; for our state-meeting did depend upon his message.   It pleased God to make his detainers let him go before the messenger of our state came to demand him.   When he came, he gave us a full information how all affairs in England stood.   The inclosed papers will show the incredible change that a few days wrought.   The city's declaration and diurnal declare in what a brave posture both the city and parliament once were in.   The other papers shew how soon all was overturned.   The army marched through the whole city by way of triumph; but staid not in it, did no violence to any; only three or four regiments keep the forts about Westminster, and guard the parliament still.   For all that, the House of Commons vote sundry things contrary to the mind of the army.   How long that courage will remain, I cannot say.   It is thought that people, when they have felt a little the burden of the army, will break that yoke by one mean or other.   The army's mind, much of it, may be seen in their propositions, a paper which I purposed to send, but now it is fallen by.   By it

I   they

they are clear enough for a full liberty of confcience, a
deftroying of our covenant, a fetting up of bifhops, of in-
thralling the King fo far, as in my judgement, he and
they will not agree, albeit many think they are agreed already. If this were, our cafe were very hard. Never
more appearance of a great difcord, both in our church
and ftate, fome few days ago ;· but, bleffed be God, the appearances are now much changed. Never affembly more
harmonious than this yet has been. Our declaration to
England, a very good piece, is paffed without a contrary
voice. An act againft vaigers [ftrollers] from their own
minifters, and a large direction for private worfhip, drawn
by Mr Robert Blair, for the correcting all the faults in
worfhip, which offended many here, is paft the commit-
mittee, without a contrary voice ; and, I think, fhall pafs
the affembly alfo, no lefs unanimoufly ; which demon-
ftrates the truth of what I faid in my affembly-fpeech,
" That for all the noife fome made, yet truly there was
" no divifion as yet in our church."

Yefterday, and this night, our ftate, after much irreconcileable difference, as appeared, are at laft unanimoufly agreed to fend the Chancellor and Lanerk to the King
and parliament of England, to comfort and encourage
both to keep our covenant, and not to agree to the propofitions of the army. No appearance, as yet, of any
ftirring in hafte in this kingdom, &c.

175. *To Mr Spang.   Edinburgh, September* 1. 1647.

Coufin,

——London has lien like a millftone on my breaft now
of a long time. The firft week we came to this town,
my heart was a little relieved. I thought God had anfwered our prayers much fooner than I expected, and had
put London in fo good a pofture for averting all our
fears as I could have wifhed ; but that joy lafted not full
eight days. Stapleton and Hollis, and fome others of the
eleven members, had been the main perfuaders of us to
remove out of England, and leave the King to them, upon
affurance, which was moft likely, that this was the only
means to get that evil army difbanded, the King and
peace fettled according to our minds : but their bent execution of this real intention has undone them, and all,

ill God provide a remedy. We were glad when Leslie was recalled from his Lieutenancy of Ireland, a creature of Cromwell's, who got that great trust for no virtue at all but his serviceableness to that faction. This was the first sensible grievance to that army. The second was the employing of Skippon and Massie, in the Irish command, and giving to Fairfax such a command in England as made him not very formidable. But when the third stroke came, of disbanding the most of the sectaries, and cashiering of their officers, this put them on that high and bold design, which as yet they follow, as, I think, not so much on great preconception, as drawn on by the course of affairs, and light heads of their leaders. Vane and Cromwell, as I take it, are of nimble hot fancies for to put all in confusion, but not of any deep reach. St John and Pierpont are more stayed, but not great heads. Sey and his son, not ————, albeit wiser, yet of so dull, sour, and fearful a temperament, that no great atchievement, in reason, could be expected from them. The rest, either in the army or parliament, of their party, are not on their mysteries, and of no great parts either for counsel or action, so far as I could ever observe. The folly of our friends was apparent, when at the army's first back-march, and refusal to disband, they recalled their declaration against their mutinous petitions. Easily might all their designs have been crushed at that nick of time, with one stout look more; but it was a dementation to sit still amazed at the taking of the King, the accusation of the eleven members, the army's approaching to the city. Here, had the city agreed, and our friends in parliament shewed any resolution, their opposites counsel might even then have been easily overturned; for all this while, the army was not much above 10,000 ill-armed soldiers. But the irrecoverable loss of all, was the ill-managing of the city's brave engagement. Had they then made fast the chief of the sectarian party in both Houses, and stopt their flight to the army; had Massey and Waller, with any kind of masculine activity, made use of that new trust committed to them; Mr Marshal, and his seventeen servants of the synod, for all Foulks and Gib's subornation, should never have been bold to offer that destructive petition to the Houses and common council, which, without any capitulation, put presently in the army's power, the parliament, city, and all England, without the last con-tradiction.

tradiction. An example rarely parallelled, if not of treachery, yet at leaft of childifh improvidence and bafe cowardice. Since that time they have been abfolute mafters
of all. Which way they will ufe this unexpected fove-
reignty, it will quickly appear. As yet they are fettling
themfelves in their new faddle. Before they got up, they
gave the King and his party fair words; but now, when
all is their own, they may put him in a harder condition
than yet he has tafted of. Their propofals, a part of
their mind, give to the King much of his defire in bringing back bifhops and books, in putting down our covenant and prefbytery, in giving eafe to malignants and Papifts; but fpoil him of his temporal power fo much, as
many think, he will never acquiefce to; albeit it is fpoken loud, that he and they are fully agreed.

Our ftate here, after long expectation to have heard
fomething of the King's own mind and defires, as yet
have heard nothing from him to account of. Although he
fhould employ their help againft his oppreffors, yet he
being ftill altogether unwilling to give us any fatisfaction
in the matter of our covenant, we are uncertain what
courfe to take; only we do refent to our commiffioners
to oppofe the propofals, and to require a fafe-conduct to
the Chancellor and Lanerk to come up to the King and
parliament. It coft many debates before it came to this
conclufion. Our great men are not like to pack up their
differences. Duke Hamilton and his friends would have
been thought men compofed of peace on any terms, and
to have caft on other defigns of embroiling Scotland in a
new war. But when all were weary of jangling debates,
the conclufion whereto the committee was brought, was
fo far to efpoufe the King's quarrel on any terms, that
Argyle and Warifton behoved to proteft againft our engagement on any fuch terms. To avoid invidious proteta-
tions, both parties agreed to pafs an act of not engagement. The proceedings of fome are not only double and
triple, but fo manifold, that as no other, fo, in my mind,
themfelves know not what they finally intend. They who
made themfelves gracious and ftrong, by making the
world believe that it was their oppofites who had brought
the country in all the former trouble, and would yet a-
gain bring it into a new dangerous war, when it came to
the point, were found to precipitate us into dangers, and
that in fuch terms as few with comfort could have under-

aken. We have it from divers good hands at London, that some here kept correspondence with Sir Thomas Fairfax, which to me is an intolerable abomination. The present sense of many is this : if the King and the army agree, we must be quiet and look to God : if they agree not, and the King be willing to ratify our covenant, we are all as one man to restore him to all his rights, or die by the way : if he continue resolute to reject our covenant, and only to give us some parts of the matter of t, many here will be for him, even in these terms ; but divers of the best and wisest are irresolute, and wait till God give more light.

David Leslie, with a great deal of fidelity, activity, and success, has quieted all our highlands and isles, and brought back our little army ; which, we think, shall be quartered here and there, without disbanding, till we see more of the English affairs. The pestilence, for the time, vexes us. In great mercy Edinburgh and Leith, and all about, which lately were afflicted with more of this evil than ever was heard of in Scotland, are free. Some few infections now and then, but they spread not. Aberdeen, Brechin, and other parts of the north, are miserably wasted. St Andrew's and Glasgow, without great mortality, are so threatened, that the schools and colleges now in all Scotland, except Edinburgh, are scattered.

While I had written thus far, by the packet this day from London I learn, that the army daily goes higher and higher, which to me is a hopeful presage of their quicker ruin. The chief six of the eleven members were coming to you, Stapleton, Esler, Hollis ; the second gentleman, for all gallantry in all England, died at Calais. I think it will be hard to the parliament and city to bear these men long ; and I hope, if all men were dead, God will arise against them. Munster is not like to be a school to them long. Cromwell and Vane are like to run on to the end of Becold and Knipperdolling's race. Northumberland has feasted the King at Swa-house ; hence he went to Hampton-court. They speak of his coming to Whitehall. If he agree no better with the sectaries than yet he does, that journey may prove fatal. He is not likely to come out of London willingly ; and if the army should draw him, that violence may waken sleeping hounds. If they let him come to London, without assurance of his accord with them, they are more bold and venturous than wise ;

wife; and if the King agree to their state-defigns, I think he is not fo confonant to all his former principles and practice as I took him.

I know you expect fome account of our affembly. Take it, if you have patience to read what I have fcribbled in hafte, on a very ill fheet of paper. I have no leifure to double ; for our commiffioners enter every day at feven, and we are about publick bufinefs daily till late at night. At our firft meeting, there was clear appearance of formed parties for divifion ; but God has turned it fo about, that never affembly was more harmonious and peaceable to the very end. The laft year, a minifter in the Merfe, one Mr James Simfon, whofe grandfire was, as I take it, an uncle or brother to famous Mr Patrick of Stirling, a forward, pious, young man, being in fuit of a religious damfel, fifter to Mr James Guthrie's wife, had kept with Mr James Guthrie, and others, fome private meetings and exercifes, which gave great offence to many. When they came before the laft general affembly and commiffion of the kirk, Mr David Calderwood and fundry other very honeft men, oppofite to malignants, were much grieved, and by that grief moved to join with Mr William Colvil, Mr Andrew Fairfoul, and fuch whom fome took to be more favourable to malignants than need were. Thefe two joined together, made a great party, efpecially when our ftatefmen made ufe of them to bear down thofe who had fwayed our former affemblies. The conteft was at the chufing of the moderator. The forementioned party were earneft for Mr William Colvil. Many were for me ; but I was utterly unwilling for any fuch unfit charge, and refolved to abfent myfelf from the firft meeting, if by no other means I could be fhifted the leet. At laft, with very much ado, I got myfelf off, and Mr Robert Douglas on the leets ; who carried it from Mr William Colvil only by four voices. God's bleffing on this man's great wifdom and moderation has carried all our affairs right to the end ; but Mr David Calderwood having miffed his purpofe, has preffed fo a new way of leeting the moderator for time to come, that puts in the hand of bafe men to get one whom they pleafe, to our great danger. We fpent a number of days on filly particulars. Mr Gillefpie came home at our firft downfitting. He and I made our report to the great fatisfaction of all. You have here what I
spoke.

spoke. Mr Calderwood was much offended with what I had spoken in the end; but my apology in private satisfied him. He, and others of his acquaintance, came with resolution to make great din about privy meetings and novations, being persuaded, and willing to persuade others, that our church was already much pestered with schism. My mind was clean contrary: and now, when we have tried all to the bottom, they are found to be much more mistaken than I; for they have obtained, with the hearty consent of these men whom they counted greatest patrons of schism, all the acts they pleased against that evil, wherein the wisdom and authority of Mr Blair has been exceeding serviceable. This yielding on our side, to their desires, drew from them a quiet consent to these things we intended, from which at first they seemed much averse. We agreed, *nemine contradicente*, to that declaration, which was committed to Mr Gillespie and me, but was drawn by him alone; also, after much debate in the committee, to the Confession of Faith; and to the printing of the Directory for government, for the examination of the next general assembly; of the Catechism also, when the little that remains shall come down; likewise for printing to that same end two or three sheets of Theses against Erastianism, committed to Mr Gillespie and me, but done by him at London at Voetius's motion; which we mind, when approven here, to send to him; who is hopeful to get the consent of your universities and of the general assembly of France to them, which may serve for good purpose. We have put the new Psalter also in a good way.———We have this day very happily ended our assembly with good concord; albeit Mr David Calderwood, serving his own very unruly humour, did oft very much provoke. He has been so intolerable through our forbearance, that it is like he shall never have so much respect among us. His importunity forced us, not only to a new ridiculous way of chusing the moderator, but on a conceit he has, that a minister deposed should not again be reposed almost in no case, he has troubled us exceedingly about the power of the commission of the kirk to depose a minister in any case; yet we carried it over him. We have obtained leave to print all our English papers, Catechism, Confession, Propositions, and Directory for government and ordination, our debates for accommodation against toleration, our papers to the grand committee, the

propositions

propofitions for government, albeit paffed both in our affembly and parliament 1643. Mr David oppofed vehemently the printing, and his grand followers, Mr John
Smith and Mr William Colvil with him, becaufe they held
forth a feffion of a particular congregation to have a ground
in fcripture, which he, contrary to his Altar of Damaf-
cus, believes to have no divine right, but to be only a
commiffion, with a delegated power from the prefbytery,
tolerated in our church for a time. With great difficulty
could we get the printing of that paper paffed for his importunity; but at laft we got all.

An exprefs from London this day tells us, that the army's parliament prefs the concurrence of our commiffioners to fend to Hampton court the propofitions to the King.
This feems to import the King's refufal of the propofals,
and difagreeing yet with the army. And what they will
do with the King, if he refufe the propofitions alfo, we
know not; only their laft remonftrance fhews their refolution to caft out of the parliament many more members,
and to take the lives of fome for example. The fpirit that
leads them, and the mercy of God to that oppreffed people, will not permit thefe tyrannous hypocrites to reft, till,
by their own hands, they have pulled down their Babel.
The Lord be with you. Let me hear of the receipt of this,
and help us with foreign news more liberally.

 Your Coufin,

   ROBERT BAILLIE.

176. *To Mr Spang.* *Edinburgh, October* 13. 1647.

——We gave in this day to the ftates a remonftrance of
the hazard of religion and covenant, if our army fhould
difband. We hope that plot, long hatched, and with too
great eagernefs driven on, fhall this day or to-morrow be
broken. Our dangers of farther confufion are great, if
God be not merciful. The perfecution at London is very
intolerable. I am very confident that party, fo much oppofite to God and man, cannot long ftand. Ere long, at
my leifure, I may give you a particular account of all our
affairs.——

177. *Lieu-*

177. *Lieutenant-General Baillie's vindication of himself for the part he acted in the battle of Kilfyth. To Mr R. Baillie.*

SIR,

AT your being here I did conceive you were defirous to know, amongft my other misfortunes, how I came to be employed in my country's fervice againft James Graham, and the other rebels who infefted this kingdom at that time; and what I could alledge for caufes, or rather means and midfes of his victories and my misfortunes in that employment; wherein, for your fatisfaction, you fhall be pleafed to know, that I believe that God Almighty doth often fuffer the wicked to profper, or go on fuccefsfully in their wicked way, for their greater punifhment when their cup is full, and for reclaiming of his own, whom he fuffereth for that end to be afflicted by them; in both which he is often pleafed to ufe ordinary means. And therefore, by his Providence, after the battle at Longmerton, and the intaking of Newcaftle, I returned to this country for doing my private bufinefs, and thereafter I went back into England; but being within twelve miles of Newcaftle, at Battle-caftle, I was overtaken by an exprefs, with letters from the committee of eftates, from the General, and fome of my noble friends, requiring my return to Edinburgh, for giving advice in bufinefs wherein the kingdom was much concerned. I immediately obeyed the order; and at my coming I found, that neither the Marquis of Argyle, nor the Earl of Lothian, could be perfuaded to continue in their employment againft thefe rebels, nor yet could the Earl of Calendar be induced to undertake the charge of that war; for which I was prefsd, or rather forced, by the perfuafion of fome friends, to give obedience to the eftate, and undertake the command of the country's forces, for purfuing its enemies: but becaufe I would not confent to receive orders from the Marquis of Argyle, if cafually we fhould have met together, after I had received commiffion to command in chief over all the forces within the kingdom, my Lord feemed to be difpleafed, and expreffed himfelf fo unto fome, that if he lived, he fhould remember it; wherein his Lordfhip indeed hath fuperabundantly been as good as his word.

I   Now,

Now, though the finding and ruining of thefe rebels have been talked of as eafy, yet you fhall know, Sir, that I was never enabled to do the fame, neither by the forces given me, nor the provifions made unto me; I never having at once and together 2000 foot, nor above 300 horfemen, before my laft difafter at Kilfyth, nor no artillery at all fit for intaking any ftrong houfe, though often demanded by me of the eftate.

Immediately after my unhappy engagement, I was commanded to march with all the infantry towards Argyle, whither the rebels had gone; but when we were at Rofneath, the Marquis [of Argyle hearing, that they were marched to Lorn and Lochaber, defired, that in regard of the feafon, (which was in the beginning of January), and fcarcity of victuals, a part of the foot only might be given to him to pine with his own in thefe parts; whilk fo foon as ordered by the committee was obeyed by me, giving to my Lord Marquis fixteen companies of foot, confifting of 1100 men; and returning with the reft to Perth, for the fecurity of thefe parts, as was commanded by the committee.   This party was ruined with the lofs of many good gentlemen more at Inverlochy, about Candlemas, as you have heard. In the end of March, the rebels returned through Murray, Aberdeenfhire, Merns, and Angus, to Dunkeld. Before whilk time, Sir John Hurrie was fent unto me, to ferve with me as General-Major; which, though I doubted nothing of his honefty, I fo difliked, that to fome, even then, I told, that I would not have recommended him to the ftate and to their fervice for my right hand, which, if I were fuperftitious, I might attribute to fomewhat elfe, having, fince our overthrow at Kilfyth, learned, that when he was fent over to   unto Perth, he was defired by fome to take heed left any thing might be atchieved where I was prefent, whereby I might have honour; which did appear clear enough, by his not charging the rebels with our whole horfe at their retreat from Dundee; nor yet would bring them up to me, from whence the rebels might have been charged in flanks, notwithftanding I did require him to it at feveral times by the Laird of Brodie and Mr Patrick Pitcairn, as they witneffed thereafter unto the parliament at Stirling; and yet, notwithftanding, he was exonered there, and I charged for their efcape.   Not long after, by order of committee, he was fent to Invernefs with fome 1200 foot and 160 horfe, where all the

VOL. II.   L l   foot

foot perifhed at Oldearn; and I after that was returned
from an unneceffary voyage into Athol by order of committee.　I was appointed by them to go the fame way with
about 2000 foot and 100 horfe.　It happening, as we
learned thereafter, that the fame day that I croffed Cairn
in the Mount, Hurrie was beat in Murray, I was appointed to leave with the Earl of Crawford his own regiment,
with Caffils's and Lauderdale's, for the defence of the low
country; and the fame day that thefe 100 horfe joined
with me, I marched from Cromar towards Strathbogie,
where the rebels were arrived the night before, and Gen.-
Major Hurrie joined with me about a mile from thence,
with 100 horfe, who had faved themfelves with him at
Oldearn.　At our approach, the rebels drew unto the places of advantage about the yards and dikes, and I ftood
embattled before them from four o'clock at night till the
morrow, judging them to have been about our own
ftrength.　Upon the morrow, fo foon as it was day, we
found they were gone towards Balveny.　We marched immediately after them, and came in fight of them about
Glenlivat, be-weft Balveny fome few miles; but that night
they outmarched us, and quartered fome fix miles from
us.　On the next day early, we found they were diflod-
ged, but could find no body to inform us of their march;
yet by the lying of the grafs and heather, we conjectured
they were marched to the wood of Abernethy upon Spey.
Thither I marched, and found them in the entry of Badzenoch, a very ftrait country, where, both for inacceffible rocks, woods, and the interpofition of the river, it
was impoffible for us to come at them.　Here we lay, looking one upon another, (the enemy having their meal from
Ruthven in Badzenoch, and flefh from the country, whereof we faw none), until for want of meal, (other victuals
we had none), the few horfemen profeffing they had not
eaten in forty-eight hours, I was neceffitate to march northward to Invernefs to be fupplied there; which done, I returned, croffed at Speymouth in boats, and came to New-
ton in Garioch.　Here Hurrie, pretending indifpofition,
left me.　There I was informed the rebels had been as far
fouth as Cupar in Angus, and were returned to Cur-
garffe, upon the head of Strathdon.　At that time I received letters from fundry of my friends of the committee
of eftates, fhewing me how I was cenfured for my flow
profecution of the war, (without confideration had of the
places

places they were to be found in, and of the forces and o-
ther provisions given me to find them out with): they
shewed me, my friends were wounded through my sides;
and that to be wary was commendable, but that delays in
subduing the rebels was a real and speedy ruin to the country, my friends, and myself; whereby I conceived they
would have persuaded me to think myself either a pol-
troon, or a traitor, or both; whereupon I desired Sir
Charles Arnot, Lieutenant-Colonel to my Lord Elcho, who
was going south for his private business, to pray my Lord
Crawford, and some others of my friends, to deal with
the state to give the conduct of their forces to some other,
and recal me. By my letters likewise I returned answer,
that I was in no ways enabled to perform that which they
required of me; that I was altogether unwilling to ruin
the forces committed to my charge in ways both against
reason and common sense; and therefore my humble intreaty was, that I might be recalled, and some one employed who would undertake more and perform better.
The next advice I had was from the Earl of Crawford, to
meet him, with the forces that were with me, at the mills
of Drum, upon Dee; which I did; and there his Lordship, with the Earl Marischal, and Major Winram of Libberton, produced the resolution and order of the great
committee, for employing the Marquis of Argyle, (who
was one of the signers of my order), in pursuance of the
rebels through the hills, or whithersoever they should go;
and to this purpose, appointed me to send to his Lordship
those who were come from Ireland with Col. Hume, who
were then some 1200 strong, the Earl of Crawford and
Lauderdale's regiments, with some four or five companies,
upon the braes of Perth and Angus, and 100 of Balcarras
horse; whereunto he was to join all such forces as he
could raise himself in the highlands. In exchange whereof, I was appointed to take unto me the Earl of Casilis's
regiment of foot, some 400 strong; whereby I was reduced to betwixt 1200 and 1300 foot, and about 260 horsemen of the Lord Balcarras and Col. Halket's regiments;
wherewith, by the same order of the great committee, I
was appointed to guard the low country from the down-
fallings of the enemy. This division being made conform
to the order, the Lords went from me southward. The
Marquis of Argyle refused the employment. His reasons
I know not. The Earl of Crawford was sent with these

L l 2

forces

forces defigned for purfuing the enemy into Athol; and I, by a letter from the committee, was commanded of new (without regard had of my weaknefs) to find out the rebels. For which purpofe, (and for a conference betwixt Seaforth and the Lord Balcarras, which failed), I marched into the Engzie, and from that back to the kirk of Keith, where, in the evening, the rebels coming from the hills, prefented themfelves to fight; and I drew our fmall forces in order above the kirk, in a place of advantage, to attend their approach; but they advanced not; but on the morrow marched unto Alford, where I arrived within two days, and was neceffitate to buckle with the enemy, who were a little above our ftrength in horfemen, and twice as ftrong in foot. The Lord Balcarras's horfemen were divided in three fquadrons; himfelf charged gallantly with two of them upon the enemy's right wing, where the horfe were; but the third, appointed for referve, when I commanded them to fecond my Lord, and charge the enemy's horfe in the flank, they went ftraight up in their comrade's rear, and there ftood until they were all broken. Our foot ftood with myfelf, and behaved themfelves as became them, until the enemy's horfe charged in our rear, and in front we were overcharged with their foot; for they had fix in file, did overwing us, who, to equal their front, had made the half ranks advance, and fo received the charge at three deep. The enemy had likewife two bodies of referve, and thir were they, who, by God's providence, did ruin me, as may be prefumed, for want of thefe men who were formerly by order taken from me; and if fuch provifions, and other forces, as fince have been plentifully furnifhed to others, whereby they have had, through God's bleffings, happy and wifhed fuccefs, mine might have been no lefs. Immediately thereafter I went to the parliament, then to meet at Stirling, where I had an exoneration and approbation for what was paft; yet in this Hurrie went before me. I would have demitted my charge there; but was not fuffered until the parliament fhould come to St Johnfton, or Perth. Many orders were for ftrengthening the forces, for the better purfuing of the rebels; but to fmall purpofe: all were ruined but thofe who had been in Athol with the Earl of Crawford, and of new none were brought in but fome 300 by the Lord Chancellor, the Earls of Caffils and Glencairn, and fome 60 horfemen under Col. Harry Barclay.

clay.   In the time of the parliament, the rebels, with their whole forces, came to the wood of Methven, and I, with the forces that were with me, (whereunto were added three new regiments out of Fife); and the whole noblemen and gentlemen convened there marched towards them from the bridge of Ern.   Upon sight of us the enemy retired to the hills.   I gave Hurrie orders to advance with Balcarras's horsemen; but he was needlesly so long in crossing the Powe, that I, with the foot, was as soon at the ford of Almond (where the rebels crossed) as he with the horse. After our return *, upon consideration of the many contests and hot disputes which were at every meeting betwixt the prime men of parliament, whereby I thought the country's service might suffer, I demitted my charge; and in open parliament it was received of me.   I was of new exonered and approven.   Nevertheless, the parliament desired I should continue with their forces, without commission, until the 8th of September; which I would have refused, alledging, that whereas I was so overcharged with aspersions while I served them with a commission, if any thing now should miscarry, I wanting commission, and serving as it were at discretion, my enemies would undoubtedly take occasion to charge me far more.   This was not satisfactory to the parliament; and my best friends did advise me to condescend to the parliament's desire; which I did, more for their satisfaction than my own; wherein I must acknowledge God's providence, and you shall find what followed in these other papers.

My Lords and Gentlemen, In obedience to your command, whereby I was required to inform you of the conduct of your forces since my demission at Perth, until that unhappy day at Kilsyth, your Lordships shall be pleased to know, that at the acceptance of my demission, the Honourable House of Parliament desired me to attend their forces until the coming of these appointed to succeed unto me; whilk I endeavoured to evade, and that because I being so highly scandalized, while I had charge, and served the estate by commission; if then, serving as it were at discretion, any thing should miscarry, or fall out amiss, undoubtedly the aspersions of the malicious, and my sufferings would be doubled.   This proved not satisfactory; and therefore, yielding unto their pressings, I was content to wait on their service a fortnight; in which time, such as were appointed for the charge, as I imagined,

* Here the three Fife regiments disbanded, and went home.

might

night both be advertised, and repair unto them, if diligence had been used. Immediately thereafter the rebels returned from the hills into Logiealmond; and I, with consent of the Lords and others of the committee who were then present, marched to the south side of the bridge of Ern, hopeful the regiments of Fife should have joined with us there. Upon the second day thereafter the rebels, having crossed Ern at or above Dinning, presented themselves before our quarters which, with consent of those who were of the committee, I had caused fortify as well as time would suffer, for which the rebels marched up towards the hills on the right hand. Upon the morrow, the rebels marched into the hills of Forth; and I, by advice of the committee, brought their forces that night to Lindores, and on the morrow to the hill of Rossie; where the regiments of Fife, for whom the Earl of Crawford had ridden to Cupar the night before, did join with us. That night, with advice of these of the committee, we lodged near unto Burleigh. The next day, by their advice, I marched and lodged that night betwixt Sauchie and the bridge of Tullibody. Upon the morrow, hearing the rebels had crossed Forth above Stirling, these of the committee then present, advised we should cross above Stirling. And a little above the park, upon the south-west side thereof, I halted with the five regiments, until those of Fife were brought up, hearing the rebels were marched towards Kilsyth. After the upcoming of those regiments, the Marquis of Argyle, Earl of Crawford, and Lord Burleigh, and with them, if I mistake not, the Earl of Tullibardine, the Lords Elcho and Balcarras, with some others, came up. My Lord Marquis asked me what was next to be done? I answered, The direction should come from his Lordship, and these of the committee. My Lord demanded what reason was for that? I answered, I found myself so slighted in every thing belonging to a commander in chief, that for the short time I was to stay with them, I would absolutely submit to their direction, and follow it. The Marquis desired me to explain myself; which I did in three particulars, sufficiently known to my Lord Marquis, and the other Lords and gentlemen then present. I told his Lordship, Prisoners of all sorts were exchanged without my knowledge: the traffickers therein received passes from others, and sometimes passing within two miles of me, did

neither

neither acquaint me with their bufinefs, nor, at their return, where, or in what pofture they had left the enemy. 2. While I was prefent, others did fometimes undertake the command of the army. 3. Without either my order or knowledge, fire was raifed, and that deftroyed which might have been a recompence to fome good deferver, for which I would not be anfwerable to the publick. Which confidered, I fhould in any thing freely give my own opinion, but follow the judgement of the committee, and the rather becaufe that was the laft day of my undertaking. From that our march to the bridge of Denny was agreed upon, and from that to the Hollandbufh, where we lodged that fame night, fome two miles and a half from Kilfyth ; where the rebels quartered likewife. On the next morning, the Marquis came to the head of our quarter, accompanied with the Lord Burleigh, or fome other, of whom I do not well remember. His Lordfhip enquired of the rebels, who, I told him, were at Kilfyth. His Lordfhip afked, If we might not advance nearer them. I anfwered, we were near enough if we intended not to fight, and that his Lordfhip knew well enough how rough and uneafy a way that was to march in. My Lord replied, we needed not keep the highway, but march over at neareft. I defired the Earl of Crawford and others might be called, who were in the next tent ; who, when they came, confented to our advancing, and I marched with the regiments through the corns and over the braes, till the unpaffable ground did hold us up. There I embattled, where I doubt, if on any quarter twenty men on front could either have gone from us or attack us. At the upcoming of the noblemen and others of the committee, whom I do not fo well remember, it was afked me by the Lords, but by whom in particular I have forgot, if we could not draw up to the hill on our right hand ? I fhewed them I did not conceive that ground to be good, and that the rebels, if they would, might poffefs themfelves of it before us. Their Lordfhips then defired that fome might be fent to vifit the ground ; which was done. In the mean time, I went with my Lord Elcho and my Lord Burleigh to the right hand of the regiments. Not long after, I was fent for by the other noblemen, and I defired the Lords Elcho and Burleigh to go with me, conjecturing they would prefs our removing ; which at our coming they did, alledging the

advantage

advantage might be had of the enemy from that field,
they being, as they fuppofed, already upon their march
weftwards.   I liked not the motion.   I told them, if the
rebels fhould feek to engage us there, I conceived they
fhould have great advantage of us ; farther, if we fhould
beat them to the hills, it would be unto us no great advantage : but, as I had faid, upon like difputes near unto
Methven and the bridge of Ern, to us the lofs of the day
would be the lofs of the kingdom.   This was not fatisfactory ; and therefore I gathered the voices of fuch of
the committee as were there, namely, the Marquis of Argyle, the Earls of Crawford and Tullibardine, the Lords
Elcho, Burleigh, and Balcarras ; who the reft were, I remember not ; but all agreed to draw unto the hill except
Balcarras.   This refolution was immediately followed.
The commanded men, with the horfemen, marched before ; the regiment on the right hand, facing to the right
hand, and fo the reft advanced to the hill ; where, I fuppofe, that was done by me which was incumbent unto me
in all that the fhortnefs of time would fuffer before we
were engaged.   Whereof, and of what was done with or
againft order, your Honours may be pleafed to confider,
by the figure in this other paper.   If I was either the laft in
the fight, or the firft in the flight, I leave to the teftimony of the Marquis's officers and Col. Hume's, and unto
General-Major Holbourn ; with whom, after thefe three
regiments were broken, I came off as on the rere of thefe
horfes of the rebels who broke the Earl of Crawford.
Thus your Lordfhips have, to my beft remembrance,
what you did require of me, whereby I hope it fhall be
evident, that I did nothing of confequence at no time, but
either with the affent or advice of thefe members of the
committee of ftate, whofe advice I was obliged to take,
and who had power to call me to an account for my ac-
ions, as likewife to govern the army, which they did
practife and make ufe of, even when by commiffion I was
in charge.   How dangerous then, I pray your Honours to
confider, had it been for me, being without commiffion,
to have flighted their advice and counfel, yea, even though
no prejudice fhould have followed thereupon ?

My Lords and Gentlemen, Being appointed by your
Honours, at your laft meeting, that I fhould enlarge my
relation concerning the advancing and engaging with the
rebels near unto Kilfyth, in all the circumftances and paf-

2   fages

sages thereof, and of every man's particular behaviour thereintill, in so far as I could remember ; you shall be pleased to know, that in my former paper, I shewed your Honours, that conform to the resolution of these of the committee who were present, I sent the commanded musketeers to the hill, and desired Major Halden to be their guide unto an inclosure which I pointed out unto him ; he did it. I followed them immediately with my Lord Balcarras and the horsemen, giving order to the foot to follow us, as I mentioned in my first paper. I desired my Lord Balcarras, that the horsemen might stay near unto the commanded musketeers ; which was done. I advanced myself, where there stood a number of gentlemen on horseback, where I found five ratt musketeers, more than a musket-shot at random before their body, without any order from me. The Earl Crawford, my Lord Burleigh, and I, galloped over the brae to see the posture of the enemy, who were embattled in the meadow, and sundry of them disbanded, were falling up the glen through the bushes. At our return to the brae-head, we found the Marquis of Argyle, with sundry others, and we saw Major Halden leading up a party of musketeers over the field, and toward an house near the glen, without any order from me ; neither did they come off when I sent Col. Arnot, and thereafter Routmaster Blair, to Major Halden, for that purpose : wherefore seeing the rebels fall up strong, I desired them to retire, and the officers to go to their charge. My Lord Balcarras and I galloped back to the regiments. He asked me what he should do ? I desired him to draw up his regiment on the right hand of the Earl of Lauderdale's. I gave order to Lauderdale's, both by myself and my adjutant, to face to the right hand, and to march to the foot of the hill, then to face as they were ; to Hume to follow their steps, halt when they halted, and keep distance and front with them. The Marquis's Major, as I went towards him, asked what he should do ? I told him, he should draw up on Hume's left hand, as he had done before. I had not ridden far from him, when looking back, I find Hume had left the way I had put him in, and was gone at a trot, right west, in among the dikes and among the enemy. I followed as fast as I could ride, and meeting the adjutant on the way, desired him he should bring up the Earl Crawford's regiment to Lauderdale's left hand, and cause the Gen.-Ma-

or Leflie draw up the regiments of Fife in referve as of efore : but before I could come to Hume, he and the o-her two regiments, viz. the Marquis of Argyle's, and the hree that were joired in one, had taken in an inclofure, rom· which (the enemy being fo near) it was impoffible o bring them off. I rode down on the rere, and return-d on their front. The rebel's foot, by this time, were pproached to the next dike, on whom our mufketiers nade more fire than I could have wifhed ; and therefore did what I could, with the affiftance of fuch of the of-icers as were known unto me, to make them fpare their hot till the enemy came to a nearer diftance, and o keep up the mufketiers with their pikes and colours ; ut to no great purpofe. In end, the rebels leapt over the dike, and with down heads fell on and broke hefe regiments. The prefent officers whom I re-nember, were Hume, his Lieutenant-Colonel and Ma-or of the Marquis's regiment, Lieutenant-Colonel Camp-ell, and Major Menzies, Glencairn's ferjeant-major, and Caffils's Lieutenant-Colonel, with fundry others, who be-laved themfelves well, and of whom I faw none careful o fave themfelves before the routing of the regiments. Thereafter I rode to the brae, where I found General-Major Holbourn alone, who fhewed me a fquadron of he rebels horfemen, who had gone by and charged the horfe-nen with Lieutenant-Colonel Murray, and, as I fuppofed, lid afterward rout the Earl of Crawford, and thefe with iim. Holbourn and I galloped through the inclofures to iave found the referve ; but before we could come at hem, they were in the flight. At the brook, that not ong before we had croffed, we overtook Major Inglis of nglifton, Captain Maitland, and fome other officers of he Fife regiments, who with me endeavoured to make iur people ftand, and maintain that pafs ; but all in vain. Thereafter we rode off together till we paft the bridge of Denny ; where we parted, and Holbourn and I went to Stir-ing, where, in prefence of the Earl of Tullibardine and the Lord Burleigh, I dealt with the horfemen that were there, o have gone with me to Clydefdale ; but loft my labour ; or they finding the bridge fhut, croffed the river at the ord of Dripp, except the officers, who thereafter went n with us into the town ; where, by advice of the Earl of Crawford, the other Lords and Gentlemen that were there,
                                                      the

the beft courfe was taken that might be for that time, for
fecuring that town and caftle.

It is objected againft me only, as if no other officer
were to give an account, neither for regiment, company,
nor corporalfhip, that on this our unhappy day there were
no lighted buits* among the mufquetry. The fire given by
the firft five regiments will fufficiently anfwer what concerns them; and for the other three, I humbly intreat
your Honours to inform yourfelves of General-Major Leflie, the adjutant, and the chief officers of the feveral regiments: if they do not fatisfy you therein, then I fhall anfwer for myfelf.   2. It is alledged we fhould have marched from the one ground to the other in battle: which was
impoffible, in regard of the ground, and our large front;
neither could we have marched with fingle regiments embattled from the north fide of the water to the hill, but
by turning a narrower flank of fix deep unto the enemy,
againft common fenfe, and in doing thereof, that fame
time that fhould have been loft drawing up upon the hill
in the ground defigned unto them, fhould likewife have
been loft, or rather more, at their imbattling upon the wa-
ter-fide. Befides, they fhould have been obliged to have
wheeled once to the right hand, and when they had come
into the ground, again to the left hand, which had been
a motion of great difficulty in that rough and unequal
ground; wherefore my order was, as I efteem it, abfolutely the beft, if it have your Honours approbation,
that our battle which fronted to the enemy, and was to
march off to the right hand, fhould by the feveral regiments face to the right hand, making the flank the front;
fo that even upon our march, the facing again to the left
hand fhould have put us in our former poiture and battle,
if the enemy had attacked us on that way.   3. It is faid,
I did neither give word nor fign. Whereunto I anfwer,
At our firft imbattling it was not yet time; then we faw
no enemy but the outer guard, neither was it refolved to
fight, but moft men thought the rebels were marching
weft. After we left our ground, we had no time to im-
battle compleatly; *which Souldatti* † thinks neceffary to be
done before the giving of word or fign, neither had it been
poffible to have given them unto all the regiments in a point
of time. Farther, it cannot be alledged, that the want of

* Matches. Flints were not then in ufe.
† Two words not clear in the MS. Whether printed right, uncertain.

hem made us lose the day, or that by the enemy's sign
ve could not be known one from another. No; the want
of points of formality was not the cause of the misfortunes
of that day; but God, for our other sins, did suffer us to
fall before our enemies, whereof the only mean and occasion is only probable to have been in our removing from
hat ground whereon we stood first embattled, being so
near an enemy who had sundry advantages of us. So by
his and my former paper, your Honours may judge of
my walking in your service since my dimission; and if
here be yet any that desires an account of the disposition
of things, and the many misfortunes of the country,
while I was in charge, I shall not shelter myself with that
approbation given at Stirling and Perth, but shall endeavour to satisfy your desire, by deducing unto you of new,
and in particular, how little I was enabled for performing
so great service as was required of me, and let you see my
care to have preserved your forces when little could have
been atchieved with them, in regard both of their numbers, of the season, and of the places where the enemy was
to be found; and, last of all, I am confident your Honours shall perceive, that the losses at Inverlochy, Aldearn,
and Alford, were not procured either through my negligence or counsel.

I being informed, that these noblemen by whom your
forces were accompanied, while in obedience to your Honours desires I waited upon them after my dimission, have
given in to your Honours a query. In what capacity they
shall be examined anent the misfortunes of that day at
Kilsyth; and not knowing what can be for their advantage, except it were that noblemen, who by their birth
and quality are members of the estate and parliament, or
the chief and prime officers of an army, are not so much
concerned in the country's good or evil, nor so much to
be charged for giving counsel in matters so much concerning the publick, when they do miscarry, as members of a
committee, which, I suppose, few or none will acknowledge; and therefore I conceive, that your Honours answer may be such, ye not knowing how and in what manner we did live together since my dimission, as thereby
some men might endeavour to infer my prejudice; wherefore my humble intreaty to your Honours is, that before
your answer, ye will be pleased to take into your consideration, that if there was any act at Perth, ordaining
                                                        your

your commander in chief to be abfolute, and without a
committee, that this act could in no ways be extended to
me, but rather to thefe appointed to fucceed me ; becaufe
in the act of my dimiffion is contained your Honours acceptance, and defire that I fhould command as of before,
which was always with a committee, who had power to
govern the army ; neither was that act of abfolute power
ever intimated to me. Next, your Honours will be pleafed
to confider, that if, in the divifion of the army, and other
things of confequence, I prefumed not to do any thing but
by advice of the committee while I had commiffion, with
a great deal of more reafon fhould I not have marched a
foot with your forces wanting a committee, and being
without commiffion employed in a manner at difcretion.
Moreover, I hope it is without controverfy, that thefe noblemen were members of that committee of ftate, to whom,
in the vacancy of parliament, all that concerns the publick
were intrufted ; witnefs Lieut.-Gen. Leflie's commiffion at
his arrival, without more power from parliament than
what they had while they were with me. They were conftantly with me, though fometimes in greater, fometimes
leffer numbers, even from the enemy's coming to Logiealmond until they were all ruined ; in which time I met daily with them. They confulted, difputed, and determined, in every thing as in committees : Inftance, the refolution taken at the Powfide, after difpute to retire to the
fouth fide of Earn ; upon the fouth fide of Earn, refolutions taken (if I have not forgot) in a formal committee,
for fome bufinefs of confequence, which I remember not ;
a refolution taken for putting our quarter in defence,
and keeping the forces within it upon the enemy's approach ; the enemy's marching into Fife ; the refolution taken, after difpute, to march to Lindores ; thereafter the refolution taken at the houfe of Burleigh, to
follow the rebels towards Stirling ; next, the refolution
taken upon the muir of Tullibody before the Chancellor
left us ; next, the refolution taken above the park of
Stirling, after fome difpute, to march to the bridge of Denny, and from that to the Holland-bufh ; and on the next
day, the refolution taken, by their perfuafion, to draw
nearer the rebels who were at Kilfyth ; and after our imbattling in a place, apparently of furety, the refolution taken to remove into another ground ; for qualification
whereof, I muft remit myfelf to the teftimony of thefe
same

ſame noblemen and gentlemen who were preſent upon the ſeveral occaſions. How then, I pray your Honours, can they be miſtaken in their own capacities, or alledge, that at any time I did any thing without them? Did they not in that capacity ſometimes command the whole, and ſometimes parties, from the army, I being in the field, without my knowledge? yea, and ſometimes ſuch acts of hoſtility, as I, without a ſpecial warrant from the eſtate, though I had been in charge by commiſſion, could not now have anſwered but at the rate of my head, as matters go?

But it ſhall be ſaid, there was not a quorum on that our unhappy day. Pleaſe your Honours, if that ſhould have been objected to me, if the ſucceſs had been good; or if through any fault of mine the reſt did not wait on, or if I did not proteſt againſt the going away of ſome of them; likewiſe your Honours ſhall be pleaſed to know, that the great committee has ſometimes approven things done without a quorum; inſtance the diviſion of the forces at Roſneath: but if there had been yet two more to have made the quorum, and theſe two of the Lord Balcarras's judgement, yet the major part had carried the unhappy point as it went. But though your Honours ſhould not look upon them as members of that committee, to whom, in the vacancy of parliament, the kingdom was intruſted, and by conſequence the country's forces, which I truſt your Honours ſound judgement will forbear, they are to be conſidered, either as noblemen, or as the prime officers of the army; and in either of thir qualities, if here had been preſent no member of committee for managing the war, I, in that exigent, the propoſition flowing from them, was obliged to take counſel from them; of the one, as of the prime men of the ſtate and parliament; and of the other, as the prime officers of the army, who ſhould have both accuſed and judged me if I had not followed their advice, my Lord Burleigh only exepted; who, for his ſincerity and known affection, for want of charge, ſhould not have been ſlighted. And if I had ſlighted the counſel given, either the givers, conſiderd as committee-men, members of ſtate and parliament, or officers of the army, I leave to your conſideration, if the nemy had marched off, as moſt men ſuppoſed, if this day ſhould have wanted accuſers, either for treaſon, or pultrony in the higheſt degree; and that in confirmation of that had been laid formerly of me.

                                         If

If nothing of all this can juftify my procedure, I will intreat your Honours to advert, that the eftates defire to me was to command as of before; and of before, the great committee of eftates declared, they remitted the carrying on of the war to the Marquis Argyle, Earl Crawford, and myfelf, which fhall be qualified upon your Honours demand.

So being confident that what I have faid fhall be taken into your Honours ferious thoughts, I recommend unto your confideration, whether or not thefe noblemens depofitions fhould be taken, as members of that great committee to whom the affairs of the kingdom was intrufted, and daily confulters with me in all things of confequence concerning the army, whofe advice and counfel I was obliged to take, in whatfoever capacity; or if on that unhappy day only, wherein all mifcarried, they are not to be thought on in that quality they had been in formerly with me, and from the beginning in profperous times.

• *Act of approbation to Lieutenant-General Baillie.*

Perth, the 4th of Auguft 1645.

The whilk day, the Lord Lieutenant General William Baillie having earneftly defired the Honourable eftates of parliament to examine his former carriage in the late truft laid upon him, and thereafter to be pleafed to liberate him, and to employ fome other in that charge, finds, That he deferves thanks and approbation for his carriage; and again renews the late act made at Stirling for that effect; and do alfo liberate him from that charge, and accepts of his dimiffion; but, in the mean time, defires him to continue in the fervice as of before, until the 8th day of September next.   Extract, &c.

Act for managing the war.

Perth, 5th Auguft 1645.

The eftates of parliament, &c. after hearing of the report made by the committee for managing of the war, and after debating thereupon, and publick voicing in the Houfe, do enact, ftatute, and ordain, That the directing of the war fhall be by the parliament, or committee of parliament;

parliament; and the actual managing and executing of the directions to be by the commander in chief, as he will be anfwerable to the parliament or their committtee. Extract.

The act doth qualify the neceffity of a committee going along with the army; and I doubt not but your Honours fhall find it without controverfy, that, by this act, nothing belonging to the war is left to the commander in chief, except the difcipline, which does chiefly confift in ordering of the march, the quarter, and the battle. The managing of the war, and directions, are folely intrufted to thefe of the great committee, whofe directions the commander in chief is to execute; and therefore, I hope, I cannot be condemned for confulting and advifing with fuch of them as were with me, I being without commiffion; and I will leave it to your Honours confideration, how it fhould have fuited with the truft repofed in them, and their duty to the country and caufe, if, upon any occafion, they fhould either have refufed, or forborn, to have given their faithful and beft counfel, yea, even tho' by me it had not been required.

178. *To Mr William Spang.* *March* 27. 1648.

Reverend and Dear Coufin,

—— He is wifer than a man who can inform what courfe our affairs here will take. This is the feventh week that I have been forced to attend in Edinburgh; and yet we fee fmall appearance of any good conclufion; but as they are I make you this account of them. After the King found himfelf difappointed of all the fair hopes made to him by Cromwell and his party, whether on their repentance, or their fear from Lilburn, Rainfborough, and their levelling friends, our commiffioners made more ferious applications, and were more acceptable than before. At the Ifle of Wight, his Majefty did live with them very lovingly, and upon great hopes on all hands. Tranair, Sir John Cheefly, Callendar, and all that came fome before them, gave it out confidently in the general, that the King had given to our commiffioners full fatisfaction. This caufed great joy, and a readinefs in all to rife in arms quickly for his deliverance. But when I found all

I   **bound**

bound up by oath, not to reveal any of the particular conceffions till the commiffioners returned, I feared the fatisfaction fhould not be found fo agreeable as was fpoken. The too ftrict fecrecy bred prejudices in the minds of the wifeft. And when we heard the report from the Chancellor and Lauderdale at their return, our fufpicions were turned into grief: for we found the conceffions no ways fatisfactory, and the engagements of fome to the King upon them fo great, as did much blemifh their reputation with many of their intimate friends. Our debates for more than a fortnight were to come to the bottom of thefe offers, and to find a way how we might be free of them. We were malecontent with our commiffioners: their fcurvy ufage by the parliament of England, their compaffion of the King's condition, Lanerk's power with Lauderdale, and both their workings on the Chancellor, made them to accept of lefs, and promife more to the King, than we would ftand to. They were content we fhould declare our diffatisfaction with the King's offers as we thought fit, both by the church and the ftate, on condition we would confent to a levy againft the faction of fectaries. To this we were not unwilling, providing we might be fatisfied in the ftate of the queftion, and might be affured, that the army fhould be put in fuch hands as we might confide in. Both thefe were promifed to us in private; but when we found no performance, the bufinefs is retarded to this day. Betwixt the Chancellor, Duke Argyle, Treafurer, Lauderdale, Lanerk, Balmerino, Wariston, Mr Robert Douglas, Mr George Gillefpie, Mr David Calderwood, Mr Robert Blair, Mr David Dickfon, Mr Samuel Rutherford, many meetings have been had, night and day, private and publick; but as yet our difcords increafe, and are ready to break out in a fearful rupture both of church and ftate. Our meetings were long in private for a ftate of a queftion. We required peremptorily to ftand to our former principles and covenant; "to have religion settled " firft; and the King not reftored till he had given fecuri- " ty, by his oath, to confent to an act of parliament for " injoining the covenant in all his dominions, and fettling " religion according to the covenant." We ftuck many days on that negative expreffion, "The King not to be re- " ftored till he had fworn the covenant." This much had both our parliament and affembly preffed upon him at Newcaftle; yet at laft we were content of affirmative

xpreſſions : " Religion and the covenant to be ſettled,
' and thereupon the King to be reſtored." The next dif-
iculty in the queſtion was about the malignants. We
vere peremptory to have none of them in our army who
hould not take the covenant, and to have all of them de-
:lared enemies who ſhould riſe in arms by themſelves for
iny end contrary to our cauſe. Here we had great ſtrug-
jling. In the writ which we called an agreement and en-
jagement, the King's offers therein, too great favour was
hown to malignants. We reſolved to beware of them ſo
nuch the more. The greateſt ſtop of all was upon the
iath. We reſolved to have theſe things put in a formal
iath, to be taken ſolemnly by all the members of parlia-
nent and officers of our army. They declined an oath
iy all means. While we are like to come to no agree-
nent about theſe things, the pulpits ſounded loud againſt
he dangers of malignants, but more ſoftly againſt ſecta-
ies. We prepare alſo a declaration of dangers and du-
ies, wherein we preſs to the full our diſſatisfaction with
he King's conceſſions in matters of religion. This gave
jreat offence to our commiſſioners. We had put them
o it to give us in writ the report what paſſed between
hem and the King concerning religion; for his Majeſty
n his letter to us had ſaid, he had offered to them what
ie was confident would give us ſatisfaction, which they are
neceſſitated to give us in writ theſe private conceſſions, and
ie content to have them, and our reaſons againſt them,
iubliſhed to the world. They were not a little offended;
iut there was no remedy. To our ſenſe, they had paſſed
he bounds of their duty, though both the committee of
:ſtates, and parliament itſelf, had, in a fair general, with-
iut examination, approved all they had done. We thought
t deſtructive to our cauſe and covenant, and ourſelves ab-
iolutely impeded from all motion for the King till theſe
jrounds of motion were publickly diſclaimed. It increa-
ed our offence, that ſo many noblemen did vex us with
lebates and votes openly in face of the commiſſion, after
ve had changed in private, for the ſatisfaction of the
Chancellor and Lauderdale, many paſſages of our writ;
ilſo that they had laboured to their power to make a party
imong the miniſters to oppoſe us, Mr Andrew Ramſay,
Mr Andrew Fairfoul, Mr Robert Laurie, Mr Andrew
Affleck, and divers others; but eſpecially Mr William
Colvil, who had in private objected againſt one paſſage,
                                        inferring

inferring the neceffity upon confcience to reftore the King prefently to the exercife of his full regal power in all his dominions, notwithftanding of all he had done, without any condition, either of covenant, religion, or propofitions; that we were obliged to do this duty unto him, and never more to oppofe till we found him abufe this power; and then we might refift, albeit no more but the abufe of this power.   I did think it enough in our fubcommittee to bring him to acknowledge fo fhameful a tenet, all of us thinking he would not have the boldnefs any more in publick to fpeak to fuch a purpofe; yet in the face of the commiffion, in a very jeering infolent way, being a little provoked by the indifcreet challenge of Mr Rutherford, he offered to reafon for fuch a conclufion.   We had not failed to have called him to an account for his malapertnefs, had not the intervention of other greater affairs diverted us.

By this time the parliament was fet.   Never fo many noblemen prefent in any of our parliaments; near fifty Earls and Lords.   Among them were found but eight or nine for our way; Argyle, Eglinton, Caffils, Lothian, Arburthnot, Torphichen, Rofs, Balmerino, Cupar, Burleigh, and fometimes the Chancellor and Balcarras.   All the reft, with more than the half of the Barons, and almoft the half of the Burgeffes, efpecially the greater towns, Edinburgh, Perth, Dundee, Aberdeen, St Andrew's, Linlithgow, ran in a ftring after Duke Hamilton's vote. That party, befides the advantage of the number of two at leaft to one, had likewife the moft of the ableft fpeakers.   For us none did fpeak but Argyle and Warifton, and fometimes Caffils and Balmerino; but they had the Duke, the Treafurer, Lanerk, Lauderdale, Traquair, Glencairn, Cochran, Lee, all able fpokefmen; yet the other party had the advantage of reputation, having from the beginning been conftant in our caufe: alfo all the affiftance the church could make was for them.   The firft pickering was for our declaration.   When, contrary to their minds, we had paffed it, they were earneft it might not be publifhed; but we had given orders, as ever had been our cuftom, to print it, even before we had communicated it to the parliament.   They had divers purpofes, either by perfuafion or violence, to have kept it in; but we let it go out on Monday, and ordained it to be read on Sunday thereafter in all the kirks of Edinburgh, and about

bout.   That which haftened it out was our irritation by
the Treafurer's challenge of Argyle on the Monday morning; an unhappy accident, that was ready to have kindled
the fire amongft us all, had not God prevented it.   Argyle's enemies had of a long time burdened him, among
many flanders, with that of cowardice and cullionry.   On
the Friday afternoon in parliament, difcourfing merrily
with the Treafurer, he faid, " He heard of a meeting
" whereat the Treafurer had been the other night."
Speaking a little of this purpofe, he apprehended, that the
Treafurer had faid, not only that the beft men of the
kingdom had been at that meeting, but alfo, that himfelf
was a better man than he.   Upon this, Argyle goes out
of the Houfe in anger, and calls for Major Innes, who
fat at both their feet, and heard their difcourfe, to know if
he had heard the Treafurer fay, that himfelf was a better
man than Argyle.   Innes did not avow the words; but
being fent to the Treafurer from Argyle, to try if he had
fpoken fo, he faid, He would not account to Argyle what
he faid; but whatever it was, he would make it good with
his fword.   Upon this, Argyle defired him to appoint
time and place; and on the Sunday, a publick faft-day,
the Treafurer fent back word, after both fermons, that
on Muffelburgh links, at feven o'clock to-morrow morning, he fhould meet him, and bring a nobleman for a fecond.   Innes, albeit no great friend to Argyle, not only
offered himfelf to Argyle for a fecond, but told him, he
would refent it as a wrong if he were not admitted; fo
Argyle, with no flefh but Innes, the Treafurer, and Lanerk his fecond, did meet.   Incontinent all were miffed,
and many ran to all quarters to fearch for them; and, by
God's providence, before they began their plea, fome fell
on them, and made them part without a ftroke.   The
council that night, with much ado, got them to a profeffed coldrife friendfhip.   We had refolved in the commiffion of the church, to have made both before the congregation acknowledge their fault; fo much the more, as
Sinclair and David Lefly, Eglinton, and Glencairn, fome
days before; and fome days after, Kenmuir and Cranfton,
had been on the like engagements: but other matters put
that out of our heads.
    The publifhing of our printed declaration put fome of
the parliament on many hard thoughts of us; but the refult of all was, the calling of fix of us to confer with fix
                                                        of

of their great committee upon a state of a question. For them were, Lauderdale, Lanerk, Humbie, Lee, Archibald Sydserf, and Sir Alexander Wedderburn, with the Chancellor: For us, Mr David Calderwood, Mr D. Dickson, Mr G. Gillespie, Craighall, Libberton, I, with the moderator Mr Robert Douglas. They produced to us a draught of a declaration, penned with a great deal of deliberation, by the counsel of many, but especially by Lanerk's pen. They had slandered us exceedingly, as opposite to all war with the English sectaries on any terms. To clear that mistake, I wrote, and put in divers hands, Lanerk's among others, the paper which herewith I send you. Their draught did endeavour to give pretty good satisfaction to most of our doubts; yet after a day's advisement, we found it so unsatisfactory, that themselves were content we should take it to our consideration to be corrected as we found expedient. Mr Gillespie and my Lord Wariston had drawn an oath of association, which pleased themselves well, but their opposites extremely ill, and their best friends but so and so, when best corrected. In our draught we took so much of their declaration, and our friends oath of association, as we thought made a state of a question which should be satisfactory to all; and here, to my great joy, were we on the very nick of a cordial agreement: but behold a most unhappy accident, which did put us to, and yet has kept us in a discord almost irreconcileable. There was a great desire in the chief that were for an engagement, to seize on Berwick and Carlisle, both for the extreme great advantage of these places, and also to begin the war, for the encouraging of our friends abroad, and wakening our people at home. This they counted no wrong, nor invasion of England; their quarrel being only against the sectaries and their adherents, for vindicating of our covenant, for the rescue of the King, parliament, and oppressed covenanters. An indiction needed not against this enemy. The towns of England, for our passing and safe retreat in the prosecution of the common cause, ought to be patent. Yet the most of us were averse from this design, and had long kept it off. In a few days we found the parliament, two thirds for one, otherwise affected than we wished. So soon as it was constitute, there was an inclination to make a close committee for the greatest affairs. Six of every state were named. So long as their power was not determined, we were not

startled;

startled; but so soon as they got an absolute power to do what was fitting for the safety of the kingdom, in relation to Berwick and Carlisle, incontinent all were alarmed. Six of the trustiest members of parliament protested against that vote. The protestation was not admitted; but the protestors thereafter kept themselves together; and albeit the least, yet they kept the reputation of the best part of the parliament. Privately and publickly we gave warning, that the passing of such a vote would break us irrecoverably; but we were believed too late. My Lord Callendar's party were so furiously earnest to possess Berwick, and to begin action, that they threatened to desert Hamilton and his friends if they delayed the vote any longer: so it passed, notwithstanding our earnest intreaties, and our friends protestation to the contrary. The issue was, we refused to confer any more on the state of a question. The protestors confirmed their union. Many of the shires sent in to supplicate against all engagement, unless the kirk were satisfied in the state of a question. David Lesly, Holburn, with the rest of the officers, declared their resolution, not to move without our satisfaction. After some days contest, we found a great change. The Chancellor that had hitherto been too far for the engagers, offended with their unreasonable proceedings, came almost wholly off them to us his old and best friends. The chief of the Duke's friends came to intreat us to accept all we could desire, to state the question according to our mind, to be assured to have such in our armies and committees as we liked, to give over the surprise of Berwick, and all acting by the close committee. These things, by the Treasurer and others, were offered to us, with many fair and earnest expressions. As yet we are not satisfied by words, and some of our leaders are likely never to be satisfied, and resolve to trust to nothing that their opposites can do or say, so long as this parliament, which they call unsound, is in being. The danger of this rigidity is like to be fatal to the King, to the whole isle, both churches and states. We mourn for it to God. Though it proceed from two or three men at most, yet it seems remediless. If we be kept from a present civil war, it is God, and not the wisdom of our most wise and best men, which will save us. I am more and more in the mind, that it were for the good of the world, that churchmen did meddle with ecclesiastick affairs only; that were they ever so able otherwise, wife, they are unhappy ftatefmen; that as Eraftianifm is hurtful to the church, fo an Epifcopal papacy is unfortunate for the ftate. If no man were wifer than I am, we fhould not make many fcruples to fettle the throne, and pull down the fectaries. Never more high and dangerous queftions in Scots hands. What the conclufion will be, a few days will declare.

While we are fticking in thefe labyrinths, one of our number, none of the moft rigid, falls on the overture to propone the commiffion of the general affembly's defires all together immediately to the parliament, wherein, if we got fatisfaction, we were to go on as they defired us, to ftate a queftion. The motion was approven. This draught of eight articles, after fome changes of it to the worfe, was paffed, and prefented, in name of the commiffion of the church, by Mr Robert Blair, Mr Robert Ramfay, and I. For anfwer, the eighteen of their firft great committee, with the addition of fix more, twenty-four in all, the prime members of parliament, were appointed to confer with us on thefe our defires. The commiffion, to thefe feven who had met before with the fubcommittee of parliament upon their declaration, added Mr Robert Blair and Mr Andrew Cant. On the Thurfday, before noon, they went through the firft five of our defires. All the fticking was on the fifth; wherein we preffed to have the malignants who fhould rife in arms by themfelves declared enemies, as well as fectaries. This was contrary to the King's agreement with fome, and their intentions, who, without the help of malignants, made the work impoffible. At laft we carried the article. In the afternoon we had almoft differed on the fixth, the King's oath to confent to an act of parliament for injoining the folemn league before his reftitution to the exercife of the royal power. We preffed him not to take the covenant; but whatever his confcience was, we conceived him bound to confent to the neceffary laws of the kingdom. Thus his good-dame Queen Mary affented to the acts of parliament for the Reformed religion. This alfo did pafs for the fubftance; only a committee was appointed to fmooth fome expreffions about the King's reftitution. We had no power to recede from any word, and fo would not be at any committee for changing any expreffion, but believed the commiffion of the kirk would not ftick at words, if the matter were well fecured. On the feventh article, for managing

aging the war by conftant hands, there was not much
lebate. We could here fall on no words which might
not be granted, and yet little for our advantage; albeit
his was the greateft of all our difficulties. Upon the con-
titution of the army depended all our human fafety,
hope, and fecurity of whatever elfe was granted. It goes
now fo, that no truft remains to any words or oaths: except therefore force were in the hands of our friends, we
refolved not to ftir; and yet we could not crave any fuch
particular, but had neceffity to have it done one way or
other. Some underhand did move to have the Duke General. Callender and his friends were careful to free us
of this fear; for generally all but the Dukes's own followers doubted much the fincerity of his intentions, either
for religion or the King; albeit I confefs, whenever I
heard him or his brother fpeak in earneft, they feemed to
me to give ample fatisfaction; but as yet they have not the
fortune to be believed by many. Ochiltree's bufinefs
ticks ftill in the throats of fome. Upon too great probability, Callender, by his own party, which is great, is
wifhed General: but his inflexibility to ferve againft Mont-
ofe, upon the fenfe of private injuries, whereby inde-
ible marks of difgrace were printed on the face of Scot-
and, and his very ambiguous proceedings in England at
Hereford and elfewhere, make us that we dare not put
our lives and religion in his hands. David Lefly and Hol-
urn are more beloved by us. The old General, for all
his infirmities, is acceptable; alfo Middleton, and the general of the artillery, will not be refufed. In private we
were affured thefe fhould be the general officers; but we
fill not be affured without fight, and our main difficulties
fill be upon the committees to govern the ftate and army
in the intervals of the feffions of parliament. If herein
hey permit them whom we count trufty, to have full
ower, when they can carry what they will in parliament,
it will be a great wonder; yet if in this we get not fatis-
action, nothing elfe will fatisfy. We expect little debate
on the eighth article, to have an oath for all this; but herein we were peremptory, and hope to obtain. It was my
wifh, that only the parliament and officers of the army
fhould fwear, and that the body of the land fhould be put
to no more oaths; but it feems this affociation muft be no
lefs fworn than our two former covenants. While thus
far we had proceeded on Thurfday, I thought we were as

2   good

good as agreed; fo I refolved to go home to-morrow; for the opening of our provincial fynod lay on me as the laft moderator; alfo a new very dangerous infection was broken up in Glafgow, and come to my very gates. Upon thefe reafons, after eight weeks ftay, I got leave from the commiffion to return; albeit very hardly, for our bufinefs was not fully clofed, and I had immediate accefs and truft with fundry of the moft leading men, with whom I was efteemed to do no evil fervice; while others, by their way, did irritate more; alfo we had refolved to have reafon of Mr W. Colvil and his followers for their great and dangerous infolency, not fo much in their open contempt, neglecting to read our declaration, as in their fermons and private negotiations, both with noblemen and minifters, to frame a faction for dividing of our church, wherein the peremptory rigidity of fome, the too great fimplicity of others, and the evil talents of more, gave them the occafion to make too great progrefs; but having ftaid till I declared my fenfe abundantly againft thefe men, and helped to bring them low, and put them in a way either to recant or be cenfured, I came away on the Friday morning, and to my own houfe at night. The college was almoft totally diffolved for fear of the plague. We are waiting on the Lord's pleafure, what he will do with Glafgow, whether yet it may be fpared from the plague, whereof I am not defperate; and what fhall be the next act of the long tragedy among us. Much fpeech of the Prince's coming: as yet our affairs are not in a condition to receive him as I could wifh; but ere long he may be welcome. I cannot, of certain knowledge, hear any thing of that youth, whereby I can conjecture, on any hand, what to hope or fear. His mother's unkindnefs to the Queen of Bohemia and her fons is vifibly retaliated in the eyes of all Europe. My beft wifhes are for the reftitution of King James's family. Before this, I fee no appearance of any folid peace, either to Germany or Britain. This long letter fhall be a ground of a challenge, if you write fo rare and fo fhort as this while bygone. Farewell.

Glafgow, March 28. 1648.

179. *To Mr William Spang.* *June* 26. 1648.

Reverend and Dear Coufin,

Since my laft, March 28th, I have heard nothing
rom you, nor long before. Our affairs fince have had a
reat progrefs, but not an inch to the better. All appear-
nce of any poffibibility to agree, daily does more and
nore evanifh. A fpirit of bitternefs, jealoufy, and mu-
ual contempt, grows on all hands, and the ftronger par-
y is begun to perfecute the weaker, and that evil is like
nuch to increafe quickly. The courfe of affairs may draw
)oth befide any intention to do the worft of that which
as been objected to either as their defign. The fectaries
nd malignants may fhortly divide the whole ifle, to the
reat danger and hurt of the King and the honeft Prefby-
erians in both kingdoms. Our ftorm is yet but waxing;
ve can make but fmall judgement of its end.

When I clofed my laft to you, as then I wrote, there
vas fome good hope of concord, a pretty good anfwer
vas expected to our eight defires; but fome unhappy men
nade all thefe hopes to flee away. The committee of
wenty-four framed their anfwer, and got it paffed in an
ct of parliament before it came to the commiffion of the
cirk. They to whom the confideration of it was com-
nitted, looked fo narrowly into every word of it, that
hey found fnares in every other line, and not one of our
:ight defires fatisfied. This much the commiffion repre-
ented in a new paper, added a new defire, to declare a-
;ainft the negative voice of the King, which the commif-
ioners papers in England had fo much preffed. This
lraught of Mr James Guthrie's, in the abfence of Mr
3. Gillefpie, was as ill taken when it came to the par-
iament as any other, and fo was as good as laid afide, till
n the large declaration they gave it an anfwer. In the
nean time they put out the act of pofture for fetting all
he kingdom in a defence againft invafion; but in a few
lays came out the act of levy, which, incontinent, a-
armed all. The firft narrative was ill taken, a danger
:rom the malignants that had taken Berwick and Carlifle.
The world knew there was no danger to us from them,
or they had been with us in Edinburgh, and their enterprife
upon

upon Berwick and Carlisle was generally believed not to have been undertaken without some of our privities. The act therefore, before publishing, was helped, grounding our levy on the danger from the army of sectaries, which these surprises would draw down on our borders; and in this there is like to be no false prophecy.

Here it was where our differences began first to be irreconcileable. We stood on the managers of the war as much as any one thing. The committees of shires, and crowners for the posture, were indifferent; but when it came to the levy, generally all the crowners of horse and foot were chosen as Duke Hamilton and Callender liked. Our friends here got very little of their will; but the cope-stone was put upon our despair, when we found Hamilton and Callender, how much contrare soever one to another, yet at last, after there had been much speech and dealing of either to join with Argyle, and that, through whose fault I know not, had miscarried at last; I say, Hamilton and Callender did join too friendly to our prejudice, and that on these terms, beside others, that the Duke should be General, and the Earl his Lieutenant. Both of them to that time had been opposite to the employment of either; and so long as they had any hope of our compliance, both professed a great deal of willingness to continue the old general officers, without any change, and each offered to mar the employment of the other; but when they could not draw our friends to engage in any terms liking them, then peremptorily they struck hands, and went on without much more notice of us.

With threats and promises they moved old Lesly to lay down his place. For a long time we had hopes the army, which we had kept from dissolving, should have been firm to us; but Middleton spoiled that our hope. All the officers had joined in a supplication to the parliament backing the desires of the kirk. Had this been stood to, the designs of others had soon been broken; but Middleton, who long had shifted subscription, at last was willing to join, with an addition of a short postscript, of the subscribers willingness notwithstanding to obey all the parliament's directions. This commentary did so enervate the text, that our friends persuaded the officers to lay aside their petition, as that which was profitable for nothing, being clearly emasculate by the postscript. From that day

re loft the army.   David Lefly, by much dealing of
many, was made willing to keep his place; yet afterward
he repented, and gave it over; and fo did Holburn, and divers more of the moft gallant of their officers, when they
faw the church's advice totally neglected.

These things did grieve much the fpirits of many, and
I believe few more deeply than my own, fo that my health
by grief for many days was impaired; yet, by the importunity of many, I was (before fully recovered) drawn
back again to Edinburgh.   Then I found that matters totally were defperate.   Lauderdale with grief, the Treafurer, with many tears, told me how fore againft their
hearts they went the way they were in, cafting the blame
on others, who yet affured me, for their parts, that they
found never any truth in the fair general offers was made
them, when it came to any particular.   However, then
the dice was caft, every fide were engaged to go on in
their own way.

The declaration, long and well ftudied, and penned
moft by Lanerk, in very plaufible terms, was offered to
us.   We appointed a committee for it.   It was my advice
to be fhort in obferving, and to pitch but on the main exceptions.   On fundry we agreed, and what fome offered
I got out of their own conceptions; yet being obliged to
take phyfic, I was forced to keep my chamber ten days.
In this interval Mr Gillefpie, without much contradiction,
got in his reprefentation whatever either himfelf or W.
or C. had collected, which made it tedioufly long, and
in fundry things needlefsly quarrelfome, and to come fo
late, that the parliament, after ten days waiting for it, at
Lauderdale's canker'd motion, commanded their declaration to go out without any more notice of what we had to
fay againft it.

At this time a meffenger went to the parliament of England with five demands, craving an anfwer peremptorily
in fifteen days.   That which they feared moft was to engage in any treaty.   This we ever preffed, but they thought
it needlefs, fince they quarrelled not with the parliament,
but with the army and their adherents, with whom they
were not obliged to treat, and lofe the feafon of the Englifh motions at home.   The rumour of our war made a
great ftir in many parts both of England and Ireland, and
put the parliament to alter much of their former way, to
                                                    grant

grant London their militia, the tower the guard of the parliament as before, the freedom of their imprisoned aldermen, the recalling of the eleven members to their places, the restoring the impeached Lords, the making Warwick admiral of the navy : the army also was forced to divide ; Cromwell to Wales, where yet he is ; Fairfax to the north : but in his march he was recalled to suppress the Kentishmen. The most of the shires were on their feet. Had not our unhappy discords marred our expedition ; had we with a small army, with any unanimity, but appeared on the border in time, appearingly, without stroke, we might have got for the King, for our friends, for ourselves, what we pleased ; but our fatal discords were as well known at London as at Edinburgh, so leisure is taken by Fairfax to quiet Kent and Essex, and by Cromwell to hold down Wales, and by others to keep in Cornwall. Lambert in Yorkshire had time to keep back Langdale from York and Lancashire, and great pains are taken to join the Presbyterians and the Independents against all the risers in the shires, and our army, as against malignants. If this conjunction go on, the King and our nation are in a hard taking.

In the mean time the parliament and commission proceed in their paper-differences. Their declaration and our representation are both printed. They go on to act, we to preach against the lawfulness of the enagagement as it was stated. The rendezvouses are appointed for the shires against the 21st of May. Many presbyteries, synods, burghs, shires, gave in supplications the 1st of June, to delay the levy till the church got satisfaction. Our poor town, still singular in that unhappiness, is made the first example of suffering. All of us the town-ministers went up to supplicate the Duke in Hamilton, in the name of the presbytery, to delay the lifting of our people till our supplications were answered by the parliament. I spoke oft, and at length, to his Grace and Excellency, as moderator of the presbytery. We got courteous and civil words enough ; but deeds very bitter. Incontinent all our magistrates and town-council, that same night, were summoned to answer to the parliament, for not keeping with their men the rendezvous ; a fault common to them with all their neighbour towns and shires, yea with the whole kingdom well near ; yet they were all cast in the tolbooth,

tolbooth, and kept there divers days; and becaufe they profeffed fcruple of confcience to further the levy, they were all deprived of their places, and a commiffion fent to the old council that before was removed, to elect new magiftrates; who made (with lefs fcruple than I wifh to fet down and name) Colin Campbell Provoft, John Anderfon, James Tran, William Neilfon, Bailies; and thefe, for a council, took the old cafhiered men with a very little change: fo great grief is among the new faction in our town, and too great contentment in the old, to fee themfelves reftored to their places by the fame men and means they were cafhiered, the parliament putting them in, and others out, only for following the advice of their minifters and commiffion of the church.

But this is not all our mifery. Before this change, fome regiments of horfe and foot were fent to our town, with orders to quarter on no other but the magiftrates, council, feffion, and their lovers. Thefe orders were exerced with rigor. On the moft religious people of our own, huge burdens did fall. On fome 10, on fome 20, on others 30 foldiers, and more, did quarter; who, befide meat and drink, wine, and good cheer, and whatever they called for, did exact cruelly their daily pay, and much more. In ten days they coft a few honeft, but mean people, 40,000 lb. befides plundering of thefe whom neceffity forced to flee from their houfes. Our lofs and danger was not fo great by James Graham.

No relief got we, but a greater mifchief. Many yeomen in Clydefdale, upon fear to be levied by force, had fled from their houfes to Loudon-hill, and there had met in a body of fome hundred horfe and foot. Sundry of the foldiers who had left the army, joined with them. Much fpeech began of a refiftance in the weft. Too many minifters, both eaft and weft, were faid to be for it, if here fhould appear a likelihood of a party. For myfelf, was clear againft all fuch thing: I thought we had neither a juft caufe nor a good authority for any fuch matter, and the fartheft we might go was no more than fuffering. While we are on thefe debates, Callender and Middleton come weft on the Saturday the 10th of June. About a fortnight before Argyle had met with Eglinton and Caffils at Irvine. This meeting gave a fhow to the ilk of a refiftance in the weft. Fife alfo feemed to look
that

that way : but it appears now well, that the named noblemen, whatever they met for, did conclude of no such
thing ; for Argyle went presently home to Inverary, and
Eglinton declared himself willing to let his men be levied.
However Callender made haste to make the west secure.
The Clydesdale men came, on the Saturday, to Mauchline to communicate. That night Callender lay at Paisley.
On Monday he made a rendezvous at Stewarton, of 1600
good horse, and above 2000 foot, at ten o'clock. From
thence he marched to Mauchline, sending Middleton before him with 300 horse.

The noblemen and gentlemen of the shire of Ayr had
sat late on the Saturday at a committee in Riccartoun :
finding that Fife had yielded, that Argyle was far off and
quiet, and Callender with an army in their bosom, they
resolved to lay aside all thoughts of resistance, and of this
advertised the people at Mauchline. They notwithstanding would not dissolve, but after the sermon in the morning of Monday, some 1200 horse and 800 foot with eight
ministers go out to Mauchline muir ; gentlemen or officers very few were among them. While they are about
to chuse some, Middleton appears. They expected no e-
nemy in haste, so they are amazed at the sight. The ministers went to Middleton, and capitulated for the safety
of all, except the soldiers who had left their colours,
whereof were 100 or 200. This written capitulation the
ministers did carry to the people, and persuaded to their
power their disbanding. The most of the men of Kyle
and Cunningham were content to go, but the soldiers and
Clydesdale men would needs fight. While they are more
than an hour in this confused uncertainty, and sundry
crying to fight, Middleton makes a few of his horse to
charge ; but the people presently fled. His soldiers abstained from killing, only a taking horse, arms, and
purses. A troop of the people fleeing to a bridge, and
missing the way, were forced to stand. They turned on
the soldiers, and fought very stoutly. Here was the most
of the slaughter ; near forty fell : some say as many of
the troopers as of the people. Middleton himself was sore
put to it by a smith. He got some wounds ; and confesses,
had he not stabbed the smith, though not deadly, while
he was bringing on him too great a stroke, he had undoubtedly killed him. Many of the people were wounded. By the time Callender and the army came up, the
                                                    people

people were difperfed. They fpeak as if the Clydefdale horfe were gone to Galloway, with a mind yet to fight; but I believe it not. There is indeed in our people a great animofity put in them, both by our preaching and difcourfe; alfo by the extreme great oppreffion of the foldiers; fo that it fears me, if Lambert be come to Carlifle with frefh men, and have put Langdale in to the town, as they fay, fo foon as our army fhall be entangled with the Englifh, many of our people rife on their backs. To prevent this, they have paffed a fevere, and, as I think, an injuft and tyrannous act of parliament, to put all the fubjects of the kingdom to fubfcribe their readinefs with life and eftate, to further the execution of the acts of this parliament, meaning, above all, the act of the levy, which the church has fo much contradicted as unlawful; alfo to declare, that the execution of the acts of this parliament, are the moft neceffary and fitteft means to remeid our troubles, and preferve religion; and that all who fhall not fubfcribe this much, without delay, are juftly to be holden enemies to the common caufe, religion, and country. We think the beft part of the land will never fubfcribe this, and fo that all of us who refufe fhall be at their mercy. If I be put to this fubfcription, as poffibly I may fhortly, I think I may once more come to you, and that to remain longer. A fervice to any of our regiments, or any company of Englifh merchants, will be very welcome to me; which you will be thinking of; for however yet they let minifters alone, and I have as much favour as any other, yet I think our troubles may fo increafe, that I may be glad to be out of Scotland. It feems many of our people may incline to venture their lives, either alone or with the Englifh army, if it come near, againft them who now are employed. I am not for any fuch matter. For fear of fectaries, we have not joined with malignants. If we fhould join with fectaries, it would be to me abominable. We who refolve neither to join with malignants nor fectaries, may fall into great inconveniencies; but the Lord's will be done.

Our approaching general affembly is like to be a dangerous one. The moderator's tafk will be hard. I am in doubt if I fhall be at his election. The laft time I was near it. I am feared more for it now, I incline by abfence to efchew it. You have here the pofture of our affairs as now they ftand. I think they fhall be much worfe before

.   2   they

they amend. It is fome refrefhment to us to look a little abroad. If Melander's death, and the worfting of the Bavarian army near Aulburg, be true, I will be glad. No prince in the world I wifh more to be humbled than that wicked fox of Bavaria. I pity the great and unexpected misfortune of Guife in Naples. What mean your Zealanders to diffent from the peace with Spain? Dream they that the French would be a better or fo good a neighbour? You never wrote to me fo rarely as thefe twelve months. Help this fault.

180. *To Mr William Spang.*   *Auguft* 23. 1648.

Reverend and Dear Brother,

WHAT is become of you fince your journey to Dantzick? I long much to hear, defiring earneftly to know your fafe return, and underftand how affairs go in thefe bounds. How things go here fince my laft, I give you this account. So foon as the motion in the weft was crufhed, which now I find had proven a very high and dangerous commotion, had Callendar delayed but two or three days to fee to it, the Duke with diligence did draw his forces together to the border, both to eafe the poor country of their free quarter and grievous oppreffion, as alfo to put Lambert from hazarding the regaining of Berwick and Carlifle. The leaguer lay long about Penrith and Appleby before the Irifh troops, and foot-regiments from the north, came to him. At laft they became a very confiderable force; the greateft that went from Scotland fince the beginning of thefe troubles, though far from the number, as I conceive, of 22,000 foot and 8000 horfe, which common report made them. Never an army was fo great a charge to the country; the foot-foldier for his levy-money, cloaths, and arms, cofting generally 100 lb. the horfemen 300 merks, and their free quarter being an unlimited plundering of many very good and pious people. Our ftate has now found, which fcarcely could have been believed, that, contrary to the utmoft endeavours of the church, and all their friends, they can raife and maintain an army, and do what they will at home and abroad. The wifdom of fome of us has made that practick to pafs, and the myftery of our weaknefs to be divulged much fooner than needed. Always what the

nd will be, a little time will try. They are now in Lancashire. Lambert has no force to look upon them. The
trained bands of the shires join not with him. Cromwell, with the few he could bring with him from Pembroke castle, having marched mid-way, is forced to return to Wales, where the Lord Biron did raise a party so
soon as he had left it. Fairfax is yet at Colchester. It
seems the Houses, city, and committee of the shires, have
of purpose withdrawn assistance, that Fairfax at Colchester, and Cromwell at Pembroke, should lie till their forces melt away, and become contemptible. If London permit the Prince to lie still in the Downs, and be master of
their trade, it cannot but breed great alterations quickly.
That the cursed army of sectaries should evanish in smoke,
and their friends in the Houses, city, and country, be
brought to their well-deserved ruin; that the King and
his family should be at last in some nearness to be restored
to their dignity and former condition, I am very glad:
but my fear is great, that his restitution shall come by
these hands, and be so ill prepared, that the glorious reformation we have suffered so much for, shall be much
endangered, and the most that shall be obtained be but an
Erastian weak Presbytery, with a toleration of Popery and
Episcopacy at court, and of divers sects elsewhere. We,
who might have been the chief instruments to have stopped this evil, are for the time so far at odds with our
state, army, and King, that the despite which all three
have at us is like to further much that evil in England,
and draw it ere long on Scotland also; but the Lord can
easily disappoint our fears. Our state, on pretence to attend the Prince, whom, by my Lord Lauderdale, according to the agreement at the Isle of Wight, they are invi-
ting hither, but really to keep down insurrections of people in the west, are levying 1500 horse more. They suspect deadly, that the dissenters in parliament, with the
help of the church, may raise the country, if their army
were once deeply engaged or worsted in England. Of this
I know no ground; but men who are conscious of occa-
sioning much grief to many, fall in needless fear, and by
the means of preventing, draw on their deservings. Our
condition for the time is sad: The pestilence in Glasgow,
Aberdeen, and Edinburgh also; the continuance of very
intemperate rain upon the corns; the irreconcileable differences of church and state, looking towards a very great
                                        persecution

perfecution of them who have been the beft inftruments both of church and ftate, are great figns of the wrath of God; efpecially the hearts of the body of the people being evidently hardened, and the minds likewife of the miniftry diverted from preffing that humiliation and mourning, which the times call for above all things elfe.

But, leaving the ftate, our general affembly fat down on Wednefday July 12th. On the Saturday before, I had been tormented with a pain in my tooth, more vehemently than ever with any other pain. This put me from preaching on Sunday, and riding on the Monday. Thus far I was glad that I had a true excufe for my not appearing the firft day in the affembly, whence I had refolved, however, to have been abfent. Mr Robert Douglas and Mr Robert Blair preached at the faft. The affembly fat till near eight at night chufing their moderator. Every man's addition of three to the moderator's lift, albeit an equitable and fatisfactory way, yet it proves very longfome. Mr Robert Douglas named for his two, Mr Andrew Cant and Mr George Gillefpie; the affembly added Mr David Dickfon, Mr Robert Blair, and Mr John Smith. Many named me; but I was well away. Mr Blair was doubtlefs the meeteft man; but becaufe lately he had moderated, he got few votes. Mr Andrew Cant got two; Mr David Dickfon none. It went betwixt Mr George Gillefpie and Mr Jo. Smith. Mr George did much deprecate the burden; as he had great reafon, both for his health's fake, and other great reafons: yet he carried it.

The feffion on Thurfday was fpent on the nomination of the committees. In all prior affemblies, fome few of us met the night before the affembly in Warifton's chamber, with Argyle, the Chancellor, and fome others of our chief and wifeft friends, to confider about chufing the moderator, committees, and chief points of the affembly. This preparation was now neceffarily omitted to our hurt. Argyle and the Chancellor were both abfent in their own houfes, to efchew the fubfcription of the bond of maintenance. Warifton did not appear, not only for that caufe, but alfo left he fhould have been preffed to have pleaded againft the minifters; for the eight minifters prefent at Mauchline muir were fummoned to anfwer as raifers of that tumult. Mr William Guthrie, Mr Matthew Mowat, and Mr Thomas Wylie, were diffuaded to appear. Mr Gabriel Maxwell, Mr John Nevo, Mr William Adair,

Mr

Mr Alexander Blair, appeared, and under their hand protefted, that, directly nor indirectly, they had perfuaded the people to meet there that day. When for divers weeks they had been put off from day to day, they were at laft difmiffed to a new citation. Always the good advocate being refolved in his mind, if he had been put to t, to have pleaded for the minifters, and not againft them, was, with much ado, moved by his friends to lurk for fome time till the ftorm went over.

The want of thefe private preparatory meetings, which the moderator's health permitted him not to attend, did make our affembly needlefsly long, and very tedious : for befides that the moderator's way of inquiring at fo many before every voice, was not for difpatch, his unacquaintance with the affairs of the committees before they came to the face of the affembly, made the reports unripe and unadvifed, and fo oft needful, after much debate in the affembly, to be recommitted. The committee of prime importance was that of publick affairs. Upon this the prime men were put ; but fo mixed, that the far moft part were of the moft rigid difpofitions. When Mr Robert Ramfay, and fome others, were moved to be added to the moderator's lift of this committee, it was peremptorily refufed, upon this pretence, that he was upon another committee. By this means, were got out of that meeting whoever the moderator pleafed, and on it whom he would.

For examination of the proceedings of the late commiffion, Mr John Moncrieff, Mr John Row, and fome who had not before been commiffioners, were named. Upon the fear, that they who had corrupted the parliament, fhould have been alike active to have procured commiffioners to our affembly conform to their minds, it was carefully provided, that in all prefbyteries they fhould be chofen who were moft zealous for the covenant, and for the proceedings of the commiffion of the kirk, and for the maintenance thereof : fo this affembly did confift of fuch whofe minds carried them moft againft the prefent engagement, which was the great and only queftion for the time. The ruling elders were, Caffils, Lothian, Balmerino, Coupar, Torphichen, Kirkcudbright, Angus, Creigh, Moncrieff, Netherpoilock, &c. Southefk and Loure were alfo commiffioners ; but Loure appeared not, and Southefk finding himfelf put on a mean committee,
appeared

appeared no more.   The chief conteſt betwixt us and the committee of eſtates, was like to be about the work of this committee for the commiſſion-book.   They ſent in Glencairn to deſire us to delay to approve the proceedings thereof, till they had prepared their conſiderations againſt them.   The cuſtom of the aſſembly, according to prior acts, was to examine with the firſt, acts of the commiſſion of the preceding aſſembly.   The exceptions the ſtate took at their proceedings were ſuch as made their perſons incapable to voice in the aſſembly till they were cleared.   Now the men were a great and chief part of this aſſembly; alſo the matter in queſtion, the engagement, was of a great concernment, and had for many months been in agitation betwixt the church and ſtate; ſo that long time needed not to ſet down any thing concerning it.   So ſoon, therefore, as the report of that committee was ready, it was thought meet, without longer delay than a night or two, to receive and vote it.   All without a contrary vote was approven.   This angered our ſtateſmen, and made them ſee, that all hope to make the aſſembly divert from the way of the former commiſſion, was deſperate.

The firſt ten or twelve days we had but one ſeſſion in the day, the afternoon being given to the committees to prepare work for the aſſembly.   In our committee for publick affairs, at our firſt meeting, I found more work cut out, and put in other hands, than I well liked.   I agreed we ſhould go on as far as the commiſſion of the church had done againſt the engagement; but I wiſhed no farther progreſs; yet it was proponed, and carried, to make a new publick declaration againſt it; yea, to have a declaration to England for the ſame effect.   The drawing of theſe was committed to a ſubcommittee of ſix, whereof I was glad to be none; but I was not content, when, to Meſſ. David Calderwood, Robert Ker, John Smith, were joined Meſſ. James Guthrie, John Livingſton, John Maclelland, Robert Blair, and David Dickſon, who were afterwards added; and I was required to be added, but peremptorily refuſed; for my mind was not very forward for the writs they were to draw.

Friday and Saturday were ſpent on trying the commiſſions.   Thoſe of the preſbyteries of Dunſe and Chirnſide were rejected; the one had choſen Mr Samuel Douglas moderator, the ſame day that a complaint of him had come to them from the commiſſion of the church;
for

for his never appearing there but once, and that to dissent from the church's declaration against the engagement. The other presbytery's commission was rejected, because they had put in a ruling elder, who had entered a written protestation in the presbytery against the causes of the late fast, relating to the late engagement. The disaffection of these two presbyteries was much spoken of; therefore it was thought fit to appoint a visitation, consisting of the most zealous brethren of Edinburgh, Lothian, and the Merse, to cognosce and censure their carriage as they found cause. The like course was taken with the presbyteries of Stirling and Dunkeld. They had not been exact enough in trying the alledged malignancy of one of their number. This occasioned a visitation of them likewise. Mr Harry Guthrie, a very bold man, but in this and the late assemblies very quiet, gave in a petition against this course; but rather than to make din in vain, took it up again. In our committee we had, these days, some reasonings about the commissions from boroughs: none of us were much for the thing, but all for tolerating of them, for fear of offending the boroughs at this time; only the commission of Edinburgh was thought to be wrong; but none offered themselves for that town. The discord betwixt their magistrates and ministers was much more than I desired to see. Their spleen against one or two of their ministers was great. The wilfulness of some rash men to have Sir John Smith out of his place has cost as dear. Since they have got the magistracy of that town, who, to their power, have carried all things there to the mind of those whom we little affected, one of their great cares has been, to keep their kirks rather vacant, than to plant them with any whom they liked not. In chusing of ministers and commissioners they took a new way. Their commissioners for the assembly they named in their town-council; also, as patrons, they elected their ministers there. They were content to propone the men elected, to the session of that church where they were to serve, but to no other. Much debate there was with them in a committee appointed for that end; but the result was, that the commissioners elected in their council should have the consent of their great session, which is their six sessions joined; also the ministers whom, as patrons, they name in the council, shall have the consent of the six sessions before they be presented to the presbytery; and in regard
of

of their neglect to supply their vacant places, now of a
long time, the assembly did vote six, whom they recommended to the great session to chuse four of them, and
to obtain their orderly transportations from the commission of the church. The men were, Mess. John Maclellan, George Hucheson, Hugh Mackell, James Ferguson, James Naesmith, and Robert Trail. All this has
added to the town of Edinburgh's offence, and is thought
will not further the plantation of their vacant places. One
of the assembly's committees I have ever been against, tho'
yet without fruit. The city of Edinburgh is supplied with
the ablest men of the kingdom; their chief service should
be in assembly-time. The custom ever has been, that so
long as the assembly sits, all these men are idle, and all
their kirks must be provided by members of the assembly.
This makes many weak and ill-accommodated country-
preachers fill these eminent places, at most considerable
times. This made the pulpits of Edinburgh be provided
for on the Sundays, and week thereafter, worse than
needed.

On Monday always we have the forenoon free, because
many go out on the Sunday to the churches about. That
time I spent in a meeting with the universities, and got
them to meet twice or thrice more, where we debated,
and concluded the most part of the overtures, whereof
you have here a double. I intreat you read the preface of
Burgess Dick to his Logicks. I find, that twenty years a-
go, the professors of Leyden, with the consent of the synods of Holland, have agreed on a course, to be taught
both in grammar-schools and colleges, which the magistrate has commanded to be every where but one. I pray
you try at Apollonius, or the schoolmaster of Middleburg, or some other, if it be so, and what that course is,
which you will set down, and send over here to me in
your first letter.

The three or four next sessions were spent much of
them in votes and debates upon papers betwixt us and the
states.

Glencairn and others presented to us a petition from
the Duke and the army for ministers, which they second-
ed. Likewise they offered all the security for religion they
were able: and for removing the present differences, they
required a conference with us. To all these they required
a present answer; at least before we past on the trial, in

order to the approbation of the commiffion's book, againft which they profeffed they had divers new exceptions. To all thefe we gave anfwers in writ. The proceedings of the commiffion were unanimoufly approven; a conference was appointed; eight minifters named, and fome elders; the army's letter was referred to our committee. The ftate neglected the conference, fince we had approven the proceedings of the commiffion, and had refolved, that no fecurity to religion was poffible fo long as the engagement did ftand; only they met once for a fafhion, and gave in a paper, craving fcripture from us for the unlawfulnefs of the engagement, and our meddling with matters of war and peace. This paper was referred to our committee. In an afternoon fome few of us met, and fet down our fcriptural grounds for both thefe points; but thought fit to put them in the declaration rather than in a feveral paper.

Mr R. Blair and Mr J. Smith were willing to draw the declaration, left it fhould fall in Mr James Guthrie's brifk hand. I obtefted Mr Blair, that he would be careful of two things; one, to be full againft the fectaries; another, to beware that his draught carried any thing which, directly or indirectly, might carry us to a refiftance of the ftate. I knew, that the moft of the leading men thought a refiftance by arms to the ways in hand lawful enough, if the diffenters in parliament, or any confiderable part of the kingdom, had courage and probable force to act; but it was my greateft care, that nothing might bear any fuch thing; and this I obtained to my great contentment. There were two points fomewhat akin to this that I obtained alfo, but with much difficulty. Sundry at divers times moved to have it determined, if it was lawful to pay any monthly maintenance, fince avowedly it was preffed for the ufe of the army, which was unlawful. I avowed the lawfulnefs of it, as of a tribute agreed upon by the ftate before this army was in being; and that Cæfar in confcience muft have his tribute, let him employ it to what ufes he thinks fit. Alfo, if this were refufed, the excife, the portion of annualrents, and all other dues, which were employed for the fervice of the army, behoved to be denied; which could not but make the ftate to take it by force, and the people to fight againft their fpoilers. At laft we agreed to lay the queftion afide. It was likewife much preffed, that fuch as had been active for the en-

gagement fhould be kept from the holy table; and, as I
did think, the defign of fome was to have our ftatefmen
put under church-cenfures for their diligence in this engagement. My mind in this you have in a paper here by
itfelf. I got it, by much fpeech and private dealing, carried according to my mind. But other things were carried over my head. It was moved, for the farther clearing of the wickednefs of the war, to make a collection
from the commiffioners of all the prefbyteries of the chief
infolencies committed by the foldiers before they went from
among us, and to put thefe in our declaration. I was
willing they fhould be collected to be complained of both
to church and ftate, and cenfured by both fo feverely as
poffible; but was averfe to have them regiftrated, for the
infamy of the very nation, into our publick declaration.
In this I was not heard. Alfo, when it was preffed that
minifters filent, who did not preach againft the engagement, fhould for this be depofed, I wifhed, if men were
modeft, and otherwife offended not, that this fault might
carry no more but a rebuke; but not only it was made
depofition, but, by the motion of two or three men at
moft, it was carried againft my mind, and of divers others,
that the prior acts againft depofed minifters for malignancy fhould be made more ftrait: 1. That none of them
fhould be ever admitted to any church whence a man for
malignancy was depofed; but alfo, that they fhould be
kept from preaching till a general affembly did find them
fit for a church; alfo, if after their depofition they meddled with any part of the ftipend or glebe, it fhould be
excommunication to them. It was preffed by fome, that
the not paying of the ftipend to the next intrant, fhould
be excommunication to the patrons or tenants, who, upon the act of parliament, paid it to him who was depofed
for adhering to the ftate. This was hardly got avoided.

It was againft the minds of fundry to make a declaration to England at all; but this behoved to be. I was
feared for Mr James Guthrie his hand, and fo I found I
had reafon. His draught was wanting of that which I
thought was the chief thing it became us to fay to them,
if fo we faid any thing, a fharp complaint againft the fectarian army, and the parliament's negligence to perform
their part of the covenant, which had brought on us all
our prefent troubles: alfo it had fome dangerous expreffions, which I thought imported the rock I defired to e-

ite, calling our ftate, " a faction ; yea, the mixed multitude that came out of Egypt ; but the diffenters from
the engagement, the nation, and the Ifrael of God."
With very much ado I got thefe helped, fome in the committee; and others in the face of the affembly.

I found the bent fail of the fpirits of fome fo much on
he engagement, that all things elfe were like to be neglected ; therefore I preffed, that the doctrinals, as moft
proper for us, which the laft general affembly had recommended to all the prefbyteries, might be taken into confideration. I got in the Catechifm, but no more. We
paffed this, both the Larger and the Shorter, as a part of
uniformity ; but we thought the Shorter too long, and
oo high for our common people and children, and fo put
t in Mr David Dickfon's hands, to draw it fhorter and
clearer. Of this he was careful, and prefented us with a
draught before the end of the affembly, which truly was
very good and exact ; but yet fo high and long, that it
was recommitted to Mr John Livingfton, who purpofed to
emit it to the miniftry of Edinburgh.

We had three things more of great concernment to have
paffed, and might eafily have concluded them all, had not
our time been worfe fpent, the Directory of government,
the Theorems againft Eraftians, and the Pfalms. The firft,
a very excellent and profitable piece, the fourth part of
our uniformity, was fhuffled by through the pertinacious
oppofition of Mr David Calderwood, and two or three
with him. Four or five things we all agreed unto, except
in that writ from our confent ; but that which grieved Mr
David was the matter of church-feffions, which he main-
tains to have no divine right in particular, but to be only
as a committee from the prefbytery, to execute thofe acts
of jurifdiction which the prefbytery thinks fit to commit
thereto. Left, in the end of the affembly, when many
were gone, we fhould come to fo grave a debate, or rather, left at a time of our fo great ftrife with the ftate,
we fhould fall a jarring among ourfelves, it was thought
beft to refer the whole writ to the next affembly. Upon
the fame grounds, the Theorems were alfo remitted. The
Pfalms were often revifed, and fent to prefbyteries. Had
it not been for fome who had more regard than needed to
Mr Zachary Boyd's Pfalter, I think they had paffed through
in the end of the affembly ; but thefe alfo, with almoft all
the

the references from the former affemblies, were remitted to the next.

One feffion was fpent in encouraging Mr David Calder-wood to perfect his Church-hiftory, and to confider Mr Andrew Ker for his good and great fervice to them. Both got a teftimony of our favour, 800 lb. yearly for Mr David Calderwood, and 1000 lb. to Mr Andrew Ker, with a gratuity of 5000 merks for bygones, were appointed by the affembly to be paid to them out of the church's L. 500 Sterling penfion ; but we cannot, for any requeft, get one penny paid by the Treafurer, and have little hopes to get any more in hafte.

Much fpeech we had of a ftory of the late troubles. In every province fome were named to gather materials to be fent in to Mr John Smith. The publick papers, in writ or print, were defired to be all put together ; but I expect no good from all thefe motions. If you would go on with your hiftory, I fhould be very glad of it.

We were troubled with the opening of the mouths of depofed minifters. Poor Mr Patrick Hamilton, in the very nick when the affembly was to grant all his defires, was rejected by his own unhappinefs. He had let fall out of his pocket a poem too invective againft the church's proceedings. This, by mere accident, had come into the hands of Mr Mungo Law, who gave it to Mr James Guthrie, who read it in the face of the affembly, to Mr Patrick's confufion. Alfo when the affembly was to have at laft, after three or four year's refufal, fhown favour to your old colleague Mr James Row, Mr Patrick Gillefpie, and his own coufins, did fo far mar him, upon tacit furmifes, as, I fufpect of fmall importance, that it is like he fhall never be permitted to preach ; yet honeft John Gillon got permiffion to preach, and for this I confefs I was forward ; for the man, though he want letters, is very pious and well-gifted, and ftrong againft all fectaries. The preparative is not dangerous, for I believe few in an age will fall to be in his cafe ; and if many fhould, I would grant them the like favour, though fome mifinterpret it.

The affembly fpent divers feffions, for fmall purpofe, upon tranfportations. Thefe I love daily worfe. The moft are evidently packed bufineffes, little for the credit either for the tranfporters or tranfported. Mr John Livingfton, refufed to Glafgow, and defigned for Ireland

Q q 2   by

by the late affembly, though earneftly fuited by my Lord
of Airds, and much ftuck to by my Lord Caffils, who,
for his refpect, had made a conftant ftipend for his
church, moft out of his own rent, though his parifhion-
ers had not been cited, yet was, at my Lord Lothian's
fuit, tranfported to Ancrum, where the benefice was
great, and the way to Edinburgh fhort. D. Colvill, called by Edinburgh to the divinity profeffion, fo willing to
come as it became a wife and modeft man, his colleagues
willing to difmifs him; yet the private refpects of a very
few, made him to be fixed to his ftation, which I regret-
ed. Mr George Hutchefon, orderly appointed by his
prefbytery to go to Ayr, yet he liking better to go to
Burntifland or Edinburgh, than to join with Mr William
Adair, and Mr William abfenting himfelf when the action
came in, was appointed to abide in his place.

I think the miforder of tranfportations will not be got
helped, till fome honeft men peremptorily refufe to obey,
which, I think, at laft, fome will do; efpecially fince the
falling of fo many places is referred to the commiffion of
the kirk, with a power almoft arbitrary, to neglect all the
rules before appointed by general affemblies for tranfpor-
ations. We were fafhed with Patrick Lefly of Aberdeen. His intemperate zeal for the levy had made him
overhale. Mr Andrew Cant gave in a foul libel againft
aim. He gave in another againft the minifters. It coft a
committee very much diligence to get this matter accommodated; for it was manifeft that Mr Andrew Cant could
hardly live in Aberdeen, if this man were enraged; fo for
the minifters caufe he was much fpared, and that matter
packed up as it might be. Some men are born, if not to
raife, yet continually to live in a fire. We had fome debate in our committee about conventicles. Some of them
we had heard of in Edinburgh, in the characters of feta-
ries. Mr Robert Knox got them in to my great contentment; for I found fome too fparing of them; and yet I
fear how far in their own time they may extend their duty of mutual edification. The whole two weeks following
were fpent on thefe things. The moft were fafhed for the
moderator's want of difpatch, and too much fticking will-
fully to his own fenfe.

Mr Robert Blair in the moft, Mr Robert Ramfay in all,
was of my mind. Mr Robert Douglas mifliked fome
mens carriage. The affembly of divines wrote to us a
general

general letter. To this, Mr R. Blair's anſwer was good
and uncontroverted. The ſubſcribing of the bond was
much againſt all our minds; but an act was drawn up a-
gainſt it in my abſence, which I much miſliked; for it
carried cenſure againſt the preſſers of it. This directly
aimed at our ſtateſmen, the contrivers of it; but, in the
face of the aſſembly, I got it to be exponed only *ad futu-
ra.* Some of my neighbours before the aſſembly were ſo
far in love with this ſubſcription, that I was forced to write
to them arguments againſt it, as you may ſee herewith.
Though in ſome parts of the country the ſubſcription
go on, yet in the chief and moſt parts it is not required of
any. ———

——— Our aſſembly drove on to the end of the fifth
week. Many, dwelling far off and ſuperexpended, ſlid
away. I ſuſpected the moderator drew long of purpoſe,
waiting for a letter from the parliament of England,
which came not. We hear now the Houſe of Commons
paſt a declaration to us; but the Lords conſented not to
it. I did not love to have any correſpondence with them
now, but others loved it too well. Another motion in
our committee I loved not, a letter to be written to the
King. It was fathered on Mr James Hamilton; and the
drawing of it put on him, though no commiſſioner. I
knew there would be a heavier load laid by us on his Majeſty than was expedient to be meddled with; alſo that
we ſhould not expreſs ſuch a ſenſe of his unjuſt ſufferings
as the world would expect; and ſo I was earneſt to let all
alone; but the moderator carried it: and though the
draught of that letter came never to our committee, but
at the firſt was taken in to the aſſembly, and ſome hours
ſpent in the moderator's publick correcting of it, yet the
thing behoved to paſs, and the wording of it to go to the
commiſſion. Many good overtures againſt the ſins of the
times did likewiſe paſs. One of them I was feared for.
It was, firſt, that all miniſters converſing with malignants ſhould be cenſured by preſbyteries. This would
have ſnared many; for the notion of the malignants now
by the engagement, is extended to very many. I got it
ſome way qualified, but not as it will be found needful.

That which ſome days in the end of the aſſembly
troubled us, was, Mr Andrew Ramſay and Mr William
Colvil's proceſs. Mr Andrew had, in preaching, often
fallen out in divers impertinencies, and contradiction to
his brethren: he had been oft admoniſhed; but the man's

weakneſs

weaknefs and age, and divers who reforted to him, permitted him not much to amend.   Not only he had fpoken for the engagement ; but in prejudice of our proceed-
ngs, and Prefbyterian government itfelf.   Much he denied ; much was proven.   He untimeoufly had fallen on
in unhappy queftion, The magiftrates power to remit
blood.   The general thefes which he profeffed to main-
ain, " That the fupreme magiftrate, when the fafe-
" ty of the commonwealth does require, may dif-
" penfe with the execution of juftice againft fhedders of
" blood," many of us declined to meddle with ; but the
noderator gladly would have had the affembly determining the negative exprefsly, which was efchewed ; only the
nan for his doctrine and carriage was fufpended till the
next affembly.   Mr William Colvill was referred to us
only for his filence about the engagement.   The man
vas generally too bufy to countenance and encourage our
ftatefmen in their way, and the chief mover of Mr Ram-
ay to his courfe ; however, he himfelf walked very can-
nily.   I was indeed offended at his malapert carriage in
he commiffion of the church, and for it, albeit it was not
ibelled, I confented to his fufpenfion ; but it was againft
ny mind that Dr Baron fhould have been cenfured for
nere filence ; yet it was carried.

One or two of your friends in our prefbytery had been,
or their filence and ambiguity about the engagement, referred to the affembly, had I not diverted and got that e-
vil kept off them ; for had they come before us, poffibly
hey had never come off.

We appointed vifitations for univerfities and hofpitals,
ind put on them the fharpeft men we had.   Likely Edinburgh will not fubmit to have either univerfities or ho-
pitals vifited, though they have moft need ; and I preffed
heir vifitation before any other ; fince, as yet, they
lave ever declined it.

The commiffioners for uniformity with England were
ontinued without change ; only Lauderdale, to my grief,
vas juftly omitted.   I was fcarce refolved to have feen
lim ; yet my Lady Warifton fent me to him, as trufting
n his friendfhip for her hufband's bufinefs.   He told me,
hat, however, to his beft knowledge, there was no defign
ither on his place or perfon for the time ; yet that he
ould not anfwer for what might be fhortly, efpecially
vhen in debate and difcourfe thefe things might efcape
                                                    him

him which might irritate them.   The good Wariston,
left by his enemies he might be brought in by violence,
thought meet to retire to Kintyre, where, for the prefent, he paffes his time with Argyle.   Lauderdale continues kind to me, and regrets much the difference betwixt us; fears it become a fountain of great evils, either the
overthrow of the defign for the King againft the fectaries,
or the putting up of the malignant party fo high, that
they will hardly be got ruled; at beft the making of the
government of the church, as we exercife it, to be abhorred by all in England and abroad, and intolerable to
our own ftate at home.   I find the Treafurer in the fame
mind; but both of them faft enough, for ought I can fee,
to our covenant and perfons, except to one or two whom
they efteem the prime caufes of this difference.   In Mr
William Colvill's cenfure, Mr David Calderwood rafhly
had faid, " he was the painfulleft minifter of Edinburgh."
This the moderator exaggerated fo far, as fome fpoke of
his removal for cenfure.   The moderator before had taken him up for his impertinencies indeed; yet too roughly, and more, as I thought, than became.   After this ren-
counter, Mr David went home, and came no more to the
affembly.   At this I grieved; it may do harm.

The ftate, on the Friday before we rofe, gave in a large
paper of obfervations on our declaration.   I take them
to be Primrofe their clerk's draught.   We appointed the
commiffion to fit and anfwer them.   They are but poor
ones.   That fame day we renewed the commiffion of the
church.   There is too great a change of the perfons, and
too great addition of men who never have been members
of any affembly; alfo their power is too much enlarged,
even to procefs all who oppofe their orders, as well as of
the general affembly.   I find divers in the mind, that if
once our army in England had got any fenfible fuccefs,
our ftate are refolved totally to fupprefs the commiffion of
the church, as a judicatory not yet eftablifhed by law;
and it is feared they will trouble the perfons of fome of
us: but the Lord's will be done.   I think indeed the carriage of fome is too high and peremptory; but if the ftate
begin to trouble any of us with imprifonment, it will be a
great ill of long and dangerous confequence.

On Saturday Auguft 12. we arofe.   In the morning I
went away, defirous, after much toil, to be at home
that night, unwilling to wait on the commiffion, to jangle
                                                      more

more with the moderator. I was glad we had all ended in peace. The matter of this unhappy enagement I hope will not laft, and fo the ground of our difference with the ftate fhall be removed. But new grounds of divifion may poffibly arife, which may make our contentions greater. Thus much I have written to you, to oblige you to write oftener and larger; fo much the more as our intercourfe with London is ftopt, and we know not what is doing either there or abroad. What you learn weekly by your gazettes, I pray, once in the month at leaft, let us have its fum, as you fhall have occafion to fend it. So I reft, your coufin, to ferve you.

ROBERT BAILLIE.

The confequences of the engagement were fatal. The army was totally routed in Lancafhire by Cromwell, the Duke taken prifoner, carried to London, and there exe-cuted.

181. *Mr William Spang to Mr Robert Baillie.*

Reverend Coufin,

SINCE my laft, the firft letter I have feen of yours was of the 4th of December, very concife, and moft of it in complaint of my long filence; of which you fhould have had no reafon, if thofe to whom I intrufted my letters to you have been honeft. I never let any occafion flip with which I have not written, and that at large. I am afraid left the freedom I have ufed in them may beget trouble to me, if they have fallen into any envious hand; and then what I wrote was but a rehearfal of the judgement, which the godly and wife, who ever affected our caufe, did pro-fefs to me both by word and letters. Moft of my letters to you were inclofed in packets to Mr George Gillefpie, of whofe death, to my great grief, I have lately heard. Certainly he was as able a man as our kirk had; of a clear judgement. That which fome mifliked, would eafily have been bettered by experience and years. I fee he has had a better opinion of thefe fectaries than he would have had, if he had lived till now, and had heard their vile perjured treacheries againft all bonds; alfo for that reproach caft upon our religion, and the truth of God, by thefe mens unparallelled proceedings, and for the prefent danger of

I

religion

religion in all the three kingdoms; yea, and the civil liberties of all who will not run to the same excess of madness with them.

Let Scotland chuse what side they please, that poor land will be the seat of war, by all appearance, this summer; for a considerable army is marching northward against you; and Cromwell assures his brethren in evil, of a more easy conquest of that kingdom than all the English kings ever had. His ground is, as I have heard from one who is of their council, that the bitterness betwixt those who were for the last engagement in England, and those who were against it, is so great, that there are no means left to reconcile parties, and he is able to crush those who have authority now in their hands, if they be alone; so that our domestic divisions are the chief stay of that party, and which will make us to fall into their hands as a conquest, or hinder us from being able to do any thing to purpose. They encourage themselves in these their hopes, by an alledged dissent entered in by some of the most eminent of our nobility against the proclaiming of our new king, which, though it be most false, yet it is enough to slander these noblemen; and because their authority is so great in our kingdom, to make many suspect it runs not so smooth and fair as is given out by us; so much the more, since no publick declaration is emitted by our clergy, to vindicate themselves from having given a precedent which these perjured Independents have followed.

I am sure it has been a matter of inconceivable grief to you all, when you heard of that bloody murdering of the late king; and it is reason, that following the example of the zealous preachers in London, you testify your utter abhorring of it, that there may be an extant testimony to the world of the loyalty of your hearts, whereby the foul mouths of Papists and malignants may be stopt, as Jacob did, Gen. xlix. 6.; and David, 2 Sam. iii. 35. 36. 37. All the ministers in this province do publickly declare their utter abhorring of it, and many have chosen select texts for that purpose, and ever with that tender respect to our country and their proceedings, as was matter of joy for us to hear, now you have proclaimed the Prince to be King; and blessed be God who hath put it in your hearts so to do. This makes your names like a fragrant smell; and if you be put to any hazard for the maintainance of that action, if you will manage your credit well abroad, ye will find real friends. But, first of all, I with care were taken to ce-

nent at home with you, and for that purpose remit of
bat rigor, in the which, if you continue, no man sees how
'e can subsist; for, be assured, the party that now is un-
ler, will rake hell to vindicate themselves, and put you
o that necessity, that you must join your forces with
hese murderers, and bring them again into the bowels of
our kingdom, yea, and to be subservient to them, and to
recal what has been done with such absolute agreements.
It were to be wished that men of all sides would now
learn to deny themselves, if they would approve their for-
ner professions for religion, king, and country.

There is arrived at Rotterdam some commissioners from
Scotland to the Prince, upon the 2d of March, N. S. a-
mongst whom their is one Sir Joseph Douglas, who intreated Mr Alexander Petrie to write to me in all haste,
that I should come thither, or to the Hague unto him;
for what errand I know not; yet I mind to-morrow, God
willing, to go thither, so much the more, because I hear
my Lord Chancellor is upon his way thither in a ship,
where, if I can serve them for any use, I shall not be failing.

The good God comfort and direct you in the right
way, that ye may enjoy the fruit of your labours in peace.
If the King will not take the covenant, and separate himself from the councils of those who have driven his father
to that misery, I foresee he and us all shall be miserable.
Let our eyes be towards God; he rules all. To his mercy ye are recommended by your cousin,

                                ANDERSON.

At my dwelling-place, 7th March 1649.

182. *Mr Robert Baillie to Mr Spang.*   *Edinburgh, Fe-
    bruary* 7. 1649.

Cousin,

YOUR bygone letter of the 12th I received, and thank
you for it. You complain of my long silence; but give
no satisfaction for your longer. In my next I shall give
you contentment about all your inquiry. This is upon a
particular and great occasion. One act of our lamentable
tragedy being ended, we are entering again upon the scene.
O! if it might be the Lord's pleasure to perform more
happy and comfortable actions than have appeared these
years bygone. To the great joy of all, in the midst of a
very great and universal sorrow, we proclaimed, on Mon-
                                              day

day laſt, the Prince, King of Britain, France, and Ireland. We have ſent the bearer, a worthy gentleman, to ſignify ſo much to his Majeſty at the Hague. We purpoſe ſpeedily to ſend an honourable commiſſion from all eſtates. The dangers and difficulties wherewith both his Majeſty and all his kingdoms at this time are involved, are exceeding great and many. The firſt neceſſary and prime one (as all here, without exception, conceive) doth put his Majeſty and his people both in a hopeful proceeding; and his Majeſty's joining with us in the national covenant, ſubſcribed by his grandfather K. James, and the ſolemn league and covenant, wherein all the well-affected of the three kingdoms are entered, and muſt live and die in, upon all hazards. If his Majeſty may be moved to join with us in this one point, he will have all Scotland ready to ſacrifice their lives for his ſervice. If he refuſe, or ſhift this duty, his beſt and moſt uſeful friends, both here and elſewhere, will be caſt into inextricable labyrinths, we fear, for the ruin of us all. We know Satan will not be wanting to ſtir up ill inſtruments to keep him off from a timeous yielding to this our moſt earneſt and neceſſary deſire; but as it is, and will be, one of all Scotland's ſtrong petitions to God, to diſpoſe his heart to do his duty without delay; ſo we will acknowledge ourſelves much obliged to any, whom the Lord may honour to be the happy inſtruments of his perſuaſion. Many here remember, and are ſenſible of your great and happy labours, for the clearing of our proceedings, from the very firſt commotions among us. We truſt you will not refuſe to be at any needful pains, at this ſo hard a time, for the ſervice of God, your King, and country, and all the churches here, in their great diſtreſs. I wiſh you made a voyage to the Hague, and dealt with our good friends, Dr Rivet and Dr Spanheim, to inſinuate to the King their wholeſome advices. Some, as Voſſius, Apollonius, and others there, underſtand ſo much of our proceedings, that a ſmall deſire from any intereſts would move them to contribute their beſt helps for his Majeſty's information.

I recommend it therefore moſt earneſtly to you, to beſtir yourſelf in a private clanculary way to further this work. If your, or any other mens labours be bleſſed of God to work the preſent, you will find all here (I ſhall anſwer for it) ready to acknowledge, as becomes your pains, by ſuch teſtimonies, in due time, as ſhall give you ſatisfaction.

What

What you do muft be done quickly; for every hour's delay prejudgeth (we know not how much) his Majefty and all his dominions.

Your Coufin,

ROBERT BAILLIE.

183. *Mr Spang to Mr Baillie.*

Tibi foli.

Reverend and Dear Coufin,

AFTER the clofing of my laft letter, which goes along with the fame bearer, my Lord Confervator, I received a letter from Mr Alexander Petrie, requiring me in all hafte to come to the Hague, and that in the name of Sir Jofeph Douglas, a commiffioner then arrived from Scotland with letters to the King's Majefty; but about what errand he did not write, neither would he. Though the weather is very unfeafonable and ftormy, and my health not the beft, as ufually it falls out with me in March, yet I chufed rather to run thefe hazards, than to be wanting to that gentleman's defires. When I came to the Hague, I inquired for him, and afking, what was the errand for which he had fent for me? he told me, he had brought over letters from the commiffioners of the kirk, and delivered them to Mr Alexander Petrie to be fent to me. So I fent an exprefs to Rotterdam for thefe letters, which, when they came to my hand, I found them a packet from you of the 7th of February. Ye defire me to haften to the Hague, and deal with fuch who are like to have credit with the King's Majefty, for perfuading him to do what you require of him, viz. to join with Scotland in both the covenants. The perfons whom you defigned were either abfent out of Holland, as Dr Rivet, Apollonius, or fuch who are not of credit with courtiers, or fuch who are known to make ufe only of the court-favour for their private ends; and therefore I did bethink myfelf of another mean to effectuate that end, which was, by addreffing myfelf to the Prince of Orange his Highnefs. For this purpofe, I took pains to inform myfelf, the beft I could, of the prefent pofture of counfels fuggefted to the King's Majefty, and the reafons for them; and I found, that all thefe defigned by our late Sovereign to be his four counfellors

fellors while he was Prince of Wales, viz. Cottington, Andover, Culpepper, and Hyde, advifed he fhould go directly for Ireland. This did James Graham urge alfo with great vehemency; and if that would not prevail, others were of advice, that the King was to come to Scotland *armata manu*, becaufe no truft could be given to fuch who were leading men in our parliament; partly, becaufe they thought there was reafon to fufpect the fincerity and reality of fome who ufed fuch a fair invitation only to get the King in their power, whofe advancement they thought never more to procure than they did his father's; partly, becaufe they thought, that though thefe who invite him do really intend, yet they are not able to maintain him against the Englifh ufurpers, if they do not recal their late acts against fuch who have had a hand in the engagement, and join all their powers together. But this, fay they, they will never do, and fo they fhall not be able to protect the King; but being ftraitened by the Englifh, will be content to buy their peace with quitting the King. And here, to make this probable, pregnant inftances are brought in of my Lord Chancellor's papers against the delivery of the King to the parliament, preffed by unanfwerable reafons, which yet were neglected altogether, by delivery of the King within few months after. The other inftance was, of the treating of our commiffioners with the late King at the Ifle of Wight, and our not performing our promife accordingly. But there is a third party, who, though they be not of the King's council, yet, out of love to him and their country, rejected the two former projects as bloody, to the utter ruining the King and all Proteftants; and did by all means labour to perfuade his Majefty to go to Scotland, upon the very fame terms they did require; that if he did not go, and that haftily, with a refolution to feal the covenants, he would alienate the hearts of all the Proteftants in all his kingdoms from him: and this was preffed by the Earls of Lauderdale, Callendar, and Lanerk, with fuch evident felf-denial of their own interefts, as being grievoufly cenfured by this prefent parliament, that had the King been left to himfelf, it was thought he could not but follow their advice. This honourable carriage of thefe three noblemen I can bear witnefs unto, as having heard them proteft it in private, and underftand it from others alfo, who are our enemies, and do curfe the hour they have been caft here to fpoil

the

the game they thought fure. Believe me, I do acknowledge the good providence of God in cafting them here at
this time. They have done more good than if they had
been fitting in parliament.

My next was, to find out whereto the Prince of Orange
was inclined. For this purpofe, I went to two of the
States Generals, of whofe intimacy with the Prince's councils all men did fpeak. I found them not only clear in
their own judgement for the King's going to Scotland,
and embracing the covenant, but that this alfo was the
Prince's mind. From them I went to fundry others; but
from none did I get furer information than from the Lord
Beverweert, Governor of Bergen-op-zoom, natural fon
to Prince Maurice, a nobleman truly pious, and of a publick fpirit, refolute to employ his credit for religion, and
of high account with the Prince, in whofe councils he
has chief influence.

Now having found whereto the Prince inclined, my
next thoughts were to underftand fo much out of his own
mouth, and to confirm in him what good refolution I
fhould find in him; efpecially to remove fome fcruples and
objections, wherewith many told me he was daily affaulted.
For this end, a countryman of ours promifed to bring me
to the Prince; but performed it not, or at leaft would
have me to wait fo long upon it, that I fhould be made to
think it fome great favour; for this court-policy I learned, which made me refolved to go in my old way, and by
the mediation of one of his Highnefs's counfellors, I was
brought in to him, and had the freedom of a long hour's
fpeech, where I found God's affiftance and blefing; his
affiftance, in enabling me both with words and matter,
for it was in Dutch; and his blefing, in making the Prince
fo attentive to what I faid, fo defirous to know the true
grounds of things, fo apprehenfive, and fo fully refolved
with us for his Majefty's going to Scotland upon the conditions proponed. I fhall give you a fhort and compen-
dious account of what paffed then.

After I had thanked his Highnefs for his favour in
granting me fo ready audience, and defired to know if I
might, with his good liking, propone what I intended in
Latin or Englifh, rather than Dutch, he defired me to
do it in Dutch. Then I firft condoled the parricide of our
late King his father; " fhewed how it was abhorred by
' the eftates of our kingdom; how, contrary to our co-
                                        " venant,

" venant, the end of which, among other things, was the
" fafety of the King's perfon; how not only the ftate had
" proclaimed his fon to be their King, but the miniftry
" in the kingdom alfo, according to their places, had
" done their duty, and had given affurance of their loyal
" affection to our prefent King, by their letters to him,
" and by their care that he may be perfuaded to fhun the
" wicked counfels which drove his late father to fuch
" counfellors; that they had given me orders to deal with
" all who could contribute any thing to the advancement
" of this good work; and that I could look upon none from
" whom I had reafon to expect more good than his High-
" nefs, who, by being inftrumental therein, would gain
" greater honour than by gaining of towns," &c.

He anfwered, " That there was nothing more accepta-
" ble to him than that he was looked upon as one who
" would employ himfelf for the advancement of religion,
" and that now, if ever, the reformed religion was in
" danger; that there were no probable means to prevent
" the utter extirpation of it, but by efpoufing the young
" King's quarrel; and that he, for his part, could not
" but pity the young King, torn as it were betwixt fuch
" contrary counfels; that the reafons produced by all par-
" ties feemed to be fpecious, yet how fair foever men did
" fhew, he thought it madnefs for a Proteftant to chufe
" rather to truft to a Papift, than a Proteftant who mind-
" ed truly."   " And if ever," faid I, " any ftate minded
" truly, it is our prefent ftate; their haftinefs in proclaim-
" ing, that chearfulnefs of all joining together, do witnefs
" this; and now their readinefs to efpoufe the King's
" caufe, if he firft will efpoufe God's caufe, though they
" know any undertakings of this kind to be joined with
" great dangers."   But what," faid he, " may be expect-
" ed of the minifters?"   And here he fpoke much of
the great influence their advice has on the eftates.   To
this I anfwered, " That whatfoever any Prince can expect
" of good fubjects, that may our King look for at the
" hands of the minifters, if he employ his power for the
" honouring of God; and that all the power they have
" in the hearts of the people will be for the King's advan-
" tage."   Here he fpoke fomething of the great precife-
nefs of our minifters, who would not be content with that
about religion which our late King had granted, and
wherewith the parliament of England was well nigh fatif-
                                                        fied.

fied. Here I was ready to have anfwered; but he paffed this, and fpoke of the conditions we require of the King, viz. his accepting and entering into the covenants. And I, at his defire, having explained what thefe covenants were, and how diftinguifhable, " Then," faid he, " he " will be eafily brought to fubfcribe this covenant which " concerns Scotland alone;" (he meant our national co- venant); " but the other covenant betwixt Scotland and " England, he feared fhould find greater difficulty: 1. Be- " caufe all the King's counfellors, viz. thefe four Eng- " lifh, would be againft it : 2. Becaufe it required a deli- " very up to juftice thofe who are called malignants : 3. " Becaufe, as by fubfcribing it the King would pleafe us, " fo he would difpleafe the Papifts in Ireland, and all fo- " reign Popifh princes, who will not be fo foolifh as to " favour him, whofe advancement is the ruin of their re- " ligion in his dominions. Other reafons," fays he, " are " urged, and I fhall propone them ere ye go." So I be- gan to anfwer; and, firft, " I fhewed, that the firft cove- " nant of Scotland only provides as great fecurity for re- " ligion as the fecond doth; and therefore the King's " counfellors, who advife him to fubfcribe the one, " and not the other, for fear of difpleafing the Pa- " pifts, fpeak they know not what; for there is not " a Papift who is not more difpleafed with the firft " than with the fecond." And he afking, " Why are " the King's counfellors fo much againft it?" I anfwered, " That they durft not do otherwife than diffuade our " young King from the folemn league, fince they had e- " ver diffuaded his father from it. If they would now " change, the young King, and your Highnefs, who are " fo greatly interefted, fhould have reafon to look upon " them as men whofe confciences did condemn them for " abufing the father." Here I took occafion to reprefent o his Highnefs, " the great inconvenience of the abode " of fuch counfellors about the King's perfon; that if a " courfe was not taken to banifh them from his prefence, " they would readily prove as unhappy inftruments to the " fon as they have been to the father; and that they, or " any who advife the King to flight the prefervation of " Scotland, and to go to Ireland, chufing rather he fhould " not reign than that they fhould not reign with him; " men of whofe religion the world, to this hour, was ne- " ver fatisfied." So far as I could mark, his Highnefs

2   feemed

seemed not to be displeased with this. " As for the King
" delivering up of all malignants to justice," I answered,
" the covenants do not require that all malignants should
" be punished, but only tried, and left to the judgement
" of the parliament." " But," says he, " ye call any man
" a malignant whom ye please, though he profess he ad-
" heres to the covenant, and all his aims are for the ends
" of it."   Here he brought in, for instance, the acts of
our present parliament, declaring all who had any hand
for the engagement incapable of any place of trust during
their whole lives; " and yet," says he, " the world did
" read their declaration, which spake very fair, and the
" parliament did own that work : I would therefore glad-
" ly know who are the malignants ; for I find, that there
" is no argument that so works upon his Majesty as that."
Here I profess I was at a strait.   For to have given him
such a character of a malignant as the commissioners of
the general assembly did give some two years since, that
would not have served the turn, the case being now altogether altered, is so far, that he is to be thought more a
malignant who approveth the bloody acts of that treacherous crew, now usurping the name of a parliament in
England, than any who did ever fight against them ; and
therefore I came to the distinguishing of malignants,
" some whose aims appeared evidently to be for their own
" selves, either that they might abide in a capacity to ty-
" rannize over their fellow-subjects, or to raise their
" fortunes, already desperate, by the publick troubles.
" Such malignants were justly unpardonable ; and they
" had none to blame for the ruin of their families
" and themselves but their own obstinacy.   As for o-
" thers, in whom it doth appear, that private and by-
" ends have not set them a work, their case is pitied ;
" and it has ever been the custom of the parliaments of
" Scotland to fail rather in too great clemency than cruel-
" ty."   " Well," says the Prince," if ye that are mini-
" sters will not employ your utmost credit for uniting of
" all your country, (I mean not," says he, " of such who
" have been bloody obstinate enemies to you), ye may lose
" both yourselves and the cause; and I know there is no-
" thing that should more confound the counsels of all
" your enemies, than to see you forget quarrels among
" yourselves ; for this, they say, How can Scotland, thus
" divided, be able to do any thing of moment, since the
VOL. II.   S f   " forces

' forces of the party which now rules are but little e-
' nough to suppress their enemies ? I therefore do as
' earnestly recommend this to you, that you would ac-
' quaint your ministers with it, as they by you do recom-
' mend their business. If I did not think it tending to the
' enabling of you to make your party good, I should not
' open my mouth about it." Here he enlarged himself
very pertinently and full upon the project of an act of oblivion; and told me, "That the party who now rules, will
' not be so ill advised as to reject this motion, if they
' would but consider how suddenly things may be chan-
' ged." I assure you he could tell me faults committed in
our private government, whereof I was wholly ignorant,
which he says he learned from the English council, when
they were debating about the very lawfulness of our Scot-
ish parliament, whether lawfully indicted, maintaining
strongly, that their committee, who called it, had no
power, because they had not subscribed the acts of the
former parliaments; "but, said he," "I quickly crushed
' such a motion in the very shell."

" But," says he, " the King, by subscribing that cove-
' nant, will disengage all Papists from his service, both in
' Ireland and elsewhere, and all but Presbyterians; for it
' obliges the King to root out Papistry every where in his
' dominions, which he is not able to do in the condition
' wherein he is." I answered, " That same argument
' our late Sovereign used; but how damageful his going
' about to please Papists was, doleful experience has
' taught, for Ireland especially. It has been that which
' has withdrawn the party of the Protestants from him
' more than any thing else. And what advantage took
' the Irish Papists at the King's weakness ? When they
' capitulated with him, what little performances did the
' King find of their big promises ? and since ever he be-
' gan to meddle with them, did not his condition decay
' daily ? That the condition of Protestants called *Pres-*
' *byterians,* in Great Britain and Ireland, is not so mean,
' but if the King would chearfully join himself to them,
' as *caput et vindex fœderis,* there would be no doubt of
' great and good success. As for the particulars, how
' much they could do, I durst not take it upon me to
' speak out. I was sure, that in all Scotland there was
' not a man who would not be for the King; and for one
' Independent, there would be found three Presbyterians;
" and

" and the reft, being either hierachical men, or Papifts,
" if they would not affift the King, they would far lefs af-
" fift the traiterous fectaries." " I perceive," fays his
Highnefs, " what ye mean ; but how many Prefbyterians
" foever there be, if ye live at a diftance, as I hear ye do
" now in Scotland, ye will be able to do nothing at all.
" It is a work fitting your calling to unite the hearts of
" all the great men whom you know to be Proteftants."
And here I fufpecting, that it might be his Highnefs did
mean Montrofe, as they call him, who is frequently at
court, and more familiar with many than welcome, I faid,
" I hoped his Highnefs did not mean of that man, whofe
" apoftacy, perjuries, and unheard-of cruelty, had made
" fo odious to all in our country, that they could not
" hear of his name." He prefently gave me to underftand, that he meant not him, or any fuch ; for by the
comportment of our Scottifh noblemen at court now, he
perceives how odious James Graham muft be at home ;
for they will not falute or fpeak to him ; nay, not look
where they think he is : and this I have obferved with my
own eyes. At laft, having anfwered all his queftions, I
repeated my defire, and humbly prayed his Highnefs to
continue in that holy and wholefome refolution ; and to
improve his credit with our King, that a fatisfactory anfwer may be given with all hafte, fhewing the danger of
delay.

" But," faid he, " when will the commiffioners come
" to his Majefty ?" I anfwered, " I thought not until
" the gentleman returned with an anfwer to Scotland."
He afked me, " If I knew who they fhould be ?" I anfwered, " I knew not." " Will any minifters come ?"
faid he. I anfwered, " That I queftioned not but fome
" would come who would be able to fatisfy all his
" Highnefs's fcruples better than I poffibly could." " I
" with," fays he, " fome minifters would come, for feve-
" ral reafons." I replied, " That they fhall come the
" more chearfully, when they fhall underftand how much
" your Highnefs doth engage yourfelf for perfuading the
" King's Majefty to go to Scotland, with a refolution to
" fubfcribe both the covenants." Then faid the Prince,
" Ye may confidently affure them, that I fhall do my ut-
" moft endeavour ; and come ye to me to-morrow, and I
" fhall tell you what you may expect."
So away went I, and to-morrow, being admitted to his

presence, he told me, " He had made it his work yester-
" night to persuade the King's Majesty, that the resolu-
" tion was taken to satisfy the desires of the parliament
" of Scotland, and that in all haste, letters were to be
" written of that in answer to what the King received."
And here again he recommended the care of uniting all our noblemen in one, in passing by what faults
have been the last year; and told me, it should be most
welcome news to him, if I should let him know that any
thing was done in reference to this.

Thus, cousin, ye have the substance of that discourse,
by which ye may see I have obtained the end of your letter, and that in a fitter way than ye prescribed. I most
earnestly intreat you, that you would represent to the reverend brethren of the commission, how much the fame
of rigidity, used by them against the last year's engagers,
is like to endanger the reputation of our kirk abroad, and
like also to make presbyterial government hateful. My
heart trembles when I think of this; for I am certainly
informed, by a printer, that that infamous person, who
goes under the name of ****, has a big volume ready,
of the late practices of the Scottish kirks in the exercise
of discipline, which ye may think are willingly furnished
to him by some banished Scotsman. 2. That all lovers of
our cause and nation do unanimously judge, that there
are no probable means of our safety, if we unite not, and
pack not up all quarrels amongst ourselves; if there be not
an amnesty for the last year's engagement; for such had
reason to challenge the English army overpowering the
parliament, for breach of covenants, and that your fears
of mischief against the King were not causeless, he is bla-
med who shall not. If there were faults in the compassing your votes, as I doubt not but there have been very
great ones, yet let not desire of justice against these cir-
cumstantial failings, lead us to seek the ruin of these men;
or, by excluding them from government, deprive the kingdom of their abilities, and weaken ourselves so, that we
shall not be able to oppose these treacherous and bloody
sectaries to purpose. If any of our reverend brethren had
been here to have been ear-witness what three of these
Lords, now put in our first classes, did here, in opposition
to the English council and Montrose, and all others who
went for Ireland, sure I am you would have blessed God
who brought them hither in this nick of time. If any
                                              commissioners

commiffioners fhall come, I entreat you, fee that fome of
the ableft of our minifters come alfo, who may be able to
ftand againft Dr Stuart and fuch like, if occafion fhould
ferve, and may ferve for the honour of our kirks with
the Dutch alfo. If the lot fall on you that ye muft come,
ye will let me know fo much, that I may attend you.
You may be fure I fhall moft willingly contribute my little
wit for the advancing this fo good a work. Oh! if the
Lord would blefs it, fo might we yet hope for light in the
midft of this darknefs wherewith we are threatened.

The 9th-19th March 1649. *In my chamber at home.*

184. *Mr Spang to Mr Baillie.*

Tibi foli.

Coufin,
I have reafon to be glad that the honeft party at home
with you have fuch a good opinion of me as one whom
they conceive willing to employ himfelf for the publick.
Let me never live longer than whilft I have a defire to improve what is in me that way, which makes me more curious in afking for the grounds of your actions than o-
therwife I would be ; and my doubts are merely proponed,
that I getting fatisfaction, may be able to fatisfy others.
With all whom I have conferred about the bufinefs for
which I went to Holland, I found none complained lefs
of the rigid feverity of the kirk and parliament's proceedings with you than thefe three noblemen, whom it moft
cencerned, as being thefe who are made to leave their
country, and to fuffer the plundering of their goods by
thefe fevere acts. I will not queftion what equity is in
your fo dealing with them, but ye will find it had condu-
ced more for the publick to have ufed greater lenity. Neither (fo far as wifer men than I am do fee) fhall ye ever
have fure peace without refcinding the laft acts, of your
ranking, whom you are pleafed to call malignants, into
four claffes. Paffion has been too great in that act ; for it
is judged a greater fin not to proteft againft that late engagement, than to be an ordinary drunkard, fince it is declared punifhable with a more fevere punifhment. Both
friends and enemies told me, that this favoured much of
the Romifh feverity, where eating of flefh being a breach
of

of man's law, is more heartily punished than notorious
transgressions of God's ; and be assured that our enemies
will proclaim quickly this, with much more to the world
by print ; yet as I have written, these three noblemen digest patiently all that is done against them, and are most
diligent and active for promoting of your ends.   You are
not disappointed of your hopes of noble Lauderdale and
Lanerk, and I assure you of the Earl of Callender, who
told me, in plain terms, that the King may with greater
assurance confide in these who now rule with you than in
others ; ye know whom I mean.   If ye come hither, and
do not bring a full rescinding of what the parliament has
decreed against them, ye will be looked upon as most ingrate
men ; and none would be more glad of your misery than
the English malignants and James Graham, because they
do and have so opposed their plots.   Likewise, it would be
needful that ye remitted much of that rigor which, in
your church-assemblies, ye use against ministers who have
proven your great friends ever before.   It will be better
to let your sails fall somewhat lower in time, before a
storm compel you ; or ye, who think God so highly glorified by casting out your brethren, and putting so many
to beggary, making room through such depositions to
young youths, who are oft miscarried with ignorant zeal,
may be made, through your own experience, to feel what it
is, which now, without pity, is executed upon others.
Generally the great power which the commission of the
kirk exercises, displeaseth all.   It is but an extraordinary
meeting, and yet sits constantly and more ordinarily than
any synod ; yea and without the knowledge of provincial
synods and presbyteries, deposes ministers, injoins, *pro
auctoritate*, what writs they please to be read, inflicts censures upon those who will not read them.   If the kirk of
Scotland look not to this in time, we will lament it when
we cannot mend it.   They say four or five rule that meeting ; and is not the liberty of the kirk come to a fair market thereby ? We have an act, that nothing shall be
brought to a greater meeting which has not first been
treated of in a smaller ; but now your compend of the
general assembly, or deputes of it, at the first instance,
judge of matters which might be better handled in lesser
meetings.   For God's sake, look this course in time be
stopped, else the commission of the kirk will swallow up
all other ecclesiastick judicatories, and such ministers who
                                                        reside

reside in and about Edinburgh, shall at last ingrofs all church-power in their hands. I know their is a piece of prudence hereby ufed, to get the power in the hands of thofe who are good; but what affurance have we but what they may change, or others, following this courfe, creep into their places? We meet with daily regrets that the ancient miniftry are condemned, and the infolence of young ones foftered, the very forerunner of Jerufalem's deftruction. The Lord make us wife in time.

Mr Samuel Rutherford is called to be profeffor of divinity and the Hebrew tongue, in the new-erected univerfity in Harderwych. You muft be well advifed at home what to do, if our kirk can want fuch a man in the great fcarcenefs of fuch. It is not his Englifh he writes that commendeth him, as his Latin treatife againft the Jefuits and Arminians. If ye had publifhed any thing in Latin, you would not be fuffered to ftay where you are; but then you would have loft your place in yearly provincial fynods. Scottifh minifters are generally looked upon by the Englifh to be fo rigid in difcipline, that there are no hopes for any of our nation to have a place among them; befides, the diffention of the nation. What a fearful judgement of God is this upon us, that what we thought fhould have joined the nations infeparably, is like to be the greateft feparator of them. It fears me many of our hearts, in the purfuit of it, have not been upright. I know not how this my freenefs may be taken by fome; but it comforts me that I am affured ye know it comes from a heart addicted to the wellfare of our kirk, no ways difcontented when the godly party have fuch a fway; only I wifh we ufed prudence, left we open a door to tyranny, while we think to fhut tyrants out of the kirk. The devil has many wiles to miflead men. That monfter of Popery walked modeftly at firft, and it was good; but imprudent men who led the way to it.

You will not do well to refufe coming hither when our commiffioners come, I wifh both wife and moderate godly men come with you. All the country's eyes here will be upon you more than thofe whom the ftate fends. I hear much of Mr Robert Douglas's moderation. Oh! we mifs now that precious fervant of Chrift, Mr Alexander Henderfon; he would have been a man fit for this purpofe. Whoever comes, fee that ye come, and bide

not

not behind. If you think I can be ufeful for you, let me be informed at your firft arrival in Holland. You will find our young Prince of Orange, one of the hopefulleft youths that ever Europe brought forth, and willing to do all good offices for the caufe. But more of this if God bring you hither, and I be alive. The Lord direct you all by his Holy Spirit.

When you fend commiffioners of ftate, let them be fuch as fpeak good French, if not Latin. It will be no great wifdom that who are fent muft be directed or made to depend upon any but their own prudence. You will do well to confider of the letter, which anno 1646, the affembly wrote to our late king; for the Independents make it a part of the rule they walked by. And, 2dly, They fay, that in your laft affembly, you have declared that thefe words of the covenant, where ye fpeak of defending the king's perfon and authority, in defence of religion and liberties, are explained to be a limitation and excluding your obedience to him, except in fuch acts. And what fay thefe bloody Independents? " Their put-" ing the King to a violent death is not againft the co-" venant; for they have put him to death, not for his " defending religion, and the parliament's liberties, but for " going about the overthrow of both." Think of this.

Since the writing of this, and the other letter of this fame date, I bethought myfelf to write another, which, if you think fit, you may communicate it to others; yea, to the commiffion, but upon the condition that no man mifconftrue my meaning. I know how ready men will be in thefe troublefome times to entertain jealoufies of their brethren, and to make men offenders for a word; therefore I remit the publication of it to others to your prudence. I only relate what I have from others, and thefe not malignants but friends. Moderate counfels ufed to be of account, and *feftina lente* was an advice never a man repented of.

I write this third letter fince Sir Jofeph Douglas his coming hither, and that I heard fuch a change in the king. I intreat you not to fpare an occafion in writing to me. With our Confervator, or the fhip of war, you will have a fit opportunity. Timeous and full information how matters ftand with you, in good earneft, may do much good, and fince our Prince of Orange is fo earneft, from time to time, to know the ftate of our affairs, that

2   he

he may be able to help us wherein he can, it is reasonable we satisfy him.   I have promised to give him notice of what I shall know.

   Your Cousin,   ANDERSON.
  March 19. 1649.

185. *The Commission's letter to the King, with Sir Joseph Douglas. Edinburgh, February* 7. 1649.

  May it please your Majesty,
  As we did always acknowledge your royal father his just power and greatness, and poured forth our supplications and prayers to God on his behalf, and do abhor these unparallelled proceedings of sectaries against his Majesty's person and life, so we do willingly and chearfully acknowledge your Majesty's most just right of succession to reign as king over these kingdoms; and do resolve, in the power of the Lord's strength, to continue in prayer and supplication for your Majesty, that you may fear the great and dreadful name of the Lord your God, and reign in righteousness and equity, and the Lord's people under you, live a quiet and peaceable life, in all godliness and honesty.
  These kingdoms, now for many years past, have been involved in many calamities and confusions, by which the Lord's work hath been obstructed and retarded, and the blood of his people shed as water spilt upon the ground; and we cannot but look upon the counsels of the ungodly as a main cause of all these evils.   It hath been the cunning of the Popish, Prelatical, and malignant party, to traduce Presbyterial government, and the solemn league and covenant, as destructive to monarchy, and with so much wit and industry they manage those calumnies, that your royal father, to our exceeding grief, was kept at a distance, in his judgement, from these things that do much concern the kingdom of Jesus Christ, the peace and safety of these kingdoms, and the establishing of the king's throne, and was estranged in his affection from them who tendered his person and authority.
  And seeing the Lord now calls your Majesty to succeed to one of the greatest and most important employments upon the earth, which is much heightened by the present condition, it is our earnest desire your Majesty, in

 VOL. II.   T t   the

the name of the Lord Jeſus, whoſe ſervants we are, that
you would not only ſhut your ears againſt calumnies,
but avoid the company, and ſhun the counſels of the ungodly, who ſtudy to involve your Majeſty's intereſt, and
that which concerns the preſervation of your royal perſon, and the eſtabliſhing of your throne with their private intereſts and ends, and to make your loyal ſubjects
odious, that they only may be gracious; and that your
Majeſty would avoid all the temptations and ſnares that
accompany youth, and humble yourſelf under the mighty
hand of God, and ſeek him early, and labour to have
your ſenſes exerciſed in his word; and that your Majeſty
would eſtabliſh Preſbyterial government, and allow and in-
join the ſolemn league and covenant, and employ your
royal power for promoting and advancing the work of u-
niformity in religion in all your Majeſty's dominions. It
is by the Lord, who bears rule in all the kingdoms of the
ſons of men, that kings do reign; and whatever carnal
policy ſuggeſt to the contrary, there is nothing can contribute ſo much for ſecuring the kingdom in their hand,
as being for his honour, and ſtudying to do his will in all
things. Therefore we know not ſo ſure and ſpeedy a way
for ſecuring of government in your Majeſty's perſon and
poſterity, and diſappointing all the deſigns of enemies,
both on the right hand and on the left.

We truſt it ſhall yet afterwards be no grief of heart to
your Majeſty to hearken unto us in theſe things, (we have
hitherto obtained mercy of God to be conſtant to our
principles, and not to decline to extremes, to own the
way either of malignants or ſectaries, and we were faithful and free with your royal father, would to God he had
hearkened to our advice). The Lord grant unto your
Majeſty wiſdom to diſcern the times, and to make uſe of
the opportunity of doing acceptable ſervice to God, and
engaging the hearts and affections of your people in the
beginning of your Majeſty's reign, by condeſcending to
theſe neceſſary things; ſo ſhall the Lord bleſs your Majeſty's perſon, eſtabliſh the throne, and our ſpirits, and
the ſpirits of all his people in theſe lands, ſhall, after ſo
many years of affliction, be refreſhed and revived, and
encouraged certainly to pray for your Majeſty, and to
praiſe God on your behalf; and in their places and ſta-
tions, by all other ſuitable means to endeavour your honour and happineſs, that your Majeſty may reign in pro-
ſperity

fperity and peace over thefe kingdoms ; which is the earneft defire and prayer of
    Your Majefty's loyal fubjects and humble fervants,
        The Commiffioners of the general affembly.

186. *Letter to the Commiffion, from Holland. Hague, April 3.*
   1649.

Reverend and Beloved Brethren,

THIS is the firft opportunity we have had of making to
you any account of our proceedings. On Tuefday, at
night, March 22d, the Lord brought us all fafe to Rotterdam. On the Friday we went to the Delft. There
we thought meet to reft till the Monday, both becaufe of
our own refolution to keep one day of humiliation in our
family for making our firft addrefs to God, and alfo becaufe of our information by fome of our friends who met
us at the Delft, that his Majefty would be taken up with
his Eafter devotions till Tuefday following. We therefore,
on the Sabbath, did preach and pray in our family, and
found the goodnefs of the Lord with us ; and on the
Monday did put our papers and affairs in order. At
night we came to the Hague, and fpoke with fome friends,
who were not many there. On Tuefday, the fecond afternoon, we came to the court, and had a favourable re-
ception. My Lord Caffils did fpeak to his Majefty in
name of the parliament and kingdom, and Mr Robert
Baillie in name of the church. So far as we could learn,
what was fpoken was taken in good part by all who heard.
The reft of that day, and the following, was fpent in vifiting the Queen of Bohemia, the Princefs-royal, the
Prince of Orange, the Princefs-dowager, and the States-
General.

The commiffioners of parliament found it neceffary to
give in, as previous to their defires, a paper, for removing
of James Graham from court. His Majefty's anfwer, under his own hand, was, That he defired and expected all
our propofitions together ; to which he hoped to give a
fatisfactory anfwer. With this we were not content ; but
preffed again our defire. The commiffioners of parliament by another paper, and we alfo by one feconded
theirs, a copy whereof we fend you herewith. The King's
          T t 2   second

ſecond anſwer was an abiding in the firſt. We had all of us ſome diſcourſe with his Majeſty about the equity and neceſſity of that our deſire; but James Graham hath ſo many and ſo powerful friends in the Engliſh council, that as yet we cannot get the King to diſcountenance him.

On Saturday morning we delivered to his Majeſty the National Covenant, the League and Covenant, the Directory, the Confeſſion of Faith, the Catechiſm, the Propoſitions for government, bound together in a book ſo handſome as we could get them. We ſpoke ſomething on the matter, and deſired of his Majeſty more frequent and private conferences; who ſhewed his willingneſs, and promiſed to ſend to us to advertiſe of his fitteſt opportunities. On the Sunday we preached in our own houſe. We thought not meet to go to the Engliſh congregation; their diſtractions amongſt themſelves for the preſent being ſo great, that our going there, we conceived, ſhould have given offence, and prejudged our affairs.

On the Monday we purpoſed to have given in our deſires in the paper, which herewith alſo we ſend, but his Majeſty was abroad in the afternoon, ſo we delayed till this day. We cannot yet make any judgement of the ſucceſs. The moſt part of the council are averſe from our deſires; yet we have our friends. His Majeſty is of a very ſweet and courteous diſpoſition. It were all the pities in the world but he were in good company. We hope he is not ſo far rooted in any principle contrary to us, but that, by God's bleſſing on our friends labours, he may be gotten to do us reaſon, whatſoever our fears be for the preſent. There is a very evil generation both of Engliſh and Scots here, who vomit out all their evil humour againſt all our proceedings. The peace of France, and an unhappy book, Εἰκὼν Βασιλική, does us much prejudice. Alſo the ſuppoſed death of Huntly is wreſted to our diſadvantage. Dr Branhall of Derry has printed the other day at Delft a wicked pamphlet againſt our church. We have no time, nor do we think it fit, to print an anſwer; but, by the grace of God, ſhall endeavour, with all faithfulneſs and diligence, to go about our inſtructions. We had much need of your prayers. The grace of the Lord Jeſus Chriſt be with you, and protect that church and kingdom from all the miſchief that the inſtruments of Satan on all hands are preparing to bring upon us; but our
hope

hope is in the name of the Lord, to whoſe protection we
commit you, and reſts,

Your brethren, and ſervants in the Lord,

CASSILS.
GEO. WINDRAM.
ROBERT BAILLIE.
JAMES WOOD.

187. *My ſpeech to the King, ſpoken at the Hague, March
27. in the King's bed-chamber, Tueſday, three
o'clock in the afternoon.*

Moſt Gracious Sovereign,

IN theſe very ſad and calamitous times, the church of
Scotland hath ſent ſome of us who are here, miniſters and
ruling elders, and others who are yet behind, in commiſſion to your Majeſty, to declare, in their name, not only
the ſincere and deep grief of that whole church for your
Majeſty's moſt lamentable afflictions, but alſo their real
and great joy for your Majeſty's ſucceſſion to the throne,
and their confident hopes, by the bleſſing of the Moſt
High, on your royal perſon and government, now at laſt
to come up out of that pit of grievous confuſions, calamities, fears, and dangers, wherein long they have been
ſinking.

According therefore to this our truſt, we do declare,
what in our own breaſts often we have felt, and generally
in the people among whom we live, have ſeen with our
eyes an mournful ſorrow for that execrable and tragick
parricide, which, though all men on earth ſhould paſs o-
ver unqueſtioned, yet we nothing doubt but the great
judge of the world will ariſe, and plead againſt every one,
of what condition ſoever, who have been either authors,
or actors, or conſenters, or approvers, of that hardly
expreſſible crime, which ſtamps and ſtigmatizes, with a new
and before unſeen character of infamy, the face of the
whole generation of ſectaries and their adherents, from
whoſe hearts and hands that vileſt villany did proceed.

We do alſo profeſs, in name of them who have ſent us
hither, the great joy of all ſorts of men in our land for
the immediate filling of the vacant throne with your Majeſty's moſt gracious and hopeful perſon, earneſtly praying, that the light of the Lord's countenance may ſhine ſo

bright

bright upon your Majefty's reign, that the very thick clouds of our prefent dangers and fears may flee away, and a new morning may fpring up, to all your three kingdoms, of greater peace and profperity, of more righteoufnefs and virtue, efpecially of more religion and piety, than hath been feen in the days of any, the moft pious, the moft juft, the moft profperous, of all your numerous anceftors.

For the prefent, we are loth to take up more of your Majefty's precious time; only we prefent the letter of our church, [p. 329.]; and what farther moft loyal defires we have in commiffion, we fhall, God willing, be ready, in all humility, to offer fo foon as we fhall know of a fit opportunity to ftand again in your Majefty's moft gracious prefence.

188. *Mr Robert Baillie to Mr R. Douglas.*   *April* 3. 1649.

Reverend and Dear Brother,

By the inclofed to the commiffion of the church, you fee the ftate of our affairs here. I wrote to Wariftoun from Rotterdam what was the pofture of our affairs, as we then were informed. As yet our fears are great of a fore ftorm to Scotland; yet yefternight I learned from a great perfon here, that our affairs, bleffed be God, are not defperate. There is no Scotfman that is of the King's council. The five or fix Englifh that are, Cottington, Culpepper, Hyde, Long, and fome more, are divided. The moft are of Prince Rupert's faction, who carefs Montrofe, and prefs mightily to have the King to Ireland. Culpepper, and fome bedchamber-men, as Wilmot, Biron, Gerard, and the mafter of the horfe, Piercy, are of the Queen's faction, and thefe are for the King's joining with us; but all of them are much averfe from the league and covenant. The Prince of Orange, and by him all the nobles here, are for the laft; and by their means we are hopeful yet to carry his Majefty to our covenant, and the moft of our defires for religion; but I dare not promife fo much: yet the greateft ftick, I fufpect, fhall be our fevere acts of parliament. It feems all here, even our beft friends, will be peremptory for a greater mitigation than, I fear, fhall be granted by you there. It were verily a great pity of the King. He is one of the moft gentle, innocent, well-inclined princes, fo far as yet appears, that

lives

lives in the world; a trim perſon, and of a manly carriage; underſtands pretty well; ſpeaks not much; would God he were amongſt us. I ſend you herewith the copy of what I ſaid to him. Becauſe it was but a tranſient ſpeech, I give out no copies of it here at all; yet that we ſpoke ſo, it did us much good; for heavy ſlanders lay upon us here, which the report of our ſpeeches helped to mitigate. Our enemies have great hopes, by the French peace, to get powerful aſſiſtance from France. I verily think, if the King and we ſhall agree, aſſiſtance ſhall be got from this ſtate, and the Marquis of Brandenburg, and ſome others, for good purpoſe. I pray God guide you there to put no more impediments to our agreeance than are neceſſary. My heart bleeds to think of a neceſſity for Scotland to have any friendſhip for the Engliſh ſectaries, the worſt of men, and a war with our King and countrymen in our own bowels. What relaxation you may grant, with conſcience and ſafety, let it be done freely and publickly with this expreſs. It will admit of no longer delay. You will communicate this to my Lord Wariſton.

Your Brother,

ROBERT BAILLIE.

189. *Mr Baillie to Mr R. Douglas.*

Reverend and Dear Brother,

THOUGH I have nothing at this time for the commiſſion of the kirk, yet to you I give this further account of our proceedings. After we had given in our chief paper, a double whereof you had in my laſt, it was thought meet we ſhould ſpeak with the King ſecretly and privately. I went to him firſt. He gave me a long and very favourable audience, from ten at night to near eleven. The contents of our free conference poſſibly I may ſend you on a ſure occaſion. At this time it is ſcarce ſafe. There is an Engliſh man of war near the Briel that ſearches all letters that come from this. As yet we cannot get it helped. In that conference I found the King, in my judgement, of a very meek and equitable diſpoſition, underſtanding, and judicious enough, though firm to the tenets his education and company has planted in him. If God would ſend him among us, without ſome of his preſent counſellors, I think he might make, by God's bleſſing, as good a
King

King as Britain faw thefe hundred years. Finding the
great ftop to be on the league and covenant, his own taking it, and affuring to pafs it for England and Ireland,
of his perfuafion of paffing all the acts of parliament,
paffed or to be paffed in Scotland, for taking of it there,
would be fatisfactory. I ftrove by many reafons to fhew
the unfatisfactorinefs of fuch a conceffion ; and the day
thereafter, but in writ, the chief of thefe my reafons,
which I gave to the Prince of Orange, whom, after two
long private conferences, I left, as it feemed, fatisfied with
every one of them, and promifed to prefs them as hard as
he could on the King. I found he had caufed tranflate
them into French, and had the fubftance of them by
heart. I found a way to acquaint his mother with them,
who is a wife and religious lady, and promifes to hold her
fon right. The moft of the counfellors are for Ireland,
and all, both they and the bedchamber-men, even they
who are our very great and real friends, are yet againft
our defire of the covenant in England; yet I am not defperate to get fome fatisfaction therein. We are looking
daily for an anfwer. I fear I muft engage with Dr Bramhall; for his Warning it doth fo much ill to the King and
all about him. We marvel ye write nothing to us, We
have been vexed thefe eight days with conftant reports
here of the north's rifing, and David Lefly's retiring.
However it be, you ought not to leave us fo long without
all information. No fcrape has any of us got fince we
faw you from any man. In hafte, I reft, Yours, &c.

By a good friend of mine, a Dutch ftatefman, I got
his double of the two papers the King gave in to the
States-General; as yet he has got no anfwer. The particular provinces are acquainted therewith, but have not
yet returned their mind. Surely, if his Majefty and we
agree not, I fee no human way either of his or our prefervation; but God is great and good. It were a thoufand
pities that fo fweet a man fhould not be at one with all his
people.

190. *For Mr William Spang.*   *September* 14. 1649.

Reverend and Beloved Brother, -
——— I thought to have fent you a particular account of
I   the

the general affembly as I had done of fome others; but the diary I wrote in the time, I loft; fo I cannot now do it; neither were there much in it worth the remembrance. The leeting of two for the moderator fell to Mr Robert Douglas, the ante penult moderator; Mr Gillefpie, the laft, was departed, and Mr Blair never thoroughly well fince his Englifh journey. He was not able to come to Edinburgh, whereof I was very forry. The two Mr Robert leeted were, Mr Andrew Cant in earneft, and Mr Mungo Law for a fafhion. The three the affembly added were, Mr Robert Douglas, Mr John Livingfton, and, by equal voices, Mr David Dickfon and me; fo, without queftion, the voices for moderation fell on Mr Douglas, whereof my heart was exceeding glad; for I was very feared for it, and it had done me great hurt. The committees were framed according to the cuftom by the moderator and clerk in private, and read at the next feffion, without any change confiderable. We fpent very much time; whole five weeks: I thought a fortnight lefs might have done our turn. Tranfportations took up much time, and depofition of minifters. There had been divers commiffions, eaft, weft, north, and fouth, who had depofed many minifters, to the pity and grief of my heart; for fundry of them I thought might have, for more advantage every way, with a rebuke, been kept in their places; but there were few durft profefs fo much; and I, for my ingenuous freedom, loft much of my reputation, as one who was inclining to malignancy.

My fpeech to the King, fpeaking fo fharply of his father's death, and the commendations I gave to himfelf, in the preface of my book, but efpecially a paffage of a letter wrote from Holland, wherein, to a familiar friend, I fpoke of the act of claffes as fo fevere, that it will be needful to difpenfe with fome part of it for the peace of the country: For thefe things, before the affembly, fundry fpoke of me all their pleafure; yet I comforted myfelf in this, that I knew I was far from the calumny impofed, and that all the wife men I knew profeffed their agreement with me in the three things named. My unacquaintance with obloquy made my fkin at this firft affay more tender than needed; for I had fo oft in print declared my fenfe againft, not fectaries alone, but malignants alfo, and that fo liberally, in my laft book, that I thought in reafon I fhould have been reputed above all fufpicion of that rime; yet I was neceffitated to drink more of that cup han I did truly deferve: for however in my fermon to he parliament I was as clear as needed, and in my report if our treaty obtained the unanimous approbation and hanks of the whole affembly, now in print; yet I beho-red, in fundry voices of the affembly, either to quit the iberty of my mind, or endure the whifperings of 'my ma-ignancy to continue. This laft, though to my great grief, behoved to chufe. I could not vote to depofe Mr William Colvil upon his libel. The man indeed had, in my udgement, been an evil inftrument in time of the engage-nent; yet all that was libelled againft him was for mere ilence in that engagement. For that alone I could depofe io man, for the reafons I gave in the committee of the ormer affembly, when that act paffed to depofe for filence lone, if continued in. My mind did never go along with hat act; though therefore I knew the whole affembly al-noft was otherwife minded, and forefaw the miftake of uy voice by fome, yet I behoved to vote his fufpenfion o continue, and no farther. As for Mr Andrew Ram-ay, more was libelled and proven againft him, and all his year he carried himfelf in a cankered untoward way; ret I told, I could not voice to depofe a man of fuch age nd parts: fo in that vote I was filent, to the peace of my >wn mind, though fome of my friends wrote fharp letters o me for it. I had alfo fome conteft with my neighbours n Mr William Wilkie's procefs, whom I judged more iotly purfued than there was caufe. But my fharpeft onteft was for the principal, whom I found fome men o purfue ftill, without any ground at all confiderable. Contrary to their defign, I got him reafonably fair off. Thefe contefts, and wrack of my friends, were very bitter o mind, and, joining with the obloquy in the ear againft ne by fome, troubled my fpirit fometimes, till I got my grief and wrong vented and poured out to God; for there vas no other whom I found able and willing to help me. t was a piece of comfort to me, that the beft of the land vere, on more probable grounds, taxed for compliance vith fectaries than I with malignants, whom yet I knew to >e innocent; and that I remembered the cloud of infamy mder which fuperexcellent Mr Henderfon lay, to my mowledge, till God and time blew it away. I have been >fter and forer afraid for the wo of Chrift to them, whom ll the world leve and fpeak good of, than I was grieved

for

for any reproachful speeches which some were begun to
mutter against me; but this now is our condition, that
the chief in church, state, and army, how innocent soever, are whispered to favour either sectaries or malignants.

In our report, when I had ended what you read
in print, my colleague Mr Wood, of his own motion,
truly gave a very ample testimony of my Lord Lauderdale and you, for your service. What was spoken
of you, all took well; but sundry were pleased to mistake
what was said of Lauderdale, albeit my Lord Caffils, in his
report to the parliament, had said as much of him; but
some men fearing a design to bring Lauderdale into employment at this very time, were not pleased with any motion of that kind, otherwise I had debated in the grand
committee much to have the satisfaction of the engagers
much fairer than it stands, and once I had got Mr Livingston, with the good liking of the committee, to a draught
near to Lauderdale's mind; yet thereafter that was can-
celled, and the act framed as it stands, to my grief. I
wished earnestly, and so did the Chancellor intreat Mr
Robert Douglas, but out of time, that the framing of the
declaration should have been committed to another hand
than that it fell in; who, how able soever, yet was generally thought to be among the most severe of the company to the King; but this could not be helped. Some
clauses we got altered in the committee; yet, as it stands,
I much fear it shall prove a division-wall betwixt the King
and us for ever. We were always expecting the promised
expresses from him, and for that end, some of us held off
all we could, determinations of every thing concerned
him; but when none did appear, and when at last William Murray had come without any letter or instruction,
either private or publick, then there was no remedy, but
the declaration and letter, in the style you see it, and the
act about the engagers, went out without contradiction,
which, as I foresaw and foretold in the Hague, puts harder and more peremptory conditions on the King than there
would have given satisfaction. We had greatest debate
for an act of election of ministers. Mr David Calderwood
was peremptor, that according to the Second Book of
Discipline, the election should be given to the presbytery,
with power to the major part of the people to dissent, upon reason to be judged of by the presbytery. Mr Rutherford

U u 2

herford and Mr Wood were as peremptory to put the power and voices of election in the body of the people, contradistinct from their eldership; but the most of us were in Mr Gillespie's mind, in his Miscellanies, that the direction was the presbyteries, the election the sessions, and the consent the peoples. Sundry draughts were offered. Mr Woods, most studied, was refused; Mr Callerwoods also. Mr Livingston came nearer our mind, yet was laid aside. Mine came nearest the mind of all, and almost had past; but for avoiding debate, a general confused draught (avoiding, indeed, the present question, but leading us into so many questions thereafter as any pleased to make) passed with my consent. But Mr D. Calderwood and Mr John Smith reasoned much against it in face of the assembly; where, against my mind, the Book of Discipline was pressed against them, and a double election made, one before trial, and another after, as if the election before, and the trial by the Second Book of Discipline, were given to the people, and that after-trial, before ordination, to the presbytery. This I thought was nothing so, but was silent, being in my mind contrary to Mr David in the main; though, in this incident debate of the sense of the Book of Discipline, I was for him. However, already we find the defect of our act; for, as I conceive and expressed it, so in my draught so much direction in this is due to presbyteries, that they ought to recommend to the session men to be elected, without prejudice of their liberty to add whom they think fit: but I find it the design now of leading brethren, that the presbyteries shall not meddle at all with any recommendations, but leave that wholly to any particular busy man of the presbytery, to whisper in the ear of some leading man of the parish, to get voices to any young man, though never heard in privy exercise, that he, by desires of the people to the presbytery, may be put on trials for such a church. This I find will be the way of our elections, which I think not orderly. However, Mr D. Calderwood entered a very sharp protestation against our act, which he required to be registered. This is the first protestation we heard of in our time; and had it come from any other, he had not escaped censure.

There was a design, at the last assembly, to have got the hands of many ministers to a supplication for moderating, in some things, the power of the commission of
the

the church, which was expounded by this assembly truly
to have been the overthrowing, in favour of the malignant party, the power of the kirk. Great din was made
for this supplication, to try what was the bottom of it,
and a very severe act was made against the thing; yet Mr
Douglas carried it so, that no man at all, even the chief
contrivers, did suffer any thing for it, upon what ground
I could never learn to my satisfaction; whether, because
to Mr Robert Laurie, the confessed penner of the principal supplication, impunity was promised for his ingenuous
and early confession, and he being secure, others less
guilty could not be got punished; or because others foreseeing what necessity there might be for themselves to do
more than supplicate a general assembly, had no will that
any supplication whatsoever, especially being only intended, and never offered, should be a ground of church-
censure. However, albeit a terrible act was made against
the thing, contrary to my mind, yet no man was to this
day called to any account for it, nor, as I hear, shall e-
ver be.

I was much afraid that the subscription required of the
engagers should have made many prime men in our land
desperate; but I am now very glad that so many offer
themselves to do all that is required, as I expect there
shall be very few who shall stick upon it, so I wish from
my heart that Lauderdale may be moved to do what I
found Callender and Dumfermline ready for, when I was
there with you; and what I saw in the assembly, Middleton very near, and others, as Galloway, Linlithgow, O-
gilvie, Baillie, Innes, Cochran, Kenmure, Fleming, &c.
actually to offer. I do not expect now above three or
four persons in Scotland who shall make scruple of that
subscription, which, I hope, may be a mean to teach that
man (for whom alone my love makes me afraid) some
more wisdom. Mr Hary Guthrie, in his appeal to the
assembly, had used some sharp and reflecting reasons, for
which they summoned him to appear, resolving to have
excommunicated him, if they did not find submission:
but quickly his spirit was daunted. In all humility he appeared, and passed from his appeal, which obtained him
favour not to be farther proceeded against. Mr William
Colvil took his sentence of deposition submissively. Mr
Andrew Ramsay professed his suffering. Some would
have been at the present processing of both, as guilty of
all

all the blood, and all the consequences of the engagement; but Mr R. Douglas quashed these motions, which otherwise easily had been carried on.

It was all our minds to have had transportations better regulated than they had been; for indeed their needless frequency was intolerable, yet Mr R. Douglas got all that shifted till Edinburgh once again be provided both of ministers and professors. For their university they moved for Mr Rutherford, but that was thought absurd. It seems they would be at Dr Colvil, but he will not be given them, as a man demi-malignant. They who judge so of that man, would give them Mr James Wood, or Mr D. Dickson; but in my mind, neither of these may be transported without greater hurt to the places they are in than benefit to Edinburgh, though they could get them; but as yet Edinburgh desires neither, and on whom they will fall yet, it does not appear. We fear they trouble us one way or other.

One day I escaped, to my sense, one of the greatest burdens ever was laid on me. Our committee, after many motions, had resolved for drawing up of the history of the times, to propone to the assembly a leet of three or four; Mr James Wood, Mr John Livingston, Mr Ja. Guthrie, and me. My profession made me secure of all danger, as I thought; and I minded it no more: but in the end of the assembly, when it came to be voiced, it ran wholly betwixt Mr John Livingston and me; and had not the opinion of my malignancy diverted some voices, I had undoubtedly been oppressed with that charge. As it was, I escaped it but by two or three voices; but I blessed the Lord for it; for to me it had all the days of my life been a burden intolerable, for many causes.

The assembly, for the full purgation of the church, as in former years, so in this also, has appointed divers committees; one in Angus, one in Stirlingshire, one in the Merse, one in Ross, one in Argyle, with most ample power. On these committees the most zealous men are put, which some few can chuse (even of very young men ately admitted ministers) for deposing such as presbyteries and synods do spare. I acknowledge the disinclination of my mind to so frequent depositions of ministers, and to all courses that further that, to me so severe an action; but this is a great part of my malignancy.

I think at last we shall get a new Psalter. I have furthered

thered that work ever with my best wishes ; but the scruple now arises of it in my mind, the first author of my translation, Mr Rous, my good friend, has complied with the sectaries, and a member of their republick. How a Psalter of his framing, albeit with much variation, shall be received by our church, I do not well know ; yet it is needful we should have one, and a better in haste we cannot have. The assembly has referred it to the commission to cause print it after the last revision, and to put it in practice.

These were the chief things of our long and tedious five weeks labour ; only we appointed a letter to be drawn for our brethren of England for their encourgement. The draught was Mr James Durham's. It was his first, but did not so fully please as to pass, but was referred to the commission to perfect. Our brethren of Ireland had sent Mr John Greg to us, to have our advice about their carriage in my Lord of Aird's defection. No publick advice was given ; but Mr Livingston and Mr Maclellan were appointed to confer with him on all his propositions.

All this while the parliament did sit, though ready to rise at our first downsitting, more than at our rising. Their main cause of sitting was to see what we brought from the King. Thereafter, being to rise, constant reports, week after week, of Cromwell's purpose to bring down the army on us before it went to Ireland, made them sit still to see to the defence of the country. To increase the levies, was to put the country to a farther burden, while the present was as great as could be borne, and caused dangerous grumbling every where ; also, if a greater army had been on foot, the world would not keep them out of England, which we did not intend, being far from any agreement with the King ; so nothing considerable was done, or could be done, though the English had come on us. They had written a letter with a messenger, to desire a treaty with us. Our answer was, that we could not acknowledge the present authority. This drew from them a paper, in reasonable soft words ; but clearly enough renouncing all former treaties as broken by our parliament's invasion, an advantage which they would openly make that use of, as to have it a breach of all their obligations to us. To this we made no reply ; for what needs paper-debates at such a time ?

' While

While there is nothing to do in our parliament, they make themselves bufinefs enough. Our weftland fhires had, in the rates of monthly maintenance in bygone times, been burthened above other fhires. Oft they had complained; but got no redrefs; they refolved therefore, now or never, to have it helped. Caffils, Ceffnock, Sir John Cheefly, and others, got it fo contrived, that an act paffed for their eafe, with the burthening of the eaftern fhires. Againft this they entered a proteftation, efpecially the commiffioners of Lothian and Fife, and well near the half of the parliament, having Burleigh, Balcarras, Liberton, Lothian, to countenance them. With their proteftation they arofe and left the houfe. This divifion was very troublefome and fcandalous. It continued near a fortnight; but was at laft accommodated; yet fo that the weftlandmen had their defire. This was not weil fettled till the boroughs fell out among themfelves in a great heat. Sundry of the boroughs had been long grudging that Edinburgh fhould bear fo fmall a proportion of the common burden, judging that for their trade and their wealth, the one half of the whole boroughs burden might be laid on them, 50 of an 100, whileas they paid but a twenty-feventh part or thereabout; fo in their convention at the Queensferry, they advanced them a third part, and diminifhed Glafgow, St Andrew's, Irvine, and fome others, a part of their proportion. This the provoft and council of Edinburgh took in an exceeding evil part, and ftormed much at it, yet could not remedy t. But the moft bitter difference was the laft day of their fitting. Caffils, and others, of a long time, had a great defire to have the annualrent fo low as might be. Many ways had been projected for the payment of your lamfons; but all had failed. The money had paid to the publick of the eighth that was due in the hundred, one and a half; it was moved to put it to fix in the hundred for the time to come, but during the troubles to keep it at eight, whereof one and a half to be paid as of before, and the other half merk to go to the lamfons. When this was going, the whole boroughs, except two or three obfcure ones, protefted, with high paffion, and went out; the reft at ftill, and for no dealing of Warifton and Mr R. Douglas, would fo much as delay the clofing of the parliament that night, for they feared, if they had delayed to the morrow, that the people fhould have been fet on them

I   with

with tumultuary supplications; so the parliament closed without the boroughs; yea, the committee of estates was made of a quorum, which should subsist without them, if they should persist to absent themselves, as they threatened they would.   Much high language passed on both sides; yet some days thereafter, the boroughs were made content to sit in the committee of estates: but all these grudges stick in the stomachs of many, waiting but an opportunity to discharge them.

By William Murray's private dealing, it seems Lothian was made willing, with Argyle's consent, to have been sent to the King, but alone.   Argyle therefore, off-hand, moved in parliament, in the absence of Wariston, and without the privity of the Chancellor, or any other of his friends of the church, to have a new address to the King, and carried it without any opposition; but incontinent many thoughts began to arise about the matter.   Some began to be jealous of Argyle, that he was inclining to a new trinketing with the King by himself; others, that the manner of his proceeding was to mar the matter of purpose.   However, the rashness of that unripe motion did no good.   Lothian's employment was shifted.   All it ended in, was a new letter to be carried by a gentleman; and in the last day he was voiced to be Liberton; who finding the letter drawn by Sir John Cheesly, though much smoother than the church's, drawn by Mr James Wood, yet to be so harsh, and the instructions so scabrous, that there was no hope of doing any good with the King thereby, has to this day shifted to go for all his call.   Yet I think it not unlike that he may be moved to go now on the great change of the Irish affairs.   His Majesty's chief hope was Ireland; and indeed it looked once pretty fair for him.   Ormond had taken in all the south but Dublin, which he had straitly besieged.   Cromwell, for all his diligence, had delayed very long to come over.   My Lord of Airds, in a very false subtle way, had put himself in the government of Ulster.   Sir Robert Stuart and George Monro had joined with him, and laid siege to Derry.   If Derry and Dublin had been got, there was no more ado but to have sent for the King, and come over with him, first to Scotland, and then to England.   This was the King's great snare all this year, to keep him off an agreement with us.   But behold how soon all this hope evanished; Jones, having got some supply of men from England, nakes an irruption on Ormond's camp fo profperoufly, hat he well near raifed the fiege. However, he encou- ages Cromwell, without more delay, to come over, hewing Ormond, for all his great force, fo eafy to be lealt with. Mackart, in the mean time, joined with Sir Charles Cutts, and coming towards Derry, made all our befiegers get away, becaufe the minifters before had breached fo much againft Aird's treachery, that few of he people had heart or hand to join him, but generally ill deferted him; wherefore he and his party, as if by Ormond's command, began to threaten the minifters, which made them altogether leave the country, and come over to us. In the mean time Cromwell, in the fouth, has put Ormond, without ftroke of fword, to his gari- fons, and keeps Prince Rupert with his fhips in Kinfale. Mackart, with his army, plunders at his pleafure in the north, and fhortly it is expected Cromwell fhall be cleat mafter of all Ireland, as he is of England; and then have at the third poor broken kingdom, more eafy than the other two to be fwallowed down. This being our cafe, likely our committee of eftates may haften Liberton to the King, to fee if, when the rotten reed of Ireland is broken, he will think better of our propofitions than he did be- fore; fo much the more as the Prefbyterians in England, by a very pithy fupplication, which they fent to me, and I to our ftate, do prefs the fame point. If either we ne- glect to feek him, or he continue to refufe our condi- tions, the ruin of both feems to be near; and though he were joined with us in our terms, yet he has delayed fo long, that our difficulties and his would be infuperable but by the hand of God. Always, we would fuffer all hard- fhips with the greater comfort, that he and we were con- oined in God againft the common enemy of God, of his houfe, and our country. If we make a new application, whoever hinders the King to condefcend to any terms we fhall or can propone, I fhall conclude them in my heart, moft unhappy, and either very malicious or very foolifh men.——In your next, let me know where the Duke, Callender, Seaforth, Sinclair, James Graham are; but above all, what Lauderdale minds to do. What is be- come of Willoughby, Maffey, Bunch alfo. Try to your power if there be any fufpicion of Captain Titus's com- pliance, either with fectaries or malignants. It concerns ne to know this quickly, if you can learn. If your in- telligence

telligence to Caffils and our ftate be fo rare as it is to me, it will be little worth. ——

191. *The following fuppofed to be wrote to Mr Chriftopher Love, beheaded on Tower-hill for correfponding with Argyle and Mr Baillie. Perth, Friday, December 20. 1650.*

Reverend and Beloved Brother,

THE letters of our friends there to Mr Douglas and to Mr Jamefon, [i. e. Mr Baillie], alfo two to the general affembly, the one of an old date, the other fince the defeat at Dunbar, came but lately to our hands. For fear of your hazard then, we thought it expedient to communicate them but to a few. At firft were called together, the Lord Chancellor, the Marquis of Argyle, the Earls of Caffils and Lothian, with Mr Douglas, Mr Blair, Mr Jamefon, and Mr Wood. One and all were very much refrefhed and encouraged by the two publick moft gracious and feafonable letters. The anfwer of them was remitted to the next meeting of the commiffion of the church the laft of this month, where we purpofe to make more publick ufe of thefe, if we fhall then find it ftand with your fafety. In the mean time, Mr Jamefon was appointed to give you fome fhort account of affairs here, which be pleafed to receive.

The whole eight days before the defeat at Dunbar, the Lord had fo difpofed, that, to the apprehenfion of moft in both armies, a victory feemed to incline to our fide ; when, contrary to all appearance, the Lord, by our own negligence, had overthrown us. We have ftill lien under that ftroke, not fo much by any active profecution of the enemy, as by the Lord's hand now upon us, our divifions. A ftrong party in the north, whom we have excluded from our army for the late engagement, did put themfelves in arms without publick order. It coft us fome time before we could quiet them. That danger was fcarce over, when another party in the weft, whom we have permitted to rife, and from whom we expected ready and happy fervice againft the enemy, fell in ways of their own, to our great and long difturbance, which we fuppofe Cromwell long before this has caufed print. Very anfwers were given, both by the church and ftate, as you

X x 2   will

will read here in the copies fubjoined : A while, not-withftanding, they purfued in their diverfe way. The ene-my fell on them, and put them to a total rout, whereby he enlarged his quarters now where he pleafes be-fouth Forth. However our grief and fhame for this defeat be great, yet the lofs of men was much within 100, and the prifoners are not fo many ; and among neither, any men of note, but Col. Ker, who is a prifoner. Strachan, in-deed, the author of all this mifchief, had before foully betrayed his truft, and fince has gone unto the enemy.

Thefe mifchiefs have laid us now lower in the duft be-fore the Lord. On Sunday next, the 22d of December, we have a general humiliation, moft for contempt of the gofpel, the fountain of all our plagues. On Thurfday thereafter, the 26th, we have another, for the fins of the King's family, old and late, which we fear may have in-fluence in the Lord's controverfy with us ; yet for all this, we have not caft away our help and confidence in the Lord ; but with more vigour than ever we purpofe, with all poffible diligence, to make ufe of all the remainder of our forces. The parliament the other week did call toge-ther the commiffion of the church, to be refolved, how far it was lawful to employ, in this cafe of extreme necef-fity, thefe who, for fome time, and while we had choice of men, were excluded from the fervice. The unanimous anfwer by them prefent you have here fubjoined. By the bleffing of God this may be a greater beginning of union among ourfelves, and of a more happy acting againft the enemy, than formerly. There are indeed fome among us againft the employing of thefe who before were excluded ; but we hope that in a little time this fhall change ; fo much the more, as in very few, in whom it is greateft, there yet appears the leaft inclination to comply with the enemy. And to guard the better againft this evil, the church, the other day, paffed the fubfequent act, which the parliament is about to confirm, with a fevere civil cen-fure againft all tranfgreffors. After our forefaid applica-tions to God on the 22d and 26th of this inftant, we have appointed to crown our King, the 1ft of January, at Scone, the ordinary place of our old coronations ; and thereafter, fo foon as we are able, to march with the ftrength of our nobility and gentry to Stirling, where it will be refolved, whether to go with the body of our army to England, lea-ving fuch a party here as to keep and guard the paffes

of

of Forth against the enemy; or, with the body of our army, to attend Cromwell here, and to send Massey to England with some thousand horse and dragoons. To the
former the most part incline; but you with the next shall
be acquainted with our conclusions. But, in the mean
time, the necessity is apparent for the extraordinary diligence of our friends there to procure to us their possible
assistance in this our so necessary undertaking for the common safety. The particular way we are thinking on, I
leave to another letter, sent herewith, and to the instructions given to the bearer, C. B. whom we have found a
faithful, wise, and diligent agent for your desires to us,
and whom we hope shall be no less such for our desires to
you. We have great need of your earnest intercession
with the Lord of Hosts for his powerful concurrence with
us in this our great extremity. Expecting this duty of
love from you and our dear brethren, I add but this one
word, that the brethren there would be careful, as we have
been, and purpose still to be, to lay, at this their new beginning, such foundations for their army and parliament,
that the leading men in both may be firm and zealous to
preserve the covenant, and our former principles, entire
without violation: also, if it shall seem good in the Lord's
eyes to bless our mutual endeavours, that our friends there
may be zealously conscientious, that what progress was made
in the assembly of divines for the reformation of religion
be not lost, but procured, until a final conclusion, and all
be ratified by King and parliament.

Your brother, and servant in the Lord,

JAMESON.

192. *The following letter was at first designed for Mr
Dickson, but was enlarged, and sent to Mr Spang.*

Reverend and Dear Brother,

I sent the inclosed to you by Mr R. Ramsay, thinking
you would have been at the meetings of Stirling and Perth,
whither I was resolved not to go, notwithstanding of many earnest intreaties to the contrary; yet, after the dissolving of the meeting at Stirling, I followed to Perth, upon
sundry letters from Stirling to me for that effect. Your
absence was not well taken by many; though I verily think
your presence would not have had more influence on the
remonstrants

remonftrants than that of Meff. Douglas, Blair, Cant, Rutherford, Durham, Wood, and others, who could in nothing prevail with them. Of the whole matter, as it comes in my mind, I will give you a fimple account, but to yourfelf alone, and after to the fire; for as in all the meetings I was filent, and a mere fpectator, except one forenoon, wherein I in fome things declared my mind, fo I would defire to meddle as little as may be with this unfortunate ftrife.

After the woful rout at Dunbar, in the firft meeting at Stirling, it was openly and vehemently preffed to have David Lefly laid afide, as long before was defigned, but covertly, by the chief purgers of the times. The man himfelf did as much prefs as any to have liberty to demit his charge, being covered with fhame and difcouragement for his late unhappinefs, and irritated with Mr James Guthrie's publick invectives againft him from the pulpit. The moft of the committee of eftates, and commiffion of the kirk, would have been content to let him go; but finding no man tolerably able to fupply his place, and the greateft part of the remaining officers of horfe and foot peremptory to lay down, if he continued not; and after all trials, finding no maladminiftration on him to count of, but the removal of the army from the hill the night before the rout, which yet was a confequence of the committee's order, contrary to his mind, to ftop the enemy's retreat, and for that end to ftorm Broxmouth-houfe as foon as poffible. On thefe confiderations, the ftate, unanimoufly, did with all earneftnefs intreat him to keep ftill his charge. Againft this order, my Lord Warifton, and, as I fuppofe, Sir John Cheefly, did enter their diffent. I am fure Mr James Guthrie did his, at which, as a great impertinency, many were offended. Col. Strachan offered to lay down his charge, being unwilling more to be commanded by D. Lefly. Some more inclined to do fo; but all were quieted by this expedient.

Mr Patrick Gillefpie, by his diligence with fome brethren of the weft, had procured a meeting, at Kilmarnock, of fome chief gentlemen and minifters of the fheriffdoms of Ayr, Clydefdale, Renfrew, and Galloway, where he perfuaded them, for the prefent neceffity, to raife a ftrength of horfe and dragoons, as they had defigned in their affociation, but far above the proportion of any bygone levy. This conclufion obtained, he perfuaded next

to

to put all under the command of four Colonels, the likelieſt men to act ſpeedily againſt the enemy, Ker, Strachan, Robin Halket, and Sir Robert Adair. They made their account to make up the old broken regiments of theſe four to the number of 4000, beſide volunteers. With this voluntary offer, Mr Pat. Gilleſpie, Sir George Maxwell, and Glanderſton, rode to Stirling. However many did ſmell, and fear the deſign of a diviſion, yet the offer was ſo fair, and promiſes of preſent acting ſo great, that eaſily, even by the Chancellor and Mr Robert Douglas's procurement, they obtained an act of ſtate for all their deſires. By this they ſtopped all mens mouths, and forced them of Renfrew and Carrick to join with them. The committee of Renfrew ſeeing the vaſt expences of the enterpriſe, (for the firſt rigging out would amount to 500,000 pounds, [L. 41,666 : 13 : 4], and the daily charge to 4000 or 5000 lib. upon the ſhires foreſaid), were generally averſe from the motion. My Lord Caſſils kept off Carrick; Galloway alſo did diſreliſh the matter; but the committee of Clydeſdale, conſiſting of a few mean perſons, who were totally led by Mr Patrick and Sir John Cheeſly, being very forward; the committee of Kyle and Cunningham being perſuaded by Meſſ. J. Nevo, Gabriel Maxwell, and a few more miniſters, the act of ſtate ſupervening, quaſhed all farther oppoſition. All of us in our pulpits, myſelf as much as others, did promove the work. In a very ſhort time 3500 horſe are got together, with hopes, by volunteers, to make them above 5000. We were all in expectation of ready and happy acting, by infalls on the enemy's quarters. But behold how all our hopes were ſoon moſt miſerably blaſted! Col. Strachan's ſcruples were not only about David Leſly's command; for in this his friends had procured him ample enough ſatisfaction, getting aſſurance, from the committee of ſtate, that David Leſly ſhould gladly permit the forces of the weſt to act apart, and never trouble them with any of his orders; but Strachan's ſcruples went much higher. Since the amendment of his once very lewd life, he inclined much in opinion towards the ſectaries; and having joined with Cromwell at Preſton againſt the engagers, had continued with them to the King's death. At that time, by Mr Blair, and our commiſſioners at London, he was ſomewhat altered; yet not ſo far as to join with us in covenant, till, by the great labours of Mr Ja. Guthrie and Mr P. Gilleſpie, his doubts

were

were fo far fatisfied or fmothered, that he was brought to content the commiffion of the church for that and divers other fcandals againft him : yet it feems that importunity has made him profefs large as much compliance with us as his heart did yield to. His eminent fervice, firft againft Plufcardie, and then againft Ja. Graham, got him the church's extraordinary favour, to be helped with 100,000 merks out of their purfes, for the mounting him a regiment; the greateft offering which ever our churchmen made at one time. This did not a little lift his fpirit, and get him the far beft regiment in the army. With the veftern recruit, it became ftronger than any two regiments in the kingdom. At this time many of his old doubts revive upon him; which, by the knavery of his Captain-Lieutenant, Govan, and frequent meffages of his late friends, Cromwell, and thefe about him, became fo high, that though extraordinary pains were taken upon him, yet he would receive no fatisfaction, fo far as to act any thing againft the enemy, except there might be a treaty. And it appeared therein, that Cromwell was not willing to retire, upon our affurance not to moleft England on the King's quarrel, whom he profeffed to be fo far fallen from all his right to England, that, for his wrongs to Scotland, he ought at leaft to be banifhed the land, or made a perpetual prifoner.

Strachan's axiom and debates put the whole army and commitee of the weft in fuch confufion and difcouragement, that all acting againft the enemy was impoffible. But the matter ftood not at this point. In our debates, at the time of the engagement, our publick profeffions were, of our clearnefs to fight againft the Englifh fectaries, for vindication of the covenant, and the King's juft rights, on the parliament's grant to us of fome few defires. Meff. J. Guthrie and Jo. Livingfton their whifperings a little in the ear to the contrary, were not then audible. It was ftrange to me thereafter, when I heard Wariftou and Mr Guthrie fpeak it out, that it would take a long debate to clear from the covenant, the lawfulnefs of an offenfive war againft Cromwell and his party; yet in a fhort time it appeared, that the quarrel of the King or covenant, or any quarrel tending to war with the Englifh, became to divers more queftionable than it wont to be. Whether a fear of the troubles of war, or a defpair of conquering the King to the publick, or their own perfonal interefts, or a defire to

I   keep

keep the government, not only in the form, but in the
hands it was in, or truly judgement of mind, drew
men to those changes of former professed principles,
I cannot say; only a great deal of zeal was begun to be
practised against all who did smell in any excess of favour
towards the King.   What strict acts of kirk and state were
made against malignancy?   What numbers were cast out
of their charges in the church, state, and army?   What
bars were put to their re-admitting?   You know too much
pleading was for the justice of beheading the King, whatever fault was in the actors.   Mr Guthrie and Mr Gillespie's debates were passionate against the proclaiming of
the King, till his qualifications for government had first
been tried and allowed.   You may remember the labour
was taken to hinder the addresses to the King; and how
like it was to have prevailed, had not the reason, authority, and diligence of Argyle, overswayed it; and, for
all that could be said, the voting of Mess. Guthrie, Gillespie, Hutcheson, and Durham, that no commissioner
should be sent till a change in the King should appear;
and when it was carried to send commissioners, I will not
forget the great study of some to make their instructions
so rigid, that few had any hope the King would ever assent to them; and when, above hope, the King had yielded to all the commissioners had required, the industry of
these same men to get new instructions posted away to
Holland, which, had they come thither before the King's
imbarking, were expected by all should have ruined the
treaty.   Yet when, by the extraordinary favour of God,
the King was brought into Scotland, to do what either
kirk or state had required; and, upon this agreeance, the
noise of Cromwell's march towards us was grown loud,
Sir John Cheesly, Hopeton, and Swinton, kept off, by
their debates in parliament, the raising of our army so
long, that we were near surprised; and when our army
was got together at Leith, the same men helped, by their
continual cross-debates, to keep all in confusion.   Their
strange affronting of the King at Leith; the putting of
him to a new declaration; and, when he stuck but at
some hard expressions, concerning the persons of his
father and mother; their procuring from the kirk and
state that terrible act of disclaiming his interest of the 13th
of August; that same night, without the kirk's knowledge, printed it, and sent it to Cromwell with a trumpet.

All thefe things bred jealoufies in the obfervers, what the intentions of fome men might be ; yet all was diffembled, till after the defeat at Dunbar thefe intentions broke out in their actions. So foon as they faw it probable that they were to have a force to be ruled by themfelves alone, it became their work to have that army fo great, and the o-her at Stirling fo fmall, as they were able.

Then, in thefe meetings with Mr Gillefpie, where Sir John Cheefly and fome three or four burgeffes did meet oft and long, propofitions of a ftrange and high nature were in hand, as Robert Lockhart, who fometimes was prefent, did fhow to Argyle and others. The firft vent of their motions was at the provincial fynod in Glafgow, where Mr Patrick, Mr Hutchefon, Ker, Strachan and o-thers, with much night-waking, brought forth that ftrange remonftrance of the fynod, where Mr Patrick, obtaining a committee to confider the fins procuring the wrath of God on the land, did put fuch men on it as he liked beft, and by them the framing of the draught was put upon himfelf, who quickly begat that pretty piece which I fent you. It doubtlefs had been the fubject of more difcourfe, had it not been drowned in the fubfequent more abfurd one on the fame head in the name of the army ; for at the very firft, it fell on the face of the geneval affembly and parliament, and condemns both for their firft treating with the King, and for the renewing of it in a fecond addrefs ; but moft for clofing of it without evidence of his real change. Then thefe moft bitter invectives againft the ftate, for which Mr Patrick had ufed fo high language with you and Mr Douglas, in face of the commiffion, at length are all brought in, with large additions to any thing was then heard. I have oft of late regretted to fee the judicatories of the church of the church fo eafily led to whatever fome few of our bufy men defigned, but never more than in the particular in hand. I am fure the moft of that writ was without the knowledge of the moft, and againft the fenfe of many, of the brethren. Yet all was voted, *nemine contradicente*, except honeft Mr W. Ruffel, Mr R. Ramfay, and Mr Jo. Bell, fpoke a little to fome words, but on the matter let all go. Fearing what was in hand, I could fpeak but little. The night before I expected nothing more fhould have been preffed but a keeping out engagers from the army. I loved not to ap-pear in contradiction to fome violent men ; yet my heart being

being againſt their concluſion, I was, after much ſoliciting and prayer, brought to a neceſſity of contradicting, and had thought on ſome reaſons for that point to have been mainly proponed for my diſſent ; although I doubt not but my impatience and canker had broken out, if I had heard, which I had never dreamed of, their invectives a-gainſt the treaties ; but the Lord, in a very ſenſible way to me, carried it ſo, that neither the ſynod was troubled with me, nor the peace of my mind by them. I once in-clined to abſent myſelf, and had indeed gone out, but be-hoved to return, not daring to take that courſe ; but be-hold, when I was ready to go to the ſynod at that diet when the remonſtrance came in, my Lord Caſſils ſent his man to call me to ſpeak with him at his lodging. While we are a little ſerious about ſundry of the publick affairs, I found that more time had gone than either of us had obſerved, and telling him that my abſence from the ſynod might be miſtaken, I took my leave, and with all haſte I got up to the church ; where I found, at my entry, that all the debates on that paper were cloſed, and after thrice reading, it was going to the vote. I adored divine providence, who truly beſide my purpoſe, but much to my content, had given me a fair occaſion to ſay nothing of a writ, whereof I never heard a line read. This, for the time, and ſince, was a ſatisfactory ground for my ſilence, to my own mind, in that remonſtrance which brought to the conſenters, let be the contrivers, but ſmall credit ; the com-miſſion of the church having ſo far diſavowed it, as for no requeſt they could be induced to countenance it to-wards the committee of eſtates ; but Mr Patrick behoved to preſent it himſelf, without the company of any from that meeting, which would have made a noiſe, had not the ſecond remonſtrance filled the ears of the whole king-dom with a louder ſound.

Mr R. Ramſay and others had preſſed that for remo-ving of jealouſies from many who were then ſpeaking their doubts of ſome mens intentions, that the officers of the army ſhould put forth a declaration of their deſigns. To me the motion favoured not. Since the raiſing of theſe forces were allowed by the ſtates, all declarations from particular officers ſeemed needleſs : yet on the ſy-nod's motion to Colonel Ker, a declaration by him and his fellows was promiſed, and preſently gone about by Mr Patrick and the chief aſſociates then preſent. But, as Mr Patrick told us, it was laid aſide by the advice ſent them

y Wariſton from Stirling, and Mr James Guthrie, be-
wixt whom and them the poſts then and thereafter ran
ery thick night and day, not ſo much on that ground, he
old us, that they thought it illegal for ſuch private per-
ons to make publick manifeſtoes, as for that, as I ſuſpect,
rhich he told us not.

About this time the King's head was filled by ſome unhappy men about him, eſpecially Dr Fraſer and Henry
ſeymour, with many extreme fears. After the affront at
Leith, they had raiſed ſuſpicions in his mind, which, up-
in the defeat at Dunbar were increaſed, but by the ſepa-
ate riſing in the weſt brought near to the head of a de-
ign to break the treaty with him, and agree upon his ex-
ences with Cromwell. Upon theſe motions the malig-
ants in the north ſtept in, and by the forenamed perſons
regan a correſpondence for the raiſing of the north for
iis preſent ſervice, under the conduct of Middleton. So
nany noblemen were on this unhappy enterpriſe. Craw-
ord was given out for its head and contriver, albeit he
profeſſed to me his oppoſition to it. Lauderdale knew of
t ; but he has ſaid ſo far to me, that I believe him he op-
oſed it to his power. However, the thing was ſo fooliſh-
y laid, and the King, by the counſels of theſe about him,
vas ſo various in giving order for that riſing, ſometimes
ommanding and then countermanding to riſe, that all
he party was put in a confuſion ; yet, by the informa-
ion of theſe foreſaid fools, the King being put in fear,
hat Lorn, going timely to bury a ſoldier, was drawing to-
ſether his regiment to lay hands on him, contrary to
iis former reſolutions ; he took horſe with ſome two or
hree, as if it had been to go a hawking, but croſſed Tay,
and ſtayed not till he came to Clowe in Angus. By the
vay he repented of the journey, and meeting with Lau-
lerdale at Diddup, and Balcarras coming from Dundee
ry accident, was almoſt perſuaded by them to return ; yet
ry Diddup and Buchan he was kept in Clowe. But when
ie came to that miſerably-accommodated houſe, and in
lace of the great promiſed forces, he ſaw nothing but a
ſmall company of highlanders, he preſently ſent for Ro-
ert Montgomery, who was near with his regiment, and
vithout more ado, did willingly return, exceedingly con-
ounded and dejected for that ill-adviſed ſtart. When it
vas firſt blazed abroad, it filled all good men with great
ſrief, and to my own heart it brought one of the moſt

ſenſible

sensible sorrows that in all my life I had felt. Yet his quick return of his own accord, and his readiness to give all satisfaction for that failure, and his kind receiving by the committee of states, among whom he ever sat after his return, (though never before), turned our grief suddenly into joy, his absence not lasting above two full days. Yet all men were not so soon satisfied.

Sundry of them who had been on the plot, fearing a discovery and punishment, flew to arms; Lewis Gordon, Ogilvie, Athol, and others, under Middleton's command, putting out a number of fair pretexts for their rising. This might have destroyed all; yet, by God's mercy, all was quickly quieted. D. Leslie, with all his horse, marched towards them; the King wrote earnestly to them to lay down. The committee of estates sent a fair act of indemnity, and so without more ado they went home. Mr Jams Guthrie had well near marred this peace; he moved Middleton's summar excommunication. Mr R. Douglas, and most number present, were against it; yet Mr James and Mr Patrick, by two or three votes of elders, obtained it. And though the committee of estates, by an earnest letter, intreated Mr James to delay a little the execution, yet on the next sabbath he executed the sentence, to the regret of many.

When the northern storm was ended, the western winds began to blow the louder. I told their declaration was kept in by advice from Stirling, as many thought, to make vantage of the new failings at court; for these were looked on with a greedy eye, and exaggerated to the height of truth. When, with a great deal of expences and trouble, our forces in the west were levied, and present action against Cromwell promised and expected, their very first march is to Dumfries, the farthest place they were able to chuse from the enemy's quarters. The pretence was to attend the motion of the enemy coming from Carlisle; but when the party which went from Edinburgh to fight them, neither in the going nor coming, was looked upon, nor any good at all done by that long march, but the hazarding the country, and the spoiling of a number of noblemen and gentlemen of their saddle-horse, and lying still at Glasgow, while Cromwell took up Glasgow. This made it visible they had some other thing in hand than to mind the enemy. By their earnest missives they had brought Wariston from Stirling to Dumfries.

fries. There, after some debate, the draught of the remonstrance is brought to some perfection, you see. It seems one main end of both remonstrances was to satisfy Strachan, and for that end they came up well near to his full length about the King and the state, the malignants and England. For in this last paper they are clear in condemning the treaty as sinful, and notwithstanding of it to suspend the King's government till he should give satisfactory evidence of his real change, whereof they were to be judges, who were never like to be satisfied, although they were never like to be troubled with the judging of these signs; for the King who had started away upon the suspicion of these things, upon the sight of them in an army-remonstrance, was not like to stay; so on this escape the government of the kingdom, and the distribution of the royal rent in new pensions, all the former being void, fell in our own hand; and if the King should have ventured to stay, then an effectual course was moved to be taken with him to keep him from joining with malignants, which could not be but by a strong guard or imprisonment; albeit this was needless, if the course against malignants had been taken to put them out of all capacity to hurt the people and cause of God; for this could not be but by executing, forfaulting, and imprisoning of the chief of them, as we thought fit.

As for our present state, so many and gross faults were pressed against Argyle, the Chancellor, Lothian, Balcarras, and others, that in all reason they behoved to be laid aside, and our state modelled of new; so that no active nobleman should have any hand therein; and as for England, they might rest secure of our armies, not only till church and state should agree on the lawfulness and expediency of that war was found, but also a clear call from England should appear; and if we could not hear the one, and Cromwell the other, yet we behoved to move nothing of bringing this King to England, whom we had found unmeet to govern Scotland, and though hereafter he should change never so much to the better, yet it was injustice for us to meddle with a kingdom not subordinate to us. Thus far the remonstrance went on, and closed with a solemn engagement on all their hearts, if God blessed their armies, to see all these things performed. I have oft marvelled that Strachan remained unsatisfied for all this; for I verily think, whatever he or
Cromwell

Cromwell could have defired in Scotland, would eafily
have followed upon the former premiffes.

While thefe things are a-doing at Dumfries, Cromwell,
with the whole body of his army and cannon, comes
peaceably by the way of Kilfyth to Glafgow. The magiftrates and minifters fled all away. I got to the ifle of
Cumray, with my Lady Montgomery, but left all my family and goods to Cromwell's courtefy, which indeed was
great; for he took fuch a courfe with his foldiers, that
they did lefs difpleafure at Glafgow than if they had been
at London, though Mr Zachary Boyd railed on them all
to their very face in the High Church. I took this extraordinary favour, from their coming alone to gain the
people, and to pleafe Strachan, with whom he was then
keeping correfpondence, and by whom he had great hopes
to draw over the weftern army, at leaft to a ceffation with
him; as indeed he brought them by his means to be altogether ufelefs; though, on a report of their march towards Edinburgh, he left the weft in a great fuddenty and
demi-diforder.

So foon as the remonftrance was perfected, and all prefent at Dumfries profeffed their affent to it, except Strachan, conceiving it to be too low for his meridian, Mr
Patrick and Mr John Stirling, with fome of the gentlemen, went along with it to Stirling, and Warifton in their
company. The commiffion of the kirk refufed to meddle
with it; only Mr Robert Douglas wrote to the prefbyteries
to fend to the next meeting at Stirling, with their commiffioners of the church, fome more of their number, of
greateft experience and wifdom, to advife in matters of
great importance. The committee of eftates, by Warifton's
means, at their firft prefenting, put no affront upon it;
but what was a very dangerous error, gave too good
words to the carriers; and, to allure them to action againft
the enemy, increafed their forces, by joining with them
the dragoons of Niddifdale and the Lennox; and over-
feeing alfo the feathers which they had drawn out of the
Stirling's wing, the putting them in hopes to get the Stirling's neft, which made them march quickly weft to Par-
tick, in order to Stirling, thinking that Lefly and Middleton fhould have been in others flefh in the north: but
to their open difcontent, the northern ftorm being compofed, and D. Lefly returned to Stirling, they turned their
heads another way.

When,

When, after my return to Glasgow, I saw their remonstrance, and Cromwell's letter thereupon, on the occasion
of Strachan's queries, requiring a treaty, which at that
same time he sent his prisoners, Mr Jaffray and Mr Carstairs, to agent, I was sore grieved, but knew not how to
help it; only I sent the copies of all, with express bearers
to Argyle and you at Inverary, and to the Chancellor at
Perth, and Mr James Ferguson at Kilwinning, with my
best advice to you all, and resolved myself to keep the
next meeting of the commission on the call of their letter,
to declare my dissent, if I could do no more. But behold,
the next presbytery-day, when I am absent, Mr Patrick
causes read again the commission's letter, and had led it
so, that by the elders votes, the men of greatest experience
and wisdom of our presbytery were the two youngest we
had, Mr Hugh Binning and Mr Andrew Morton. Then
when it was pressed that I might be, but added to them, it
was, by a vote, refused, upon supposition it was needless,
being clear I would doubtless go howsoever. These despite-
ful votes wrought so on my mind when I heard of them, that
I resolved not to go, for all that could be said to me by
many of the brethren; yet the clerk of the commission,
at the moderator's direction, writing a pressing letter to
me from Stirling, I went along to Perth; where, by
God's good providence, I have staid since for many good
purposes.

At the meeting of Stirling, there was a conference appointed of the chief members of the committee of estates,
and commissioners of the church, on the remonstrance;
wherein there were many high words about it betwixt Wariston and Mr R. Douglas, Mr R. Ramsay and Mr P.
Gillespie, Mr James Wood and Mr James Guthrie, and
others. No appearance there was of any issue. The time
of parliament at Perth drawing near, the King, by his letter, invited the meeting of church and state to Perth. The
desire of many was but to have some agreement before, if
no other way were possible, as none appeared, that the
remonstrance might be laid aside, and much of the matter
of it be pressed in an orderly way by the commission of
the kirk, and the forces of the west be joined with these
at Stirling; since, for so long a time, they had acted nothing apart, and never like to act any thing for any purpose alone. The remonstrants were averse from these motions; so all was laid aside till they came to Perth: at
2   which

which time a new conference was appointed, and four whole days kept in Argyle's chamber. I then, and thereafter, was witnefs to all, and little more than a witnefs; for not being a commiffioner, I thought meet to be filent. For the one fide, Mr Patrick and Wariston fpoke moft; for the other, Argyle, the Chancellor, the Advocate, and Mr Douglas: but Mr Wood fpoke moft, and to beft purpofe. Mr Rutherford and Mr Durham faid fome little for fundry points of the remonftrance. Mr James Guthrie, moft ingenuoufly and freely, vented his mind; for the principal point, (as he avowed he had oft before maintained), "That the clofe of our treaty was a fin, to promife " any power to the King before he had evidenced the " change of his principles; and the continuing that power " in his hand was finful till that change did appear;" though it was vifible, that every day the kingdom languifhed under thefe debates, which impeded all action. There was no remedy. By no perfuafion the remonftrance could be taken up; yea, the gentlemen gave in a petition to the eftates at Perth, in the prefence of the King, urging the anfwer thereof; from which petition they would not pafs: yea, when they were moft earneftly dealt with to conjoin their forces, all that could be obtained, both by publick and divers private entreaties of their beft friends, Argyle and others, there was a willingnefs to join on two conditions: The firft was, an exprefs laying afide of the King's quarrel in the ftate of the queftion; the other, to keep none in the army of Stirling but according to the qualifications in the act of parliament. When in thefe two all of the gentlemen and officers were found peremptory, the conference on Friday, the fourth day of it, was broken off as fruitlefs; though, for their fatisfaction, the parliament had been fhifted from the Wednefday to the Friday, and from the Friday to the Tuefday again, for all the iffue of blood, and ftarving, that was every day vifible over the kingdom. Before the meeting, the remonftrants had a folemn meeting at Glafgow, by Mr Patrick's call, where, the fubfcribing of the remonftrance was much preffed on the great committee of gentlemen and officers, by the minifters, who fat apart in the tolbooth, and called themfelves the prefbytery of the weftern army. That fubfcription was generally declined, and by no perfuafion any more could be obtained, nor a warrant, fubfcribed by Crofbie, the prefident of the committtee, to

ome few commiffioners, to prefent the remonftrance to
he ftate. Mr Robert Ramfay, fore againft my mind, of-
:red, in his own and my name, once and again, to come
nd debate, in their prefence, with the brethren, the inju-
ice of that remonftrance. This offer was told them in
he committee. All the anfwer it got was, that no man
ras excluded to come and propone what they pleafed.
Jpon fuch entertainment we let them alone. Here it was
here Strachan, before having laid down his charge, was
ommanded to go no more to the regiment; but he told
hem exprefsly, he could not obey. Some would have
een at laying him faft, for fear of his going to the ene-
ay; but left that Ker and many more, fhould thereby
ave been provoked, they let him alone. Govan, for his
:nown correfpondence with the enemy, was cafhiered,
nd their fcout-mafter Dundafs alfo. Sundry of the offi-
ers were fufpected to be of Strachan's principles, albeit
he moft went not beyond the remonftrance.

When the conference was broken off, the committee of
tate went about their anfwer to the petitioners, and there
egan debate. The moft found the matter high treafon;
he divefting the King of his authority; the breaking of
he treaty approven by kirk and ftate; the flandering high-
y of the judicatories; and engaging of private men to
hange the government. The deepnefs of thefe crimes
roubled the judges; the refpect the moft of them had to
he perfons guilty, moving them to go far lower than the
vrit's deferving, and all of them being refolved to make
10 more of it than was in the committee's power to par-
lon; they went therefore no higher in the cenfure than
rou have in the fentence; from which yet near fifteen
liffented for one or other word, though all profeffed their
lifallowance of the writ. This diffent was in the King's
orefence. If he had been abfent, as fome would have
oerfuaded him, the diffenting might have been greater;
or Wariston was very long and paffionate in his exhorta-
ion to wave it fimply, which had been very unhandfome,
ince the parties peremptorily refufed to take it up. At
he fentence, the gentlemen ftormed, but the minifters
nuch more. It came next to the commiffion of the
:hurch. The ftates had given in their fenfe to them, and
equired the kirk's judgement. Here came the vehement
oppofition. The remonftrants petitioned to have the pre-
ent confideration thereof laid afide, left the parties fhould
be

be difcouraged to act againft the enemy. Mr Rutherford
preffed this with much more paffion than reafon, and Mr
Guthrie alfo. Here it was where I fpoke but fo much as
declared my fenfe againft the thing. Much dealing was
ftill to take it up. Meff. Cant, Blair, Rutherford, and
Durham, were fent to perfuade them; but Mr Patrick
was peremptory to fhew their willingnefs to quit their life
rather than their teftimony. So when there was no remedy, at laft, by Mr Douglas and Mr James Wood's indu-
ftry moft, it came to that mild fentence which you fee
here fubfcribed. With it the parties were highly offended,
and entered their loud proteftation. Mr Blair came in the
hinder end. He and you, by your letters, had fignified
your judgement much averfe from the remonftrance;
which in a fcolding way was cried out by Mr John Nevo
in Mr Blair's face: to which he replied nothing. Mr David
Bennet and Mr Hugh Peebles expreffed themfelves bitter-
ly, and were anfwered accordingly by others. Our Provoft, George, fpoke in his proteftation of fomething like
fealing the remonftrance with his blood. All of them
went out of town highly difcontent; though as little occafion was given them as poffibly could be, either by church,
or ftate, or any perfon. I thought the feparation exceeding unhappy, both to our weft country and to the whole
kingdom, but remedilefs, God giving over the chief mif-
leaders, who had oppreffed, to my grief, many others, to
follow their own fenfe in that which the reft of us thought
a high and dangerous fin.

Mr Patrick and Mr James Guthrie, where-ever they
came, uttered their paffion. I heard one who had married Mr Patrick's fifter's daughter, report to Mr Douglas,
that Mr Hugh Binning, with Mr Patrick, in Kirkaldy,
had fpoke like a diftracted man, faying to Mr Douglas's
own wife, and the young man himfelf, and his mother-in-
law, Mr Patrick's fifter, " That the commiffion of the
" kirk would approve nothing that was right; that a hy-
" pocrite ought not to reign over us; that we ought to
" treat with Cromwell, and give him fecurity not to trou-
" ble England with a King; and whoever marred this
" treaty, the blood of the flain in this quarrel fhould be
" on their heads!" Strange words, if true. Always behold the fearful confequence of that pride of ftomach.
The ftate fent Col. Robert Montgomery weft, to join the
beft part of the horfe they had with the weftern forces, or

any part of them that would join with him.   For this end, he fpoke with the commiffioners of the weft, at Stirling, who had been at Perth; but they fhewed great averfenefs at any fuch junction.   He wrote alfo to Ker for this effect, and marched towards Glafgow.   On the Sunday at night he came to Campfie; but on the Saturday, Ker, with all his forces, lying at Carmunock, refolves to prevent Col. Robert's approach, and by themfelves to make an infall on the Englifh before day.

Our intelligence was, that the Englifh at Hamilton were but 1200; but Lambert lay there, with above 3000 of their beft horfe.   They called ours above 1500; but fome double the number: for of all their forces, there was not above four or five of Strachan's troops away.   Some fpeak of treachery; for Govan, for all his cafhiering, was readmitted by Ker on fair promifes.   Strachan was not far off.   It is certain when, at four o'clock in the morning, December 1. our men came to fet on, the enemy were ready to receive them, having founded to horfe half an hour before, as it were for a march to Glafgow.   All fpeak of a great rafhnefs, as in an anger, or what elfe, to caft away thefe forces.   Lieut.-Col. Ralfton, with a fmall party of horfe, entered Hamilton, and moft gallantly carried all before him, killed fundry; fome fpoke of hundreds, other are within fcores; however, he cleared the town of the enemy.   Col. Ker, with fewer than 200, feconded him well; but at the end of the town, where the body of the Englifh drew up again in the field at the back of a ditch, when Ker faw it not eafy to pafs, he retired a little, which they behind took for a flight, and all turned their backs; yea, the whole reft fled apart; not one would ftay.   The Englifh purfued as far as Paifley and Kilmarnock that day; yet very few were killed.   Some fay, fcarce twenty; not above eighty prifoners, whereof Col. Ker made one; as fome fay, deadly, as others, flightly wounded.   Argyle faid to me, he might have efcaped if he would.   The next day, 200 or 300, who rallied in Kyle, by Strachan's perfuafion difbanded; and himfelf, as fearing to be taken by us, went in to Cromwell, with Swinton, whofe firft work was, to agent the rendering the caftle of Edinburgh, with their dear comrade young Dundafs, who moft bafely, and, as yet it is taken, treacheroufly, gave over that moft confiderable ftrength of our kingdom.   But of this more certainly afterwards.

The

The miscarriage of affairs in the west by a few unhappy men, put us all under the foot of the enemy. They presently ran over all the country, without any stop, destroying cattle and corn, putting Glasgow and all others under grievous contributions. This makes me yet to stick at Perth, not daring to go where the enemy is master, as now he is of all Scotland beyond Forth, [i. e. besouth Forth], not so much by his own virtue as our vices. The loss of the west, the magazine of our best-forces, put the state presently to new thoughts. We had long many debates about employing malignants in our armies. Some were of opinion that the acts of church and state were unjust, and for particular ends, from the beginning. All agreed, that common soldiers, after satisfaction to the church, might be taken in ; but as for officers, noblemen and gentlemen volunteers, that we were not to take them in at all, at least not without an eminent degree of evident repentance. The most thought they might be employed as soldiers, on their admittance by the church to the sacrament and covenant. As for places of counsel and trust, that this was to be left to the state's discretion. However, when the case was clearly altered, and now there was no choice of men, the parliament wrote to Mr Robert Douglas to call the commission extraordinary. A quorum was got, most of these of Fife. The question was proposed, of the lawfulness of employing such who before were excluded. The question was alledged to be altered from that which Mr Gillespie writes of, and that whereto Mr Guthrie had solemnly engaged, a defence of our lives and country, in extreme necessity, against sectarians and strangers, who had twice been victors. My heart was in great perplexity for this question. I was much in prayer to God, and in some action with men, for a concord in it. The parliament was necessitated to employ more than before, or give over their defence. Mr Samuel Rutherford and Mr James Guthrie wrote peremptory letters to the old way, on all hazards. Mr Douglas and Mr D. Dick had of a long time been in my sense, that in the war against invading strangers, our former strictness had been unadvised and unjust. Mr Blair and Mr Durham were a little ambiguous, which I much feared should have divided the commission ; and likely had done so, if with the loss of the west, the absence of all the brethren of the west had not concurred.

However,

However, we carried unanimoufly at laft the anfwer herewith fent to you.   My joy for this was foon tempered
when I faw the confequence, the lothing of fundry good
people to fee numbers of grievous bloodfhedders ready to
come in, and fo many malignant noblemen as were not
like to lay down arms till they were put into fome places
of truft, and reftored to their vote in parliament   A-
gainft this neceffity for our very being, and hope that the
guides of our ftate would, by their wifdom and virtue,
and adherence of the church and good men, get kept
what they had of authority, the Chancellor oft remembering us, that in this there was a great alteration of the cafe,
that the King being now in covenant, the moft whofe ma-
ignancy ftood in their following the King againft the covenant, were no more to be counted malignants, the
fountain of that evil being ftopped in them, there was
juft ground why that blot and name of diftinction in that
refpect fhould be now abolifhed.   Another inconvenience
was like to trouble us, a feed of Hyper-Brounifm, which
had been fecretly fown in the minds of fundry of the foldiers, that it was unlawful to join in arms with fuch and
fuch men, and fo that they were neceffitated to make a
civil feparation from fuch, for fear of fin, and curfing of
their enterprifes.   The main fomenters of thefe doubts
feemed not at all to be led by confcience, but by intereft ;
for the officers of our ftanding army, fince the defeat at
Dunbar, being fent to recruit the regiments in the northern fhires, little increafed that number, but taking large
money for men, and yet exacted quarters for men which
were not ; this vexed the country, and difappointed the
fervice.   The officers, by the new levies, thought it eafy
to be recruited at their pleafure ; but an act paffing, that
the new levies fhould not recruit the old regiments, they
ftormed, and gladly would have blafted the new way for
their own ends.   Under thefe evils we wreftle as yet, but
hope for a good end of thefe divifions alfo.   In the
mean time Cromwell is daily expected to march towards
Stirling to mar the coronation, which, fore againft my
heart, was delayed to the firft of January, on pretence of
keeping a faft for the fins of the King's family on Thurfday next.   We mourned on Monday laft for the contempt of the gofpel, according to Mr Dickfon's motion,
branched out by Mr Wood.   Alfo you fee in the printed
papers, upon other particulars the commiffion at Stirling
                                                    whi...

which appointed thefe fafts, could not agree. The remonftrants preffed to have fundry fins acknowledged
which others denied, and would not now permit them to
fet down as they would what caufes of faft they liked.
Surely we had never more need of mourning, be the caufes,
what God knows, vifible or invifible, confeffed or denied,
feen or unfeen, by all but the moft guilty. It cannot be
denied but our miferies and dangers of ruin are greater
than for many ages have been ; a potent victorious enemy
mafter of our feas, and for fome good time of the beft
part of our land ; our ftanding forces againft this his imminent invafion, few, weak, inconfiderable ; our kirk,
ftate, army, full of divifions and jealoufies ; the body of
our people befouth Forth fpoiled, and near ftarving ; the
be-north Forth extremely ill-ufed by a handful of our
own ; many inclining to treat and agree with Cromwell,
without care either of King or covenant ; none of our
neighbours called upon by us, or willing to give us any
help, though called. What the end of all fhall be, the.
Lord knows. Many are ready to faint with difcouragement and defpair ; yet divers are waiting on the Lord, expecting he will help us in our great extremity againft our
moft unjuft oppreffors.

I hope you received my laft inclofed in Callender's packet. You have here a large narration of many of our
proceedings. When I began to write it, my intention
was for Mr D. Dick ; but a little after I had begun, finding this bearer going towards you, I enlarged my letter.
For your hafte and want of good inftruments for the
time, makes the writ, I fear, illegible ; but guefs at it as
you may. You have with it the copy of a letter of mine
to our friends in England, which for a time keep fecret
to yourfelf alone. I fend you alfo a copy of divers other
writs, which I think you may defire to fee.

This day we have done that what I earneftly defired,
and long expected, crowned our noble King with all the
folemnities at Scone, fo peaceably and magnificently as if
no enemy had been among us. This is of God : for it
was Cromwell's purpofe, which I thought eafily he might
have performed, to have marred by arms that action, at
leaft the folemnity of it. The remonftrants, with all
their power, would have oppofed it : others prolonged it
fo long as they were able. Always, bleffed be God, it is
this day celebrated with great joy and contentment to all

honeft-

honeft-hearted men here. Mr Douglas, from 2 Kings xi.
Joafh's coronation, had a very pertinent, wife, and good
fermon. The King fware the covenant, the league and
covenant, the coronation-oath. When Argyle put on
he crown, Mr Douglas prayed well; when the Chancel-
or fet him on the throne, he exhorted well; when all
were ended, he, with great earneftnefs preffed fince-
ity and conftancy in the covenant on the King,
lelating at length King James's breach of the cove-
iant, purfued yet againft the family, from Neh. v. 13.
God's cafting the King out of his lap, and the 34th of
feremiah, many plagues on him if he did not fincerely
keep the oaths now taken. He clofed all with a prayer,
ind the 20th pfalm.

Dundas and Major Abernethy have moft bafely delivered the caftle of Edinburgh to Cromwell. All the mi-
iifters faw the treachery, and protefted againft it. Wa-
ifton, Sir John Cheefly, and the Provoft of Edinburgh,
vho put them in that truft, contrary to the minds of o-
hers, have little credit by it.

Now the parliament having, by the needlefs length of
ome, fat fo long, ended their feffion on Monday after
welve at night. None of the remonftrants are on the
ommittee of eftates. Warifton, with great difficulty,
vas got on. All dilligence will now be ufed to get up an
rmy. The Lord be with us. Our greateft danger will
e from famine. Now get victuals to ftarving Ireland.
t were an happy benefit if your Hollanders would bring
s in victual for money. The Spaniard, nor any other,
ould never, by their perfuafion nor force, hinder them
o trade where-ever they find gain. Is not this a ftrange
avery now, our love to the Englifh murderers, that they
or their pleafure fhould give over all trade with us their
rethren and well-deferving friends? Though we fhould
ever be able to revenge their ingratitude, yet there is a
iod who will fee to it. Our cafe will be exceeding hard
, before the fummer, your Zealanders, on piety and
ity, be not moved to bring us victuals for all the money
e have refting; though it may be the Lord may be plea-
d to open fome other door which yet is not vifible to
s.

Perth, January 2. 1651.

P. S. I think to-morrow we fhall give order to excommunicate

municate Strachan, and relax Middleton the next sabbath. By the coming of some, all engaging officers and noblemen were all purged out of our army; but now I think all of them, without any considerable exception, are received. On this necessary conclusion, some turbulent men are like to be factious; but to-morrow a warning is to be put out for their reclaiming if possible. By God's blessing, our affairs shortly may be in a better posture. Our great troublers, both in church and state, have set themselves aside. If God give us over to Cromwell, we expect little good from these men but a violent executing of all in their remonstrance; but otherwise I think they may be brought quickly to repent their needless quarreling. However, the Lord's will be done, who has begun to comfort us with the smallest appearance of better hopes.

193. *For his Reverend and Dear Brother, Mr Calamy, minister at London.* Glasgow, July 27. 1653.

Reverend and Dear Brother,

THIS my third to you is only to give thanks for your kind acceptance, and answering indeed, of my two former. Mr Wilkie, our commissioner, has reported so much of your care to us, to promove to the uttermost of your power the charitable supply of our distressed people, that all of us are much obliged to bless God in your behalf, who has made you instrumental to procure a liberal support, both in your own congregation, and over all the city, to the many families of this wracked people with that strangest fire that ever was heard of in our land. I am confident enough of your readiness to go on for the perfecting of what is so well begun, even to give your best advice and assistance to this same gentleman, whom we have sent again, with some others, to receive, in the city and country, what shall be freely offered by the pious benevolence of those whose hearts God shall stir up, by you and your brethren, to contribute to that work of compassion and charity.

At this time I have no more to add, but this one word, to let you know, That on the 20th of July last, when our general assembly was set in the ordinary time and place, Lieutenant-Colonel Cottrell beset the church with some rattes of musqueteers and a troop of horse. Himfelf (after our faft, wherein Mr Dickfon and Mr Douglas had two gracious fermons) entered the affembly-houfe; and, immediately after Mr Dickfon the Moderator his prayer, required audience; wherein he inquired, If we did fit there by the authority of the parliament of the commonwealth of England? or of the commanders in chief of the Englifh forces? or of the Englifh judges in Scotland? The Moderator replied, That we were an ecclefiaftick fynod, an fpiritual court of Jefus Chrift, which meddled not with any thing civil; that our authority was from God, and eftablifhed by the laws of the land yet ftanding unrepealed; that by the Solemn League and Covenant, the moft of the Englifh army ftood obliged to defend our general affembly. When fome fpeeches of this kind had paffed, the Lieutenant-Colonel told us, his order was, to diffolve us. Whereupon he commanded all of us to follow him; elfe he would drag us out of the room. When we had entered a proteftation of this unheard-of and unexampled violence, we did rife, and follow him. He led us all through the whole ftreets a mile out of the town, encompaffing us with foot-companies of mufqueteers, and horfemen without; all the people gazing and mourning as at the faddeft fpectacle they had ever feen. When he had led us a mile without the town, he then declared what further he had in commiffion, That we fhould not dare to meet any more above three in number; and that againft eight o'clock to-morrow, we fhould depart the town, under pain of being guilty of breaking the publick peace: And the day following, by found of trumpet, we were commanded off the town, under the pain of prefent imprifonment. Thus our general affembly, the glory and ftrength of our church upon earth, is by your foldiery crufhed and trode under foot, without the leaft provocation from us, at this time, either in word or deed. For this our hearts are fad, our eyes run down with water, we figh to God againft whom we have finned, and wait for the help of his hand; but from thofe who oppreffed us we deferved no evil. We hear a noife of further orders, to difcharge all our fynods and prefbyteries, and all prayer for our King. Many the moft moderate reckon fuch orders will make havock of our church, and raife againft many the beft men we have, a fore perfecution; which, God willing, we purpofe to endure with all patience and faith, giving juft offence to none.

I

I detain you no more. The Lord mind his Zion in these lands, and bless you, who for the time stand in the most eminent pinnacle thereof. Thus rests,

Your Brother to serve you,

ROBERT BAILLIE.

194. *To Mr William Spang.   July* 19. 1654.

Cousin,

I think you marvel not at my long and universal silence. War being flaming betwixt the lands of our abode, though neither you nor I have any interest therein, yet the passage being stopped, or difficult, and all correspondence betwixt any in these and thir parts being liable to misconstruction, I chose rather to be silent than for that time to write any. But now the peace being subscribed, and ready to be proclaimed, I resume my old way of letting you know the true condition of myself, our college, church, and country; expecting the like from you of your affairs there, and of the world abroad, at your first opportunity.

As for our church-affairs, thus they stand. The parliament of England had given to the English judges and sequestrators a very ample commission to put out and in ministers as they saw cause, to plant and displant our universities. According to this power, they put Mr John Row in Aberdeen, Mr Robert Leighton in Edinburgh, Mr Patrick Gillespie in Glasgow, and Mr Samuel Colvill they offered to the Old College of St Andrew's. This last is yet held off; but the other three act as Principals. All our colleges are quickly like to be undone. Our churches are in great confusion. No intrant gets any stipend till he have petitioned and subscribed some acknowledgement to the English. When a very few of the remonstrants and Independent party will call a man, he gets the kirk and the stipend; but whom the presbytery, and well near the whole congregation, calls and admits, he must preach in the fields, or in a barn, without stipend. So a sectary is planted in Kilbride, another in Lenzie, [or Kirkintilloch], and this guyse will grow rife, to the wrack of many a soul.

We thought at the general assembly to have got some course for this; but Colonel Lilburn, the commander in chief, gave orders to soldiers to break our assembly before

: was conftituted, to the exceeding great grief of all, ex-
ept the remonftrants, who infulted upon it; the Englifh
iolence having tryfted with their proteftation againft it.
iince that time we have had no meeting for the whole
:hurch, not fo much as for counfel, though the remon-
trants have met oft, and are like to fet up a commiffion
md affembly of their own for very ill purpofes.   They are
noft bitter againft thofe who adhere to their covenant in
he matter of the King and affembly.   They are as bent
is ever to purge the church.   To punifh men truly defer-
ring cenfure, we are as willing as they; but their purging
is, for common, a very injurious oppreffion.   Sundry of
:hem fall openly to the Englifh errors, both of church
md ftate, and many more are near to that evil; yet Lord
Warifton, Mr James Guthrie, and others, ftill profefs
their great averfion to the Englifh way: however, their
great averfion of the King, and of the late affemblies, and
their zeal to make up the church and army, and places of
truft, only of the godly party, (that is, their own confidents), make them dear and precious men to the Englifh,
do or fay what they will, and their oppofites but rafcally
malignants.   This makes them exceeding bold, knowing
of their back; and were it not for a few more moderate
men among them, they, before this, would have played
ftrange pranks.   However, they are going on pretty faft.
Their wracking of the congregation of Lenzie, and dividing of the prefbytery of Glafgow, their doing the like in
the congregation and prefbytery of Linlithgow, you heard
long ago; alfo what they have done in Bathgate, and fundry parts of the fouth.   I will only give fome account of
their laft dealings.

From their meeting in Edinburgh they were inftructed
to have monthly fafts and communions.   They excluded
more than the half of thefe who were ordinarily admitted.
Six or feven minifters, leaving their own congregations
defolate, were about the action.   Numbers of ftrangers
flocked to thefe meetings.   At their fafts, four or five minifters of their beft preachers in the bounds exercifed from
morning to even.   The great defign of this was evidently
but to increafe their party; whereof yet in moft places
they miffed.   Always the word went, that they purpofed
to put up committees, for purging and planting every
where as they thought fit.   I was fo charitable as not to
fufpect them of any fuch purpofe, when the land was full
of

of confufion and danger; yet I found myfelf difappointed; for at our fynod, the moderator's fermon ran on the neceffity of taking up the too-long neglected work of purging. The man's vehemency in this, and in his prayer, a ftrange kind of fighing, the like whereof I had never heard, as a pythonifing out of the belly of a fecond perfon, made me amazed. To prevent this foolifh and cruel enterprife, we preffed, in the entry of the fynod, that in thefe times of confufion we might be affured of peace till the next fynod, as we had been in the three former fynods. We intimated our great willingnefs to caft out of the miniftry all whom we conceived either unfit for weaknefs, or fcandalous; but a fynod fo divided in judgement as we were, we conceived very unfit for any fuch work. When we found our defire flatly refufed, and perceived a clear defign to fet up prefently their tyrannous committees, we, as we had refolved beforehand, and were advifed by the miniftry of Edinburgh, and others of our mind, required them, that our fynod might be rightly conftitute; that minifters cenfured by the general affembly, and elders notorioufly oppofite to the laft three general affemblies, might have no voice. When this was flatly refufed, we fhewed we were neceffitated to fit by ourfelves, and leave them in their feparation from the general affembly and church of Scotland. When, by all we could fay, nothing could be obtained, all of us who adhered to the general affembly, went to the Blackfriars, and there kept the fynod, leaving our proteftation with them. Some brethren travelled all the next day for an union. We offered it gladly, on condition, that they would be content for this time of the land's trouble and danger, to leave all meddling with things controverted, or elfe to conftitute according to the act of the general affembly. When neither could be obtained, (as you may fee in the paper of mediation), we conftituted ourfelves in a fynod by an act; and when we had appointed a faft, we clofed, to meet at Irvine the next diet. To our abfent brethren we fent a letter, and an information of our proceedings to the neighbouring fynods of Lothian, Galloway, Argyle; alfo Fife, Perth, and the Merfe.

The remonftrants chofe Mr William Guthrie for their moderator, and one James Porter, a devoted fervant of their party, for clerk; named a committee of their moft forward men to go immediately to Lanerk, to purge and
plant

plant as they found cause; sent two of their gentlemen, Sir George Maxwell and Walkingshaw, with the help of their good friend Bogs, and Commissary Lockhart. Mr Somerville, and Mr Jack; and, when they prevailed not, two of their ministers, Mr William Somerville, and Mr William Jack, went to the Governor of Glasgow, Col. Couper, for a troop of horse to guard them at Lanerk and Douglas. Some of them, to their power, fomented a very injurious scandal on Mr Robert Hume, whom we had made minister at Crawfordjohn contrary to their mind; their committee laboured to their power to try that their own invention; but failed therein. There is an old man, Mr John Veitch, minister of Roberton, they sent two or three ministers of their number to hear him preach. In their report, they pronounced a sentence of deposition on him as insufficient. But their chief work was at Douglas. The noblemen, gentlemen, whole heritors, people, and session, unanimously had called Mr Archibald Inglis, a very good and able youth, to his father's place. They stirred up some of the elders, who subscribed a call to the young man, to desire his trials might be before the united presbytery, and not before our part of it, from which the remonstrants had separated. This motion they so fomented, that these few elders, with a very few of the people, were moved by them, contrary to all the congregation, to give a call to a silly young man, a mere stranger, from Fife, one Mr Francis Kidd, who had never been heard or seen in the bounds. This man they bring to the kirk on the Sunday. When the people refused to let him or them enter, he preached on a brae-side to some strangers and a few of the people of Douglas, and even these run away from hearing of him, except a very few of them. Sermon ended, they sent one to read an edict at the church-door, who refused to give a copy of what he read. Without more ado, on Monday morning, they passed all his trials in one hour, and came to the church of Douglas in the afternoon to give him imposition of hands. The body of the people and heritors hindered their coming into the church and church-yard; whereupon they sent once and again for their English guard. By all their importunity they could get none of the troop to countenance them, except twelve, with the Lieutenant. By the power of their sword, as was avowed on all hands, on a brae-side, without preaching, they admitted him minister of
Douglas:

Douglas: An abominable example, generally much abhorred, which shews what we may expect from that party. Our synod appointed some to join with the true presbytery of Lanerk; which met the week thereafter; tried, with all accuracy possible, what could be found in the scandal of Mr Hume; found nothing but malice of some parties, fomented by ministers; with the unanimous consent of the people of Roberton, strengthened the minister, and appointed a helper to be settled there in an orderly way; admitted to the church of Douglas Mr Archibald Inglis, after all trials duly performed, with the blessings and tears of the congregation. Possibly they will procure an order from the English, that the stipend and church shall go to Mr Kidd, and his twelve or sixteen followers, and Mr Inglis shall be tolerated, with much ado, to preach to the whole congregation, Marquis of Douglas, Earl of Angus, whole heritors and people, in the fields, or a barn, without a sixpence of stipend.

In this glass see our condition. It is so in sundry congregations already, and like to be so in many more; not so much through the violence of the English, as the unreasonable headiness of the remonstrants, which for the time is remediless; and we, for fear of worse from their very evil humour, give way to permit them to plant divers churches as they like best. This formed schism is very bitter to us, but remediless, except on intolerable conditions, which no wise orthodox divine will advise us to accept: We must embrace without contradiction, and let grow, the principles of the remonstrants, which all Reformed divines, and all states in the whole world abhor; we must permit a few heady men to walk our church with our consent or connivance; we must let them frame our people to the Sectarian model; a few more forward ones joined among themselves by privy meetings to be the godly party, and the congregation, the rest, to be the rascally malignant multitude: so that the body of our people are to be cast out of all churches; and the few who are countenanced, are fitted, as sundry of them already have done, to embrace the errors of the time for their destruction. Against these abominations we strive so much, and so wisely, as we can. Mr R. Douglas, Mr Dickson, and others, have yet got Edinburgh right. The faction which Mr Robert Traill and Mr John Stirling have there is inconsiderable. Mr R. Blair and Mr J. Wood keep St Andrew's

drew's and Fife pretty right. Mr Rutherford, to the uttermoft of his power, advances the other party. Mr John
Robertfon and Mr William Rate get Angus and Dundee
right; but the naturally heady men of Aberdeen are come
to the full defign too foon; yet the body of the people
and country are right. In this Mr J. Guthrie in Stirling
comes but fmall fpeed: albeit his confident Sir William
Bruce of Stenhoufe be made the Englifh fheriff in Linlith-
gowfhire, they have ufed great violence, imprifoned their
chief oppofite Mr John Waugh, forced a filly man into
the miniftry of Linlithgow, and another on Bathgate,
contrary to all the fynod of Lothian could do; yet the
body of the people there is flat againft them. Their greateft prevalency is with us in Glafgow, which comes much-
more by Mr James Durham's profeffed neutrality, but
real joining with moft of the other's defigns, and Mr John
Carftair's zeal, than any thing that Mr Patrick Gillefpie
had done, or could do, by himfelf. This is the pitiful
condition of our church, which is but going on from evil
to worfe till the Lord remeid it.

As for our ftate, this is its cafe. Our nobility are well
near all wracked. Dukes Hamilton, the one executed, the
other flain; their eftate forfeited; one part of it gifted to
Englifh foldiers; the reft will not pay the debt; little left
to the heretrix; almoft the whole name undone with debt.
Huntly executed; his fons all dead but the youngeft:
there is more debt on the Houfe than the land can pay.
Lennox is living as a man buried in his houfe of Cobham.
Douglas and his fon Angus are quiet men, of no refpect.
Argyle, almoft drowned in debt, in friendfhip with the
Englifh, but in hatred with the country. He courts the
remonftrants, who were and are averfe from him. Chancellor Loudon lives like an outlaw about Athol; his lands
comprifed for debt, under a general very great difgrace.
Marifchal, Rothes, Eglinton and his three fons, Crawford, Lauderdale, and others, prifoners in England; and
their lands all either fequeftrated or forfaulted, and gifted
to Englifh foldiers. Balmerino fuddenly dead, and his
fon, for publick debt, comprifings, and captions, keeps
not the caufey. Warifton, having refunded much of
what he got for places, lives privily in a hard enough condition, much hated by the moft, and neglected by all, except the remonftrants, to whom he is guide. Our criminal judicatories are all in the hands of the Englifh; our

I

civil

civil courts alfo; only fome of the remonftrants are ad-
joined with them.   In the feffion are Craighall, and his
brother Hopeton, Mr A. Pearfon, Southall, Col. Lockhart, and Swinton.   The only clerks to the feffion are
Mr John Spreul and William Downie.   The commiffariot
and fheriff courts are all in the hands of Englifh foldiers,
with the adjunction in fome places of fome few remonftrants.   Strong garrifons in Leith, Edinburgh town and
caftle, Glafgow, Air, and Dumbarton, Stirling, Linlithgow, Perth, Dundee, Burntifland, Dunnotter, Aberdeen,
Invernefs, Inverary, Dunftaffage, &c.

Of a long time no man in the whole ifle did mute.   All
were lulled up in a lethargick fear and defpair; only the
other year, Glencairn and Balcarras, underftanding of an
order to apprehend them as correfponding with the King,
retired to the hills of Athol.   Kenmure having efcaped
from England, when his houfe was burnt and his rents
feized upon, got to the Lennox with a few horfe.   Lorn
being but coarfely ufed by his father, joined with Kenmure.   To thefe fundry did affociate, Glengary, Athol,
Seaforth, not fo much to do any thing againft the Englifh,
as to make fome noife of a party, to encourage the King's
friends abroad to fend him fupplies of men, arms, and
money.   At once a great animofity did rife in every fhire
of the land.   Very many young gentlemen made bold
with all the ferviceable horfes they could find about them,
and notwithftanding of all the diligence the Englifh could
ufe to prevent, great numbers came fafe to the hills.   The
war with Holland, and rumour of great help from over-
feas, did increafe daily both the number and courage of
this party.

But behold inward divifion doth hazard all at the very
beginning.   The irreconcileable difcord betwixt Argyle
and Hamilton had undone the ifle, and almoft both the
families.   Glencairn, Hamilton's coufin, did much mif-
truft and flight Lorn.   Ralfton, and the remonftrant-
gentlemen of Kintyre, feemed ready to arm for the Englifh, againft the King's party.   Lorn and Kenmure, with
the men they had raifed, went to Kintyre to fupprefs
thefe.   They, on hope of the Englifh affiftance from Ayr,
fortified the caftle of Lochead.   But when neither Argyle nor the Englifh appear in their defence, they render
the houfe to Lorn's difcretion.   Kenmure thinking the
befieged better ufed by Lorn than they deferved, fell in a

miscontent, and went from Lorn to Glencairn with many
complaints. Balcarras also unwilling to have Glencairn
above him, and conceiving it was best for the advancing
of the King's affairs, that till the King himself, or one of
authority from him, should come, the party should be
ruled by a committee without any supreme officer, and
that all admitted to councils and command in the army
should declare for the Solemn League and Covenant.
For these ends he dealt with Lorn, Seaforth, and Athol;
till Glencairn produced a commission under the King's
hand to be general, till himself or some from him should
come to take the command. This unexpected commission
put all to a submissive silence, but increased heartburnings.
Lorn professing all firmness to the King and cause, was
not willing to take orders from Glencain, till he knew
more particularly the King's pleasure. For this end, he
Balcarras, and others, wrote to the King their discontent
with Glencairn's command. These letters were intercepted, and brought to Glencairn ; whereupon he gave order to Glengary to apprehend Lorn to answer for his se-
dition. Lorn hardly enough escaped Glengary's pursuit.
Balcarras retired ; and, a little after, with his lady, went
disguised through England to the King. Notwithstanding
of all these pitiful and shameful debates, Glencairn's party still increased, and his conduct became considerable.
The whole highlands, isles, and much of the north, and
numbers from the lowlands, were come unto him ; so it
was thought, at Middleton's coming, he had here and
there 8000 or 9000 foot, and 2000 or 3000 horse, of very
stout and resolute men as ever we had on the fields, the
most of them old soldiers. But at Middleton's coming,
when neither the King, nor his brother, nor any foreign
forces did appear, the hearts of many began to doubt ;
and when, after his coming, some months, notwithstanding of all the reiterated promises, no foreign assistance at
all did come ; but on the contrary, the Holland peace
was proclaimed ; the treaty of the Protector with Sweden
went on ; the French ambassador at London was solemnly
received, as the Spanish and Portugal had been ; all human hope began much to fail, especially after Monk's
coming down as general, the proclamation of the Protector, the act of union, and the ordinance of grace,
which forfeited and deeply fined so many, and subjected
the whole privileges of the nation to the Protector and his
                                        council's

council's pleasure, with the abolition of royalty, the whole branches of the family-royal, and all Scots parliaments and conventions of estates; the taking of Kinnoul, Lieutenant-Colonels Heriot, Wishart, Forsyth, and sundry more of our Scotsmen, unhappily : all these were so hard presages, that the most gave all the King's affairs for gone, and many thought that the King, whether through their weakness, or the treachery of the few counsellors about him, or the cross aspect of all Europe towards him, had so far disappointed the expectation of his friends, that while he lived he was not like to get such a party for his service in Scotland.

So for the time the case of our land is most sad. Monk, by sea and land, is to beset Glencairn and his party, and with much severity to crush them, and for their sakes to lie more heavily on the whole subjected country, beginning with the best of the ministers ; who, after mutual advice, find themselves in conscience necessitated to keep the King still in their publick prayers. They have been very careful to give the English no other offence at all ; for in all this northland rising, to my best knowledge, there is no minister in Scotland who has had the least hand or any meddling. However, for this our great treason of naming the King in our publick prayers, (as we conceive our duty, covenant, and directory of worship do require, as you will see in the papers herewith sent you), we are like to suffer heavy things. For all this our eyes are towards the Lord. We expect protection from him; and if so he think meet, we are willing to seal our testimony, in faith and humble modesty, with all the sufferings which the injustice of men may be permitted of our heavenly Father to impose upon us.

Being called the other week to confer with the brethren of Edinburgh, I was comforted to find all that met, fully in my sense about prayer for the King, and affairs of our divided synod, divided presbytery, troubled college, and all else we spoke of. But it was a sad sight to see the general affliction at the proclamation of the Protector, of the act of union, the act of forfaultry and deep fining of so many, the preparations of Monk by sea and land presently to swallow up the northern party, destitute of all hope of the oft-promised foreign supplies, as common fame surmised. As our miseries, (without a kingdom wholly, without any judicatories to count of of our own, without a church well near), are great; so we expect they shall increase, and the next heavy dint shall fall on the chief of the ministry. At once it will not be safe to have any audible complaints of these things either to God or man.

Postscript, July 20. 1654.

While I waited long for a bearer, I add further, our triumviri, Mess. Livingston, Gillespie, and Menzies, staid long at London without much access to the Protector. He thought it good to write for Mess. Douglas, Blair, and Guthrie. Mr Blair excused his health. Mr Guthrie, by a fair letter, declared his peremptoriness not to go. Mr Douglas, by Monk's friendly letter, got himself also excused. On their not coming, Mr Livingston got leave to return, and is at home. Mr G. and Mr M. are expected. The business of the plot gave not the Protector much leisure for auditing of them. Only we fear that our church shall be cast under such a committee as now guides all ecclesiastical affairs in England, absolutely as the Protector thinks fit, the most whereof are Anabaptists, Independents, and gentlemen of no ecclesiastical relation. We thank God that persecution on the ministry is not yet begun, except what the remonstrants draw from the English on some few. Mr John Waugh and Mr Robert Knox were long prisoners for naming the King in their prayers; yet now they are at their liberty, and at their charges, to our great joy.

As to our anti-synod, after the pranks in Lanerk they met synodically very frequent at Glasgow, fell on a committee for purging all the presbyteries. I alone went up to them, intreated them with many fair words to delay any such work, and for that end gave them in a large paper, which a very gracious and wise brother, somewhat a mid-man betwixt us, had drawn for that end, which I send to you, that from it you may more fully learn our present temper. All this labour procured little; for notwithstanding they proceeded in their work, and appointed their purging and planting committees; but with this proviso, that they should have, at their next meeting, a conference with any I pleased of my mind before they proceeded. Against their day I had our part of the synod met, and full information of the brethren of Edinburgh

burgh and others for our proceeding. We presently set
up a purging and planting committee as well as they, and
of these we appointed a number to confer with them.
With much ado we got them to stay till the first of August, upon a new conference : against that day Mr James
Ferguson drew up a paper of his overtures for our re-
union, and I drew up another. You have both here.
What the issue shall be you may hear afterward ; only
these things lie heavier on my heart than any man's else I
know, for usually at the times of these comfortless janglings, I am sick and distempered with grief and discontent, though every one of them gives me more respect
than to any other ; yet for the remediless breach I am
heavily oft troubled in my own mind, which I use to pour
out before God, and get then courage and strength to go
on, and bear the burden.

General Monk went to the fields in the beginning of
June, thinking and professing that the discussing of the
northern Tories would cost him but a few weeks labour ;
and we indeed expected no other ; for the English in men,
horse, money, and all things they could desire, had the
clear advantage : yet we cannot hear of any great progress
he has made. So soon as Glencairn had rendered his
commission to Middleton ; on a jar between Monro and
Glengary, Glencairn speaking for Glengary, got a challenge from Monro ; which he answered, and beat Monro,
to his great commendation. This affront, not so much
resented by Middleton as need had been, together with
the King's too much neglect, as some say, in his late commissions, of Glencairn's very great services, upon the information, as it is thought, of Lorn and Balcarras, he left
Middleton, and came with a small party to the Lennox.
The noise of this malecontentment exceedingly discouraged
many ; but at once Glencairn carried it so, that all this
discouragement was quickly changed ; for with the small
party he had he defended the pass of Aberfoyle so well a-
gainst Monk's frequent assaults, and sent out, for good
purpose, so many small parties to Clydesdale, Renfrew,
Cunningham, Kyle, Carrick, and Galloway, as retarded
a while Monk's march to the north ; and when he went
north, notwithstanding of all the garrisons, and beside
them one full regiment of foot and another of horse, left
at Glasgow and Kilsyth, the party sent out from Glencairn, ran up and down the whole country, and did what
they

they liked, without great impediment. Monk found his march to the north very troublesome. The people carried all out of his way; stragglers were snapped up; the hills made sundry both horse and men sicken and die. It was oft printed, that Morgan had Middleton so inclosed in Sutherland, that he could not escape to the south; yet when Middleton thought it time, he divided his men in parties, and passed by, with ease, both Morgan and Monk, coming to Perthshire and Argyle, notwithstanding all they could do to impede him. Colonel Brian's regiment from Ireland, landing in Lochaber, was lighted on by the country-people, and near 100 of them slain: for this Monk did cause burn all the lands of Lochaber, Glengary, and Seaforth, as he came through. Glenorchy had been too great an intelligencer to the English, and sided with Argyle against Lorn his son; so Middleton caused burn much of his land. This burning, now begun on both hands, may ruin the whole country. It is thought the English have their full of the highland hunting, and that the flux is fallen among them, which make them speak already of quartering. It seems Middleton minds no fighting in any body, but shifts till he see what time may bring forth. The country every where suffers much; yet is patient, for they see no remedy; also the victual all this year is at 4 lb. the boll, a greater appearance of the continuance of this greater plenty than has been seen in our days.

What the world abroad is doing, we know no more than the London Diurnal tells us. What the mystery may be of the Queen of Sweden's dimission, and why her last act should have been (without all necessity) a strict friendship with the Protector, is much marvelled; also, why, for the Protector's friendship, (contrary to the mind of the other provinces), these of Holland should have cast off the Prince of Orange; and if Spain be with the Protector upon a league offensive and defensive, how comes it that both France and Portugal should, by their ambassadors, be begging his friendship? What all this may mean, we understand not, nor what our King's journey to the sea imports. You possibly may make us understand these things. Is Salmasius dead? What is become of Blondell? What new books are among you? Try to get me what of chronology is lately come out. Dr Strang, your good friend, having to do in Edinburgh with the lawyers, concerning the unjust trouble he was put to for his stipend,

after

after a few days fickneſs, did die, fo fweetly and gracioufly, as was fatisfactory to all, and much applauded over all the city, his very perſecutors giving him an ample teſtimony: His treatiſe *Dei circa peccatum,* he has enlarged, and made ready for the preſs.   Be careful to get it well printed, according to the conſtant friendſhip that was always betwixt you and him.   They hope you will get it printed freely, for the piece is likely to fell; but if you muſt give any money for its printing, they will bear the charge.   Let me know with the firſt, your anſwer herein; for they will fend you the copy fo foon as your mind is known, and your advice given.   How is your condition in Middleburg?   The Engliſh congregations uſe to be very fickle and hard to be kept by their miniſters.   If your lot be better with yours I will be glad.   This letter is after my old faſhion.   It deſerves a long anſwer.   My love to your wife and children.   I reſt, in the Lord,

        Your Couſin,

                        ROBERT BAILLIE.

That you may know the way of planting our churches, have this late practice.   Mr John Galbraith of Bothkennar was depoſed for tippling and other faults, fome three or four years ago.   When Mr James Guthrie continued to preach in Stirling, after his depoſition by the general aſſembly, Mr Galbraith followed his example, and returned to his pulpit.   His people loved him better than Stirling did the other.   Of the preſbytery of Stirling, Mr James Simpſon, of Airth, likewiſe depoſed, and Mr Jo. Hogg, of Larber, adhered to Mr Guthrie, and theſe three made one preſbytery.   Mr R. Wright and other two or three adhering to the aſſembly, made themſelves another preſbytery.   Mr George Bennet and other two were neutrals, and abſtained from both.   Mr Guthrie began a proceſs of excommunication againſt Mr Galbraith; but he boaſted fo faſt to excommunicate Mr James if he proceeded againſt him, that this was left off.   Mr James profeſſes to have no meddling with the Engliſh at all, and to be much averſe from all compliance with them, yea to miſlike Mr P. Gilleſpie's way; yet Sir William Bruce of Stonehouſe, his ſpecial and intimate friend to this day, has taken the ſheriffſhip of Stirling from the Engliſh, and continues ruling elder in Mr James's preſbytery.   By his means an order is procured from the Engliſh, that Mr

John

John Galbraith shall give over preaching. This he is forced to obey. They whole parish gives an unanimous call to Mr William Galbraith, a good young man; but an order comes from the English to hinder his plantation; and the whole parish's supplication oft presented to the English, could not get it helped; for the judges are fully for the remonstrants, though General Monk seems to dislike them. Thereafter one Mr John Blair, never heard nor seen by the parish, is named by Mr Guthrie's presbytery to be minister of that kirk; for that people having adhered to a deposed minister, must be counted malignant, and so lose their right to call, and the right of calling must fall in the hands of the presbytery; so an order is procured by the presbytery's ruling elder, Sir William Bruce, from the English to admit that Blair. Mr Ja. Guthrie causes convene a great number of this faction from divers parishes about, and gets Mr Robert Trail from Edinburgh, and Mr John Carstairs from Glasgow, and others, to spend a day in preaching and prayer at his admission. The whole people of the parish meet, and keep the other out of the kirk; the tumult begins; dry strokes are distributed; some fell upon the sheriff's neck. The gentlemen-parishioners, so soon as the sheriff produced his English orders for the admission, ceded; but the people continued all day casting stones and crying: yet they went on with their work, and thrust in the man. For all this, Mr Guthrie has no dealing with the English, and does no wrong. Our oppression is great and crying.

At Glasgow, Mr Andrew Gray, a youth of twenty-two years at most, lately laureate at St Andrew's, upon one sermon or two at Glasgow, Mr P. Gillespie and his friends will have him admitted to his place. I refused to consent; the youth being so young, and utterly a stranger to us; his trials of expectant being hastily passed in the presbytery of Hamilton; and none of the ministers either of Edinburgh, or St Andrew's, the places of his residence, being acquainted with him, as he professed; also his voice being so weak, that the most in our kirks heard him not. The magistrates and town-council being utterly against his admission, dealt with him earnestly not to trouble them. At first his modesty was so very great, that a small impediment seemed enough to scar him from accepting of any charge; but so soon as our session (which is but the echo of what our brethren speak) had given him a call, with-

2   out

out scruple he went on to his trials, and, over the belly of the town's protestation, was admitted by their part of the presbytery minister of Glasgow. His voice is not yet so good as to be heard by divers. He has the new guise of preaching, which Mr Hugh Binning and Mr Robert Leighton began, containing the ordinary way of expounding and dividing a text, of raising doctrines and uses; but runs out on a discourse on some common head, in a high, romancing, and unscriptural style, tickling the ear for the present, and moving the affections in some, but leaving, as he confesses, little or nought to the memory and understanding. This we must misken, for we cannot help it. This faction grows much among us. I fear the issue. The King's restitution, or his party's thriving, they seem to fear. Their piety and zeal is very susceptible of schism and error; I am oft afraid for their apostasy. Many conferences has been among them, Argyle, and Col. Lockhart, for taking up arms against the northern party; yet nothing of this kind is done, though divers mints have been made. Time will clear the honesty and dishonesty of many. Our life here is a warfare; yet God supports us, and we faint not. Blessed be our Father, who, through all these confusions, will bring his children to glory.

One of our friends wrote to us some scruples against the constitution of our separate synod; to which I returned the inclosed answer. On the 1st of August some of both sides met, but could come to no agreement. We gave them in our overtures, cast in another mould; and they theirs, as our inability to deal with the English, and their continual assistance from that power, (sought or unsought, I cannot say, and many affirm), make us daily lose, and them gain, and many incline to their thriving side.

After some refreshment from a fruitless journey through the hills, Monk is again to the fields. He, Couper, Twislington, and Argyle, are at Dumbarton, advising on a hard and sorrowful work, what houses and what corns to burn. This work is begun on both sides already. We know not where it will end.

195. *To Mr William Spang.* *Anno* 1655.

Cousin,

I go on to give you an account of our affairs where I
left

left off in my laft long letter. The Lord has given myfelf above this twelve months much more peace than I had before, and than I expected upon this occafion. You heard the overtures we proponed for the union of our fynod, which were the leaft we could receive before we could join. Though among ourfelves unanimoufly we had agreed to keep up our part of the fynod, if the fubftance of all thefe were not granted, and the brethren at Edinburgh, to whom I went for advice, had approven that our refolution; and the chief of the prefbyteries of Ayr and Irvine, with whom I had met alfo at Irvine, had agreed to adhere to thefe overtures; and if they, being *minimum quod fic*, fhould be refufed, they concluded to fet up their two prefbyteries in a fynod by themfelves, according to their ancient privilege acknowleged in all our late general affemblies; alfo, when we met at our fynod, thefe on our fide agreed again to act here according to former refolutions. Notwithftanding, when the brethren of the other fide had peremptorily refufed our overtures, and drawn on a new conference, to try if two of each fide, particularly, Mr James Fergufon and Mr George Young for us, Mr James Durham and Mr P. Gillefpie for them, could fall on any other overtures which might unite us, thefe four among themfelves condefcended to the inclofed paper, and engaged themfelves to do their beft to perfuade others thereto. When I faw the paper, I found clearly, that the final determination of all things was left in the fynod, whereof remonftrators were the plurality; and that no remeid was left us againft the oppreffion, either in purging or planting, that was for any purpofe; and that this agreement was a clear receding from our former determination. I did not yield to it: yet fear from the remonftrants violence, and love of peace, and hope, by yielding, to make them more moderate, made the moft declare their contentment to accept of it; all of Glafgow except one, and of Dumbarton except two, of Irvine except two. Finding it fo, I was glad at my heart that fo fair a door to my private peace was opened; for not being willing to accept of the terms of that agreement, I had a clear reafon to abfent myfelf from the fynod and prefbyery, united on fo unjuft terms. The brethren of my former mind finding me refolute not to join with them, were defirous to keep with me, efpecially the author of the late overture, Mr Fergufon, and Mr Young. But this by no means I would permit; for that having declared almoft all their

their willingness to unite on these mean terms, I would not
have them draw back, contrary to their minds, upon my
diffent: fo with much ado I got them to join, and let me,
and a few more, ferve my own mind of abftaining from
their united meetings.   This hitherto I have done, to the
great quietnefs of my own mind, and freedom of the very
frequent and vexatious janglings, wherewith, in all meetings, I was wont exceedingly to be troubled : only I am
grieved to fee my predictions too truly to come to pafs ;
the remonftrants, as unqueftionable mafters, to do within the bounds of the fynod whatever they think expedient.
Mr Archibald Dennifton, without any confiderable fault,
they depofed.   When he fled to the Englifh, Mr P. Gillefpie, as I forefaw, by his greater credit, ftopped all
hearing there.   Mr David Adamfon, though of many libelled fcandals they got not one proven, yet ftill they keep
in the pannel ; and our moft regular plantation of Mr
James Ramfay, Mr Archibald Inglis, and one in Roberton, they will have annulled, and the moft irregular plantations of their men to ftand.   At their next diet they will
fall on whom they pleafe without controul.   However,
being free of publick debates without, as, I think, my
own procurement, but the rafh imprudence, if not the
too much wifdom of others, I am glad.

I was like to have been more troubled by another defign
of a larger union.   Mr Durham going through St Andrew's to the houfe of Purie, he fell with Mr Blair to refume his old counfels of a general union with the remonftrants, by an overture of oblivion of bygones.   For this
end, Mr Blair and he deal with Mr Wood to be content
of a conference at Edinburgh upon that fubject, together
with the other purpofes we were much vexed with, prayer
for the King, and admiffion of compliers to the communion ; alfo they went to defign the conferrers.   For us
they named Mr Robert Douglas, Mr David Dickfon, Mr
Hugh Mackell, Mr W. Rate, Mr W. Douglas of Aberdeen, Mr Jo. Robertfon of Dundee, Mr Ja. Wood, Mr
Ja. Fergufon, and me.   For the other, Mr J. Guthrie,
Mr P. Gillefpie, Mr Jo. Livingfton, Mr S. Rutherford,
Mr R. Traill, Mr Jo. Carftairs, Mr Sa. Auftin, and fome
three more.   So foon as I heard of this motion fo far advanced, I was much feared for the confequence of it, and
therefore wrote to Mr Dickfon to beware of the danger ;
and being welt, called Mr Jo. Bell, Mr W. Ruffel, and

Mr

Mr Ro. Wallace, to advise on it. All of them were afraid
of the issue; yet none would be at the pains of riding to
Edinburgh to consult about it. This I behoved to do myself. When I came there, I found the brethren not at all
minding the matter; but setting the hazard before their
eyes, I got them roused to look about them, and to com-
missionate me to bring from the west whom I thought fit
for that conference, to write themselves to Mr Knox and
Mr Jameson, with others in the south, and to Mr Robert
Young, Mr James Sharp, and others in the north, to be
present. When we came to the meeting, I was glad the
danger was not so great as I apprehended. The remonstrants had as little a mind to unite with us as we with
them. Mr Gillespie and Mr Carstairs, and a few others,
were for capitulating; but Wariston, Mr Guthrie, and o-
thers, were as rigid as ever; yea, whatever by their con-
triving or otherwise, it was so, that we could have no conference. We had drawn up an overture, as we thought,
very favourable, so far as we could go, according to the
assembly's late overture for union, and by the hands of the
trysters, Mr Blair, and Mr Durham, sent in to their
meeting. Also the trysters had given us both their overtures to be thought upon; but the remonstrants told us,
in regard of Mr Rutherford and Mr Livingston's absence,
they could not at that time engage in a conference; and
therefore desired a new meeting. We were not content
that they had made us travel in vain, and thought not fit
to appoint a meeting, till they met among themselves, and
considered the paper we had given them; if they would
acquiesce to it, or send us any better whereto we could acquiesce, upon the advertisement of some probability of accommodation from Mr Dickson to us, and Mr Traill to
them, there might be a meeting so soon as they thought
fit. So, after a little prefacing by delegates from both
meetings, we parted before we entered in a conference.
We understood, that our overture was laughed at by their
high stomachs; and as for that of Mr Blair, we were offended all of us with it, as granting to the remonstrants almost all their unreasonable desires. For this we expostu-
lated sharply enough with Mr Blair, and he with us. But
he was much more offended with the other; and both he
and Mr Durham said, that so long as Wariston and Mr
Guthrie guided that party, there could no peace be
possible. Though the great and much-talked-of errand of
                                                    our

our meeting had evanished; yet we conferred among ourfelves, and Mr Blair, Mr Durham, Mr Traill, Mr Stirling, and Mr Carftairs, on other things for good purpose.
For a number of years, the communion had not been celebrated in Edinburgh, Glafgow, St Andrew's, Dundee,
&c. moft becaufe all the magiftrates were fo deep in complying with the Englifh, that they were excluded from the
table by the act of our church, and long conftant practice,
except they declared their repentance; which they would
not do, nor durft we crave it of them: alfo they were fo
importunate to have the communion, and impatient to be
longer excluded, that they were on heady and evil defigns
againft us, if we gave them not fatisfaction herein. The
minifters of Edinburgh inclined to admit them on very
fmall acknowledgement. We in Glafgow were all for
that, except Mr Durham and myfelf, albeit we were both
much modified at that time; but thefe of St Andrew's
were very averfe from their admiffion, except on conditions not to be expected from them. For this end, they
had fent us a long paper; yet, after fome days conference,
we came to agree to admit them on a general teftimony in
our doctrine againft their compliance, and private admo-
nifhing of them to repent for it, laying it on their confciences to come or not as they thought good. We
thought, indeed, time had much altered the cafe; and I
drew Mr Blair by, and told him roundly, it was very dif-
concordant, not to quarrel Mr Livingfton's and Mr Gillefpie's celebration, notwithftanding their voluntary moft
grofs and avowed compliance, and to controvert the admiffion of magiftrates for compelled compliance in a far
lefs degree. This ftopped his mouth, and he contradicted
no more. As for prayer for the King, we fpake not
much of it in publick; but in private I found, that moft
of the company thought it might be forborn, were it not
for the proclamation to forbear it under the penalty of lofing our ftipends; that leaving of it now would occafion a
great fcandal. While we were in private conferring on
this, Mr Wood overtured, that a way might be found to
fatisfy the Englifh, and keep ftill our prayer for the King.
I thought this impoffible; and before I could learn it from
him, he was neceffitated to go home. Thereafter I found
that Mr James Sharp had perfuaded him and Mr Douglas
to go with Monk's recommendation to the Protector, to
intreat for our fparing in this confcientious practice; and
                                                        for

for the freedom of our assemblies, on promise of peaceable behaviour. How far the remonstrants provocations
put on such a resolution, I know not; but no such thing
is yet done, and to me it is a matter of a very doubtsome
nature. It is true, all the estates of the kingdom, yea,
every particular person of note, have submitted, and on
occasion of civil rights, have acknowledged the present
power, except some of us ministers; and that our protest-
ing brethren, of their own accord, ever since Worcester,
having put the King out of their prayers, have provoked
hereby the English to persecute us; yet if all be true what
some of us have written for this duty, how we shall for a-
ny trouble leave it, it is hard to say. I sent you three papers for the continuance of this practice; and Mr Hut-
chieson wrote a fourth, which I did not see, better, as I
heard, than all the former. For myself, I never wrote a
line on that question, but adhered to the thing without
scruple; albeit what ye wrote from Voetius stumbled me,
and the general practice of all our brethren of England
and Ireland more. What we shall do in the end we do
not know. This is the greatest difficulty that sticks in our
stomach; albeit in mine, Mr Dickson's, Mr Durham's,
Mr Smith's, and others, more; in Mr Douglas, Mr Blair,
Mr Wood, and Mr Ferguson, and most of others, less.
It is our present deliberation: the Lord direct us in it. I
hear the King himself would gladly permit us to forbear
it, and our flocks would earnestly request us to the same;
but for myself I know not yet how to do it. Mr Ja. Ferguson and Mr Alexander Nisbet, by the malevolence of
some of their neighbours, were sorely persecuted, and
chased some weeks from their flocks, and with very much
ado obtained some forbearance of the General. How long
we shall be spared, we cannot tell.

I wrote to some of the ministers at London to cause
some friends to represent our case to the Protector; but
the answer I got promised little: yet (by what means I
know not) to this day the storm is holden off, whether
conscience, or pity, or fear, or diversion by other affairs,
has helped it, is uncertain.

When Mr Gillespie was with Cromwell, he assisted and
pleasured sundry in the matter of their fines. All the
three preached once or twice in the chapel. Cromwell
was kind enough to them all; but Mr Livingston came
first away. Mr Gillespie and Mr Menzies, for the two
colleges

colleges of Glasgow and Aberdeen, obtained sundry favours; the superiorities of Galloway as the bishop had them, and 2900 merks a-year out of the customs of Glasgow, for maintenance of bursars at our own nomination, with the town's maintenance for the use of the poor who were hurt by the burning. For this service the town gave Mr Patrick a gratuity of 30 pieces, which he took: and having regretted to us his great charges in that half-year, that it had exceeded L. 250 Sterling, and all that he had received from Cromwell was L. 100, I was content the college should allow him L. 100; but it was carried by votes to 3000 merks. His stipend that year, I think, was 2000 merks, and his deburfements for us about one thing and another, another 1000 merks, befides 1000 merks for books to the liberary. For all this I think he was no gainer: his journey and way of living at London was sumptuous. Yet all this would have been well taken, had not the last half of his gift contained an order to the judges to allow no intrants any stipend but thefe who had the testimony of so many of the remonstrant faction in every diocefs as they fat down. There were only a few of our mind joined, who would have carried nothing against the other, fo the planting of all the churches was, in effect, devolved on that faction. The claufes in the order appointed the judges to affift them in the ejection of all thefe they should declare fcandalous, as you may read in the order itfelf printed by the council. So soon as this was known, however, the remonftrants in our bounds; and in the fouth were glad, and began to make ufe of it, yet generally it was cried out upon; the minifters of Edinburgh preached much against it; the prefbytery of Edinburgh and fynod of Lothian declared against it; the fynods of Fife and the Merfe did the like: yea, Mr Guthrie wrote fharply against it, and the minifters of Edinburgh gave in to Monk a paper, to be communicated to the Protector, as both the fynod and prefbytery of Edinburgh had declared before against it. And in a meeting of the remonftrants, Wariston carried a vote of a teftimony against it: but this was fuppreffed, for fear of dividing their party, who in other things alfo did not well agree; for fome of them were much more complying with the English than Wariston or Mr Guthrie allowed. Yet Mr Guthrie's way became doubtful on this much talked occafion. His colleague, Mr David Bennet, had under his hand engaged

gaged himself some more to the assembly of Dundee, than agreed with his former rashness, and Mr Guthrie's way : though after the breaking of the land Mr David retracted somewhat of this, yet so much stuck of it as made him not fully of Mr James's judgement. The people liked neither well, but Mr David best of the two : thence emulation and some contests in the session began to arise ; but Mr David being on his death-bed, and advising to plant his place with a man peaceable, not factious, Mr James and the town fell in a strife about that matter immediately after his death. Mr James had formed the session to his own mind ; whoever opposed his way, were removed, on divers pretences. The remainder were but few, who were persuaded to call to Mr Bennet's place, one Mr Rule from Angus. To this election the body of the town was opposite ; but when Mr James, neglecting their opposition, went on to admit him, the people, tumultuously, with cries, and shouts, and strokes, opposed it ; yet Mr James admitted the man, and caused summon above 60 of the chief burgesses before the English criminal court at Edinburgh for a riot. Being all put to an assize, to the judges open dissatisfaction, they were all absolved once and again. Their advocate publickly served Mr James with very coarse language ; but the judges favoured him all in their power. This all misliked in Mr James as a dangerous preparative to the whole land. However, it made his people irreconcileable to him. The synod of Perth met at Dumblane. When they were about to declare against the violent intrusion of Mr Rule, Mr Guthrie appeared with a declinature of their judicatory. This irritated them so far as they appointed some of their number to go to Stirling, and intimate his sentence of deposition by the general assembly, the nullity of Mr Rule's admission to Stirling, and of Mr Blair's to Bothkennar, to elect a new session for calling of ministers to Stirling, and to approve that as the presbytery of Stirling, from which Mr James had separated. This provoked the remonstrant party to meet at Edinburgh, where, what course of revenge they have resolved upon, I fear we shall hear in time. There is a talk of sending propositions to Cromwell for investing the church-government in their party's hands. However, Mr Rutherford was sent to Stirling to preach against the synod's proceedings, though Mr Rule was a known fornicator. There was another

2　　　　　　　　　　　　　　　　　other

other very erroneous practice of our brethren? A good
and able young man, Mr Jo. Jameson, being planted, almoft unanimoufly, in the parifh of Eccles by the whole
prefbytery of Dunfe, fome few of the remonftrant-fide give a
call to Mr Andrew Rutherford.   Mr John Livingfton, with
two of the prefbytery of Chirnfide, admit him to his trials
in reference to that church.   The brethren of Edinburgh
hearing of it, earneftly wrote to Mr John to beware of
fuch a clear overturning of our fundamental difcipline.
However, they go on with all fpeed with the trial; and,
with an Englifh order and guard, force him on the people.
When the fynod were about to declare againft this unheard-of intrufion, Mr John and his friends gave in a
ftrong proteftation.   The fynod declared againft them; and
they, by the Englifh force, keep out Jamefon, and put in
Rutherford.   The prefbyteries of Edinburgh and St Andrew's, and, as I think, the fynods of Fife and Lothian,
declared againft this fhameful ufurpation; but our brethren regard little either prefbyteries or fynods when oppofite to their defires.   This fynod of Lothian, in a well-
framed act, opened Mr William Colvill's mouth.   Thefe
fatal divifions which wracked England and our kingdom,
firft and laft, which with our eyes we have feen, the only
confiderable means of the ruin of thofe who are down, and
rifing of thofe who are up, are like to put in the hands of that
unquiet faction of our brethren, or elfe into the hands of
Eraftian ftatefmen, all church-jurifdiction; fo at once we
fhall have no difcipline to look after, but to preach, pray,
and celebrate the facraments, and be glad to be tolerated
to go about that without controul.   When Quakers fall
a-railing on all the miniftry, in the face of our congregations, on the Sabbath-day, they are not punifhed at all;
nor, for ought I know, is there any church difcipline at
all to this day any where in England.   The minifters
there, are herein fo heartlefs and difcouraged, that they
dare fpeak nothing which may be interpreted to give the
leaft offence.   I marvelled, that when I fent my anfwer to
Cotton and Tombes, to Mr Calamy for his *Imprimatur,*
yea, a dedicatory epiftle, he was no feeble-minded as to
refufe both my dedication and his own *Imprimatur*; yea,
with a great difficulty could I get his *Imprimatur* to my
very catechifm: A ftrange change of times, and great
feeblenefs of men!

Concerning our commonwealth, how it is conceived
here I give you this account.   The rifing of the highlands

Vol. II.   3 D   has

has proven, as the moſt of wiſe men ever expected, hurtful to us. The country was much oppreſſed by it; the
King's party much weakened; the English imbittered the
more againſt us; and their inward diviſions and factions
holden in ſo long as that party ſtood conſiderable. It
grew indeed to a greater height than any could have imagined; yet the Holland peace, and the King's diſappoint-
ment abroad, with their own fooliſh pride and diviſions,
brought them to nothing, and made them capitulate one
after another, till at laſt all are come in. John Graham of
Duchray is the laſt, who indeed was among the moſt honeſt,
ſtout, and wiſe men of them all. The English gave tolerable terms to them all; and by this wiſdom have got them all
quiet. Glencairn led the way to the reſt, as of going out,
ſo of coming in; for which much blame lies on him. A-
thol's friends brought him off with the firſt; Seaforth alſo became wiſe in time. Lorn's difference with his father kept him longer out; yet he is at laſt perſuaded to
come in, albeit he and his father are not like to be good
friends. His father, leſt he give any occaſion to the Engliſh to ſuſpect his colluſion with his ſon, keeps the greater
diſtance from him, albeit the moſt think the domeſtick diviſions between them are ſo real and true as makes both
their lives bitter and uncomfortable to them, and the
great burthen of debt puts their very houſe in hazard to
ruin, if the Engliſh be no more kind to them than they
have been, or it ſeems they will be. The father ſought a
garriſon to lie in Argyle, to keep it from his ſon's violence;
but when it was on the way, he repented, and got a new
order for their return: yet they would go on; yea, took
up his own beſt houſe of Inverary, made the kirk and
ſchool their ſtables, and hardly at this very time have
been got removed. The people's great hatred lies on him
above any one man, and whatever befals him, few do
pity him. At this time his eſtate is very ſtaggering. The
Chancellor got better conditions in his capitulation than
any expected, albeit his debts and infamy lie very heavy
upon him.
  For this time, all Scotland is exceeding quiet, but in a
very uncomfortable condition; very many of the noblemen and gentlemen, what with impriſonments, baniſh-
ments, forfeitures, fines, as yet continuing without any
releaſement, and private debts from their former troubles, are wrecked or going to wreck. The commonality
                                                are

are oppreffed with maintenance to the Englifh army. Strange want of money upon want of trade, for our towns have no confiderable trade ; and what is, the Englifh have poffeffed it. The victual is extraordinary cheap, in God's mercy, but judgement to many. Want of juftice, for we have no baron-courts ; our fheriffs have little fkill, for common being Englifh foldiers ; our lords of feffion, a few Englifh, unexperienced with our law, and who, this twelvemonth, have done little or nought : great is our fuffering through want of that court. After long neglect of us as no nation, at laft a fupreme council of ftate, with power in all things, is come down to fix or feven Englifh foldiers and two of our complying gentlemen, Colonel Lockhart and Swinton. We expect little good from them ; but if an heavy excife, as is faid, be added to our maintenance, and the paying of all the garrifons lie on us, our condition will be infupportable ; yet be what it will, it muft be borne, we have deferved it. But we hope the Lord will look down on the affliction of the unjuftly afflicted by men.

The other year, when the good parliament fat down, we were in great fear. Their firft declarations were fo pious, but to me fo full of the Anabaptiftick ftrain, that I was afraid of them. They were elected abfolutely by the officers of the army, and the minifters of their cabal, fully according to the mind of the Sectarian party ; but they were no fooner fet, than they flew fo high, as to mind nothing but a fifth monarchy upon earth, to overthrow all magiftracy and miniftry as it ftood, and put all in a new mould of their own, wherein publickly fome fomented them for their own wife defigns. However, they were far on in overturning all remaining foundations of church and ftate. The General, with fome of his confident friends of the army, diffolved them by force, left they fhould have overwhelmed him, themfelves, and all, in their new Babel, and took on himfelf the office of Protector, with a power, to him and his council-fupreme, beyond, as it feemed to many, the regal line ; yet neceffary for the time, and quietly acquiefced in without contradiction. To mollify it, a parliament was called after the old way, but of men engaging to the new way of government. There went from Scotland thirty, and from Ireland as many. Our and their chufers were men who, for peace, were refolved to do or fay any thing they found tolerable

3 D 2

o their own large mind, and, I think, were all so complying with the Protector as he could have wished : yet many of the chief in this meeting were so dissatisfied with one above a parliament, (a true and high royalty as they conceived), that at their very first downsitting they set themselves to overturn the new building for their love of their too much-fancied republick, in a free and absolutely supreme parliament. An unhappy dream ! unfit for the government of the people of this isle at any time, and most is now disposed. The Protector finding it so, made no scruple to discipline them, and, without much more ado, to purge the House presently of all who, under their hand, did not engage again to preserve the model of government appointed by the Protector and his friends. When many of the most stirring heads, by the refusal of this engagement, were put out of the House, it was expected, that the rest would have so fully complied as they had written with their hands ; yet, for what causes we know not, the Protector found them all so undermining of his government, that he thought it fit to dissolve them. Hence all were filled with new discontents : but the Protector had so far with his wit and diligence provided for all, that there was no confiderable stir. Lambert and the chief of the army were made, by hopes, so fast, that they concurred chearfully in all things. Lieut.-Col. Lilburn, a most turbulent man, whom I thought no force nor skill would ever have got quiet, was so cunningly conveyed to Jersey, and there so strictly kept, that there has been nothing more heard of him than he had been dead. Capt. Joyce was put in the same condition. General-Majors Harrisons and Overton, with sundry other officers of the army, both in Scotland and England, are close prisoners for designs to turn the army against the Protector. A number of the royal party rising in a very confused imprudent way in many shires, were all easily scattered, and the chief of them made fast, and sundry executed for their conspiring ; albeit in what, and how far, we know not. We are glad, that no Scotsman was found accessory to any of these designs. It seems our people were so ill burnt, that they had no stomach for any farther meddling ; only Crawford, Lauderdale, and David Lesly, when the Tower was filled with new prisoners, were sent to farther and worse prisons, for no new fault that we hear tell of.

These stirs make the Protector more vigilant. The fall
out

out of his coach, and the attempts more than once for his life by Gerard the tailor, and others, shew the violence of some spirits.   The raising of all the three last parliaments ; the speaking of a crown, and title of a King or Emperor, which some think is not vain ; the putting of the government of Ireland under his son Henry, and Scotland under a council of some six or seven officers of the army, and chiefly of his nieces, Robin a sewster's husband, the young Lord of Lee, make great malecontentment in the heart of the most.   To help this, all possible courses are taken to satisfy England ; but Scotland is not worth the minding.   In England L. 60,000 Sterling a month, the half of the maintenance is diminished ; but we fear the new excise shall double our maintenance ; albeit excising in England seems to have been great, yet few have suffered, and we hear of few forfeitures or fines there ; but many of our nation are sent to the plantations, our fines are many and great, and our grievances much neglected.   For satisfying the people of England, the two great navies, the one, on the coast of Africa, Italy, and Spain, under Blake ; the other, in the West Indies, under Penn, served much for a time : for it was thought at first, that the navy under Blake to assist the Spaniard against the French, invading by sea, both Naples and Catalonia, besides the securing of the ships and cannon, should have had assurance from the Spaniard for pay 200,000 pounds Sterling ; and thereafter, that their design was to free all the English captives at Tunis, Algiers, and Salee, and to intercept the Spanish plate at Cadiz.   Also that Penn's great army of 12,000 men had been, not only to have taken St Domingo in Hispaniola, but also Mexico in New Spain. These high and advantageous designs did much please the spirits of the vulgar ; but now miscontentments are feared, even on that ground also, to rise, that so huge expence has been laid on the people for fruitless designs ; and that in their far voyages, many lives have been lost for no purpose.   Since this time Blake has lived on the English charge, the Spaniard has borne no expences.   The burning of the Turkish ships at Tunis is said to have provoked the Turks at Constantinople, and elsewhere, to rob many English of life and goods ; that none of the Spanish fleet is yet gotten, and if meddled with, it were a breach with Spain, which were a beginning of a needless war at an unseasonable time ; that Penn's great navy and army

have

have done no service at all, but in Hispaniola have got a great affront. These things from the Diurnals : the discontent royalists blaze far ; but the Protector is wise enough to see to all these murmurings of silly people. In quieting of malecontents he has a strange both dexterity and skill.

For church-matters, there is no ecclesiastick government at all that we can hear of ; yet the hand of power is not heavy on any for matters of religion, no not on Quakers, who are open railers against the Protector's person ; yea, we hear of little trouble of Papists, who grow much in the north of Scotland, more than these eighty years, without any controul. We expect our council of state will see to it.

For things abroad, they are thus represented to us : That the French totally neglect our King, the Cardinal being unwilling in the King's minority to undertake a war with England, for the marring of the great advancement of the French interest against their chief enemies, the Spanish and Austrian ; that for this end they pass by the daily taking of numbers of their ships.

The defeat of the royal navy in its way to Dunkirk, whereupon alone followed the loss of Dunkirk ; the taking from them the plantations of Canada, and St Christopher's, and others ; that all these the French dissemble, and seek the English friendship, till they have done their business elsewhere, as daily they make so good progress ; that Conti takes in town after town in Catalonia, which is interpreted the great weakness of Spain, that is not able in Spain itself to crush a little French army ; in Italy also, the Spanish in Milan is put hard to it, when the French, with all the power of Savoy and Modena, and the neutrality of the Venetian, Pope, Florence, and Genoa, deals with him ; only it is marvelled what folly moved the French, in their passage through Savoy, to fall on the quiet Protestants of the vallies. If this massacre be the half of the thing it is called, it were enough, not only before God, but with men, to mar the full career of the French victory. But many here suspect the matter not to be so great ; not so much because the French King, Pope, and Savoyard, disclaim it as none of their deeds ; but because so many diurnals insist so much upon it, and so much noise is made of it here, the royalists say, that of the blood of the saints this politick use is made, to make

people

people fee the happinefs of our prefent government, wherein we live in peace, free from the cruelty of Papifts ; and
if Charles Stuart came here, the people had caufe to fear,
from him and his mother, thefe incredible murders which
the Proteftants of Savoy find from the Duke, the King's
coufin-german, by the advice of his mother, the Queen's
true fifter.   But we fear too much of this perfecution be
true, let any exaggerate or abufe it to what end they think
fit.   But the terrible progrefs of the French, and moft to
our prejudice, is in Flanders, where the Englifh junction
with Spain, if in time, might eafily have ftopped ; but if
to the conqueft of Lorain and Alfatia, they add Flanders,
and get of Spain the Low Countries, their neighbourhood,
both to England and Holland, will be more formidable
than ever Spain was ; and whatever progrefs the French
make this year againft Spain, many impute it to the Englifh, who have hindered the Spanifh filver-fleet to come
home, whereby the Spanifh have been difabled to keep
the fields againft the French any where, let be in Flanders
againft the King in perfon, with the great royal army.

Poftfcript, December 1. 1655.

While Mr Wood, rector of the univerfity of St Andrew's, had oft to do with Gen. Monk for the univerfity,
and always got civil hearing, it was thought fit, that Mr
Douglas and he fhould reprefent to the General the manifold and increafing grievances of the church ; which they
did in a paper.   The General profeffed himfelf willing,
but unable to remedy them ; only undertook to fend them
to the Protector, with whom yet they keep together, with
their reprefentation againft Mr Gillefpie's charter, as they
call it.   The General oft fpoke concernig prayer for the
King.   Mr Douglas, and others, fhewed their utter un-
willingnefs to quit it fo long as the proclamation ftood ;
and when the fheriff was fent to trouble them, had he not
given over his begun procefs, they had prepared protefta-
tions.   The General declared his inability to take off the
proclamation for the time ; but hoped the new council,
when it came down, fhould do it.   At their coming, the
Prefident Broghill, having a good impreffion from his
fifter, the Lady Clotworthy, of Mr Douglas and Mr Dickfon, dealt kindly with them ; and underftanding their ftick

at

at the proclamation, albeit with some difficulty, got the council to take it off, shewing withal to the ministers the strictness of his instructions against all who continued publickly naming the King. After much deliberation, they thought it fit to give it over. They once purposed a declaration, and a paper for removal of objections; but foreseeing the offence from these writs would have been equal to the continuance of their practice, they abstained, and only drew a paper, which they sent to me, and no other. Mr Wood's larger answer to objections I have not yet got. The example of these in Edinburgh is like to be followed by all. Some yet stick. Our remonstrants grieved and mocked at this change. Some of our people, from whom we did not expect it, were offended; but, above all, General Monk was irritated against us, as if we had yielded to Broghill what we denied to him: and from that day, on all occasions, befriended openly the remonstrants, to our prejudice, as men to be trusted beyond us, their principles being opposite to the interests of their enemy Charles Stuart, whom we did affect still, notwithstanding of our silence in our publick prayers. Mr Traill, who conversed much with him, wrote in the time of our last synod a long letter to Mr Gillespie, which he read publickly to a grand committee of his mind, as if we had uttered to the General and President very many calumnies against them, especially their averseness from all peace with us their brethren.

On occasion thereafter, both the President and General, to their own faces, witnessed our innocency; affirming, that in all our speeches to them we had never spoke one word to their prejudice. However, the remonstrants of our synod, stirred up by Mr Traill's calumnious letter, sent to Mr Gillespie and others to clear them of our imputations, and to desire, that the ministers of Edinburgh might call a meeting for union, if possible; or, if not, that it might be seen by whose fault the discord continued. The meeting was called, and kept November 8. by a number of both sides from all the parts of the kingdom. It was not long before it was clear who were the men that made the union desperate, except on intolerable conditions. Our meetings appointed nine on every side to confer. Theirs were Wariston, Sir John Cheesly, Col. Ker, Mr Rutherford, Mr Guthrie, Mr Gillespie, Mr Naesmith, Mr Traill, Mr Gabriel Maxwell: Ours were, Mr Douglas, Mr Dickson,

2

fon, Mr Wood, Mr Ker, Mr Fergufon, Mr Robert
Young, Mr Mackell, Mr Smith, and myfelf. Mr Blair
and Mr Durham appeared as midfmen; albeit of our
judgement for the main, and in the whole debate, grieved
with the other. Their papers were all framed by Mr
Guthrie's hand of my Lord Warifton's materials. The
firft to us was fo high and abfurd, that we could fcarcely
believe our own apprehenfions of it, and refolved, by queries, to try their pofitive mind anent it. I drew a paraphrafe on it, and Mr Fergufon another; out of which Mr
Wood drew this third, which we gave them to anfwer.
To be even with us, they, November 13. gave us queries
on our overture the 1ft of June; and withal, an anfwer
to our queries. Having pondered thefe, we returned an
anfwer to their queries, and our fenfe of their overture.
Our conceffions were fo many and great, that Mr Gillefpie, Mr Carftairs, and others of their meeting, not Mr
Durham and Mr Blair only, feemed fully fatisfied therewith, and we began to hope for a concord. But Warifton and Mr Guthrie carried it fo in their meeting over
Mr Gillefpie, that this very captious paper was given to
us; which Mr Gillefpie denied openly to be the fenfe of
their meeting, and Mr Guthrie affirmed it was; and hardly by diftinctions could they be brought, even in our
meeting, to agree among themfelves about that paper.
However, we agreed to give it a foft unreflecting anfwer,
though much provoked; yea, to gain them, we gave in a
reprefentation. At laft they gave us their clear and final
fenfe; with which Mr Gillefpie refufed to join, but deferted their meeting. Mr Wood was here called from us
to fee his father die; but we gave them the laft paper, of
Mr Fergufon's hand; and fo, after twenty-three days ftay,
we clofed the meeting. We heard in the midft of our
conference, they had voted the fetting up of twenty-four
minifters and fix elders, thirty of all, even their part of
the commiffion of the affembly 1650, with abfolute power
of a full jurifdiction over the whole kirk of Scotland, on
fuppofition we fhould not agree to their defires; and likewife had agreed on a fupplication to the council for affiftance to that their moft prefumptuous and unreafonable
committee which ever our church did fee.

At our fynod of Glafgow, where this conference for
union was hatched, there were other two dangerous motions. Warifton and Mr Guthrie had fallen on a new

conceit, to put all the godly of the land, of their faction, under the band of a new covenant, which Mr Guthrie had drawn in some sheets of paper, from which he had cut off all the articles of our former covenants which concerned the King, parliament, or liberties of the land, or mutual defence. At this motion the council was highly offended, and spoke threatening words of Wariston and Mr Guthrie for this attempt: yet after their apology, were so well pleased, that the General gave Wariston a visit in his house, which I know not if he hath yet done to any other of the nation; and Mr Guthrie hath that familiarity with him, that when both are in town, he sends his mind to him in closed epistles, which I doubt if any other of the nation has yet made bold to do. In their meeting at Edinburgh, January 1st, they proponed this covenant. The English agents, Mr Gillespie, and Mr Livingston, disputed against it in vain. Mr Gillespie, so soon as he went west, called a meeting at Kilmarnock to crush it if he could. Wariston hearing of his design, sent Sir John Cheesly to keep that meeting, where there were bitter and reflecting words betwixt Sir John and Mr Patrick; yet Mr Patrick carried it over Sir John, that all should declare their mind concerning the covenant; where all, except four or five of little weight, dissented, yet so that they should inquire the sense of the godly of the bounds anent it, and report at the next synod. Sir John, foiled in this, prevailed against Mr Patrick in another vote of their mind, for erection of the commission for purging the kirk. These interferings put us in hopes that faction would divide among themselves. At Glasgow, the report was, that all the godly in these parts misliked the motion of the covenant; however, the godly in Fife and Lothian were said to like it; yet, on the west's mislike, the motion for the time was laid aside. But behold, from some of the sessions of Glasgow it was moved, that the ordinance for testifying, notwithstanding of all the contradiction had been made to it, seemed very innocent and exceeding good to be practised. To this Sir John opposed, and Mr Patrick avowed he knew nought of the motion; but so soon as he went to Edinburgh to seek a conference for union, the president and other counsellors, of their own proper motions altogether, without his knowledge, as he affirms, resolved to proclaim his ordinance, and did it after his departure; but after his

preaching

preaching to the council, and keeping of their kirk the whole sabbath, and going with the president in his coach to dinner, these things made us not at all to understand Mr Gillespie's meaning; yet this was visible, as Mr Gutharie wrote sharply against his ordinance, so he opposed his covenant and commission, and looked towards an union with us; but for what end many did doubt. A little time will clear more mysteries. You will perceive in the papers, as is evident in the conference, that our remonstrants first resolution is, 1. Not to rest content with an oblivion of what is past, of enjoying their own judgement in peace, and taking off their censures; but will have us consent to their liberty of prosecuting their protestations in posterior assemblies, not only for condemning of the publick resolutions, (which we in conscience judge necessary truths, the grounds of our apology to foreign churches, and the world, for our innocence in all these fearful scandals which our brethrens tenets and practices have occasioned to be cast upon the face of our church and nation), but also for condemning the two last general assemblies for ever, which for constitution cannot be more lawful than these two. 2. That whatever necessity we may have of a general assembly, or whatever desire we may have of one, or liberty from the English to get it; yet we must never have it till they be willing to join with us to seek it in their terms. 3. That as peace with them may not be had, except during the paucity of their party, compared with the multitude of their opposites in the presbyteries and synods, (for sundry whole synods will not have any of them, as Angus, Moray, Argyle; and I think sundry other divers synods have but very few of them; as Fife but seven, whereof two only considerable; Perth at most fourteen, whereof but one considerable; Lothian, if ye except them of Lithgow and Biggar, but three), the whole synods and presbyteries of the kingdom will be content to surcease from their jurisdiction, and devolve it on a committee for the bounds of every synod, of the number whereof they shall make the equal half, to judge and determine all matters of planting and purging, and whatever falls to be controverted, whose acts the synods shall have no power to reverse without the previous advice of a general consultatory committee out of all the synods, whereof also the equal half shall be of their judgement, and nominated by them.

When

When we in the fynod of Glafgow defired fomething like this in a far other cafe, we being the right-conftitute fynod, and they a fchifmatick faction, we juftly fearing their unjuft violence, and more diffimilitudes apparent in our cafe, of their demand for the whole land, yet they paffionately cried down our motion, and rather chofe to reject all peace with us than to hear of any fuch overture. 4. All plantations muft be taken from the congregations and feffions, to be put in the hand of a few whom they count the godly party; for they avow that the plurality of all congregations in the land are fo ignorant and fcandalous or ungracious, that they are to be excluded from the communion and voice in chufing of a minifter. By this device they hope quickly to fill all vacant places with intrants of their faction, as they are careful to do wherever they have any power to do it. 5. Though we fhould yield to them all their defires, yet do they exprefsly deny to us that which we count the effence of Prefbyterial fubordination, a fubmiffion to the fentence of our judicatories for time to come. They feem to be for the thing in general, but not for a fubmiffion to our judicatories in their prefent corrupt conftitution of fo many unfit members. In this cafe of the church they plead for a liberty both of judgement and practice, both to diffent and contradict the fentences of the beft fynods of Scotland, fuch as Lothian and Fife, in any planting and purging that is contrary to their mind. And a 6th now they are come to, a few of them to name fome twenty-nine of their faction which were of the commiffion 1650, to be a fettled judicatory, with abfolute jurifdiction over the whole church, ever while they think time to call a general affembly. This to us is worfe than Mr Gillefpie's ordinance, which they fo much cry down; for it was alone for ftipends in order to planting; but this is an ufurpation of the whole immediate jurifdiction; worfe than Independency, that encroaches not on others, but exempt only their own adherents from other's jurifdiction; worfe than Epifcopacy, that never made fuch havock, and fo caufelefsly of all prefbyteries and fynods at once. The event, is feared, will be the forfeiture of all our ecclefiaftick liberties, in taking them out of both our hands, to be depofited in an Eraftian ftate-committee, till our remonftrants think fit to join with us; whereof I have no hopes, as things now

go

go in the land.   Near two years ago I drew up the ftate of the queftions they had then ftarted.

For matters of ftate at home and abroad, we meddle not at all with them ; only we obferve the footfteps of divine providence as they offer themfelves to the eyes of all beholders.   Admiral Blake's navy has coft a vaft charge, without any profit.   The expedition of Hifpaniola, as I read it in a London defcription, is full of fhame and lofs, both of charges and men, has drawn on an open war with Spain which will hurt our trade.   Our empty coffers will not be furnifhed with all the ordinary incomes, though great, and much greater than before, nor by this new preffure of the cavaliers, the feparating of them from others, even thofe againft whom no new tranfgreffion is alledged, only for the holding down, as is profeffed, the great and reftlefs faction of the royalifts, we fear do more harm than good, albeit Lillie's prognoftick we count merely knavifh.

Since I came from Edinburgh, there are two or three papers more paft betwixt us and the remonftrants, which make our wounds wider, efpecially fince by violence they avow openly to opprefs us ; one part of them under Warifton and Mr Guthrie's patronage, though difallowed by others, puts into their hand the power of making all the churches void.   They look by their fupplicating of the Englifh for erecting of themfelves in a commiffion for purging, againft which the prefbytery of Edinburgh has given an honeft teftimony.   Another part, under the patrociny of Meff. Gillefpie and Livingfton, by the Englifh ordinance, takes the power of planting all with their own friends, though paffionately difclaimed by the other.   Againft thefe fearful oppreffions we have no human help. We cannot make fuch cordial application to the Englifh as they do ; fo we fear they fhall lend their power to the other for our hurt ; whereof, and other things, you fee how I exprefs myfelf to a friend at London ; the return to which you have here alfo.   I break off here till the next occafion.   My fervice to your kind wife.

Your Coufin,

ROBERT BAILLIE.

December 31. 1655.

196. *For*

196. *For Mr Spang, at Middleburg. September 1. 1656.*

Reverend and Dear Coufin,

——— As to our plantations, I am glad my hand is free
of them totally. Mr James Ramfay, a very able and fufficient youth as we have of his age, planted by us in Lenzie, to the great fatisfaction of all, except a very few, who
chofe an Englifh fectary, to whom they promifed the ftipend ; when, after two year's trouble, the Englifhman
removed, our brethren Meff. Gillefpie, Durham, Carftairs, all much obliged to Mr Robert Ramfay for their
own places, would not for any intreaty be pleafed to let
his fon live in peace ; fo we let him go to Lithgow, where
he is much better than he could have been where he was :
but in his place they have put one evidently of far meaner
parts, Mr Henry Forfyth, lately a baxter-boy, laureated
within thefe two years ; a little, very feckless-like thing in
his perfon, and mean in his gifts. To him the parifh,
weary of ftrife, wherein by the Englifh power they were
always oppreffed, yielded in filence without oppofition.
In Campfie likewife, one Mr Archibald Dennifton, depofed by them without any confiderable caufe, much to my
grief, and againft the hearts of his parifh, who loved him,
they have planted Mr J. Law within thefe three years,
brought from a pottinger to be laureate. In Rutherglen,
againft the people's heart, they have planted a little mani-
kin of fmall parts, whom I never faw ; and forced old Mr
R. Young, albeit as able yet as ever, to give over his miniftry. In Cathcart, where they had planted an Englifhman againft my mind, having, after two or three years
trial, enough of him, they fhuffled him over to Ireland ;
and are to plant another young thing lately laureate, with
fmall contentment to the people. In Glafgow, Mr A.
Gray being dead of a purple fever, of a few days roving,
the magiftrates would have been at the calling of Mr James
Furgufon, one of the moft excellent young men of our
and ; but to this Mr Durham and the reft were fo averfe,
that they were ready publickly to have oppofed it : fo the
magiftrates, knowing their inability to carry any call con-
rary to their mind, yielded to let them call whom they
pleafed. Mr Durham would have been at Mr J. Law be-
ore they put him on Campfie ; but Mr Patrick carried it
to.

to Mr Robert Macward, who lately, for inability of body, had left his charge in the college, and evidently was unable for such a charge as Glasgow : yet they put him in *nemine contradicente*, and that without all the ordinary trials, being unable for his health to have undergone them. Appearingly the burthen shortly will crush him, except he go on to do so as he has done yet, frequently to let his place vaik. Through the violence of that party, our church in these parts is in a hard condition, and for the time remediless. They got a little stop lately from whence it was not expected. At Blantyre, Mr John Heriot, of seventy-eight years, having admitted Mr James Hamilton his helper, with two parts of his stipend, because he would not thereafter give over the whole, the presbytery of Hamilton intented a process against him, for small inconsiderable clauses, and deposed him. When he is charged to remove from his house and all he has there, his son, by the friendship of Swinton, get the English to take notice of the violent oppression ; who, after a full hearing, decerned the old minister to enjoy all, even what before he had been content to quit. This preparative is dangerous for our whole church ; but the unhappy violence of these unadvised men, draws on these evils on themselves and others.

This is like now to be the refuge of all they oppress ; but a miserable one. It puts all our church-causes in the hands of the English, who defire to be judges of them according to their Erastian principle, though ordinarily our brethren have the ear of the English to do with them what they please. With much ado your old friend, a right honest and able man, more than the most of his neighbours, Mr Allan Ferguson of Drymen, escaped their hands. The last synod had put a committee to the presbytery of Dunbarton to try a number of slanders noised upon him. When, beside all his elders, ninety-four witnesses are sworn and tried, nothing at all is found against him. This process, and another of his neighbour Mr David Adamson of Fintry, where also, after much noise, nothing was found, has made their fervour of purging in our bounds much to relent ; for, as oft I told them, they will find on trial, that the men to be purged out, are on their side, not on ours, if there were any justice. At that same synod, the deposition of Mr R. Hume was ratified, as I was informed, very unjustly. In the other parts of
the

the land we fee no relenting of our brethrens fervour.
Mr Livingſton, notwithſtanding of all the trouble about
the planting of Eccles, has gone on to the like enormous
practice at Sprouſton, coming in on the preſbytery of
Dunſe, with two or three of the neighbour preſbyteries,
and planting Mr S. Row, one of their party, contrary to
the mind of all the preſbytery. Mr Guthrie is ſtill in
conteſt with the people of Stirling, but in more vexation
than formerly; for his colleague Mr Matthias Simpſon is
as heady and bold a man as himſelf, and has good hearing with the Engliſh, ſo that he is like get the ſtipend,
and Mr Rule to live perquire. Mr James and Wariſton
are on their old deſign ſtill, to ſet up their commiſſion for
tyrannizing over the kirk; but it is like the Engliſh will
not countenance them, the thing is ſo extremely and evidently unjuſt; alſo ſome of us are fallen in with the Engliſh far enough.

The Preſident Broghill is reported by all to be a man
exceeding wiſe and moderate, and by profeſſion a Preſbyterian. He has gained more on the affections of the people than all the Engliſh that ever were among us. He has
been very civil to Mr Douglas and Mr Dickſon, and very
intimate with Mr James Sharp. By this means, we have
an equal hearing in all we have ado with the council; yet
their way is exceeding longſome, and all muſt be done firſt
at London. It is but the other week that Mr Gilleſpie's
abſurd orders for ſtipends was got away. He puts us in
hopes of more favour. That much-talked-of reſpect to
Mr Wood, (though I have not yet inquired it of himſelf),
as I hear, was this: Mr Rutherford's daily bitter contentions with him, made him weary of his place exceedingly.
The Old college being long vacant, and he the eldeſt maſter of it, and for ſundry years employed to overſee it almoſt as Principal, was wiſhed by ſundry who loved it and
him to be placed there; and there is no doubt he was the
fitteſt man living for that charge. But here was the inſuperable difficulty: A fair call could not be got. The five
maſters who had power to call were divided. One Campbell, a remonſtrant, minded the place, and, by his party,
was not unlike to have carried it from the Engliſh. One
Martin, the oldeſt maſter then in charge, alledging it to be
his right to ſucceed, with the conſent of other two maſters,
went to the Engliſh to ſuit their favour. The Preſident,
I think, on Mr Sharp's information, moved the council,

without Mr Wood's knowledge, to make choice of him
for the place. They write a peremptory letter to the
ministers and masters of St Andrew's to admit Mr Wood
Principal to the Old college without delay. When the
university is convened, and the letter read, Mr Campbell
protested. The other three were moved to invite him, in
obedience to the English command, but not to call him.
He accepted the charge. I am glad he is in it, or any other
place where he is contented; for indeed he is the most
serviceable man our church now has: but I am not yet satisfied of his accepting that place on the English command;
for if, in divine providence, they who had right to call,
for their own base and hurtful designs refused to call
him, I think it was hard for him, upon whatever causes,
to meddle with it. I love not that we should justify or
harden the English in their usurpations in our university-
rights; but these things I will debate with himself at
meeting.

Another passage of ours I was not satisfied with. Swinton was excommunicated for his early compliance with the
English. Sundry of his friends were earnest to have him
relaxed, that in their necessary affairs they might have the
more liberty to employ his help. He was either so proud,
or so feared to offend his masters, that he would neither
acknowledge a fault, nor petition for favour. When his
friends dealt with the presbytery of Edinburgh, they sent
two to confer with him. All that they reported from
him was, that he was very willing to live and die in the
communion of our church; and that the reason of his
not appearance when cited to the commission of Perth,
was not contempt, but just fear of his life. Upon this report, without any supplication, he is relaxed the next
Sabbath by Mr Ja. Hamilton. This I did not like at all,
as a mere scorn of our discipline. Our brethren would
not long be behind with us: for at once the presbytery of
Ayr relaxed good William Govan, who was, at least, on
the scaffold at the King's execution, if no more, excommunicated on the like occasion; yea, the synod of Glasgow and Ayr took the censure off Mr Gillespie and Mr
Naismith, without any acknowledgement of a fault, or
desire to be relaxed. To this strange enormity all formally
voted; only Mr Ferguson, Mr Kirkaldie, Mr G. Young,
were absent. Mr J. Bell and Mr Alexander Nisbet removed themselves; but no dissent was entered.

Our ſtate is in a very ſilent condition. Strong garriſons ver all the land, and a great army both of horſe and oot; for which there is no ſervice at all. Our nobles ly-ng up in priſons, and, under forfaultries, or debts, pri-ate or publick, are for the moſt part either broken or reaking. No more word of delivering Crawford, Lau-lerdale, Eglinton, Montgomery, Ogilvie, Mariſchal, and aany more, than was the firſt hour. Glencairn lies ſtill n the caſtle of Edinburgh; Col. Borthwick betrayed him. The letter he brought to him from the King, he delivered o Monk before it came to Glencairn's hands, and his an-wer of it alſo before it came to the King; and yet, under he moſt fearful imprecations can be deviſed, the villain vrote unrequired, that he had done no ſuch thing. Some ay it would have ſtood hard with Glencairn's life, had it ot been the Preſident's favour procured by Mr Sharp.

The dyvour-act, of lands for creditors at twenty years purchaſe, has made much clamour; albeit none who have any credit have made uſe of it. All the advocates are re-turned to the bar. Balcolmy and Ker make ſome more diſpatch in cauſes than was before. The great ſeal of Scotland, with Cromwell's large ſtatue on horſeback, *Oli-verius, Dei gratia, reip. Angliæ, Scotiæ, et Hiberniæ, Protector*, under the arms of Scotland, *Pax quæritur bello*, is given to Deſborough; the ſignet, with the great fees of the ſecretary's place, to Col. Lockhart; the regi-ſters to Judge Smith, and the reſt of the places of ſtate to others. The expences, delays, and oppreſſions in law-ſuits, are ſpoken of to be as great as ever.

This Spaniſh war has wracked many of our merchants; albeit, in God's mercy, as little loſs has befallen on our neighbours of this town as on any of the iſle; for except one little ſhip taken by the Biſcayners near Bourdeaux, and James Bell's ſhip, which, with himſelf, by a pitiful miſguiding, was blown up almoſt in the harbour, we had no more loſs this year, whileas a world of others have been wracked; many more in a few months than was all the time of your war. It is much talked, that it is both your men and ſhips that ſerve the Spaniards in all theſe ſpoils. Our fleet, waiting in vain on the coaſt of Spain, does little good to the merchants on theſe coaſts; and yet the taxes with us are great. The maintenance was to-wards L. 10,000 Sterling a-month. They ſay the exciſe will be double; ſo that the revenue will be above 300,000 pounds

pounds Sterling a-year, the half whereof is never together among us. The truth is, the money was never so scarce here, and grows daily scarcer; and yet it is thought this parliament in September is indicted mainly for new taxations. What England may bear, to whom the Protector remitted the half of their monthly maintenance of L. 120,000 Sterling, I know not; but Scotland, whose burden has been triple, besides the fines, forfeitures, debts, and other miseries, seems unable to bear what lies on already. Wise men think the Protector wiser than to desire the empty title, when he has much more already than the thing. No man looks for any good from this parliament, but fear evil; yet all who are wise think, that our evils would grow yet more if Cromwell were removed. They think his government, as it is, will be far better than a parliament, or any thing else they expect; only all think this war with Spain needless and hurtful, and hope by the parliament it will be taken away.

There was never such solicitation for votes to be chosen commissioners as now among us. It is like there shall be none of the whole number more cordial for all the Protector's desires, be what they may, than these that come from Scotland. It is said, Mr Guthrie and Wariston, with their friends, have been sitting more than this fortnight in Edinburgh, drawing their papers, to be sent by some of their number to the Protector or parliament. They were so absurd, that Mr Gillespie, who was expected to have been sent up to agent them, turned his back, and left them: yet they will not want agents. We think my Lord Broghill, commissioner for the city of Edinburgh, will cross their injustice and irrational violence. However, our minds will be in no peace till we see what this parliament will bring forth. No man I know expects any good from it, and that is our condition for the present, that we can be hardly worse.

Through God's mercy our town, in its proportion, thrives above any in all the land. The word of God is well loved and regarded, albeit not as it ought, and we desire; yet in no town of our land better. Our people have much more trade in comparison than any other. Their buildings increase strangely both for number and fairness. It is more than doubled in our time. I pray God to increase his blessing on this place of our birth, albeit I am afraid for it; for on Sunday was eight days, at four

n the morning, August 17. there was a sensible earth-
quake in all the parts of the town, though I felt it not.
Five or six years ago, there was another, in the afternoon,
which I felt, and was followed with that fearful burning,
and all the other shakings has been among us since.   The
Lord preserve us from his too-well-deserved judgements.

The King is so far forgot here, that not one, so far as
I know, keeps any correspondence with him; nor do we
hear at all what he does or intends.   Yet I think divers
pray to God for him, and wish his restitution.   But if men
of my Lord Broghill's parts and temper be long among us,
they will make the present government more beloved than
some men wish.   From our publick praying for the King,
Broghill's courtesy, more than his threats, brought off
our leading men.   About the time of abstaining I was a
more earnest supplicant for him than ever; whereupon
some of my good neighbours deferred me to the council
as an earnest prayer for the King.   This was false; for in
doctrine I struck not on that string; only, so long as I
might do it without scandal, or reflecting on my wiser
and better brethrens omitting it, I never passed by it in
prayer.

When in that we had yielded, we were like to be put
farther to it.   Our unhappy remonstrants still occasioned
trouble.   Mr Livingston made no bones to preach and
pray publickly with the English, and persuaded Mr Gil-
espie to begin before him; so that Mr Patrick, when he
came to Edinburgh, made no scruple to preach in that
English church to their council and judges, and go home
in coach with the President, and say grace at his table;
yea, in Glasgow to preach to their circular court, and
feast the judges in his house.   This made the council endeavour to have so many of our best preachers appointed
by turns to come to Edinburgh, and preach to them.
When my opinion was craved in this unhappy motion, I
gave it an answer, and, by God's blessing, got it crushed
for the time; but how long, I know not; for Mr Livingston being solicited to go to Ireland, was sent over there
by his remonstrant brethren to make a visit and return.
It has been their design this long time to fill Ireland with
their party; and they have come too good speed.   I did
what I could to help that evil; albeit not with that success
I would.   Mr John, so soon as he went over, he goes immediately to Dublin, and there is content to be employed
to

to preach to the ftate. What evil this will work, we know not; efpecially Wariſton and Mr Guthrie's impatience to be out of work, and kept down, inclining them, as fome fay, to come nearer the Engliſh than they did: yet their defign being evident to play the tyrants in the whole church, and to put the magiftracy of the whole land in their party's hand, which they call the godly, fo many will be againſt them, as it is hoped they will not prevail. Mr Gillefpie found their defign fo unfeafonable and irrational, that he left their meeting difpleafed this laſt week: yet Sir George Maxwell, who with him is all one, thought the week before to have carried by a number of blue caps of that party, the commiffion of the fheriffdom of Ayr and Renfrew to himfelf, on purpofe, as they fay, to have been that party's agent with the Protector in all their defires. But my Lord Cochran's diligence and wifdom broke Sir George's defign. Time will let us know more of mens fecret contrivances, which are yet covered.

This fect of Quakers is like to prove troublefome. They increafe much among the Engliſh both in England and Ireland. They in a furious way cry down both miniftry and magiftracy. Some of them feem actually to be poffeffed with a devil, their fury, their irrational paffions, and bodily convulfions, are fo great. Lieut. Ofburn, one of our firſt apoſtates to the Engliſh, and betrayers to his power of our army, for which he had great favours and rewards from Cromwell himfelf, is an open leader to them in the ſtreets of Edinburgh, without any punifhment. Sundry in Clydefdale, of the moſt zealous remonftrant-yeoman, have turned fo, and their increafe is feared, which is the juſt recompence of admitting the beginnings of error. They are patient as yet of ſtrokes; but if the Fifth-monarchy-men of the late parliament had prevailed, or if their party go on in its growth, their fury is like to go to unmerciful killing (with their predeceffors) of their oppofers.

Our church-ſtrifes are not like to end. The remonftrants make it their endeavour to put themfelves, as the commiffion 1650, or under fome fuch notion, in a committee to purge and plant all Scotland, with the Engliſh allowance to them as the godly party; one of the vileſt, moſt ſhameful, and tyrannick tricks, that ever was heard of in any church in any time. To prevent this, our brethren there-eaſt fent up, with Broghill, our profeffed friend Mr James Sharp, to Cromwell; with what inſtructions,

ions, I know not; but I hear very fair and honest. The remonstrants cry out on this message, though alone to guard against and prevent their mischievous designs. They will not be long a-sending one after him, to desire openly, what long, by their letters and secret agents, they have been dealing for. This strife at this time is shameful and dangerous. I love it not. My advice was never sought to it; but on our part it seems necessary. I wish it may end better than I fear. My love and service to your kind wife, oft remembered by Harry, and all your three daughters, whom I pray God to bless.

      Your Cousin,

           ROBERT BAILLIE.

197. *To Mr Spang.*

Cousin,

THAT which oft I promised you, a large account of our affairs this twelvemonth, you have it, but in a confused way for want of leisure. Our church has been pretty quiet; our troubling remonstrants not having yet prevailed with the English to get authority from them to exercise their tyranny among us. The great instrument of God to cross their evil designs, has been that very worthy, pious, wise, and diligent young man, Mr James Sharp. The purpose of the few brethren that were on the advice of his going to London, upon my Lord Broghill's desire, you may see in his instructions, subscribed, and at first seen, only by three, Mess. Douglas, Dickson, and Wood. The remonstrants agreed not very well among themselves. My Lord Wariston, Mr Gillespie, and Mr Guthrie, these three restless heads, looked not one way. But after the affronts Mr Gillespie received from the synod of Lothian, and Wariston's domestick straits, had made him content, contrary to his former resolutions, to embrace his prior place of register from his Highness; and Mr Guthrie's continual vexation by Mr Simpson his colleague; and Mr Simpson of Airth being provoked by the synod of Perth's meddling with the great scandal of the fatherless child, reflecting so on him, they resolved at last to go up together, and openly petition his Highness for all their desires.

When the synod of Glasgow had taken off the censure

                            of

of the general assembly from Mess. Gillespie and Naismith, in the strange way I wrote to you of before, that party thought it advantageous to them to have that act of Glasgow acknowledged by other synods. For this end they resolve to send Mr Gillespie correspondent from Glasgow to the synod of Lothian. They thought they would not refuse him for many causes; and if they admitted him, it was a leading case to the other synods to pass from the act of the general assembly in its censure without all satisfaction. That message was not much to the mind of Mr Gillespie himself, but Mr Carstairs and others would needs have it put upon him. When he came, his commission was scrupled at by Mr John Smith and others, and laid aside to be cognosced upon. They gladly would have shifted the matter, and eschewed all din, being unwilling to enter in contest. But Mr Gillespie's high humour would not permit it; but he must needs have their positive answer to admit or reject his commission. They lenified the question, and since he would have it put, they made it, *Admit* or *Commit.* When the votes almost of all was for referring it to a committee to be cognosced on, he took it so ill, that he broke out in railing, telling them, " Their sword was but of wood, and their arm was " broken," and much more evil language; to which Mr Douglas gave sharp and stout replies. I knew this irritation would not be easily forgot. It was a spur for their voyage to London. There was a very foul scandal broke out on Mr James Simpson of Airth. A young woman, familiar with him, and oft in his house, was found with child. She granted the child; but denied she had known any man. Mr James, with the advice of his presbytery, Mr James Guthrie, and other two or three (for their number is no greater in the remonstrant-presbytery of Stirling) take the woman's confession, in face of the congregation, that she was with child, and withal her purgation by oath, that she knew no man. For this Mr James and she are both cited to answer to the synod of Perth. Both of them send in to the synod a declinature (both written by Mr James Simpson's hand) as of a corrupt judicatory. While this is in agitation, Mr Guthrie is sent to London to wait on till his four fellow-commissioners should be ready to come. Their commission I did not see; but it was such as some of their own, as Mr Carstairs and others, refused to subscribe. We may know it by their

their proposals, which to the very laſt they preſſed to obtain from the Protector, viz. 1. An order from him, that within the bounds of every ſynod, there ſhould be named a committee of equal number of aſſembly-men and remonſtrants, who ſhould have power to determine all differences in planting and purging in all the preſbyteries of the bounds. 2. That there ſhould be a committee of delegates from all the ſynods, of equal number of aſſembly-men and remonſtrants, to determine finally all differences ecclefiaſtick in the whole land. 3. That the Protector ſhould nominate a committee to plant kirks, and that the power of giving of ſtipends in all vacant churches ſhould be in this committee. 4. That the parliament ſhould renew the act of claſſes, to the end the places of civil power ſhould be in the hand of their party. The laſt they obtained for Lieut.-Gen. Lambert, and the General-Majors in the parliament were much their friends, and others, whom their diligent agents Garſland and Tweedale made for them. At firſt their motion was rejected; but thereafter, when our friends were out of the houſe, they got it paſt in an additional propoſition. It was intended chiefly for the changing of our Glaſgow magiſtrates; whereupon I moved our brethren of Edinburgh to write to Mr Sharp many reaſons to ſtop the thing if he could. He wrought it ſo that it paſſed with much difficulty, and however got private aſſurances it ſhould do no harm; and ſo that act of parliament lay as good as dormant, till of late they obtained, on a ſupplication of procured hands in this town, a letter from the Protector to ſuſpend the new election of magiſtrates in our burgh till farther order. Our late magiſtrates, with the concurrence almoſt of all the burghs of Scotland, are dealing with the Protector to get the privileges of their burgh reſerved. What will be the iſſue, we will ſee ere long.

For the other three deſires, Mr Sharp, in divers conferences before the Protector, made them appear ſo unreaſonable, that after more than half a year's importunate ſolicitation, they could obtain nothing at all. One of the cauſes of fruſtrating their hopes was, that the London miniſters were flatly for us againſt them. You ſee that information I wrote up to Mr Aſh, a prime city-miniſter, to be communicated to all our Preſbyterian friends; alſo to my ancient Mr Rous, one of the council of ſtate. Mr Rutherford wrote to Mr Aſh an information

2   tion

tion in favour of his party; but after both his and mine
were read, and Mr Sharp with his five oppofites had
been heard at length in divers meetings of the city-minifters, all of them profeffed their difiatisfaction with the
way of the remonftrants, and fatisfaction with our proceedings. Mr Wood had drawn a reprefentation of our
differences, which Mr Hutchefon, in his fmoothing, to
my fenfe, had fomething enervated, not only in its fharp-
nefs, but vigour. This Mr Sharp printed at London,
which (fince thefe two ready fcribes have not anfwered)
did us much good with all intelligent men. The remonftrants finding no Prefbyterian friends, plied the Sectaries
hardly, prayed oft with them both publickly and privately; fo that with all their power thefe befriended them, I
mean Dr Owen, Lockier, and Caryl, and other Independents. Lambert and Fleetwood, with the great officers of
the army, moftly Anabaptifts, were affectionately for
them. At laft, the Protector being wearied, named a
duodenary committee to hear both, and report their
judgement to the council. Mr Sharp refufed to appear,
as being a mere private man, having no commiffion to
tranfact any thing of publick concernment to the church
of Scotland; but being charged at the fecond meeting, he
appeared, and gave fuch anfwers to his oppofites challenges, that they could get nothing there for a good time.
Of the twelve, fix were conceived to be Prefbyterians, and
the reft enemies to our church-difcipline. Of the firft
fort none kept but one, Mr Manton; the other kept very
well, and were ready at laft to report to the council their
advice, all the defires of the remonftrants, as they had
reafon, being avowed adverfaries to our church government. When it was at this nick, Mr Afh, by his letters,
procured Mr Godfrey, and Mr Cooper, two Prefbyterians,
who had been named on the committee, to meet; they,
with Mr Manton, after a new full hearing, were fo well
fatisfied with Mr Sharp's replies, that they drew up their
judgement by way of teftimony againft the remonftrants
defires. This wrought fo upon the council, that they refolved not to interpofe in our debates, only to write a
letter to the minifters of Edinburgh, Meff. Douglas, Dickfon, Trail, Stirling, to agree at home among ourfelves.
Yet in this letter, by canny conveyance of their friend
Mr Scobel, I think, clerk to the council, they had got foifted
in a very hurtful claufe, that where there was difference

bout stipends, it should be determined by the testimony
of four named in Mr Gillespie's orders, which the parliament had expresly abolished. That clause was repre-
ented both to the Protector and counsellors to be so unreasonable, that it is like there shall no letter at all be
sent us. The storm we were afraid for, by God's mercy,
for a time is put by ; but how soon it will waken again we
do not know. Mr Guthrie left them before they came to
their greatest contest, whether, for want of monies, or
difference among themselves, I know not ; though they
put all the ministers in our bounds of their mind to pay,
at the first, forty shillings Sterling, for their maintenance,
and all of their party, men and women, to a voluntary
contribution ; whence out of Glasgow, some say, there
went up L. 180 Sterling ; yet their charge was so great,
and their friends charity after the first fervour so cold,
that all of them were straitened enough for money, as I
was informed. Also, they say, they agreed not so well
among themselves. Certain it is that Mr Guthrie opposed my Lord Wariston's resuming his place of register. If
it had been upon both their professed principle, of the unlawfulnefs to take places subordinate to an unlawful
power, I would the better have excused it ; but Mr Guthrie, (as one who should have known it with the best, informed me), with all his power, did labour secretly to
get that place to his confident friend Swinton, with the
burden of a yearly pension of L. 300 Sterling out of it to
Wariston. I know not what to say to it. However, Mr
Guthrie left them in the midst, having obtained nothing
but a pension of L. 100 Sterling to his colleague Mr Rule,
out of the treasury of vacant stipends, the spoil of other
churches, which now is dried up. Wariston is now also
returned, having with his place obtained the most of the
registers which were carried out of the betrayed (as many
say) castle of Edinburgh to the tower of London. Mr
Gillespie remains there sorely sick, some think in displea-
sure that his desires were not granted. However, at his
last going to Hampton-court, he got no speech of the
Protector ; but he went immediately from Hampton-court
to Wombleton, Lambert's house, being Saturday at
night ; and having engaged to preach on Sunday's morning, before sermon he had five stools ; and after his pain-
ful preaching, fourscore before he rested. Thereafter,
for many days, a great flux and fever, together with the
breach

breach of an ulcer in his guts, put him to the very brink of death. Many thought it the evident hand of God upon him, and would not have sorrowed for his death. For myself I was grieved, foreseeing the hurt of our college by his removal.

While these debates at London continued, the restless humour of that party at home was somewhat quiet, waiting for the issue. Our synod of Glasgow, whether for want of matter, or being deserted and contemned by many, have passed this year without din. Mr Robert Semple of Lesmahago's foul process has been referred to a committee, and little done in it, the man being one of their side. Mr John Hamilton of Innerkip, a prime man among them, of a long time under very gross scandals, is not so much as challenged. Mr Henry Semple, a busy agent for them, prevented his process by death. The synod of Lothian and Perth have been careful to try accurately the challenges of sundry.

The Quakers make some trouble among us, and increase in Lenzie, Douglas, and other places, most where that faction have been troublesome. Thus does our church-affairs stand.

For our state, all is exceeding quiet. A great army in a multitude of garrisons abides above our heads, and deep poverty keeps all estates exceedingly at under. The taxes of all sorts are so great, the trade so little, that it is a marvel if extreme scarcity of money, end not, ere long, in some mischief. What came out of the doors of the parliament was this. All who came thither were complying and confident men, and none more ready to serve his Highness in every thing, than all that came from Scotland. If any were doubted, they were held off till their commissions were well examined. The maliciousness of the faction with us kept out Commissary Lockhart, commissioner for Glasgow, a large month; yet at last, by Ambassador Lockart's letter from France, he got in. The great work at first was, to settle the excise, and maintenance for the army. A vast sum of money was requisite for the garrisons in England, Scotland, and Ireland, for the navies in Spain, at Dunkirk, and Jamaica, for the army in France, for the Protector's court. When this was agreed to, without all contradiction, it was so laid by a few of the Protector's safest friends, not above five, that the city should petition the parliament to advise the Pro-

:Ctor to take upon him the government, and title of King, fter the way which, in a long paper of advice, was fet lown. To this none did oppofe but the officers of the rmy. To take them off, one of the articles of government was, the erection of a Houfe of Peers, to be nominated by the Protector, who doubtlefs was to make Lords he chief of thefe officers : yet the thing was fo far againft ll that was profeffed, and fo oft printed before, that it ould not go down at firft with them. That which made ome of them, efpecially their head, Lambert, fo averfe, vas his own evident intereft ; for in all mens eyes he was he heir-apparent to the Protector's power, but the kinghip cut him off clearly from that hope. About this, nany fharp debates were in and out of the houfe by the officers. All other were to give the Protector whatever ne defired ; not fo much for recent accidents, which were thought either invented or directed as opportune for that end, viz. the feizing of a number of gentlemen in and about the city, as if Charles Stuart had employed them for a prefent difturbance of the peace, which fear quickly evanifhed as totally groundlefs. Alfo Sundercomb's plot to kill the Protector with a blunderbufs. The man's denial of all, and poifoning of himfelf for fear of quartering quick, made not this to appear. The feizing of the declaration and ftandard of the Fifth-monarchy fools, the imprifoning of Sir Henry Vane in Carifbrook caftle, and General-Major Harrifon, did quickly evanifh. But that which inclined the moft to further the Protector's kinghip, was their expectation of a regular government thereby, without the perpetuating of a military rule by the fword, to which fo vaft and arbitrary charges would always be neceffary ; befide that all expected a more moderate and meek ruling from the Protector and his children, than from Lambert, or any of all the army. Some alfo were glad of a profeffed and open royalty, hoping, in time, it might further the return of thefe whom they counted the lawful heirs of the crown.

When the Protector, as they faid, was willing to have come, and declared his willingnefs to accept, after much debate, private and publick, of the article of kingfhip, as well as the reft of the advice, that fame morning his fon-in-law Fleetwood came to him, with fome papers, affuring of a ftrong combination in the army to oppofe that motion. Upon the which affrightment, his Highnefs went

to

to the painted chamber, and called the House to shew
them, that he accepted the government according to the
petition and advice in all the articles, except the title of
King, which he could not digest. His best and most intimate counsellors, Broghill and Thurloe, thought this a
great error ; yet it seems the best expedient ; for at that
time Lambert and the General-Major's power was so great,
both in the House and army, that if their obstinacy had
continued, they might have overturned all. To prevent
this mischief, a few days thereafter he adjourned the parliament from June 27th till October.

In the last day of the parliament, June 27. he was most
solemnly installed supreme magistrate in a canopy of state
and throne, with a royal purple, furred robe, a sword of
state, a sceptre, and a Bible in place of a crown, by the
Speaker of the House, Widdrington, and was graced with
a sermon and feast. In all the action, the French and
Dutch ambassadors stood on his two hands, congratulating in their master's name. The hearts of many were sorry to see in effect all the kingship established on Cromwell
in peace. Yet this did not satisfy ; for quickly Lambert
was called for to a privy conference, wherein declaring
himself unwilling to comply in all things, his commission
was called for, and he made a man most private. The
chief of the army, in a supplication, expressed their adhering to his way. Broghill got passed in parliament a right
of L. 1000 a-year for his good service. All men expected, that when so easily Lambert was quashed, the next
session of parliament would have quickly made Cromwell
king ; yet it did not sooner meet, but great miscontentments were apparent. The House of Lords, according to
the petition and advice, did sit. Manchester and many
would not sit. Cassils disdained it. There were no more
peers for Scotland but Wariston and Lockhart : yet the
chief of Cromwell's friends were taken out of the House
of Commons to fill the other House ; and many then
came to the House of Commons, who were excluded before, no great friends to him, Scot, Haselrig, Lambert,
and many more, who quickly began to move high questions about the power of the militia, the name and power
of the other House, to whom the supreme magistrate was
to be answerable. Upon their stickling so high, after a
few days sitting, they were dissolved ; the Protector calling
to God to judge betwixt him and them, and they saying,
Amen.

Amen. In his speech he attested God he had rather chosen, at a wood-side, to have kept sheep, than have undertaken the office he had, if the love of the people's peace had not constrained him. He assured of Charles Stuart's readiness to come from Flanders with an army, and sundry listing men for him in London.

A storm after this was expected, some prodigies seeming to foretell it: A little after his instalment, a magazine of powder blowing up many houses and persons; about the house in Fogo-muir and Dunse-law, in December, an army of pikemen appearing to many; and some days after, some thousands of cannon, in a formal shape, for many days being seen by many, both English and Scots, made of the snow without the hand of man. For all this, nothing to this day is seen but a deep peace.

It is expected a new parliament may be called, and sundry shires are said to be forming petitions to his Highness to accept of the title of King. Many in the army, both in Scotland and England, are cast out; but who remain, write up their supplication, encouraging the Protector to proceed. It is thought, on the council's act and army's petition, the crown shall be put on, and confirmed by the next parliament. They speak of my Lord Fairfax and Lambert's committing. In a late speech of the Protector to the mayor and aldermen of London, it is still averred, that Charles Stuart is ready to come from Ostend, with 5000 men and 7000 arms. All marvel how this can be; for the English navy is ready about that place to sink all that come that way; and the design of raising men in England is so poor, that none value it, especially when it is so well known by the Protector in every circumstance; besides that the most who profess themselves for the King among us, or over sea, are of so exceeding ill principles and humour, that few wish to be under their power.

I was called to Edinburgh, December 30. to hear Mr Sharp's report. He gave us a very notable relation of every passage, how, by the good hand of God, he had got all the designs of the exceeding busy and bold remonstrants defeated; that the Protector had dismissed him with many good words, assuring he should be loth to grant any to our prejudice. He commended himself in his last speech to four of us in particular, and by name Mr Douglas, Mr Dickson, Mr Blair, and me, professing his sorrow that he was a stumbling-block to us. The reason of this kindness nefs I take to be, 1. My Lord Broghill and Secretary Thurloe's reports of us; 2. That the Prefbyterian party in England who adhere to us is exceeding great and ftrong, and, after the army, is the Protector's chief ftrength againft the fectaries, who generally are out of conceit of him; 3. That our adverfaries are found but inconfiderable, and a heady party, much joining with the way of his adverfaries. However, we bleffed God that by Mr Sharp's labours was kept off us for a time a much-feared ftorm. At his coming from London, he appointed a correfpondence with one Major Beak, a zealous Prefbyterian, for affifting us in what we might have to do. We appointed Mr Wood to draw a fhort declaration of our willingnefs to have any tolerable peace with the remonftrants, if fo, for time to come, they would promife to be fubmiffive to the eftablifhed government. This now is printed; but they carp at all we can do or fay for peace, except we fubject ourfelves to their good pleafure. There was fomething moved in our laft meeting of a few, to do a little more for engaging the Protector. I crufhed the motion at the beginning, inveighing againft it; fo for the time it is dead.

The Earl of Rothes is put in the caftle on a moft fhameful occafion. My Lord Howard's fifter, married with my Lord Balgony, Rothes's fifter's fon, General Leflie's grandfon; this Howard's wife, a very light woman, came to make a vifit to Fife, where her carriage every where was exceeding wanton. Rothes openly bore her too much company, to the offence of many. However, about that time fhe is got with child, which fhe bears at London. Her hufband finding, that he had not been near her for three or four months from her conception, falls in an outrageous jealoufy with her, fufpects my Lord Belafis, whom his brother fights in that quarrel; but fufpects Rothes more; and in a rage pofts towards Scotland to fight Rothes. The Protector hearing of it, caufes follow and apprehend Howard, and fends an order in hafte to fecure Rothes in the caftle of Edinburgh, where yet he lies in great infamy.

We are fometimes in fear for your ftates. Their unkindnefs to the Britifh family and that of Orange; their needlefs provocations oft of Sweden, by open favouring of all his enemies, and drawing to their power Brandeburg from him; alfo their too ftrait alliance with Spain, and neglect of France, portends no good, though their fuccefs

againft

against the Portugal ſhips in the very bay of Liſbon, and
their boaſting of the Biſhop of Munſter unto a peace with
the city, were very pleaſant to us.   They are a very noble
member of the Reformed church, which we pray God to
help and bleſs; albeit their ſtate ſeems to ſtand but on
tottering props, and they have loſt much of the love and
reputation ſometimes they had both at home and abroad.
It ſeems the Spaniſh patience has ſent home the Engliſh
navy, without all fruit of their three or four years ſumpt-
uous attendance, but the loſs of Blake their admiral.   As
for the burning ſome veſſels in the Canaries, it was no
great buſineſs; ſince now all the plate ſeems to be come
home without impediment.   Mr Patrick Gilleſpie preached before the Protector in his velvet rarely cut caſſock,
a very flattering thankſgiving for that ſignal ſervice, thank-
ing God for the great reformation of the church.

· But he whom all men begin to look moſt on is Charles
of Sweden.   In his quarrel with Poland, many were not
ſatisfied; and generally all here, for his league with the
Protector, did malign him.   For myſelf, ſince the battle
of Leipſick, I have loved the houſe of Sweden to this day
above all foreigners; and, by the ſtrange ſucceſſes God
gives to their valour, I expect more good to the church
from them than any other.

Keep all theſe things to yourſelf.   They are the inſide
of all our affairs, which I deſire none to know from me
but yourſelf alone.

Your ſorrowful Couſin,

ROBERT BAILLIE.

198. *To Mr Spang.*   *November* 1658.

Couſin,

———— Our church lies as it did.   The repreſentation
printed by Mr Sharp at London, they durſt never eſſay to
anſwer; but our late declaration of new deſires of peace,
they anſwered a part of it with a very bitter pamphlet; to
which Mr Rutherford printed a preamble in his preface to
late anſwer to Hooker.   Being deſired, I ſent my obſer-
ations on that preamble to Mr Douglas; but on that and
their whole pamphlet, Mr Hutcheſon has written a very
accurate and ſolid review, with ſome additions of Mr
Wood's; all which I think are now on the preſs.   It is ve-

2   ry

ry like the end of this obftinate difference will be a formal feparation : the fooner the better for the kirk ; for
they abide among us only to increafe their party ; and if
they were formally feparated, they could do us the lefs
harm.

'The country lies very quiet ; it is exceeding poor ; trade
is nought ; the Englifh have all the money.   Our Noble
families are almoft gone : Lennox has little in Scotland
unfold ; Hamilton's eftate, except Arran and the barony
of Hamilton, is fold ; Argyle can pay little annualrent
for 700,000 or 800,000 merks ; and he is no more drowned in debt than in publick hatred, almoft of all, both
Scots and Englifh ; the Gordons are gone ; the Dou-
glaffes are little better ; Eglinton and Glencairn on the
brink of breaking ; many of our chief families eftates are
cracking, nor is there any appearance of any human relief for the time.   What is become of the King and his
family we do not know.   Some talk, that he fhould be in
the Hague.   Many take his unkindnefs to Balcarras very
ill ; efpecially that he fhould oppofe his Lady's provifion to
the overfight of the little Prince of Orange.   His obftinate
obfervance of Hyde offends all ; but what he minds, no
man here knows, and few care.   The Protector's death
was unexpected : the way of it we do not learn ; men
fpeak as they lift.   What fome fpeak, of troubles of body
and mind, and, after a fwoon, the crying out of the devil and a northern army, muft be but a fable.   We were
afraid for trouble after his death ; but all is fettled in
peace.   We doubted what might become of the officers of
the army their petition for the generality of Fleetwood :
if they infift in it, it cannot but breed evil blood ; but
they are wifer than to differ when fome would be glad of
it.

In Edinburgh, at their election, they fell on a paffage
againft the mind of many.   Sir Andrew Ramfay, a right
fharp young man, but very proud, had carried himfelf
for two years in the place of Provoft, very haughtily ; and
in his abode at London had been at vaft charges to the
town for no profit ; yet was ftill in hope to have got from
the Protector what might have done the town good in
their exceeding low condition.   Mr Thompfon, the clerk,
who had brought him to his place, became very ungracious to him, by the fuggeftion moft of Bailie Jaufie, who
defiring to have his fon conjunct clerk with Mr W. Thomp-

on, was refufed, on fear that fuch a conjunction fhould
ut himfelf to the door. Upon this difference, the Pro-
oft, and that Bailie, did what they could to bear down
he clerk, and were ready, when able, to have fhifted him
rom his place. The clerk, and all the town, would moft
ladly have had Archibald Sydeferf for Provoft, the far
itteft for the charge: but Ramfay kept Sydeferf from the
eets, according to the late act of the Englifh parliament,
or his guilt of the engagement; and got on the leets him-
elf, Bailie Jaufie, and (being perfuaded that none would
ive him a vote) Sir James Stuart. Thompfon finding it
o, he wrought underhand, that any living might be cho-
en before his enemies Ramfay or Jaufie. Thus Sir James
arried it. This offended many, and feared them, left
the man being very wife and active, and an open favour-
r of the remonftrants) it might make a great change in
Edinburgh and all the land for that party's advancement.
When I met with Thompfon, my good friend, I railed on
im, that for revenge of his private fuit, and fpleen againft
Ramfay, he had betrayed the publick intereft into the
ands of a proteftor. I was impatient of all apologies;
et I hear Sir James has given affurance enough to Mr
Douglas, and others, and denies his remonftrantifm. For
myfelf, I do not well believe, nor much truft him; but
ear the great evil of this prank of the clerk: Sir James
nce caft him out of his place; if he do it again, no man
rill pity him.

Being weary, I have now laid afide my chronology. I
ave drawn the facred and profane ftory fhortly from the
ountains through the Old Teftament, in feven epochas,
o every one of which I have fubjoined the moft of the or-
inary queftions of chronology: and, after a pretty free
ebate with all forts of men, determine them after mine
wn mind. I have alfo fet down the ftory of the New
Teftament, the firft epocha of it to the death of John the
Evangelift, and at the back of it, feventeen of the chiefeft
ueftions. Being tired, I fubfide. It may be I revife it,
nd add more queftions, efpecially from the Apocalypfe.
Therefore what you find of new books that may further
ne in this defign, let the College have them. I think we
ant few of the old. This year's ftudy I caft it upon the
hole head of juftification, moft to meet with Bifhop For-
es, printed lately at London by Mr Thomas Sydferf, Bi-
iop of Galloway, and our moderate mid-men, whom I
have

have esteemed, ever since I knew them, real Papists in the most and main; also to meet with Baxter, whom, albeit I highly esteem for piety and learning, yet I think a very unhappy broiler, a full avowed Amiraldist, and a great confounder of the head of justification. I pray you in your first to Voetius, remember my hearty service to him, and tell him from me, that many his lovers here long for a third volume of his Disputations; also, that they exceedingly desire some Exercitations from him on the way of Amirald, and that the heads of justification were vindicated by him, from Baxter and Forbes, and all other adversaries. We love here very well Maresius's writs, all but his bitter flytings with Voetius. We long to hear, that these two very eminent and useful men were better friends. What you sent us of Jesuit Semple is but a preface to his *Dictionarium Mathematicum*, which we pray you search for.

Your Cousin,

ROBERT BAILLIE.

199. *To Mr Spang.* *January* 31. 1661.

Cousin,

I long much now to hear how it goes with you and your family, and what is become of Dr Strang's book; for it is long since I have heard from you. As you desired, and as my custom is, I give you here an account of our affairs since my last long letter; though you possibly know all, yet it is not unfit you should know our sense and conception of them also. We expected this year for great quietness at home, and for trouble abroad; but God, who governs all, has much disappointed both our hopes and fears, making far more confusion at home and quietness abroad, than was expected. When the Portuguese had defeated the Spanish army at Elvas, and Turenne had possessed so many places in the midst of Flanders; the English being master of Dunkirk, and, with their navy on the coast of Spain, scaring the plate-fleet from coming home; the Swedes being ready to swallow up Denmark, and thereafter, with his French and Dutch friends, to fall on the Emperor, a child; the prosperous fight of Ragotsi, of the Venetians, and the Bassa of Aleppo, increasing the tumults in Constantinople: these things

made

made us expect great changes abroad. But before we were
ware the scales turned. France, in the midst of his victo-
ies, stopped; on what 'true motive we cannot dream. His
lliance with his cousin of Spain seemed not so desirable,
he Lady being so far in years beyond the King, and no
great matter for tocher offered, as we can hear. How Pie-
mentilli, who cheated the poor Queen of Sweden out of
her religion, her kingdom, and reputation, should have
got the Cardinal of France so far enchanted as to lay down
arms, when they most prospered, we marvel, and wait for
he end. In the mean time, Spain has got time to breathe;
he riches of his safe-landed fleet, the death of Modena,
he discontent of Savoy for the French refusal of his sister,
after the interview at Lyons; Arch-Duke Sigismund's
readiness to march to Flanders with the Imperial army;
he changes in England drawing our thoughts home for
he time; the Pope's obstinate adherence still to the Spaniard against Portugal; the Queen of Spain's two sons
have put that old languishing King once again on his feet;
your states beating of the Swedish navy; Sweden's repul-
ses from his too furious and unreasonable assaults of Copenhagen; the Imperial, Brandeburg, and Polish army,
falling on Pomerania; the Dutch league of Cologne,
Mentz, and others, making no diversion; France lying
off; the English navy's going home, make the valour of
Sweden to be overpowered, and also doubtful of the e-
vent; for we do not expect any agreement of Denmark
without all his confederates; and that they will never put
Denmark in the poor terms of Roschild's capitulation.
However, the fearful ruining of all Denmark's country,
and the stopping of Sweden in all his designs through the
strong armies leagued against him, seems to be the work
chiefly of your states, on some reasons of their own, more
than yet are visible to the world. We bless God, that less
blood is yet shed in these bounds than we feared. We are
sorry for the ruining of the Prince of Holstein and Cour-
land. The Turks also seem to be in a much better condition; the Persian invasion of Babylon being a mere fable; Bassa of Aleppo and all his party ruined; Ragotsi
put to depend on the Emperor for a subsistence; the Vizir,
by sea, putting in Candia what men he will; the Musco-
vites victory against the Tartars and Cossacks being of no
consequence: so where we expected a quick overturning of
states

ftates and empires in a fhort time, affairs are fo turned a-
bout, that what was fhaking is more firmly eftablifhed.

But with us all contrary: our very firm-like foundations
in a moment overturned. The Protector Oliver endea-
vouring to fettle all in his family, was prevented by death
before he could make a teftament. He had not fupplied
the blank with his fon Richard's name by his hand, and
fcarce with his mouth could he declare that much of his
will. There were no witneffes of it but Secretary Thurloe
and Thomas Goodwin. Some did fearfully flatter him as
much dead as living. Thomas Goodwin, at the faft before his death, in his prayer, is faid to have fpoke fuch
words: " Lord, we pray not for thy fervant's life, for
" we know that is granted ; but to hafte his health, for
" that thy people cannot want." And Mr Sterry in the
chapel after his death, " O Lord, thy late fervant here is
" now at thy right hand, making interceffion for the fins
" of England." Both thefe are now out of favour at
court as court-parafites. But the moft fpoke, and yet
fpeak, very evil of him ; and, as I think, much worfe
than he deferved of them. His burial was large as mag-
nificent as any king of England. Richard immediately
fat down on his chair ; and, after a moft folemn in-
ftalment, got addreffes almoft from all the fhires, cities,
regiments of the armies in England, Scotland, Ireland,
Dunkirk, from the navy, from the miniftry, Prefbyterian and Independent, Anabaptiftick, all ftriving who
fhould be firft and moft promifing. All neighbour-ftates,
of France, Holland, Sweden, Denmark, Brandeburg,
Hamburg, Portugal, congratulating his fucceffion. No
appearance of the fmalleft air of oppofition, till the officers of the army began to petition for a general, and payment of their arrears. For their fatisfaction, a parliament
was fummoned againft the 27th of January. This did
meet frequently. Some fay it was pretty well chofen, of
men who for the moft had good defigns for the publick,
and aimed at a folid fettlement both of church and ftate ;
but among them were men for contrary defigns. The
firft fencing was about the act of recognition: tor albeit,
at the entry in the Houfes, every one took the oath in the
humble petition and advice ; yet when it came to an act of
recognition, many and fharp debates arofe. It was carried to acknowledge Richard for Protector ; but withal,
that the bill could not pafs till the limitations of his power,
the

the full security of the privileges of parliaments, and liberty of the subjects, should pass in the same act. A committee was appointed for that work, and Sir Harry Vane set in the chair. The House of Lords did pass it, but in a poor and slighting way of another House. In the mean time, Opdam, with the Dutch fleet, passed to the Sound. All were alarmed with this; and in a very short time, the Protector, with the consent of all, sent Montague with as great a fleet, to wait upon them. All did expect a present breach betwixt us and you; but since your fleet did nothing but supply Copenhagen with some men and victuals, and did not transport any of the confederate army to raise the siege; the English and Holland instructions have been, not to fight, and so to do but little service to either party all this long summer. Whether you will do so still, when the English are returned, we will shortly see.

The parliament's next work was about pay to the army. This was, and yet is, a business almost inextricable. The land-armies in Scotland, England, Ireland, Flanders, and Jamaica, with the navy, reckoning every frigate of 40 guns to a regiment of foot, could not be within 100,000 men of daily pay; the revenue being all exactly counted, did not amount to L. 1,900,000 Sterling; the necessary charge of the army and state was above 2,200,000; it was no marvel then that the arrears of the army should exceed 2,500,000, and the Protector's debt many hundred thousand pounds also: how all this should be paid without the country's ruin, was the parliament's great care. While they are about this, the officers of the army have their daily meetings in Fleetwood's lodging or Wallingford-house. The Anabaptistick and Republican party had, by many papers, which now are printed, been secretly, for a long time, plying Fleetwood and the officers in conscience, to return to their first principles, to overthrow Oliver's selfish innovations, to abolish the other house, and all government by one, under whatsoever name. The parliament finding these people's addresses take much with the officers, and that such meetings on such high consultations could not stand with their authority, resolved an act for dissolving the meeting of Wallingford-house, and to command all the officers to attend their several charges in the three kingdoms, and to take an oath of obedience to the present parliament. While the

other

other house is advising on that vote, the Protector joins
with it, and accordingly commands the officers to be gone
to their charges. He and the house supposed that they
had so great a part of the army and city for them, that
there was no hazard of any force : but they found themselves quickly mistaken ; for the officers, with all speed,
making a rendezvous at the back of St James's park in the
Pall-Mall, at eleven o'clock at night, before the Protector had provided any thing for opposition, they came
immediately to Whitehall, and made the Protector consent, under the great seal, not to the adjourning, (which
at first would have satisfied), but the dissolution of the parliament. To this most hardly he did consent; but his
uncle Desborough, and brother Fleetwood, drew him to
it with firm promises of the army's readiness still to serve
him. When the officers saw the parliament so easily dissolved, they found themselves not secure, till, contrary to
Fleetwood and Desborough's mind, they made the Protector lay down his place, and took, for a time, the government of all into their own hands. To this also the
Protector did quietly submit, and, from a very great
prince, did descend to a very private and quiet gentleman.
The officers immediately put down the council of state ;
removed all the Protector's confidents out of the army ;
the regiments of the Protector, Ingoldsby, Whally, Goff,
Falconbridge, Howard, and others, were given to Lambert, Overton, and such whom Oliver had outed. The
tower was taken from Barkstead, the great seal from Nat.
Fiennes, and a great change made. But the officers were
quickly weary of the burden of the parliament. After
much advisement, they fell on a very unexpected overture, to sit down with a parliamentary power, so many
of the long parliament that remained not cast out, when
the Protector, in the year 1652, had dissolved them. Of
these they found in the city and about it, about forty ; who,
with Lenthal their speaker, they moved to sit down in
the house, the 6th of May ; who since that time have
ruled as a parliament. At the very first, all the army's
proposals passed in acts of parliament. A council of state of
thirty-one was constituted. All this was done without any
din, except what Mr Prin and some other sharp pam-
phleteers made ; which they misregarded. For the city of
London, and the most of all the regiments in the three nations, sent them congratulatory addresses, so full of good
words

words as ever were made to either of the Cromwells;
whose names by many were then torn in the worst language, pictures, and pamphlets, that could be. Some ftir
was expected from Henry in Ireland, Monk in Scotland,
and some other of the Protector's friends; but all came to
juft nothing.

The new old parliament's firft and chief work was, to
conftitute the army. A committee of nomination was
to nominate every officer in every regiment; the Crowner,
Lieutenant, Major, even Captain, Enfign, &c. All thefe
were appointed to come to the bar of the Houfe, to receive
their new commiffions, and make their oath there to the
parliament. This was a long and fafhious work, and is
not yet ended. Many officers were left out without any
accufation. Nothing of this was the work of the General,
which many took for a flighting of him. The army en-
dured all this as coming from the hands of their trufty
friends. But another work of the parliament ftartled them
more; the eftablifhing of the militia of the counties in fuch
hands as the parliament nominated. Thefe went, if com-
plete, to the number of 20,000 horfe and 80,000 foot,
to be paid by the counties when they were in fervice.
This was a vifible curb to the army's power, and a hazard to their pay; for the country was unable to pay
both: but it feems the country-militia was but for a time.

While thefe things are in doing, there arifes a general
nifcontent among the people every where in England;
which bred a confpiracy in many fhires, to take arms at
everal rendezvoufes the 18th of Auguft. But before the
ft of Auguft all was revealed: Maffey, Titus, and others,
rom the King, were faid to have been for divers months
t work in the city and country to make a party. The
hief ftickling was where leaft expected, in Chefhire and
Lancafhire. Sir George Booth had drawn moft of the
people after him. The report of this flew every where,
nd increafed the number and ftrength of the confpira-
ors hugely above truth; for when it came to the proof,
hey were found inconfiderable. Fleetwood and the mi-
tia of London kept down the city, the rifing whereof
as moft feared. A few old troops, and the new militia
f the fhires, prevented, and eafily fuppreffed, the rendez-
oufes in Kent, Hertfordfhire, Gloucefterfhire, Notting-
am, Darby, Leicefter, Shropfhire, and other places.
Lambert, with 4000 or 5000 horfe and foot, making a

2   quick

quick march northward, met with Sir George Booth at a bridge some miles from Chester: his 10,000 horse were become 2000 horse and foot. The dispute was nought, scarce half an hour. Sir George had not 30 killed, and Lambert hardly one. Chester, Manchester, Preston, Liverpool, rendered on the first summons; Sir George, fleeing towards London in womens apparel, was taken at Newport Pagnel, the Earl of Darby in Shrewsbury. In a very few days all was composed without blood. Sir George Booth's confessions, they say, are so liberal, that many talk he has been but an emissary of purpose to discover who were disaffected to the parliament, to have them crushed; but others, who know the gravity of the gentleman, and consider his declaration, do not believe this, nor his rumoured confessions. At the first, many of the Presbyterian ministers in the city and country were said to be on this plot; but this likewise appears now to be a vain report. Ere long, doubtless, we will hear of all the bottom of the business; for the time we know no more but what the Diurnal tells us.

So soon as this was over, the army was careful to cause the parliament dissolve, and pay off the county-militia, that it might not stand when there was more use for it than to be a visible curb to them. Yet the people's general miscontentment remains: for though the decay of trade has increased the poverty of the country, yet the necessities of the army and navy increase the taxations very much, nor is yet any government established. The parliament and army agree against all monarchy, whether of Kings or Protectors, and against a House of Lords; but what form of republick to settle, this they differ on. Some are for the perseverance, if not the perpetuity, of this part of the old parliament that now sits; others for a new parliament of Commons, chosen according to the qualifications which this parliament shall agree upon; others for a parliament of 2000 or 3000 of the people, with a co-ordinate power of a senate, to be a check to the people's extravagancies. What of these shall be determined, we expect to hear. Some think that difference in the parliament not like to be agreed. Prevalence of the Quakers and Fifth-monarchy men so far, that they have obtained James Naylor, that monstrous blasphemer, out of prison; and have moved some wise Presbyterians, Independents, and more sober Anabaptists, to syncretism against their

anger, will force the army once more to raise the parliament, and fupplicate Lambert, a very wife, ftout, active,
fober gentleman, to take the government upon him: but
that the end of all will be, we refer it to God.

Scotland's condition for the time is not good: exhaufted in money; dead in trade; the taxes near doubled;
fince the 6th of May without all law, nor appearance of
any in hafte. My Lord Warifton was called to the Houfe
of Peers by the laft Protector. When the parliament was
diffolved, his old friend Sir Henry Vane got him in the
council of ftate, and the moft ordinary chairman thereof.
All the weight of Scots affairs lies on him alone. Argyle, although he went thither a commiffioner from A-
berdeenfhire, and fat in the Houfe of Commons, complying with the Protector fo long as he ftood, and with
the new parliament fo much as any defired; yet was mif-
regarded, and, for fear of arreftment for debt, flipped a-
way home with fmall credit or contentment. The reft of
the Scots commiffioners, Swinton, Garfland, Major Barclay, Earl of Linlithgow, Earl of Tweeddale, &c. comply
as they pleafed, fignified little thing; but Warifton was
ill. He was made to believe, that our union would be a
fhort bufinefs; and that it was better to want law than to
have it before the union: but that conceit has made us to
want the fummer feffion, and may be the winter alfo; for
the debates of the union grew fo long, that they fay it is
laid afide till they have once agreed on the government of
England, to which we are to be united. No man pays
any debt but of his own accord. That which much retarded our union, was a petition from many hands in our
country, put on by Garfland, young Dundafs, our Quakers, and many others, for a full toleration to be infert-
ed in the act of our union. This was fo well backed by
fome of the officers of the army, that till it be fatisfied
nothing can be got done, though Warifton do his uttermoft againft it.

Upon fufpicion that fome in Scotland might be on the
Englifh plot, the General called all who had been in
arms, and were under bonds, to take a new oath, of renouncing the Stuarts, and adhering to the prefent government. Who refufed, were laid up in prifons; Montrofe,
Callender, Lorn, Selkirk, Kenmure, Didup, Loudon,
David Lefly, Sir James Lumfden, and others. Some took
it, as Glencairn, and, as they fay, Rothes, Montgomery,
                                                      &c.

&c. But it is thought there was no Scots flesh on this design, whether because not trusted, or not desired by the English, who would do it all their alone, is not known; but, however, it is thought none of our nation were upon it. What was talked of Kinnoul and General-Major Montgomery landing in our highlands, was found a mere fable. Our people are so ill bit, and so exceedingly low, that though there were no garrisons to hold them down, they have neither mind nor ability to make any noise.

Our church lies as it was, full of grief for inward divisions, and outward hazards. As yet the English trouble us not: and truly they have no cause; for whatever be our thoughts, yet in all expressions we are as quiet and peaceable as they could wish. Being afraid for Wariston's incessant designs, the brethren of Edinburgh moved Mr Sharp to go up again to attend his motions. The Protector Richard took very well with him, and sundry members of parliament; but when these were put down, Wariston deferred him to the council, as corresponding with Massey and Titus. Being upon this called to the council, Sir Henry Vane and Mr Scot were sent out to confer with him; to whom he gave abundant satisfaction; and a little after was sent home in peace.

Our town has been in more peace than formerly. Mr Gillespie's four months absence, want of publick judicatories has helped to it; but no good-will in some is inlacking to keep in the fire. The last trick they have fallen on to usurp the magistracy, is, by the diligence of their sessioners to make factions in every craft, to get the deacons and deacon-conveener created of their side: and herein they have much prevailed; but with such strife as sometimes it has come to strokes. But this Lent way does not satisfy. It is feared, by Wariston's deligence, some orders shall be procured by Mr Gillespie, to have all the magistrates and council chosen as he will. These in place have guided the town so moderately and wisely, that none are expected to do it better: notwithstanding of their huge charge to defend themselves against Mr Gillespie's pleas, they have still kept the town free of all taxes, when all our other boroughs are wracked with them. They have built a fair meal-market, which has been near 3000 merks; a fair bridge at Colin's port, which will be above 1000 merks; a very fair merchant-hospital near the bridge, which will be a great sum; and is most done by contribution.

—— My

—— My Lord Belhaven, without any example I ever eard of in Scotland, with his lady a very witty woman's dvice, feigned death, and for seven years was taken by ll for dead, yet now appears again safe and found in his wn house. He was much engaged for Duke Hamilton : earing the creditors might fall on his person and estate, nd knowing, if he were reputed dead, his wife, by conunct fee, and other wife, would keep his estate, he went, /ith his brother and two servants, towards England. These returned, affirming, that in Solway fands my Lord /as carried down by the river, and they could not recue him. His horse and hat they got, but when all earch was made, his body could not be found. His lady nd friends make great dool for him, and none controerts his death. In the mean time he goes beyond Lonon, and farms a piece of ground, and lives very privatey there. He had but one boy, a very hopeful youth and retty scholar ; he is struck with a fever, as his mother aid, but as others, with a fall from his horse, whereof n a few days he dies. In this real death, by God's hand, /ho will not be mocked, the hope of that house perished. So soon as the Duke's debts were satisfied by selling his wn lands, the secret journeys of my Lord to his own louse were spied, and so much talked of, that he now at aft appears in publick, for his great disrepute ; and though le disposes of his estate to his good-son Silverton after lis death, yet many think both their estates will go.

Thus far I had written with my former long letter nuch of a year ago ; but it lay beside me, that I might fee ome settling of these extraordinary and happy changes, /hich the hand of God, above all human hope or reaon, has wrought its alone. After Sir George Booth's lefeat, all did almost despair of human help from our vils. I hear sweet Balcarras at the Hague died of grief or that calamity. His body his lady brought home, and aufed bury honourably at his parish-church. Without loubt that was one of the most brave and able gentlemen >f our nation, if not the most able.

It was the parliament's work, especially Vane, Haslerig, and Scot, to search out all the accomplices of Sir George Booth ; and doubtless, if God had not, in answer o the prayers of the choice ministers and people of Lanashire, given them somewhat else to do, they had made nuch execution of many good and honest men. But behold,

hold, while they are running to fuck all this blood and spoil, the Lord casts another bone in their teeth. The officers who had defeated Sir George, lifted up with that deserving, expected from the parliament all they could desire. With this confidence they approach the city. Many of them subscribe a petition, to get all the general officers established; and when this did not relish well in the house, (for Haslerig and Vane were very jealous of Lambert), they press it harder: whereupon the house, trusting to the late oaths of obedience from all the officers, makes bold to cashier Lambert, Ashfield, Cobbet, and divers others. Upon this affront, the officers went to the house, and with threats dissolved them. In this new confusion, all was put to a stand, not knowing what to do. A judicial blindness fell among them. All were malecontent, and raised in mind, to expect and desire a change; but none durst venture on any more action.

Our noblemen, very secretly, most by the mediation of my Lady Wemys, a witty active woman, whose daughter Buccleugh was in Monk's custody at Dalkeith, did oft solicit him to attempt for the King; but doubts and fears still kept him off: yet when Haslerig and others had importuned him from England to assist the parliament against the violence of Lambert and his party, he called the most of the army to draw near to Edinburgh. He sent for commissioners from every one of our shires, and desired them to advance six months maintenance. Though this in our deep poverty was to us almost unfeasible, yet on good hopes it was chearfully and quickly done. He had of his own above L. 50,000 Sterling, which helped him to give good satisfaction to his soldiers, while the army in England was put to live on free quarters, all the shires refusing to pay any more money till a free parliament did command it. There went a strong remonstrance amongst the most of the shires, against an arbitrary sword-government, and all taxes till a free parliament; but to sugar it, there were two clauses put in, one against the Stuarts and all monarchy, another for full liberty of conscience to all sectaries. This encouraged Monk to declare to the officers of the army at London his desires of a free parliament. This did much startle them; and when many papers passed among them, and Monk continued resolute to march into England for that end, Fleetwood sent down to him M. Caryl, Col. Whally, Goff, and his brother-in-law Dr Clarges. These wrought him

to

to a treaty, for which he sent three of his officers to London, Cloberry, Wilkes, and Knight. These were so laboured on by their friends, that they made an accord, and subscribed it. But Monk being more and more encouraged both from Scotland and England, and having purged his army from Cobbet, Young, Sorrie, Holms, and many Anabaptists, filling their places with a number of Scottish old soldiers, he refused that accord, as done contrary to his instructions. Finding him grow in strength and resolution, they sent to the north Lambert with 5000 of their best horse, and some 3000 or 4000 foot, with which he came to Newcastle on free quarter. Monk came to Berwick in the midst of December, and lay on the fields in a very cold winter near Coldstream, with 6000 or 7000 good foot, and within 2000 horse. Many of our noblemen came to him at Berwick, and offered to raise quickly for his service all the power of Scotland ; but the most of his officers refused it, fearing the stumbling of their army and friends in England ; for as yet all of them, in their right-well penned papers, did declare as positively as ever, with divine attestations, against all kings and monarchy, and for a free parliament, and all former principles. Lambert was the far strongest, and easily might have cut in pieces all Monk's party, and made havock in our poor land, as they say it was their purpose, designing the chief of the nobles and ministers for the scaffold, and many ministers for Jamaica, whereof I heard myself was one ; but blessed be the Lord who kept us from their bloody teeth. Monk resolved to keep his ground at Coldstream, and if he was beat, to retire to Stirling, and take our help. Our nobles, by his allowance, but without all engagement, sent Major Bunten to Breda, where the King was, with his sister, in a very hard condition. He had gone to Bayonne, conferred with the Cardinal and Du Haro, to get his interest considered in the treaty. He got from both courteous words ; but, in effect, was by both neglected. Coming back with a perplexed heart, with his brother York, through France and Flanders, to his sister at Breda, scarce tolerated by the States-General's connivance, to abide in the Prince of Orange's bounds, he is much refreshed by what he heard from Scotland. About the same time Broghill and Sir Charles Cutts send Sir Arthur Forbes to him from Ireland, and some from England make him hopeful of

Lambert.

Lambert. This puts him to an uncertainty to what party first he fhould apply himfelf. Hyde inclined moft to Lambert. Lauderdale's letters, and thofe from Scotland, advifed to truft Monk or Scotland. However, Ormond inclined to accept the Irifh offers. All the meffengers he difmiffed kindly, with good anfwers. But in the mean time Col. Wotham invited Haflerig, and fome of the militia of the late parliament, to Portfmouth, where he commanded. Here, incontinent, forces are gathered, fome 4000 or 5000 men, who march directly to London. The people favoured them rather than their oppofites. But Fleetwood with his forces in the city, and Defborough with his cannon from the tower, held the city at under. Yet fo foon as Haflerig came near with his forces, reported to be far above the truth, both Fleetwood and Defborough retired, and Haflerig entered; who incontinent fat down in the laft parliament, fent letters to Monk to hafte up, and emitted an act of indemnity to all who fubmitted. Lambert was not any longer able to keep his people in order, fo retired fpeedily towards London, and, with Fleetwood and the reft, accepted the act of indemnity, and retired to their houfes.

On the 1ft of January 1660, Monk marched orderly, and at leifure, to London. Where-ever he came, he was received as an angel; bells and bonfires welcomed him. All declared their earneft defire of a free parliament, and gave him great encouragement to procure it. He was civil to all, but referved himfelf to fee farther. Mr Douglas and Mr Sharp had been free with him in Scotland. On his letter, Mr Sharp followed him, and overtook him. So foon as he reached London, he was to him the moft wife, faithful, and happy counfellor he had; and if it had not been for God's affiftance to Mr Sharp, Monk was divers times on the point of being circumvened, or of himfelf to have yielded to deftructive counfels. The parliament fent two, and the city three, to meet him at Nottingham with many fair words, and great honours; but joined three with him in commiffion to curb his power. They had put Vane, Whitlock, and others, out of the Houfe; they were fecure of Fleetwood, Lambert, and the reft of the army: their only fear was Monk. They defired he fhould not bring his army to the city: he quartered about it; but himfelf came to the Houfe, and got many good words, and gave as many. Sundry fhires petitioned

titioned for a new free parliament. Several of the petitioners were laid up for this. Monk at all this was silent and ambiguous. There had fat long in the city, very secretly, a committee of two from every shire, and four of the city, advising how to caft off the yoke of flavery. When they found the rump of the long parliament, also the petition of 250 members, unjuftly by Cromwell caft out, to be re-admitted; and all that could be obtained from Haflerig, who then ruled all, was to fupply the House againft fuch a day with members of many qualifications, which they made, and whereof they would be judges, chiefly that all fhould fwear againft the Stuarts, and all government by one. The people, almoft defperate, met in common council, and voted no more addreffes, nor more payment, ill a new free parliament did fit. Herewith the House is enraged, and vote the uncitying of London, a-cafting down of all their gates, pofts, and chains; for walls they had none fince Cromwell pulled down their lines of communication. The common council was abolifhed, and a new one appointed to be chofen. Monk was commanded o fee thefe votes executed, and fo become moft odious to he people, that the more eafily they might deftroy both. Monk was in a very hard taking, yet obeyed; and the people permitted him patiently to do all he pleafed. The gates and pofts are pulled down, the common council is hanged; but behold a prefent change. The fool Haflerig had wiped the city and Monk's nofe to the blood. Monk, by conference with the fecluded members, Pref-byterian minifters, and chief citizens, is encouraged to write a fharp letter to the parliament, of his refentment of heir feverity to the city, and dallying with Fleetwood, Lambert, Vane, Ludlow, and others, though declared a-ainft; farther, of his own engagement to the city, that within five days they fhould iffue letters for calling a new ree parliament againft the 25th of April.

In the mean time, Haflerig, Scot, and others, fent ma-y meffages to him; and near had gained him to come out f the city, and lie at Whitehall. But Mr Sharp's night-abours here were happy. On the 20th of February, Monk went to the House, and fet down the fecluded mem-ers. At this the city and country's joy was inexpreffi-le; bells and bonfires every where; Monk made Cap-ain-General of all forces by fea and land of the three ingdoms, and General-Major of the city-militia; Hafle-

2   rig.

rig, Secretary Scot, and others of the rump, sneaked a-
way to the country; Lambert and Overton were put in
the Tower; a council of state of thirty-two, Lewis, Hollis, Crew, Knighton, Pierpoint, and such; the covenant
appointed to be hung up in the House, also in every
church, and to be read once solemnly every year; Sir
George Booth and all his party were let free; also Lauderdale, Crawford, and all of ours, were freed of their
long prisons. Commissioners from our shires, Glencairn,
Durie, Carden, William Thompson, with Monk's good
allowance, came to London. Frequent private messengers
went to the King. He, from Breda, sent over Sir John
Greenville and Dr Morley, with a very gracious message to
both Houses, to the City, and to the General, which satisfied
all. An order of parliament was given to proclaim the
King May 8. which was done over all England most solemnly. A committee of six Lords, twelve Commons,
three Aldermen, nine Common-Counsellors, with sundry
city-ministers, Calamy, Manton, Reynolds, &c. sent to
Breda to haste the King home; 50,000 pounds Sterling
sent him in money, 10,000 in gold; to his brother, York,
10,000 in money, one in gold; to Gloucester five in money, one in gold. Landing at Dover, he stayed Sunday
in Canterbury, Monday in Rochester; Tuesday, May 29.
his birth-day, came to the city, with the most solemn shew
and heartiest joy, that, I think, was ever in England. At
Whitehall, Manchester and Grimeston, the Speakers of
the two Houses did welcome him in more cordial than e-
loquent speeches. He had from Breda given full security,
on his word, to men of all professions, to live in peace;
for satisfaction to the soldiers of their arrears; for keeping them in possession of the crown and church lands till
they were satisfied; for pardoning of all bygones, except a
few, whom the parliament might except, for their eminent hand in his father's murder. The first morning he
came to Whitehall, he issued a proclamation against profanity, swearing, and healths. Thanksgiving to God for
this his own work, with bells and bonfires, went quickly
through all the three kingdoms. Monk was made Baron,
Earl, and Duke of Albemarle, Master of the Horse, one
of the Privy Council, General of all the forces under the
King; Ormond, Steward of the House; Manchester,
Chamberlain; Lauderdale, a Gentleman of the Bedcham-
ber; Hyde, Chancellor; Nicholas and Culpepper, Secre-

aries; Reynolds, Calamy, Manton, Baxter, chaplains; the country-militia put in hands confident; the King, Duke of York, Ormond, the moft of the courtiers, made Colonels of the ftanding regiments, the Colonels willingly ceding to be Lieutenants. But quickly the parliament fell on a better way, with all poffible fpeed to difband all forces by fea and land. For this end, befide the maintenance and excife, a poll-money was appointed to defray arrears; great fums came in, and a chearful enough difbanding was made; fo that before this, except a few garrifons, and a very few horfe and foot, are all peaceably difbanded in the three kingdoms: a mighty unexpected work.

The King, in wifdom, moderation, piety, and grave carriage, giving huge fatisfaction to all; the parliament reftored him the power of the militia, his negative voice, the determination of all ecclefiaftick differences, and whatever he could have wifhed; took a courfe for buying back his revenues, and much augmented them. He endeavoured carefully to relieve all that had been fufferers for him or his father. He preffed the Houfes to hafte the bill of indemnity. They excepted a very few from it; fcarce a dozen executed: in which the people had much more fatisfaction than he; for he would have been induced to have pardoned all; but it was the juftice of God that brought Peters, Harrifon, and others, to a fhameful death; to hang up the bones of Oliver, Bradfhaw, Ireton, Pride, on the gibbet at Tyburn; to difgrace the two Goodwins, blind Milton, Owen, Sterry, Lockiers, and others of that maleficent crew.

The moft of our nobles, with very many of our gentry, run up to Whitehall. All were made welcome. Old places were reftored to Crawford, Caffils, and others. No wonder the Chancellor and Secretary's places were taken from Loudon and Lothian, and given to Glencairn and Lauderdale; yet with recompence enough to them both, whom fome thought deferved little. Loudon had his penfion of L. 1000, and gift of annuities continued. Lothian got his fecond fon director of the chancery, which Sir John Scot was thought not to deferve. Montrofe's Marquifate was confirmed; the cuftoms of Glafgow given to him till he was paid of a great fum; Argyle is ordained to refund him a great fum. Selkirk made Duke Hamilton, and out of the cuftoms of Leith L. 20,000 Sterling affigned. Marfhal got L. 10,000 Sterling out of the cuftoms of Aberdeen.

Aberdeen, Didup, Earl of Dundee, a sum out of the customs of Dundee. The King gave among them all he had in Scotland, and much more. For judicatories, he appointed the committees of estates of the year 1650 to sit down, and the parliament December 12. For a Commissioner, by our nobles consent, lest strife should be for it, the Lord Middleton, Earl of Fettercairn, was nominated; who was not very acceptable to many; especially not keeping the day of the parliament, but causing it to be adjourned to January: yet when he is come down, his wisdom, sobriety, and moderation, has been such, as makes him better beloved and reputed for that great charge, as fit as any other we could have got. So far it went every where, to the great joy of all.

But as nothing is perfectly blessed on earth, some water was quickly poured in the wine of many; I am sure in mine, as I expressed it in a sharp and free letter to Lauderdale. Bishops and liturgies were every where set up in England and Ireland without contradiction; our league and covenant, by a number of printed pamphlets, was torn to pieces. This was the more grievous, that at the beginning it appeared most easy to have been remedied. His gracious Majesty was ready to have been advised by his parliament; the leading men there were avowed covenanters and Presbyterians; Lauderdale and Mr Sharp, both at Breda and London, had very much of the King's ear; Monk was for us in that at the beginning firm enough; the Queen and her party was on our side; the Episcopal men were sundry of them as evil as before; Bramhill, Wren, Heylin, Thorndyke, Cossings, Sydserf, Hammond, Pierce, none of the best or most orthodox; Juxon and Duppa smallily learned; Sheldon, Morley, able indeed, and very wise men; but the overturning of all the reformation of England, without a contrary petition, to me was strange, and very grievous, and I suspect we know not yet the bottom of that mystery. I with all our friends, Scots and English, have been honest and faithful. Sure they have not been so prudent and industrious as, I think, they should have been. However, as this was the original of all our late troubles, I think it will not fail in time to procure new commotions, if petitions and remonstrances do not prevent them.

It is like the general joy for the King's happy return, and the general abhorrence of our late confusions and miseries,

eries, together with fear left any juftling, even by peti-
ions, might give occafion to thefe who were watching for
t to make fome new commotions, made our friends eafy
o be prevailed with not to oppofe the King's defires; efpecially the King promifing, by conference with the chief
Prefbyterians and Epifcopals, to do his endeavours for
their agreement; as indeed he laboured much in this, and,
oy his declaration, drew both fome nearer than they were;
out for little fatisfaction of either of the parties: the Epifcopals, not having all they were wont, were difcontent: the
Prefbyterians found the other had got too much, and more
than in confcience they could ever affent to; yet, for love
o the King, they were filent, when all the bifhops were
folemnly inftalled, and the liturgy every where reftored,
clean contrary to our covenant, and acts of the Englifh
parliament fince 1641. Chancellor Hyde was thought the
great actor in this Epifcopal bufinefs, while a few hours
treaty, or but a petition from the Houfes, General, and
city, fent with the commiffioners to Breda, might eafily
have freed us, for the great good of them, and of all thefe
vexations.

It was a huge grief alfo to us, and more to the King,
that the Lord was pleafed to remove that moft excellent,
and exceeding hopeful Prince, the Duke of Gloucefter, in
a few day's ficknefs, of the meafles or fmall pox; and
what came on the back of it, the noife of the Duke of
York's clandeftine marriage with the Chancellor's daugh-
er, was to the King and his loving people a very great
grief; efpecially that third heavieft ftroke following, the
death of that moft excellent Princefs, and exceedingly be-
oved both of the King and all his fubjects. I wifh what
fome fpeak of her clandeftine marriage with Harry Jer-
nyn's brother's fon may be found to be a falfe lie. However, thefe moft fad accidents did temper our exceeding
great and juft joy. Alfo there were fome fears of the fec-
arian party's plots; but, bleffed be God, they are come
o nought. That bloody mad fpirit of Munfter lodges in
many of them. The Chancellor's fpeech clofing the par-
iament, fhews their defign, on the 25th of December, to
have fired the city, feized on Whitehall, the King, York,
Albemarle, and others. Overton, Ludlow, Whyte, and
many, are taken for this: yet many did not believe it. But
fomething of it did actually appear fince; for while the
King is convoying his mother to Portfmouth, fome of
                                                    thefe

thefe fanaticks did rife two divers times in the night; but
were eafily, by the mayor of the city alone, fuppreffed,
without any confiderable bloodfhed, bleffed be God; for
fure it is, that party is yet too ftrong, but likely their own
madnefs will fhortly annihilate them.

· The Bifhop of London baptized Charles the Duke of
Cambridge at Worcefter houfe; the Lady Ormond was
godmother. The Queen entertained that night the Duchefs
of York at her table, and to-morrow the King entertained
her and her hufband, his brother, at his table. The
Queen went immediately with her daughter towards France,
to agent her marriage with Monfieur Duke of Anjou; albeit fome think difcontent at her fon's marriage did further her journey.

· For us in Scotland, thus things have went among us.
After Monk's march, fome ftickling there was in the weft
to have had meetings in fhires for new commiffioners.
They liked not Glencairn's employment. They fpake of
Lauderdale and Crawford; but their defign was, Lockhart
and the remonftrator's intereft. My Lord Lee, Sir John
Cheefly, Sir George Maxwell, my Lord Stair, Mr Gillefpie, and others, were faid to be the contrivers. They
laboured to have had Selkirk and Caffils with them; but
this was foon crufhed by Monk and Morgan; for they
were informed of their inclination to Lambert more than
to them. When the committee of our eftates, to our
great joy, had fat down in our parliament-houfe to prepare matters for our parliament, Mr James Guthrie having met before at Edinburgh, and elfewhere, with divers
of his party, did tryft it fo, as he and they met in Robert
Simpfon's houfe, the next door almoft to the meeting of
eftates, and did draw up a petition to the King, making
many profeffions of their joy for his return, but withal
remembering him of his covenant to fupprefs bifhops and
ceremonies in England, and to beware to put the government of Scotland into the hands of malignants. They alfo write letters to Mr P. Gillefpie, and the chief of their
party in the weft, to meet them at Glafgow the next week,
with fo many as they could bring with them. The committee hearing of this, immediately fent fome of their
number to them, feized on their papers, brought them before their court. They were forry, at their firft downfitting, to have to do with minifters; but Mr Guthrie's reftlefs and proud infolence, irritated, efpecially when all
their

their number, Meff. Robert Traill, Jo. Stirling, Alexander Moncrieff, John Semple, John Murray, Gilbert Hall, and fundry others, abfolutely refufed to acknowledge any fault. Surely they had no warrant to meet, being no kirk-judicatory, and their ill band of remonftrance could give them no privilege in a body to admonifh the King, how to govern England, and tax him for making malignants members of judicatories. Upon their obftinacy, all were fent to the caftle at once. Mr Thomas Ramfay went ftark mad. He was always but a weak foolifh thing. Sundry of them fell fick, and were fent to their own houfes, as at laft all were fent to their lodgings in Edinburgh. Mr James Guthrie was confined to the tolbooth of Dundee, and Mr Gillefpie to the caftle of Stirling; Mr James Simpfon to the tolbooth of Edinburgh; as alfo Mr John Dickfon, minifter of Rutherglen, for many odious fpeeches in pulpit againft the ftatefmen. Mr James Naefmith alfo, for fpeeches in pulpit, was confined to his chamber in Edinburgh. But, above all, Mr Rutherford was difgraced; his book, *Lex Rex*, burnt by the hand of the hangman at the crofs of Edinburgh and St Andrew's; himfelf confined to his chamber, his ftipend fequeftrated, and himfelf cited before the parliament. Mr Andrew Cant preaching againft Mr Rutherford's hard ufage, was accufed before the magiftrates of treafon. He demitted his miniftry, and came to his fon at Liberton, where both live very quietly. The Commiffioner ufed the old man very courteoufly, and likely will protect him from trouble. Sir James Stewart and Sir John Cheefly were fent prifoners to the caftle, where yet they abide. Wariston fled; whereupon he was declared fugitive, and all his places void. His poor lady could not obtain to him a pafs from the King to live in banifhment; fo he lurks daily in fear of his life. Argyle, by his fon Lorn's letter, being advertifed that the King took kindly with all men, ventured to go to London: but in the chamber of prefence, before he faw the King, a warrant under the King's hand meets him to be carried to the Tower clofe prifoner: yet when his Lady came up, fhe got free accefs to him; but could not obtain to him a hearing before the King. Swinton, who, either by a ftrong hypocrify or temptation, had turned Quaker, was taken at London, and fent to Newgate. Argyle and he were fent to the parliament by fea in one fhip, by a great guard of citizens. Both were carried on foot, and

Swinton

Swinton discovered, through all the streets of Edinburgh, Argyle to the castle, and Swinton to the tolbooth, close prisoners. Capt. Govan was cast in the tolbooth for a long time in irons; Jaffray of Aberdeen, Osborn the Quaker, were likewise put in the tolbooth; the chief of the remonstrants were cited, and were made to subscribe their renouncing the remonstrance, and appearing before the parliament, and something else whereat they stumbled at the beginning; but at once Greenhead, Sir George Maxwell, Mr John Harper, and others, subscribed all. Our folks, Mr John Graham, Mr John Spreul, lay long in the tolbooth of Edinburgh for refusing; but at last they, John Johnston, and Thomas Paterson, subscribed it. James Porter, our Catholick clerk, was confined to his house, and referred to our magistrates, to be disposed on as they pleased. That whole party was clear run down, to the contentment of the most; for they have been ill instruments of irreconcileable division for twelve years, both in kirk and kingdom. For myself, I rejoiced not at the hurt of any of them; but wished all of them might have been spared, on their good behaviour in time to come, which now is like will be easily obtained, though before it was desperate. The pity and favour of many is turning towards them, by the insolent behaviour of some, who are suspected may make a new party among us. Our state is very averse to hear of our league and covenant. Many of our people are hankering after bishops, having forgot the evil they have done, and the nature of their office. An exceeding great profanity, and contempt both of the ministry and religion itself, is every where prevalent. A young fry of ministers in Lothian, Fife, and elsewhere, look as if they intended some change, without any fear or reverence to the older ministers, who lately put them in their places. The wisest and best are yet quiet till they see whither these things will go.

The goodness of the King himself is the only hope we have to get any thing to go right. For our private matters in the college, this twelvemonth we have been at peace, our unrest [Mr P. Gillespie] being quieted. He sent his wife to London, to offer all service to the King, as Sinclare said to Glencairn, and he to Mr Sharp, who wrote it to Mr Douglas: he offered to do his endeavours for Episcopacy, though this he denies. However, she got no access nor countenance, only occasioned the King to remember me,

and

and name me to his place. Lauderdale wrote to me, that it stuck only at a form of presentation, which he desired Mr James Sharp, when he came home, to send up to him. The interveening of other things makes it stick yet there; for myself, I never moved in it, directly nor indirectly, nor purpose to do. Ten years ago I might have had it with the liking of all who had interest; but I settled it upon good Mr Robert Ramsay, by an act of the general assembly. Since his death, Mr Gillespie intruded himself by the English power. At his coming we were large L. 1000 Sterling to the fore; this day we will be as much in debt, and a number of confused businesses in our hands, which few who know will be very willing to undertake: yet, on the report of my refusal, sundry are busy seeking it by their friends, far and near. Many of my friends deal with me to take it. I have promised, when the presentation comes, to advise before I can either accept or refuse.

I have now my piece ready for the press. Because it is in Latin, and long, I will not get it printed here. I debate sundry questions, modestly, but roundly, with Dr Walton, and sundry of the chief Episcopal men; so I despair to get it printed at London. Most of my matter is new and pleasant. I have sent you the *summa*, to be communicated to whom you will. I hope you may get it printed there freely. If you advise, I shall send the book with the next. Keep these sheets clean; for they must be put in the book, either in the beginning or end.—— Ragotsi's calamity has grieved us sore. That gallant brave prince should not have been left to the Turkish fury. I fear his states shall turn Turkish or Austrian. Still we marvel what Mazarine can mean by his Spanish peace, when West Flanders, Catalonia, and Milan, were likelier to have been conquered by the French than these many years. Conde is brought home to France. Portugal is totally deserted. What can the end of this be? The people are nothing eased of their taxes; the clergy complain as much of their oppression. The Prince of Orange, too well deserving of the house of France, spoiled in his minority, by treachery, of his patrimony. The Venetians not assisted either by France or Spain with any conderable help more in their peace than war; but the Venetians put in a worse case after their help than before. However guide as they will, blessed be God for the peace

2   of

of the churches abroad, and the happy restoration of our
King, when all the world absolutely, and at home also,
well near had deserted him.   At last I break off.
     Your Cousin,
                              ROBERT BAILLIE.
     January 31. 1661.

               200. For Mr Spang.

   Cousin,
   I hope ere now you have received my book, and that
ere long I shall have your sense of the printing of it.
Since my last long letter, thus our affairs went, so far as
I understand and remember.   The Commissioner was met
at Musselburgh with 1000 horse.   The parliament sat
down at the beginning of January on the Tuesday.   It
rode in a very magnifick way : few of the nobles were absent.   The Chancellor had so guided it, that the shires
and boroughs should chuse none but these that were absolutely for the King.   Divers were cited to the parliament,
that they might not be members.   The parliament's pulse
was quickly felt : for when Cassils moved, that the election
of a President should be by vote of parliament, the Commissioner obtained, that the Chancellor should preside by
virtue of his office, as before it wont to be.   The oath of
allegiance was appointed next to be taken by all the members.   There was inserted in the midst of it, the main
clause of the oath of supremacy : " That the King was su-
" preme governor over all persons in all causes."   About
this sundry did scruple ; yet when the Commissioner and
Chancellor declared, that they intended thereby no eccle-
fiastick power to the King in word, sacraments, or discipline, but a supreme civil power to put churchmen in all
things to their duty ; all were satisfied, and took it in that
sense : only Cassils and Kilburnie refused, because they
could not obtain that sense to be expressed in writ.
Therefore it was appointed, that all members of parliament,
all officers of state, lords of session, and others in shires
and boroughs should take it.   The ministers of Edinburgh desired a word to be added, which would have satisfied all, " Civil supreme governer ;" and without that word
Civil they seemed peremptor to refuse it.   At this I was
very sorry : for I feared it should occasion trouble, and a
     VOL. II.   3 L   new

ew fchifm, without great caufe, as I wrote to them when he act of parliament came out, of putting all intrants in he miniftry to it; and, as I hear, they will put all maters of colleges to it. For myfelf, I took the oath of alegiance and fupremacy thirty-four years ago, when I enered regent, and yet never fcrupled it. My Lord Caffils, vithout doubt the truly beft man of our nobility, and s loyal as any, for this fcruple is as good as removed rom parliament: and though he be fince at London, and has avour and countenance enough of the King, as well ne deferves; yet it is like to put him from the exercife of ll his places, of Juftice-General, Lord of Council, Seffion, ınd Exchequer. The fhire of Ayr had elected Sir James Dalrymple of Stair with the laird of Blair, the Chancelor's brother-in-law; but their fcrupulofity being feared, ı new election was made of Kilburnie and Haflehead. Kilburnie following Caffils's vote, appeared no more in parliament.

Their next work was about the prerogative. With very little or no difficulty, all was given to the King he defired; fole power of peace and war; of militia by fea and and; of calling and raifing of parliaments, and all things elfe was in queftion, which lately were called the liberies of the nation, and privileges of parliament. At firft t was only fpoken to annul the parliament 1649, which had annulled that of 1648, and had fent for the King on ın unreafonable treaty. This paffed eafily. But at once :he defign appeared of annulling all the former parliaments fince 1633, which had given any civil fanction to :he general affembly of Glafgow 1638, or any after affembly, which ratified our folemn league and covenant or :hurch-goverment, and all we had been doing thefe years bygone. This caufed a great noife and grief over the whole land; fo that for a while the motion was retired, ınd all fuch intention denied: but when things were better prepared, it was openly preffed, and carried, fcarce forty appearing in the contrary. While the prefbytery of Edinburgh, fynods of Lothian, Fife, Glafgow, and others, were preparing petitions againft this, they were fore threatened, and that of Fife raifed by Rothes, that of Lothian by Callender, Dumfries by Annandale, &c. When, by our own privy ways, we had got the King informed of all this, we were once in good hopes of a remedy; but yet that appears not. Lauderdale, in whom we we trufted, being overpowered and diverted by the great-er court of Chancellor Hyde, and the great zeal that fun-dry here have to his fervice. However, we are filled with grief and fear of troubling both the inward and out-ward peace of our church. His Majefty's letter to the prefbytery of Edinburgh, confirmed our hopes that no change fhould be made in our church; but feeing what is paft fince, we know not now what to fay, who defire moft gladly to get any true ground of apologifing for all the King and ftate's actions. Some fpeak of a dangerous improvidence in thefe acts, as if all poffibility of any fo-lid agreement betwixt the King and his fubjects were thereby taken away, if any difcord, which God forbid, fhould ever again fall out : for what fecurity is left to the King to give to his people, when treaties confirmed by King and parliament, in all due forms, are not binding, but fo eafily reverfed on the alledgeances of fears, temp-tations, inconveniencies, and the like, which will never be wanting ?

The moft of the parliament's work was on delinquents proceffes. The great one was Argyle. Many hearings had he on his long libel. His defences were very preg-nant. The Advocate was fometimes uncivilly tart to him ; the Commiffioner alfo fharp enough. Sir John Gilmour in many things reafoned for him. There was no inlack of full hearing, and debates to the uttermoft. His act of indemnity kept him from all that was libelled before the year 1651 ; all the odious clamours of his cruelty againft the Lamonds, Macdonalds, and others, were cut off ; al-beit in all thefe he gave fair anfwers. Much of that guilt lay on his depute George Campbell, and on his friends Ardkinglafs, Macconochie, and others. Thefe appeared not when cited, and therefore were forefaulted. George appeared, and was made clofe prifoner : yet a par-don came from the King to him, procured, as was thought, by his purfe ; for many are poor, and he was very rich. His mafter's chief indictment was, compliance with the Englifh, his fitting in the parliament at London, his affifting Monk againft Glencairn and Middleton on the hills.

When his libelled crimes appeared not unpardonable, and his fon Lord Neil went up to fee his brother Lorn at London, and fpake fomewhat liberally of his father's fa-tisfactory anfwers, Monk was moved to fend down four or five of his letters to himself and others, proving his full compliance with them; that the King should not reprieve him. The Chancellor and Rothes went to court to shew the hazard of his escape. The man was very wise, and questionless the greatest subject the King had, sometime much known and beloved in all the three kingdoms; it was not thought safe he should live. The condemnatory sentence he took well; supped the night after chearfully; parted with his gracious lady that Saturday at night Christianly. Mr Douglas and Mr Hutcheson preached to him in the tolbooth on the Sunday. Mr Dickson prayed with him all Sunday night, except a little time of his sleep. On the Monday he breakfasted and dined; about two o'clock he went through the streets, with his hat on, with his friends; very chearfully mounted the scaffold at the cross; spoke well at the corners of the scaffold; prayed twice. Mr Hamilton and Mr Hutcheson waited on him. He blessed the King and his family; attested God of his freedom from all designs against the King or his father; gave some pieces to the executioner; laid down his head on the block very courageously; at the stretching out of his hand, the sign agreed on, the maiden quickly struck off his head. However he had been much hated by the people, yet in death he was much regretted by many, and by none insulted over. His friends, in the night, in Marischall's six-horse coach, carried him through Falkirk and Glasgow, and thence to Kilpatrick, where they put him in a boat for Dunoon, and buried him with his fathers in the kirk of Kilmun. His head was set up on the west end of the tolbooth, where Montrose's head had stood. At the beginning of the parliament, Montrose's head and body, buried in the borough-muir, was appointed to be carried honourably to the Abbey church; whence, on the King's charges, he was carried to St Giles's to be entombed there, with a greater solemnity than any of our Kings ever had at their burial in Scotland. His son is a good, modest gentleman, has given no offence to any, neither at London nor in the parliament. The King's liberality, with his lady's portion and virtue, are like to put him in a better condition than was any of his predecessors.

Argyle long to me was the best and most excellent man our state of a long time had enjoyed; but his compliance with the English and remonstrants, took my heart off him these eight years; yet I mourned for his death, and still
                                                        pray

pray to God for his family. His two fons are good youths,
and were ever loyal. The ruin of the family may prove
hurtful to the King and kingdom. Without the King's
favour debt will undo it. When Huntly's lands are rendered, and Montrofe paid near 100,000 pound, his old
debts of 400,000 or 500,000 merks will not be got paid.
Many wonder of his debt, and think he muft have money, for he got much, and was always fober and fparing.
My good-fon, Mr Robert Watfon, was with his lady in
Rofneath the night the King landed in England. He told
me, all the dogs that day did take a ftrange howling and
ftaring up to my Lady's chamber-windows for fome hours
together. Mr Alexander Colvill, juftice-depute, an old
fervant of the houfe, told me, that my Lady Kenmure, a
gracious lady, my Lord's fifter, from fome little fkill of
phyfiognomy, which Mr Alexander had taught her, had
told him fome years ago, that her brother would die in
blood.

After Argyle's procefs, thefe of the minifters took up
moft of the parliament's time. Mr James Guthrie's libel
was tartly drawn, and wittily anfwered : yet he defended
all he had done ; juftified the matter of the remonftrance,
proteftation, caufes of God's wrath, and fathered all on
the difcipline of the church and acts of affemblies, even
his declinature of King and parliament at Perth, when
cited for treafonable preaching. After many days hearing, perfifting obftinately, he was condemned to be hanged, and his head to be fet on the Netherbow. Though
few approved of his way, yet many were grieved to fee a
minifter fo feverely ufed. Mr Rutherford, had not
death prevented, was in the fame hazard. Mr Gillefpie
had gone the fame way, had not his friends perfuaded
him to recant his remonftrance, proteftation, compliance
with the Englifh, and to petition the King and parliament
for mercy. All agreed to fupplicate the King for him ;
and now he has obtained liberty to abide at Ormifton, and
fix miles about it, to the firft of March. Mr James Naefmith, Mr John Dickfon of Rutherglen, Mr John Stirling, and Mr Traill, did follow his way : but Mr R. Mack-
ward, Mr Rutherford's fervant at London four years,
made minifter at Glafgow the way I wrote to you before,
in a fet fermon of purpofe, declared his grief for the parliament's hard ufage of the covenant, wherein all honeft
men did concur with him ; but in fo high language, as entering

tering a proteftation in heaven againft the parliament's
deed, whereof he took all his hearers for witneffes. Such
terms none approved; yet for all that either one or other
could fay, he obftinately ftood to all : which provoked
them to pafs a fentence of banifhment upon him.

All the reft of the imprifoned minifters are fet free,
fome upon one fatisfaction, and fome upon another. How
long their or our liberty fhall laft, we know not; for the
parliament feems to have fmall regard of any of us. They
took a way to nominate to themfelves preachers. Mr
Douglas, indeed, began; but was no more employed.
Mr Dickfon, Mr Hamilton, and others of the minifters of Edinburgh, were paft by; as all we of the
weft, except Mr James Hamilton of Cambufnethan,
and Mr Hugh Blair: but in all the nooks of Scotland
men were pitched out who were thought inclinable to
change our church-government, and according to our invectives, againft what we were lately doing, were printed good or weak divines, at the pleafure of a very rafcal
Thomas Sydferf, a profane atheiftical Papift, as fome
count him. Mr Blair, Mr Dickfon, and Mr Hutchefon,
were, without all caufe, mifchantly abufed by his pen,
without the refentment of the ftate, till his Majefty himfelf commanded to filence him. To myfelf I found the
Commiffioner very courteous. With much ado I got
myfelf fhifted of preaching. Mr Wood and Mr Colvil
did their duty very honeftly. Divers of the northern minifters, and fome others, played the fycophants; divers
are ftaggering: but what his Majefty was informed, that
the moft part of the miniftry, efpecially the moft grave,
wife, and learned, were for Epifcopacy, is utterly falfe;
for the moft and far beft part are lying in the duft before God, for what they fee, and for which they fear,
the great plague of God, even for the increafing abominations of burgh and land.

Many blame Mr Sharp, as the great court-minifter, by
whofe fole advice the King and ftatefmen, both Scots and
Englifh, are put on, and directed in thefe meddlings with
our church; but I have found him always fo kind a friend
to myfelf, that I will be loth to admit fuch thoughts of
him. Indeed the Chancellor and Prefident of the Council, when the parliament fent them to the King for removing the garrifons, took him up with them, as fome
thought, to be an agent betwixt them and Lauderdale,
who was faid to be colder in purfuing Chancellor Hyde's
                                    defigns.

defigns in Scotland than fome others; yet we hear not but Lauderdale and they agree well enough, and that he keeps fully his court.

The parliament laid on no taxation, for the land is ex-haufted, and very poor; yet they laid on a greater bur-den than many parliaments before them thefe many years, L. 40,000 Sterling a-year during the King's life; but to be lifted in a way not very burdenfome, a moderate excife on drink alone. When all this alfo is diftributed among well-deferving men, the neceffities of many, and greed of fundry, will not be got fatisfied.

At the beginning of the parliament there were many brave defigns for fifhing, and more ufe of trade; but after fome empty talk, all feems to be vanifhed, the boroughs fticking abfolutely to their old job-trot for their own hurt. The charge of the parliament was great. It had fat long for no very pleafant purpofes. The moft defired it to rife without adjournment, and chofe rather to be governed fimply by the King's good pleafure, who was an equitable and wife prince. While it was adjourned from July 10. to March 1. it was not very acceptable. They feared the interval was but for the ripening the defigns of bringing in books and bifhops, either in whole or in part, as prepara-tory to all was in England; alfo to fine many for fmall faults, to fupply the waftry of undeferving men. The act of debitor and creditor was very heavy to thefe that had to do with it. It was a pity, when the King intended no-thing but to eafe his people, and make the hearts of all that loved him rejoice, it fhould fall out, through the im-providence, at leaft, of fome, to the contrary. Our good town was particularly grieved, that the nineteenth part of the excife fhould be laid on them alone, notwithftanding of all their very diligent commiffioner, John Bell, could do to the contrary. The town of Edinburgh got a part of their excife to defray their prefent burdens: but get what they will, it does little good; for their debt, it is a-bove 900,000 merks, though ftill they be ftenting their town for their needlefs prodigality. They fay the dinner they gave to the Commiffioner in the College-hall coft them large L. 500 Sterling.

In England and Ireland thus affairs are. After the King had diffolved the parliament at London, Decem-ber 29. all things being done abundantly to the King's contentment, the day of coronation was appointed to be

April

April 28. St George's day. The ceremony was very folemn, as ever any coronation before. Our only grief was, that the bifhops, in anointing, crowning, and all, had fo deep a hand. It was thought the former parliament, how bountiful to the King foever, had one defect in the legality, that it was not fummoned by the King, but called by the former parliament. To remedy this, another was called to meet May 8. Great care was had to get, in all the fhires, men commiffionate according to the heart of the court. The Prefbyterians made fome ftickling for this, but to no purpofe ; for the Chancellor was fo active, as the moft affectionate of the old cavalier party were generally chofen. When they met, the Chancellor's fpeech advertifed them to beware of the Prefbyterian minifters, as peftiferous incendiaries. This grieved us fore. But when the Houfe of Commons did not only vote the bifhops into the Houfe of Lords, but the folemn league and covenant to be burnt by the hand of the hangman, all our hopes were turned into defpair.

The parliament of Ireland, which fat down the fame 8th of May, was not behind, but put bifhops in the Houfe of Lords ; yea, chofe Bifhop Bramhall to be Speaker in the Houfe of Peers, though Mr Davis of Derry was ready to challenge him of many adulteries, and other odious crimes. The perfecution of Prefbyterian minifters began to be very hot. Almoft all of them, both in England and Ireland, were put from their charges. The King, before the parliament, after fundry conferences with the chief of the Epifcopal and Prefbyterian parties, had emitted a declaration, albeit full enough for books and bifhops, yet it had fundry limitations for the eafe of the Prefbyterians ; but all was neglected. The bifhops and books were fully eftablifhed as of old, without *ifs* or *ands*. This caufes a very great mifcontentment in many. What the end will be, the Lord knows ; only for the time, thoufands, who heartily pray for all good to the King, do cry to Heaven for help againft the Epifcopal oppreffors, who little regard their prayers, knowing that they have neither any will, nor any power, to ufe any force againft them. Pamphlets on both fides flee thick abroad. The King declared to all his three parliaments the unanimous advice he had got from all his counfellors, to marry the Infanta of Portugal ; and all his parliaments gave their hearty confent to it, though it was vifible it brought with it a prefent war with

I   Spain.

Spain. This was little regarded; especially since Holland adhered to our King, and submitted to him all their differences with Portugal. The great conditions, which yet are secret, and the great hopes of the Princess's readiness to be of the King's religion, make all to like the match well, and to pray for a blessing to it. The parliament at London would gladly have been, as they say, at changing the act of indemnity; but the King's peremptory adhering to it, made them let it alone; only some more executions, and forfaultries of them in the Tower, are expected. It was much, that Sir Henry Mildmay and Robert Wallop escaped, with drawing to Tyburn with ropes about their necks on hurdles. They speak of Sir Henry Vane and Lambert as to be tried for their lives. They are two the most dangerous men in England. Their execution will be well enough taken by all generally; yea, though Solicitor St John's should be added to them. The King desires the parliament to adjourn till winter, that he may go to his progress towards Worcester, the place of his deadly dangers, to visit all who had been there friends to him.

After the adjourning of our parliament, sundry of our nobles posted to court, the Commissioner, Duke Hamilton, Montrose, the Treasurer, Athol, Aboyne, and others. There were there before, the Chancellor, Rothes, Lorn, and more.

It is thought their agreement will be scarce good upon their private interests, and especially about Lorn, whether he shall be restored or not; but I fear they shall agree too well to trouble our poor church. The King's late declaration is no ways satisfactory. It continues our church-discipline only during pleasure, and discharges any preaching, petitioning, or meddling with the church-government. Mr Sharp is the only man with whom the King advises; and many say he is corrupted by Hyde; which I wish be false; otherwise we are in an exceeding hard taking: yet the Lord ever lives.

I have got sundry of yours lately, two yesterday together, May 3. and July 4. for which I thank you. I think before this you have got sundry of mine also. I long to hear if you received my book, and your sense of it. My speech at my entry to my place, you have herewith. If you think fit, I would put it at the end of my book, as a publick testimony of my loyalty, also my prayer and exhortation at the laureation.——Our Queen's etiring out of England, with her daughter Henrietta, ome thought was more on miscontent for Chancellor Hyde's too great power, than for any reality of a match vith the Duke of Anjou. The match of the Prince of Florence with the second daughter of Orleans, might well iave served the eldest. God be thanked your state is in so good terms with all their neighbours. We hope Spain, in iis old age, and infancy of his son, will be loth to ven- ure on a war with England.

When the King was going to his progress, and the par- iament to adjourn, July 20. they changed, as we hear, heir resolution. The parliament sat still. The King gave over his progress for this year. He is not to send for his Queen in haste. What may be the reason of this change, ve yet do not know. I am glad to find you continue just n my sense of our publick affairs.

201. *For Mr William Spang.*   *Glasgow,* May 12. 1662.

> Dear Cousin,

My last was by the hand of my lad Harry. I have kept ny chamber these six weeks, and yet do keep it, through rose in my leg; but, blessed be God, I now walk up ind down my chamber and yard. The doctor thinks I iave a scurvy. I find an universal weakness, especially of ny stomach. It were a favour to me to be gone; yet I am willing to abide my appointed time, and take my part vith others in these very hard times. It was one of my pecial desires to have my book printed, which you, of our singular kindness, have procured fully to my mind. will not be able to return you this special favour. It is n fine paper, a brave letter and volume; I could not have vished it better. Only I would intreat you would hasten t so much as may be, that it be not *opus posthumum.* As ou have sent me the first sheets, I wish you sent me like- vise what since are cast off. The corrector had need, for he credit of the press, to be more careful. In these two heets you see what gross faults are escaped, which makes olecisms and nonsense. Do your best to help this.

The publick affairs you know them as well and better han I. Our kirk, all the English times, had been very aithful to our King, and so instrumental as we could for is restitution. We had lost much blood at Dunbar, Worcester,

2

Worcester, and elsewhere, and at last our liberty, in his cause. We firmly expected, at his restitution, a comfortable subsistence to ourselves, and all our Presbyterian brethren, in all the dominions; and believe the King's intention was no other; but, by divine permission, other counsels thereafter prevailed, and now carry all. When the King was at Breda, it was said he was not averse from establishing Presbytery; nor was the contrary peremptorily resolved till the Saturday at night in the cabinet-council at Canterbury. At the beginning it went on softly. Calamy, Baxter, Manton, Reynolds, were made chaplains. But at once it altered. This came from our supine negligence and inadvertence; for the parliament there, consisting of the secluded members, the city, Monk also, and the army, were for us. Had we but petitioned for Presbytery at Breda, it had been, as was thought, granted; but fearing what the least delay of the King's coming over might have produced, and trusting fully to the King's goodness, we hasted him over, without any provision for our safety. At that time it was, that Dr Sheldon, now Bishop of London, and Dr Morley, did poison Mr Sharp, our agent, whom we trusted; who, piece and piece, in so cunning a way, has trepanned us, as we have never got so much as to petition either King, parliament, or council. My Lord Hyde, the great minister of state, who guided all, and to whom, at his lodging in Worcester-house, the King, weekly, and ofter, uses to resort and keep counsel with him some hours; and so, with the King, Mr Sharp became more intimate than any man almost of our nation. It seems he has undertaken to do in our church that which now he has performed easily, and is still in acting.

He had for co-operators the Commissioner, Chancellor, and Rothes. Lauderdale and Crawford were a while contrary; but seeing the King peremptory, they gave over. His Majesty's letter to us at first, penned by Mr Sharp, promised to keep up our church-government established by law, and to send for Mr Douglas and others to confer about our affairs. The last Mr Sharp hindered; for with himself alone it pleased his Majesty to confer: and the sense of the first, few of us dreamed till it came out thereafter. We were amazed at the proclamation, discharging all petitioning against Episcopal government, established by law, as it was in the year 1633; of putting down our synods, presbyteries, and sessions; of calling up Mr Sharp,

Ir Fairfoul, and Mr Ja. Hamilton of Cambufnethan, lfo Mr Leighton, then at London, to be confecrated by he Englifh bifhops ; which, after fome time, they were y the Bifhops of London and Worcefter, and others, vith many Englifh guyfes. Their feaft to all the Scots, nd many of the Englifh nobility, was great. They ftaid here fome months longer than was expected, that they night be fufficiently inftructed in the Englifh way. When hey came down, they were received by a number of no-lemen, gentlemen, and the magiftrates of Edinburgh. The Commiffioner's lady feafted them and the nobility hat night magnificently, as the Chancellor did the mor-ow thereafter. Mr Sharp bought a fair new coach at London, at the fides of which two lacqueys in purple does run.

. The parliament of England did all things for the King he pleafed ; augmented much his revenues beyond what any King in England ever had before. After fome conferences at Worcefter-houfe betwixt the bifhops and a few of the Prefbyterians, where it was hoped his Majefty would bring the bifhops to a great condefcenfion, at laft it was found they would yield in as good as nothing : fo the Houfe of Commons formed a bill of uniformity, that all fhould be put from their charges who did not conform to the bifhops orders. On this the Houfe of Lords made fome demur, and yet does ; but we doubt not of their agreement to it at laft ; and from thenceforth a fearful per-fecution is expected, for the prevalent party of the Epifco-pal faction are imbittered, and, both in doctrine and party, it feems, fully of the old Canterburian ftamp. God be merciful to our brethren, who have no help of man, nor any refuge but in God alone. We fear our cafe fhall be little better. Our parliament was adjourned from the 10th of March to the 8th of May. The Commiffioner and our nobles were defired not to leave London till they had feen the Queen. Alfo much talk was of difcord be-twixt the Commiffioner and Treafurer about the collection of the new revenue of L. 40,000 Sterling. The Trea-furer pleaded it might come into the exchequer, and the other had obtained a gift of collecting it to his good-bro-ther Lord Lyon. The Secretary partied with the one, and my Lord Hyde with the other. The ftrife was more long and loud than was fit. The King agreed them at laft as it might be. The Commiffioner came from London on

the

the Wednesday, and came hither on the Sunday morning. The archbishops consecrated other five on the Wednesday in the Abbey-church; Mr Haliburton to Dunkeld, Mr Paterson to Ross, Mr Murdoch Mackenzie to Moray, Mr Forbes to Caithness, Mr Robert Wallace to the Isles; Dr Wishart, designed for Edinburgh, and Mr David Mitchell, for Aberdeen, are not yet come out of England; nor old Sydserf, appointed for Orkney. Mr David Fletcher, whose patent was for Argyle, refused it, the rent being naught. The Commissioner gave the feast after consecration, as his Majesty had defrayed liberally all their charges in England.

Our bishop, the other week, took a start to come to Glasgow. The Commissioner convoyed him, with Montrose, Linlithgow, Callender, and sundry more noblemen and gentlemen, with a number of our town's folk, both horse and foot, with all our bells ringing, brought them to the tolbooth to a great collation. He preached on the Sunday, soberly and well; but Mr Hugh Blair in the afternoon, ridiculously worse than his ordinary. Some of my neighbours were earnest that the Chancellor and he should have a collation in the college on Monday morning. Against this I reasoned much; but was overvoted, to our great and needless charge: 200 pound paid not our charge. Mr John Young made to the bishop a speech of welcome, beside my knowledge. The Chancellor, my noble kind scholar, brought all in to see me in my chamber, where I gave them sack and ale the best of the town. The bishop was very courteous to me. I excused my not using of his styles, and professed my utter difference from his way; yet behoved to intreat his favour for our affairs of the college; wherein he promised liberally. What he will perform, time will try.

The council called for Mr Robert Blair some months ago, but never yet made him appear. We think they have no particular to lay to his charge, but the common quarrel of Episcopacy; only will not have him abide in St Andrew's to be a daily eye-sore to his Grace. Also they called Mr John Carstairs, that he should not sit in Glasgow, to preach after his manner against the times, to bear him company. Mr James Naesmith is likewise written for, as is thought, that the deanry of Hamilton may vaike for Mr James Ramsay, and with him Mr William Adair of Ayr, the two ministers of Kilmarnock, Mr

John

John Veitch of Mauchline, and Mr Alexander Blair of Galstone. The guyse now is, the bishops will trouble no man, but the state will punish seditious ministers. We are in the most hard taking we have seen at any time. It is the matter of my daily grief, and I think it has brought all my bodily trouble on me, and I fear it shall do me more harm.

I pray you hasten my book. I intend no other preface than it has. I purposed a dedication for Lauderdale; but it seems it now will not be welcome to him. I wrote to him of it, but he did not answer. However, that will be the last sheet. For verses here I intend none. I care not for vanities. Let me have my count with you, that I may know what English money to send you. My hearty service to your dear kind wife and all your sweet children. I rest, after the old fashion,

      Your Cousin, to serve you,

                ROBERT BAILLIE.

GLOS-

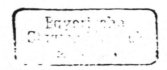

GLOSSARY.

always — however, nevertheless
allenarly — only
anent — concerning
azhort — among, or through
attour — over and above
aughtin — owing
backing — partisans, assistants, followers
bardish — impertinent
baxters — bakers
benfail — bias, propenfity
blephum — mere pretence
blue bore — fair appearance
bonny — elegant, fine, handfome
bruckle — brittle
bruik — enjoy
boaft — threaten
brae — declivity of a hill
by, — befides, vol. 1. p. 339. lin. 41.
bygone — time paft
blink — flight perufal; fometimes fhine
blythe — glad
broaching — hatching
caged — imprifoned
caufey — ftreet
cuttedly — haftily
cummer — goffip
cracking — credit decreafing
compear — appear
caufey-cloaths — fashionable drefs
canny — prudent
clatters — uncertain reports
cefsing — taxing
compefced — defeated
coldrife — lukewarm
cullionry — pultrony
caulms — moulds
coupers — horfe-jockeys
coinzie-houfe — mint-houfe
cap — falute
curious — anxious to know
curler — a diverfion on ice
ding — beat
divot — turf
dorlacks — dagger or fhort fword
driffling — fmall rain
dicted, dyted — dictated
dilled down — died away
Dodracenifm — an afferter of the articles of the fynod of Dort
dainties — a rare thing
disjune — breakfaft
dyvour — bankrupt

dool — grief, mourning
decerned — adjudged, gave judgement
decreet — decree or fentence
dittay — accufation
deaved — deafened
drumly — muddy
demented — diftracted
expone — expound
excemed — exempted
eke — add
evited — fhunned
ergh — fcare
ferd — fervour
feus — quitrents
foreanent — oppofite to
flit — remove
frequent numbers — great numbers
flyting — fcolding
flought — flame, combuftion
field-coming — coming abroad
foregainft — oppofite to
fashious — troublefome
fashrie — trouble
grip — hold
guyfes — fashions, ceremonies
gloom — frown
good-dame — grandmother
good-brother — brother-in-law
good-fon — fon-in-law
galliard — brifk, lively
hofe-net — fnare
here-yefterday — the day before yefterday
haunflit — eagerly catched
bows — difficulties
haill — whole
borning — denouncing a man a rebel
interlocutor — decifion
inkling — diftant hint
ilk — each
inlack — want
kythe — appear
lent fire — flow fire
laigh — low
libel — indictment
lathnefs — laxnefs
leet — lift
let be — much lefs
mint — attempt
mifter — want
malifon — evil wifh, curfe
mifken — let alone
mifchant — mifchievous

mifhappens

GLOSSARY.

ifhappens — unfortunateneſs
ill he would be — whether he would or not
otars — attorneys
eaves — fiſts
otour — publickly known
ur fault of you — our want of you vol. 2. p. 146. l. 42.
ndicle — appendage
aſch — Eaſter
ropone — propound
erquire — diſtinctly
hraſe — pretence
reveen — prevent
iiked — drubbed
oceſs — proſecution
ock — bag
tata — turf, fewel
ek — ſmoke
meid — remedy
poned — replaced
adily — poſſibly
oved — clinched
ed — lop
ant — few
eat — inundation
a — ſo
eired — aſked
iil hoſt — main army
lebroſities — roughly
unk — ſpark
ored — threatened
ck — ſtop, ſtab
kerly — ſurely
klike — ſuchlike
on or ſyne — ſooner or later
nk — ſtrong
aith — harm
atching — drubbing
oops — ſupporters, pillars

fetter of tacks — letter of leaſes
tacks — leaſes
traiked — weakened by fatigue
tint — loſt
tyne — loſe
thereanent — concerning it
traſh — refuſe, lumber
twenty ſhilling — twenty pence
tolbooth — priſon, gaol
thir — theſe
thrawart — backward
terned — cholerick
the morn — to morrow
tocher — dowry
tryſt — appointment
targe — ſhield
tirlies — trellis or rails
there-eaſt — in the eaſt
trewſmen — highlanders
unpaunded — unpledged
uncanny — miſchievous
unwell — ſick, not well
unkent — unknown
unfriends — enemies
unlaws — laws of no force
while — till
whiles — ſometimes
win — get in
wyte — blame
water-brae — river-bank
whilkas — whichas
whinger — hanger
vaike — to be vacant
vaiking — becoming vacant
voice — vote
Zuill — Chriſtmas

one lib. Scots is 20 pence Sterling.
one merk Scots is 13 ¼ d.

The End of the Second Volume.

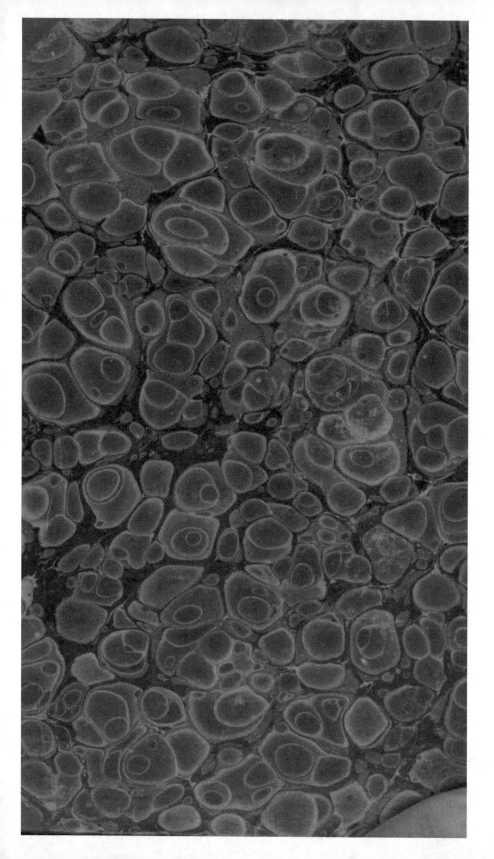

Check Out More Titles From HardPress Classics Series In this collection we are offering thousands of classic and hard to find books. This series spans a vast array of subjects – so you are bound to find something of interest to enjoy reading and learning about.

Subjects:
Architecture
Art
Biography & Autobiography
Body, Mind &Spirit
Children & Young Adult
Dramas
Education
Fiction
History
Language Arts & Disciplines
Law
Literary Collections
Music
Poetry
Psychology
Science
…and many more.

Visit us at www.hardpress.net

Im The Story
personalised classic books

"Beautiful gift... lovely finish.
My Niece loves it, so precious!"

Helen R Brumfieldon

★★★★★

UNIQUE GIFT

FOR KIDS, PARTNERS
AND FRIENDS

Timeless books such as:

Kids

Alice in Wonderland · The Jungle Book · The Wonderful Wizard of Oz
Peter and Wendy · Robin Hood · The Prince and The Pauper
The Railway Children · Treasure Island · A Christmas Carol

Adults

Romeo and Juliet · Dracula

Highly Customizable   **Change** Books Title   **Replace** Characters Names with yours   **Upload** Photo (for inside page)   **Add** Inscriptions

Visit
Im The Story .com
and order yours today!

CPSIA information can be obtained
at www.ICGtesting.com
Printed in the USA
BVHW080811120819
555626BV00009B/1625/P